ASTER FAMILY FLOWER (COMPOSITE)

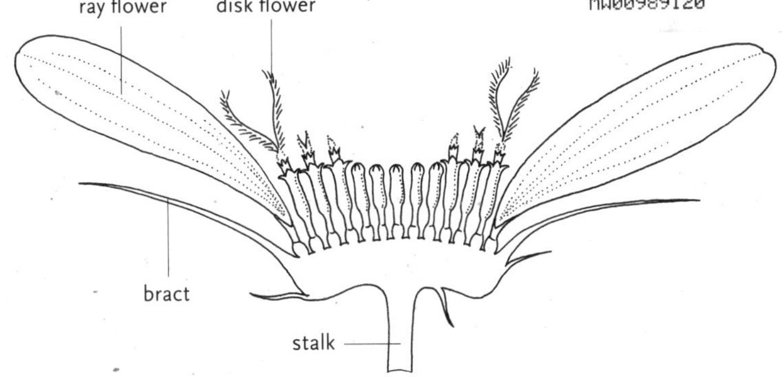

INFLORESCENCES

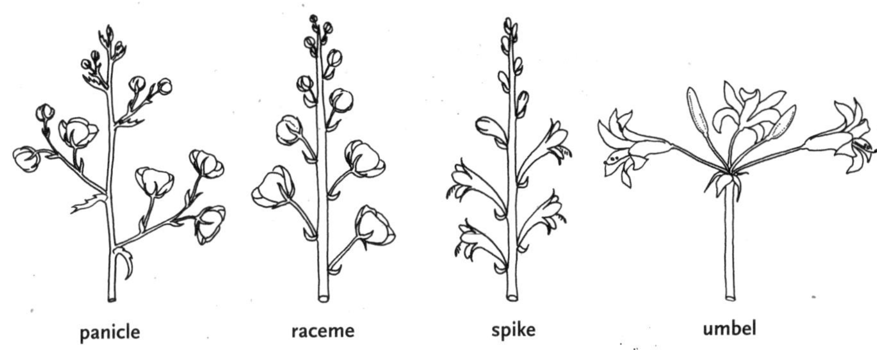

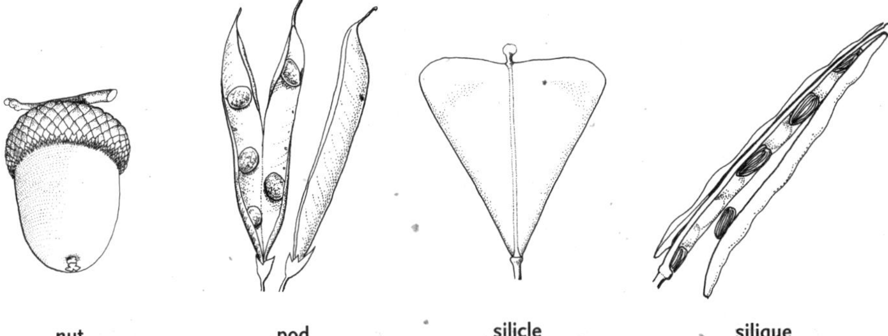

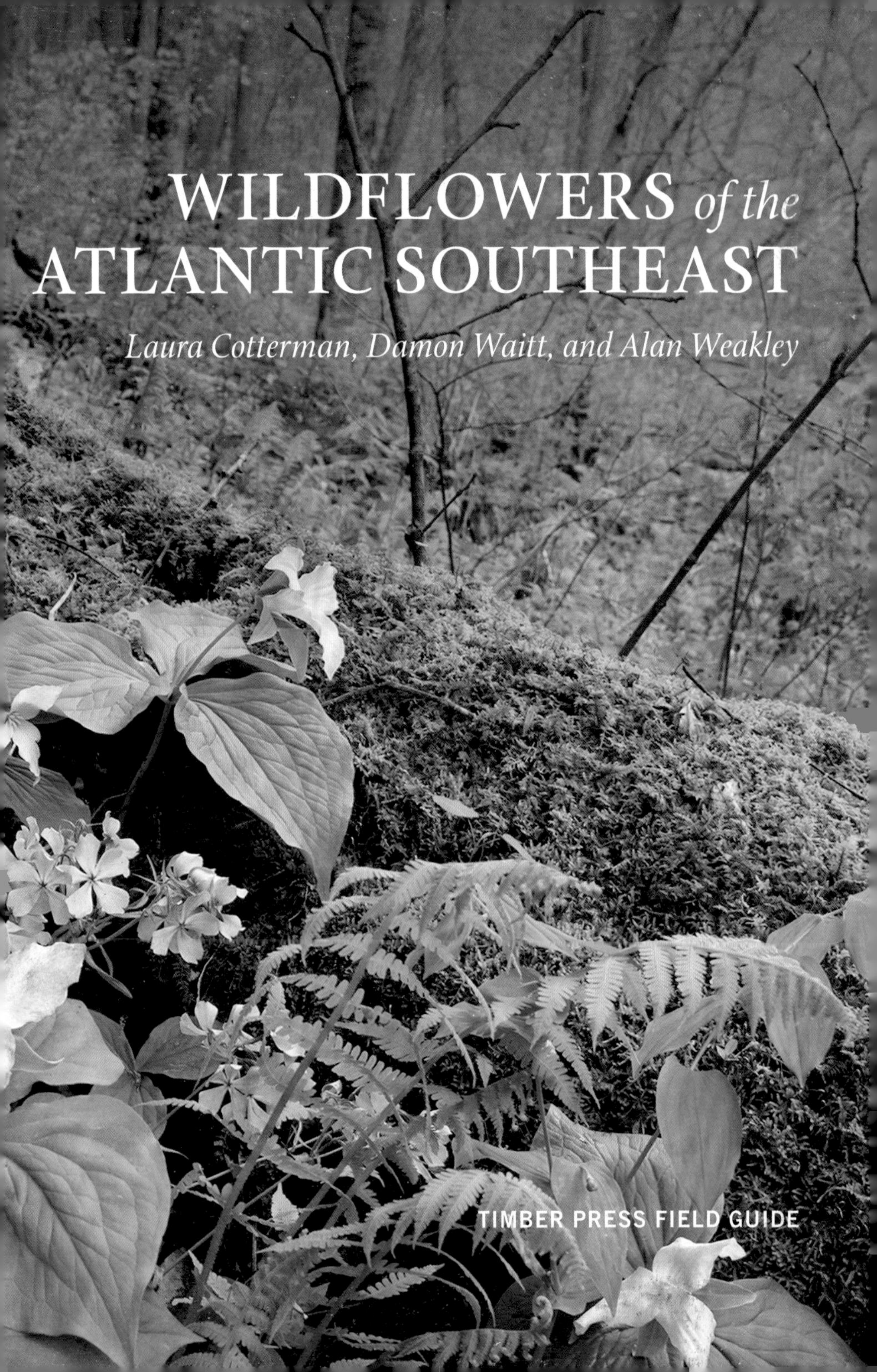
WILDFLOWERS of the
ATLANTIC SOUTHEAST
Laura Cotterman, Damon Waitt, and Alan Weakley
TIMBER PRESS FIELD GUIDE

Published in 2019 by Timber Press, Inc.

Endpapers by Alan Bryan
Maps by Michael Lee
Frontispiece: *Arisaema triphyllum* (Jack-in-the-pulpit) by Alan M. Cressler
Title page: Trilliums and friends by Anthony Heflin

Timber Press
The Haseltine Building
133 S.W. Second Avenue, Suite 450
Portland, Oregon 97204-3527
timberpress.com

Printed in China
Cover and text design by Susan Applegate

ISBN: 978-1-60469-760-5
A catalog record for this book is available from the Library of Congress.

CONTENTS

PREFACE

Welcome to *Wildflowers of the Atlantic Southeast* (or as it has become affectionately known to its authors, *WOTAS*). This easy-to-use field guide is your introduction to more than 1200 wildflower species found in the Atlantic Coastal states (and West Virginia) from New Jersey south to Georgia. This region is home to one-fifth of the U.S. population, and these plants surround us in our daily lives in the urban and suburban areas where most of us now live.

The ability to differentiate the greenness that surrounds us has to start somewhere—and that somewhere is usually a good wildflower guide that shows us that plant identification is not an unknowable mystery revealed only to botanists. It is something anyone can learn with a little practice and patience. Our hope is that this new resource will help improve your "botanical literacy" and start you down the path to a sustainable relationship with nature through a better understanding and appreciation of plants.

Botanic gardens have a long history of involvement in plant exploration, carrying out education and research programs, and developing resources like this guide. The North Carolina Botanical Garden has been a leader in native plant conservation and education in the southeastern United States for more than 50 years. As part of the University of North Carolina at Chapel Hill, we further the university's teaching, research, and public service mission through our own mission to inspire understanding, appreciation, and conservation of plants and to advance a sustainable relationship between people and nature. The North Carolina Botanical Garden maintains and protects over 1100 acres of garden and conservation areas, curates the largest herbarium in the southeastern United States, safeguards rare and endangered plant species from extinction, educates new generations of botanists and scientific leaders, and offers a remarkable natural environment to more than 100,000 visitors each year along with extensive educational programming focused on North Carolina's native flora, horticulture, ecology, conservation, and botanical art. Today, we are recognized as the nation's most comprehensive center of knowledge on the regional flora of North Carolina and the southeastern United States.

We hope that in addition to using this field guide, you will take the time, in your travels, to visit botanical gardens, arboretums, and nature centers to learn more about the plants, animals, pollinators, and habitats with which all our lives are intertwined.

ACKNOWLEDGMENTS

This book is a natural outgrowth of decades, even centuries, of botanical exploration in the southeastern and mid-Atlantic states. As such, the many individuals who came before us and made numerous contributions to our knowledge of the flora of this expansive region must be acknowledged. Though they are too numerous to name, we are mindful of our debt to them.

It takes a village to raise a field guide, and the authors are deeply grateful to the photographers who generously contributed images to make this guide possible. All photographers are credited by their initials at the end of each photo caption or species description; see the photographer list on page 488 for a key to these initials. Photographers retain all rights to their photos. Please contact the photographer if you would like to obtain the right to use a photo for another purpose. We are especially grateful to Alan Cressler (AMC), Gary Fleming (GPF), Bruce Sorrie (BAS), Will Stuart (WS), and Richard and Teresa Ware (RTW) for their substantial contributions of images to this book.

We are indebted to our colleague Michael Lee, who prepared the plant distribution maps as well as the regional map. In addition, Michael's programming and data management support in the Flora of the Southern and Mid-Atlantic States project of the UNC Herbarium (North Carolina Botanical Garden) has been integral to the development of this field guide.

Many thanks to Kathleen Strakosch Walz and Andy Windisch, who reviewed the descriptions of New Jersey natural community types and helped us find sources for photographs illustrating those communities. Finally, gratitude to North Carolina Botanical Garden volunteers Paula LaPoint and Fran Whaley, who researched and wrote more than 100 wildflower descriptions for this guide.

INTRODUCTION

Our intention for this field guide is to support wildflower enthusiasts in identifying and appreciating the more common, and a few rare, herbaceous plants encountered in a region encompassing the Atlantic Coastal states (plus West Virginia) from New Jersey south to Georgia. The region has about 6200 species of native and naturalized vascular plants (plants with advanced conducting tissues). This guide includes only about one-fifth of those! Many plants that grow in our area are deliberately excluded as not being "wildflowers": woody plants of all forms (trees, shrubs, woody vines), ferns, clubmosses, and graminoids (grasses, sedges and rushes, and other grass-like plants with small, inconspicuous, mostly wind-pollinated flowers). These important parts of our flora are covered, or will be covered in the future, by other field guides.

To make this a portable, usable volume, we had to exclude some plants. Our selection of wildflowers was weighted toward those which you are most likely to encounter—plants that are common at least somewhere in the area of coverage and that are likely to be found by people interested in native and naturalized wildflowers that grow in parks, game lands, and preserves as well as in suburban and, even, urban areas.

It is worth noting that plants do not respect state boundaries. This is one reason we provide information about natural communities: some of these habitats occur outside of our defined Atlantic Southeast region, and so do the wildflowers known to occur in those habitats.

The habitat, distribution, and descriptive information for the wildflower species covered here have been distilled from many sources. Decades of data compilation by author Alan Weakley and many colleagues for the Flora of the Southern and Mid-Atlantic States project form the foundations of this guide. Ultimately we have used information obtained from herbarium specimens, published literature (scientific papers, flora manuals, other field guides), online sources, Natural Heritage Program databases, and personal communication with a regional network of botanists and taxonomic experts.

Yet our understanding of the taxonomy and ecology of plants continues to grow. Scientific names change, and new species are discovered; in addition, extinction is an ongoing and in fact accelerating process. The information in this field guide cannot be assumed to be static and unchanging, but we trust that it will take you on an interesting journey. We look forward to hearing about discoveries made by people who use this guide; there is really no end to the possibilities!

CLIMATE, GEOGRAPHY, AND NATURAL COMMUNITIES: READING THE LANDSCAPE

Observing and identifying wildflowers, in addition to being an aesthetic pleasure, can be an initiation into a wider exploration of the landscape. Curiosity about wildflowers often leads to curiosity about the many ways that climate, geology, water, soils, fire, and human history create the mosaic of habitats in our world. Whether you have already experienced the pleasures of wildflower study or are embarking on a new hobby, this book will be an informative guide.

Wildflowers, like all plants and animals, are inseparable from their habitats. Before we introduce you to a selection of wildflowers of this region, we provide an overview of the ecological factors that determine where plants grow, and discuss how those factors combine to create recognizable habitats or natural communities, which you will see referenced in the species profiles that form the heart of this guide.

Ecological Factors that Determine Where Plants Grow

Sun and shade. Light is a critical resource for nearly all plants. It is the basis for their manufacture—through the process of photosynthesis—of starches and sugars, which plants metabolize and on which we, as animals, are directly (by eating plants) or indirectly (by eating meat or other animal products like milk, cheese, and eggs) dependent. But that does not mean that all plants grow in blazing sun! Trees, shrubs, and woody vines have the ability to grow tall because they have the supporting structure of wood; and in temperate climates like ours, most natural communities are dominated by these tall plants, which shade the ground and the herbaceous plants growing there. Our wildflowers (defined here as herbaceous plants lacking woody growth) get access to sufficient light by a variety of means: (1) by growing in the relatively unusual situations where trees or shrubs are absent, sparse, or form only an open or translucent canopy; (2) with adaptations that enable them to thrive in low-light situations (though this usually results in an evolutionary trade-off, whereby the species cannot thrive in strong light); (3) by "time-shifting" their life cycles, or at least photosynthesis, to seasons when deciduous trees are bare (the basis for winter annual wildflowers and many of our early spring ephemeral perennials); or by employing a combination of these strategies. This means that we can expect to find some wildflowers in sunny situations and others in partial or full shade.

Temperature. The Atlantic Southeast region covers a substantial north-south distance: over 11 degrees of latitude, or about 760 miles (almost one-eighth of the way from the equator to the North Pole). Obviously, northern New Jersey and southern Georgia experience different extremes of climate. The USDA Plant Hardiness Zone Map, very familiar to gardeners, is an effort to create a simple and relatively crude guide to cold temperature tolerance for cultivated plants. Northern New Jersey is currently mapped as Zone 6a (minimum winter temperatures of -10 to -5°F), while southeastern Georgia is Zone 9a (minimum winter temperatures of 20 to 25°F). But the temperature tolerance of a given plant species is more complicated than extreme winter cold tolerance. Plants in the wild must do more than *survive*: they must complete their life cycle—that is, grow and compete with other plants in their shared habitats under a particular climatic regime. Other factors, in addition to latitude, determine temperature at a location, including the direction a slope faces and its steepness, and proximity to the coast or other large water bodies (water and humidity act as insulators and thermal sinks, so areas near the coast average cooler in summer and warmer in winter). In eastern North America, elevation is an additional, very important factor influencing the temperature of various plant habitats.

Elevation. Mountains in the Atlantic Southeast rise to a maximum of 6684 feet above sea level, providing cooler habitats that support a different array of plants than found in lowlands at the same latitude. Elevation further interacts with coastal amelioration, such that at the same latitude in North Carolina, for instance, the USDA Hardiness Zone varies from 8b on the Outer Banks to 5b in the Blue Ridge Mountains—with corresponding differences in the natural communities and wildflowers present.

Rainfall. This guide covers a region with a relatively moist climate: generally, rainfall is equitably distributed through the year. Annual precipitation is greatest in the higher mountains (particularly in the Blue Ridge) and along the Blue Ridge/Piedmont escarpment near the Georgia/South Carolina/North Carolina triple-corner. Areas of high rainfall and cloud immersion support northern disjunct and endemic plant species associated with specialized high-elevation natural communities, such as spruce-fir forests and grassy balds. The constant moisture seen at specialized habitats, such as the "vertical bogs" of spray cliffs, supports a mix of northern and tropical plants.

Hydrology, water chemistry, and soil moisture. Areas that are regularly saturated or flooded for even short amounts of time generally support different natural communities and wildflowers, compared with areas that do not flood or are drier. Plants need specialized adaptations to survive and thrive in conditions in which their roots are saturated, so many plants grow only in wetlands or only in uplands, though other species can tolerate or even thrive in both settings.

The specific ways in which areas are wet matters to plants—the length of time and seasonality of the wetness, whether the wetland is isolated and surrounded by uplands or connected along a watercourse or by groundwater, and the chemistry of the water. Some areas are permanently or semi-permanently flooded ("ponded") with water and support aquatic plants (note that few truly aquatic plants are covered in this guide). Other areas are flooded seasonally—for long periods of time from winter into spring—but then dry out with the increase in evaporation and transpiration. Still other areas (especially in floodplains) are flooded temporarily (typically for a few days or less), when heavy rain events cause overbank flooding of a watercourse, but may even be rather dry when not flooded.

A quite different and important situation is created when the water table is at or near the ground surface all or much of the year, but is rarely or ever above the ground. Such saturated conditions are particularly prevalent in flat landscapes of the outer Coastal

Plain, and in sloping landscapes where the water table is forced toward the surface by a layer of rock or clay. Saturated wetlands (bogs, fens, seeps) are often dominated by peat moss (*Sphagnum*), which absorbs and slowly releases water, helping maintain saturation.

The chemistry of the water flooding or saturating a landscape is another critical determiner of natural communities and their composition. Most waters in the region covered by this guide are relatively acidic, and particular areas of the Coastal Plain (e.g., the New Jersey Pine Barrens and the Carolinas) support large saturated wetlands and blackwater streams stained brown with organic acids.

Water matters to plants growing on upland sites too, shaping the natural communities and determining the specific places where particular species may be found. Ridges and upper slopes are generally more dry (xeric), while lower slopes near streams are more moist (mesic)—though, again, this topographic effect may be overridden at high elevations by higher rainfall. Less obviously, south- and southwest-facing slopes are hotter and drier, while north- and northeast-facing slopes are cooler and more moist. Because moisture is such an important determiner of plant habitat, habitat descriptors regularly include such terms as "mesic," "dry-mesic," and "xeric."

Substrate—rock and sediment. Soils are derived by complex processes involving plants, fungi, and microorganisms; but parent material—the weathered rock or sediment from which soils develop—remains a critical and dominant factor for fertility as well as moisture- and nutrient-holding capacities of soil. Sedimentary rocks (predominant in the Ridge and Valley and Appalachian Plateau physiographic provinces, but also present in limited areas of the Coastal Plain, Piedmont, and Blue Ridge) range from calcareous to siliceous in composition, with calcareous rocks weathering to higher pH, more fertile, and "rich" soils, and siliceous rocks weathering to lower pH, more sterile, and "poor" soils. Metamorphic and igneous rocks, predominating in the Blue Ridge and Piedmont physiographic provinces, vary from mafic through intermediate to felsic, with mafic rocks weathering to higher pH, more fertile soils, and felsic rocks weathering to lower pH, more sterile soils. (Ultramafic rocks, such as serpentine, have unusual chemistry and create interesting barren communities, notably in the Piedmont of Maryland and Pennsylvania and in the Blue Ridge of North Carolina and Georgia). Most of the rocks and sediments in the Atlantic Southeast region are on the acidic, sterile, "poor" end of the spectrum. In our habitat descriptions, we mention this essentially "default" condition less often than calcareous, mafic, or "rich" conditions, because the latter are encountered less frequently and are notable for supporting special habitats.

Fire. Many of the natural communities and species in our region evolved with fire and are dependent on it for their health, reproduction, and continued existence. Fire was an important evolutionary force here, ignited by lightning and by Native American activity. Fire-maintained habitats primarily occur today on public lands, where they are managed through prescribed burning. Fire-maintained natural communities are known to occur throughout the geographical area of this guide but are especially extensive in the Coastal Plain and southward. Some major landscapes

Prescribed fire at St. Marks National Wildlife Refuge, Wakulla County, FL. AMC

and ecosystems, such as the New Jersey Pine Barrens and the longleaf pine ecosystem of the Coastal Plain from southeastern Virginia south through the Carolinas and Georgia, are strongly shaped by fire. Fire regimes (from infrequent to near-annual) and intensities (from stand-replacing to light ground fires) shape the structure and plant composition of many natural communities and promote a high diversity of wildflowers. Many species, including many showy wildflowers, bloom only or primarily after a fire.

Coastal processes. The near-coastal environment has a number of unique processes that are unimportant inland, and as such these areas support natural communities and wildflowers that are strikingly different from those inland. These processes relate to tidal movement of water, the presence of salt (which has strong impacts on plants), and active shaping of the land itself by wind, hurricanes, nor'easters, and other storms. Lunar and wind tides create regularly to irregularly flooded marshes and forests (with waters of varying salinity), immediately near the coast but also tens of miles inland from the actual coastline in estuaries, sounds, and estuarine river-mouths, some of the largest being Sandy Hook, Raritan Bay, Barnegat Bay, and Great Bay (in New Jersey); Delaware Bay (in Delaware and New Jersey); Chesapeake Bay and the Potomac River (in Virginia, Maryland, and the District of Columbia); and Pamlico, Albemarle, Core, and Bogue Sounds (in North Carolina). Salt is ubiquitous near the Atlantic Ocean and haline estuaries, and is distributed by wind and water. In substantial concentrations it presents a challenge for plants lacking specific adaptations to its drying effect on their cells, and particularly where concentrated (as in salt marsh pannes), limits the flora to a specialized cohort. Trees and shrubs at the coast are literally shaped by salt stunting and wind pruning. Coastal natural communities are also notable in being highly dynamic, with everyday and especially storm winds and water reshaping dunes and islands and resetting primary succession.

Human activity. Human activity has had profound impacts on the modern landscape, especially influencing which plants grow where. We have managed the land around us for thousands of years; as population numbers and technologies multiply, the scope and depth of landscape alteration intensifies. Some alterations are obvious to even the casual eye (a forest converted to a field, suburban neighborhood, highway, or city), but others are more subtle (a grass native to Asia dominating a forest's ground layer). Because of our deliberate or inadvertent introduction of species not native to the eastern United States, many more plant species grow in our region than were present 500 years ago—about a third again as many (quite a few naturalized, non-native wildflowers are included in this guide). For most of our native species, though, the habitat available to them has decreased, sometimes drastically so. Shade-loving woodland species have suffered from the clearing and conversion of forestland to intensive human uses. But perhaps less obvious, most sun-loving native wildflowers have declined as a result of fire suppression. It is interesting to note that when well managed with occasional bush-hogging or mowing, roadsides and utility corridors can provide good to excellent habitat for these sun-loving wildflowers.

Natural Communities and Habitats

Physiographic provinces—large-scale regions defined by geologic history and landform—provide a foundation for discussing the ecoregions, natural communities, and associated plant and animal life in our region. As broadly defined for this field guide, the Atlantic Southeast includes five major physiographic provinces (these are sometimes further subdivided): the Coastal Plain, Piedmont, Blue Ridge, Ridge and Valley, and Appalachian Plateaus. These provinces occur as broad, roughly parallel bands across the region and parallel to the Atlantic Ocean shoreline (see map). Our discussion of natural communities and habitats of wildflowers is organized by physiographic province, because most of the natural communities we discuss are limited to or concentrated in a single physiographic province. For the purpose of enumerating natural communities, we have combined Blue Ridge, Ridge and Valley, and Appalachian Plateaus provinces into a single Mountain province; you will see this same Mountain province on the individual plant species distribution maps. We recommend that you first determine the physiographic province in which you are botanizing, and then read about the primary natural communities associated with that province. Just as most natural communities are limited to a single physiographic province, most wildflower species are limited to one or a few natural communities (though some are generalists that can be seen in a wide range of settings). If you want to see a diversity of plant species on a trip, in a year, or through a lifetime, a good general principle is to diversify your experience: visit many different habitats, in a diversity of physiographic provinces, across different seasons!

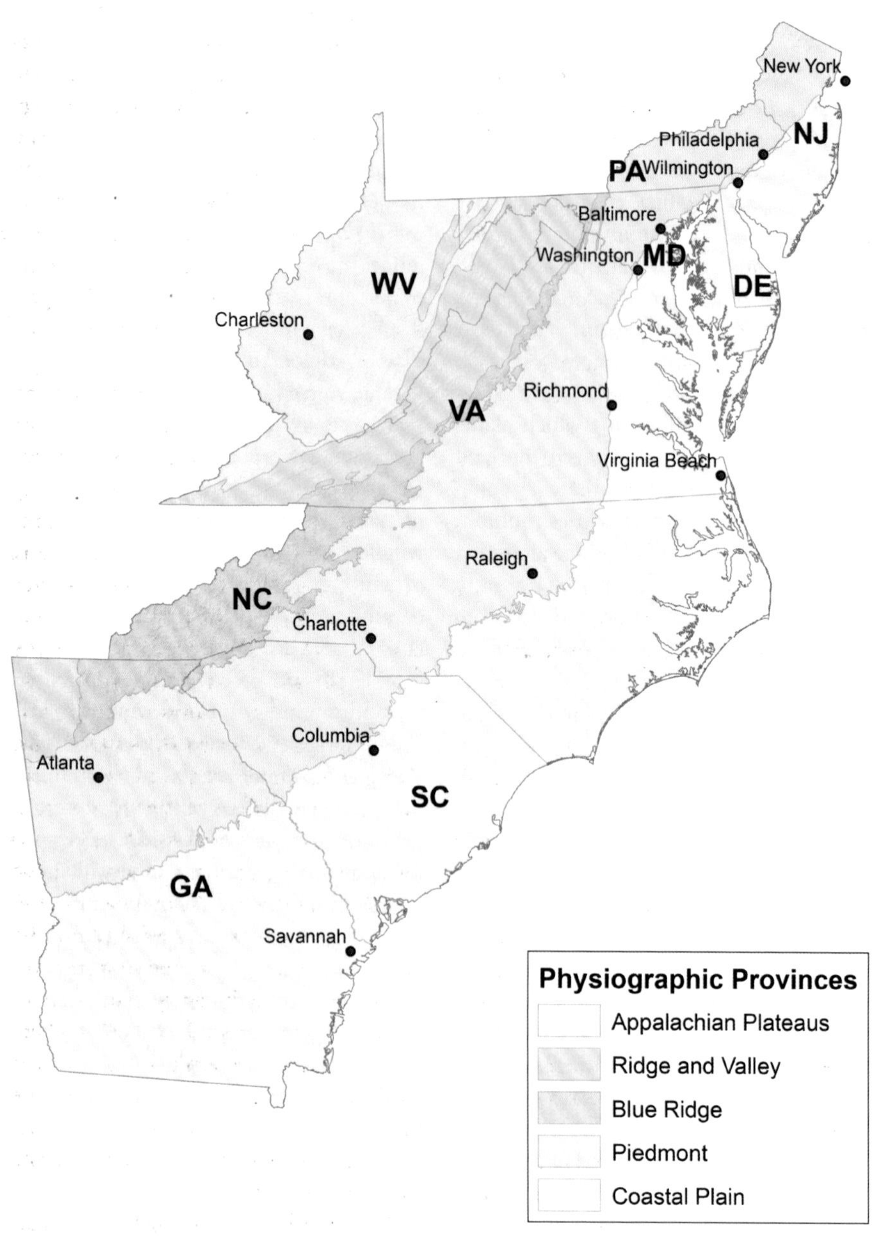

The Atlantic Southeast region and associated physiographic provinces.

Coastal Plain

The Coastal Plain stretches from central New Jersey south through Delaware, eastern Maryland, eastern District of Columbia, eastern Virginia, eastern North Carolina, eastern South Carolina, and eastern and southern Georgia. Outside the Atlantic Southeast, as we have defined it here, the Coastal Plain also extends into southern Alabama, northern Florida, and Long Island, New York—areas where this guide will be useful but incomplete in coverage.

The Coastal Plain consists largely of unconsolidated sediments (sand, silt, and clay particles that once were rock) weathered off the Appalachian Mountains for hundreds of millions of years and transported toward the Atlantic Ocean. The oldest parts of the Coastal Plain are of Cretaceous age and occur along its inland boundary; to the east the land surface is younger. Topography varies from rolling hills inland—especially in the fall-line Sandhills, which extend from south-central North Carolina through South Carolina and Georgia along the Piedmont boundary (and consist largely of coarse sands that have been reworked into old dune fields)—to more subdued and even flat areas eastward. What the Coastal Plain lacks in topographic and altitudinal diversity, it makes up for in hydrologic and soil diversity, with soils that range from excessively drained, through moist, to constantly saturated (bogs), and to seasonally, tidally, or permanently inundated soils of floodplains, depression ponds, estuaries, and coastal marshes. Rainfall is relatively high and on average equitably distributed through the year, though hurricanes and tropical storms can cause widespread flooding. Prior to extensive alteration and fragmentation of the Coastal Plain landscape in the last several hundred years, fire was a nearly pervasive shaper of Coastal Plain natural communities and flora; the high frequency of lightning-ignited fires and the flat landscapes with few natural barriers allowed an individual fire to spread over a large area. Most upland areas of the Coastal Plain experienced fire once every few years, and thus the flora there is highly adapted to and dependent on fire as a natural disturbance.

Dunes, beaches, and maritime grasslands. Treeless communities occur on the most-exposed and shifting parts of barrier islands all along the coast from New Jersey to Georgia. Annual herbs grow on upper beaches, newly deposited sand dunes, and overwashed sand flats, while grasses—such as sea oats (*Uniola paniculata*) southward, beach grass (*Ammophila breviligulata*) northward, and salt hay cordgrass (*Sporobolus pumilus*) throughout—form sparse to dense maritime grasslands on dunes and flats. These communities consist of distinctive salt tolerant and sun-loving wildflowers.

Maritime forest and scrub. Maritime forest and scrub occurs in more sheltered situations: farther from the ocean or sheltered by dunes. From southeastern Virginia southward, these communities are dominated mostly by evergreens, such as live oak (*Quercus virginiana*), yaupon (*Ilex vomitoria*), and southern bayberry (*Morella cerifera*); northward, the dominants are more likely to be deciduous species, including northern bayberry (*M. pensylvanica*) and American beech (*Fagus grandifolia*).

Tidal marshes and swamp forests. Areas with tidal hydrology support marshes and, upstream, shrub-dominated and forested swamps. The dominant species and diversity are especially dependent on the salinity

Maritime grassland on dunes at Candler Beach, Cumberland Island National Seashore, Camden County, GA. AMC

Maritime forest with live oak (*Quercus virginiana*), covered with resurrection fern (*Pleopeltis michauxiana*), and saw palmetto (*Serenoa repens*). Jekyll Island, Glynn County, GA. AMC

Salt marsh, Brunswick River, Jekyll Island Causeway, Glynn County, GA. AMC

of the water, which is largely determined by distance, through inlets and estuary mouths, from the Atlantic Ocean; some tidal areas are tens of miles from saline ocean water and are essentially freshwater marshes. Areas exposed to regular (twice a day) flooding by tides of standard ocean salinity are dominated by saltmarsh cordgrass (*Sporobolus alterniflorus*) or, if flooded less deeply, by black needlerush (*Juncus roemerianus*), with few flowering plants present. Tidal marshes with lower salinity are more diverse and have more wildflowers. Salt pannes and high salt marshes, flooded by spring and neap tides and with salinity concentrated by evaporation, develop peculiar communities dominated by saltgrass (*Distichlis spicata*), saltworts (*Salicornia*), and Carolina sea-lavender (*Limonium carolinianum*)—all able to tolerate the salt content of the soils. Upstream along rivers and large streams with tidal hydrology, marshes give way to shrub and forested swamps, with tree species relatively similar to those in brownwater bottomland forests and swamps, but also with grasses and wildflowers more characteristic of freshwater tidal marshes. Tidal marshes with little or no salinity support a distinctive and diverse flora, including water-hemp (*Amaranthus cannabinus*), spatterdock (*Nuphar advena*), and narrowleaf cattail (*Typha angustifolia*).

Estuarine aquatic beds. Truly aquatic communities—that is, those submersed permanently or semipermanently in tidal waters—are not covered in this book, as the flowering plants that occur there have inconspicuous flowers that are unlikely to be seen by the wildflower seeker.

Pine savannas. Moist longleaf pine savannas were once the dominant or "matrix" community (in which all other communities were embedded) of the outer Coastal Plain from southeastern Virginia southward. A scattered to open canopy of longleaf pine (*Pinus palustris*), or also slash pine (*P. elliottii*) in South Carolina and Georgia, allows plenty of sunlight to reach the diverse ground layer of grasses, shrubs, and wildflowers, including orchids (Orchidaceae), carnivorous plants (pitcher-plants, sundews, butterworts, Venus' flytrap, bladderworts), meadow-beauties (*Rhexia*), and many others. Typical grass and sedge species include wiregrass (*Aristida stricta*), toothache grass (*Ctenium aromaticum*), and beaksedges (*Rhynchospora*). Pine savannas have a mesic to saturated hydrology, usually acidic soils, and very frequent (but low-intensity) fires as sustaining ecological features. This natural community has been reduced to a small fraction of its former extent as a result of activities by the naval stores industry, conversion to other intensive human uses, and suppression of fire. Most remaining areas are on federal, state, or private conservation or multiple-use lands managed by professional staff who conduct prescribed burns. Many of the wildflower species are so dependent on fire that you are likely to see them in flower only shortly after a burn (a month to a year following fire).

Longleaf pine sandhills. Like pine savannas, longleaf pine sandhills are dominated by longleaf pine (*Pinus palustris*), wiregrass (*Aristida stricta*), and other grasses, such as little bluestem (*Schizachyrium scoparium*) and pineywoods dropseed (*Sporobolus junceus*). Longleaf pine sandhills are more prevalent inland, especially in the inland-most section, often referred to as the fall line sandhills; but they do extend to the coast (even sometimes on barrier islands) interspersed with longleaf pine savannas.

Longleaf pine savanna, Green Swamp Nature Conservancy Preserve, Brunswick County, NC. AMC

Longleaf pine sandhills occur on dry, acid sand deposits and, like the more moist pine savannas, are exposed to frequent (but low-intensity) fires. A subcanopy or shrub layer (depending on fire regime) of scrub oaks (e.g., *Quercus laevis, Q. marilandica, Q. stellata*) is characteristic. Shrubs of the heath family (Ericaceae) are common, especially blueberries (*Vaccinium*) and huckleberries (*Gaylussacia*). There is a distinctive set of wildflower species with adaptations to xeric conditions and not typically found in other natural communities. Like longleaf pine savannas, longleaf pine sandhills have been tremendously reduced in extent by the naval stores industry, conversion to intensive human uses, and suppression of fire. Most remaining areas are on federal, state, or private conservation or multiple-use lands managed by professional staff using prescribed burns.

New Jersey Pine Barrens. In southern New Jersey, strongly acid, dry sands and frequent fires shape the Pine Barrens, a unique ecosystem dominated by pitch pine (*Pinus rigida*) and oaks (*Quercus*). The dwarf pitch pine plains, a remarkable forest of stunted trees, is restricted to areas of highest fire frequency. Short-stature pitch pines, with multiple dominant and low basal stems, basal sprouting, and a crooked or flat-topped growth form, dominate these plains; shrubby oaks (*Q. marilandica* and *Q. ilicifolia*) co-dominate. Heath shrubs like black huckleberry (*Gaylussacia baccata*), blueberries (*Vaccinium angustifolium, V. pallidum*), and sand myrtle (*Leiophyllum buxifolium*) are also common. While the canopy is short and dense, intense fire creates open areas where light reaches the sandy ground, supporting dwarf flowering shrubs like pyxie-moss (*Pyxidanthera barbulata*),

Longleaf pine (*Pinus palustris*) and turkey oak (*Quercus laevis*) sandhill barren, Emanuel County, GA. AMC

teaberry (*Gaultheria procumbens*), and kinnikinnick (*Arctostaphylos uva-ursi*), and unburned areas that remain open can support broom crowberry (*Corema conradii*). An underlying pristine, 17-trillion-gallon aquifer in the pinelands supports wetlands in headwaters and along streams: Atlantic white-cedar swamps, leatherleaf bogs, riverside savannas, pitch pine lowlands, and isolated intermittent ponds. Many flowering herbaceous species are associated with each of these habitats, particularly the wetlands.

Pine barren riverside savannas. The New Jersey Pine Barrens support a unique type of open herbaceous wetland, found along beautiful, meandering, tannin-rich streams and rivers bordered by Atlantic white-cedar swamp. These pine barren riverside savannas, saturated by groundwater, are globally rare peatlands that feature a high diversity of peat moss (*Sphagnum*), grasses (*Danthonia, Andropogon, Muhlenbergia*), sedges (*Cladium, Carex, Rhynchospora*), and wildflower species, with scattered shrubs and trees. Like other Coastal Plain wetlands from New Jersey to Georgia, these are acidic and nutrient-poor systems supporting carnivorous plants such as pitcherplants (*Sarracenia*), sundews (*Drosera*), and bladderworts (*Utricularia*). A notable endemic wildflower is bog asphodel (*Narthecium americanum*) and a notable fern is curlygrass fern (*Schizaea pusilla*). Other conspicuous flowering plants include golden crest (*Lophiola aurea*), ten-angled pipewort (*Eriocaulon decangulare*), and lanceleaf violet (*Viola lanceolata*). Most of these sites are accessible only by canoe and are protected on state-owned land.

Coastal Plain bogs and pocosins. This category encompasses a diversity of communities, with different structures, fire

Dwarf pitch pine barrens, New Jersey Pinelands National Reserve. JFB

Pine barren riverside savanna, New Jersey Pinelands National Reserve. TC

regimes, and composition, tied together by saturated hydrology and the usual presence or abundance of peat moss, which stabilizes the saturation of the mineral to organic soils. Communities included here include ones referred to in the region as peat dome pocosins, streamhead pocosins, sandhill seepage bogs, Atlantic white-cedar swamps, pond pine woodlands, and sea-level fens. Geomorphically, these communities can be associated with high water tables along small streams, as well as places where seepage saturates the substrate in large peat-filled Carolina bays; or they form as extensive peat domes in the flat landscape of the outer Coastal Plain. Despite being wetlands, nearly all these communities are shaped by fire—frequent, low-intensity burns in some places, and less frequent but high-intensity (stand-replacing) burns in others. When trees are present, they are wetland-adapted species, including pocosin pine (*Pinus serotina*), Atlantic white-cedar (*Chamaecyparis thyoides*), and the bays: sweetbay magnolia (*Magnolia virginiana*), swamp redbay (*Persea palustris*), and, south of Virginia, loblolly bay (*Gordonia lasianthus*). Bog-adapted shrubs, especially heaths (Ericaceae) and hollies (*Ilex*), can be dense.

Seasonal ponds. This natural community occurs in natural ponds with seasonally determined drawdown water regimes. These sites are most common in the Coastal Plain, but also occur in the other physiographic provinces. With a water table that fluctuates but is generally at its highest in winter, subsequently lowering through the growing season, the sloping margins (like a very shallow bowl) are gradually exposed, resulting in a succession of annual and perennial grasses, sedges, and wildflowers. Such vegetation patterns vary according to geography of each pond and its annual drawdown pattern. Upper margins can be rarely flooded (and even dry), while the center of the pond may be permanently or semi-permanently flooded (though many ponds do not retain water in all or even any years), resulting in concentric vegetation zones. These seasonal ponds are seen in the Coastal Plain from New Jersey to Georgia, sometimes occupying geomorphic features referred to as Carolina bays or Delmarva bays, or (northward) in glacial freeze-thaw basins called pingos. In the Coastal Plain and elsewhere, the ponds also can originate in the collapse and subsidence of underlying carbonate rocks (limestone or dolomite)—for instance, karst ponds or dolines—or simply by differential erosion of rock near the surface. When embedded in a larger matrix of fire-maintained natural communities, as most ponds in the Coastal Plain are, these communities burn periodically when water tables are low—the late-summer fire season. In addition to hosting diverse and interesting flora (expressed differently each year, so visits in successive years can yield very different results!), these natural communities are important amphibian breeding habitats. Their seasonal hydrology usually prevents the establishment of predatory fish populations, allowing amphibians to lay eggs in late winter, which will hatch as larvae prior to pond drawdown.

Bottomland forests and swamps. Rivers, streams, and their associated floodplains make up a substantial proportion of the land area of the Coastal Plain. These natural communities are riparian and affected by overland flooding from the associated stream, though the most elevated areas in the floodplain (ironically, often the natural levee nearest the river) may flood quite infrequently and for very short durations.

Seasonal pond, Florida panhandle. FG

Most of the floodplain, however, experiences wetland hydrologies varying from temporary flooding (occasional flooding of short durations generated by rain events), through seasonally flooded (swamps flooded for lengthy periods, especially in winter), to semi-permanently flooded. Larger rivers tend to have mosaics of the different hydrologies, while smaller streams have smaller and less complex floodplains, often lacking areas with any hydrology wetter than temporarily flooded. Shorter hydroperiod areas tend to be dominated by a diversity of mainly deciduous hardwood trees, especially oaks but also American sugarberry (*Celtis laevigata*), American sycamore (*Platanus occidentalis*), and river birch (*Betula nigra*), and often lush and diverse herbaceous layers. These areas are referred to as bottomland hardwood forests. Areas with seasonal or longer hydroperiods tend to be dominated by gums or tupelos (*Nyssa aquatica, N. biflora, N. ogeche*) or bald-cypresses (*Taxodium distichum, T. ascendens*) and have few herbaceous species. These are referred to as swamp forests. Two major subsets of bottomland hardwood forest and swamp forest natural communities relate to the source and chemistry of the water source: blackwater and brownwater.

Blackwater bottomland forests and swamps occur along rivers and streams with their headwaters in the Coastal Plain, and with extensive areas of Coastal Plain bogs and pocosins supplying acidic waters stained to tea or coffee color with tannins and humic acids. Characteristic trees include swamp tupelo (*Nyssa biflora*), swamp redbay (*Persea palustris*), and swamp red maple (*Acer rubrum* var. *trilobum*). Trees, shrubs, and vines are often evergreen, with many heaths (Ericaceae), often an abundance of

Bottomland swamp forest, Congaree National Park, Richland County, SC. AMC

blaspheme-vine (*Smilax laurifolia*), and with considerable overlap of composition with Coastal Plain bogs and pocosins.

Brownwater bottomland forests and swamps occur along rivers and streams with their headwaters in the more western, "hard rock" provinces of the Piedmont and Mountains. These rivers carry more sediment and less organic acid, and deposit the sediment in their floodplains, creating moderately to very rich soils. The flora is more deciduous, less heath-prominent, and less "boggy." Typical tree species include swamp laurel oak (*Quercus laurifolia*), overcup oak (*Q. lyrata*), and green ash (*Fraxinus pennsylvanica*). In less deeply and frequently flooded parts of the floodplain, herbs, including many sedges (*Carex*), can be diverse and dense.

Mesic hardwood and dry-mesic oak forests (hammocks). Mesic hardwood forests are characterized by a diversity of hardwood species, typically including American holly (*Ilex opaca*), tulip tree (*Liriodendron tulipifera*), maples (*Acer*), and the more moisture-loving oaks, such as swamp chestnut oak (*Quercus michauxii*). Dry-mesic oak forests are more obviously oak-dominated, with a broader set of oaks, including black oak (*Q. velutina*), southern red oak (*Q. falcata*), and post oak (*Q. stellata*). In the Coastal Plain, these upland hardwood forests are common only in the Delmarva, giving way in New Jersey and south of the James River in Virginia to fire-maintained, acidic pine-dominated natural communities. In these pineland landscapes, mesic hardwood and dry-mesic oak forests are less typical and were limited in the natural landscape to fire-protected steep slopes along rivers, and stream and upland "islands" in bottomland hardwood forests and swamps. Farther south, fire-protected hardwood and oak forests are often termed "hammocks." With general fire suppression and fragmentation of the landscape by intensive human uses, areas in the Carolinas and Georgia that were formerly pinelands (longleaf pine sandhills or pine savannas) have succeeded to hardwood dominance, and are particularly likely to be dominated by sand laurel oak (*Q. hemisphaerica*) and/or water oak (*Q. nigra*). Where natural mesic hardwood forests and dry-mesic oak forests occur in the Coastal Plain, they tend to have wildflowers similar to those found in similar habitats farther inland.

Coquina, marl, sandstone, and shell exposures. While the Coastal Plain consists largely of unconsolidated sediments, there are small areas of poorly to strongly consolidated limestone or sandstone that support specialized natural communities. Glade-like communities occur on flat exposures of sandstone (Altamaha grit) in the Coastal Plain of Georgia. A variety of unusual situations produce specialized calcareous natural communities and habitat for unusual calcium-loving wildflowers; these include vertical exposures of calcareous rock along streams in Georgia, South Carolina, and southeastern North Carolina, ravines cut into marl and shell hash deposits in Virginia, and Native American–deposited shell mounds associated with islands in tidal marshes in southeastern North Carolina, South Carolina, and Georgia. These calcareous sites support a specialized flora, including Venus'-hair fern (*Adiantum capillus-veneris*) and other lime-loving ferns, as well as some species that are more characteristic of Piedmont or Mountain areas, such as eastern columbine (*Aquilegia canadensis*).

Limestone exposure, Hale County, AL. AMC

Altamaha grit glade, Broxton Rocks Nature Conservancy Preserve, Coffee County, GA. AMC

The Piedmont

The Piedmont is the easternmost of the inland "hard rock" provinces and runs the full length of our region, from northern New Jersey to west-central Georgia. It is characterized by a gently rolling landscape of low elevations and low to moderate relief (the variation from valley bottoms to hilltops is usually a few hundred feet or less). Greater relief occurs in the western end of the province in the form of outlying foothills of the Blue Ridge. The Piedmont is geologically old and complex, with an extreme diversity of rocks—metamorphic and igneous rocks of all chemistries (felsic, mafic, and ultramafic) and sedimentary rocks also of all chemistries and textures (limestones, shales, sandstones). This geologic diversity translates, through weathering and soil-forming processes, to a corresponding diversity of soils, natural communities, and wildflowers. The Piedmont is the driest province in our region, lacking the elevation-induced precipitation of the Mountain province and the thunderstorms and hurricanes of the Coastal Plain; nevertheless, it experiences relatively frequent rainfall throughout the year. Although fire historically occurred with less frequency here than in the Coastal Plain, it remained an important force shaping upland communities.

Dry-mesic oak forests. Dry-mesic oak forests form the matrix in the dissected, low-relief landscape of the Piedmont, occupying middle to upper slopes and ridges across the region. In felsic or acidic landscapes, which cover most of the Piedmont, characteristic and dominant tree species include white oak (*Quercus alba*), northern red oak (*Q. rubra*), and mockernut hickory (*Carya tomentosa*). The driest areas support a more dry- and fire-adapted canopy, with oaks such as post oak (*Q. stellata*) and blackjack oak (*Q. marilandica*) more prevalent. A distinctive subcanopy is typically present, including trees such as flowering dogwood (*Cornus florida*), sourwood (*Oxydendrum arboreum*), and black gum (*Nyssa sylvatica*). Dry-mesic oak forests usually have a ground layer of scattered heath (Ericaceae) shrubs and sparse wildflowers. In mafic or calcareous landscapes, composition is relatively similar, but other canopy and subcanopy trees may be present, for example, southern shagbark hickory (*Carya carolinae-septentrionalis*) in the Carolinas and Georgia. Viburnums may be more important in the understory, and wildflowers may be more abundant and diverse. Historically, and especially in southern parts of the region, dry-mesic oak forests experienced occasional fire and were, therefore, open-canopied, minimally shrubby, and with a diverse ground layer of grasses and wildflowers. Few examples of this natural community type are managed with fire today, but the sun-loving flora once characteristic of these forests can now be found as relicts on road banks and powerline rights-of-way, where periodic bush-hogging partially simulates the effects of burning.

Mesic hardwood forests. Downslope from dry-mesic oak forests are mesic hardwood forests, found on lower, moist slopes and streamside flats in headwater areas where flooding is very rare or absent. While oaks (especially the moisture-loving species) may be present, the canopy is dominated by a more diverse set of hardwoods: American beech (*Fagus grandifolia*), tulip tree (*Liriodendron tulipifera*), American holly (*Ilex opaca*), sugar maples (*Acer saccharum* northward, *A. floridanum* and *A. leucoderme* southward). Wildflowers are often diverse

Mesic hardwood forest, Cobb County, GA. AMC

and lush, especially over mafic or calcareous rocks, with many spring-blooming species rivaling the spectacular early spring wildflower displays of rich cove forests in the mountains.

Bottomland hardwood forests. Flowing through the Piedmont's matrix of dry-mesic oak forests and mesic hardwood forests are rivers and streams that drain the Piedmont toward the Atlantic Ocean (or, in the western half of Georgia, the Gulf of Mexico). These natural communities are similar to the brownwater bottomland forests and swamps of the Coastal Plain, but they have shorter flooding regimes, including areas only rarely and occasionally flooded for a few days or less (temporarily flooded). Soils are often rich and deep, replenished by flood deposits, and some areas have showy and diverse wildflower displays in the early spring before trees have fully leafed out.

Rock outcrops. Because the Piedmont is a relatively old landscape with a substantial history of erosion, and it has a humid climate and mostly forested landscape, outcrops of exposed rock are relatively rare, primarily found along stream and river bluffs. Crevices and shallow soil edges or islands on these outcrops often support specialized floras adapted to the lack of competition. These communities vary tremendously, based on the chemistry of the rock and the soil developed from it (pH can range from 3 on quartzite to 8 on limestone), as well as its exposure (sun or shade), shape and geometry, and geographic location within the region.

Granite flatrocks and domes. Specialized outcrop communities found only in the Piedmont. Where granite, granite-like rocks, or metamorphosed granites (granitic gneisses) are exposed in the Piedmont,

Piedmont bottomland hardwood forest, White Oak Creek, Coweta County, GA. AMC

Granite flatrock, Putnam County, GA. AMC

they tend to form either flat, pavement-like exposures or sloping domes with few cracks. This form results from spalling, the unique way in which granite weathers. These rock exposures range from an acre or two to hundreds or thousands of acres. From south-central Virginia, through the Carolinas to Georgia and (just outside our area) east-central Alabama, granite flatrocks and domes support several dozen plant species that are limited to this natural community and have a variety of specializations for growing in thin soil mats with seasonal moisture. This natural community type reaches its best development in and around Atlanta, where it can be observed in well-known parks, including Stone Mountain, Arabia Mountain, and Panola Mountain.

Mafic barrens, glades, and prairies. Scattered throughout the Piedmont are barrens, glades, and prairies developed on mafic or ultramafic rock types, such as serpentine, gabbro, or diabase. These rocks weather to clayey soils with chemistry and texture issues that make them challenging for plant growth, leading to specialized natural communities with a very open to somewhat open structure (trees few and stunted). This open structure is often influenced (at least historically) by fire regimes that help prevent dominance by trees and shrubs. These sites have little or no exposed rock, but the shallow and challenging soils support diverse and interesting natural communities, featuring many sun-loving species of wildflowers and grasses. A few of these are endemics, but most are disjunct species, more characteristic of grasslands to the west of our area, including midwestern and Great Plains prairies, barrens, and glades. Some of these species are too rare to be

Piedmont depression pond, Bartow County, GA. AMC

included in this guide, but many others, especially the more common sun-loving wildflowers, are included. This is a very heterogeneous group of natural communities, varying by rock type and geographic location, but including serpentine barrens along the Pennsylvania/Maryland border and in Georgia, diabase barrens and glades in central North Carolina, and gabbro barrens in north-central South Carolina.

Bogs, seeps, and depression ponds. Even rarer than in the Mountains, bogs and seeps are small features in the mature landscape of the Piedmont. As wetland areas with saturated hydrology, they support a group of species that would otherwise be absent from the Piedmont, including orchids (Orchidaceae) and pitcherplants (*Sarracenia*). Depression ponds, which have a seasonally ponded water regime, also provide unique habitats in the Piedmont; they are often dominated by willow oak (*Quercus phellos*) and provide important amphibian breeding habitat.

The Mountains: Blue Ridge, Ridge and Valley, and Appalachian Plateaus

The Blue Ridge physiographic province extends from southern Pennsylvania to northern Georgia and encompasses the highest elevations in eastern North America. Peaks rise to over 4500 feet elevation in southwestern Virginia and western North Carolina to northeastern Georgia. The greatest concentration of high peaks is in southwestern North Carolina, in the ranges of the Great Smoky Mountains and the Great Balsams. The topographic diversity of this province creates great variations in climate, with cool summits supporting natural communities and wildflowers reminiscent of New England, and elevation-induced precipitation creating hyper-humid gorges and waterfalls populated with relict flora of both boreal and tropical affinities. Northward (especially north of Shenandoah National Park in Virginia), the Blue Ridge gradually narrows to a single and lower elevation ridge and is less distinct from the Piedmont in its natural communities and wildflowers. Like the Piedmont, the Blue Ridge's diversity of rock types reflects its ancient and complicated geologic history and includes nearly the full range of possible rocks and derived soils. The steep, rugged terrain of the Blue Ridge, especially in the broader, more complex southern end, has helped protect the forests types and other natural communities from conversion to intensive human use. This ecoregion is one of the most intact in eastern North America.

West of the Blue Ridge and south to northwestern Georgia is the Ridge and Valley province. Geologically younger than the Piedmont and Blue Ridge, the Ridge and Valley is characterized by folded layers of sedimentary rock, with alternating ridges of sandstone and valleys of limestone or shale. Elevations are generally lower than in the Blue Ridge, though a few ridges exceed 4000 feet. Although rock type diversity is lower than in the Piedmont and Blue Ridge, stark contrasts in soils are a feature of the Ridge and Valley, with nutrient-poor and acidic soils derived from quartzitic sandstones and acid shales, and circumneutral and basic soils derived from limestone and dolomite. In eastern West Virginia, the Allegheny Front or Allegheny Mountain section (not mapped here) has the highest elevations west of the Blue Ridge (locally reaching over 4000 feet); because of its elevation and relatively northern position, it

Spruce-fir forest, Clingmans Dome, Great Smoky Mountains National Park, Sevier County, TN, and Swain County, NC. AMC

includes some of the most boreal natural communities of the Atlantic Southeast, in places like Dolly Sods, Spruce Knob, and Canaan Valley.

Like the Ridge and Valley, the Appalachian Plateaus province consists of younger, sedimentary rocks, yet differs in being flat-bedded rather than folded. This lack of folding has a profound influence on the geomorphology, topography, and landscapes in this physiographic province and its constituent ecoregions. Rather than long, narrow, parallel ridges and valleys, plus streams with trellis drainage patterns, the province consists of a dissected plateau—primarily of resistant sandstone—with dendritic gorges cut through the sandstone caprock and exposing layers of limestone, dolomite, coal, siltstone, and shale along gorge walls and slopes.

Spruce-fir forests. The dominant forested natural community type at the highest elevations in the Mountains, spruce-fir forests are the result of cooler conditions. The lower elevation limit of this type is also determined by latitude: the farther south, the higher the elevation needs to be. Conifers with pointed crowns (the better to shed snow) dominate—red spruce (*Picea rubens*), balsam fir (*Abies balsamea*, from central Virginia northward), and Fraser fir (*A. fraseri*, in southwestern Virginia, western North Carolina, and eastern Tennessee)—though hardwood species, notably yellow birch (*Betula alleghaniensis*) and American mountain-ash (*Sorbus americana*), are also present. Shrubs or herbs can predominate below the canopy, and include many species characteristic of New England or eastern Canada, as well as

Northern hardwood forest, Rich Mountains, Gilmer County, GA. AMC

High-elevation granite dome, Whiteside Mountain, Macon and Jackson Counties, NC. AMC

many Central and Southern Appalachian endemics.

Northern hardwood forests. This natural community occurs at slightly lower elevations than spruce-fir forests. Instead of dominance by conifers, it is characterized by a mixture of deciduous hardwoods, including (variable by location within our region) cherry birch (*Betula lenta*), yellow buckeye (*Aesculus flava*), and northern sugar maple (*Acer saccharum*). Northern hardwood forests show a greater diversity of shrubs and herbs than spruce-fir forests but are similar in having many of the same shrub and herbaceous species, with a similar mixture of northern species and Central/Southern Appalachian endemics.

High-elevation rocky summits. In the Blue Ridge (especially in North Carolina), high-elevation peaks often have north-facing cliffs with a very specialized flora, including many species limited to this habitat, such as cliff avens (*Geum radiatum*). In addition to supporting narrowly endemic species, this natural community retains relict northern species from the Pleistocene Ice Age, when higher-elevation areas of the Southern Blue Ridge were occupied by a tundra landscape with species we might now find in Labrador or Alaska. The rarity, intrinsic ruggedness, and restrictive conservation management of these sites limits public access.

High-elevation granite domes. High-elevation granite domes occur primarily in southwestern North Carolina (south of Asheville) and in adjacent parts of northwestern South Carolina and northeastern Georgia. They have broad sloping surfaces, which weather from granite or granite-like rocks via spalling, with soil

Grassy bald at Round Bald, Roan Mountain massif, Pisgah and Cherokee National Forests, Mitchell County, NC, and Carter County, TN. AMC

Heath bald, Craggy Pinnacle and Craggy Gardens, Blue Ridge Parkway and Pisgah National Forest, Buncombe County, NC. AMC

mats and a distinctive flora often dominated by twisted-hair spikemoss (*Selaginella tortipila*), with other annual and perennial wildflowers.

Grassy balds. Some of the most scenic and popular areas in the Southern Appalachians are the grassy bald natural communities, best represented in the Roan Mountain massif area of North Carolina and Tennessee. Though they are not true alpine grasslands (found above timberline), these natural communities nevertheless support some northern alpine species with distributions centered in arctic and alpine areas of North America, as well as characteristic species of the Southern Appalachians. Dominated by grasses and sedges, grassy balds also support a range of sun-loving plants otherwise scarce in the wooded landscape of the Blue Ridge.

Heath balds. Heath balds are treeless (or nearly so) habitats on high-elevation ridgelines and summits in the Blue Ridge. They reach their most classic and most extensive development in Great Smoky Mountains National Park. Heath balds are dominated by shrubs of the Ericaceae, such as Catawba rhododendron (*Rhododendron catawbiense*), mountain andromeda (*Pieris floribunda*), and mountain fetterbush (*Eubotrys recurvus*). Herbaceous species are uncommon.

Montane oak forests. Montane oak forests can be considered the matrix (or dominant) forest type in the Mountain region, in that they occupy much greater acreage than other natural communities. They also have a more diverse flora, depending on geography, elevation, slope, rockiness, geologic substrate, and recentness of fire. Tree species vary, with northern red oak (*Quercus rubra*) dominating at the highest elevations (up to 5000 feet in the southern portions of the Mountains, lower northward). Hardwoods other than oaks can be important, including pignut hickory (*Carya glabra*), sand hickory (*C. pallida*), and red hickory (*C. ovalis*). On calcareous substrates, such as limestone, calcareous shale/siltstone, and dolomite, mainly in the Ridge and Valley and Appalachian Plateaus, other species, especially chinquapin oak (*Q. muehlenbergii*) may be prominent or dominant. These communities can have shrubby, grassy, sedgy, ferny, or herbaceous ground layers and can be good sites for seeing a diversity of wildflower species. They occur in many mountain natural areas and parks, such as along extensive sections of the Skyline Drive and Blue Ridge Parkway.

Pine-oak/heath woodlands. Pine-oak/heath woodlands occur on drier, more extreme sites than montane oak forests, especially at low to middle elevations and on dry ridges. Because of their position in the landscape, they are subject to hot, stand-replacing fires. Dominant trees tend to be a mixture of pines and oaks, including Table Mountain pine (*Pinus pungens*), shortleaf pine (*P. echinata*), rock chestnut oak (*Quercus montana*), and scarlet oak (*Q. coccinea*). Shrub species are heaths, such as mountain laurel (*Kalmia latifolia*), and bear oak (*Q. ilicifolia*). The usual shrubbiness of these communities limits the diversity and cover of wildflowers, though they do hold some unique species unlikely to be found in other habitats.

Rich cove forests. Rich cove forests occur in coves (downslope areas surrounded on

Rich cove over periglacial boulderfield, Sosebee Cove, Chattahoochee National Forest, Union County, GA. AMC

Hurricane Creek Bog, Upper Nantahala River, Nantahala National Forest, Macon County, NC. AMC

three sides by slopes or ridges) and especially over intermediate, mafic, or calcareous substrates. The canopy is dominated by species such as cherry birch (*Betula lenta*), yellow buckeye (*Aesculus flava*), and northern sugar maple (*Acer saccharum*). The herbaceous layer is usually lush and diverse, with species such as doll's-eyes (*Actaea pachypoda*), bloodroot (*Sanguinaria canadensis*), Canada violet (*Viola canadensis*), and many others. These are typically considered some of the premier wildflower areas in the Atlantic Southeast.

Acid cove forests. These natural communities occur in landforms similar to those of rich cove forests (along streams and with slopes above them in three directions) but tend to be on more acidic geology and with steeper (more ravine-like) slopes. Canopy composition is similar, but there is greater birch dominance, and eastern hemlock (*Tsuga canadensis*) is often present, sometimes even co-dominant. A dense heath shrub layer is typical; great rhododendron (*Rhododendron maximum*) and mountain dog-hobble (*Leucothoe fontanesiana*) are characteristic dominant species. Prized and interesting wildflowers in these habitats include Oconee bells (*Shortia galacifolia*) and largeflower heartleaf (*Hexastylis shuttleworthii*).

Bogs, fens, and seeps. These communities (especially well-developed bogs and fens) are rare and of small extent in the Mountains. Seeps are more common but always small. These saturated wetlands are largely groundwater-fed (even when occurring on the edges of floodplains) and have a distinctive flora adapted to saturated hydrology. Most have peat moss (*Sphagnum*), often with extensive coverage. Orchids, heath shrubs, and carnivorous plants are

Serpentine barren at Buck Creek, Nantahala National Forest, Clay County, NC. AMC

characteristic and common. While these communities have always been rare in the landscape, they have also been substantially reduced in extent by accidental (roads affecting hydrology) and deliberate (ditching, draining, and filling) impacts stemming from human uses of the landscape matrix around them.

Rock outcrops. Two specialized types of rock outcrops, high-elevation rocky summits and high-elevation granite domes, were discussed earlier. This category is something of a catch-all for other rock outcrop communities in the Mountains, occurring on various rock types, often of small extent, and with a less distinctive flora. Different rock types, shade or sun, and geographical location within our region all determine the plants present, often including species not present in other habitats in the local area. Rock outcrops are always worth exploring (cautiously!) for plants not found in deeper soils away from exposed rock.

Glades, barrens, and prairies. In the Mountains, glades, barrens, and prairies historically occurred on thin soil areas, especially over calcareous rocks in the Ridge and Valley, but also on serpentine or other ultramafic rocks and other rock types. These communities have few trees or at least open canopies, allowing a diversity of sun-loving plants to thrive. Many were also kept open and sunny by periodic fire in the past. Rare communities in the modern landscape, these offer excellent opportunities to see a diversity of wildflower species, including some species not likely to be encountered in other habitats.

Spray cliffs. These natural communities are a kind of hybrid of a rock outcrop and a bog: a vertical, saturated wetland! Spray and high humidity created by a waterfall ensure

Spray cliff, Dry Falls of the Cullasaja River, Nantahala National Forest, Macon County, NC. AMC

near-constant moisture of the rock surfaces and soil-filled crevices and ledges around the waterfall. The high humidity also acts as a temperature buffer, so spray cliffs rarely freeze or get excessively hot, providing microhabitats that support an odd mixture of plants with tropical and boreal affinities. The greatest development and frequency of these communities is near the triple-corner of Georgia, South Carolina, and North Carolina, where the highest annual rainfall amounts in eastern North America are recorded. Waterfalls are abundant along the tributaries and main watercourses of the Toxaway, Horsepasture, Thompson, Eastatoe, Chattooga, and Cullasaja Rivers.

Montane riparian forests. Similar to the bottomland hardwood forests of the Piedmont, montane riparian forests occur in riverine corridors in the Mountains. Because they are at low elevations and connect directly into lower-elevation areas (for instance, the Piedmont to the east), montane riparian forests have floras similar to Piedmont bottomland hardwood forests and often have equally rich wildflower displays.

Human-dominated Habitats

Much of the land area of our region, and where most of us spend most of our time, has been converted from the natural communities present centuries ago to intensive human uses: residential neighborhoods, shopping centers, manufacturing, agriculture, pine plantations, roads and highways. These human-dominated habitats have their own distinctive sets of plants able to take advantage of the particular growing conditions. Such habitats are more influenced by human activity than they are by the geographic characteristics that determine natural communities. We have chosen, therefore, to discuss them here as a group, without reference to physiographic province. That is not to say, however, that a pasture on limestone in the Ridge and Valley of West Virginia will have the same plants as a pasture on Coastal Plain sand in eastern South Carolina.

Urban areas. Cities may seem like the ultimate "no wildflower" place; yet if you look, you will find plants growing uncultivated in even the most urban situations—in cracks in sidewalks, at the bases of street trees, and as "weeds" in landscaped areas. (Cultivated plants are not included in this guide, but some of the weeds that colonize flower beds and other landscaped areas are). Many of the non-cultivated plants that grow in urban settings are now widely, even globally, distributed "weeds"; a few species might even be findable in Washington, London, Tokyo, Cape Town, Buenos Aires, and Sydney. The homelands of these plants are similarly diverse, including natives of our area but especially plants that co-adapted with human cities in Europe and Asia.

Suburban woodlands. As wildflower habitat, suburban areas are something of a transition. One can expect some native species characteristic of the natural landscape that preceded land conversion, as well as alien, introduced species. Horticultural species (grown in landscaped areas) are especially prone to naturalizing in suburban areas—that is, to start reproducing and spreading spontaneously, in some cases becoming problematic invasive species. Many of these species are treated in this guide; others may be familiar to the gardener or home improvement store shopper. The process of naturalization of horticultural species in semi-natural and remnant natural areas in our region is ongoing and probably accelerating, raising concern that we may be headed toward a homogenized worldwide temperate flora.

Roadsides and rights-of-way. Rural and suburban roadsides and utility corridors (powerline rights-of-way) are often very interesting plant habitats. Though they may seem to be strongly altered habitats maintained for human use by mowing and herbicides, under current management many of them support a relict flora of sun-loving native plants that were once more common and widespread in landscapes with regular canopy-opening natural fires.

Cropped fields and pastures. Cropped fields and pastures support a set of plants adapted to the conditions on such sites. They vary across the region, based on soils and geography, but in general, plants of crop fields are "weeds" that are adapted to the annual plowing and exposure of fresh bare soil. Many are European species, but native eastern North American weeds can also be common. Pasture plants are a little different, in that they experience a different disturbance regime—primarily herbivory by grazing animals. Pastured animals essentially select what they like to eat and avoid, as much as possible, plants that are unpalatable because of texture (barbs or spines), low quality, or bitter/poisonous compounds. When grazed too intensively, pastures can become overrun by monocultures of grazing-adapted plants.

Pondshores and ditches. Artificial ponds, lakes, ditches, and other water bodies provide accessible habitat for wetland plants. Plants tolerant of variable water levels, especially weedy species, will thrive in amphibious or seasonally ponded situations.

EXPLORING FOR WILDFLOWERS

Where can you go to see wild plants, not those growing in a garden and planted and tended by people? Almost anywhere! Backyards, vacant lots, pastures, old fields, roadsides, pavement cracks—all are places where native and naturalized plants grow and thrive. Even so-called weeds are fun to identify and learn about, with their interesting backstories that involve human history and culture and changes to the biosphere around us.

Most people will use this book to identify plants in "natural areas"—forests and other habitats that have vegetation more or less similar to what would have been seen in our region a few hundred years ago. If you do not own such land, you will need to seek out places to explore.

Parks, game lands, and nature preserves owned and managed by land trusts usually allow public access but with specific rules, times, and conditions necessary for the safe and effective management of the property. Please respect these constraints so as not to endanger yourself, the resources being protected, the land management activities (such as prescribed burning) undertaken by the manager, or future access by you and others.

For a region as large as we cover in this field guide, it is not practical to provide many specific suggestions, but the information below will help the neophyte. We suspect many of you already have your favorite places to botanize!

Private Land

Most of the natural area remaining in the Atlantic Southeast region is in private land, which you do not have the right to access without landowner permission. *Please respect landowner rights and do not botanize where you do not have permission to be.*

National Park Service Land

The National Park Service (NPS) manages over 84 million acres nationwide, and while the largest units and bulk of the acreage is in the western United States (especially Alaska), significant units exist in the Atlantic Southeast. Units managed by the National Park Service offer great opportunities for botanizing. In addition to national parks, the NPS manages areas with many other names, including national seashores, national scenic trails, parkways, national monuments, national historic sites, national military parks, and others. Some of the largest and best-known NPS units in our region provide prime opportunities for botanical exploration: Shenandoah National Park (VA), Great Smoky Mountains National Park (NC and TN), Blue Ridge Parkway (VA and NC), and the New Jersey Pinelands National Reserve (NJ). Even NPS units with a primary purpose of interpreting historic events (like national battlefields) often have diverse habitats available for botanizing.

U.S. Fish and Wildlife Service Refuges

The U.S. Fish and Wildlife Service (USFWS) manages over 150 million acres nationwide, including extensive areas from New Jersey to Georgia. The bulk of these lands are coastal, and include many areas that receive extensive visitation for hunting and birding; but they also offer great opportunities for botanizing and nature observation. Note that these often have areas closed to public access, at least in particular seasons to prevent disturbing wildlife species at sensitive times of the year.

National Forests of the U.S. Forest Service

The U.S. Forest Service (USFS) manages over 192 million acres of land nationwide. In our region, national forests provide prime opportunities for observing wildflowers. From north to south, the national forest units are Monongahela (WV); George Washington and Jefferson (VA); Pisgah, Nantahala, Uwharrie, and Croatan (NC); Francis Marion and Sumter (SC); and Chattahoochee and Oconee (GA).

State Park Agencies

The states covered by this guide each have a state park system, with missions that include biodiversity conservation, historic preservation, education, and outdoor recreation. Information about park units, visitation, etc., can be obtained from the agency.

State Wildlife Resource (Fish and Game) Agencies

All the states covered by this guide have agencies that manage lands for wildlife, often with a focus on hunting and fishing. These lands often represent excellent botanizing opportunities, and non-hunting recreational uses are increasingly promoted by these agencies as a way to broaden their constituency. Information about gameland units and visitation should be obtained from the agency.

Other State Conservation Agencies

The states in our region have additional conservation agencies that own and manage lands for conservation purposes. Examples include North Carolina Plant Conservation Preserves, South Carolina Heritage Preserves, Virginia Natural Area Preserves, and New Jersey Forest Service lands. Consult the managing agency directly or online to determine the locations and features of their managed lands and their visitation policies.

Land Trust and Private Conservation Preserves

The land trust movement has grown tremendously in recent decades, and many international, national, and local non-governmental organizations (NGOs) have acquired and now manage natural areas for a variety of purposes, including conservation, public open space, and recreation. The Nature Conservancy has lands throughout the Atlantic Southeast, while hundreds of other NGOs operate in a particular state, region, or county. Consult the managing organization directly or online to determine the locations and features of their managed lands and their visitation policies.

Roadside Rights-of-Way

Roadside areas in rural and suburban parts of our region can be very fruitful for viewing wildflowers, especially those requiring sunny habitats. Maintenance of these areas by mowing and bush-hogging mimics the periodic fires that maintained open woodlands, savannas, and even prairies in our region. Roadside habitats have some obvious positive and negative features for wildflower-viewing: they are readily accessible by car (though parking may be a challenge) but also dangerous because of proximity to traffic. Be aware, as well, that private land adjoining a roadside may begin just a few yards from the roadway edge. Also, be aware that other motorists or law enforcement may stop to ask what you are doing or if you need assistance.

HOW TO USE THIS BOOK

Plant descriptions in this guide are organized by flower color. It is important to note here that flower color can be quite subjective: we don't all see colors in the same way, and in nature, there are many gradations of shade and tone that are difficult to encompass with basic color names. For that reason we suggest flexibility when trying to determine which color category your specimen falls into. For instance, the Red Flowers chapter includes species whose flowers may be perceived as pink, scarlet, or even reddish-purple. But if the wildflower you are trying to identify is purplish, you may want to also check in the Blue Flowers chapter, which covers many shades of blue as well as bluish-purple. Also keep in mind that some flowers change from their initial bloom color as they mature. Some whitish flowers, for instance, may start out greenish-white and mature to mostly white, while other may have more green than white. Thus, you may need to check in both the White Flowers and Green Flowers chapters.

Flipping through a chapter searching for a photo and descriptive text that matches your plant is one way of using this guide, but that is a time-consuming approach. We have provided an alternative. A Key to Wildflowers, beginning on page 48, begins with flower color and then leads you through some mostly simple choices regarding flower and leaf characteristics. In combination, your selection of the leaf and flower characteristics matching the plant you are identifying will lead you to a book section with plants that are similar to one another—that is, possess similar characteristics. Your selection may lead you to a single wildflower species, to several alternatives, or (at most) to a few dozen. Most of the time, comparing your plant to the possibilities will lead you to a tentative identification. You can come to greater confidence about your choice by comparing your plant to the listed description, habitats, geographic location, and time of bloom. If your plant does not seem to fit any of the possibilities, which can happen on occasion, it may be an odd example (plants vary!), or you may need to reconsider your choices of characteristics that led you to a particular section of the book: is there anything you may have misinterpreted, especially features that may be ambiguous? Finally, you could have a wildflower species that we did not include in this guide. The flora of the Atlantic Southeast region is diverse, and many of the plants here identified have relatives (in the same genus) that are similar. In some cases, reference to complete and more technical manuals (see "Resources for Learning More") is the only way to be really certain of the identification of your plant to the species level.

How to Identify a Plant

The procedure for observing a plant's characteristics is similar for all types of plants—woody, herbaceous, grass, fern—but here we give a brief overview of what to look for when identifying herbaceous wildflower species. We have tried to use as few technical terms as possible but have also provided a glossary at the end of the book, as well as a visual glossary on the endpapers inside the front and back covers.

A first thing to consider is overall appearance, often called the plant's habit. Is the growth form erect, leaning or ascending, sprawling, clambering? Does it grow singly, in clumps, in extensive colonies or mats? Without excessively disturbing the plant, you might be able to note whether it arises from a bulb, rhizome, or taproot. You might also note whether there are runners/stolons.

Next examine the stems: are they stiff or weak, are they leafy or naked, do they branch or not? Does stem color depart from "green," or are there woody sections or even shredding bark? There may be ridges, angles, spines, and various types of hairs or glands.

The next step is to look at leaves—their arrangement on the stem (or there may be a basal rosette only); their stalks (petioles) and stipules (if any); their shape, size, and any division into segments (also notice the arrangement of those segments); margins and texture; and not least, surface embellishments—hairs, glands, vein patterns, etc. Note that plants that have their largest and most prominent leaves basal, but which nevertheless have reduced leaves (not tiny bracts) up the stem, are treated in the Key to Wildflowers according to the arrangement of the leaves on the stem: alternate, opposite, or whorled. In other words, even if most of the leaves are basal, if there are a few well-developed leaves on the stem, we have placed the plant in the section based on the arrangement of leaves on the stem. Finally, examine the flowers and determine if symmetry is radial or bilateral (see the glossary). Take special note if the "flower" seems to be radial but is a composite of many tiny flowers (florets) organized into a kind of "head." Composite flowers (members of the aster family) often have ray florets that can be mistaken for simple petals, but usually these florets, each with a single "petal," encircle a center disk of tubular florets. Next, how are flowers or heads arranged on the plant? Compare with the several inflorescence types (including composite heads) illustrated in the endpapers of this book. Count the number of petals and sepals, if possible, and note if either of these are missing. Observe shape of these parts as well as number and shape of the reproductive parts—stamens and pistil. Color of petals/tepals is important (and sometimes ambiguous, as just outlined) but so may be markings on petals, or the texture, surface, and embellishments of any flower part. If fruit are present, try to characterize these, again using the endpapers. A hand lens with 10× magnification is very useful for closely examining hairs or other embellishments on leaves, stems, and flower parts. Remember that flower size (width or length) may vary within a species and even on an individual plant. Similarly, leaf size can vary a great deal. Sizes given in the descriptions should not be taken as absolute.

Another important observation to make is of the plant's habitat. Is it growing in a forest/woodland or out in the open? Does the site show a lot of human disturbance or does it seem fairly natural? Do soils seem wet or dry, and is there anything that suggests the presence of especially rich (fertile) soils? Observe rocks in the vicinity. If the plant is in a floodplain or a wetland, that is significant, too. Clues about habitat can come from observing what other plants are present. Knowing the physiographic region and habitat you are in will help you narrow the possibilities as you try to identify a wildflower. (If you haven't yet read the earlier section on climate, geography, and natural communities, this would be a good time to do so.) We give a description of habitat at the beginning of every plant profile in the color chapters, and an accompanying map indicates which physiographic regions and states that species is currently known from.

How to Use the Key

Step 1. Determine flower color: white, yellow, red, blue, orange, green, brown. Remember that some flowers have ambiguous coloration, or they may have more than one color present. If the color is ambiguous between two categories, you may need to try each, sequentially. If several colors are present in the flower, the plant is placed by the predominant or most obvious color.

Step 2. Determine flower symmetry: bilateral, radial, composite heads, petals indistinguishable. The latter category is used for plants that do not have petals or petal-like colored sepals, or have very small floral parts not readily distinguishable with the naked eye (this is somewhat subjective; in some cases you may need to consider two possible answers).

Step 3. Determine number of petals (radial flowers only): 2, 3, 4, 5, 6, 7 or more. For flowers with undifferentiated sepals and petals (tepals), the count should be based on number of tepals.

Step 4. Determine leaf type: simple, deeply divided. "Deeply divided" refers to leaves with either true leaflets (separate leaflets not connected by flattened leaf tissue), or lobes/segments that are divided more than halfway to the base of the leaf (palmately divided leaves), or more than halfway to the midrib (pinnately divided leaves), or leaves that are finely divided into many linear or elongate parts.

Step 5. Determine leaf arrangement: alternate, opposite, whorled, basal, absent/scalelike/needlelike. The last category includes plants that do not have any larger leaves. Remember that plants with most leaves basal are keyed as alternate or opposite if they have any well-developed leaves on the stem.

Step 6. Determine leaf margin: entire, toothed or lobed. Entire leaves may have hairs (cilia) along the margin but do not have actual teeth on the leaf tissue itself. Teeth can be quite small (less than 1/16 of an inch) on the leaves of some plants. Larger or more deeply cut teeth can grade into lobes, but remember that when the lobes are really well developed, with cuts more than halfway to the midrib or base of the leaf, the leaf is considered deeply divided (see Step 4).

Let's walk through an example. Making your way along a seepy area by a stream, you come across a 3-foot-tall plant with a terminal spike of white flowers tinged with pink at the tip. The flowers are bilaterally symmetric and tubular, opening to 2 lips. Leaves are opposite, simple and lance-shaped, with toothed margins. Here is a summary of your observations:

- Flower color: White
- Flower symmetry: Bilateral
- Petal number: [not used for bilateral flowers]
- Leaf type: Simple
- Leaf arrangement: Opposite
- Leaf margins: Toothed

Checking the Key to Wildflowers, you find the page in the White Flowers chapter where plants with these characteristics—Flowers bilateral; leaves simple, opposite, toothed or lobed—begin. In the White Flowers chapter, 13 wildflower species are described on pages under this heading (the heading is found in the page's marginal color stripe). By reading the descriptions and examining photos and maps, you conclude that what you have seen is *Chelone glabra*.

Chelone glabra. AMC

The Species Descriptions

The descriptive information for each wildflower species, in its respective color chapter, was composed to help you identify plants you might encounter in explorations of this region. In most cases there will be one photograph for each wildflower species. Photos were selected to show as many identifying characteristics as possible, with an emphasis on flowers. Occasionally you will find a second inset photo providing a closer view of some important feature. Most images were captured in the plant's natural habitat, but you will see a few that were taken in gardens or even indoors as specimens. The photo(s) will certainly give you a feel for the plant, but you will need to read the descriptions carefully as well. A map showing distribution and abundance (common vs. uncommon/rare) of each species in the Atlantic Southeast region is very useful, in that you may be able to eliminate a species as a possibility if you see that it is not known to occur where you are exploring. On the other hand, new discoveries are possible, so don't dismiss a potential identification too swiftly.

The heading of each description gives current scientific name, a recent synonym (if any, and if space allows), family name, and common name. Below that are the species' bloom months and approximate height range (length, for vines) in inches (in.) or feet (ft.). Because the Atlantic Southeast region, as defined here, covers a broad range of latitudes from north to south, one can generally assume that the earlier months in a given range of bloom months apply to the more southerly parts of the region. The entry continues with a sentence on habit, duration (annual, perennial, or biennial) and habitat, plus place of origin for non-native species; notable characteristics concerning leaves—arrangement, petioles, shape, length, divisions (if any), venation (if notable), margins (entire if not otherwise noted), thickness/texture, color (if other than green), and surface features; and a description of flower arrangement (inflorescence), color, size, shape, and details about various parts of the flower, as deemed significant. Where available, we note fruit type. At the end of the entry there may be additional brief comments about similar taxa, pollinators, traditional uses, or other interesting facts.

A Note about Plant Names

Each plant has a unique scientific name composed of at least two parts: genus and species. There can also be a third subspecies (ssp.) or variety (var.) name, though for the purposes of this guide, we have mostly merged subspecies and varieties into their main species. Plant names do change over time as a result of botanical research, so we have sometimes listed recently used synonyms to help you find information if you consult other sources. The first name listed is considered correct and current by the authors as of the time of publication of this field guide (sometimes taxonomy is in flux and for a time there is no one, uncontroversial correct name).

A common name is listed for each wildflower. Assignment of common names is notoriously inconsistent and spelling varies widely, making the choice of name a fluid and inexact exercise. Readers who are familiar with some of the wildflower species included in this guide may notice that their favorite common name is missing. Forgive these "lapses" and understand that there are no hard and fast rules governing the application of common names.

A Note about the Maps

The maps accompanying each description show that species' distribution, abundance, and native status in each combination of state and broadly defined physiographic province (Coastal Plain, Piedmont, Mountains). Map color indicates whether the species is native (purple), introduced (orange), or unknown (white) from a region. The degree of shading indicates whether a species is common (darker shading) or uncommon/rare (lighter shading). Note that a species can be native to one region and introduced in another. Maps are based on published distribution maps in other floras, amended and improved by herbarium specimens and published records.

KEY TO WILDFLOWERS

White Flowers

Flowers bilateral

Flowers radial with 2 petals

Flowers radial with 3 petals

Flowers radial with 4 petals

Flowers radial with 5 petals

Flowers radial with 6 petals

Flowers radial with 7 to many petals

Flowers composite

Flower petals indistinguishable

Yellow Flowers

Flowers bilateral

Flowers radial with 3 petals

Flowers radial with 4 petals

Flowers radial with 5 petals

Flowers radial with 6 petals

Flowers radial with 7 to many petals

Flowers composite

Flower petals indistinguishable

Red Flowers

Flowers bilateral

Flowers radial with 3 petals

Flowers radial with 4 petals

Flowers radial with 5 petals

Flowers radial with 6 petals

Flowers radial with 7 to many petals

Flowers composite

Flower petals indistinguishable

Blue Flowers

Flowers bilateral

Flowers radial with 3 petals

Flowers radial with 4 petals

Flowers radial with 5 petals

Flowers radial with 6 petals

Flowers radial with 7 to many petals

Flowers composite

Orange Flowers

Flowers bilateral

Flowers radial with 4 petals

Flowers radial with 5 petals

Flowers radial with 6 petals

Flowers composite

Green Flowers

Flowers bilateral

Flowers radial with 3 petals

Flowers radial with 4 petals

Flowers radial with 5 petals

Flowers radial with 6 petals

Flowers composite

Flower petals indistinguishable

Brown Flowers

Flowers bilateral

Flowers radial with 3 petals

Flowers radial with 5 petals

Flowers radial with 6 petals

Flower petals indistinguishable

UNDERSTANDING PLANT FAMILIES AND GENERA AS AN AID TO PLANT IDENTIFICATION

Like other living organisms, angiosperms (flowering plants) are classified in a hierarchical scheme based on degree of relationship. The most fundamental unit is the species, a group of individuals that are sufficiently genetically similar to interbreed; this degree of genetic similarity also means that individual plants of the species closely resemble one another in nearly all characteristics. Sometimes species themselves are subdivided into two or a few groupings that grow in different geographic areas or different habitats, or that have different genetic or morphologic features that in combination suggest they are "incipient species"—that is, while not separate at this time, they appear to be in the evolutionary process of splitting apart into separate species. In this book we have only rarely included or referred to this level of differentiation below the species.

Above the species level are two hierarchical ranks that provide useful information about the species included in them and that offer an excellent aid to the identification of newly encountered plants. Immediately above species rank is the genus, the importance of which is shown by its inclusion as the first part of the scientific name of any plant (or other organism). In the scientific name *Baptisia australis*, *Baptisia* is the genus, *australis* is the specific epithet, and *Baptisia australis* is the species name. Note that *australis* is not the name of a species (many different species have *australis* as a specific epithet); only in combination with the genus name does the specific epithet name a particular species.

As you become more interested in and adept at identifying wildflowers, you will find that the genus and the characteristics that hold it together, so to speak, will become more important to you. Once you have seen several *Baptisia* species, for instance, you will start noting the similarities between them, either unconsciously ("I think I'm getting a sense of what a baptisia looks like!") or consciously ("*Baptisia* has leaves with 3 leaflets or sometimes reduced to 1; the flowers are pea-like and white, cream, yellow, or blue, borne in an unbranched raceme, and form tough woody or leathery beans that often turn black"). We do not describe genera (the plural of genus) in this book; and because we have grouped plants by superficial characteristics, such as flower color, several species of a genus, though treated here, will be found in different chapters or sections. If you want to study genera, you can do so with this guide by finding examples in the index. Alternatively, more technical botanical manuals/floras will group together the species of a genus and describe the features that help distinguish that genus. Using online search engines is another way to view multiple images of the members of a genus and learn the similarities (and diversity) within the genus.

The next standard classification level above genus is family. Each family includes from one genus to more than a thousand genera (in a few very large families), but the number is usually from 2 to 20. Just as the genus brings together species that are closely related to one another by common ancestry and shared visible characteristics, the family brings together genera that are related to one another by common ancestry and that share various visible characteristics—at a broader and more general level.

As you learn to identify wildflowers, you will find that getting a sense for the characteristics of different plant families will help. Some families in particular have distinctive sets of features that are diagnostic; learning these will help to reduce the number of possibilities and hasten your path to a successful identification. For that reason, we provide here short accounts of the distinctive features, and list the constituent genera, for families represented in this guide. Here, we have organized the families into three groups that also represent (at a higher level) evolutionary relationships and morphological similarities: magnoliids, monocots, and true dicots. Within each group, families are ordered so that related families are next to or near one another, aiding in the comparison of related families, which often show similarity in features.

Magnoliids

Magnoliids encompass the earliest diverging evolutionary branches of the flowering plants. Traditionally considered dicots and having two cotyledons (seed leaves) like true dicots (now called "eudicots"), these plants differ from the eudicots in fundamental ways and show a mixture of dicot and monocot characteristics. Floral parts (sepals, petals, stamens, and carpels) typically occur in an irregular number greater than 6 but are sometimes in multiples of 3 (a monocot characteristic), as in Cabombaceae and Aristolochiaceae. The flowers are usually solitary.

Cabombaceae (Coontail Family). Aquatic plants with elliptical floating leaves and underwater parts covered with a thick, transparent layer of slime, the flowers purplish-brown with 6 tepals and many stamens and pistils. Genus: *Brasenia*

Nymphaeaceae (Water Lily Family). Aquatic plants normally rooted underwater, with large, usually floating (or emersed) leaves and large, showy, solitary flowers composed of 6 (yellow) or many (white/whitish) tepals. Genera: *Nuphar, Nymphaea*

Aristolochiaceae (Dutchman's Pipe Family). Heart-shaped leaves and brownish flowers consisting of 3 fused sepals, no petals. Genera: *Asarum, Endodeca, Hexastylis*

Saururaceae (Lizard's-tail Family). Wetland (usually temporarily or seasonally flooded) plants with alternate, heart-shaped leaves and small white flowers arrayed in a curved raceme. Genus: *Saururus*

Monocots

With very few exceptions, the monocots have their floral parts in 3s or 6s. Monocot leaves are usually narrow and elongate (somewhat to extremely longer than broad), except for some members of Alismataceae, Trilliaceae, Dioscoreaceae, Stemonaceae, and Pontederiaceae, and have parallel venation (main veins parallel to one another from base to tip of leaf).

Acoraceae (Sweetflag Family). Marsh plants with sword-like leaves. Our only genus has a yellow, cigar-shaped, spadix inflorescence held at an angle from a flattened, leaf-like stem. Genus: *Acorus*

Araceae (Arum Family). Characterized by a spadix inflorescence with a thick, unbranched axis in which are embedded numerous small flowers (green, yellow, or brown). The spadix is partially and loosely enclosed (except in *Orontium*) by a spathe (usually green or brown). Most of our genera are wetland plants, except *Arisaema*, which is unique among our monocot wildflowers in having compound leaves (3 leaflets). Genera: *Arisaema, Orontium, Peltandra, Symplocarpus*

Alismataceae (Arrowhead Family). Marsh or wetland plants with narrow to broad basal leaves and white, 3-petaled flowers borne in a branched inflorescence, the branching often in whorls of 3. Genera: *Alisma, Echinodorus, Helanthium, Sagittaria*

Tofieldiaceae (Tofieldia Family). Plants of saturated wetlands, with equitant (iris-like) basal leaves and whitish flowers composed of 6 tepals and borne in a raceme. Genera: *Pleea, Tofieldia, Triantha*

Liliaceae (Lily Family). Leaves are broad and either basal, on the stem and whorled, or on the stem and alternate. Flowers are 6-tepaled and showy (medium to large) with white, yellow, orange, or red tepals. Genera: *Clintonia, Erythronium, Lilium, Medeola, Prosartes, Streptopus*

Colchicaceae (Autumn-crocus Family). Our one genus with broad, alternate leaves on a once-forked stem. Flowers are yellow, bell-shaped, and of medium size, composed of 6 tepals, and borne terminally or axillary to the leaves. Genus: *Uvularia*

Xerophyllaceae (Turkeybeard Family). Our single species has a dense basal rosette of many, long, tough, grass-like leaves and raceme of small, white, flowers with 6 tepals. Genus: *Xerophyllum*

Heloniadaceae (Swamp-pink Family). Our single species is rare and grows in saturated wetlands; with a rosette of basal leaves and raceme of small pink flowers with 6 tepals. Genus: *Helonias*

Chionographidaceae (Devil's-bit Family). Our single species with oblong-oval leaves and a raceme of small, white to creamy flowers with 6 tepals (male or female only on an individual plant). Genus: *Chamaelirium*

Melanthiaceae (Death Camas Family). Leaves basal but often also alternate up the stem, and linear or broader (elliptical). Flowers small to medium-sized, with 6 tepals and usually white (sometimes greenish or brownish). Genera: *Amianthium, Anticlea, Melanthium, Stenanthium, Veratrum, Zigadenus*

Trilliaceae (Trillium Family). Leaves in a single whorl of 3, flowers solitary, with 3 sepals and 3 petals. Genus: *Trillium*

Asparagaceae (Asparagus Family). Our single genus with stiff linear "leaves" along an upright stem and small greenish-yellow bell-shaped flowers with 6 tepals. Genus: *Asparagus*

Ruscaceae (Lily-of-the-valley Family). Our species with elliptical leaves borne on the stem (or basal in *Convallaria*) and white or pale yellow flowers borne in small clusters in leaf axils (*Polygonatum*) or terminally in panicles or racemes (*Maianthemum, Convallaria*). Genera: *Convallaria, Maianthemum, Polygonatum*

Agavaceae (Agave Family). Plants with basal, linear leaves (broader and fleshy in *Agave*) and racemes of medium-sized flowers with 6 tepals. Genera: *Agave, Camassia, Schoenolirion*

Hyacinthaceae (Hyacinth Family). Plants with linear basal leaves and racemes of small to medium-sized flowers with 6 tepals. All our examples are planted exotics that sometimes escape. Genera: *Muscari, Ornithogalum*

Alliaceae (Onion Family). Plants from bulbs, usually with an onion odor from all parts of the plant; leaves basal and linear (and either flat or hollow) and flowers with 6 tepals and borne in an umbel. Genera: *Allium, Nothoscordum*

Amaryllidaceae (Amaryllis Family). Plants from bulbs, with linear basal leaves; flowers large, white (in the species in this guide), 6-tepaled, solitary or in an umbel. Genera: *Hymenocallis, Zephyranthes*

Iridaceae (Iris Family). Leaves equitant (oriented edgewise to the stem and each leaf tucked into a pocket-slit in the leaf below) and primarily basal, with a few alternate leaves on the stem. In *Iris*, the flower generally has a specialized structure—consisting of "falls" (often with beards), "standards," and style "arms and crests"—familiar from its use in horticulture and art (the *fleur-de-lys*). *Sisyrinchium* has smaller flowers with 6 tepals. Genera: *Iris, Sisyrinchium*

Hypoxidaceae (Yellow Stargrass Family). Our single genus has linear, ascending, basal leaves and an inflorescence with a few yellow, medium-sized flowers with 6 tepals. Genus: *Hypoxis*

Orchidaceae (Orchid Family). Leaves linear to broader; best recognized by the bilaterally symmetric flowers, typically with 1 petal modified as a broad lip (usually borne lowermost, but sometimes the reverse, so as to be uppermost), and the other 2 petals and 3 sepals usually also "petaloid." Flowers often brightly colored, and often also varicolored, though some species have single-color flowers and some orchids are drab (greenish or brownish). All our species are at least partially dependent on fungi for their nutrition, and a few are strictly so, lacking green leaves (*Corallorhiza, Hexalectris*). In the tropics, many orchid species are epiphytes, but only *Epidendrum* is epiphytic in the area covered by this guide. Genera: *Aplectrum, Arethusa, Calopogon, Cleistesiopsis, Corallorhiza, Cypripedium, Dactylorhiza, Epidendrum, Epipactis, Galearis, Goodyera, Habenaria, Hexalectris, Isotria, Liparis, Listera, Malaxis, Platanthera, Pogonia, Ponthieva, Spiranthes, Tipularia, Triphora*

Hemerocallidaceae (Daylily Family). Commonly planted (and sometimes escaped or persistent) plants with linear leaves and large brightly colored flowers with 6 tepals. Genus: *Hemerocallis*

Burmanniaceae (Burmannia Family). Small plants with scalelike leaves and a cluster of small flowers at the top of a wiry stem. Genus: *Burmannia*

Nartheciaceae (Bog Asphodel Family). Plants mainly of saturated wetlands (*Aletris* sometimes in drier sites), with linear leaves and yellow or white flowers with 6 tepals. Genera: *Aletris, Lophiola, Narthecium*

Stemonaceae (Baibu Family). An odd monocot, with broad leaves (smilax- or yam-like) and small, yellowish-green, axillary flowers with 4 tepals. Genus: *Croomia*

Dioscoreaceae (Yam Family). Broad leaves with palmate venation, 5–9 primary veins arising at the base of the leaf and arcing toward the tip. Flowers are small, borne in axillary racemes or panicles, and whitish-green to yellow-green with 6 tepals. Genus: *Dioscorea*

Commelinaceae (Spiderwort Family). Plants with narrow leaves on the stem, the flowers pink or blue and with 3 petals (in *Commelina*, 2 of the petals are larger and more brightly colored than the other, making the flowers bilaterally symmetrical). Genera: *Commelina, Cuthbertia, Murdannia, Tradescantia*

Haemodoraceae (Bloodwort Family). Our single genus with iris-like (equitant) leaves, blood-red roots, cream-yellow hairy inflorescences, and flowers with 3 petals. Genus: *Lachnanthes*

Pontederiaceae (Pickerelweed Family). Wetland or aquatic plants with broad leaves and usually bilateral white or blue flowers with 6 petals. Genera: *Eichhornia, Heteranthera, Pontederia*

Bromeliaceae (Bromeliad Family). Our only species is epiphytic and unique in appearance: festoons of curly gray stems with yellowish-green 3-petaled flowers. Genus: *Tillandsia*

Typhaceae (Cattail Family). Aquatic plants with long, strap-like leaves and flowers aggregated into green spherical clusters (*Sparganium*) or brown cylinders (*Typha*). Genera: *Sparganium, Typha*

Eriocaulaceae (Pipewort or Hatpins Family). Plants usually of saturated or wetter areas, with many radial basal leaves that taper to pointed tips and a leafless stalk bearing a button-like head with many very small white, gray, or yellowish flowers. Genera: *Eriocaulon, Lachnocaulon, Syngonanthus*

Xyridaceae (Yellow-eyed Grass Family). Leaves basal and iris-like (equitant); flowers borne in an ellipsoid, tan or brown, cone-like structure at the end of a scape, the individual flowers with 3 yellow (or whitish) petals. Genus: *Xyris*

Mayacaceae (Bogmoss Family). A distinctive aquatic or bog plant with very many small, narrow leaves along the stem and a small white to pink flower with 3 petals. Genus: *Mayaca*

True Dicots

Most of our wildflowers are true dicots (in other words, the dicots other than the magnoliids). In general these plants have broad leaves with the primary veins in a pinnate (a single central vein down the long axis of the leaf, with secondary veins branching off it) or palmate (3–9 nearly equal veins branching from a single point at the base of the leaf) pattern. Finer veins branch in a further and elaborately interconnecting (netted) pattern. With very few exceptions (e.g., Berberidaceae, Limnanthaceae), true dicots do not have floral parts in 3s or 6s; flowers usually have 4–5 petals, 4–5 sepals, and usually 4–5 stamens (or stamens in multiples of 4 or 5). Except in a few families (notably the Ranunculaceae, Hydrastidaceae, Saxifragaceae, Crassulaceae, Penthoraceae, and some members of the Rosaceae), the carpels (the female parts in the center of the flower) are fused into a single pistil. Flowers are much more likely than those in the Monocots to have bilateral symmetry and to have fusion of parts (petals connate to one another, sepals connate to one another, stamens adnate to the petals, etc.).

Ranunculaceae (Buttercup Family). This family shows some "primitive" features reminiscent of the magnoliids, with some members having whorled floral parts in large numbers (more than 5). Leaves mostly compound or deeply lobed. Flowers usually radial (but bilateral in *Aconitum* and *Delphinium*), with many pistils, each pistil usually with a hooked or curved tip. The non-female whorls in the flower (sepals, petals, and stamens) are sometimes missing or highly modified in non-standard ways (such as no petals and the sepals brightly colored, or the stamens brightly colored and flattened). Some members of this family are easy to mistake for Rosaceae and vice versa, because of similar features (e.g., many pistils, many stamens, lobed or compound leaves). Genera: *Aconitum, Actaea, Anemone, Anemonidium, Aquilegia, Caltha, Clematis, Coptis, Delphinium, Enemion, Ficaria,*

Hepatica, Myosurus, Ranunculus, Thalictrum, Trautvetteria

Hydrastidaceae (Goldenseal Family). The lone member of this family is often placed in the Ranunculaceae and has some features in common with that family (many separate pistils, many stamens), but it also shows similarities to the Berberidaceae, with its 1–2 palmately lobed, large leaves. Genus: *Hydrastis*

Berberidaceae (Barberry Family). Plants of moist forests with either compound leaves of many broad leaflets with coarse rounded teeth (*Caulophyllum*), bilobed leaves (*Jeffersonia*), or 1–2 palmately lobed to cleft leaves (*Podophyllum, Diphylleia*). Flower parts usually in whorls of 3 or multiples of 3 (unusual for a dicot). Genera: *Caulophyllum, Diphylleia, Jeffersonia, Podophyllum*

Papaveraceae (Poppy Family). Characterized by pinnately or palmately lobed or divided (cleft) leaves, colored sap (white, yellow, orange, or red), and 4 petals (or multiples of 4), which are separate, radial, and typically white, yellow, orange, or red. Stamens many (more than 5). Genera: *Chelidonium, Papaver, Sanguinaria, Stylophorum*

Fumariaceae (Fumitory Family). Sometimes merged into the Papaveraceae but has distinctive features. Leaves finely divided into many small and narrow segments; flowers bilaterally symmetric with 2 sepals and 4 petals. Genera: *Adlumia, Capnoides, Corydalis, Dicentra*

Nelumbonaceae (Lotus-lily Family). The single, odd genus is an aquatic plant with large, blue-green umbrella-like leaves floating on the water's surface or held a few inches above water. Flowers have many tepals, many stamens, and the female part of the flower is a curious, flat-topped cone. Genus: *Nelumbo*

Buxaceae (Boxwood Family). Our only genus has toothed evergreen leaves borne near the end of the stems (seeming whorled) and inconspicuous, separate male and female flowers borne in spikes at ground level. Flowers have no sepals or petals, and the stamens (male flowers) are white. Genus: *Pachysandra*

Saxifragaceae (Saxifrage Family). Plants with small white (or greenish) flowers with parts in 5s (4s in *Chrysosplenium*). Leaves (except in *Chrysosplenium*) primarily or strictly basal. Carpels are unfused (as 4–5 separate pistils). Genera: *Astilbe, Boykinia, Chrysosplenium, Heuchera, Micranthes, Mitella, Tiarella*

Crassulaceae (Stonecrop Family). Succulent plants with thickened, water-storing leaves, typically in thin soils of rock outcrops, though *Sedum ternatum* is often found in moist forest soils. Flowers small and white, pink, or yellow, with sepals, petals, and pistils in 4s or 5s and stamens usually twice that. Genera: *Diamorpha, Hylotelephium, Sedum*

Penthoraceae (Penthorum Family). Similar to Crassulaceae, but *Penthorum* is not succulent and grows in wetlands (including ditches). Flowers white. Genus: *Penthorum*

Oxalidaceae (Wood-sorrel Family). Small plants with palmately compound leaves of 3 notched leaflets arranged at 120° angles to one another. Flowers 5-petaled, yellow or pink. Genus: *Oxalis*

Parnassiaceae (Grass-of-Parnassus Family). Our single genus grows in saturated wetlands. Plants completely smooth and hairless, with waxy, rounded, basal leaves on long petioles. Flowers white with prominent tracery of green veins and borne singly on a stem (which can have a few bracts). Genus: *Parnassia*

Euphorbiaceae (Spurge Family). A large family in our region, especially southward. Male and female flowers separate and with small, greenish, inconspicuous petals; ovaries (and fruits developed from them) are distinctive, being roundish but 3-lobed. Some members of the family (e.g., *Euphorbia*) exude bitter, white sap from broken stems or leaves. *Euphorbia* has a specialized inflorescence, with many tiny male flowers and a single female flower borne in a tiny cup (cyathium), which often has bright white gland flanges that are mistaken for petals (and serve a similar function in attracting insect pollinators). Genera: *Acalypha, Cnidoscolus, Croton, Euphorbia, Stillingia, Tragia*

Phyllanthaceae (Leaf-flower Family). Similar to Euphorbiaceae and traditionally often included in it. Single genus treated here is weedy in flower beds and landscaping; has small alternate leaves and inconspicuous greenish flowers in the leaf axils. Genus: *Phyllanthus*

Hypericaceae (St. John's-wort Family). Plants with opposite leaves sessile or on short petioles. All parts typically with translucent or dark dot-like glands. Flowers considered radial, with 5 sepals and 5 petals (yellow or dull reddish), and many stamens. Individual petals often each slightly curved in the same direction, giving the flower a pinwheel (rather than truly radial) aspect. Genera: *Hypericum, Triadenum*

Violaceae (Violet Family). The main genus in our area, *Viola*, with many species, low-growing, with leaves basal or on short stems and simple, toothed, or lobed (usually heart-shaped). Flowers bilaterally symmetric with 5 sepals and 5 petals, and typically mainly blue, white, cream, or yellow, but often with patches or lines of contrasting color, or bearded patches of colored hairs. *Cubelium* has taller stems, alternate lance-shaped leaves with entire margins, and axillary greenish-yellow flowers that are subtly bilateral. Genera: *Cubelium, Viola*

Linaceae (Flax Family). Our only genus with small radial flowers composed of 5 sepals and 5 petals (yellow in all the species treated in this guide, though rarer species in our region have blue petals). Plants are wand-like, with few branches below the inflorescence and small alternate or opposite, entire leaves sessile or on short petioles. Genus: *Linum*

Passifloraceae (Passionflower Family). Vining herbs with highly distinctive flowers and (in our species) trilobed leaves. Flowers with 5 sepals and 5 petals (sepals often similar in color to petals, but usually smaller or deflexed) and a conspicuous corona of many thread-like segments. Genus: *Passiflora*

Fabaceae (Pea or Bean or Legume Family). One of the largest families in our region, easy to learn and important to recognize. Nearly all have compound leaves, consisting of 3 or more separate segments; in a few species, compound leaves have been evolutionarily modified to a single leaflet, appearing to be simple leaves. All have a legume (pea-pod) fruit, which usually resembles a pea-pod. An additional, subtle feature of the family is that the leaf-stalk has a distinctly swollen base, the pulvinus. Most of our members are in the subfamily Papilionoideae (pea) and have bilateral flowers with distinctive "banner," "wings," and "keel," thus resembling flowers of garden peas and beans. *Mimosa* has twice pinnate leaves and flowers grouped together in a spherical cluster, with long and brightly colored stamens giving the cluster a pompom-like appearance. *Chamaecrista* flowers are more subtly bilateral, with separate yellow petals. Genera: *Amphicarpaea, Apios, Baptisia, Centrosema, Chamaecrista, Clitoria, Crotalaria, Dalea, Desmodium, Erythrina, Galactia, Hylodesmum, Kummerowia, Lathyrus, Lespedeza, Lotus, Lupinus, Medicago, Melilotus, Mimosa, Orbexilum, Pediomelum, Phaseolus, Pueraria, Rhynchosia, Securigera, Senna, Sesbania, Strophostyles, Stylosanthes, Tephrosia, Trifolium, Vicia, Zornia*

Polygalaceae (Milkwort Family). Plants with bilateral flowers with a complex and specialized structure, typically with 8 stamens fused to the petals, and 2 of the sepals brightly colored (petal-like) and splayed out as the "wings" of the flower. Genera: *Asemeia, Polygala, Polygaloides*

Rosaceae (Rose Family). A large and important family in our region (its many trees and shrubs not treated in this guide) and long famous among botanists for the difficulty in simply characterizing it! Leaves almost always alternate and with toothed margins, and often compound or lobed. Stipules (leaf-like structures at the base of the petiole) often prominent. Flowers radial, the sepals and petals usually 5 each; stamens often in multiples (often high multiples) of 5. In *Agrimonia, Aruncus, Filipendula, Fragaria, Geum, Gillenia, Potentilla,* and *Sibbaldia,* carpels are separate (with 2, 5, or many individual pistils). Some members are easy to mistake for Ranunculaceae and vice versa, because of similar features (e.g., many pistils, many stamens, lobed or compound leaves). Genera: *Agrimonia, Aphanes, Aruncus, Filipendula, Fragaria, Geum, Gillenia, Potentilla, Sanguisorba, Sibbaldia*

Moraceae (Mulberry Family). Most members are trees; our only "wildflower" is a recently introduced weed species. Flowers are in clusters and inconspicuous. Leaves look like those of its relative, the mulberry tree. Genus: *Fatoua*

Urticaceae (Nettle Family). Plants with oval leaves on petioles, usually with 3 main veins from the base of the leaf. Flowers are small and greenish, with floral parts not readily distinguishable. Some genera have stinging hairs. Genera: *Boehmeria, Laportea, Parietaria, Pilea, Urtica*

Cucurbitaceae (Cucumber Family). Herbaceous vines with tendrils. Separate male and female radial flowers with 5 fused sepals and 5 fused white or yellow petals (6 in *Echinocystis*). Leaves are shallowly or deeply lobed, with palmate venation and toothed margins. Genera: *Echinocystis, Melothria, Sicyos*

Geraniaceae (Geranium Family). Plants with palmately or pinnately lobed or divided leaves and radial flowers with 5 sepals and 5 pink to white petals. Genera: *Erodium, Geranium*

Lythraceae (Loosestrife Family). Plants mostly of wetlands, with leaves opposite and entire. Radial flowers white or pink with 4, 6, or 8 petals. Genera: *Cuphea, Lythrum, Rotala*

Onagraceae (Evening-primrose Family). Plants with alternate or opposite leaves on short petioles. Radial flowers with 4 sepals, 4 petals (yellow, pink, or white), 8 stamens with straight anthers, and the stigma 4-lobed (*Circaea* with 2 sepals, 2 white petals, 2 stamens, and stigma not 4-lobed). Genera: *Chamaenerion, Circaea, Epilobium, Ludwigia, Oenothera*

Melastomataceae (Melastome Family). Plants usually of saturated or ponded wetlands (or mesic longleaf pine savannas), with opposite leaves (3 veins from the base) sessile or on very short petioles. Radial flowers with 4 roundish petals (pink, yellow, or white) and sepals fused into a flask-shaped hypanthium, which remains in the capsular fruit; stamens strongly curved in most species. Genus: *Rhexia*

Brassicaceae (Mustard Family). Plants with leaves usually toothed or pinnately lobed. Radial flowers with 4 sepals, 4 petals (usually white or yellow, rarely pink), usually strongly narrowed to the base ("clawed"), and 6 stamens of 2 different lengths. Fruit capsular, with seeds attached to a translucent, papery replum between the 2 outer valves of the capsule. Many species in our area are alien and weedy, seen along roadsides or in cultivated fields or pastures. Genera: *Alliaria, Arabidopsis, Barbarea, Boechera, Brassica, Capsella, Cardamine, Draba, Hesperis, Lepidium, Nasturtium, Planodes, Raphanus, Rorippa, Sisymbrium, Thlaspi*

Cleomaceae (Cleome Family). Similar to and in the past often included within the Brassicaceae. The genus included here has pink (fading to white) flowers with 4 slightly bilaterally arranged petals and very elongate capsules borne on long stalks. Genus: *Tarenaya*

Malvaceae (Mallow Family). Plants in our region with alternate, toothed (sometimes also deeply or shallowly lobed) leaves. Flowers with 5 sepals (sometimes fused), 5 petals (not fused, usually pink, yellow, or white), and many stamens fused into a hollow tube. Ovaries and fruits radially segmented. There is often an epicalyx (additional whorl of green bracts) below the sepals. Genera: *Abutilon, Hibiscus, Kosteletzkya, Malva, Modiola, Ripariosida, Sida*

Limnanthaceae (Mermaidweed Family). Our lone member a small plant with divided leaves and small radial flowers with 3 petals. Genus: *Floerkea*

Cistaceae (Rockrose Family). Short, bushy plants with small alternate (sometimes whorled on short shoots) leaves. Petals 5 and yellow in *Crocanthemum* and *Hudsonia* and obscure (often dark) in *Lechea*. Genera: *Crocanthemum, Hudsonia, Lechea*

Caryophyllaceae (Pink Family). Usually small plants with opposite leaves, with nodes often swollen. Flowers with 5 separate petals often deeply notched ("pinked"), sometimes so much as to suggest 10 or more petals; 5 sepals usually fused into a tube. Genera: *Arenaria, Atocion, Cerastium, Dianthus, Holosteum, Mononeuria, Paronychia, Sagina, Saponaria, Scleranthus, Silene, Stellaria, Stipulicida*

Phytolaccaceae (Pokeweed Family). Our single species is a distinctive plant with thick, pink stems and flowers in racemes borne opposite the alternate leaves. Small 5-petaled, white flowers develop into purple-black, juicy berries. Genus: *Phytolacca*

Amaranthaceae (Amaranth Family). Plants mainly weedy and found in disturbed habitats. Leaves often deep green and somewhat fleshy or rubbery in texture; small flowers in clusters and with obscure floral parts. Genera: *Alternanthera, Amaranthus, Froelichia*

Chenopodiaceae (Goosefoot Family). Similar to the Amaranthaceae and sometimes combined into it. Small flowers with obscure floral parts and often deep green leaves. Includes members that have strongly succulent stems and/or leaves (*Salicornia, Suaeda*). Species mainly weedy (in disturbed areas) or in salty coastal habitats. Genera: *Chenopodium, Dysphania, Salicornia, Suaeda*

Aizoaceae (Stone-plant Family). The sole genus similar to some of the Chenopodiaceae in being succulent, coastal plants of saline habitats. It has opposite leaves and radial flowers with 5 sepals and 5 pink petals. Genus: *Sesuvium*

Molluginaceae (Carpetweed Family). With a single species in our area, *Mollugo* *verticillata*, a small prostrate, weedy plant with whorled leaves of irregular lengths and small radial flowers with 5 petal-like sepals. Genus: *Mollugo*

Montiaceae (Miner's-lettuce Family). Historically included in the Portulacaceae, with features generally similar to the casual observer. Our genera with elongate, somewhat fleshy and flat leaves (*Claytonia*) or very succulent and thick leaves (*Phemeranthus*), and pink to purple small-medium flowers with 2 separate sepals and 5 separate petals. Stamens 5 (*Claytonia*) or many (*Phemeranthus*). Genera: *Claytonia, Phemeranthus*

Portulacaceae (Purslane Family). The only genus treated here has alternate, entire leaves with fleshy texture and small yellow or pink flowers with 2 separate sepals, 5 or more separate petals, and many stamens. Genus: *Portulaca*

Droseraceae (Sundew Family). Small plants with leaves basal (or low on the stem) and adapted as active insect traps (snap-traps in *Dionaea*, with sticky-tipped tentacular hairs in *Drosera*). The flowers are radial, with 5 sepals and 5 white or pink petals. Genera: *Dionaea, Drosera*

Polygonaceae (Knotweed Family). Small to medium-sized plants with many small flowers aggregated into inflorescences. Leaves alternate (except often whorled in *Eriogonum*), simple, and with entire margins. Flowers lack true petals but have 5–6 white or pink (rarely greenish) sepals. Seeds are typically 3-sided in cross-section. Genera: *Eriogonum, Fallopia, Persicaria, Polygonum, Rumex*

Plumbaginaceae (Leadwort Family). Our only genus, plants of tidal marshes, with basal rosette of entire leaves and diffusely branched inflorescence composed of many small lavender-blue flowers with 5 petals. Genus: *Limonium*

Balsaminaceae (Touch-me-not Family). Our only genus has alternate leaves with scalloped margins and bilaterally symmetric yellow or orange flowers. Fruits explosively dehiscent, hence the common name. Genus: *Impatiens*

Polemoniaceae (Phlox Family). Plants with simple, opposite, entire leaves (*Phlox*) or alternate, pinnately divided leaves (*Ipomopsis, Polemonium*). Radial flowers (pink, red, white, or blue) have 5 united sepals and 5 petals united into a narrow tube and then expanded into a flat face. Genera: *Ipomopsis, Phlox, Polemonium*

Primulaceae (Primrose Family). Leaf arrangement variable (basal, alternate, opposite, or whorled), but leaves are simple with entire margins. Flowers small to medium-sized, radial, usually with 5 sepals, 5 petals, and 5 stamens (usually 7 each in *Lysimachia borealis*). Genera: *Lysimachia, Primula, Samolus, Trientalis*

Diapensiaceae (Diapensia Family). All members of this family in our region are really dwarf shrubs. *Pyxidanthera* has creeping woody stems and white to pinkish flowers in early spring; *Galax* and *Shortia* have a short stem with many glossy, evergreen, near-basal, toothed leaves. Flowers are small to medium in size, radial, with 5 sepals, 5 petals, and 5 stamens. Genera: *Galax, Pyxidanthera, Shortia*

Ericaceae (Heath Family). A major family in our area, with many shrubs (especially) important in many habitats, but with fewer herbs and ambiguous herb-like dwarf shrubs. Heaths treated here fall into three groups, two of which have sometimes been treated as separate families: the monotropoids and pyroloids. The monotropoids (*Hypopitys, Monotropa*, and *Monotropsis*) are mycoheterotrophs; their stems have reduced scalelike bracts and are white, tan, red, violet, or brown, with 1 or several 5-petaled flowers usually with coloration similar to stems and bracts. The pyroloids (*Chimaphila*, *Orthilia*, and *Pyrola*) are dwarf shrubs often considered to be herbs (and so treated in this guide), with a few evergreen leaves and white, waxy flowers with 5 separate petals. *Gaultheria* and *Epigaea* are also dwarf shrubs, but petals are fused. Genera: *Chimaphila, Epigaea, Gaultheria, Hypopitys, Monotropa, Monotropsis, Orthilia, Pyrola*

Sarraceniaceae (Pitcherplant Family). Unique in our flora, plants with tubular leaves that catch insects as pitfall traps, and large, nodding, 5-petaled flowers with an umbrella-like style disc. Genus: *Sarracenia*

Solanaceae (Nightshade or Potato Family). Plants with alternate, simple leaves with entire margins or (often) few, irregular and rounded teeth. Flowers small to large, radial, with 5 fused sepals, 5 fused petals, and 5 stamens, which are usually fused at their bases to the petal bases. Genera: *Datura, Nicandra, Physalis, Solanum*

Convolvulaceae (Morning-glory Family). Mainly twining or sprawling vines. Flowers small to medium and funnel-shaped, radial, with 5 fused sepals, 5 fused petals, and 5 stamens (fused to the petals). A star-shaped crease pattern (frequently of a different color) is often visible on the petals. Genera: *Calystegia, Convolvulus, Cuscuta, Dichondra, Ipomoea, Stylisma*

Hydroleaceae (Hydrolea Family). Similar to and not readily distinguished from the Solanaceae based on obvious characteristics. Our single genus holds wetland plants (contrasting with the Solanaceae) and has blue flowers. Genus: *Hydrolea*

Rubiaceae (Madder or Coffee Family). One of the largest plant families, especially diverse in the tropics and in woody plants. Plants in our region are small with simple and entire-margined leaves, opposite or whorled on the stem. Flowers with 4 petals united into a tube, the free tips usually spreading in a plane. Genera: *Diodia, Edrastima, Galium, Hexasepalum, Houstonia, Mitchella, Richardia*

Gentianaceae (Gentian Family). Small or medium plants (*Frasera* large) with simple, opposite, entire leaves (alternate in some *Bartonia* species, whorled in *Frasera*). Flowers have 4–5 separate sepals, 4–5 fused petals, and 4–5 stamens that are fused basally to the petals. Flower colors mainly pinks and blues. Genera: *Bartonia, Frasera, Gentiana, Gentianella, Obolaria, Sabatia*

Apocynaceae (Dogbane or Milkweed Family). Most members exude a milky sap when a stem or leaf is broken. Flowers radial, with sepals, petals, and stamens 5 each and fused. Three of our genera (*Amsonia, Apocynum*, and *Asclepias*) are medium-sized plants with usually opposite leaves (less typically alternate or whorled). The others are twining or prostrate vines with opposite leaves. *Asclepias* has a highly distinctive flower structure: 5 reflexed corolla lobes and a central crown—composed of 5 2-parted appendages ("hood" and "horn")—surrounding a complex structure of fused anthers and style. Other members of the family also have unusual, though less elaborate, flower structures. Genera: *Amsonia, Apocynum, Asclepias, Cynanchum, Gonolobus, Matelea, Pattalias, Thyrsanthella, Vinca*

Loganiaceae (Strychnine Family). Plants with simple, opposite, entire leaves. Flowers radial and tubular, with fusion of the 5 sepals, 5 petals, and 5 stamens. Genera: *Mitreola, Spigelia*

Hydrophyllaceae (Waterleaf Family). Sometimes merged into the Boraginaceae, but has distinctive features. In our area, small plants with basal and alternate leaves divided into lobes or segments. Flowers typically white, blue, or pink to maroon, radial, with 5 fused sepals, 5 fused petals, and 5 stamens fused to the petals. Fruits are capsules. Genera: *Hydrophyllum, Nemophila, Phacelia*

Boraginaceae (Borage Family). Our plants have simple, alternate, entire leaves and radial flowers with 5 fused sepals, 5 fused petals, and 5 stamens fused to the petals. Stems and foliage often with stiff, calcified or silicified hairs that are harsh to the touch. Fruit typically a cluster of 4 nutlets. Genera: *Andersonglossum, Buglossoides, Echium, Hackelia, Lithospermum, Mertensia, Myosotis*

Tetrachondraceae (Tetrachondra Family). Our single species with linear opposite leaves on prostrate stems, and small radial flowers with 4 white petals. Genus: *Polypremum*

Plantaginaceae (Plantain or Veronica Family). The scope of this family has greatly increased in recent decades, with the addition of many genera formerly placed in the Scrophulariaceae. All have bilateral flowers. *Plantago* has simple, basal, entire leaves and spikes of whitish or greenish flowers composed of 4 fused sepals, 4 fused (often translucent) petals, and 4 stamens. Other genera mostly have simple, opposite (but some are alternate), and often toothed leaves, and flowers with 4–5 fused sepals; 0, 4, or 5 fused petals; and 1, 2, or 4 stamens. Flower colors primarily white, pink, or blue. Fruits are capsules. Genera: *Callitriche, Chelone, Gratiola, Linaria, Mecardonia, Penstemon, Plantago, Sophronanthe, Veronica, Veronicastrum*

Scrophulariaceae (Figwort Family). Many genera traditionally placed in the Scrophulariaceae have been parsed out to other families, especially the Plantaginaceae and Orobanchaceae. Remaining in the family and treated in this guide are *Scrophularia*, with opposite leaves and bilateral, brownish flowers with 5 fused sepals, 5 fused petals, and 5 stamens; and *Verbascum*, yellow or white bilateral flowers with fused sepals, petals, and stamens in 5s. Fruits are capsules. Genera: *Scrophularia, Verbascum*

Orobanchaceae (Broomrape Family). Once limited to wholly parasitic plants (lacking green pigment), this family now includes a much broader suite of plants (most formerly placed in the Scrophulariaceae) that are semi-parasitic but do have chlorophyll. Our genera all have bilateral and tubular flowers (often yellow or pink), usually with 5 sepals, 5 petals, and 4 stamens (stamens in pairs and usually included in the flower tube). The holoparasitic genera *Aphyllon, Conopholis*, and *Epifagus* lack chlorophyll and have scalelike leaves. Fruits are capsules. Genera: *Agalinis, Aphyllon, Aureolaria, Buchnera, Castilleja, Conopholis, Epifagus, Melampyrum, Pedicularis, Seymeria*

Mazaceae (Mazus Family). Our sole genus holds small plants with simple, basal and opposite, toothed leaves and bilateral, tubular blue flowers and capsular fruits. Genus: *Mazus*

Linderniaceae (False-pimpernel Family). Our sole genus is very similar to and can be confused with *Mazus* in the Mazaceae. Small plants with simple, basal and opposite leaves and bilateral, tubular, blue flowers and capsular fruits. Genus: *Lindernia*

Phrymaceae (Lopseed Family). Plants with simple, opposite, toothed leaves. Flowers bilateral and tubular, with 5 fused sepals, 5 fused petals, and 4 stamens fused to the corolla. Fruit is a capsule in *Mimulus* and an achene in *Phryma*. Fruits of *Phryma* are distinctive, bent down ("lopped") against the axis of the inflorescence. Genera: *Mimulus, Phryma*

Acanthaceae (Acanthus Family). Plants with simple, opposite, entire leaves and tubular flowers composed of 5 fused sepals, 5 fused petals, and 2 or 4 stamens fused to the petals. Flowers of *Dicliptera* and *Justicia* are distinctly bilateral (2-lipped); those of *Ruellia* are radial or nearly so. *Justicia* and *Dicliptera* occur in bottomlands; *Ruellia* typically grows in upland sites. Fruit is a capsule. Genera: *Dicliptera, Justicia, Ruellia*

Lentibulariaceae (Bladderwort Family). Small, carnivorous plants; aquatic or in saturated wetlands. *Pinguicula* with a rosette of basal leaves that lie flat on the ground and have a viscous upper surface that traps insects. *Utricularia* with specialized bladders that trap small crustaceans in the water or wet interstices in saturated soils; aquatic species of *Utricularia* lack leaves, but terrestrial species have small leaves that emerge from the ground away from the stalk base and are often overlooked. Flowers bilateral and tubular, with 2, 4, or 5 fused sepals, 5 fused petals (and also have a spur), and 2 stamens fused to the petals. Fruit is a capsule. Genera: *Pinguicula, Utricularia*

Verbenaceae (Vervain Family). Plants with simple (divided in *Glandularia*) opposite, toothed leaves. Flowers radial to slightly bilateral, tubular, with 5 fused sepals, 5 fused petals, and 4 stamens fused to the petals. Flowers usually blue, pink, or white; petals often flared abruptly from the tube and with scalloped lobe margins. Genera: *Glandularia, Phyla, Verbena*

Lamiaceae (Mint Family). A large and distinctive family (though its members have similarities to other, related families, such as Verbenaceae and Phrymaceae). Leaves simple, opposite, and usually toothed (rarely more deeply lobed). Stem often square, but this can be undetectable in some genera. Flowers bilateral, tubular, and usually 2-lipped, with 5 fused sepals, 5 fused petals, and 2 or 4 stamens fused to the petals. Many genera distinctly aromatic (tested by crushing or rubbing a leaf). Genera: *Agastache, Blephilia, Clinopodium, Collinsonia, Cunila, Glechoma, Hedeoma, Hyptis, Lamium, Leonurus, Lycopus, Monarda, Nepeta, Perilla, Physostegia, Prunella, Pycnanthemum, Salvia, Scutellaria, Stachys, Teucrium, Trichostema*

Apiaceae (Carrot or Umbel Family). Divided leaves with broad or narrow segments or leaflets (leaf modified into jointed quills in *Harperella, Lilaeopsis,* and *Tiedemannia*), the petiole typically expanded and clasping the stem (like the base of a celery stalk). Flowers always very small and usually arranged in simple or compound umbels (these sometimes modified into heads, as in *Eryngium*). Ovary inferior (below attachment of sepals and petals). Genera: *Angelica, Centella, Chaerophyllum, Cicuta, Conium, Cryptotaenia, Cyclospermum, Daucus, Erigenia, Eryngium, Foeniculum, Harperella, Heracleum, Ligusticum, Lilaeopsis, Osmorhiza, Oxypolis, Pastinaca, Ptilimnium, Sanicula, Sium, Taenidia, Thaspium, Tiedemannia, Torilis, Zizia*

Araliaceae (Ginseng Family). Closely related to the Apiaceae, and sharing many similar features, such as usually compound leaves and small flowers borne in umbels. *Aralia* and *Panax* have compound leaves with broad leaflets; *Hydrocotyle* has small umbrella-like (peltate) leaves. Ovary inferior. Genera: *Aralia, Hydrocotyle, Panax*

Caprifoliaceae (Honeysuckle Family). The few wildflowers in this primarily woody family are difficult to characterize. Leaves alternate (*Valerianella*) or opposite and fused basally around the stem (*Dipsacus* and

Triosteum). Sepals, petals, and stamens variable in number but show fusion into bilateral, tubular flowers. Ovary inferior. Genera: *Dipsacus, Triosteum, Valerianella*

Campanulaceae (Bellflower Family). Plants with simple, alternate, toothed leaves. Sepals, petals, and stamens are 5, with fusion. In *Lobelia*, flowers bilateral and tubular (2-lipped) and pale to deep blue; in other genera, flowers radial and blue (*Campanula, Wahlenbergia*) or pink (*Triodanis*). *Lobelia* has milky sap, and the teeth are tipped with whitish calluses. Ovary inferior. Genera: *Campanula, Lobelia, Triodanis, Wahlenbergia*

Asteraceae (Aster Family). One of the three largest families of flowering plants and abundantly represented in our flora. This is one of the most important and helpful families to learn to recognize. While variable in leaf arrangement, flower color, and many other features, the Asteraceae is distinctive in having small flowers aggregated together into heads; few other families ever have small flowers arrayed on a flat, conical, or hemispherical receptacle. Examples of "non-Asteraceae heads" include *Eryngium* in the Apiaceae, some members of the Lamiaceae (e.g., *Blephilia, Hyptis, Pycnanthemum*), and the Eriocaulaceae. Some aster family members have two kinds of flowers (also sometimes of different colors): ray flowers (florets) with a conspicuous enlarged petal around the edge of the head, and smaller disk flowers (florets) in the center of the head. Look for flowers aggregated into a head, the head with green bracts at its base, the top of the head usually with small tubular flowers with 5 lobes, and if the head has a large enough number of flowers, they will be arranged in intersecting spirals. Ovary inferior. Genera: *Acanthospermum, Achillea, Ageratina, Ambrosia, Ampelaster, Antennaria, Anthemis, Arctium, Arnica, Arnoglossum, Artemisia, Balduina, Berlandiera, Bidens, Bigelowia, Boltonia, Borrichia, Brickellia, Carphephorus, Centaurea, Chaptalia, Chrysogonum, Chrysopsis, Cichorium, Cirsium, Conoclinium, Coreopsis, Croptilon, Doellingeria, Echinacea, Eclipta, Elephantopus, Erechtites, Erigeron, Eupatorium, Eurybia, Euthamia, Eutrochium, Gaillardia, Galinsoga, Gamochaeta, Helenium, Helianthus, Heliopsis, Heterotheca, Hieracium, Hypochaeris, Ionactis, Krigia, Lactuca, Leucanthemum, Liatris, Marshallia, Nabalus, Oclemena, Packera, Parthenium, Pilosella, Pityopsis, Pluchea, Polymnia, Pseudognaphalium, Pterocaulon, Pyrrhopappus, Rudbeckia, Rugelia, Sclerolepis, Senecio, Sericocarpus, Silphium, Smallanthus, Solidago, Sonchus, Symphyotrichum, Taraxacum, Tetragonotheca, Trilisa, Tussilago, Verbesina, Vernonia, Xanthium, Youngia*

Platanthera blephariglottis

(Habenaria blephariglottis)

ORCHIDACEAE | **white fringed orchid**

Jul–Sep, 1½–2½ ft. Erect perennial of boggy streamhead margins and seepages, pitcherplant bogs, and sandhill-pocosin ecotones. Stems unbranched, smooth. Leaves sessile-sheathing, strongly ascending, broadly lance-shaped, 2–13 in. long (reduced to bracts above) and folded lengthwise. Flowers 20–45 in a dense, cylindrical terminal raceme; each flower snowy white, about ¾ in. long, with 2 small upper petals plus 1 of 3 sepals forming a small hood, beneath which projects a deeply fringed lip petal bearing a curved spur (longer than the lip, ½–1 in.). Fruit an elliptical capsule. WS

Platanthera clavellata

(Habenaria clavellata)

ORCHIDACEAE | **small green wood orchid**

Jun–Sep, 4–18 in. Erect perennial of seepages, mossy streamheads, bogs, swamps, and other wet places. Stems unbranched, smooth. Leaf single near base of stem (small bracts above), ascending, sessile-clasping, lance-shaped with blunt tip, 2–7 in. long, with parallel veins. Flowers 5–15 on short, often twisted stalks, in a cylindrical terminal raceme; each flower white or yellow to pale green, about ½ in. long, with 2 petals plus 1 sepal forming a small hood, 2 more winglike sepals, and a subtly lobed lip petal bearing a ½-in.-long spur. Fruit an elliptical capsule. FG

Platanthera lacera

(Habenaria lacera)

ORCHIDACEAE | **green fringed orchid**

Jun–Sep, 1–2½ ft. Erect perennial of swamps, bogs, and seepages. Stems unbranched, smooth. Leaves (1–4) alternate, sessile with sheathing base, lance-shaped to oblong-elliptical, 2–8 in. long (reduced to bracts above), with parallel veins, smooth. Flowers 20–40 in a cylindrical, spikelike terminal raceme; each flower greenish-white or greenish-yellow, ¾ in. long, with an upper sepal and 2 upper petals forming a small hood, 2 lateral sepals that usually curve backward, a 3-lobed lip petal below, all lobes deeply fringed, and a slender, curved spur. Fruit an erect, elliptical capsule. WS, JED

Platanthera nivea
(Habenaria nivea)
ORCHIDACEAE | **snowy orchid**

May–Sep, 1–3 ft. Erect perennial of wet savannas, bogs, and seeps. Stems unbranched, smooth. Leaves (1–3) alternate, erect-ascending, sessile with sheathing base, narrowly lance-shaped, 4–12 in. long (reduced to bracts above), often withered by flowering time. Flowers 20–50 in a conical-cylindrical terminal raceme, blooming from the bottom up; each flower bright white, about ½ in. wide, with 2 spreading sepals, 2 spreading petals, and a narrow lip petal at the top (unlike most of our other *Platanthera* species). None of the petals are fringed, and the long, thin spur extends backward. RTW

Spiranthes cernua
ORCHIDACEAE | **nodding ladies'-tresses**

Jul–Nov, 5–16 in. Erect perennial of bogs, swamps, and ditches; usually in acidic situations with sphagnum moss. Stems somewhat fleshy, unbranched, smooth below, minutely downy above. Leaves (3–6) basal and erect, linear to narrowly lance-shaped, 2–10 in. long, smooth; may or may not persist through blooming. Flowers 10–50 in 2–4 overlapping, dense spirals on a terminal spike covered with white, gland-tipped hairs; each flower waxy-white, often vanilla-scented, about ⅓ in. long, tubular, with a total of 5 petals and petal-like sepals, including an upper downward-curving hood (its 3-lobed tip curled up) and a lower lip with crinkled edge. Fruit an elliptical capsule. AMC

Spiranthes lacera var. *gracilis*
ORCHIDACEAE | **southern slender ladies'-tresses**

Aug–Sep, 6–26 in. Erect perennial of fields, meadows, pastures, and woodlands. Stems unbranched, smooth but may be sparsely hairy above. Leaves (2–4) basal, oval, smooth, usually withered by bloom time. Flowers 10–35 in a narrow, tightly spiraled spike; each flower white, ¼ in. long or less, tubular, with a total of 5 petals and petal-like sepals, the lowest of which forms a downcurved lip with crinkled edges and has a green patch in its center. Fruit a tiny, elliptical capsule. AMC

Spiranthes tuberosa

ORCHIDACEAE | **little ladies'-tresses**

Jun–Sep, 2–12 in. Erect perennial found in a wide variety of habitats, especially relatively well-drained woodlands and fields, sandhills, dry hammocks, and dry pine flatwoods. Stems from a tuberous root, unbranched, smooth. Leaves (3–5) basal (reduced to bracts above), short-petioled, oval, ¾–2 in. long, overwintering but withering before flowering. Flowers 10–35 in a hairless, narrow, spiraled spike; each flower pure white, less than ¼ in. long, with 5 petals and petal-like sepals, including a lowermost pure-white lip with crinkled edges. Fruit an elliptical capsule. AMC

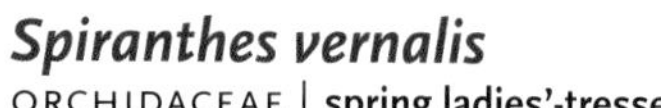

Spiranthes vernalis

ORCHIDACEAE | **spring ladies'-tresses**

Mar–Jul (early Sep, mountains), 8–35 in. Erect perennial of savannas, bogs, marshes, and fairly dry fields. Stems unbranched and densely hairy above. Leaves (4–5) basal (upper leaves reduced to bractlike sheaths), linear or narrowly lance-shaped, 2–10 in. long, smooth and persisting through flower bloom. Flowers 12–50 on a hairy (nonglandular), slender, spiraled spike; each flower white to cream, ¼–½ in. long, with 5 petals and petal-like sepals, including 2 linear lateral sepals and a lower lip with crinkled edges and a cream-yellow center or 2 brown spots. Fruit a tiny, elliptical capsule. Flowers are fragrant. FG

Triphora trianthophoros

ORCHIDACEAE | **three birds orchid**

Jul–Sep, 4–12 in. Erect, sometimes colonial perennial of humid forests, swamps, and rhododendron thickets, often on rotten logs or humus. Stems from a tuber, fleshy, unbranched, maroon-tinged, smooth. Leaves sessile and clasping, oval, concave, ½–¾ in. long (smaller and scalelike below), sometimes maroon-tinged, smooth. Flowers 1–3(6), nodding from upper leaf axils; each white to pale pink, ⅓–⅔ in. long, with 3 petal-like, lance-shaped sepals and a central column of 3 partially fused petals, the lowest curved downward and with a green-bumpy-striped patch at the base and the upper ones bearing a purplish-pink, specialized pollen-carrying structure. AMC

Polygala senega

POLYGALACEAE | **Seneca snakeroot**

Apr–Jun, 4–16 in. Erect-ascending perennial from stout roots, found in woodlands and openings, especially over calcareous or mafic rocks. Stems simple or branched, rough-hairy. Leaves crowded, lance-shaped, sometimes minutely toothed; middle and upper leaves 1½–3 in. long, but lower leaves much smaller and scalelike. Flowers in a spike-like terminal raceme, white tinged with pink or green, less than ¼ in. long, often closed, with 2 spreading (when open), rounded "wings" (sepals) and 3 joined petals forming a small, white tube. Fruit a rounded capsule. Superficially resembles *Polygonum* species, but stems lack joints. BAS

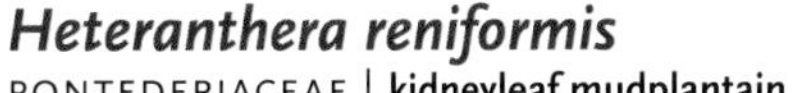

Heteranthera reniformis

PONTEDERIACEAE | **kidneyleaf mudplantain**

Jun–Oct, to 3½ in. Mat-forming annual/perennial of shallow, stagnant water of floodplains, and lake and pond edges. Nonflowering stems creeping, branched and submerged or above water; flowering stems erect and above water. Leaves 1–1½ in. long, glossy green, with prominent parallel veins; sessile leaves linear to lance-shaped and thin-textured; petiolate leaves floating or extending above water and kidney-shaped with a notched base. Flowers 2–8 on a spike arising from a spathe, all opening the same day; each with a short corolla tube (glandular-hairy on outside) with 6 spreading, unequal, linear to lance-shaped lobes, one of which bears 2 yellow or green spots at the base. BAS

Oenothera simulans (*Gaura angustifolia*)

ONAGRACEAE | **southeastern gaura**

May–Sep, 3–5 ft. Erect to ascending annual found in open woodlands, sandy fields, and roadsides, primarily in the outer Coastal Plain. Stems slender, widely branched, stiff-hairy. Leaves basal and alternate, sessile and sometimes in clusters, lance-shaped, to 3 in. long (reduced above), with a few vague teeth, smooth or stiff-hairy. Flowers in branched terminal spikes, white (aging to pink), with 3–4 oblong-oval to spoon-shaped petals that tend to cluster at 1 side of the flower; 4 reddish-pink sepals are severely swept backward. Fruit a sessile, sharply 3- or 4-angled, oval pod. KB

Verbascum blattaria

SCROPHULARIACEAE | **moth mullein**

May–Jun, 2–5 ft. Erect biennial of fields, roadsides, disturbed areas; forms large basal rosette in first year. Native to Eurasia, widespread in NoAm. Stems ribbed, unbranched (rarely 1–2 branches). Lower and basal leaves sessile-clasping, oblong-lance-shaped, 6–8 in. long, doubly toothed, smooth; stem leaves alternate, clasping, to 6 in. long (smaller upward), toothed, mostly smooth. Flowers in loose, glandular-hairy, 2-ft. terminal raceme; each white or yellow with purplish-red center, 3/4–1 1/2 in. wide, with 5 spreading, rounded petals of slightly differing size, 5 purple-hairy stamens with orange anthers, and 5 glandular-hairy, lance-shaped sepals. Fruit a rounded capsule. RTW

Viola arvensis

VIOLACEAE | **European field pansy**

Mar–Jul, 4–12 in. Erect to leaning annual of roadsides, fields, and other disturbed habitats. Native to Europe. Stems 1–several from crown, ridged, hairy throughout. Leaves with large, leaflike, lobed stipules at the petiole base; lower leaves round to oval, upper ones oblong to elliptical; 1/2–2 in. long; with rounded, coarse teeth, hairy margins, and hairs on veins beneath. Flowers solitary on long stalks from upper leaf axils, creamy to yellowish-white with a darker yellow patch (sometimes light purple), 1/3–3/4 in. wide, with 5 unequal petals, the lowest largest and extending behind, in a spur. Fruit a 3-celled capsule. Roots give off wintergreen odor when crushed. BAS

Viola canadensis

VIOLACEAE | **Canada violet**

Apr–Jul, 6–16 in. Erect to spreading perennial of rich cove forests, floodplains, and other rich, moist situations. Stems unbranched and smooth or very finely hairy. Stem leaves on petioles with narrowly lance-shaped stipules at the base, narrowly to broadly heart-shaped, 1–6 in. long, with rounded to pointed teeth, hairy or smooth. Basal leaves similar but larger and broader. Flowers solitary from leaf axils, white with yellow throat and purple veins on lower 3 petals (back of petals purple-tinged), about 1 in. wide, with 5 unequal petals, the 2 lateral ones bearded. Fruit a 3-celled oval capsule. Closed, self-pollinating flowers may be briefly present. WS

Viola striata

VIOLACEAE | **cream violet**

Mar–Jun, 6–13 in. Erect, rhizomatous perennial of moist forests and woodlands as well as disturbed areas. Stems erect to leaning but becoming prostrate; branching after flowering, mostly smooth. Leaves on petioles with conspicuously toothed, lance-oval stipules; round to oval with a notched base; to 2½ in. long; round-toothed and smooth. Flowers solitary on smooth, long stalks from upper leaf axils; each flower creamy white, about ¾ in. wide, with 5 unequal petals, the lowest with purple veins and a short, blunt, backward-pointing spur, the 2 lateral ones bearded at the base. Fruit an oval capsule. Closed, self-pollinating flowers often present. AMC

Gratiola amphiantha

PLANTAGINACEAE | **pool-sprite**

Apr, 2–5 in. Aquatic annual found in shallow, flat-bottomed depressions on granitic outcrops that are inundated for a time in early spring and where soil is thin and gravelly. Stems submerged, thin. Floating leaves in pairs at the ends of thin stalks, oval, less than ¼ in. long; submerged leaves in a rosette at the top of the underwater stem, oblong with a pointed tip, less than ¼ in. long. Flowers held between the floating leaves and also among the submerged rosette leaves; each flower white to pale lavender, less than ¼ in. long, with a short corolla tube and 5 spreading, slightly notched lobes. Fruit a somewhat flattened, 2-lobed capsule. AMC

Chelone glabra

PLANTAGINACEAE | **white turtlehead**

Jul–Oct, 2–5 ft. Erect perennial of streambanks, seeps, and swamp forests. Stems simple or sparingly branched, smooth. Leaves short-petioled or subsessile, lance-shaped tapering to a sharp tip, 4–7 in. long, toothed. Flowers in dense terminal spikes, each resting on a leafy bract that mostly conceals the stalk; each flower white but pink-tinged at the tip, 1–1½ in. long, inflated-tubular and with a hoodlike upper lip, a 3-lobed lower lip bearing a white or yellowish beard, 4 fertile stamens, and a single green-tipped sterile stamen. Fruit a broadly oval capsule. AMC

Gratiola neglecta

PLANTAGINACEAE | **clammy hedge-hyssop**

Mar–Oct, 4–15 in. Erect annual of bottomlands, ditches, pool margins, upland depression ponds, and other wet areas. Stems short-branched above, sometimes branched below, sometimes succulent, sticky-hairy. Leaves sessile, oblong to oblong-lance-shaped or oblong-oval, ½–2 in. long, toothed or entire, hairy when emerging but later smooth. Flowers solitary on long stalks from leaf axils, with a pair of small leafy bracts at the flower base; each flower cream to white but yellow or green within, about ⅓ in. long, the tubular corolla opening to several spreading, short, rounded lobes. The calyx is tubular but shorter, with 5 lobes. Fruit an oval capsule with pointed tip. BAS

Gratiola ramosa

PLANTAGINACEAE | **branched hedge-hyssop**

May–Jun, 4–12 in. Erect to ascending perennial of wet pine savannas, marshes, pond margins, and ditches. Stems somewhat succulent, usually simple but occasionally branched, smooth to slightly hairy above. Leaves sessile-clasping, narrowly lance-shaped, ¼–¾ in. long, entire or with a few teeth toward the tip, smooth. Flowers solitary on stalks from leaf axils, white but yellow at the base (outside and inside), where also marked with brownish-purple veins, ⅓–½ in. long, the tubular corolla opening to 4 unequal, spreading lobes (bottom one largest). A much shorter calyx tube has 5 linear-lance-shaped lobes and is finely hairy. Fruit a tiny, nearly round capsule. AMC

Gratiola virginiana

PLANTAGINACEAE | **Virginia hedge-hyssop**

Mar–Oct, 4–16 in. long. Sprawling annual of sluggish streams, bogs, ditches, and other wet areas. Stems succulent, simple but often rooting at leaf nodes and sending up erect branches from there, reddish, smooth to slightly glandular-hairy. Leaves sessile (not clasping the stem), elliptical to lance-shaped, to 2 in. long, with entire, undulate, or sharply toothed margins. Flowers solitary in leaf axils, on short stalks or sessile, white or pink-tinged and marked on the inside with purple lines, about ½ in. long, with a tubular corolla opening to 4 unequal, spreading, notched lobes and the calyx with 5 narrowly lance-shaped sepals. Fruit a tiny, round capsule. BAS

Gratiola viscidula

PLANTAGINACEAE | **Short's hedge-hyssop**

Jun–Nov, 4–20 in. Erect to sprawling perennial of bogs, marshes, ditches, pond margins, and other wet areas. Stems somewhat succulent, unbranched, hairy or glandular-hairy. Leaves sessile and somewhat clasping, oval to oblong-lance-shaped, with variously toothed margins, hairy (sometimes glandular). Flowers solitary on short, glandular stalks from leaf axils; each flower white to cream or pink-tinged and marked on the inside with purple lines and a yellow center, about ½ in. long, with a tubular corolla opening to 4 unequal, spreading, wavy-margined lobes (the lowest largest) and a calyx with 5 elliptical to lance-shaped sepals. Fruit a tiny, round capsule. PHA

Mecardonia acuminata

PLANTAGINACEAE | **common axil-flower**

Jul–Sep, 4–20 in. Erect perennial from a slightly woody crown, found in marshes, ditches, wet pine savannas, bottomland forests, and wet disturbed areas. Stems 4-angled and winged, simple or branched, smooth. Leaves sessile, elliptical to lance-shaped and tapering to a narrow base, to 2 in. long, toothed on the upper half. Flowers solitary on stalks from leaf axils, white (sometimes with purple tinge or veins), about ⅓ in. long, with a tubular corolla opening to 5 spreading lobes, the lower 3 slightly larger and the upper 2 bearded at the throat. 5 linear-lance-shaped sepals are of unequal widths and nearly as long as the corolla. Fruit an elliptical capsule. BAS

Penstemon digitalis

PLANTAGINACEAE | **tall white beardtongue**

May–Jul, 2–4 ft. Erect perennial of low meadows and forest edges where the soil is moist and sandy, moist fields, clearings, and other open, disturbed areas. Stems unbranched, smooth or finely hairy. Leaves sessile, lance-shaped or oval, 2–8 in. long, finely toothed, smooth or with fine hairs on the midvein beneath. Flowers in a moderately compact, terminal panicle, with branches angled upward; flowers white (occasionally tinged purple), 1¼ in. long, tubular with an abruptly swollen throat and 2 lips, the upper lip 2-lobed and of equal length to the lower, which is 3-lobed. Corolla throat white with purple lines inside. Fruit a capsule. AMC

Penstemon laevigatus

PLANTAGINACEAE | **eastern smooth beardtongue**

May–Jul, 1–4 ft. Erect perennial of bottomlands, forest edges, hammocks, and moist, low meadows. Stems 1–several but generally not branched above base, smooth or minutely hairy. Leaves sessile, variable but mostly oblong-lance-shaped, to about 5 in. long, toothed, mostly smooth. Flowers many, in a narrow terminal panicle, with glandular-hairy branches angled upward; each white (becoming violet-purple), ½–¾ in. long, tubular and abruptly swollen above the middle, with 2 lips, the upper lip 2-lobed and mostly equal to the lower, which is 3-lobed. Corolla throat with faint (or no) purple lines and a barely protruding yellow-bearded tongue. BAS

Sophronanthe pilosa (*Gratiola pilosa*)

PLANTAGINACEAE | **shaggy hedge-hyssop**

Jun–Sep, 4–28 in. Erect perennial of marshes, wet pine savannas, seeps, and seasonally wet clearings. Stems tufted, from a slightly woody crown, unbranched, hairy. Leaves sessile, oval to lance-oval, to ¾ in. long, toothed toward the tip, with long hairs and pebbly texture on upper surface. Flowers mostly sessile in leaf axils, white, about ¼ in. long, with a tubular corolla (hairy inside) opening to 5 tiny, spreading lobes that may be veined with purple. There are 5 hairy, unequal, linear-lance-shaped sepals about as long as the corolla tube. RTW

Veronica peregrina

PLANTAGINACEAE | **purslane speedwell**

Apr–Aug, 3–12 in. Erect-ascending annual of fields, roadsides, and disturbed areas. Stems simple or branched, somewhat fleshy, smooth. Leaves sessile or short-petioled, spoon-shaped to oblong with bluntly rounded tip, to ¾ in. long; may be irregularly toothed. Flowers in leafy-bracted, loose, terminal racemes; each flower white (sometimes pink-tinged), less than ¼ in. wide, with a tiny corolla tube opening to 4 slightly unequal, oval lobes. 4 green sepals are visible between corolla lobes. Flowers wilt quickly. Fruit a tiny, heart-shaped capsule. BE

Veronica serpyllifolia

PLANTAGINACEAE | **thymeleaf speedwell**

Apr–Aug, 4–12 in. Creeping perennial of meadows, lawns, roadsides, and other disturbed areas. Native to Eurasia. Stems several from base, prostrate but ascending at tips where flowers are produced, finely hairy. Leaves short-petioled to sessile, elliptic-oblong to oval, ¼–¾ in. long, vaguely toothed and smooth. Flowers in narrow, terminal racemes 2–7 in. long, sometimes in pairs within a raceme, and on a short stalk subtended by a leafy bract. Each flower white to pale blue with dark blue lines, ¼ in. wide, with 3 rounded petals and 1 narrower petal, 2 stamens bearing purplish-blue anthers, and a single style. Fruit a flattened, heart-shaped capsule. RTW

Phyla nodiflora (*Lippia nodiflora*)

VERBENACEAE | **turkeytangle**

May–Oct, to 4 in. Rambling-spreading perennial of sandy lawns and roadsides and other disturbed areas. Stems sprawling, branched and rooting at the nodes, smooth. Leaves short-petioled, oval to wedge-shaped (widest above middle), to 2½ in. long, generally with 5 (3–7) teeth per side, semi-evergreen, red-tinged in cool weather, smooth. Flowers in dense, cylindrical heads about ⅓ in. long, on stalks from upper leaf axils; each white to rose-purple with a yellow or pinkish-red eye, tiny, with a tubular corolla opening to 2 spreading lips, the upper notched, the lower larger and 3-lobed. KB

Verbena urticifolia

VERBENACEAE | **white vervain**

May–Nov, 1½–8 ft. Erect annual/perennial found in floodplain forests, moist and dry upland forests, and disturbed habitats. Stems 4-angled, with ascending branches, long-hairy. Leaves long-petioled, oval to lance-shaped, to 6 in. long, toothed (sometimes doubly), rough-hairy. Flowers in slender spikes, 4–10 in. long, on stems arising from upper leaf axils, only a few flowers opening at a time; each flower white, less than ¼ in. wide, with a short corolla tube opening to 5 slightly unequal, spreading petals, the lowest notched. The 5-parted calyx tube is nearly as long as the corolla. RTW

Polygala ambigua

POLYGALACEAE | **loose milkwort**

Jun–Sep, 4–13 in. Erect to ascending annual found in fields, woodlands, and openings. Stems subtly 4-angled, slender, branched, smooth. Leaves whorled above and alternate below, linear to narrowly elliptical, smooth. Flowers in narrow, spikelike racemes ¾–2 in. long at ends of branches, these racemes becoming interrupted below through persistence of the fruits on the axis; each flower white or greenish-white (occasionally pinkish), with 2 spreading oval wings (sepals) and 3 joined petals forming a small tube. AMC

Veronicastrum virginicum

PLANTAGINACEAE | **Culver's root**

Jun–Sep, 2–4 ft. Erect perennial of streambanks, bogs, wet meadows, and dryish soils in areas with prairie affinities. Stems branched above in inflorescence, smooth or hairy. Leaves whorled, short-petioled, lance-shaped to oval, to 6 in. long, toothed, smooth above and very hairy beneath. Flowers in several crowded, erect spikes at tips of branches, resembling a candelabra; each flower white (rarely pink-tinged), to ¼ in. long, tubular, with 4 tiny corolla lobes and 2 protruding stamens bearing orange or brown anthers. RTW

Pinguicula pumila

LENTIBULARIACEAE | **small butterwort**

Mar–Jun, 6–8 in. Scapose, carnivorous plant of pine savannas and wet pine flatwoods. Stem a single, hairy flowering scape. Leaves basal, in a rosette about 1½ in. wide, oval with curled-up margins, smaller than leaves of other *Pinguicula* species, somewhat fleshy, yellowish-green and oily feeling. Flowers held singly at tip of scape, often angled with opening upward; the flower whitish to pale violet, less than ½ in. wide, tubular and with 5 spreading, notched corolla lobes, a hairy lump on inside bottom of the throat, and a backward-pointing spur. Insects are trapped on the upper surface of leaves, which secrete a musty-smelling mucilage and digestive fluids. FG

Calopogon pallidus

ORCHIDACEAE | **pale grass-pink**

May–Jun, 8–20 in. Erect perennial of pine savannas and sandhill seeps. A Coastal Plain endemic. Stem slender, smooth. Leaf single, erect, linear, grasslike, 3–12 in. long, folded lengthwise. Flowers 2–12 in a loose, terminal raceme, opening successively from bottom to top, white to pale pink, less than 1 in. wide, with 3 spreading, pointy-tipped sepals (the upper 2 strongly curved upward and back), 2 spreading-curved, blunt-tipped petals that project slightly forward, and an erect lip petal with widened tip, darker pink patch, and golden crest; a protruding, spoon-shaped column holds the reproductive parts. Fruit an erect, oblong capsule. Flowers vaguely fragrant. AMC

Goodyera pubescens

ORCHIDACEAE | **downy rattlesnake-orchid**

Jun–Aug, 4–15 in. Erect, rhizomatous perennial of dry to moist forests and woodlands. Stem an unbranched, glandular-hairy flowering scape with a few bracts. Leaves (3–8) in a basal rosette, petiolate, oval to elliptical, to 2½ in. long, bluish-green with prominent white midvein and side veins, evergreen, smooth. Flowers in a narrow, dense terminal spike covered with glandular hairs (flowers on all sides of spike); each flower white, about ¼ in. long, hairy, with 2 petals and 1 sepal forming a hood over a lower, saclike lip petal and 2 flanking, tiny sepals. Fruit a round to elliptical capsule. WS, BAS

Goodyera repens

ORCHIDACEAE | **lesser rattlesnake-orchid**

Jun–Sep, 4–9 in. Erect, rhizomatous perennial of moist forests, usually found under conifers and rhododendrons. Stem an unbranched, glandular-hairy flowering scape bearing a few bracts. Leaves (3–7) in a basal rosette, petiolate, oval to oblong-elliptical, ½–1¼ in. long, dark green with light green midvein and side veins. Flowers in a narrow, lax terminal spike covered with glandular hairs, mostly on 1 side of the spike; each flower white (may be green-tinged), ¼ in. long, hairy, with 2 petals and 1 sepal forming a hood over a lower, saclike lip petal with downward-pointing tip and 2 flanking white sepals. Fruit an oval capsule. AMC

Platanthera orbiculata (*Habenaria orbiculata*)

ORCHIDACEAE | **dinner-plate orchid**

Jun–Sep, 4–23 in. Erect perennial of moist hardwood forests and seeps, especially over amphibolite. Flowering scape unbranched, smooth. Leaves in a pair at base of plant, flat against ground (a few bracts above), broadly oval to rounded, 2–8 in. long, with parallel veins and a central crease, shiny dark green and smooth. Flowers 10–30 in a cylindrical terminal spike, greenish-white, about 1 in. long, with 3 oval sepals, a pair of sickle-shaped lateral petals, a narrowly elongate lip petal at the bottom and, pointing backward, a slender, drooping, ½- to 1-in.-long spur. Fruit an erect, slender, elliptical capsule. JF

Ponthieva racemosa

ORCHIDACEAE | **shadow witch**

Sep–Oct, 6–18 in. Erect perennial of bottomlands, floodplains, and moist ravines, nearly always over marl or coquina limestone. Stems unbranched, purplish to green, hairy. Leaves (3–8) in a basal rosette (bracts above on stem), short-petioled, narrowly oblong-oval with bluntish tips, ¾–5 in. long, lustrous green above. Flowers (to 30) in a loose, terminal raceme, each positioned horizontally on a hairy stalk; flowers greenish-white, about ½ in. wide, with obliquely triangular petals and a sepal at one end, a deeply concave and clawed lip petal at the other end, and 2 oval sepals like wings to each side. Fruit an ascending, elliptical capsule. RTW

Plantago virginica

PLANTAGINACEAE | **Virginia plantain**

Mar–Jul, 4–8 in. Erect annual/biennial from a basal rosette, found in fields, pastures, roadsides, disturbed rock outcrops and other clearings. Stems 1–several woolly-hairy, leafless flowering scapes, often red-tinged at the base. Leaves on winged and often purplish petioles, oblong-lance-shaped to oval with blunt tip, to 6 in. long, with 3–5 parallel veins and woolly (longer hairs on veins). Flowers densely crowded in a narrowly cylindrical spike on the upper ⅔ of each scape; each greenish-white, tiny, with a narrow, papery corolla with 4 erect lobes and a calyx with 4 sepals. The corolla becomes tan-brown at maturity; the sepals remain green and hairy. BAS

Micranthes petiolaris *(Saxifraga michauxii)*

SAXIFRAGACEAE | **cliff saxifrage**

Jun–Aug, 4–15 in. Erect, rosette-forming perennial found in crevices in exposed high-elevation rock outcrops, other moist to dry rock outcrops, periglacial boulder fields, rocky seeps. Leaves sessile, spoon-shaped, coarsely and unevenly toothed, often red-tinged, hairy. Flowers in a wide-branching cluster, with a few leaflike bracts and sticky glands on the stalk; each ½ in. wide, with 5 spreading, lance- to spoon-shaped petals, the 3 largest with basal claws and 2 yellow spots, the 2 smallest lacking both. There are 5 green to reddish, recurved sepals and 6–10 stamens with orange anthers. Fruit an oval capsule. AMC, RTW

Viola blanda

VIOLACEAE | **sweet white violet**

Apr–May, 1–10 in. Erect-ascending perennial of northern hardwood forests, cove forests, and other moist to sub-moist forests. Stemless, with creeping runners rooting at nodes or tip. Leaves on reddish petioles (color often extending into the midrib and larger veins) with lance-shaped stipules, 1–3½ in. long and wide, heart-shaped with a narrow notch at the base, bluntly toothed, smooth to finely hairy and with a satiny sheen on upper surface. Flowers solitary on reddish stalks, 5-petaled, ½ in. wide, with brown-purple veins on the lower 3 petals, the lowest often the largest and spurred, the 2 upper ones curled backward. Fruit an oval capsule. RTW

Viola lanceolata

VIOLACEAE | **lanceleaf violet**

Mar–May, 2–10 in. Low-growing perennial of wet habitats, including pitcher-plant seepage bogs, small swamp forests, depression ponds, and interdune swales and ponds. Stemless, the flowering scapes and leaves arising from slender, creeping rhizomes and stolons. Leaves in a basal cluster, on typically reddish petioles with lance-shaped stipules, lance-shaped with a tapering base, 1–6 in. long, shallowly toothed and smooth. Flowers solitary on reddish stalks, white with a greenish throat, about ½ in. wide, with 5 petals, the lowermost with prominent purple veins and a blunt, backward-pointing spur. Stolons bear many closed, self-pollinating flowers. RTW

Viola primulifolia

VIOLACEAE | **primrose-leaf violet**

Mar–Jun, 2–10 in. Erect, creeping perennial of bogs, wet savannas, pocosins, and moist organic soils along small streams. Stemless; underground, horizontal rhizomes produce numerous stolons that terminate in crowns of leaves. Leaves petiolate, often with the tapering base of the blade continuing as petiole wings, elliptic-oblong to oval, ½–4 in. long, entire or shallowly toothed, smooth or hairy. Flowers solitary on slender, smooth stalks arising from leaf crown; each flower white with purple lines on lower petal(s), about ⅓ in. wide, with 5 unequal petals, the lowest with a backward-pointing spur. Fruit a green, narrowly oval capsule. JF

Baptisia albescens

FABACEAE | **spiked wild indigo**

May–Jul, 2–3 ft. Erect perennial of dry, open woodlands and woodland borders, pine flatwoods, and roadsides. Stems 1–several from a crown, stout, unbranched, blue-green to gray-purple and with a waxy coating, smooth. Leaves alternate; on petioles with small stipules at the base; divided into 3 elliptical leaflets with rounded tips, each ½–2½ in. long. Flowers in 1–several long, erect, terminal spikes extending above foliage; each flower white or cream with yellow, less than ¾ in. long, with typical pea-flower shape, including an erect banner petal. Fruit an erect, yellowish-brown and leathery, narrowly cylindrical seed pod. BAS

Galactia erecta

FABACEAE | **erect milkpea**

May–Jul, 8–16 in. Erect perennial of dry longleaf pinelands, especially where regularly burned. Stems slender, sparingly branched, sparsely hairy. Leaves few, alternate, long-petioled, divided into 3 narrow leaflets, each 1–2 in. long, smooth. Flowers in small clusters of 1–6 from leaf axils, white, turning red or maroon, about ½ in. long, with typical pea-flower shape. BAS

Hylodesmum glutinosum (*Desmodium glutinosum*)

FABACEAE | **clusterleaf tick-trefoil**

Jun–Aug, 1–4 ft. Erect perennial of moist forests, especially nutrient-rich ones. Stems unbranched, sparsely to moderately hairy. Leaves alternate to almost whorled, long-petioled, divided into 3 broadly oval leaflets, the terminal one slightly larger at 2½–5½ in. long; leaflets green on both sides, often with stiff hairs above and soft-hairy beneath. Flowers in a terminal panicle above the leaves, white to purplish-rose, about ¼ in. long, with typical pea-flower shape. Fruit a flattened pod divided into 1–4 U-shaped segments and covered with hooked hairs that stick to clothing and fur. AMC

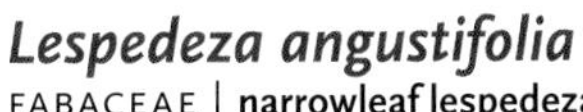

Lespedeza angustifolia

FABACEAE | **narrowleaf lespedeza**

Aug–Oct, to 4½ ft. Erect to ascending perennial of sandhill-pocosin ecotones, dry to moist savannas, and mountain bogs. Stems mostly unbranched, covered with thin, longitudinal lines and close-pressed hairs. Leaves on short petioles with linear stipules that soon drop, divided into 3 narrowly linear leaflets, each ½–1½ in. long and often hairy. Flowers in dense cylindrical to spherical spikes (⅓–1 in. long), on stalks from upper leaf axils; each flower yellowish-white to cream, about ¼ in. long, resembling pea-flower structure. Fruit a hairy, flattened, elliptical to oblong pod containing a single seed. BAS

Lespedeza capitata

FABACEAE | **bush-clover**

Aug–Oct, 1½–5 ft. Erect perennial of woodlands and woodland borders, wet meadows, fens, prairies. Stems 1–several, stiff, smooth below, branched and covered with dense, close-pressed silvery hairs above. Leaves petiolate with needlelike stipules that soon drop, divided into 3 narrowly elliptical to oblong leaflets, each ¾–1¼ in. long, blunt-tipped, usually silvery-hairy. Flowers in dense, nearly spherical racemes from upper leaf axils (the raceme stalks longer than leaves); each yellowish-white, less than ½ in. long, with typical pea-flower shape, the banner petal bearing a central purple spot. Fruit a hairy, flattened-elliptical pod with a short point and a single seed. BAS

Lespedeza cuneata

FABACEAE | **Chinese lespedeza**

Jul–Sep, 2–5 ft. Erect short-lived perennial/annual of road banks, disturbed areas, floodplains, creek banks; also invading other natural habitats. Native to e Asia, brought to NoAm to control erosion and for wildlife food plots. Stems slender and ridged or grooved, branched and covered with dense, upwardly pressed hairs. Leaves crowded, short-petioled, divided into 3 blunt-tipped, narrowly oblong leaflets, each to 1 in. long, gray-green, covered with dense, short, white, close-pressed hairs. Flowers 1–4 on tiny stalks from upper and middle leaf axils, creamy-white, 1/3 in. long, with typical pea-flower shape, the banner petal bearing purple veins. BAS

Lespedeza hirta

FABACEAE | **hairy lespedeza**

Aug–Oct, 1½–3 ft. Erect perennial of woodlands, woodland borders, clearings, roadsides. Stems few-branched above; covered in tawny, spreading hairs. Leaves on short, hairy petioles with a pair of narrow stipules, divided into 3 widely oval leaflets, each to 2 in. long, finely hairy above, soft-hairy beneath. Flowers in short, dense racemes 1–3 in. long on hairy stalks from upper leaf axils; each flower cream-colored, 1/3 in. long, with typical pea-flower shape, the erect banner petal streaked with purple at the base. Conspicuous, narrow, hairy calyx lobes, longer than the flower, eventually turn brown. Fruit a flattened, hairy, elliptical to oval pod containing a single seed. JG

Trifolium arvense

FABACEAE | **rabbitfoot clover**

Apr–Aug, 4–16 in. Erect annual/biennial of disturbed areas and shale barrens. Native to the Mediterranean region. Stems branched, hairy. Leaves on short, hairy petioles with a pair of tiny stipules, divided into 3 elliptic-oblong leaflets, each ½–1 in. long and sparsely silky-hairy. Flowers in dense, pinkish-gray, fuzzy-hairy cylindrical clusters ½–1½ in. long, at ends of branches and from leaf axils; each flower about ¼ in. long, with a white corolla of 5 petals, a greenish-red calyx with 5 bristly lobes, several inserted stamens, and a pistil with a single style. Fruit an oval pod. BAS

Vicia caroliniana

FABACEAE | **pale vetch**

Apr–Jun, 1–5 ft. long. Sprawling or climbing rhizomatous perennial of dry or occasionally moist forests, woodlands, disturbed areas. Stems several, hollow, slightly winged, mostly smooth. Leaves on short petioles with stipules, pinnately divided into 4–25 pairs of narrowly elliptical to oblong-lance-shaped leaflets with a tiny spine at the tip and dense hairs above and beneath. Tendrils extend from leaf ends. Flowers in stalked, 1-sided racemes 3–4 in. long, arising from leaf axils; each oriented parallel to the ground or nodding, white to pale lavender, 1/4 in. long, tubular, typical pea-flower shape. Fruit a flattened oblong pod with a long-beaked tip. BAS

Torilis arvensis

APIACEAE | **field hedge-parsley**

May–Jun, 1–2 ft. Erect annual that may sprawl when in fruit; found on roadsides, fields, disturbed areas. Native to Europe. Stems slender, branched above middle, somewhat rough-hairy. Leaves petiolate, oval to lance-shaped in outline but 2–3 times pinnately divided into lance-shaped, toothed or lobed leaflets that are sparsely white-hairy above. Flowers in terminal compound umbels 2–3 in. wide, each with about 8 umbellets of about 8 flowers each. Flowers white, less than 1/4 in. wide, with 5 tiny, unequal petals and 5 stamens. Fruit a rose-colored to whitish-green, oblong and burlike (covered with bristles) seed that turns brown. RTW

Melilotus albus

FABACEAE | **white sweetclover**

Apr–Oct, to 6 ft. Erect annual/biennial found in agricultural fields, roadsides, and other open, disturbed areas. Native to Eurasia. Stems lanky, branched, smooth to slightly hairy. Leaves on petioles with a pair of tiny, linear stipules at the base, divided into 3 grayish-green, narrowly oval leaflets (center one stalked), each 1/2–2 in. long, toothed and smooth. Flowers in numerous, erect, slender racemes 1 1/2–5 in. long, on stalks from upper leaf axils; each flower white, 1/3 in. long or less, angled downward, with typical pea-flower shape, including a nearly erect banner petal. Fruit an oval pod with a beak at the tip. KB

Trifolium hybridum

FABACEAE | **alsike clover**

Apr–Oct, 6–22 in. Erect to weakly erect perennial of lawns, fields, roadsides, and other disturbed areas. Native to Europe. Stems hollow and soft, somewhat branched, smooth to hairy. Leaves alternate; on petioles with a pair of lance-shaped stipules at the base, palmately divided into 3 oblong-oval leaflets, each about ½ in. long, finely toothed and mostly smooth. Flowers in dense, pompom-like clusters about ½–¾ in. wide, on stalks from upper leaf axils; each flower white or pink, tiny, with typical pea-flower shape. RTW

Trifolium reflexum

FABACEAE | **buffalo clover**

Apr–May, 8–20 in. Erect to ascending annual/biennial of open woodlands, woodland edges, and dry habitats over limestone and shale. Stems branching from the base, smooth but hairy toward the terminus. Leaves on petioles with a pair of hairy stipules, divided into 3 oval leaflets, each ½–1 in. long, (usually) hairy and very finely toothed. Flowers in dense, pompom-like clusters about 1 in. wide, at stem ends and from upper leaf axils; each flower white tinged with green, becoming pinkish-red then brown, about ½ in. long, with typical pea-flower shape. Each flower on its own tiny stalk, starting out erect but soon spreading to reflexed. RTW

Trifolium repens

FABACEAE | **Dutch clover**

Apr–Nov, 4–12 in. Erect and creeping perennial of lawns, roadsides, and other disturbed areas. Native to Eurasia. Stems branched, smooth or hairy, creeping and rooting at nodes. Leaves on long petioles with a pair of stem-clasping stipules at the base, palmately divided into 3 oval to oblong-oval leaflets, each about ¾ in. long and with finely toothed margins and a white or light green chevron mark on the upper surface. Flowers in stalked, dense, pompom-like clusters of 20–50 flowers each and about ¾ in. wide, held above leaves; each flower white or pinkish, ⅜ in. long, with typical pea-flower shape. BAS

Trifolium virginicum

FABACEAE | **Kates Mountain clover**

May–Aug, 4–6 in. Erect, clumped perennial of shale barrens; also on outcrops or glades over limestone, diabase, and ultramafic rocks. Stems mostly prostrate but not rooting at the nodes; densely hairy. Leaves arising from a woody crown on hairy, reddish petioles with stem-clasping stipules at the base, palmately divided into 3 narrowly oblong leaflets that are 3–7 times as long as wide, finely toothed, silky-hairy beneath and with a white chevron mark above. Flowers in dense, pompom-like clusters about 1 in. wide, borne on long, hairy stalks arising from crown; each flower creamy white with purple veins, about 1/4 in. long, with typical pea-flower shape. JB

Adlumia fungosa

FUMARIACEAE | **Allegheny-vine**

Jun–Sep, to 12 ft. Vining biennial of cliffs, talus, rocky slopes, rich bottomland forests, cool rocky forests, burned areas, especially over calcareous or mafic rocks. Stems climbing (even into trees), smooth; essentially stemless in its first year, with several erect leaves. Leaves petiolate, 2 times pinnately divided; reduced in size at the upper reaches of the vine, where leaves act like tendrils. Flowers in drooping clusters from leaf axils, white to pale pink, 1/2–2/3 in. long, tubular and shaped like upside-down vases with a pair of tiny, scalelike bracts at the flower base (which is on top) and 2 spreading lobes at the mouth of the vase. Fruit a narrow, oval capsule. JG

Aconitum reclinatum

RANUNCULACEAE | **trailing wolfsbane**

Jun–Sep, 1–3 ft. Sprawling perennial growing in rich cove forests, particularly along brook banks, in seepages, and in periglacial boulder fields with seepage, primarily over mafic rocks. A Southern Appalachian endemic. Stems weak, sparsely branching, smooth. Leaves petiolate, roundish in outline, to 6 in. wide, palmately divided into 3–7 coarsely toothed, wedge-shaped segments. Flowers in loose, elongate panicles from upper leaf axils and stem end; each flower yellowish-white or cream, with 5 yellowish-white petal-like sepals, the uppermost one shaped like a hood or helmet, that enclose 2 smaller petals. Fruit a beaked, elliptical follicle. GPF

Gillenia trifoliata (*Porteranthus trifoliatus*)

ROSACEAE | **mountain Indian-physic**

Apr–Jun, 2–3 ft. Erect perennial found in moist forests, forest edges, and on road banks. Stems 1–several from woody root crown, branched, thinly hairy. Leaves alternate; nearly sessile and with linear stipules (about ¼ in. long); divided into 3 oblong-oval to lance-shaped, finely toothed leaflets (to 4 in. long); thin and smooth to hairy. Flowers on reddish stalks in a widely branched, open, terminal cluster; each flower white (sometimes pink-tinged), 1–1½ in. wide, with 5 widely spreading, unequal, linear petals and a reddish, tubular, 5-lobed calyx that persists after petals drop. WS

Dicentra canadensis

FUMARIACEAE | **squirrel corn**

Apr–May, 4–12 in. Erect, colonial perennial found in rich, moist forests, especially mountain cove forests. Stems hollow at maturity, smooth. Leaves petiolate, 4–12 in. long, finely divided into many narrow segments (fernlike), bluish-green. Flowers dangling from a leafless stalk arched above the foliage, white, to ¾ in. long, tubular, with 2 upward projecting, rounded spurs—suggesting a heart-shape—and 2 small, spreading corolla lips at the bottom of the "heart." Fruit a green, narrowly oval, beaked capsule. Plants arise from small, round, yellow tubers that resemble corn kernels. Flowers fragrant. WS

Dicentra cucullaria

FUMARIACEAE | **Dutchman's breeches**

Mar–May, 4–12 in. Erect-spreading, colonial perennial found in rich, moist forests, especially mountain cove forests. Stems hollow at maturity, smooth. Leaves finely divided into many narrow segments (fernlike), silvery-green. Flowers dangling from a leafless stalk arched above the foliage, white, about ½ in. long, tubular, with 2 upward-projecting, narrow spurs (the "breeches") and 2 small, yellow, spreading lips at the tube opening, which faces downward. Fruit a slender, tapering, beaked capsule. Foliage very similar to *D. canadensis*, but the spur shapes differ, and *D. cucullaria* is not fragrant. RTW

Aphyllon uniflorum (*Orobanche uniflora*)

OROBANCHACEAE | **ghostpipe**

Apr–May, 2–8 in. Slender, leafless perennial, found throughout NoAm in a wide range of forest habitats, from sandy floodplain forests to rich/acid cove forests and dry to moist mixed oak and oak-hickory forests. Stems essentially underground and sending up furry, tan-brown, leafless flower stalks. Flowers solitary at top of stalk, nodding or held horizontally, white with pale bluish-purple lines, 1 in. long, tubular, with 5 spreading lobes. Fruit an oval capsule. Lacks roots and chlorophyll, instead deriving water and nutrients from host plants, including goldenrods and sunflowers. AMC

Conopholis americana

OROBANCHACEAE | **bearcorn**

Mar–Jun, 4–10 in. Erect perennial lacking chlorophyll, found in rich, moist forests under oak trees. Stems leafless, thick and fleshy (to 1 in. thick), yellowish- to pale brown, covered with brown scales and often growing in clumps. Flowers densely packed into a spike that occupies ½ or more of the plant, pale yellow, to ½ in. long, tubular with 2 lips. Fruit an oval to round capsule. The whole plant, which is parasitic on the roots of oaks, resembles an ear of corn and later, as it turns dry and brown with age, a pine cone. WS

Circaea alpina

ONAGRACEAE | **alpine enchanter's-nightshade**

Jun–Sep, 3–10 in. Delicate, erect perennial of moist organic soil at high elevations (especially in spruce-fir and northern hardwood forests), rocky or gravelly seepages, in spray behind waterfalls, and at dripping cliff bases. Stems weak, unbranched, smooth; upper stem may be glandular-hairy. Leaves on winged petioles, triangular to oval, ¾–2 in. long, coarsely toothed, thin, shiny and smooth. Flowers in a terminal raceme on ascending, smooth stalks (spreading to deflexed when in fruit); each flower white to pale pink, less than ¼ in. wide, with 2 deeply notched petals (appearing as 4) and 2 smooth, green sepals. Fruit a hairy, flattened capsule. LADI

Circaea canadensis

ONAGRACEAE | **Canada enchanter's-nightshade**

Jun–Aug, 10–30 in. Delicate-flowered, erect perennial of moist, nutrient-rich forests. Stems with few to no branches, smooth or hairy. Leaves petiolate, in pairs at 90° to each other, oval, 2–4 in. long, irregularly toothed and mostly hairless. Flowers in an open terminal raceme, each on a spreading, ½-in.-long, finely hairy stalk; flowers white, less than ¼ in. wide, with 2 small white, deeply notched petals (appearing to be 4) and 2 green, hairy sepals. Fruit a bristly, grooved-and-ridged capsule. AMC

Trillium grandiflorum

TRILLIACEAE | **great white trillium**

Apr–Jun, 6–20 in. Erect perennial of rich coves and moist slopes; less typically on ridges over rich rock types. Stems stout, unbranched, pale green to pale reddish-green, smooth. Leaves 3 in a whorl at top of stem, sessile to short-petioled, broadly oval, 2½–6½ in. long, smooth. Flower solitary on an ascending stalk to 4 in. long emerging from center of leaf whorl, waxy-white and turning pink with age, about 3 in. wide, widely funnel-shaped, with 3 spreading elliptical petals that overlap at the base, 3 green narrow sepals, 6 straight yellow anthers, and a white ovary. Fruit a pale green, oval, berrylike capsule. WS

Trillium pusillum

TRILLIACEAE | **dwarf trillium**

Mar–May, 3–8 in. Erect, colonial perennial of the ecotones between calcareous savannas and swamp forests. Stems slender, unbranched, smooth. Leaves 3 in a whorl at stem top, short-petioled, oblong to narrowly lance-shaped, 1–3 in. long, usually with rounded tip, with 3–5 parallel veins, maroon-tinged when young. Flower solitary above leaves, on a stalk or sessile; white aging to rosy-pink, with 3 spreading-ascending oblong to narrowly lance-shaped, thin-textured petals with wavy margins, 3 spreading, oblong-lance-shaped, green-with-maroon-undertones sepals just below the petals, 6 stamens, and a 3-parted style. Fruit a berrylike capsule. Highly variable species. RTW

Trillium rugelii

TRILLIACEAE | **southern nodding trillium**

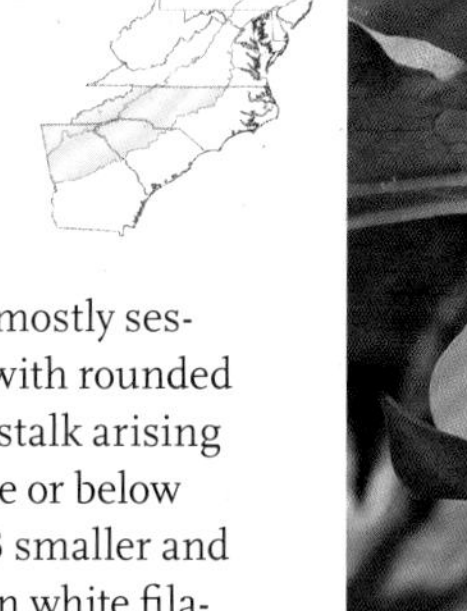

Apr–May, 6–16 in. Erect perennial of rich woodlands and forests over mafic or calcareous rocks. Stems stout, unbranched, smooth. Leaves 3 in a whorl at top of stem, mostly sessile, diamond-shaped (broadest at middle) with rounded angles, 2½–6 in. long. Flower solitary on a stalk arising from center of leaf whorl and nodding above or below leaves, white, with 3 oval, recurved petals, 3 smaller and green sepals, 6 stamens (maroon anthers on white filaments), and a white ovary that may be maroon-tinged. Fruit a maroon, 3-celled, fleshy capsule resembling a berry. RTW

Trillium simile

TRILLIACEAE | **sweet white trillium**

Mar–May, 11–23 in. Erect, rhizomatous perennial found in very rich soils of slopes and coves over mafic or calcareous rocks; often also in or near seepage. Stem scapelike, with a single whorl of 3 leaves and flower stalk at the top, smooth. Leaves sessile, roughly diamond-shaped, 4–7 in. long by 4–8 in. wide, solid green, with prominent major veins. Flower solitary, erect to leaning on a stalk emerging from center of leaf whorl, creamy white, 1½–3½ in. wide, with 3 ascending, broadly oval petals with slightly recurved tips, 3 shorter sepals, and 6 stamens surrounding a purplish-black pyramidal ovary. Flowers have a faint green-apple smell. JF

Trillium undulatum

TRILLIACEAE | **painted trillium**

Apr–May, 8–16 in. Erect perennial found on acidic soils of ridges, slopes, and bog margins, mostly at high elevations and often associated with rhododendron, hemlock, pine, or spruce species. Stems slender, unbranched, smooth, green to purplish. Leaves 3 in a whorl at top of stem, short-petioled, broadly oval, 2½–5 in. long. Flower solitary on an erect stalk arising from center of leaf whorl, white with red markings and with 3 long (1–2 in.) elliptical to oblong-lance-shaped petals with undulating margins and a red, inverted-V mark, 3 smaller pointed sepals, 6 lavender anthers, and a white ovary. Fruit a red, 3-celled, fleshy, oval capsule resembling a berry. WS

Alisma subcordatum

ALISMATACEAE | **southern water-plantain**

Apr–Nov, to 3 ft. above water. Aquatic perennial of marshes, ponds, and stream edges. Leaves emergent, arising in a cluster from an underground stem, long-petioled, oval, sometimes with a heart-shaped base, sharp-tipped, 2–8 in. long, smooth. Flowers in an emergent, open, much-branched and many-flowered panicle on a stalk arising from the underground stem; each flower white, less than 1/4 in. wide, with 3 round petals, 3 green sepals visible between them, a central ring of green ovaries, and 6–9 stamens. Fruit a tight cluster of tiny achenes. AMC, BAS

Echinodorus cordifolius

ALISMATACEAE | **creeping burhead**

Jun–Nov, to 3 ft. above water. Prostrate to erect aquatic perennial of swamps, ditches, and wet thickets, especially on base-rich substrates. Stem underground, sending up separate flowering scapes and leaves. Leaves clustered, erect and rising above water surface on long, 3-sided petioles, oval to heart-shaped with a sharp tip, 2–8 in. long, fleshy and smooth. Flowers in widely spaced whorls along a single, arching scape that often leans onto the ground and roots at the nodes and tip; flowers 1 in. wide, with 3 spreading and rounded petals, 3 sepals, and a central compound ovary ringed by stamens. Fruit a brown, compact cluster of short-beaked achenes. BAS

Helanthium tenellum (*Echinodorus tenellus*)

ALISMATACEAE | **mud-babies**

Jul–Oct, 2–4 in. Erect, rhizomatous perennial of drawdown zones of Coastal Plain ponds, pineland ponds, blackwater river banks, and ponds in the Mountains. Stem underground, sending up flowering scapes and leaves. Leaves basal, long-petioled, linear to elliptical, 1/2–1 in. long, submerged leaves narrower and lacking a distinct blade. Flowers on drooping stalks in whorls of 2–8 at top of flowering scapes, white to pinkish-white, less than 1 in. wide, with 3 spreading and rounded petals, 3 sepals, and a central compound ovary ringed by stamens. Fruit a reddish-brown, compact cluster of beakless achenes. AMC

Sagittaria australis

ALISMATACEAE | **Appalachian arrowhead**

Jun–Oct, 8–30 in. Erect aquatic perennial of marshes, swamps, river shores, backwaters, and margins of ponds and lakes. Flowering stems (scapes) and leaves arising from underground stem and held above water surface. Leaves clustered basally on long, 5-angled petioles, arrowhead-shaped with broad basal lobes, 4–10 in. long, smooth. Flowers in whorls of 3 along an erect, 6-angled scape, male and female flowers separate; flowers white, about 1 in. wide, with 3 spreading, rounded petals. Male flowers with bushy yellow stamens and female flowers with mounded, green compound ovary. Fruit a brown, compact cluster of beaked achenes. RTW

Sagittaria calycina

ALISMATACEAE | **hooded arrowhead**

May–Sep, 2–6 in. Aquatic annual/perennial of ponds, pools, and impoundments, on seasonally exposed shores and flats. Stemless; leaves and flowering scapes arise from underground rhizomes. Emersed leaves on long, spongy petioles, nearly triangular to arrowhead-shaped or elliptical, to 8 in. long; submersed leaves (rare) primarily linear, lack petioles. Flowers stalked, in 3–12 whorls on an erect or curved scape, male flowers above, perfect flowers below, their bulbous yellow-green center of tiny carpels ringed by yellow stamens; flowers (sometimes pink-tinged) ¾ in. wide, each round petal with a yellowish-green basal spot. Fruit a brown, compact cluster of beaked achenes. GPF

Sagittaria engelmanniana

ALISMATACEAE | **Engelmann's arrowhead**

Jun–Oct, 8–30 in. Erect aquatic perennial of blackwater stream banks, sphagnum bogs, pocosins, beaver ponds. Leaves and flowering scapes, both held above water surface, arise from an underground stem. Leaves clustered basally on long petioles, narrowly arrowhead-shaped with nearly linear basal lobes, 4–8 in. long, smooth. Flowers in 2–4 whorls of 3 flowers each, spaced along upper half of scape, upper whorls male, lower whorls female. Each flower about 1 in. wide, with 3 spreading and rounded petals, 3 reflexed sepals, 15–25 bushy yellow stamens (male flowers) or a mounded, green compound ovary (female flowers). Fruit a brown, compact cluster of beaked achenes. BAS

Sagittaria graminea

ALISMATACEAE | **grassy arrowhead**

May–Nov, 1–3 ft. Erect aquatic perennial of marshes, ponds, freshwater and saltwater tidal marshes. Flowering scapes and leaves, mostly held above water surface, arise from an underground stem. Leaves clustered basally: linear to narrowly lance-shaped leaves on petioles and to 7 in. long are both submerged and above water; narrower, grasslike leaves to 14 in. long are above water. Flowers in 1–10 whorls of 3 flowers each along an erect scape, upper whorls male, lower whorls female. Flowers ½–1 in. wide, with 3 spreading, rounded petals; male flowers with bushy yellow stamens, females with a mounded, green compound ovary. Fruit a brown, compact cluster of achenes. JF

Sagittaria lancifolia

ALISMATACEAE | **bulltongue arrowhead**

May–Jun, 2–3 ft. Aquatic perennial from tuber-producing rhizomes, found in freshwater to brackish marshes and in swamps. Flowering scapes and leaves, mostly held above water surface, arise from an underground stem. Leaves clustered basally, blades gradually tapered to a stout petiole, lance-shaped with pointed tip, 4–16 in. long. Flowers in 4–12 whorls of 3 at top of the erect scape, upper whorls male, lower whorls female; each flower to 1¼ in. wide, with spreading, rounded petals; male flowers with bushy yellow stamens, females with mounded, green compound ovary. 3 reflexed to spreading sepals persist in fruit. Fruit a brown, compact cluster of beaked achenes. WS

Sagittaria latifolia

ALISMATACEAE | **broadleaf arrowhead**

Jul–Oct, 4–8 in. Erect aquatic perennial of marshes, swamps, farm ponds, ditches, and bogs. Flowering scapes and leaves, mostly held above water surface, arise from an underground tuber. Leaves clustered basally on spongy stalks, arrowhead-shaped with long, spreading basal lobes, to 12 in. long, smooth. Flowers in well-spaced whorls along a scape that is about as tall as the leaves, upper whorls of male flowers, lower whorls female; flowers to 1½ in. wide, with 3 rounded, spreading petals and 3 reflexed sepals. Male flowers with bushy yellow stamens, female flowers with a mounded, green compound ovary. Fruit a brown, compact cluster of beaked achenes. PHA

Floerkea proserpinacoides

LIMNANTHACEAE | **false-mermaid**

Apr–Jun, to 1 ft. Sprawling to sub-erect annual of moist, rich floodplain forests and adjacent lower slopes. Stems branched, somewhat succulent, smooth. Leaves long-petioled, pinnately divided into 3–7 linear to elliptical leaflets or segments, which are also sometimes 2- to 3-times divided. Flowers solitary on long stalks from leaf axils, white, about 1/4 in. wide, with 3 tiny petals, 3 green and lance-oval sepals, 6 stamens (usually), and a single style. Fruit a brown, tiny cluster of 1–3 achenes. GPF

Mayaca fluviatilis

MAYACACEAE | **bogmoss**

May–Jul, to 2 ft. long. Floating aquatic perennial found in marshes, streams, swamp forests, shores of natural lakes (rarely in artificial impoundments), and seepage areas; in saturated soil or variously submersed, from South America to the s U.S. Stems floating in water or matted and mosslike on the shore, whitish-green and very leafy. Leaves spiraled around and perpendicular to the stem, dense, needlelike, 1/4–1/2 in. long, shiny pale green. Flower solitary on a slender, erect stalk, whitish to pink or white-and-pink, about 1/2 in. wide, with 3 spreading oblong-oval petals, 3 pointed green sepals showing between the petals, and 3 stamens with yellow anthers. WS

Arabidopsis thaliana

BRASSICACEAE | **mouse-ear cress**

Mar–May, 1–20 in. Annual herb from basal rosette, growing in disturbed areas, fields, roadsides, and lawns. Native to Eurasia, widespread in NoAm. Stem a flowering stalk with reduced leaves, branched from base, hairy in the lower half, smooth in upper half. Basal leaves to 1½ in. long, oval to spoon-shaped with a few shallow teeth; the few alternate stem leaves are not toothed. Flowers in a dense terminal raceme that becomes more open as it elongates, white, 1/4 in. wide and with 4 tiny rounded petals. Fruit an erect, smooth, linear green pod. BAS

Diamorpha smallii (*Sedum smallii*)

CRASSULACEAE | **elf-orpine**

Apr–May, 3⁄4–4 in. Short, fleshy, erect to prostrate annual growing in very thin soil of periodically wet depressions on granite flatrocks and outcrops. Stems branching, succulent, red (rarely green) and smooth. Leaves sessile, blunt-tipped, less than 1⁄4 in. long, succulent (round in cross-section), red and smooth. Flowers in branching clusters, white, about 1⁄4 in. wide, with 4 spreading petals, 8 stamens with red anthers, and a white, 4-segmented pistil. Fruit a 4-celled capsule. WS

Maianthemum canadense

RUSCACEAE | **Canada mayflower**

May–Jul, 1½–7 in. Short, erect, colonial perennial found in moist forests, especially at high elevations. Stems smooth, unbranched, sometimes seeming to zigzag. Leaves sessile with clasping base, oval to lance-shaped, 1–4 in. long, shiny; typically only 1–3 per plant. Flowers in a single, narrow, terminal raceme to 1½ in. long, white, with 4 tiny, slightly reflexed, short-lived, pointed tepals and protruding, persistent stamens. Fruit a red-mottled-with-green, round berry. WS

Alliaria petiolata

BRASSICACEAE | **garlic mustard**

Apr–Jun, 1–3 ft. Erect, colony-forming biennial weed, highly invasive in moist forests, in bottomlands and on slopes, where it aggressively outcompetes native species. Native to Europe. Plants form only a basal rosette of rounded to kidney-shaped leaves, to 4 in. long, the first year. Stem leaves alternate, petiolate (petioles reduced above), triangular, 1–3 in. long, coarsely toothed. All leaves with prominently incised veins. Flowers, 1⁄4–1⁄2 in. wide, in short, dense terminal racemes that elongate as flowers and fruit develop. Petals spreading, oblong. Fruit an erect-ascending, green, linear-cylindrical pod. Crushed leaves and stem emit odor of garlic. BAS

Boechera canadensis
(Arabis canadensis)

BRASSICACEAE | **Canada rockcress**

May–Jul, 1–4 ft. Erect biennial with rosette of leaves its first year and a tall raceme of tiny white flowers the second year; grows in thin soils around rock outcrops (especially mafic or calcareous) and in dry to moist, nutrient-rich, often rocky woodlands over mafic or calcareous rocks. Stems grayish-green, hairy below. Basal leaves to 8 in. long, lance-shaped with widely spaced teeth; stem leaves smaller, alternate, clasping. Flower petals slightly longer than the 4 green sepals. Fruit a flattened, slightly curved pod that droops when ripe; lower pods form while upper flowers are still blooming. AMC

Boechera laevigata
(Arabis laevigata)

BRASSICACEAE | **smooth rockcress**

Apr–May, 1–3 ft. Erect biennial with rosette of leaves its first year and a tall raceme of tiny white flowers in second year; grows in limestone barrens, shale barrens, and other dry, rocky habitats. Stems smooth, simple or branched above, with a white-waxy coating. Basal leaves spoon-shaped to narrowly oblong-lance-shaped, to 4½ in. long, varying from toothed to pinnately lobed. Stem leaves larger and notably clasping at base. Flowers, less than ¼ in. wide, on ascending stalks in a terminal raceme, petals slightly longer than the 4 green sepals. Fruit a spreading-ascending linear, narrowly winged pod. BAS

Cardamine bulbosa

BRASSICACEAE | **bulbous bittercress**

Mar–May, 6–20 in. Erect perennial of swampy forests and bogs, primarily in circumneutral soils over limestone or mafic rocks. Stems mostly simple, arising from a barely buried rhizome. Basal leaves long-petioled, oval to nearly round, to 1¼ in. long, withering before full flowering; stem leaves alternate, widely spaced, short-petioled to sessile, oblong-oval, to 2 in. long, wavy-margined to blunt-toothed. Flowers on spreading-ascending stalks in a short terminal raceme, white (rarely pink), about ½ in. wide, with 4 white (rarely pink) petals that form a cross; 4 sepals (green turning yellow), 6 stamens, and a pistil with single style. Fruit a thin, linear green pod. AMC

Lepidium campestre

BRASSICACEAE | **cow cress**

Mar–Jun, 8–18 in. Erect annual/biennial of disturbed areas. Native to Europe, widely naturalized in NoAm. Stems 1–several arising from a basal rosette, sometimes branching at the base, grayish-green, covered with fine hairs. Basal leaves narrowly oblong-oval, shallowly toothed to entire; stem leaves alternate, numerous, clasping with small "earlobes" at the base, lance-elliptical, to 3 in. long (but reduced in size upward); all leaves fuzzy like the stems. Flowers on spreading stalks in dense terminal racemes, white, less than 1⁄4 in. wide, with 4 tiny petals. Fruit a dry, flattened, oval pod that is notched at the tip. JG

Thlaspi alliaceum

BRASSICACEAE | **garlic pennycress**

Mar–Apr, 8–22 in. Erect annual of fields, spreading very aggressively along roadsides and other disturbed areas. Native to Europe. Stems branched from the base, smooth above and with a white-waxy coating, a few hairs and red-tinged at the base; with a garlic odor when crushed. Leaves widely spaced, sessile with clasping basal lobes, oblong-lance-shaped, 1⁄3–1 in. long, shallowly toothed, soon withering. Flowers on stalks in a compact terminal raceme (elongating in fruit), white, less than 1⁄4 in. wide, with 4 spoon-shaped petals, 4 green sepals (shorter than petals), 6 stamens, and an ovary with a short, thick style. Fruit a green, round to oval, minutely winged pod. JG

Thlaspi arvense

BRASSICACEAE | **field pennycress**

Mar–Jun, 8–30 in. Erect annual of fields and other disturbed areas. Native to Europe. Stems ribbed and sometimes winged, branched, smooth. Leaves alternate (a rosette of basal leaves may form first), mostly sessile with clasping lobes at the base, lance-shaped to narrowly oval, to 4 in. long, wavy-margined to blunt-toothed, smooth. Flowers on stalks in terminal racemes, which elongate during blooming (flowers at top open first); each flower white, less than 1⁄4 in. wide, with 4 tiny spoon-shaped and round-tipped petals, 4 green sepals, 6 anthers, and a green ovary. Fruit a green, round to oval, minutely winged pod. JG

Obolaria virginica

GENTIANACEAE | **Virginia pennywort**

Feb–Jun, 1–6 in. Inconspicuous perennial growing in the leaf litter of nutrient-rich, moist to dry forests. Stems short, fleshy, simple (very occasionally branched) with an overall purple-green coloration. Leaves opposite and sessile, roundish, less than ½ in. long, thick-textured, the lower leaves bractlike. Flowers solitary, or in clusters of 3, in upper leaf axils; each flower white to lavender, tubular, but cleft to the middle of the tube into 4 diamond-shaped lobes. This spring ephemeral is often barely visible above the leaf litter; it has little chlorophyll and is believed to be a mycoheterotroph. WS

Rotala ramosior

LYTHRACEAE | **toothcup**

Jun–Oct, 2–15 in. Erect to reclining annual of marshes, ditches, exposed drawdown muds and silts. Stems 4-angled, freely branched (sometimes unbranched), smooth, turning red over time. Leaves opposite or whorled, linear-oblong, petiolate, ½–1¼ in. long, smooth. Flowers solitary in leaf axils, red, to ¼ in. long, tubular with 4 tiny, white-pink corolla lobes. Fruit a rounded, 4-sectioned capsule tipped with 4 teeth. RTW

Clematis ochroleuca

RANUNCULACEAE | **curlyheads**

Apr–Jun, to 3 ft. Erect perennial of dry woodlands and woodland borders, generally over mafic or calcareous rocks. Stems simple or branched from nodes, furry and at times a little woody. Leaves sessile, oval, to 5 in. long, occasionally shallowly lobed, somewhat leathery. Flowers solitary and nodding at top of stem, purple- or blue-tinged on the outside and creamy yellow inside, shaped like an upside-down urn (to 1⅓ in. long) and composed of 4 thick sepals (no true petals) with strongly recurved tips. Fruit a golden, feathery, curved seed. A lesser known native species of *Clematis* with habit more like a shrub than a vine. WS

Diodia virginiana

RUBIACEAE | **large buttonweed**

Jun–Dec, 4–18 in. Prostrate annual/perennial of ditches, wet fields, and other moist to wet habitats. Stems 4-sided, sprawling, branched from root crown, hairy at least on angles. Leaves sessile with linear stipules at the base, lance-shaped to narrowly oval, to 2½ in. long, entire. Flowers solitary in leaf axils, white (occasionally pink), about ¼ in. long, funnel-shaped, with 4 spreading, pointed corolla lobes that are densely hairy inside. Fruit a green, 8-ribbed, elliptical drupe with persistent calyx lobes. BAS

Edrastima uniflora (*Oldenlandia uniflora*)

RUBIACEAE | **oldenlandia**

Jun–Oct, 5–18 in. Ascending to leaning annual of pondshores, muddy drawdown shores, Coastal Plain streamheads, and other moist to wet places. Stems weak, loosely branched, hairy. Leaves nearly sessile, oval to broadly lance-shaped, to ¾ in. long, hairy. Flowers in small, sessile clusters of 3–10 at stem tip and in leaf axils; creamy white; with a tiny corolla tube opening to 4 triangular lobes, and a very hairy, green calyx surpassing the corolla. Fruit a rounded, 2-celled capsule enclosed by the persistent calyx. BE

Hexasepalum teres (*Diodia teres*)

RUBIACEAE | **poorjoe**

Jun–Dec, 6–18 in. Prostrate to erect annual of dunes, sandy roadsides, glades, hardpans, and other dry to moist habitats. Stems bluntly 4-sided, branched from base, sometimes red-tinged, minutely hairy. Leaves sessile, linear to narrowly lance-shaped, to 1½ in. long, stiff, with margins rolled slightly downward; a stipule connecting the bases of opposing pairs of leaves bears reddish, erect bristles. Flowers solitary in axils of middle and upper leaves, white to pale purple, to ¼ in. long, funnel-shaped with 4 spreading, pointy corolla lobes. Fruit a green (turning brown), dry, rounded drupe with stiff hairs. BAS

Houstonia longifolia

RUBIACEAE | **northern longleaf bluet**

Jun–Aug, 4–10 in. Tufted, erect perennial of dry woodlands, barrens, road banks, other dry sandy or rocky habitats. Stems branched above in inflorescence, smooth or hairy. A small rosette of basal leaves withers early; stem leaves sessile, linear to narrowly lance-shaped with sharp or blunt tips, to 1¼ in. long, smooth. Flowers in small, stalked clusters at top of stem and in upper axils; each flower white to lavender (lacking a yellow center), ¼–⅜ in. wide, consisting of a conspicuously hairy (inside) tubular corolla with 4 spreading to recurved lobes and a green calyx with 4 linear-lance-shaped lobes. Fruit a 2-celled, round capsule. JG

Houstonia procumbens
(Hedyotis procumbens)

RUBIACEAE | **creeping bluet**

Jan–Dec, to 12 in. long. Low-growing, semi-succulent perennial found on beach dunes and in moist to wet, sandy pinelands. Stems creeping along ground, rooting at nodes. Leaves sessile, oval to round, about ⅓ in. long, somewhat succulent and with tiny hairs on the margins. Flowers solitary on short, erect stalks from leaf axils; each flower white, ⅓ in. wide, with a short corolla tube and 4 spreading, oval, pointed lobes. AMC

Houstonia tenuifolia

RUBIACEAE | **diffuse-branched bluet**

Apr–Jul, 6–12 in. Slender, erect to ascending perennial found in dry, often rocky (especially mafic rocks) or sandy woodlands. Stems thin, weakly 4-angled and obscurely winged, widely branched, hairy on angles. Basal and lower leaves petiolate, oval, to ¾ in. long; upper stem leaves linear, bluntly pointed, with a prominent vein. Flowers on thin stalks in open clusters terminating branches; each flower less than ¼ in. long, white to purple, funnel-shaped with 4 spreading, triangular-tipped corolla lobes. Fruit a green, rounded and compressed capsule. BAS

Mitchella repens

RUBIACEAE | **partridge-berry**

May–Jul, to 4 in., trailing ½–1 ft. Prostrate, loosely mat-forming, evergreen perennial of deciduous and coniferous forests, streambanks, heath balds, and maritime forests. Stems branched, trailing and rooting at nodes, minutely hairy or smooth. Leaves short-petioled, oval and truncate to rounded at the base, to 1 in. long, leathery, dark green and noticeably veiny. Flowers in pairs in leaf axils, white (sometimes pink-tinged), ½ in. long, tubular, with hairs inside and opening to 4 recurved, pointed corolla lobes. Fruit a bright red, round drupe. WS

Polypremum procumbens

TETRACHONDRACEAE | **rustweed**

May–Oct, to 12 in. long. Ascending to reclining annual/perennial found in fields, pastures, roadsides, dunes, riverside sandbars, and disturbed areas. Stems much-branched and spreading radially in a circular mat from a central crown, the branches usually orange near the crown. Leaves sessile and connected to the stem by a stipule-like membrane, linear to needlelike, to ¾ in. long, smooth. Flowers solitary and sessile in leaf axils, or in small stalked clusters, white, less than ¼ in. wide, with 4 rounded petals and a tuft of white hairs in the center. RTW

Sedum glaucophyllum

CRASSULACEAE | **cliff stonecrop**

May–Jun, 2–6 in. Tufted, erect, sprawling perennial of sedimentary rock outcrops with basic chemistry. Stems fleshy, smooth; nonflowering shoots prostrate, rooting at nodes, forming dense leaf rosettes; flowering branches erect. Leaves alternate but so crowded they appear whorled; sessile, oblong to spoon-shaped, narrowed at base, smooth, succulent, somewhat flattened, pale to bluish green often with a whitish coating (rosette leaves more oval-shaped, not flattened). Flowers in branching, spreading to recurved, terminal clusters; each white, star-shaped, with 4 (sometimes 5) widely spreading, lance-shaped petals, 4–5 sepals, and stamens with reddish-purple anthers. JS

Sedum ternatum

CRASSULACEAE | **mountain stonecrop**

Apr–Jun, 3–6 in. Mat-forming perennial with both prostrate and erect stems, found in moist forests, coves, bottomlands, and on shaded rock outcrops. Stems fleshy, smooth; nonflowering stems lie on ground but are turned up at the tip, where there is a rosette of whorled leaves; flowering stems erect. Leaves in whorls of 3 or alternate, oval to spoon-shaped with rounded tips, to 1 in. long, succulent and smooth. Flowers in a 2- to 4-forked terminal cluster, white, about 1/2 in. wide, with 4 (sometimes 5) spreading, narrowly lance-shaped petals, 4(5) sepals, 8 stamens with red anthers, and a 4-parted ovary. Fruit a small cluster of 4 erect-spreading, beaked capsules. RTW

Galium aparine

RUBIACEAE | **cleavers**

Apr–Jul, to 5 ft. Prostrate annual that sprawls over other plants, often forming dense mats and found in meadows, thickets, disturbed areas, and forests. Stems 4-angled, hollow, branched and covered with stiff, downcurved prickles. Leaves whorled (6–8), sessile, oblong-lance-shaped to linear, to 3 in. long, with stiff, downcurved hairs on midvein and margins. Flowers in small clusters of 1–3 on forking stalks arising from leaf whorls, white, less than 1/4 in. wide, with a short tube and 4 spreading, long-tipped petals. Fruit a green (turning brownish-black) capsule composed of 2 round lobes covered with curved bristles and containing 1 seed per lobe. AMC

Galium bermudense (*G. hispidulum*)

RUBIACEAE | **coastal bedstraw**

Jun–Aug, 6–24 in. Erect to sprawling perennial of maritime forests, sandhills, and dry sandy forests. Stems 4-angled, branched, finely hairy. Leaves in whorls of 4, elliptical, 1/4–3/4 in. long. Flowers at ends of branches, white, tiny, tubular with 4 corolla lobes. Fruit a green (turning purplish-black) capsule composed of 2 round lobes covered with curved bristles and containing 1 seed per lobe. KB

Galium circaezans

RUBIACEAE | **forest bedstraw**

Apr–Jul, 6–22 in. Wiry, erect to ascending perennial of moist to dry forests. Stems 4-angled, sometimes branched at the base, light green, sparsely hairy on angles. Leaves in whorls of 4, sessile, oval to lance-oval, to 2 in. long, with 3 prominent veins, sparsely hairy above and beneath. Flowers in a branched terminal cluster and sometimes also in smaller branched clusters from leaf axils; each flower yellow-green to greenish-purple, less than ¼ in. wide, with 4 spreading, pointed petals. Fruit a black or dark brown capsule composed of 2 round lobes covered with curved bristles and containing 1 seed per lobe. JG

Galium mollugo

RUBIACEAE | **hedge bedstraw**

May–Jun, 1–2½ ft. long. Sprawling, rhizomatous perennial of moist roadsides, fields, and other disturbed areas. Native to Europe. Stems usually sprawling, weakly branched, smooth or hairy only at lower end. Leaves in whorls of 7–8, sessile, linear to oblong-lance-shaped (widest above middle) with sharp tip, ½–1½ in. long, smooth but with slightly rough margins. Flowers in large branching terminal cluster; each flower white, less than ¼ in. wide, with a short tubular corolla with 4 spreading, elliptical, pointy-tipped lobes. Fruit a smooth, dark brown, kidney-shaped seed with dry covering. JG

Galium obtusum

RUBIACEAE | **bluntleaf bedstraw**

Apr–Jul, 6–18 in. Ascending to sprawling, sometimes bushy or matted, perennial of wet to moist soils of marshes and swamps. Stems 4-angled and shallowly furrowed, mostly smooth except at nodes. Leaves in whorls of 4–6, sessile, ascending to spreading, elliptic-oblong, ½–1¼ in. long, with stiff hairs along margins and veins beneath. Flowers in dichotomously branched clusters of 2–4 at stem and branch ends, white, less than ¼ in. wide, with 4 lance-triangular corolla lobes, a tiny pair of pistils, and 4 stamens. JG

Galium tinctorium

RUBIACEAE | **southern three-lobed bedstraw**

Apr–Jun, 6–30 in. Sprawling, rhizomatous perennial of swamps, marshes, and ditches. Stems 4-angled, ascending or reclining, simple or weakly branched, with tiny downward-pointing bristles on angles. Leaves in whorls of 4–6, narrowly elliptical to oblong, to 3/4 in. long, with short, stiff hairs on margins. Flowers in terminal and upper axillary clusters of 1–3, white, less than 1/4 in. wide, with a 3-lobed (rarely 4-lobed) corolla, a 2-celled ovary with a pair of styles, and 3 (less often 4) stamens. Fruit a smooth, dry, black capsule composed of 2 round lobes and containing 1 seed per lobe. BAS

Galium triflorum

RUBIACEAE | **sweet-scented bedstraw**

May–Sep, 1–3 ft. Sprawling, rhizomatous perennial of moist to dry upland forests, floodplain forests, seepage swamps, old fields, disturbed areas; usually on base-rich soils. Stems 4-angled, simple or with forking branches toward the end, with downward-pointing bristles on angles. Smooth vanilla-scented leaves to 2½ in. long in whorls of 6, sessile, elliptical to oblong-lance-shaped, with toothed tip and rough hairs on margins and midrib beneath. 1–3 flowers clustered on stalks from middle and upper leaf nodes, greenish-white, tiny, petals pointy-tipped. Fruit a dry, brown or black capsule composed of 2 round lobes covered with hooked bristle, 1 seed per lobe. BAS

Draba verna (*Erophila verna*)

BRASSICACEAE | **whitlow-grass**

Feb–Apr, 3/4–6 in. Rosette-forming annual/biennial of barren soils, including granite flatrocks, lawns, and pastures. Native to Europe, common in NoAm. Stems leafless, slender, arising from center of a rosette of leaves, which often emerge in winter. Leaves basal, oblong-lance-shaped to spoon-shaped, to 1 in. long, often toothed toward the tip, furry. Flowers 4–30 on ascending stalks in a loose terminal raceme, white, less than 1/4 in. wide, with 4 spreading, deeply cleft petals. Fruit a tiny oblong to elliptical pod. AWF

Capsella bursa-pastoris

BRASSICACEAE | **common shepherd's purse**

Mar–Jun, 4–20 in. Erect annual of fields, roadsides, gardens, and disturbed areas. Native to Europe, occurs throughout NoAm. Stems arising from winter rosette of basal leaves about 9 in. across, sometimes branched, hairy. Basal leaves elliptic-lance-shaped, to 4 in. long, most of them deeply pinnately divided; stem leaves smaller and widely spaced, clasping the stem and toothed or entire. Flowers in cylindrical terminal racemes to 12 in. long, those at the bottom opening first; each flower white, less than ¼ in. wide, with 4 tiny petals. Fruit a flattened, heart-shaped pod on a long stalk. ER

Cardamine flagellifera

BRASSICACEAE | **Blue Ridge bittercress**

Mar–May, 4–10 in. Erect perennial with stolons found in seepages, on streambanks, and in moist cove or bottomland forests, mainly at mid to low elevations. Stems hairy below, often purplish. Basal leaves oval to round, petiolate, divided into 1–2 pairs of rounded leaflets plus a terminal leaflet, usually purple beneath. Stem leaves 2–5 in a whorl, each divided into 3–5 toothed or lobed oval or round leaflets. Flowers on ascending stalks in a short terminal raceme, white, about ½ in. wide when fully open, with 4 oval petals. Fruit a thin, linear green pod; pods ripen on lower flower stalks while upper flowers are still blooming. AMC

Cardamine hirsuta

BRASSICACEAE | **hairy bittercress**

Feb–May, 3–15 in. Erect annual of fields, gardens, and other disturbed areas. Native to Europe, naturalized in much of NoAm. Stems sparingly branched, light green to dull purple, somewhat hairy at the base. Basal leaves, in a rosette up to 8 in. wide, are petiolate (petioles may be hairy), to 4 in. long and pinnately divided into 5–9 rounded or oval leaflets with wavy margins. Stem leaves 2–6, alternate, smaller, divided into 2–3 pairs of narrow leaflets. Flowers in short terminal racemes, less than ¼ in. wide, with 4 oval petals, 4 light green to dull purple sepals (shorter than petals), 4 stamens, and a pistil with a single style. Fruit a thin, linear green pod. JF

Cardamine parviflora var. *arenicola*

BRASSICACEAE | **sand bittercress**

Mar–May, 3–15 in. Erect to prostrate winter annual/biennial/short-lived perennial, primarily of seasonally wet areas with shallow soil or sand; also in glades on mafic outcrops and nutrient-rich granite. Stems slightly angular, smooth. Leaves numerous; basal leaves pinnately divided into 4–5 pairs of roundish leaflets, and the alternate stem leaves divided into 2–6 pairs of much narrower leaflets. Flowers on ascending stalks in a short terminal raceme, white, less than ¼ in. wide, with 4 tiny oval petals, 4 lance-shaped sepals, several stamens, and a pistil with a short stout style. Fruit a thin, linear green pod. GPF

Cardamine pensylvanica

BRASSICACEAE | **Quaker bittercress**

Mar–Jul, 6–22 in. Erect, early-blooming annual/biennial found in various wet habitats, especially swampy depressions, streambanks, and small woodland seeps. Stems may be branched from the base; smooth but hairy near the base. Leaves alternate (a few basal leaves), petiolate, 1½–4 in. long and pinnately divided into 3–13 oval to lance-shaped leaflets, each with 2–3 rounded teeth or lobes. Flowers on spreading-ascending stalks in a short terminal raceme, white, ¼ in. wide or less, with 4 tiny oval petals, 4 light green sepals, several stamens, and a stout pistil. Fruit a linear green pod; pods ripen on lower flower stalks while upper flowers are still blooming. KB

Lepidium virginicum

BRASSICACEAE | **poor man's pepper**

Apr–Jun (Dec), 4–20 in. Erect annual from a basal rosette, found on roadsides and other disturbed areas. Stems smooth or thinly hairy, much-branched in upper reaches. Leaves of basal rosette to 4 in. long, oblong-oval to spoon-shaped and pinnately divided into toothed lobes, withering by flowering; stem leaves alternate, smaller, toothed but not lobed. Flowers on short, spreading stalks of cylindrical terminal racemes, the lower flowers opening first; each flower white, less than ¼ in. wide, with 4 tiny petals. Fruit a flat, rounded pod with a tiny notch at the top. BAS

Nasturtium officinale

BRASSICACEAE | **watercress**

Apr–Jul, 6–30 in. Reclining, floating, or submerged perennial of streams, springs, and seepages. Native to Eurasia, found throughout NoAm. Stems grooved, succulent, rooting at nodes. Leaves petiolate, 2–8 in. long, pinnately divided into 3–11 elliptical to oblong-oval leaflets, the terminal leaflet usually larger than lateral ones; leaves somewhat fleshy. Flowers in compact, branching, terminal racemes; each flower white, less than 1/4 in. long, with 4 tiny, rounded petals. Fruit narrow, green, slightly curved and erect pod; seeds have sharp, peppery smell. JG

Planodes virginicum (*Sibara virginica*)

BRASSICACEAE | **Virginia-cress**

Feb–Jun, 6–18 in. Erect to ascending annual of roadsides, fields, disturbed areas. Stems 1–several from a basal winter rosette, unbranched, hairy below and smooth above. Leaves mostly basal, petiolate, to 6 in. long, pinnately lobed, slightly succulent, smooth and sometimes red-tinged; stem leaves similar but reduced, the uppermost lance-shaped and without lobing. Flowers in terminal racemes, which are compact during flowering but elongate in fruit; each flower white, less than 1/4 in. wide, with 4 petals, 4 green or reddish-green sepals, a central pistil, and a few stamens. Fruit a narrow, flattened, hairless seed pod. JG

Cardamine angustata (*Dentaria heterophylla*)

BRASSICACEAE | **slender toothwort**

Mar–May, 4–16 in. Short, spring-flowering perennial found in rich, moist forests. Stems smooth (occasionally hairy), often red-tinged. Basal leaves divided into 3 diamond-shaped to oval, toothed leaflets; midstem leaves also divided into 3 leaflets, these narrowly lance-shaped to linear and toothed or entire. Flowers on spreading stalks in a short terminal raceme, white (often tinged with purplish-pink), nearly 1 in. wide, with 4 petals forming a cross pattern. Fruit a linear green pod; pods ripen on lower flower stalks while upper flowers are still blooming. SJB

Cardamine diphylla
(Dentaria diphylla)

BRASSICACEAE | **toothwort**

Apr–May, 6–15 in. Erect, spring-flowering perennial found in rich, moist forests. Stems smooth, arising from a branching rhizome near the soil surface. Basal leaves to 10 in. long and divided into 3 oval, toothed leaflets with pale veins; often evergreen. Stem leaves, in a single pair at midstem, resemble basal leaves. Flowers in a short terminal raceme, white, nearly 1 in. wide when fully open, with 4 oval petals that later turn pink. Fruit a thin, linear green pod that rarely produces seeds. BAS

Cardamine concatenata
(Dentaria laciniata)

BRASSICACEAE | **cutleaf toothwort**

(Jan) Mar–May, 8–12 in. Erect, spring-flowering perennial found in rich, moist forests. Stems arising from a jointed rhizome, mostly smooth (hairy near top). Basal leaves to 3 in. long and divided into 3–5 narrow, toothed leaflets; may be seen without or separate from the flowering stem. On flowering stems, 3 similarly sized leaves are at midstem in a whorl. Flowers on spreading-ascending stalks in a short terminal raceme, white to pale pink, $\frac{1}{2}$–$1\frac{1}{2}$ in. wide, with 4 oblong-lance-shaped petals forming a cross. Fruit a thin, linear green pod; pods ripen on lower flower stalks while upper flowers are still blooming. BAS

Bartonia paniculata

GENTIANACEAE | **screwstem bartonia**

Aug–Oct, 4–16 in. Erect to sprawling, slender annual of swamps, bogs, pocosins, sphagnous seepages, and sinkhole ponds. Stems smooth, twisted, and tinted with purple; sometimes twining or sprawling on other plants. Leaves mostly alternate, scalelike and greenish-purple. Flowers in a sparse narrow panicle, green to creamy white (occasionally pink-tinged), tiny, with 4 lance-shaped, pointed petals; flowers often remain closed. Fruit a tiny, oval capsule. *Bartonia* species are believed to be at least partly dependent on a fungal association (mycorrhizae) in the soil. BAS

Bartonia verna

GENTIANACEAE | **white bartonia**

(Nov) Jan–Apr (Jun), 2–8 in. Wiry, erect annual of wet pine savannas, shores of Coastal Plain depression ponds, interdune swales, and other moist sandy habitats. Stems smooth, slightly twisted and usually reddish-tinged. Leaves opposite, minute and scalelike. Flowers in a narrow, sparse panicle; each flower white, about 1/4 in. long, with 4 oblong to oblong-oval petals, which are widely spreading in full bloom, and 4 prominent orange stamens around a yellowish-green ovary. Fruit a tiny, oval capsule. AMC

Bartonia virginica

GENTIANACEAE | **Virginia bartonia**

Jul–Oct, 4–16 in. Wiry, erect annual of bogs, swamps, savannas, pocosins, and dune swales. Stems stiff and often twisted, smooth. Leaves opposite, scalelike. Flowers erect in a narrow, racemelike panicle; each flower creamy white to yellowish-green, less than 1/4 in. long, egg-shaped in that they are essentially closed, with 4 oblong petals that are typically pressed against the ovary and 4 short, lance-shaped sepals. Fruit a tiny, oval capsule. AMC

Harperella nodosa *(Ptilimnium nodosum)*

APIACEAE | **harperella**

Jun–Aug, 6–36 in. Erect, semi-aquatic annual with quill-like leaves found in rocky river beds, upland depression ponds, and seepages on granite flatrocks. Stems slender, ridged, branched, smooth. Leaves on petioles with a sheathing base, round in cross-section and tapering to a point, to 12 in. long (reduced above). Flowers in flat-topped, compound umbels at top of stem and from leaf axils; flowers white, tiny, with 5 petals that curve up and strongly inward, 5 stamens with dark pink anthers, and a 2-part ovary. Fruit oval, with a joined pair of elliptical, ridged seeds. AMC

Tiedemannia filiformis
(Oxypolis filiformis)

APIACEAE | **water dropwort**

Jul–Sep, 1½–6 ft. Erect to ascending perennial of wet pine savannas, sandhill seepages, cypress ponds, and wet ditches. Stems stout, finely ribbed, few-branched, covered with a white-waxy coating. Leaves few, with expanded bases that clasp the stem, linear and tubelike (round in cross-section), hollow, the largest (to 2 ft. long) at stem bottom (reduced above); retained through flowering. Flowers in a flat-topped, compound terminal umbel, white, less than ¼ in. wide, with 5 tiny petals that mostly curve up and inward and 5 stamens. Fruit a joined pair of flattened, oblong, slightly winged seeds. RTW

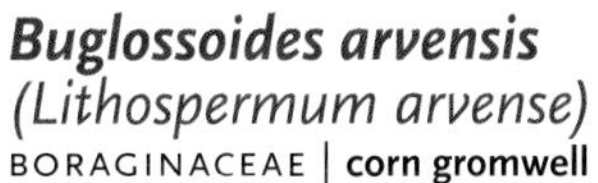

Buglossoides arvensis
(Lithospermum arvense)

BORAGINACEAE | **corn gromwell**

Mar–Jun, 6–20 in. Erect annual/biennial. Native to temperate Eurasia, widespread in NoAm along roadsides and in dry disturbed areas and sandy fields. Stems slender; simple to sparsely branched; with stiff, close-pressed hairs pointing in one direction. Leaves sessile, linear to lance-shaped, to 1½ in. long, with a single prominent vein. Flowers nearly sessile in axils of upper leaves, white to bluish, about ¼ in. long, funnel-shaped, 5-parted, the corolla scarcely longer than the hairy calyx. Fruit a tiny, pale brown to gray nutlet. SJB

Hackelia virginiana

BORAGINACEAE | **Virginia stickseed**

Jun–Sep, 2–4 ft. Lanky biennial of rich forests and woodlands. The first year, plant produces only a rosette of basal leaves; in the second year, a tall stem, branched above and rough-hairy. Leaves sessile, oval to lance-shaped, 1½–8 in. long, with curving veins, dark green and with stiff hairs above, medium green and more densely hairy beneath. Flowers in spreading, hairy racemes that branch off the stem, usually on 1 side of the raceme rachis; flowers white to pale blue, less than ¼ in. wide, with a short tube and 5 flat-spreading lobes. Fruit a brown, oval to round, burlike nutlet covered with small barbs. GPF

Myosotis macrosperma

BORAGINACEAE | **bigseed forget-me-not**

Apr–May, 6–18 in. Erect to lax annual/biennial of bottomland forests and alluvial fields, probably associated with nutrient-rich soils. Stems slightly angled in leafy portion, loosely branched, rough-hairy. Leaves sessile, oblong to linear-oblong (basal ones spoon-shaped), to 2¼ in. long, furry. Flowers arranged in a coiled raceme that straightens as flowers open and fruit ripen, white, tiny, funnel-shaped with 5 spreading-ascending corolla lobes and a furry calyx tube with 5 lobes. Fruit a brown, furry capsule containing 4 nutlets. JG

Calystegia sepium (*Convolvulus sepium*)

CONVOLVULACEAE | **European bindweed**

May–Aug, to 7 ft. long. Twining herbaceous perennial vine of openings, fields, fencerows, and woodland edges. Stems trailing over the ground or twining over other plants, smooth or hairy. Leaves petiolate, arrowhead-shaped, 2–4 in. long, smooth or hairy. Flowers from middle and upper leaf axils, often in pairs, white or pink and with a yellow throat, 2–3 in. wide, funnel-shaped, with 5 fused petals; 5 light green sepals surround the corolla base but are largely hidden by a pair of large bracts. Fruit an oval capsule. BAS

Convolvulus arvensis

CONVOLVULACEAE | **field bindweed**

Jun–Nov, 2–4 ft. Trailing or climbing herbaceous perennial vine of fields, roadsides, and other disturbed areas. Native to Europe. Stems freely branched, often forming tangled mats, short-hairy or nearly smooth. Leaves long-petioled, often narrowly arrowhead-shaped (shape may vary), 1–2 in. long. Flowers 1–3 on slender stalks from leaf axils, white or pink-tinged and with a yellowish throat, to 1 in. wide, with a funnel-shaped corolla, 5 small sepals, 5 stamens, and a pair of small bracts up to 1 in. long below the flower. Fruit an oval, 2-celled capsule. JG

Dichondra carolinensis

CONVOLVULACEAE | **Carolina ponyfoot**

Mar–Sep, 1–2 in. Creeping, mat-forming perennial of lawns, roadsides, and moist pinelands; rarely seen in natural habitats. Stems horizontal below and above the soil surface, rooting at the nodes, green or purplish-red, soft-hairy. Leaves petiolate, rounded or kidney-shaped, 3/8–1 1/4 in. wide, palmately veined, with principle veins raised on the lower surface, commonly hairy. Flowers solitary in leaf axils, greenish-white, less than 1/4 in. wide, with a bell-shaped corolla with 5 rounded lobes and a calyx with 5 longer sepals bearing long hairs on the outer surface. Fruit a tiny, 2-lobed capsule. BAS

Ipomoea pandurata

CONVOLVULACEAE | **wild sweet potato**

May–Sep, 4–16 ft. Herbaceous perennial vine from a large tuberlike root, growing in sandhills, other dryish forests and woodlands, rocky-gravelly river bars and shores, and road banks and other disturbed areas. Stems trailing or slightly twining, smooth to slightly hairy. Leaves on often reddish-purple petioles, broadly oval or violin-shaped or heart-shaped with a notch at the base, to 6 in. long, smooth or hairy. Flowers in long-stalked terminal clusters of 1–7, white with a purple-maroon throat, 2–3 in. wide, tubular-funnel-shaped with 5 shallow lobes at the rim. Fruit an oval capsule. WS

Stylisma humistrata (*Bonamia humistrata*)

CONVOLVULACEAE | **southern dawnflower**

Jun–Sep, 1–4 ft. long. Mostly prostrate herbaceous perennial vine found in sandhills, dry hammocks, and other dry woodlands, especially on dryish stream terraces. Stems slender, trailing to slightly twining, much-branched and hairy. Leaves short-petioled to sessile, oblong to elliptical with a rounded to notched base, to 2 1/4 in. long, slightly hairy. Flowers 1–7 on long stalks from leaf axils, white, 1/2–1 in. long, funnel-shaped, with 5 long-pointed, smooth, green sepals surrounding the base. Fruit an oval capsule. Flowers close quickly in direct sun. RTW

Stylisma patens (*Bonamia patens*)

CONVOLVULACEAE | **common dawnflower**

Jun–Aug, 1–4 ft. long. Prostrate herbaceous perennial vine of sandhills and other relatively dry sandy areas. Stems slender, spreading across ground. Leaves short-petioled to sessile, linear to narrowly elliptical, to 2 in. long, covered with short and close-pressed hairs. Flowers solitary on erect, slender stalks from leaf axils, white, ¾ in. wide, funnel-shaped with 5 corolla lobes that are hairy on the outer surface; 5 hairy, pale green, much shorter calyx lobes; and 2 short, dark green bracts below the calyx. Flowers open in morning; remain open for a day. WS

Pyxidanthera barbulata

DIAPENSIACEAE | **pyxie-moss**

Mar–Apr, 1–2 in. Mosslike, mat-forming, evergreen perennial of wet sands and peaty sands in pine savannas, pine flatwoods, pocosin margins, and edges of sandhill seepage bogs. Stems branched, smooth or hairy. Leaves sessile, narrowly oblong with a hardened, sharp point, to almost ¼ in. long, generally smooth. Flowers solitary at ends of short leafy branches, white or rose-colored, ¼ in. wide or less, with a tiny, cup-shaped corolla tube splitting into 5 spreading oblong-oval lobes. Fruit a rounded capsule. WS

Epigaea repens

ERICACEAE | **trailing arbutus**

Feb–May, 4–6 in. Prostrate, shrubby perennial of various moist to dry habitats on acidic soils, including heath balds and exposed banks in rocky or sandy woodlands. Stems creeping, reddish-brown, slightly woody and densely hairy. Leaves short-petioled, oval, 2–3 in. long, leathery-evergreen, rough in texture, covered in rust-colored hairs when new. Flowers in short clusters from axils of terminal leaves, often concealed beneath leaves; each flower white to pink, to ½ in. long, trumpet-shaped with 5 spreading corolla lobes, fragrant. Fruit a pea-sized berrylike capsule that changes from green to red, then purple; contains hundreds of tiny brown seeds. BAS

Euphorbia corollata

EUPHORBIACEAE | **eastern flowering spurge**

Jun–Sep, 1½–3 ft. Erect perennial of dry upland woods and forests. Stems 1–several, wiry, branching in the inflorescence, smooth (rarely hairy); exude milky sap when broken. Leaves short-petioled to sessile, angled upward, linear-oblong, to 2½ in. long, with prominent midvein, somewhat leathery, light gray-green to medium green, smooth. Flowers in an open, terminal panicle; each about ⅓ in. wide, consisting of a green cup holding tiny male and female parts and, attached to its rim, 5 white (to greenish or pink), round petal-like bracts (sometimes notched) with green glandular appendage at the base. Fruit a 3-lobed capsule on a drooping stalk. RTW

Euphorbia pubentissima

EUPHORBIACEAE | **southeastern flowering spurge**

Mar–Jul, 11–22 in. Erect to leaning perennial of dry forests, woodlands, and clearings. Stems branched above, green to sometimes reddish, smooth or hairy, leaking milky sap when broken. Leaves mostly petiolate, angled downward, linear to oblong or elliptical with rounded tips, ¾–2½ in. long, thin-textured, smooth. Flowers in an open, terminal panicle; each ¼ in. wide or less, consisting of a green cup holding tiny male and female parts and, attached to its rim, 5 white (to greenish or pink), round petal-like bracts with green glandular appendage at the base. Fruit a smooth to sparsely hairy, round, 3-lobed capsule on a stalk. FG

Phytolacca americana

PHYTOLACCACEAE | **common pokeweed**

May–Nov, 3–10 ft. Coarse, erect perennial of a wide variety of natural and disturbed habitats, and usually associated with exposed mineral soil. Stems stout, branched, light green to pinkish or dark red, smooth. Leaves petiolate, oval to lance-shaped, 3–12 in. long, with prominent veins, smooth. Flowers stalked and in elongated racemes (2–8 in. long) that nod from leaf axils, about ¼ in. wide with 5 spreading white to pinkish sepals (no petals) and a bright green ovary. Fruit a shiny dark purple, slightly flattened-round berry with reddish-purple juice. Stems, leaves, and berries toxic to humans. ER, TLJ

Samolus parviflorus

PRIMULACEAE | **water-pimpernel**

Apr–Oct, 6–18 in. Erect to sprawling perennial found in freshwater and brackish tidal marshes, streambanks, pools in floodplains, calcareous seepage swamps, and interdune ponds. Stems with long flowering branches, smooth. Leaves basal and alternate, short-petioled, spoon-shaped to oval, to 3 in. long, glossy and smooth. Flowers in slightly zigzagging racemes (typically 1–2) at branch ends, each on its own spreading, ½-in.-long, wiry stalk, each less than ¼ in. wide, with 5 white, oval, gently notched petals and 5 stamens in the center of a short corolla tube. Fruit a minute, round to oval capsule. AMC

Hydrocotyle americana

ARALIACEAE | **American water-pennywort**

Jun–Sep, 2–5 in. Creeping to weakly erect, often colonial perennial found in bogs, marshes, seepages, and cliffs and ledges that are wet from seepage or waterfall spray; sometimes in roadside ditches. Stems slender, branched, smooth. Leaves long-petioled, round to kidney-shaped, ¼–2¼ in. wide, notched at base, blunt-toothed, shiny and smooth. Flowers in small (2–7 flowers) sessile clusters along the stem at the bases of petioles; each flower white to greenish-white, less than ¼ in. wide, with 5 tiny petals and 5 stamens. Fruit flattened, ribbed, greenish-brown. GPF

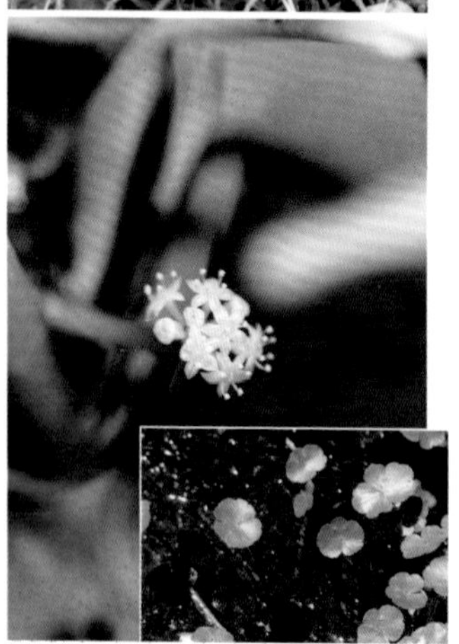

Hydrocotyle ranunculoides

ARALIACEAE | **swamp water-pennywort**

Apr–Jul, 4–12 in. Creeping, fleshy, aquatic to semi-aquatic perennial growing in stagnant to, less commonly, swiftly flowing waters of swamps, pools, backwaters, and blackwater streams. Stems thick, fleshy, floating or creeping, rooting at the nodes, pale green and smooth. Leaves petiolate, round to kidney-shaped, to 3 in. wide, palmately lobed, scallop-edged, lustrous green and smooth. Flowers in stalked, round-topped umbels about ½ in. wide (4–10 flowers) arising from leaf axils; each flower greenish-white or greenish-yellow, minute, with 5 spreading petals, 5 stamens, and a divided style. Fruit flattened, ribbed, greenish-brown. JG

Hydrocotyle sibthorpioides

ARALIACEAE | **lawn water-pennywort**

Mar–Sep, 2–5 in. Creeping, mat-forming perennial growing in lawns, pond margins, and cracks between paving stones. Native to Asia and Africa. Stems slender, branched, rooting at nodes, smooth. Leaves petiolate, round to kidney-shaped, notched at base, shallowly palmately lobed, scallop-margined, light green. Flowers 3–10 in tiny, stalked umbels arising from leaf axils, greenish-white, minute. BE

Hydrocotyle umbellata

ARALIACEAE | **marsh water-pennywort**

Apr–Oct, 3–8 in. Floating-creeping aquatic perennial of marshes, shores of rivers or lakes, and other moist areas. Stems fleshy, branching, smooth. Leaves on long petioles attached near the center of the blade, round to kidney-shaped, scalloped-edged, shiny and smooth. Flowers in erect, stalked umbels of 10–35+ arising separately from leaves and sometimes overtopping them; each flower white, less than 1/4 in. wide, with 5 spreading petals, insignificant sepals, and 5 stamens. BAS

Hydrocotyle verticillata

ARALIACEAE | **whorled water-pennywort**

May–Jul, 3–8 in. Creeping aquatic to semi-aquatic perennial of swamp forests and pools. Stems slender, branched, rooting at nodes, smooth. Leaves on long petioles attached at the center of the blade, round, shallowly lobed to scallop-margined, shiny. Flowers in 2 or more small, few-flowered umbels arranged along an erect stalk arising separately from leaves; flowers sessile, white, minute, with 5 spreading petals and 5 erect stamens. BAS

Ipomoea imperati *(I. stolonifera)*

CONVOLVULACEAE | **beach morning-glory**

Aug–Oct, 6 in. (to 75 ft. long). Prostrate herbaceous perennial vine found on beaches, dune blowouts, and foredunes. Stems trailing, rooting at nodes, smooth. Leaves petiolate, oblong, to 2 in. long, usually lobed, leathery and smooth. Flowers solitary on stalks from leaf axils, white with yellow throat, to 2 in. long, tubular-funnel-shaped and with 5 united petals (there is a suggestion of separate petal lobes at the rim); 5 elliptic-oval sepals with toothed tips surround the base of the flower, and 5 stamens and a style are visible in the corolla throat. Fruit a nearly round capsule. AMC

Ipomoea lacunosa

CONVOLVULACEAE | **white morning-glory**

Jul–Dec, 2–10 ft. Herbaceous annual vine of riverbanks, marshes, swamps, fields, roadsides, and disturbed areas. Stems twining or trailing, smooth to slightly hairy. Leaves petiolate, heart-shaped with a deep notch at the base or angular to 3-lobed, 2–4 in. long, with scattered white hairs above. Flowers in clusters of 1–5 from leaf axils, white (occasionally pink or pale purple), 5/8–1 in. wide, with a funnel-shaped corolla with 5 short lobes at the rim, a calyx of 5 hairy, lance-shaped sepals, and 5 stamens with purple anthers. Fruit a round capsule. RTW

Sicyos angulatus

CUCURBITACEAE | **bur-cucumber**

Jun–Nov, to 25 ft. long. Annual vine of moist forests and thickets on floodplains and in disturbed areas. Stems light green, angled, hairy and climbing over other plants with branched tendrils. Leaves petiolate, nearly round in outline but palmately 3- to 5-lobed, to 8 in. long and wide, finely toothed, rough-hairy above. Female and male flowers separate: female in round, densely flowered clusters on short stalks and male in few-flowered, long-stalked clusters. Flowers greenish-white, about 1/3 in. wide, typically with 5 (rarely 6, as shown) spreading, pointed lobes. Fruit a yellowish, oval berry covered in sharp bristles and grouped in round, compact clusters. RTW

Chimaphila maculata

ERICACEAE | **pipsissewa**

May–Jul, 4–8 in. Short, erect evergreen perennial found in forests and woodlands, usually of a drier, more acidic type. Stems slightly woody, unbranched, pinkish above the leaves, smooth. Leaves alternate to whorled, petiolate, oval to lance-shaped (broadest below middle), to 4 in. long, sharply toothed, leathery and variegated with white along veins. Flowers 2–5 on short, nodding stalks branched from top of stem, waxy-white (sometimes pink-tinged), about 1/2 in. wide, with 5 spreading concave petals surrounding a prominent green ovary and 10 stamens. Fruit a ribbed, round capsule on an erect stalk. AMC

Chimaphila umbellata var. *cisatlantica*

ERICACEAE | **prince's-pine**

May–Jun, 4–10 in. Short, erect evergreen perennial found in dry, acidic forests and woodlands. Stems semi-woody, pinkish above the leaves, smooth. Leaves alternate to whorled, short-petioled, oblong-lance-shaped, to 4 in. long, sharply toothed, leathery and solidly glossy green. Flowers 4–8 on short, nodding stalks branched from top of stem, whitish to waxy-pink, about 1/2 in. wide, with 5 spreading, concave petals surrounding a prominent green ovary and 10 stamens. Fruit a ribbed, round capsule on an erect to recurved stalk. AMC

Gaultheria procumbens

ERICACEAE | **teaberry**

Jun–Aug, 2–6 in. Rhizomatous, colonial perennial of heath balds, woodlands, openings, and bogs, usually on acidic (often dry) sites. Stems unbranched, somewhat woody, smooth or hairy. Leaves alternate but clustered toward the top of the short stem, elliptical, 1–2 in. long, with widely spaced bristle-tipped teeth, evergreen-leathery and shiny. Flowers 1–several dangling from leaf axils, white to pink, 1/4–1/2 in. long, urn-shaped with a bell-shaped, shorter calyx. Fruit a bright red, many-seeded, persistent berrylike capsule. Leaves and fruit with strong wintergreen fragrance and flavor, used in teas, chewing gum, candy, and medicines. WS

Hibiscus moscheutos

MALVACEAE | **eastern rose-mallow**

Jun–Sep, 4–6 ft. Tall, shrublike perennial of marshes, swamps, and river sandbars. Stems few to many arising from a single crown, fuzzy-hairy. Leaves long-petioled, oval to lance-shaped, shallowly toothed, smooth to furry above and densely furry with white hairs beneath. Flowers on long stalks from upper leaf axils, white to pink with maroon throat, 5–8 in. wide, funnel-shaped, with 5 rounded petals, a central column of fused stamens around a style, all surrounded by a 5-lobed calyx and an outer whorl of 10–15 very narrow green bracts. Fruit a smooth, oval capsule with tapering, pointy tip. LMC

Penthorum sedoides

PENTHORACEAE | **American penthorum**

Jun–Oct, 12–32 in. Erect perennial of pondshores, drawdown zones, moist forests, floodplain forests, ditches, and other moist, disturbed areas. Stems simple or bushy-branched above, green or red, smooth with glandular hairs on upper half. Leaves short-petioled, lance-shaped to elliptical, to 7 in. long, finely toothed, the midvein white or red-tinged. Flowers on terminal and some axillary branches, on 1 side of each curving, glandular branch; flowers greenish-white to yellowish-green, ¼ in. wide, with 5 sepals (no petals) and 10 white stamens. Fruit a red, 5-parted, 5-horned capsule. BAS

Boykinia aconitifolia

SAXIFRAGACEAE | **brook-saxifrage**

Jun–Jul, 6–32 in. Fuzzy, erect perennial of streambanks, riverbanks, crevices in spray cliffs around waterfalls, and seepages. A Southern Appalachian endemic. Stems branched above in inflorescence, covered with gland-tipped hairs. Basal leaves long-petioled, round or kidney-shaped, sharply divided into 5–7 toothed lobes; stem leaves similar but smaller. Flowers on glandular-hairy stalks in compact, terminal panicle that elongates with time; each flower white, to ½ in. wide, with 5 oblong-oval petals, 5 reddish-green sepals, and 5 stamens. Fruit a 2-sectioned capsule. WS

Datura stramonium

SOLANACEAE | **jimsonweed**

Jul–Sep, 2–5 ft. Rank-smelling annual found in fields and other disturbed areas, especially in severely overgrazed pastures. Presumably introduced from Mexico or Central America. Stems stout, coarsely branched, and often marked with purple. Leaves petiolate, lance-shaped, 2–8 in. long, with large, irregular teeth. Flowers solitary in branch axils, white to lavender, 2–4 in. long, trumpet-shaped and with a ridged, green calyx tube that is 1–2 in. long. Fruit a distinctive spiny, oval capsule containing black seeds. All parts are toxic and cause hallucinations. BAS

Solanum carolinense

SOLANACEAE | **Carolina horse-nettle**

May–Oct, 1–3 ft. Prickly, rhizomatous perennial with small yellow fruits resembling tomatoes, found in fields, gardens, and other disturbed areas throughout much of the U.S. Stems simple or weakly branched, greenish-purple and hairy, with scattered white to yellowish spines. Leaves petiolate, triangular to oval with irregular, angled lobes that often seem more like teeth; undersides with spines along the midvein. Flowers on hairy stalks in a small terminal cluster, white to light violet, about 3/4 in. wide, star-shaped, with 5 petals that are united at the base and 5 prominently protruding, elongated, yellow anthers. Fruit, a round, dull yellow berry, is toxic. RTW

Solanum ptychanthum

SOLANACEAE | **American black nightshade**

May–Dec, 1–3 ft. Erect annual of upland forests and woodlands, shaded rock outcrops, well-drained floodplain forests, open fields, disturbed areas. Stems branched, smooth or rough-hairy. Leaves petiolate, partially winged, oval to triangular with a wedge-shaped base, 3 in. long, irregularly blunt-toothed, slightly hairy, becoming smooth. Flowers (3–10) in stalked clusters from mid to upper leaf axils, each 1/4 in. wide, star-shaped, with 5 recurved-spreading, lance-shaped corolla lobes and a central column of yellow anthers enclosing the pistil. 5 green, lance-oval sepals are connected at their bases and persist on the fruit, a round berry, green maturing to shiny black. RTW

Sesuvium maritimum

AIZOACEAE | **small sea-purslane**

May–Dec, 4–7 in. Prostrate (rarely erect), mat-forming annual of barrier island beaches and salt flats; rarely also inland in disturbed areas. Stems branched, succulent, smooth. Leaves sessile-clasping, oblong-lance-shaped with blunt tips, ½–1 in. long, succulent and smooth. Flowers essentially sessile in leaf axils, pinkish-white, with 5 sepals with spinelike appendage near the tip and multiple stamens with pink anthers. Fruit a capsule enclosed by the persistent calyx. KB

Apocynum androsaemifolium

APOCYNACEAE | **spreading dogbane**

Jun–Aug, 1–3 ft. Erect to ascending bushy perennial of moist to dry forests, woodlands, and clearings. Stems with loosely ascending branches, smooth. Leaves loosely spreading or drooping on slender petioles, oval to oblong-oval, to 3½ in. long, smooth. Flowers in large clusters at tips of branches and smaller ones in leaf axils, flowering simultaneously; each flower white often pink-tinged or pink with red stripes inside, less than ½ in. long, tubular-bell-shaped with 5 spreading to recurved corolla lobes, fragrant. Fruit a dangling pair of cylindrical-linear, slightly curved follicles containing silky-tufted seeds. GPF

Apocynum cannabinum

APOCYNACEAE | **hemp dogbane**

May–Jul, 1–4½ ft. Erect to ascending perennial that branches as it ages; found widely in forests, woodlands, roadsides, pastures, disturbed areas. Smooth reddish-green stems leak milky sap when broken. Leaves smooth, oval to lance-shaped, 5 in. long by 2 in. wide, with a notably pale midvein and whitish coating, leaking milky sap when torn. Flowers in loose clusters at tips of branches and in leaf axils, white to pinkish-white, less than ¼ in. long, tubular-bell-shaped with 5 erect to spreading lobes with recurved, pointy tips. Fruit paired drooping, slender, linear, slightly curved follicles containing silky-tufted seeds. Milky sap of stem and leaves is toxic. JG

Asclepias perennis

APOCYNACEAE | **smoothseed milkweed**

Jun–Aug, 1–2 ft. Erect to ascending perennial found in swamp forests. Stems several from a woody crown, mostly unbranched, dark purplish-green, smooth below, with a line of hairs above between leaf nodes; leak milky sap when bruised. Leaves petiolate, elliptical to lance-shaped, 2½–5½ in. long, waxy-white beneath. Flowers in umbels at stem top and from upper leaf axils, white (may be tinged pale lavender), about ¼ in. long, with 5 reflexed corolla lobes and a central crown surrounding the fused anthers and style. Fruit a follicle containing tufted seeds. The tips of flower buds are pink. AMC

Asclepias variegata

APOCYNACEAE | **white milkweed**

May–Jul, 2–3 ft. Erect perennial of upland forests and woodland edges. Stem solitary, stout, weakly hairy; leaks milky sap when bruised. Leaves usually in 2–6 pairs (lowermost pair reduced in size), petiolate, oval to widely elliptical, to 5½ in. long, dark green and smooth above, pale green and hairy beneath. Flowers in a crowded, globe-shaped terminal umbel; each flower white, about ⅜ in. long, with 5 spreading-reflexed corolla lobes and a central crown with a purple ring at the base surrounding the fused anthers and style. Fruit an erect, spindle-shaped follicle containing tufted seeds. Nectar is favored by skippers and other butterflies, bees, wasps, and ants. WS

Cynanchum laeve *(Ampelamus albidus)*

APOCYNACEAE | **sandvine**

Jul–Sep, 9–30 ft. long. Vining perennial of bottomlands, streambanks, and various moist to wet disturbed areas. Stems branching, twining and climbing, often reddish and with lines of hairs, oozing milky sap when broken. Leaves petiolate, oval with long tip and heart-shaped base, to about 4 in. long, smooth or hairy. Flowers in furry-stalked, axillary umbels; each flower white, about ¼ in. long, with 5 erect corolla lobes and a 5-parted, erect “crown,” as well as 5 shorter, green calyx lobes. Fruit a teardrop-shaped follicle containing tufted seeds. RTW

Pattalias palustre (*Cynanchum angustifolium*)

APOCYNACEAE | **swallow-wort**

Jun–Jul, to 10 ft. long. Herbaceous perennial vine of coastal hammocks and edges of marshes, generally on barrier islands. Stem twining over other plants, slender, smooth. Leaves drooping downward, linear, 1–3 in. long, evergreen. Flowers in long-stalked clusters from leaf axils, greenish-white (often rose-tinged), about ¼ in. wide, with 5 ascending, pointed petals and a short central crown composed of 5 rounded "hoods" encircling the greenish-yellow, fused reproductive structures. Fruit a dangling, slender follicle containing tufted seeds. PIP

Arenaria serpyllifolia

CARYOPHYLLACEAE | **large thyme-leaved sandwort**

Mar–Jun, 2–10 in. Erect to sprawling (but with upturned tips) annual found in the dry soil of fields, woodland edges, outcrops, and various disturbed area. Native to Eurasia. Stems multiple from plant base, rather wiry, branched, dark purple and finely hairy. Leaves in pairs spaced widely along stems, oval with pointed tips, about ¼ in. long, sparsely rough-hairy. Flowers in small clusters at upper ends of stems, 1–2 blooming at a time; each flower white, less than ¼ in. wide, with 5 unnotched petals, 5 longer and more sharply pointed green sepals, 10 stamens, and 3 styles. Fruit a dry, oval capsule. JG

Cerastium fontanum ssp. *vulgare*

CARYOPHYLLACEAE | **common mouse-ear**

Mar–Jun, 2–18 in. Semi-erect to sprawling, mat-forming annual/short-lived perennial found widely in fields, gardens, and many disturbed areas. Native to Europe. Stems slender with swollen nodes, branching from base, rooting at nodes and covered with white hairs. Leaves sessile, oval to elliptical (lower ones usually spoon-shaped), 1 in. long or less, densely hairy. Flowers in compact clusters at ends of branches, white, with 5 deeply notched petals (each appearing to be 2), 5 hairy green sepals, 10 white stamens, and 3 styles. Fruit a slightly curved, cylindrical capsule. BE

Cerastium glomeratum

CARYOPHYLLACEAE | **sticky mouse-ear**

Mar–May, 2–18 in. Semi-erect to sprawling annual of fields, roadsides, and other disturbed habitats. Native to Europe. Stems tufted, branching basally, light green to dark purple, covered with white, mostly gland-tipped hairs. Leaves sessile-clasping, broadly oval to elliptical or lance-shaped, to 1 in. long, covered with long white hairs on both surfaces. Flowers in compact clusters at tips of branches, white, about 1/4 in. wide, with 5 deeply notched petals, 5 hairy, green, pointed sepals, 10 white stamens, and a pistil with 5 styles. Fruit a cylindrical capsule. BAS

Cerastium nutans

CARYOPHYLLACEAE | **nodding chickweed**

Apr–May, 4–16 in. Reclining to ascending annual of alluvial forests, bottomlands, and other moist forests. Stems weak, branching from the base, sticky-glandular. Leaves sessile-clasping, lance-oblong to lance-shaped, 1/2–2 in. long, hairy. Flowers on glandular-hairy stalks at tips of branches (nodding in bud), and at the base of each pair of inflorescence branches is a pair of leafy bracts. Flowers white, 1/4 in. wide, with 5 ascending-spreading petals that are notched at the tip, 5 slightly shorter, green sepals, 5–10 stamens and an ovary with 5 styles. GPF

Holosteum umbellatum

CARYOPHYLLACEAE | **jagged chickweed**

Mar–Jun, 2–10 in. Erect to ascending annual starting out as a winter rosette, found in fields, on roadsides, and in other open, disturbed areas. Native to Europe. Stems several from the base, unbranched, with swollen nodes, smooth below but with gland-tipped hairs above. Leaves opposite (basal leaves tufted), sessile to short-petioled, oblong to lance-shaped, to 1 in. long, with tiny, stalked glands along the margins. Flowers 3–15 in terminal umbels, on long stalks that turn downward in fruit; flowers white to pinkish, with 5 fringed, partially open (but not spreading) petals, and 5 shorter, pointy sepals with thin, dry margins. Fruit an oval to cylindrical capsule. BH

Mononeuria caroliniana

(Minuartia caroliniana)

CARYOPHYLLACEAE | **Carolina sandwort**

Apr–Jun, to 1 ft. Erect to ascending perennial of deep white sands of barren sandhills. Stems branched, densely glandular hairy (occasionally smooth). Leaves sessile, closely spaced and overlapping, linear, less than 1/2 in. long, smooth. Flowers in small clusters at tips of branches, white, 1/2–3/4 in. wide, with 5 spreading petals and 5 short oval sepals visible between the petals. Fruit a small triangular capsule. AMC

Mononeuria glabra

(Minuartia glabra)

CARYOPHYLLACEAE | **Appalachian sandwort**

Apr–May, 3–10 in. Erect to ascending, tufted annual of granitic flatrocks and other outcrops of granite, granitic gneiss, or other felsic gneisses and schists; in the Mountains restricted to low to mid elevations. Stems slender, simple or branched, smooth. Leaves sessile, linear, 1/4–1 in. long, soft and somewhat fleshy. Flowers 5–12 on threadlike stalks of branching terminal cluster; flowers white, about 1/3 in. long, with 5 ascending oblong-oval, delicately pleated petals, which are surrounded by 5 shorter sepals. Fruit a 3-celled, oval capsule. AMC

Mononeuria uniflora

(Minuartia uniflora)

CARYOPHYLLACEAE | **one-flower stitchwort**

Apr–May, 2–8 in. Tufted, colonial annual found on granitic flatrocks and outcrops of Altamaha grit. Stems wiry thin, unbranched, smooth. Basal leaves lance-shaped, 1/4 in. long, somewhat fleshy; stem leaves few, opposite, spreading and smaller than basal ones. Flowers held singly at the top of threadlike stalks (to 2 in. long), white, about 1/3 in. wide, with 5 spreading, oval petals with blunt, slightly scalloped tips. BAS

Paronychia argyrocoma

CARYOPHYLLACEAE | **silverling**

Jul–Sep, 2–10 in. Prostrate perennial of thin soils of rock outcrops, especially on mountain summits at mid to high elevations; also disjunct to a few Piedmont monadnocks. Stems from a woody taproot, forming tufts or mats, branching at the base, covered in silvery-silky, close-pressed hairs. Leaves linear to lance-linear, to 1 in. long, covered in silvery-silky hair, with conspicuous oval to lance-shaped stipules. Flowers in small, dense clusters at branch tips, mostly concealed by bracts; each flower greenish-white, less than 1⁄4 in. long, with 3–5 hairy sepals with white margins and awned tips (petals lacking). EB

Sagina decumbens

CARYOPHYLLACEAE | **eastern pearlwort**

Mar–Jun, 1–6 in. Erect to ascending annual of disturbed ground, fields, and cracks in pavement. Stems slender, tufted, simple or slightly branched, smooth. Leaves sessile, pairs joined at the base where they encircle the stem, linear, to 1⁄2 in. long, bristle-tipped, smooth. Flowers on threadlike stalks in loose racemelike clusters at top of stem and from leaf axils, white, with 5 spreading thin petals, 5 sepals shorter than and visible between the petals, 3–10 stamens, and a green ovary with 3 stigmas. Fruit an oval capsule. BAS

Saponaria officinalis

CARYOPHYLLACEAE | **soapwort**

May–Oct, 1–2½ ft. Erect, rhizomatous perennial of disturbed areas, fields, roadsides. Native to Europe. Stems essentially unbranched, smooth. Leaves sessile or clasping, broadly oval or lance-shaped, 3⁄4–43⁄4 in. long, strongly 3-veined, smooth. Flowers in dense, oblong-pyramidal, terminal clusters; each flower white or light pink, 1 in. wide, with 5 spreading oblong petals with slightly notched tips, a green or red-tinged calyx tube, 10 protruding stamens, and usually 2 styles. Fruit a cylindrical capsule. AMC

Silene latifolia (*Lychnis alba*)

CARYOPHYLLACEAE | **white campion**

May–Jul, 1–3 ft. Spreading (seldom erect) annual to (more often) biennial/short-lived perennial, found in fields, roadsides, and other disturbed areas. Native to Europe. Stems loosely branched, hairy and sticky. Leaves petiolate, broadly lance-shaped, 1–4 in. long, hairy. Flowers fragrant, opening in the evening in branching panicles, white to pinkish, 1 in. wide, with 5 deeply notched petals spreading outward from an inflated calyx tube that is hairy and bears 10 reddish veins in male flowers and 20 reddish veins in female flowers. Fruit a golden brown capsule. KB

Silene noctiflora

CARYOPHYLLACEAE | **sticky cockle**

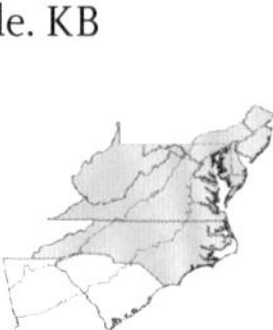

Jun–Aug, 8–47 in. Erect annual of fields and other disturbed areas. Native to Europe. Stems few-branched near the base, coarsely stiff-hairy below and with sticky glandular hairs above. Leaves sessile, 2–6 in. long; basal leaves spoon-shaped, stem leaves lance-shaped. Flowers open at night in loose, branching terminal clusters; each white or pinkish, ¾–1 in. wide, with 5 deeply 2-lobed petals bearing a ruffled basal appendage (creating a ruffled circle at the mouth of the corolla throat) and a glandular-hairy, inflated, cylindrical calyx tube bearing 10 prominent green ribs that branch and rejoin, the tube splitting into 5 narrow lobes at the top. Fruit an oval capsule. KL

Silene ovata

CARYOPHYLLACEAE | **mountain catchfly**

Aug–Sep, 1–5 ft. Erect perennial found in woodlands and forests on circumneutral soils, especially over mafic or calcareous rocks. Stems branched, hairy. Leaves sessile, oval to elliptical, tapering to a sharp point, 2–4¾ in. long. Flowers in panicle-like terminal clusters, white, with 5 petals, each ¼–⅝ in. long and divided into 8 linear segments, and a hairy, tubular calyx about ⅜ in. long and bearing 10 conspicuous veins. Fruit an elliptical capsule. AMC

Silene vulgaris (*S. cucubalus*)

CARYOPHYLLACEAE | **bladder campion**

May–Aug, 6–24 in. Ascending to reclining perennial of fields, roadsides, and other open, disturbed areas. Native to Europe. Stems branched near the base, smooth to slightly downy, with a waxy coating. Leaves sessile or clasping, elliptical to oval and pointed at the tip, ¾–3 in. long. Flowers in an open, branching panicle; each flower white, ½–¾ in. wide, with 5 deeply notched petals, a smooth, greenish-pink, inflated calyx tube bearing 20 prominent veins and a network of secondary veins, and 10 protruding stamens and a pistil. Fruit a capsule. RTW

Stellaria graminea

CARYOPHYLLACEAE | **common stitchwort**

May–Aug, 8–18 in. Erect to spreading perennial of fields, roadsides, pastures, and other open, disturbed areas. Native to Europe. Stems weak, 4-angled, branched or unbranched, smooth (sometimes rough on prominent angles). Leaves sessile, linear to narrowly lance-shaped and broadest at the base, ½–2 in. long. Flowers arranged in open forking branches on upper stems, white, ⅛–½ in. wide, with 5 deeply cleft petals, sepals as long as or shorter than the petals and bearing 3 distinct veins, and 10 stamens. Fruit a narrowly oval capsule. RTW

Stellaria media

CARYOPHYLLACEAE | **common chickweed**

Jan–Dec, 4–16 in. Erect or reclining, mat-forming annual of disturbed areas, gardens, fields, bottomlands, and moist forests. Native to Europe. Stems much-branched and 4-angled with 1–2 rows of fine hairs. Leaves sessile on upper stem and petiolate on lower stem, oval, ¼–1 in. long. Flowers solitary or in open leafy clusters at the ends of branching stems, white, about ¼ in. wide, with 5 spreading, deeply cleft petals (giving the appearance of 10 petals) and 5 hairy, lance-shaped sepals longer than and showing between the petals. Fruit an oval capsule. RTW

Stellaria pubera

CARYOPHYLLACEAE | **star chickweed**

Apr–Jun, 4–16 in. Erect to ascending or reclining perennial of bottomland forests, moist slopes, coves, and hammocks. Stems 4-angled, branching, with 2 lines of fine hairs. Leaves sessile to short-petioled at lower stem, oval or lance-shaped, ¾–4 in. long (the larger ones on nonflowering stems), usually hairy above. Flowers in open, leafy clusters at ends of stems; each flower white, ¼–⅝ in. wide, with 5 spreading petals that are so deeply notched they appear to be 10, and 10 reddish-tipped stamens. Fruit a round capsule. RTW

Sabatia calycina

GENTIANACEAE | **coastal rose gentian**

Jun–Oct, 4–15 in. Erect short-lived perennial of swamp forests and riverbanks. Stems vaguely 4-angled and simple or with alternate, divergent branches; the stem base may be woody, and leafy basal offshoots may be present. Leaves sessile to short-petioled, elliptical, 1–2 in. long, sometimes with a short spine at the tip. Flowers solitary or in few-flowered clusters borne in upper leaf axils, white to pale pink, with 5–7 spreading, oblong-oval petals with yellowish-green tint at the base, the same number of longer lance-shaped sepals showing between petals, a split yellow stigma, and 5–7 stamens. Fruit a rounded capsule. FG

Sabatia difformis

GENTIANACEAE | **lanceleaf rose gentian**

May–Sep, 18–32 in. Stiffly erect perennial of pine savannas, bogs, and pocosins. Stems several from a short rhizome, 4-angled above, with opposite branching in the inflorescence. Leaves sessile and angled upward, lance-oblong to elliptical, to 1½ in. long (reduced above). Flowers at ends of upper branches, white, about 1 in. wide, with 5–6 spreading oblong-lance-shaped petals and 5 needlelike sepals. Fruit an elliptical capsule. WS, FG

Mitreola petiolata (*Cynoctonum mitreola*)

LOGANIACEAE | **Caribbean miterwort**

Jul–Sep, 4–32 in. Erect annual of alluvial swamps, marshes, peaty pond margins, seasonally exposed river shores, ditches, and other wet habitats. Stems somewhat 4-angled, branched above in inflorescence, smooth. Leaves petiolate, elliptical to oval and tapered at both ends, to 3 in. long. Flowers arranged along 1 side of ascending, terminal branches and in similar, smaller clusters from leaf axils, the branches slightly coiling at the tip; each flower white, tiny, funnel-shaped with 5 spreading, pointy lobes. Fruit a tiny, deeply 2-lobed capsule. PIP

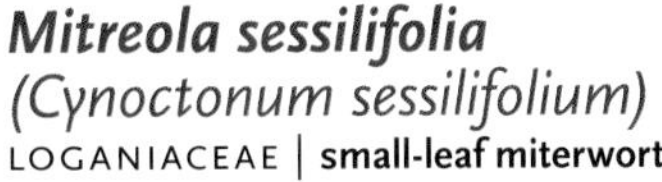

Mitreola sessilifolia (*Cynoctonum sessilifolium*)

LOGANIACEAE | **small-leaf miterwort**

Jun–Aug, 4–18 in. Erect annual of wet savannas, pocosins, ditches, and margins of dolines. Stems vaguely 4-angled, simple or with a few erect branches above. Leaves usually sessile, oval to widely elliptical with a rounded base, to 3/4 in. long and entire. Flowers in branching clusters on long ascending stalks/branches from upper leaf axils, white, less than 1/4 in. long, funnel-shaped with 5 spreading, pointed petals. BAS

Valerianella radiata

CAPRIFOLIACEAE | **beaked cornsalad**

Apr–May, 4–18 in. Erect perennial found in moist forests, bottomlands, and disturbed areas. Stems 4-angled, with forked branching in the upper half, often hairy on angles. Basal leaves spoon-shaped and forming a rosette in winter; stem leaves opposite, usually clasping, oblong with rounded tips, to 3 in. long, often toothed near base of leaf. Flowers in terminal, flat-topped clusters, less than 1 in. wide and surrounded by lance-shaped, hairy-margined bracts; flowers white, tiny, with 5 petals and 3 protruding stamens. Has a tendency to form colonies through reseeding. RTW

Mitella diphylla

SAXIFRAGACEAE | **two-leaved miterwort**

Apr–Jun, 8–16 in. Erect, rhizomatous perennial of moist rocky forests, rocky seeps, seepage swamps, especially over mafic or calcareous rocks. Stems thin, sparsely hairy below, glandular-hairy above. Leaves mostly basal, with a pair of stem leaves and sometimes a third leaf just above; petiolate to sessile, oval to round, 1–3 in. long, each with 3–5 shallow lobes (the terminal lobe prolonged), palmately veined, toothed. Flowers 5–20 in a narrow terminal raceme, less than 1/4 in. wide, snowflake-like, the tiny petals pinnately divided into minute, obliquely ascending segments. Calyx is bell-shaped. Fruit a 2-beaked capsule containing numerous, tiny seeds. BAS

Asclepias verticillata

APOCYNACEAE | **whorled milkweed**

May–Sep, 8–24 in. Erect to ascending perennial of barrens, sandhills, dry woodlands, rock outcrops, especially mafic rocks. Stem solitary, branched in upper portions, bearing vertical lines of hairs above, leaking milky sap when bruised. Leaves in whorls of 3–6 (opposite at some nodes), linear, 1–3 in. long, with margins noticeably rolled downward, sparsely hairy. Flowers in small, dense terminal and upper axillary umbels; each white to greenish-white, 1/3 in. long, with 5 strongly reflexed green-suffused-with-purple corolla lobes and a whitish central crown surrounding the fused anthers and style. Fruit a narrowly spindle-shaped, erect follicle containing tufted seeds. AMC

Silene stellata

CARYOPHYLLACEAE | **starry campion**

Jul–Sep, 1–4 ft. Erect to ascending perennial of dry to moist forests and rock outcrops. Stems stiff, branched from the base, smooth to densely hairy. Midstem leaves in whorls of mostly 4 (opposite on upper and lower stem); sessile to short-petioled; lance-shaped or oval and tapering to a sharp point; to 4 in. long; finely hairy beneath, smooth to rough above. Scentless flowers in open panicles, often closed during the bright light of midday; each 3/4–1 in. wide, petals deeply and unevenly divided into 8–12 segments, giving flowers a fringed appearance. Bell-shaped calyx tube, slightly inflated, smooth to hairy, with 5 triangular lobes. Fruit a rounded capsule. WS

Mollugo verticillata

MOLLUGINACEAE | **carpetweed**

May–Nov, to 5 in. Sprawling annual of fields, disturbed areas, and drawdown zones on the shores of rivers and ponds. Native to the Neotropics, widespread in NoAm. Stems prostrate and much-branched, forming mats; smooth. Leaves in whorls of 3–8, oblong-lance-shaped to linear, 1⁄3–1 in. long, smooth. Flowers on stalks from leaf nodes, 2–5 per node; each flower white, to 1⁄4 in. wide, with 5 petal-like sepals (often with pale green lines), 3–5 white stamens, and a large green ovary with a 3-parted style. Fruit a capsule. BAS

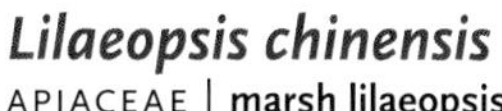

Lilaeopsis chinensis

APIACEAE | **marsh lilaeopsis**

May–Jun, 4–10 in. Prostrate-creeping aquatic perennial. Stems creeping, rooting at nodes, smooth. Leaves lacking a real blade, linear to narrowly club-shaped with round tip, flattened, hollow and segmented. Flowers in simple umbels on long stalks from leaf axils, 4–9 flowers per umbel, white, tiny, with 5 petals. Fruit a joined pair of oval, curved, ridged seeds, each with a flat side facing the other. KB

Parnassia asarifolia

PARNASSIACEAE | **brook parnassia**

Jul–Oct, 4–16 in. Erect, rhizomatous perennial of bogs, sphagnous seeps, brook banks; generally in more acidic habitats than *P. grandifolia*. Stems essentially lacking; leaves and slender, smooth flowering scape (with 1 small, clasping leaf halfway up) arise from the rhizome. Leaves primarily basal, long-petioled, kidney-shaped with a notched base, 1–2 in. long, 4 in. wide, with conspicuously curved veins. Flowers solitary, 1 1⁄3 in. wide, with 5 oval petals with clawed bases and 11–15 green/tan veins, 5 sepals, 5 stamens with large whitish-tan anthers, 5 orange-tipped sterile stamens divided into 3 lobes each, and a whitish ovary. Fruit a 4-celled capsule. RTW

Parnassia caroliniana

PARNASSIACEAE | **savanna parnassia**

Sep–Dec, 8–20 in. Erect, rhizomatous perennial of sandhill seepage bogs and wet longleaf pine, pond pine, or pond cypress savannas, especially where shallowly underlain by coquina limestone. Stems essentially lacking; leaves and thin flowering scape arise from the rhizome. Leaves nearly all basal (1–2 smaller leaves on flower scape), long-petioled, broadly oval with notched base, 3⁄4–21⁄2 in. long, fleshy, with curving parallel veins. Flowers solitary, 11⁄2 in. wide, with 5 oval petals with 9–18 prominent greenish or tan veins, 5 sepals, 5 stamens with large white or brown anthers, 5 sterile stamens divided into 3 lobes each, and a whitish ovary. Fruit a 4-celled capsule. FG

Parnassia grandifolia

PARNASSIACEAE | **limeseep parnassia**

Aug–Oct, 4–20 in. Erect, rhizomatous perennial of fens, gravelly seepages, pineland seepage bogs, usually over calcareous, mafic, or ultramafic rocks. Stems essentially lacking; leaves and flowering scape arise from rhizome. Leaves primarily basal (1 smaller leaf clasps the flower scape), long-petioled, broadly oval, 2–3 in. long, fleshy, with parallel veins. Flowers solitary, 1 in. wide, with oval to oblong petals with 7–9 green or tan veins (including short side veins extending to petal edge, the tips of veins dilated), 5 sepals, 5 stamens with reddish-brown anthers, 5 longer sterile stamens divided into 3 lobes each, and a greenish ovary. Fruit a 4-celled capsule. JF

Primula meadia (*Dodecatheon meadia*)

PRIMULACEAE | **eastern shooting star**

Mar–Jun, 6–20 in. Scapose perennial of rich forests, woodlands, and rock outcrops, primarily calcareous or mafic ones with nutrient-rich seepage. Stem a leafless flower stalk. Leaves basal, elliptical to lance-shaped, 3–12 in. long, smooth, sometimes red-tinged at the base. Flowers 3–many in an umbel; each flower on a curved stalk, white to lilac-pink, with 4–5 strongly recurved and backward-pointing petals, which are united at the base, and 5 stamens united into a tube pointing downward. Fruit a reddish-brown, narrowly oval capsule on a now-straightened stalk. Flowers are buzz-pollinated by bees. RTW

Myosurus minimus

RANUNCULACEAE | **mousetail**

Mar–May, 2–6 in. Erect, rosette-forming annual mostly seen in disturbed areas, such as fields in floodplains. Nativity uncertain. Stems 1 or more leafless, unbranched and smooth flowering stalks. Leaves basal, linear, blunt-tipped, 2–4 in. long and shorter than to slightly exceeding the scapes, smooth. Flowers solitary and terminating each scape, whitish- to yellowish-green, with 5 spreading, lance-oblong sepals, each with a downward-pointing, narrowly triangular, spurlike extension, 5 tiny petals, 5–10 stamens, and an elongated, cylindrical ovary bearing multiple pistils. Fruit a conical, spikelike cluster of multiple flattened, rectangular achenes. JG

Centella asiatica (*C. erecta*)

APIACEAE | **coinleaf**

Jun–Aug, 1–6 ft. long. Prostrate perennial of wet savannas, pondshores, ditches, and a wide variety of other moist to wet habitats. Stems slender, smooth or hairy, spreading across ground, with clumps of leaves arising from widely spaced nodes. Leaves on reddish petioles in clusters along stem, heart-shaped with rounded tips, ½–2 in. long, toothed, slightly succulent, dull green, hairy or smooth. Flowers in small rounded umbels on erect stalks arising with leaf clusters, white to greenish-white (tinged with rosy pink), tiny, with 5 pointed petals. SH

Hydrocotyle bonariensis

ARALIACEAE | **dune pennywort**

Apr–Sep, 6–10 in. Creeping, mat-forming perennial of beaches, dunes, and other moist sandy areas. Stems fleshy, branched, rooting at nodes, smooth. Leaves on long petioles that attach to center of leaf, round, 1–4 in. wide, blunt-toothed or scalloped, shiny and somewhat succulent. Flowers in rounded-pyramidal, compound umbels, 2–3 in. wide, at ends of branches; each flower white to greenish-white, minute, with 5 oval petals. BAS

Galax urceolata (G. aphylla)

DIAPENSIACEAE | **beetleweed**

May–Jul, 8–15 in. Low-growing, colonial evergreen perennial spreading by rhizomes, found in mountain forests, around rock outcrops, and on moist to dry slopes. Stem consists of underground rhizomes. Leaves emerge directly from rhizomes, usually in extensive colonies, round, leathery and shiny green, turning reddish-bronze in winter. Flowers in a spike occupying upper third of a slender, leafless flowering stalk; each white, 1/4 in. wide or less, with 5 tiny ascending petals. Overcollecting of leaves for the florist trade is a significant threat to the plant, which can be detected by its skunklike smell. AMC

Shortia galacifolia

DIAPENSIACEAE | **Oconee bells**

Mar–Apr, 4–8 in. Erect, rhizomatous and often colonial evergreen perennial of moist slopes, creek banks, and rock outcrops in humid escarpment gorges with high rainfall, generally in deep shade under *Rhododendron maximum* and *R. minus*. An underground rhizome sends up a rosette of leaves and separate flowering stalks. Leaves basal, petiolate, nearly round, 1–3 in. long, with toothed margins, thick and glossy, smooth. Flowers solitary, nodding on individual reddish stalks; each flower white, 3/4–1 in. long, bell-shaped and with 5 frilly-margined petals, 5 shorter pinkish-red sepals, and 5 stamens. WS

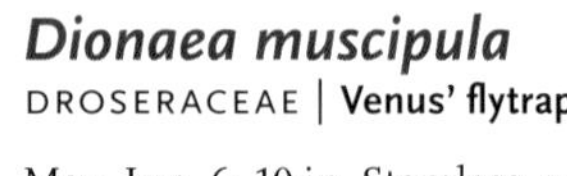

Dionaea muscipula

DROSERACEAE | **Venus' flytrap**

May–Jun, 6–10 in. Stemless, carnivorous perennial found in wet savannas and sandhill seepages over a very restricted range. Stems underground and bulblike; a flowering scape arises from the center of a basal rosette. Leaves basal, uniquely shaped with a flat, winged petiole-like portion and folded 2-lobed, reddish bristly-margined blade, which attracts insects and folds closed to trap them; when folded, the "trap" is clam-shaped. Flowers in an umbel-like cluster atop a single stalk, white, 1/2–3/4 in. wide, with 5 spreading, oval, delicately veined petals and 5 sepals. Fruit an oval capsule containing shiny black seeds. MK, RL

Drosera brevifolia (*D. leucantha*)

DROSERACEAE | **dwarf sundew**

Apr–May, 1–3 in. Low-growing, carnivorous annual/perennial of pine savannas and other wet sandy sites, and rarely in seepage over rock outcrops. Stems are slender, smooth flowering scapes covered with gland-tipped hairs that emerge from a small (about 1 in. wide) basal rosette. Leaves basal on short dilated petioles, oblong to spoon-shaped, greenish to reddish and densely covered with hairs exuding a clear, sticky liquid that attracts and traps insects. Flowers several in small cluster at top of scape, opening one at a time, white to rose-pink, with 5 spreading, nearly round petals. FG

Drosera intermedia

DROSERACEAE | **spoonleaf sundew**

Jun–Sep, 1–3 in. Low-growing, carnivorous perennial of savannas, ditches, bogs and pocosins, pool or stream margins; often in standing water. Stems short, unbranched, reddish; smooth flowering scape separate. Leaves basal and alternate, the latter close together and appearing basal; short-petioled; spoon-shaped; about ¾ in. long; the upper surface covered with red, sticky-tipped glandular hairs that attract and trap insects. Flowers 3–8 in a 1-sided, coiled raceme that unfurls as flowers open one at a time from the bottom up; each white, ⅓ in. wide, with 5 spreading, rounded petals, 5 yellow-tipped stamens, and a single pistil with 3 styles. Fruit an oval capsule. FG

Drosera rotundifolia

DROSERACEAE | **roundleaf sundew**

Jun–Sep, 3–12 in. Low-growing, carnivorous perennial found in mountain bogs and fens, seepage slopes, vertical seepages on rock or clay, and in northern parts of our range in Coastal Plain wetlands. Stems are slender, smooth flowering scapes that emerge from a basal rosette (about 4 in. wide) of leaves. Leaves on flattened petioles, nearly round and covered with red, gland-tipped hairs that attract and trap insects. Flowers 3–15 in a 1-sided, coiled raceme at top of scape; each flower white (rarely pink), about ¼ in. wide, with 5 oval petals and 5 sepals as long as or longer than the petals. Fruit an oval capsule. AMC

Orthilia secunda (*Pyrola secunda*)

ERICACEAE | **one-sided shinleaf**

Jun–Jul, 3–8 in. Erect evergreen perennial of cool, moist forests. Stem a single smooth flowering scape arising from a small rosette of leaves and bending just below the flowers. Leaves basal and essentially whorled, petiolate, round to elliptical, 3/4–1½ in. long, entire to finely toothed, smooth and shiny. Flowers in a 1-sided raceme bent nearly horizontal to the ground; each flower cream-white to greenish-white, 1/4–3/8 in. long, urn-shaped with a straight, stout, green style protruding. Fruit a flattened-round capsule. JASA

Pyrola americana

ERICACEAE | **rounded shinleaf**

May–Aug, 4–12 in. Rhizomatous evergreen perennial of dry to moist, mostly acidic woodlands and forests. Stem a single flowering scape covered with dry, brown scales, arising from a small rosette of leaves. Leaves basal, petiolate, round with truncate to slightly wedged base, obscurely wavy or toothed, leathery and shiny-smooth. Flowers in a narrow raceme occupying upper half (or less) of scape, nodding on short stalks; each flower white, ½–3/4 in. wide, with 5 petals, 5 sepals, 10 protruding stamens, and a pale green style curving down below the lower petals like an elephant trunk. Fruit a nodding, 5-parted, round capsule containing many seeds. AWF

Pyrola elliptica

ERICACEAE | **elliptic shinleaf**

Jun–Aug, 4–10 in. Rhizomatous perennial of moist to dry forests, including rich northern hardwood forests. A single flowering scape covered with dry, brown scales rises from a basal leaf rosette. Leaves petiolate, oval with round tip, tapering slightly at base, to 3 in. long, dull green and thin, with barely noticeable teeth. Flowers in a narrow raceme occupying upper half of scape, nodding on short stalks; each white, 1/3 in. wide, with 5 concave, oval petals, a cluster of orange-tipped stamens under the upper petals, and a pale green style curving down like an elephant trunk. Fruit a brown, flattened-round capsule with style persistent at the bottom. GPF

Heuchera parviflora

SAXIFRAGACEAE | **cave alumroot**

Jul–Sep, 4–18 in. Erect, tufted perennial of grotto floors, cliff bases under overhangs, and behind waterfalls (but not in the spray zone), nearly always in deep shade. Flowering stems unbranched, leafless, spreading-hairy. Leaves basal, on hairy petioles, round to kidney-shaped with notched base, 1–5 in. long, palmately cut into broadly rounded and toothed lobes, sometimes velvety-hairy beneath or furry above and reddish beneath. Flowers in a narrow, loose terminal panicle; each less than ¼ in. wide, white to pink, the 5 tiny petals attached to a white-hairy conical calyx tube with 5 protruding stamens. Fruit a round to oval capsule with 2 persistent styles. AMC

Heuchera villosa

SAXIFRAGACEAE | **rock alumroot**

Jun–Oct, 8–12 in. Erect, tufted perennial of rocky forests, boulder fields, outcrop crevices. Flowering stems unbranched, furry with rust-colored hairs and a few small bracts. Leaves basal, on hairy petioles, broadly oval with notched bases, 2–10 in. long, palmately divided into 5–9 triangular, pointy-tipped and toothed lobes, smooth or glandular-hairy. Flowers often nodding in a tall, narrow panicle, which starts out crowded but elongates with time; each flower white to pinkish, with 5 tiny, often twisting petals attached to a hairy, conical calyx with minute teeth. There are 5 protruding stamens with orange anthers. Fruit an oval capsule with 2 persistent styles. WS, JG

Micranthes careyana

SAXIFRAGACEAE | **Carey's saxifrage**

May–Jun, 4–15 in. Erect, rosette-forming perennial of moist rock outcrops and cliffs, often in moist soil at the base of a vertical or overhanging rock outcrop. A Southern Appalachian endemic. Flowering stems branched above, furry with glandular hairs. Leaves basal on winged petioles, oval to oblong-oval with wedge-shaped base, to 5 in. long, coarsely toothed, fleshy-thick, green above and purple mottled beneath, furry on both surfaces or only beneath. Flowers in a wide-branching, glandular-furry panicle with some leaflike bracts; each flower white, with 5 tiny petals, 5 partially fused minute sepals, and 10 stamens. Fruit a 2-parted oval capsule. KB

Micranthes micranthidifolia

SAXIFRAGACEAE | **brook saxifrage**

May–Jun, 10–20 in. Erect, rosette-forming perennial, sometimes occurring in small colonies. Flowering stems slender, branched above, somewhat sticky. Leaves basal, on winged petioles, oblong-lance-shaped, 3–12 in. long, sharply toothed and each tooth with a sharp, hard tip, usually smooth. Flowers in a loose panicle, the slender branches subtended by small bracts; each flower white, less than ½ in. wide, with 5 spreading to recurved, minute, oval petals with yellow spots at the base, 10 club-shaped stamens, and a 2-lobed ovary. Fruit a 2-lobed, pointed oval capsule, the 2 parts fused only at the base. KB

Micranthes pensylvanica

SAXIFRAGACEAE | **swamp saxifrage**

Apr–Jun, 11–30 in. Erect, rosette-forming perennial of forested seeps and seepage swamps and fens, usually over mafic or calcareous rocks. Leaves basal, short-petioled, elliptical to lance-shaped and tapering at the base, 4–10 in. long, shallowly toothed, with conspicuous midrib, sparsely hairy or smooth. Flowers in a dense panicle that elongates and loosens with age, bracts subtending the stout sticky-hairy branches; each flower white to yellow or greenish-purple, to ¼ in. wide, with 5 tiny lance-shaped petals, 10 thin orange-tipped stamens, and a 2-lobed conical ovary. Fruit a 2-lobed, pointed oval capsule, the 2 sections widely spreading at maturity. GPF

Micranthes virginiensis

SAXIFRAGACEAE | **early saxifrage**

Feb–Jun, 4–18 in. Erect, rosette-forming perennial found on rock outcrops, moist alluvial and slope forests, and streambanks. Flowering stems arising from a basal rosette, stout, branched above, with a few bracts, sticky-hairy. Leaves basal, on widened petioles edged with hairs, oval to spoon-shaped, ½–3 in. long, bluntly toothed, fleshy, often purplish-red beneath, smooth or hairy. Flowers in a compact, sticky-hairy terminal panicle that elongates with age; each flower white, about ⅓ in. wide, with 5 spreading, oval petals, 10 yellow-tipped stamens, and a 2-lobed ovary. Fruit a 2-parted, teardrop-shaped capsule. RTW

Tiarella cordifolia

SAXIFRAGACEAE | **heartleaf foamflower**

Apr–Jun, 10–12 in. Rosette-forming, colonial perennial of rock outcrops and moist, cove, and well-drained bottomland forests. Flowering stems unbranched, hairy. Leaves long-petioled, broadly oval to nearly round, to 5 in. long, 3- to 7-lobed, palmately veined, sometimes mottled pale green or brown, toothed, hairy above; evergreen in areas with mild winters. Flowers in a crowded, glandular-hairy, terminal raceme that elongates and loosens with age, opening from the bottom up; each flower white to pinkish-white (buds pink), 1/3 in. wide, with 5 spreading, pointed petals with basal claws, 10 long stamens, and a conical ovary. Fruit a conical capsule. Spreads by runners. AMC

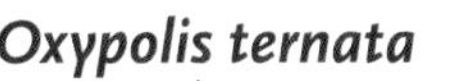

Oxypolis ternata

APIACEAE | **savanna cowbane**

Sep–Oct, 1–3 ft. Erect perennial of wet pine savannas and sandhill seepages. Stems slender, few-branched, smooth. Leaves few (1–3), alternate, on long petioles with sheathing bases, palmately divided into 3 very narrow segments up to 8 in. long (though upper leaf may be undivided) with parallel veins and smooth surface. Flowers in a flat-topped, compound terminal umbel, white, less than 1/4 in. wide, with 5 tiny petals, 5 stamens with white anthers, and an ovary with style. Fruit a joined pair of oval, ridged seeds that are flat on 1 side. BAS

Angelica triquinata

APIACEAE | **mountain angelica**

Aug–Sep, 2–6 ft. Coarse, erect perennial of grassy balds, brook banks, and moist forests at mid to high elevations. A Southern Appalachian endemic. Stems stout, purplish, smooth. Leaves basal and alternate, with broadly sheathing petioles, 1–2 times pinnately divided, the largest leaflets 3–6 in. long (reduced above). Flowers in compound terminal umbel to 6 in. wide, with smaller umbels from upper leaf axils, the umbellets slightly dome-shaped; greenish-white flowers with tiny, incurved petals appear to intoxicate bees and wasps and are thought to be mildly poisonous. Fruit green to reddish-pink, striped, flattened and winged seeds. SG, AMC

Angelica venenosa

APIACEAE | **deadly angelica**

May–Aug, 2–6 ft. Erect perennial found in dry forests and woodlands, woodland borders, longleaf pine sandhills, hammocks, and prairies. Stems unbranched and finely hairy, especially above. Leaves on broadly sheathing petioles, divided into many elliptical, somewhat leathery, toothed and finely hairy leaflets; leaves reduced above. Flowers in large, compound terminal umbel (to 5 in. wide) and umbels from upper leaf axils, the umbellets domed and on slender, hairy stalks; flowers greenish-white, with 5 white petals and 5 long, white stamens. Fruit a green, flattened, winged seed. Roots are highly toxic (hence the specific epithet). WS

Chaerophyllum procumbens

APIACEAE | **spreading chervil**

Mar–Apr, 6–18 in. Reclining-sprawling or erect annual of alluvial forests. Stems angled, usually branched near base, smooth or sparingly hairy. Leaves on petioles with sheathing bases, oval in outline, 1–4½ in. long, finely divided (3 times pinnately compound) into many narrowly elliptical segments, smooth or with some hairs on nerves and margins. Flowers in compound umbels from leaf axils, each umbel with about 3 umbellets; each flower white, less than ¼ in. wide, with 5 spreading, rounded petals. Fruit a joined pair of elliptic-oblong, ridged seeds. When crushed, gives off parsleylike scent. SJB

Chaerophyllum tainturieri

APIACEAE | **southern chervil**

Mar–Apr, 1–3 ft. Erect annual of fields, roadsides, disturbed areas. Stems slender, round but with longitudinal lines, densely hairy in lower half, branched in upper, very leafy. Leaves on petioles with clasping-sheathing bases, oval in outline, to 4½ in. long, finely divided (3 times pinnately compound) into tiny narrow segments, which often have reddish margins and a minute orange spot near the tip; leaves hairy. Flowers in flat-topped, compound umbels to 2½ in. wide from leaf axils; each umbellet with 3–10 white, minute flowers with 5 spreading, rounded petals. Fruit a joined pair of elliptic-oblong, ridged seeds. When crushed, gives off sweet carrotlike scent. AMC

Cicuta maculata

APIACEAE | **water-hemlock**

May–Aug, 2–6 ft. Coarse, erect perennial found in marshes, bogs, seepages, ditches, and swamp forests. Stems stout, hollow, pale greenish-pink, smooth. Leaves short-petioled with sheathing bases, to 1 ft. long and 1 ft. wide, 2–3 times pinnately divided into lance-shaped and sharply toothed leaflets. Flowers in numerous flat-topped umbels at ends of stem and branches; each flower white, less than ¼ in. wide, with 5 petals that are narrow at the base and notched at the tip, 5 white stamens, and a divided style. Fruit a joined pair of green, flattened, winged seeds. An extremely toxic plant. RTW

Conium maculatum

APIACEAE | **poison-hemlock**

May–Jun, 3–7 ft. Coarse, erect biennial of ditches, roadsides, streambanks, disturbed areas. Native to Eurasia, widespread throughout NoAm. Stems stout and hollow, ribbed with longitudinal veins, branched, usually purple-spotted, smooth. Leaves on petioles with sheathing bases, triangular, 8–16 in. long and finely divided (3–4 times pinnately compound) into many sharp-toothed, fernlike, smooth segments. Flowers in a large compound terminal umbel (2–5 in. wide) and smaller lateral umbels; umbellets contain 8–25 white, ¼-in.-wide flowers with 5 spreading, tiny, oblong-oval petals. Fruit a joined pair of curved, elliptic-oblong, ridged seeds. All parts are extremely poisonous. RTW

Cryptotaenia canadensis

APIACEAE | **honewort**

May–Jun, 1–3 ft. Erect perennial of moist, nutrient-rich forests, such as alluvial, bottomland, slope, and cove forests. Stems slender, branched, smooth. Leaves on petioles with sheathing bases, divided into 3 oval or diamond-shaped, toothed leaflets that are 1½–3 in. long (these sometimes further lobed) and smooth. Flowers in open, sparsely flowered umbels at top of stem and from upper leaf axils, white, minute, with 5 tiny petals. Fruit a joined pair of blackish, very slender, ribbed seeds. RTW

Cyclospermum leptophyllum

APIACEAE | **marsh-parsley**

Apr–Jun, 4–18 in. Erect to reclining annual of freshwater marshes, roadside ditches, disturbed areas. Probably native to the Neotropics, widespread in se U.S. Stems slender, branched, smooth. Leaves on petioles with sheathing bases, ½–3½ in. long (reduced above), finely divided (2–3 times pinnately compound) into many linear, almost needlelike segments, smooth. Flowers in compound, terminal and axillary umbels containing 2–3 umbellets; umbellets ¼–½ in. wide and composed of 5–15 tiny, white, 5-petaled flowers. Fruit a joined pair of asymmetrically elliptical seeds that are flat to slightly concave on 1 side and convex and conspicuously 3-ribbed on the other. KB

Daucus carota

APIACEAE | **Queen-Anne's-lace**

May–Sep, 1–6 ft. Erect biennial of fields, roadsides, disturbed areas, with only a rosette of leaves the first year. Native to Europe, widespread in NoAm. Stems stiff, hollow, with long white hairs. Leaves oval-lance-shaped to oblong, 2–4 in. long, finely divided (2 or more times pinnately compound) into narrow sharp-tipped segments, sometimes hairy below and along margins. Flowers in a 2- to 5-in. wide, flat to dome-shaped compound umbel with 20–90 umbellets (each of 15–60 tiny flowers; the middle flower may be maroon) and in a few smaller, axillary umbels; petals have incurved tips. Fruit a joined pair of reddish, elliptical, slightly flattened, very bristly seeds. BAS

Erigenia bulbosa

APIACEAE | **harbinger-of-spring**

Jan–May, 3–10 in. Erect to sprawling annual of moist, nutrient-rich forests, over calcareous substrates or on very rich alluvial deposits (e.g., riverbanks). Stems 1–3 from a tuber, thick, unbranched, longitudinally ridged, light green to reddish, smooth. Leaves 1–2 on sheathing petioles, broadly oval in outline, divided into 3 leaflets, each further divided 1–2 times, the ultimate segments oblong to elliptic-oblong or lance-shaped, smooth. Flowers in a compound terminal umbel of 1–4 umbellets; each flower ¼ in. wide, with narrow petals, 5 dark red stamens that turn black, and a divided white style. Fruit a joined pair of minute, curved, ridged seeds. RTW

Heracleum maximum

APIACEAE | **cow-parsnip**

May–Jul, 3–10 ft. Large, rank-smelling perennial of road banks, meadows, and forest openings. Stems coarse, hollow, ribbed/grooved, light green and covered with spreading, white hairs. Leaves large and coarse, on petioles with conspicuous purple-veined sheaths, and ternately divided (lower leaves may be pinnately divided), the leaflets oval and irregularly toothed or cleft. Flowers in a large (to 8 in. wide) compound terminal umbel as well as in smaller umbels from upper leaf axils, each flower with 5 tiny white petals. Fruit a joined pair of hairy, flattened-elliptical seeds. WS

Ligusticum canadense

APIACEAE | **American lovage**

Jun–Jul, 2–6 ft. Tall, celery-scented perennial from a large taproot, found in moist to dryish, nutrient-rich forests and woodlands. Stem stout, green with white-waxy coating. Leaves to 14 in. long; lower leaves 3–4 times ternately compound, but upper leaves less divided or even simple. Leaflets lance-shaped to oblong, thin-textured and serrate-edged to toothed. Flowers in compound terminal umbels, the umbellets with about 15 flowers each; flowers 1/4 in. wide, composed of 5 tiny white petals. Fruit a joined pair of flattened, oval seeds. BAS

Osmorhiza claytonii

APIACEAE | **hairy sweet cicely**

Apr–May, 1–3 ft. Erect perennial of cove and other moist, rich forests. Stems stout, branched above, light green to reddish-green, hairy. Lower leaves petiolate, upper sessile, widely oval in outline but 2–3 times divided into 3 leaflets, the ultimate leaflets pointy-tipped and toothed with hairs on the margins. Flowers in sparse compound umbels at top of stem and from upper leaf axils, white, less than 1/4 in. wide, with 5 petals with incurved tips, 5 white stamens, and an ovary with a very short, divided style. Fruit a joined pair of narrowly elliptical, 5-ridged seeds that are slightly bristly along their ribs. Unlike *O. longistylis*, this species is lacking in scent. EB

Osmorhiza longistylis

APIACEAE | **anise-root**

Apr–May, 1–2½ ft. Erect perennial of moist, rich forests. Stems stout, branched above, light green to reddish-green, smooth with hairs only at nodes or densely hairy. Lower leaves petiolate, upper sessile, widely oval in outline and 2–3 times divided into 3, the ultimate leaflets pointy-tipped and toothed with hairs on veins beneath. Flowers in sparse compound umbels at top of stem and from upper leaf axils, less than ¼ in. wide, with 5 petals with incurved tips, 5 white stamens, and an ovary with a divided style that is longer than the petals. Fruit a joined pair of narrowly elliptical, 5-ridged seeds that are slightly bristly along their ribs. All parts anise-scented. BAS

Oxypolis rigidior

APIACEAE | **cowbane**

Aug–Oct, 2–5 ft. Erect perennial of bogs, seepages, swamps, wet meadows, streambanks. Stems stout or slender, few-branched, smooth. Leaves on long petioles (reduced above) with sheathing bases, to 12 in. long, once pinnately divided into 5–11 oblong to lance-shaped segments with netted veins and widely spaced teeth toward the tip, smooth. Flowers in flat-topped, compound umbel (3–5 in. wide) at top of stem, with a few smaller umbels from upper leaf axils; each less than ¼ in. wide, with 5 upcurved to spreading petals, 5 stamens with white anthers, and an ovary with style. Fruit a joined pair of oval, ridged seeds that are flat on 1 side. Poisonous to livestock. BAS

Ptilimnium capillaceum

APIACEAE | **Atlantic bishopweed**

Jun–Aug, 6–60 in. Slender, erect annual of ditches, marshes, and other wet places. Stems loosely branched, at least above, smooth. Leaves on short petioles with sheathing base, to 4 in. long, divided into 3 leaflets that are further divided into many smooth, threadlike segments. Flowers in flat-topped, compound umbels (to 2 in. wide) at tips of branches, each umbellet with 4–20 flowers, and the umbel surrounded by a whorl of bracts that resemble small versions of the leaves. Flowers white, tiny, with 5 incurved petals and stamens with pinkish-purple anthers. Fruit a joined pair of oval, ridged seeds. BAS

Sanicula canadensis

APIACEAE | **Canada sanicle**

Apr–May, ½–4 ft. Erect to ascending perennial of dry to moist forests. Stems branched above, light green, smooth. Leaves petiolate (petioles and blades reduced above), ¾–2½ in. long, palmately divided into 3–5 narrowly oblong-oval leaflets with sharply toothed margins, smooth. Flowers in compound umbels to 2½ in. wide on grooved stalks at stem ends, each umbellet pompom-like and with 3 perfect flowers and 1–15 male flowers, all on short stalks. Flowers greenish-white, with 5 tiny petals and 5 shorter sepals, and in the perfect flowers, a prominent ovary covered in rows of hooked bristles. Fruit a round, burlike cluster of 2 bristly seeds. JG

Sanicula marilandica

APIACEAE | **Maryland sanicle**

May–Jun, 1–4 ft. Erect to leaning perennial of moist to semi-moist, nutrient-rich forests. Stems branched in inflorescence, smooth. Leaves basal and alternate, petiolate (uppermost leaves nearly sessile), palmately divided into 5–7 lobes or leaflets, each oblong-oval with toothed margins and smooth. Flowers in compound umbels at ends of stems, each umbellet bristly and pompom-like with 3 perfect flowers and many male flowers, all sessile to short-stalked. Flowers greenish-white, tiny, with 5 petals, 5 sepals of equal length, and protruding stamens with greenish-white tips that turn brown with age. Fruit an oval, burlike cluster of 2 bristly seeds. GPF

Sanicula smallii

APIACEAE | **southern sanicle**

Apr, 1–2½ ft. Erect perennial of moist to semi-moist forests. Stems branched in inflorescence, smooth. Leaves basal and alternate, petiolate (uppermost leaves with short, flaring petioles), palmately divided into 3 or 5 leaflets, the segments lance-elliptical with toothed margins and smooth. Flowers in compound umbels at ends of branching stems, each umbellet on a grooved stalk, bristly and pompom-like with 3 perfect flowers and 5–6 male flowers on short, thick stalks. Flowers white to greenish, tiny, with 5 petals, 5 sepals, 5 protruding stamens, and a bristly ovary with a pair of long styles. Fruit an oval, burlike cluster of 2 bristly seeds. BAS

Sanicula trifoliata

APIACEAE | **beaked sanicle**

May, 1–2½ ft. Erect biennial of cove and other moist, nutrient-rich forests. Stems branched in inflorescence, smooth. Leaves basal and alternate, long-petioled (sessile above) and palmately divided into 3 leaflets, each widely elliptical to oblong-oval, 2½ in. long or more, sharply toothed and smooth. Flowers in open compound umbels at ends of branches, the umbellets with 3 sessile, perfect flowers and 3–5 male flowers on short stalks. Flowers white, tiny, with 5 petals, 5 sepals that are longer than the petals, and a bristly ovary. Fruit an oval to oblong, burlike cluster of 2 bristly seeds. GPF

Sium suave

APIACEAE | **water-parsnip**

Jun–Aug, 2–6 ft. Erect perennial found in freshwater marshes, brackish marshes, and swamp forests. Stems stout, hollow, longitudinally ribbed, branching above middle, smooth. Leaves pinnately divided into 5–17 lance-shaped, sharply toothed leaflets that are ½–6 in. long; submerged leaves, when present, are 2–3 times divided. Leaf surface smooth. Flowers in generally flat, compound umbels (2–5 in. wide) at ends of branches, the umbellets with 20–35 flowers each; flowers white, to ¼ in. wide, with 5 petals with incurved tips, a short calyx, 5 protruding stamens, and a 2-celled ovary with a pair of divergent styles. Fruit a joined pair of oval, ridged seeds. GPF

Aralia racemosa

ARALIACEAE | **spikenard**

Jun–Aug, 3–5 ft. Erect, somewhat woody and bushy-appearing perennial of rich woodlands, trail margins, and roadsides. Stems stout, branched, dark maroon, smooth to slightly hairy. Leaves few, alternate, long-petioled, to 30 in. long, pinnately divided or first divided into 3 and then leaflets pinnately divided; ultimate leaflets oval with heart-shaped bases (these sometimes asymmetric) and toothed and slightly furry. Flowers in a long (1–1½ ft.) spike rising above leaves and composed of numerous rounded umbels; flowers greenish-white, less than ¼ in. wide, with 5 petals, 5 sepals, and 5 protruding stamens. Fruit a reddish to dark purple, round berry. WS

Cnidoscolus stimulosus

EUPHORBIACEAE | **spurge-nettle**

Mar–Aug, 20–40 in. Erect to reclining perennial of sandhills, dry sandy woodlands, and other sites with dry sandy soils. Stems branched, covered in stinging hairs. Leaves long-petioled, round in overall outline, to 8 in. long, deeply palmately lobed, the 3–5 lobes entire to sharply toothed; with stinging hairs. Flowers in loose, fork-branched, terminal clusters, with the central flower usually female and lateral flowers male; flowers white, about 1 in. wide, with 5 spreading, elliptical petal-like sepals (true petals absent) from a ½-in.-long tube. Fruit a spiny, 3-parted capsule. BAS

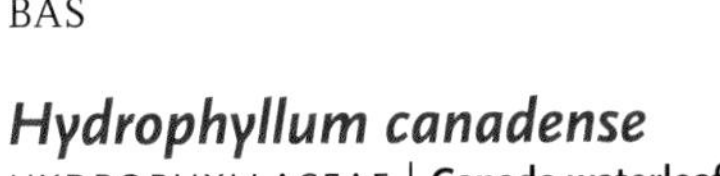

Hydrophyllum canadense

HYDROPHYLLACEAE | **Canada waterleaf**

May–Aug, 8–28 in. Erect-spreading, rhizomatous perennial of cove hardwood forests and other moist, nutrient-rich forests, rocky streambanks, seepy limestone cliffs. Stems branching, smooth to slightly hairy. Stem leaves alternate, long-petioled, palmately divided into 5–9 lobes, toothed and sparsely hairy; basal leaves (overwinter and die back in spring) elongated in comparison, pinnately divided and with silvery-white blotches. Flowers in 1–3 branching terminal clusters, white to pale pinkish-purple, to ½ in. long, bell-shaped, with 5 corolla lobes and fringelike appendages between them, a 5-parted calyx, and 5 prominently long stamens. AMC

Hydrophyllum macrophyllum

HYDROPHYLLACEAE | **hairy waterleaf**

May–Jun, 1–2½ ft. Erect, rhizomatous perennial of cove forests and other moist rocky forests, especially over calcareous or mafic rocks. Stems tending to zigzag, branched, furry-hairy. Leaves petiolate, elliptical to oblong, to 6 in. long, pinnately divided into 7–13 toothed segments, blotched with grayish-white when young (resembles a water stain) and slightly hairy. Flowers in 2–3 floppy, terminal clusters, the branches and stalks covered with long hairs; flowers usually white, ¾ in. wide (fully open), bell-shaped, with the corolla divided into 5 spreading lobes and the hairy calyx divided into 5 triangular lobes. RTW

Hydrophyllum virginianum

HYDROPHYLLACEAE | **eastern waterleaf**

Apr–Jun, 8–34 in. Weakly erect, rhizomatous perennial of cove hardwood forests, moist rocky forests, alluvial forests. Stems branched, smooth or with close-pressed hairs. Leaves petiolate, broadly oval to triangular, to 6 in. long, pinnately divided into 5–9 coarsely toothed and pointy segments, with scattered whitish spots that fade with age; sometimes slightly hairy. Flowers in 1–2 rounded clusters on a terminal stalk, white to pale purple or purple-maroon, ½ in. long, tubular-bell-shaped with 5 erect corolla lobes, 5 hairy and linear calyx lobes with feathery edges, and 5 hairy stamens bearing pale yellow anthers that turn brown with age. Fruit a round capsule. GMP, BAS

Nemophila aphylla

HYDROPHYLLACEAE | **eastern baby-blue-eyes**

Mar–Apr, 2–15 in. Tufted, weakly erect annual of moist, nutrient-rich floodplain forests and slope forests. Stems weakly spreading, succulent and rough-hairy. Leaves alternate (at least above), petiolate, broadly triangular in outline, ⅓–1 in. long, deeply pinnately divided into 3–5 oval segments, which are usually lobed or toothed and hairy. Flowers solitary on short stalks from leaf nodes, white to pale lavender, ¼ in. wide or less, the corolla with a short bell-shaped tube and 5 spreading, oval lobes and the calyx with 5 prominent, hairy, lance-shaped lobes and tiny, reflexed, earlobe-like appendages between. Fruit a tiny, hairy, rounded to oval capsule. AMC

Phacelia covillei

HYDROPHYLLACEAE | **eastern buttercup phacelia**

Apr, 4–8 in. Erect-spreading annual/biennial found in the rich soils of floodplains and nearby terraces and slopes. Stems weak, simple or branched from the base, lower parts rough-hairy. Leaves petiolate, oblong-oval in outline, 1–3 in. long, deeply pinnately divided into 1–6 segments that may be further lobed; blade and petiole are rough-hairy. Flowers in loose, branching, and sometimes weakly coiled, axillary clusters of 1–6; each flower blue, less than ¼ in. wide, tubular, with 5 tiny, ascending corolla lobes. BAS

Phacelia fimbriata

HYDROPHYLLACEAE | **Blue Ridge phacelia**

Apr–May, 4–12 in. Spreading-ascending annual found in moist forests on slopes and floodplains at all elevations, often over circumneutral soils; often locally abundant. Stems weak, branched from the base and covered with stiff, spreading hairs. Leaves petiolate (uppermost sessile), pinnately divided into 5–9 lobes that are blunt or pointed and sparsely rough-hairy. Flowers in branched clusters of 5–15 at tips of branches, white, nearly ½ in. wide, the corolla bowl-shaped and opening to 5 spreading, rounded lobes with prominently fringed margins. 5 stamens are attached to the petals. KB

Hibiscus aculeatus

MALVACEAE | **comfort-root**

Jun–Aug, 3–6 ft. Erect, shrublike perennial arising from a woody crown, found in pine savannas and dry sandy or loamy soils of maritime forest edges. Stems mostly simple, rough-hairy. Leaves petiolate, to 3½ in. long, with 3–5 deeply cut lobes, coarsely toothed and rough-hairy. Flowers solitary on stalks from leaf axils, cream-white (turning pink with age) with a dark red center, 4½ in. wide, with 5 overlapping scalloped-edge petals, a 5-lobed calyx, and an erect central column of red stamens surrounding a red pistil. The flower rests on a whorl of 10–15 very narrow green bracts. JP

Ripariosida hermaphrodita (*Sida hermaphrodita*)

MALVACEAE | **Virginia-mallow**

Jul–Aug, 3–6 ft. Erect perennial of sandy or rocky areas along riverbanks. Stems tough-woody, branched, smooth, but hairy when young. Leaves on petioles with stipules, oval, 4–7 in. long and deeply cut into 3–7 lobes (middle one longest), serrate to toothed, smooth but with some hairs along veins. Flowers numerous in panicles at ends of branches, white, ¾–1 in. wide, with 5 slightly incurved petals surrounding a central cluster of white stamens (in bundles of 5) and styles. Fruit a ring of about 10 joined podlike, kidney-shaped segments, each with 1 beak, the ring surrounded by persistent, triangular calyx lobes. GPF

Enemion biternatum

RANUNCULACEAE | **false rue-anemone**

(Jan) Mar–Apr, 8–16 in. Delicate, erect perennial of rich forests, often in dense patches on natural levees with very nutrient-rich sediments or on slopes with underlying mafic rocks. Stems slender, sparingly branched, reddish-tinged, smooth. Leaves alternate and basal, petiolate, divided into 3 leaflets up to 1 in. long, these again divided into 3 bluntly rounded lobes; the terminal leaflet is longer stalked than the 2 lateral leaflets. Flowers solitary, or in groups of 2–3, on thin stalks from leaf axils; each with 5(6) petal-like sepals, several slender stamens with yellow anthers, and a few green pistils in the center. Fruit a small cluster of beaked follicles. FG

Fragaria virginiana

ROSACEAE | **wild strawberry**

Apr–Jun, 1–3 in. Low-growing, tufted perennial of grasslands, roadsides, pastures, woodlands, grassy balds. Essentially stemless, except for hairy, slender runners, which spread across the ground, forming new plants at nodes. Leaves tufted, long-petioled, divided into 3 oval, coarsely and sharply toothed leaflets to 2 in. long. Flowers in small branching clusters on hairy stalks, white, about ¾ in. wide, with 5 round to oval petals, 5 green, hairy, pointed sepals (visible between petals), and a cluster of about 20 stamens around a green, conical center bearing multiple tiny pistils. Fruit an edible, fleshy, round berry with tiny seeds shallowly embedded in the surface. BAS, AMC

Geum canadense

ROSACEAE | **white avens**

Apr–Jul, 1½–2½ ft. Weakly erect perennial of moist slope, bottomland, and swamp forests. Hairy stems arise from a 6-in. basal rosette. Basal leaves on petioles with basal stipules, variably shaped from unlobed to 3-lobed or palmately divided into diamond-shaped segments; stem leaves alternate, to 4 in. long, 3- to 5-lobed or divided; upper stem leaves usually sessile, undivided and smaller. Flowers in a terminal leafy panicle, 1–3 flowers per primary branch; each ½ in. wide, with 5 spreading oblong petals, 5 slightly shorter triangular sepals, and numerous stamens surrounding a green domed ovary covered with styles. Fruit a bristly, round head of many beaked achenes. BAS

Geum geniculatum

ROSACEAE | **bent avens**

Jun–Aug, 1½–2½ ft. Erect-ascending perennial of seeps, grassy balds, cliff bases, streambanks, apparently restricted to the highest peaks of nw NC, ne TN. Basal leaves petiolate, pinnately divided into 3–5 major and 2–5 minor leaflets, the terminal largest; stem leaves smaller, sessile-subsessile, divided into 3 leaflets or with 3 lobes, with deeply lobed basal stipules. Flowers 5–15, nodding on densely hairy stalks in branching terminal cluster; creamy white to pinkish, with 5 erect, oblong-oval petals with blunt-rounded tips, 5 erect-spreading, hairy, greenish-maroon lance-shaped sepals, and a cone-shaped compound ovary with kinked styles. Fruit a bristly head of achenes. WS

Geum laciniatum

ROSACEAE | **rough avens**

Jun–Jul, 1½–3 ft. Erect perennial of fens and wet meadows, especially over calcareous or mafic rocks. Stems densely hairy. Basal and lower leaves on long petioles with lobed or toothed stipules, simple and round or pinnately divided into 5 or more sharply toothed leaflets/lobes; upper stem leaves smaller and simple or divided into 3. Flowers 1–3 at top of stem, each on a stalk to 3 in. long and covered with spreading hairs; flowers white or cream, to ½ in. wide, with 5 spreading petals, 5 lance-shaped sepals that are significantly longer, and several stamens surrounding a cone-shaped compound ovary bristling with elongated styles. Fruit a bristly, round head of achenes. GPF

Sibbaldia retusa

ROSACEAE | **mountain-cinquefoil**

Jun–Aug, 4–12 in. Rhizomatous, semi-shrubby perennial of grassy balds, rock outcrop crevices, high-elevation glades. Stems trailing, branched, hairy. Leaves on petioles with lance-shaped stipules, palmately divided into 3 leaflets (each ½–1 in. long) bearing 3–5 teeth at the squared-off tip, somewhat leathery, shiny green above, pale green beneath, evergreen, turning bright red in winter. Flowers in stalked, branching, few-flowered clusters; each to ½ in. wide, with 5 spreading oval petals, a bowl-shaped calyx with 5 short triangular lobes, a dense cluster of pistils, and 20–30 stamens. Fruit a cluster of achenes. WS

Panax quinquefolius

ARALIACEAE | **American ginseng**

May–Jun, 1–2 ft. Erect perennial of moist hardwood forests; formerly abundant but now reduced to small populations of scattered individuals, the spindle-shaped forked roots overharvested for the herbal trade. Leaves 3 (1–5) in a whorl at top of smooth, solitary stem, long-petioled, palmately divided into 3–5 elliptical to oblong-oval leaflets that are 2½–6 in. long, toothed, pointy-tipped and smooth, the 2 lower leaflets smaller. Flowers 6–20 in an umbel to ¾ in. wide rising from the center of the leaf whorl; each greenish-white, less than ¼ in. wide, with 5 spreading petals, an insignificant calyx, 5 stamens, and a divided style. Fruit a bright red, round berry. EB, AMC

Panax trifolius

ARALIACEAE | **dwarf ginseng**

Apr–Jun, 4–8 in. Erect perennial found in cove forests, bottomland forests, and other nutrient-rich forests. Stem solitary, unbranched, smooth. Leaves 3 in a whorl, long-petioled, divided into 3 elliptical to narrowly oblong leaflets that are ¾–2 in. long, deeply toothed and smooth. Flowers 15–30 in a single, rounded umbel at top of stem above leaf whorl; each flower white fading to pink, less than ¼ in. wide, with 5 spreading petals, 5 protruding white stamens, and 3 styles. Fruit a yellow-green, rounded but 3-angled berry. ER

Anemone lancifolia

RANUNCULACEAE | **lanceleaf anemone**

Mar–May, 4–11 in. Erect, rhizomatous perennial of rich, moist soils on slopes or in bottomlands and seepage swamps; also occasionally in nutrient-poor soils. Stems unbranched, smooth to sparsely hairy. Basal leaves petiolate, solitary, divided into 3 leaflets; stem leaves 3 at top of stem just below flowering stalk, divided into 3 narrowly diamond-shaped to elliptical, toothed leaflets. Flowers solitary on a smooth, slender stalk from top of stem, white, with 5 (4–7) oblong-elliptical, very veiny petal-like sepals encircling a small domed compound ovary and numerous stamens. BAS

Anemone quinquefolia

RANUNCULACEAE | **wood anemone**

Mar–May, 2–12 in. Erect, rhizomatous perennial of rich, moist forests and grassy balds; sometimes forms sizable colonies on woodland borders. Leaves include a single, long-petioled basal leaf and a whorl of petiolate stem leaves below the flower. Leaves to 3 in. long, divided into 3 oval to oblong, toothed, pointy-tipped leaflets (can appear to be 5 if lateral lobes are deeply incised). Flower solitary on a slender, usually hairy stalk at top of mostly smooth stem, white (sometimes pink-tinged), 1 in. wide, with 5 (4–10) veiny, oval, petal-like sepals encircling a small, green compound ovary and many white stamens. Fruit a small cluster of minutely hairy achenes. RTW

Anemone virginiana

RANUNCULACEAE | **thimbleweed**

May–Aug, 1–3 ft. Erect perennial found in rich forests and rocky woodlands, especially on circumneutral soils. Stem solitary, loosely hairy. Leaves basal, and 1–2 whorls of similarly shaped leaves toward top of stem, below the flower scapes; palmately divided into 3- (sometimes 5-) parted, toothed, lance-shaped and hairy segments with purple stalks. Flowers solitary on 2 or more hairy, terminal scapes, white, to 1½ in. wide, with 5 petal-like sepals encircling a green, bristly, cone-shaped compound ovary and ring of bushy stamens. Fruit a thimble-shaped cluster of brownish achenes. BAS

Anemonidium canadense (*Anemone canadensis*)

RANUNCULACEAE | **Canada anemone**

May–Aug, 8–24 in. Erect, colonial, rhizomatous perennial of moist forests. Stems slender, branched, semi-hairy to quite furry. Basal leaves petiolate, roundish in outline, ½–4 in. long, and palmately divided into 5–7 lobes that are usually further sharp-lobed, prominently veiny and hairy beneath; stem leaves just below flowers are sessile, smaller, 2- to 3-parted, and sharply toothed. Flowers 1–3 on stalks from top of stem, white, 1–1½ in. wide, with 5 petal-like oval sepals of unequal size and shape (½–⅔ in. long) surrounding a green, compound ovary and numerous yellow stamens. Fruit a rounded cluster of tiny achenes. WS

Oxalis montana

OXALIDACEAE | **American wood-sorrel**

May–Jul, 3–6 in. Erect, often colonial perennial of spruce-fir forests and northern hardwood forests, at high elevations. Leaves and flowering stalks separate, arising from creeping rhizome. Leaves long-petioled, divided into 3 cloverlike, heart-shaped leaflets ½–1 in. wide each and sparsely hairy. Flowers solitary on a hairy stalk slightly taller than leaves, white to pale pink veined with pink or purple, about ¾ in. wide, with 5 petals, each with a scalloped tip and a yellow spot along with a pink band near the base; there are 5 sepals with flat tips and 10 unequal stamens. Fruit a smooth, rounded or flattened capsule that splits and flings seeds when mature. AMC

Stipulicida setacea

CARYOPHYLLACEAE | **Coastal Plain wireplant**

May–Aug, 2–10 in. Erect annual/short-lived perennial found on xeric sands of sandhills, dry pine flatwoods, and maritime forests. Stems smooth and wiry, with many rigid, forking branches that are so fine the tiny flowers may seem to hover above the ground. Basal leaves in an overwintering rosette, petiolate, spoon-shaped, to ¾ in. long and withering by flowering time. Stem leaves opposite, tiny, triangular scales. Flowers in small clusters at tips of branches, white, less than ¼ in. wide, with 5 spreading, round petals and 5 pointed, reddish-brown sepals. Fruit a broadly elliptical capsule. BAS

Cuscuta gronovii

CONVOLVULACEAE | **swamp dodder**

Jul–Nov, to 6 ft. long. Herbaceous annual vine lacking roots and chlorophyll, parasitic on a wide variety of herbaceous and woody plants; found on streambanks, in bottomland forests, bogs, marshes, swamps, wet fields, and wet disturbed areas. Stems threadlike, yellow or orange, climbing, forming twining networks, with numerous small suckers (haustoria) that attach to the host plant. Leaves tiny and scaly or absent. Flowers in compact clusters and lacking surrounding bracts, white, less than ¼ in. wide, the corolla bell-shaped with 5 spreading to reflexed, round-tipped, oval lobes. Fruit a rounded capsule with a thickened ridge around the tip. SG

Cuscuta pentagona

CONVOLVULACEAE | **five-angled dodder**

May–Nov, to 6 ft. long. Herbaceous annual vine lacking roots and chlorophyll, parasitic on a wide variety of mostly herbaceous host plants; found on roadsides and in fields and other open, disturbed areas. Stems threadlike, yellow to bright orange, climbing, forming twining networks, with numerous small suckers (haustoria) that attach to the host plant. Leaves tiny and scaly or absent. Flowers short-stalked in small clusters, white, less than ¼ in. wide, the corolla bell-shaped with 5 spreading, triangular lobes with pointed tips; the calyx is conspicuously 5-angled. Fruit a rounded capsule, depressed in the center, cupped by the withered flower. AMC

Cuscuta rostrata

CONVOLVULACEAE | **Appalachian dodder**

Jul–Sep, to 6 ft. long. Herbaceous annual vine, parasitic, lacking roots and chlorophyll; found in high-elevation hardwood forests and thickets. Stems coarsely threadlike, yellowish-green to bright orange, climbing, forming twining networks, with numerous small suckers (haustoria) that attach to the host plant. Leaves tiny and scaly or absent. Flowers clustered in small umbels, lacking surrounding bracts, white, to ¼ in. wide, the corolla bell-shaped and with 5 broadly triangular to oval lobes, very fragrant. Fruit a broadly oval, beaked capsule surrounded by the withered flower. AMC

Monotropa uniflora

ERICACEAE | **ghost flower**

Jun–Oct, 2–12 in. Translucent-white (all parts) perennial growing in clumps in a variety of moist to dry forest types throughout NoAm. Stems smooth, usually several clumped, changing from translucent-white (tinged with pale pink) to black after fruiting. Leaves clasping, small and scale-like, sharp-tipped. Flowers solitary at ends of stems, translucent white (same as whole plant), nodding or slightly raised, bell-shaped, about ½ in. long, with 3–6 petals and 10 stamens. Fruit a capsule that turns brown and erect with time. A mycoheterotroph. AMC

Chamaelirium luteum

CHIONOGRAPHIDACEAE | **fairy-wand**

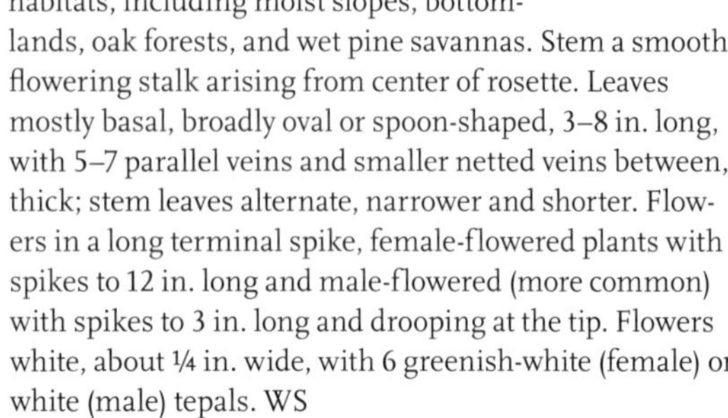

Mar–Jun, 1–4 ft. Erect perennial from a basal rosette, found in a wide variety of habitats, including moist slopes, bottomlands, oak forests, and wet pine savannas. Stem a smooth flowering stalk arising from center of rosette. Leaves mostly basal, broadly oval or spoon-shaped, 3–8 in. long, with 5–7 parallel veins and smaller netted veins between, thick; stem leaves alternate, narrower and shorter. Flowers in a long terminal spike, female-flowered plants with spikes to 12 in. long and male-flowered (more common) with spikes to 3 in. long and drooping at the tip. Flowers white, about 1⁄4 in. wide, with 6 greenish-white (female) or white (male) tepals. WS

Dioscorea villosa

DIOSCOREACEAE | **wild yam**

Apr–Jun, to 23 ft. long. Perennial herbaceous vine of moist hardwood forests. Stems angled, twining, light green or reddish, smooth to sparsely hairy. Leaves alternate (sometimes whorled at base of vine), petiolate, heart-shaped with long tip, to 5 in. long, with 7–11 curved parallel veins, smooth above and short-furry beneath. Flowers all male or all female on a single plant, in panicles (male) or racemes (female) from leaf axils, whitish-green to yellow-green, less than 1⁄4 in. wide; male flowers with 6 tepals and 6 fertile stamens, females with 6 tepals, 6 infertile stamens, and a large ovary. Fruit a golden green, 3-winged, elliptical capsule, papery tan in winter. BAS

Prosartes maculata (*Disporum maculatum*)

LILIACEAE | **nodding mandarin**

Apr–May, 1–2½ ft. Leaning, erect perennial of moist, nutrient-rich forests, especially cove forests. Stems lightly red-tinged, with forking branches, stiffly hairy. Leaves (relatively few) alternate, oblong to oval-oblong, 1½–6 in. long, with prominent parallel veins, sparsely hairy above but with stiff, spreading hairs beneath. Flowers single or in a pair, dangling on stalks from leaf axils, mostly at ends of branches; creamy white spotted with purple, with 6 lance-shaped tepals. Fruit a 3-lobed, rough-hairy, yellow berry. RTW

Streptopus amplexifolius

LILIACEAE | **white mandarin**

Apr–Jun, 10–36 in. Erect to leaning perennial found in moist forests and seepages at high elevations. Stems simple or with forked branches, zigzagging and mostly smooth. Leaves sessile, oval to lance-shaped with a heart-shaped, clasping base, 2–6 in. long. Flowers solitary and dangling on thin, kinked stalks from leaf axils, greenish-white (sometimes rose-tinted), bell-shaped and with 6 recurved, lance-shaped tepals. Fruit a red, elliptical berry. KL

Amianthium muscitoxicum

MELANTHIACEAE | **fly-poison**

May–Jul, 1–4 ft. Scapose perennial from a thick bulb, found in a wide variety of moist to dry forests, pine savannas, sandhills, and meadows, from 18 to at least 5250 ft. elevation. Stem an unbranched, slender, smooth flowering scape. Basal leaves clustered, straplike, to 24 in. long and 1 in. wide, with a deep channel down the center and purplish sheath at the base; stem leaves alternate, much reduced. Flowers on short stalks in a dense, conical raceme, white to occasionally pink (turning green or purplish at maturity), 1/3 in. long, with 6 unfused, rounded and widely spreading tepals. Fruit a 3-lobed capsule with 3 persistent styles. WS

Anticlea glauca

MELANTHIACEAE | **mountain death-camas**

Jul–Aug, 9–36 in. Erect perennial of calcareous woodlands, glades, cliffs, outcrops. Stems from a bulb, bluish-green with a white-waxy coating. Basal leaves 4–12 in. long, 1/4–1/2 in. wide, smooth, faintly lined, with keeled midrib beneath; stem leaves clasping to basal sheathing, smaller and folded lengthwise. Flowers in an open, terminal panicle up to 1 ft. long, each creamy white, 1/2–3/4 in. wide, with 6 oval tepals that are greenish-bronze to purple on the outside and with a thick, greenish-yellow, heart-shaped gland on the white inside surface; central cone-shaped style is split into 3 arching stigmas and surrounded by 6 stamens. Fruit an erect, 3-celled, oval capsule. GPF

Melanthium hybridum (*Veratrum hybridum*)

MELANTHIACEAE | **crisped bunchflower**

Jul–Sep, 1–4 ft. Erect perennial of moist to dry forests, usually in base-rich soils. Stems hollow, mostly unbranched, thickened at the base, hairy. Leaves mostly basal, petiolate-clasping, elliptical to oblong-oval, 10 in. long or more, with prominent parallel veins; stem leaves few, sessile and greatly reduced. Flowers in a narrow panicle about 1 ft. long, off-white to yellowish, about ½ in. wide, with 6 spreading, undulate-margined, triangular tepals with tapered, incurved tips and 2 tiny glands at the base just above the abruptly tapered claw. Fruit a 3-lobed capsule with 3 persistent, beaklike styles. BAS

Melanthium virginicum

MELANTHIACEAE | **Virginia bunchflower**

Jun–Aug, 2–5 ft. Erect perennial of savannas, bogs, wet streamheads, and wet forests. Flowering stems arise from a leaf rosette, unbranched, densely hairy above, smooth below. Leaves both basal and (smaller) alternate, arching, with sheathing petioles (lower leaves only), broadly linear, 3–30 in. long, folded lengthwise. Flowers in branching terminal panicle to 2 ft. long; lower flowers perfect, upper ones male; greenish-white to cream-colored fading to green or purple, ¾–1 in. wide with 6 spreading, oblong-oval tepals, narrowed abruptly at the base, bearing stiff hairs on the outer surface and 2 small glands on the inner surface toward the base. Fruit a 3-lobed capsule. AMC

Stenanthium densum (*Zigadenus densus*)

MELANTHIACEAE | **crow-poison**

Apr–Jun, 1–4 ft. Erect perennial from a bulb found in pine savannas and pine flatwoods. Stem smooth, unbranched, with a few small bracts. Basal leaves crowded, ascending, grasslike, 4–20 in. long and less than ½ in. wide, with lengthwise crease; stem leaves few, short, alternate. Flowers in a dense, cylindrical raceme to 6 in. tall at top of scape, opening successively from the bottom up; creamy white to greenish (turning pink with time); about ⅓ in. wide; with 6 oval, nearly blunt-tipped tepals, a white, conical ovary, and 6 stamens. Fruit a conical, 3-lobed capsule. WS

Stenanthium gramineum

MELANTHIACEAE | **featherbells**

Jul–Sep, 2–6 ft. Erect perennial from a bulb found in moist to dry forests and woodlands, grassy balds, serpentine barrens, wet meadows, and acidic fens, to at least 5500 ft. elevation. Stems unbranched, smooth. Basal leaves numerous, ascending, grasslike with lengthwise crease; upper leaves alternate and reduced. Flowers in a pyramid-shaped panicle, white to green (at times bronze-purple), ½ in. wide or less, nodding, each composed of 6 lance-shaped, sharp-tipped tepals; flowers on side branches of the panicle are mostly male, those on the main part are perfect or female. Fruit an oval, 3-parted capsule with spreading beaks; turns black with time. WS

Stenanthium leimanthoides (*Zigadenus leimanthoides*)

MELANTHIACEAE | **pinebarrens death-camas**

Jul–Aug, 3–5 ft. Erect perennial from a bulb found on high-elevation rock outcrops and seepage areas, shrub balds, fens, and in the Coastal Plain in sandhill bogs and wet pine savannas. Stems unbranched, smooth with a whitish coating. Leaves mostly basal and clustered, linear/grasslike, 8–22 in. long, with a sparse whitish coating; stem leaves gradually reduced above. Flowers in a terminal panicle, white to greenish-white, about ⅓ in. wide, with 6 spreading, oblong-oval tepals with rounded to blunt tips, each with a single yellowish gland at the base. Fruit an oval-conical, 3-lobed capsule with spreading beaks. BAS

Zigadenus glaberrimus

MELANTHIACEAE | **large death-camas**

Jun–Sep, 1–3½ ft. Erect perennial from a blackish horizontal rhizome, often growing in clumps, in sandhill seepage bogs, pine savannas, and on pocosin edges. Stems obscurely 3-angled and smooth. Leaves mostly basal, ascending, lance-shaped, 3–5 in. long and keeled on the underside; stem leaves rapidly reduced above. Flowers in a loosely pyramidal panicle with smooth, ascending branches; off-white; composed of 6 oval to lance-shaped, sharp-tipped tepals, each with 2 distinctive dot-shaped glands near the base. Fruit an oval to conic capsule that becomes reddish brown and persists through winter. WS

Maianthemum racemosum (*Smilacina racemosa*)

RUSCACEAE | **eastern Solomon's-plume**

Apr–Jun, 10–24 in. Ascending-arching perennial of moist to dry forests. Stem solitary, usually arching and with a slight zigzag, hairy or smooth, with a few sheathing bracts at the base. Leaves nearly clasping, elliptical to lance-shaped and often with a long tip, to 3 in. long, with 3–5 main parallel veins, smooth or hairy above, hairy beneath. Flowers in a plumelike terminal panicle 2–5 in. long, white, fragrant, tiny, with 6 pointed tepals and 6 wide, flat stamens surrounding the white ovary. Fruit a round berry starting out coppery green and turning bright red. BAS

Maianthemum stellatum (*Smilacina stellata*)

RUSCACEAE | **starry Solomon's-plume**

Apr–Jun, 8–24 in. Erect-arching perennial of alluvial forests, calcareous fens, and seepage swamps. Stems with a slight zigzag, finely hairy or smooth. Leaves sessile to clasping, lance-shaped, 2–6 in. long, with prominent parallel veins, finely hairy beneath. Flowers 6–15 in a spikelike, terminal raceme, white, 1/4 in. long, with 6 tepals and 6 stamens with pale yellow tips. Fruit a round berry, at first green with red stripes but turning solid red-purple. GPF

Xerophyllum asphodeloides

XEROPHYLLACEAE | **beargrass**

May–Jun, 1–4 1/2 ft. Erect perennial from a clump of grasslike leaves, found on dry ridges and slopes, primarily strongly acidic sites that burn periodically, such as pine/heath woodlands and forests, heath balds, and xeric oak forests. Basal leaves linear, to 30 in. long and arching from crown; stem leaves alternate, similar but progressively smaller upward. Flowers in a compact, cylindrical terminal raceme that elongates with age, blooming from the bottom up, white, 1/2 in. wide or less, with 6 widely spreading, lance-shaped tepals and 6 stamens encircling an ovary. Fruit a 3-lobed capsule. WS

Echinocystis lobata

CUCURBITACEAE | **wild cucumber**

May–Oct, 2–10 ft. long. Annual vine of bottomland forests and thickets. Stems angular, smooth, with 3-forked tendrils arising from leaf axils that entwine surrounding vegetation. Leaves long-petioled, to 7 in. wide, palmately 3- to 7-lobed, rough on upper surface. Male and female flowers separate, white to cream, ½ in. wide, with 6 long-tapering, fringed petals. Male flowers in 4- to 8-in.-long erect racemes arising opposite the leaves, with a short central column of pale-yellow-tipped stamens; females, 1 to few, short-stalked, at the base of the male flower cluster, consist of a short, blunt stigma and bloated, spiny ovary beneath the petals. Fruit a spiny, oval pod. BMP

Lythrum lineare

LYTHRACEAE | **narrowleaf loosestrife**

Jul–Oct, 1½–4 ft. Erect perennial of nearly fresh, brackish, and saline marshes. Stems 4-angled, branched, smooth. Leaves sessile, linear to lance-shaped, ½–1½ in. long. Flowers solitary in upper leaf axils; white to pale purple; ¼ in. wide; with 6 spreading, widely spaced, oblong-lance-shaped petals, a tubular calyx, 6 slender stamens, and a style. Fruit a 2-sectioned, many-seeded, cylindrical capsule. JG

Richardia brasiliensis

RUBIACEAE | **Mexican-clover**

May–Nov, to 4 in. Reclining-spreading (20 in. or more) annual/perennial, with thickened, woody rootstock, found in fields, roadsides, vacant lots, urban and other disturbed areas. Native to South America. Stems prostrate, 4-angled when young, much-branched and white-hairy. Leaves petiolate and joined across the stem by a small green, bristled stipule, elliptical to oval, ½–2 in. long, strongly veined and hairy on both surfaces. Flowers in dense, sessile clusters at tips of branches; white (rarely pink or bluish), less than ¼ in. long, tubular and opening to 6 spreading, triangular lobes. Visible in the corolla tube are 6 yellow stamens and a style with 3-part stigma. KB

Eriogonum tomentosum

POLYGONACEAE | **sandhill wild buckwheat**

Jul–Oct, 1–3 ft. Erect perennial of sandhill turkey oak scrub and longleaf pinelands, usually in white sand, primarily in the fall-line Sandhills area and on riverine dunes in the middle and upper Coastal Plain. Stems branched above, densely hairy. Basal leaves numerous, in a rosette, petiolate, elliptical to oblong with rounded tips, to 4¾ in. long, dark green and smooth above, densely hairy beneath; stem leaves smaller in widely spaced whorls of 3–4. Flowers at branch ends in tight clusters of 10–20, stalks and bracts densely tan-hairy; white to pinkish-white, to ½ in. wide, bell-shaped when open, with 6 petal-like sepals of 2 sizes and 9 pink stamens. RTW

Allium cernuum

ALLIACEAE | **nodding onion**

Jun–Aug, 12–15 in. Erect, scapose perennial found in open woodlands or around outcrops of shale or mafic, ultramafic, or calcareous rocks, mostly at low elevations in the Mountains. Stem a smooth flowering scape arising from a cluster of reddish-purple bulbs. Leaves basal, linear and flattened, 4–15 in. long, with a whitish cast and limp appearance. Flowers on relatively thick stalks within a dense umbel at the "shepherd's crook" terminus of the scape, white or pink to purplish, widely bell-shaped and downward-pointing, to ¼ in. long, with 6 petaloid tepals. Fruit a 3-lobed capsule containing black seeds. All parts have an onion smell and flavor. EO

Allium cuthbertii

ALLIACEAE | **Cuthbert's onion**

May–Jun, 8–24 in. Erect, scapose perennial occurring rarely in sandhills, and on granitic flatrocks. Stem a smooth flowering scape arising from a bulb with a cross-hatched fibrous covering. Leaves basal, flattish and solid, 8–15 in. long. Flowers on stalks in a dome-shaped, compact umbel (no bulbils), which begins with a saclike, membranous covering, dried remnants of which usually persist at the base of the inflorescence. Flowers white, sometimes streaked with pink, and with 6 spreading, sword-shaped, pointy tepals, 6 stamens, and a striking emerald-green, bumpy-surfaced ovary. Fruit a 3-lobed capsule containing black seeds. WS

Allium tricoccum

ALLIACEAE | **ramps**

Jun–Jul, 6–11 in. Erect, scapose perennial of cove and other moist slope forests. Stem a leafless flowering scape, papery sheath at the base, reddish to pale green, smooth. Leaves 2–3 in early spring, withered by bloom time, often with reddish sheaths at the base, oval to broadly lance-shaped, 6–12 in. long, glossy-green with prominent parallel veins. Flowers in a rounded umbel at top of scape, white or pale yellow, 1/4 in. wide, bell-shaped, with 6 translucent tepals, 6 stamens with pale yellow anthers, and a light green to pale yellow ovary with a white style. Fruit a 3-lobed capsule containing black seeds. Foliage and strong-scented bulbs are popular wild edibles. JF

Nothoscordum bivalve (*Allium bivalve*)

ALLIACEAE | **grace garlic**

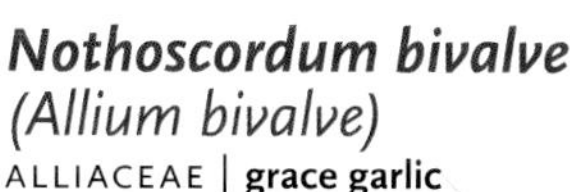

Mar–May, Sep–Dec; 4–16 in. Erect perennial from a bulb, found around granite flatrocks, in glades and barrens of various kinds, in open woodlands, and also weedy in fields and along roadsides. Stem a slender, smooth, hollow flowering scape. Leaves 2–5 in a small basal rosette, linear, 4–12 in. long, smooth. Flowers 4–8 in a simple terminal umbel, white, 1/2–1 in. wide, with 6 tepals with greenish-yellow base on the inside and greenish-brown vein on the outside, 6 stamens, and a greenish-yellow ovary with single style. Fruit a round to oval, 3-lobed capsule. Onionlike plant, but generally lacking the onion odor. WS

Hymenocallis coronaria

AMARYLLIDACEAE | **shoals spiderlily**

May–Jul, 1–4 ft. Colony-forming perennial from a bulb, found among rocky river shoals, often with *Justicia americana*. Stem a smooth, slightly flattened scape with whitish coating, arising from a basal rosette. Leaves erect, straplike, 14–30 in. long, leathery. Flowers fragrant, 3–10 in a cluster at top of scape, opening sequentially, white with a yellowish-green eye, to 8 in. wide, with a green tube that flares out to a white, membranous, funnel-shaped corona with irregular margins and 6 white spider-leg-like extensions; 6 stamens are attached to the margins of the corona. Once-abundant populations now extirpated by impoundments. AMC

Hymenocallis occidentalis

AMARYLLIDACEAE | **hammock spiderlily**

Jul–Aug, 1–1½ ft. Colony-forming perennial from a bulb, growing on moist soils of slopes and floodplain forests, gabbro glades, and other mafic upland flats. Stem a smooth, slightly flattened scape arising from a basal rosette. Leaves straplike, 14–24 in. long, sprawling, waxy blue-green. Flowers 3–10 in a cluster of top of scape, white, to 8 in. wide, with a green tube that flares out to a 2-in.-wide white, membranous, funnel-shaped corona with irregular margins and 6 white spider-leg-like extensions; 6 stamens are attached to the margins of the corona. Each flower blooms for a day or less, first opening in late afternoon/evening. FG

Zephyranthes atamasco

AMARYLLIDACEAE | **Atamasco lily**

Mar–Apr, 6–8 in. Colony-forming, scapose perennial from a bulb, found in bottomland forests and adjacent road shoulders, wet meadows, and sometimes in upland forests over mafic rocks. Stem usually a single, hollow flowering scape that may be red-tinged. Leaves basal, linear and grasslike, 6–18 in. long, sprawling, shiny and slightly succulent. Flower solitary on the flowering scape, white, 2–4 in. wide, funnel-shaped, with 6 spreading tepals that turn pink after pollination, fragrant. Fruit a more or less round, 3-sectioned capsule. AMC

Ornithogalum umbellatum

HYACINTHACEAE | **star-of-Bethlehem**

Mar–May, 4–10 in. Scapose perennial from a rosette and bulb, commonly cultivated and found in lawns, old fields, bottomlands, and forests. Native to Europe. Stem a flowering scape arising from a basal rosette. Leaves basal, linear, fleshy-thick and channeled, with a pale green or white line down the middle. Flowers erect on stalks in a modified, umbel-like, spreading-branching raceme; each flower white, about ¾ in. wide, with 6 spreading-ascending, oblong-lance-shaped tepals bearing a green stripe on the outside, 6 stamens, and a single pistil. The fragrant flowers usually open in morning and close by noon. RTW

Clintonia umbellulata

LILIACEAE | **speckled wood-lily**

May–Jun, 8–16 in. Erect perennial from a basal rosette, found in red oak and other oak forests on moist to dry ridges and slopes. Stem a slender, leafless flowering scape. Leaves in a basal rosette, oblong to elliptical, 6–12 in. long, with strongly inset and hairy midvein, shiny-green, with long hairs on margins. Flowers 5–25 in a compact, rounded umbel terminating the scape, white to greenish-white, with 6 spreading tepals with purple or green speckles. Fruit a dark blue to black berry. Less commonly seen in northern hardwood forests and generally occurs at lower elevations than *C. borealis*, though the species can co-occur. WS

Erythronium albidum

LILIACEAE | **white trout lily**

Mar–May, 4–8 in. Early-blooming, colony-forming, scapose perennial growing in leaf litter of rich, moist forests over calcareous substrates, or in very nutrient-rich alluvial soils. Stem a red-tinged, smooth flowering scape. Leaves basal and spreading-ascending, sessile, elliptical to lance-shaped, to 7 in. long, smooth, fleshy, and usually with purplish-brown mottling. Flowers solitary, nodding at the tip of the scape, white, 1–2 in. long, trumpet-shaped, with 6 reflexed tepals and 6 dangling stamens bearing yellow or brown anthers. Fruit a green, rounded capsule held above the ground surface. EO

Aletris farinosa

NARTHECIACEAE | **mealy colic-root**

Apr–Jul, 1–3½ ft. Scapose, rhizomatous perennial of pine savannas, pine flatwoods, seepage bogs, mafic fens and barrens, upland woodlands, road banks. Stem an unbranched flowering scape with a few small bracts, arising from a basal rosette. Leaves spreading-ascending, lance-shaped, 1½–7½ in. long, yellowish green. Flowers in a spikelike raceme occupying the top 4–14 in. of the scape, each ¼–⅜ in. long, cylindrical to urn-shaped, composed of 6 fused petals that at full bloom flare into 6 pointed lobes; the tube is slightly constricted just below the lobes, and its outer surface is granular-bumpy. Fruit a beaked, oval capsule containing tiny reddish-brown seeds. WS

Convallaria pseudomajalis (*C. majalis* var. *montana*)

RUSCACEAE | **American lily-of-the-valley**

Apr–Jun, 6–11 in. Erect perennial of mountain forests, particularly in rocky woodlands or on or near ridge tops under oaks at 3000 to 5000 ft. elevation. Stem a flowering scape with 2–3 basal leaves, smooth. Leaves erect, on petioles with a sheathing base, oblong to widely elliptical, 6–12 in. long, smooth, yellowing in late summer. Flowers in a raceme on a slender scape that is less than half as long as the leaves, nodding, white, ¼–⅓ in. long, with 6 tepals that are almost completely joined to form a bell-shaped corolla, each with a tiny recurved tip. Fruit an orange-red berry. WS

Pleea tenuifolia

TOFIELDIACEAE | **rush-featherling**

Sep–Oct, 1–2½ ft. Tufted, erect perennial from a thick rhizome, found in wet savannas and pocosin margins, usually in peaty soil; may be locally abundant. Stems scapelike, with 0–4 progressively smaller leaves, unbranched, smooth. Leaves mostly basal, whorled or 2-ranked, with overlapping bases, linear, 4–12 in. long, evergreen. Flowers 3–8 in a terminal raceme, each 1 in. wide, surrounded by 3 overlapping bracts, with 6 narrowly lance-shaped tepals (the outer 3 slightly longer and wider than the inner 3), 6 stamens about a third as long as the tepals, and a green, conical, 3-celled ovary with 3 styles at the top. Fruit a 3-celled, oval capsule. JF

Tofieldia glabra

TOFIELDIACEAE | **Carolina bog asphodel**

Aug–Nov, 1–2 ft. Erect, rhizomatous perennial of savanna-pocosin ecotones, wet savannas, and seepage bogs. Stems scapelike, unbranched, smooth. Leaves mostly basal, erect, grasslike, 3–12 in. long and less than ⅓ in. wide, rapidly reduced in size up the stem, smooth and with a succulent texture. Flowers in a dense terminal raceme, with a single flower at each node; each flower white, less than ½ in. wide, with 6 spreading, oblong-lance-shaped tepals with rounded tips, 6 erect stamens equal to or slightly shorter than the tepals, and a white, 3-celled ovary. Fruit a 3-celled capsule. WS

Triantha racemosa (*Tofieldia racemosa*)

TOFIELDIACEAE | **Coastal Plain bog asphodel**

Jun–Aug, 8–24 in. Erect, rhizomatous perennial of savanna-pocosin ecotones, seepage bogs; dolines in VA mountains. Stems scapelike, unbranched, covered with granular glands. Leaves mostly basal, erect, grasslike, 14 in. long, 1/4 in. wide; the few stem leaves smaller, bractlike. Flowers on glandular-hairy stalks in a terminal cylindrical cluster, 3–7 per node (1 per node at top); each white (drying orange), 1/3 in. wide, with 6 spreading, blunt-tipped, oblong-lance to spoon-shaped tepals (the inner 3 narrower and longer) and 6 stamens surrounding a greenish-white, 3-celled ovary. Fruit an oval capsule. WS

Diphylleia cymosa

BERBERIDACEAE | **umbrella-leaf**

May–Jun, 1–3 ft. Erect, colony-forming Southern Appalachian endemic found in seepages and brook banks in northern hardwood or cove hardwood forests, at mid to high elevations. Stem single, unbranched; may start out hairy but becomes smooth. Leaves 2 per plant, to 20 in. long and wide, divided into 2 lobed and toothed, kidney-shaped segments; the petiole is connected to the blade off-center. Flowers in a 4-in.-wide terminal cluster borne on a stalk that rises above leaves from the leaf fork; each flower white, about 1 in. wide, with 6 spreading petals and 6 prominent stamens surrounding a green ovary and single style. Fruit a dark blue berry on a reddish stalk. RTW

Coptis trifolia

RANUNCULACEAE | **goldthread**

Apr–Jul, 3–6 in. Erect, rhizomatous perennial of moist forests, bogs, swamp edges, often on mossy hammocks. Leaves basal, petiolate, evergreen and shiny, palmately divided into 3 oval or fan-shaped, toothed, smooth leaflets (1/2–1 in. long). Flower solitary at top of naked scape, 1/2 in. wide, with 5–7 narrowly elliptical petal-like sepals surrounding a bushy cluster of white-tipped stamens and bright green styles with curled tips; alternating with the sepals are short, golden yellow, club-shaped petals with cup-shaped tips that hold nectar; the white sepals drop early. Fruit a candelabra-like array of 5–7 tiny, stalked pods, each with a long-tapering tip. AH

Nymphaea odorata

NYMPHAEACEAE | **American white waterlily**

Jun–Sep. Aquatic perennial of ponds and other sluggish waters, the stems growing toward the water surface from thick rhizomes in the bottom mud. Leaves floating, round with a deep cleft at the base, to 11 in. wide, green above with a waxy coating, reddish-brown beneath. Flowers floating, fragrant, borne singly, white or pink, 3–5 in. wide, with many lance-shaped petals and many prominent yellow stamens in the center. Flowers open by day and close at night. Fruit a fleshy, globular berry that matures underwater. The species is polymorphic, with numerous subspecies and varieties. JP

Trientalis borealis (*Lysimachia borealis*)

PRIMULACEAE | **northern starflower**

May–Jun, 3–10 in. Erect perennial from a slender, creeping rhizome, found in northern hardwood forests and rich slope forests, often in second-growth areas. Stems unbranched, smooth. Leaves 5–10 in a single whorl at top of stem, short-petioled or sessile, lance-shaped, unequal, 1½–4 in. long, minutely wavy-edged, glossy; 1–2 small, scalelike leaves may be alternate on the midstem. Flowers usually 1–2 on slender stalks from center of leaf whorl, white, ¼–½ in. wide, with 7 spreading, oval to lance-shaped, pointy-tipped petals and 7 stamens. Fruit a rounded capsule. JF

Podophyllum peltatum

BERBERIDACEAE | **may-apple**

Mar–Apr, 1–1½ ft. Rhizomatous, colonial perennial of rich forests, bottomlands, slopes, and pastures. A single, smooth stem emerges in early spring from a rhizome bearing distinct annual increment scars. Leaves 2 (only 1 on young plants), opposite, round, to 8 in. wide or more, palmately divided into 5–9 lobes, unfurling as stem lengthens, to finally stand horizontally erect at the forked tip of the stem. Flower single, nodding on a stalk below the leaves, waxy-white, 1–2 in. wide, with 6–9 rounded, overlapping petals, many prominent yellow stamens, and a yellow-green ovary. Fruit a fleshy, oval, lemon-colored berry. Roots, leaves, and unripe fruit are highly toxic. LMC

Anemone berlandieri

RANUNCULACEAE | **eastern prairie anemone**

Mar–Apr, 8–18 in. Erect perennial growing on thin, circumneutral soils around rock outcrops and calcareous glades. Stems unbranched, woolly. Basal leaves (1–3) 1/3–1 in. long and wide, divided into 3 oval segments, those segments irregularly lobed, toothed and hairy; a few whorled or opposite stem leaves resemble basal ones, with segments linear to lance-shaped. Flowers solitary at top of stem, white (rarely pale blue to rose), with 7–20 narrow and round-tipped, petal-like sepals encircling a conical, compound ovary and multiple stamens. Fruit a cylindrical cluster of densely woolly achenes. MK

Thalictrum thalictroides (*Anemonella thalictroides*)

RANUNCULACEAE | **windflower**

Mar–Jun, 4–8 in. Delicate, erect perennial of moist upland forests and well-drained floodplain forests; in the Coastal Plain, somewhat restricted to base-rich soils. Stems slender, smooth and often purple-tinged. Leaves few, 2–3 times divided into 3, the leaflets bluntly 3-toothed; green and smooth above, pale beneath. Flowers 1–6 in a small terminal umbel, white, 3/4 in. wide, with 6–10 white (pink-tinged) petal-like sepals surrounding a small, green compound ovary (5–15 carpels) and multiple stamens; sepals drop early. Fruit a cluster of tiny achenes. RTW

Hepatica acutiloba (*Anemone acutiloba*)

RANUNCULACEAE | **sharp-lobed hepatica**

Jan–Apr, 2–8 in. Low-growing, stemless perennial of moist forests, especially over calcareous or mafic rocks. Leaves basal, petiolate, kidney-shaped, to 2 3/4 in. long and 4 in. wide, 3-lobed but with the lobes pointed, leathery, usually variegated (2-tone green or green and purple-brown), turning bronze and persisting into winter. Flowers solitary on softly hairy stalks, white or pink to blue, 1/2–1 in. wide, with 5–12 petal-like sepals surrounding a green, conical, compound ovary and bushy stamens; 3 hairy, pointed, oval bracts sit just below the flower. Fruit a cluster of tiny, beaked achenes. WS

Jeffersonia diphylla

BERBERIDACEAE | **twinleaf**

Mar–Apr, 6–11 in. Stemless perennial of moist and extremely nutrient-rich forests, usually over calcareous or mafic rocks or very rich alluvium. The flower and leaves are on separate, smooth stalks. Leaves divided into 2 identical, shallowly lobed to entire, palmately veined segments, which are sometimes bluish-green. Overall, a leaf resembles an open-winged green butterfly. Flower solitary at the top of a leafless stalk, white, about 1 in. wide, with 8 elliptical to oblong-oval petals, 4 elliptical sepals that eventually drop off, and 8 stamens. Fruit an oblong to pear-shaped green capsule, turning brown and eventually releasing seeds that are dispersed by ants. WS

Sanguinaria canadensis

PAPAVERACEAE | **bloodroot**

(Jan) Mar–Apr, 6–12 in. Stemless, often colonial perennial of moist, nutrient-rich forests. Underground stem (rhizome) sends up leaves and flower stalks in early spring. Leaves at first wrapped around the smooth, red-tinged stalk but soon expand to 5 in. wide or more; they are kidney-shaped, irregularly palmately lobed (3–9 lobes), waxy-green and wavy-margined. Flower solitary on a naked stalk, bright white, 1–2 in. wide, with 7–12 elliptical petals surrounding a center of many yellow stamens and a single green ovary. Fruit an erect, waxy-green, spindle-shaped capsule that splits lengthwise. Stem/rhizome exudes orange-red sap if broken. WS

Antennaria plantaginifolia

ASTERACEAE | **plantain pussytoes**

Mar–May, 2½–8 in. Erect, colony-forming perennial of dry forests, barrens, meadows, road banks; spreads by runners. Flowering stalk unbranched, white-hairy, from a basal rosette. Basal leaves petiolate, spoon-shaped, to 3 in. long, with 3 major veins, green above, densely white-hairy below; stem leaves smaller, ascending, clasping, hairy above. Male and female flowers on separate plants, in compact umbel-like, terminal clusters; heads creamy white (or pink-tinged), ¼–½ in. wide, each with a dense cluster of tiny florets (males with brownish, tubular anthers; females fluffy white with multiple styles) surrounded at base by whorls of light green, white-tipped bracts. BAS

Antennaria solitaria

ASTERACEAE | **southern single-head pussytoes**

Mar–May, 7–11 in. Erect, colony-forming perennial of moist to semi-moist forests and woodlands, often on bluffs and streambanks; spreads by runners. Flowering stalk from a basal rosette is covered with long white hairs. Leaves mostly basal, oblong-oval to spoon-shaped, 2–3 in. long, 3- to 5-veined, white-furry beneath, furry to smooth green above. Male and female flowers on separate plants, in solitary terminal heads; heads white or pink, ½–¾ in. wide, with a tight clump of tiny florets surrounded at the base by whorls of green or brown, white-tipped bracts. Male florets with reddish-brown, tubular anthers; female florets fluffy white with multiple styles. BAS

Antennaria virginica

ASTERACEAE | **shale-barren pussytoes**

Mar–May, 4–8 in. Erect, colony-forming perennial of shale barrens and other dry, rocky habitats; spreads by leafy runners. Flowering stalk from a basal rosette is covered in white hairs; sometimes red-tinged. Basal leaves spoon-shaped to oblong-lance-shaped, ⅓–1 in. long, mostly 1-veined, greenish-gray and moderately hairy; stem leaves linear. Male and female flowers on separate plants, in compact terminal clusters of 3–9 heads; heads white, ¼–½ in. wide, each with a dense clump of tiny florets surrounded at the base by whorls of greenish-white to straw-colored bracts. Male florets with brownish, tubular anthers; female florets fluffy white with multiple styles. GPF

Arnoglossum ovatum

ASTERACEAE | **broadleaf Indian-plantain**

Jul–Oct, 1½–8 ft. Erect perennial of bottomlands, bay forests, wet savannas (especially over coquina limestone), and other moist to wet forests. Stem stout, branched in inflorescence, sometimes purple-tinged. Basal leaves petiolate, oval to lance-shaped, entire or toothed, smooth and with a light white-waxy coating; stem leaves alternate and similar but progressively smaller and sessile. Flower heads in flat-topped, branched, terminal cluster; heads about ⅓ in. tall, with 5–9 greenish-white, tubular disk florets with a pinkish interior. Whitish (sometimes purple-tinged), narrow bracts surround each head. Very variable. BAS

Boltonia caroliniana

ASTERACEAE | **Carolina doll's-daisy**

Aug–Oct, 4–6 ft. Erect, somewhat bushy perennial of bottomlands, ditches, roadsides and prairies. Stems diffusely branched. Leaves sessile, linear to narrowly oblong-lance-shaped, 3–5 in. long, bluish-green and smooth. Flower heads daisylike, numerous, in a spreading-branching inflorescence; heads about 1 in. wide, with 25–36 white to lilac, narrow ray florets encircling a yellow center disk composed of numerous tiny, tubular florets. 2–3 series of light green, linear bracts surround the base of each head. GPF

Doellingeria infirma (*Aster infirmus*)

ASTERACEAE | **Appalachian flat-topped white aster**

Jun–Sep, 1½–3½ ft. Erect perennial of woodland borders and dry to semi-moist woodlands and glades. Stems solitary or several from a woody crown, slender, slightly zigzagged, mostly smooth. Leaves mostly sessile, elliptical with somewhat pointed tips, to 5 in. long (lower leaves smaller), smooth to rough above. Flower heads in a widely branched, terminal cluster; heads to 1 in. wide and with 5–9 well-spaced white ray florets encircling a center disk of pale yellow tubular florets. Several series of green, narrow bracts surround the cup-shaped base of each head. AH

Doellingeria sericocarpoides (*Aster sericocarpoides*)

ASTERACEAE | **southern flat-topped aster**

Jul–Oct, 3–6 ft. Erect to ascending perennial of peaty soils in sandhill ecotones, streamhead pocosins, and other acidic seeps and swamps. Stems 1–few from a root crown (not creeping-rhizomatous as in *D. umbellata*), branching above, sometimes reddish or brownish, smooth. Leaves short-petioled, elliptical to broadly lance-shaped, 1½–4¼ in. long, stiff. Flower heads in branched, mostly flat-topped terminal cluster; heads about 1 in. wide, with 2–7 white ray florets encircling a center disk of 4–14 yellow (turning purplish) tubular florets. WS

Doellingeria umbellata (*Aster umbellatus*)

ASTERACEAE | **northern flat-topped white aster**

Jul–Oct, 2–6 ft. Erect, rhizomatous perennial of wet meadows, pastures, bogs, fens, marshes, stream floodplains, and road banks. Stems scattered and from creeping rhizomes, very leafy, branched above, smooth or sometimes hairy. Leaves sessile, oval to lance-shaped with pointed tips, to 6 in. long (uppermost leaves smallest), prominently veiny beneath, rough or smooth above. Flower heads (30–300) in a crowded terminal cluster with stiffly ascending branches; heads ½–¾ in. wide, with 7–14 white ray florets encircling a mounded central disk of tiny, yellow tubular florets. BAS

Marshallia obovata

ASTERACEAE | **Piedmont Barbara's-buttons**

Apr–Jun, 1–2 ft. Erect, sometimes colonial perennial of clay flats, woodland borders, and dry woodlands. Stems often with longitudinal lines, unbranched, leafless above. Leaves, occupying only the bottom quarter of the plant, are alternate, petiolate or sessile, oblong-oval to spoon-shaped, 1–7 in. long, and smooth. Flower heads solitary at top of stems; heads about 1 in. wide, with 20 or more white (rarely pinkish), 5-lobed disk florets. Green bracts with bluntly rounded tips surround the base of each head. WS

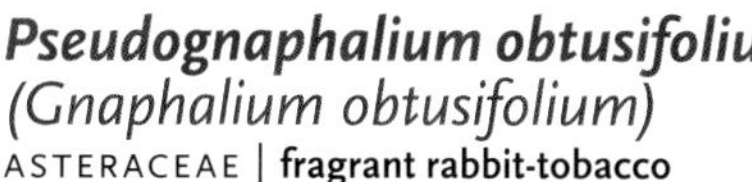

Pseudognaphalium obtusifolium (*Gnaphalium obtusifolium*)

ASTERACEAE | **fragrant rabbit-tobacco**

Aug–Nov, 8–36 in. Erect annual/biennial of openings, woodlands, coastal dunes, sandy pinelands, disturbed areas. Stems unbranched, woolly-hairy (may be smooth at base). Leaves sessile, linear-oblong, 1–4 in. long, wavy-margined, woolly and white beneath, smooth and green (or slightly hairy) above, fragrant; first-year rosette leaves spoon-shaped. Flower heads in clumps of 1–5 in branching terminal cluster; heads about ¼ in. wide and pointed or flat-topped, with white or yellow-tinged, tubular disk florets (no ray florets) tightly enclosed by several series of brownish-white, papery and woolly bracts. WS

Pterocaulon pycnostachyum

ASTERACEAE | **blackroot**

May–Jun, 8–30 in. Erect to leaning perennial from large, black roots found in sandhills, dry pinelands, and pine flatwoods. Stems unbranched, prominently winged and covered with white or rust-colored hairs. Leaves sessile with leaf bases continuing down the stem as wings, elliptical or lance-shaped, to 4⅓ in. long, dark green and nearly smooth above, white and densely hairy beneath. Flower heads densely packed in a terminal spike (1–3 in. long), which may nod; heads less than ¼ in. wide, with tiny, white (pink-tinged) tubular disk florets and protruding styles. Tiny greenish-white bracts tightly surround the cylindrical base of each head. RTW

Sericocarpus linifolius *(Aster solidagineus)*

ASTERACEAE | **narrowleaf white-topped aster**

Jun–Jul, 8–24 in. Erect perennial of dry woodlands, barrens, and sandhills. Stems branched above, smooth. Leaves mostly sessile, rigid, linear to narrowly elliptical, to 3 in. long, smooth. Flower heads in a flat-topped, branching terminal cluster; heads about 1 in. wide, with 3–6 long-petaled, white ray florets encircling a small center disk of tiny, white to cream tubular florets. Several series of green-and-white bracts surround the cylindrical to oblong base of each head. RTW

Sericocarpus tortifolius *(Aster tortifolius)*

ASTERACEAE | **twisted-leaf white-topped aster**

Aug–Oct, 2–3 ft. Erect perennial of dry woodlands, dry to moist sandhills, and roadsides. Stems slightly woody, branched above, hairy. Leaves mostly sessile, oval, rough-hairy and slightly sticky-resinous; many leaves are twisted at the base, resulting in an orientation perpendicular to the ground. Flower heads in a flat-topped, branching terminal cluster; heads about ½ in. wide, with 2–5 white ray florets encircling a center disk of 6–11 tiny, dull white, tubular florets. Several series of tiny, green-tipped whitish bracts enclose the cylindrical base of each head. BAS

Symphyotrichum dumosum

ASTERACEAE | **long-stalked aster**

Aug–Oct, 1–4½ ft. Erect perennial of old fields, pastures, and other disturbed areas. Stems 1–many forming a clump, smooth to minutely hairy, often arching, with 10–30 leaf nodes below the spreading-ascending branches. Leaves sessile, linear to narrowly elliptical, ¾–4 in. long (much smaller bracts on branches and branchlets), stiff, often with rolled-under margins, usually smooth above and beneath. Flower heads in a wide-branching panicle; heads about ½ in. wide, with 9–30 pale lavender or bluish (rarely white), narrow ray florets encircling a center disk of 15–30 yellow or brown (becoming reddish-purple) tubular florets. Fruit a white-tufted achene. MHV

Symphyotrichum lanceolatum

ASTERACEAE | **white panicle aster**

Jul–Oct, 1½–6 ft. Erect, rhizomatous, colonial perennial of floodplain forests, alluvial swamps, fens, riverbanks, and moist meadows. Stems 1–several, stout, sometimes with ascending-spreading branches, smooth or hairy. Leaves sessile and somewhat clasping, linear-lance-shaped to elliptical, 3–6 in. long, sometimes sparingly toothed, smooth or sometimes rough above. Flower heads in a large, open, leafy panicle; heads ¾–1 in. wide, with 16–50 narrow, white to pale blue ray florets encircling a center disk of yellow (becoming reddish-purple) tubular florets. Fruit a white-tufted achene. GPF

Symphyotrichum pilosum

ASTERACEAE | **hairy white oldfield aster**

Sep–Nov, ½–4½ ft. Erect perennial of old fields, disturbed areas, woodland borders. Stems 1–several, stout, white-hairy, sometimes excessively so, with 10–15 leaf nodes below branches. Basal leaves petiolate, oblong-lance- to spoon-shaped, ¾–4½ in. long, sometimes toothed, white-hairy; stem leaves alternate, sessile, lance-linear, reduced in size upward, somewhat rigid, entire to slightly toothed, white-hairy. Flower heads in a diffuse panicle with stiffly ascending or spreading branches; heads ½–¾ in. wide, with 16–35 white (rarely pink or purple) narrow ray florets encircling a central disk of 20–40 yellow to reddish tubular florets. Fruit a white-tufted achene. AMC

Symphyotrichum racemosum

ASTERACEAE | **small white aster**

Aug–Oct, 1–3 ft. Erect, rhizomatous perennial of alluvial swamps and marshes, floodplain forests. Stems 1–3, clumped, minutely hairy. Leaves short-petioled, elliptical to lance- or linear-lance-shaped, 1/3–2½ in. long, entire or toothed, smooth or sometimes minutely hairy beneath. Flower heads in a diffusely branched, wide terminal panicle; heads about ¾ in. wide, with 7–20 narrow, white (or purplish-pink) ray florets encircling a center disk of yellow tubular florets. Several series of close-pressed, greenish-white lance-shaped bracts surround the cylindrical base of each head. Fruit a light-brown-tufted achene. BAS

Eryngium yuccifolium

APIACEAE | **northern rattlesnake-master**

Jun–Aug, 2–4 ft. Stiff, erect perennial of diabase barrens and glades, olivine barrens, pine savannas, pine flatwoods over loamy or clay soils, prairies and other open sites with at least periodic moisture. Stems stout, branched above, pale green. Leaves alternate but mostly clustered toward stem base, sessile, straplike, to 40 in. long (reduced above), with parallel veins and widely spaced bristles on margins, thick and leathery, smooth. Flowers in 1-in.-wide compact, rounded heads at branch tips and top of stem, each head surrounded by small, sharp-tipped bracts; flowers greenish-white, less than ¼ in. wide, with 5 tiny petals, 5 green sepals, and tiny, sharp bractlets. WS

Arnoglossum atriplicifolium

ASTERACEAE | **pale Indian-plantain**

Jun–Oct, 3–8 ft. Coarse, erect perennial of moist forests, woodland edges, clearings, prairies, meadows. Stems faintly ribbed, unbranched, pale green and waxy, often reddish-purple above, smooth. Leaves basal and alternate, petiolate, oval to kidney- or fan-shaped, 2–7 in. long, to 12 in. wide (reduced above), thick, with pointed lobes or coarse teeth, green above, pale green to white beneath. Flower heads in clumps of 4–15 in a large, flat-topped, compound terminal cluster; heads on light green stems, cream to greenish-white or pale purple, about 1/3 in. long, with 5 cylindrical disk florets with protruding split styles. A tube of light green bracts surrounds each head. Fruit a white-tufted, oblong achene. WS

Arnoglossum reniforme

ASTERACEAE | **great Indian-plantain**

Jun–Oct, 3–8 ft. Coarse, erect perennial of cove forests, rich oak-hickory forests, northern hardwood forests and clearings at mid to high elevations. Stems conspicuously 6- to 8-grooved, unbranched, sometimes red-tinged, smooth. Leaves petiolate, 2–10 in. long; lower leaves broadly kidney-shaped with widely notched base and round-toothed margins, upper leaves kidney- to oval-shaped, notched to nearly flat at base, with sharply toothed margins. Flower heads in a many-branched, terminal cluster; heads greenish-white, to 1/4 in. wide, with 5 tubular disk florets, each with 5 tightly curled corolla lobes. Fruit a dark brown to purple, oblong achene with tuft of white hairs. JG

Brickellia eupatorioides

ASTERACEAE | **Flyr's false-boneset**

Jun–Oct, 1–5 ft. Erect, clumped perennial of dry slopes, shale barrens, dry woodlands and thickets. Stems 1–many, branched above, hairy to mostly smooth; may be burgundy-tinged. Leaves alternate (lowest may be nearly opposite), short-petioled, lance-shaped, 1–4 in. long, with 3 prominent veins and toothed margins, gland-dotted beneath, softly hairy. Flower heads in a much-branched terminal cluster; heads 1/3 in. tall, cylindrical and with 6–15 creamy white, tubular disk florets surrounded by several series of narrow, green or purplish bracts. Flowers open in the early evening and close by mid-day, presumably an adaptation for pollination by nocturnal insects. AMC

Erigeron annuus

ASTERACEAE | **annual fleabane**

May–Oct, 2–5 ft. Erect annual of roadsides, gardens, and other disturbed areas. Stems occasionally branched above, leafy, covered with sparse, spreading hairs. Leaves on winged petioles (lower leaves) to sessile (upper leaves), elliptical to oblong-lance-shaped or oval, to 4 in. long, sharply to coarsely toothed toward tips (upper leaves), hairy toward base and on midrib. Flower heads daisylike, in a branching terminal cluster, 1/2–3/4 in. wide, with 80–125 white (occasionally pinkish), threadlike ray florets encircling the greenish-yellow center disk of tiny, tubular florets. BAS

Erigeron canadensis (*Conyza canadensis*)

ASTERACEAE | **common horseweed**

Jul–Nov, to 6 ft. Erect, bushy annual of fields, gardens, roadsides, and other open, disturbed areas. Stems branched above the middle, hairy or smooth. Leaves narrowly lance-shaped, ¾–4 in. long, margins toothed and fringed with small hairs or entire. Flower heads on wide-spreading branches of upper plant; heads about ¼ in. long, cylindrical to urn-shaped and with 20–45 tiny, white ray florets surrounding a center disk of yellow tubular florets. Several series of narrow, green-tipped bracts surround the base of each head. Fruit a cluster of tiny flattened achenes with tufts of white or tan hairs. BAS

Erigeron philadelphicus

ASTERACEAE | **Philadelphia-daisy**

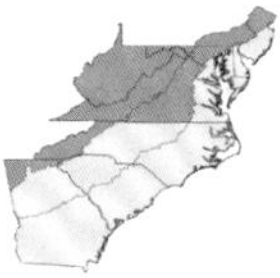

Apr–Aug, 6–30 in. Erect, stoloniferous biennial/perennial of moist to wet roadsides, meadows, and other disturbed areas. Stems ribbed, branched above, usually very hairy. Basal leaves petiolate, spoon- to lance-shaped, to 4½ in. long, toothed, shaggy-hairy; stem leaves alternate, sessile-clasping, oval to lance-shaped and shorter, usually hairy. Flower heads in a branching terminal cluster; heads 1 in. wide, with threadlike white or pale pink ray florets encircling a yellow center disk of tiny, tubular florets. 2–3 series of narrow, pointed green bracts surround the base of each head. RTW

Erigeron quercifolius

ASTERACEAE | **oak-leaved fleabane**

Apr–Jun, 4–26 in. Erect annual/biennial/short-lived perennial of sandy roadsides, clearings, and other open, disturbed areas. Stems slender, branched above, hairy. Basal leaves in a rosette up to 6 in. wide, oblong-lance-shaped to oblong-oval, to 5 in. long, wavy-margined to lobed (reminiscent of oak leaves); stem leaves few, alternate, sessile-clasping, shorter and often lobed. Flower heads 1–many on terminal branches, about ¼ in. wide, with many very narrow, white to bluish-lavender ray florets surrounding a yellow center disk composed of tiny, tubular florets. BAS

Erigeron strigosus

ASTERACEAE | **common rough fleabane**

Apr–Oct, 1–4 ft. Erect annual (rarely biennial) of open woodlands, roadsides, and disturbed areas. Stems slender, branched above, ribbed and with short hairs pressed up against the stem. Leaves linear to spoon-shaped, ½–4 in. long, toothed or entire, rough-hairy; basal leaves usually withered by flowering, toothed near the tip. Flower heads daisylike at ends of branches, ½ in. wide, with 40–100 white to pale pink, threadlike ray florets encircling a yellow center disk composed of tiny, tubular florets. Several whorls of hairy, green, narrow bracts surround the saucer-shaped base of each head. BAS

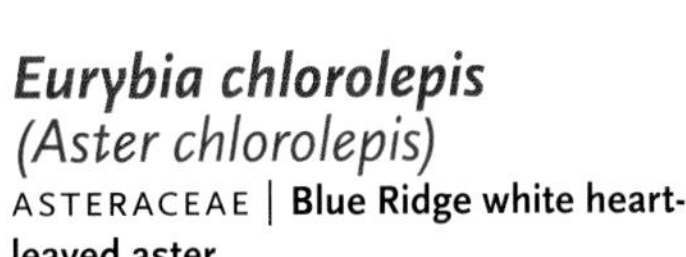

Eurybia chlorolepis
(Aster chlorolepis)

ASTERACEAE | **Blue Ridge white heart-leaved aster**

Aug–Oct, 8–30 in. Erect, colony-forming, rhizomatous perennial of northern hardwood forests and spruce-fir forests, mostly at elevations higher than 3940 ft. Stems 1 per plant, branched above, smooth or hairy in the inflorescence. Leaves petiolate, oval to lance-oval (upper ones elliptic), 1–7 in. long, sharply toothed, smooth or slightly rough above. Flower heads in branched, terminal clusters; heads about 1½ in. wide, with 10 or more long, white ray florets (may be tinged lilac) encircling a center disk of tiny yellow (turning red with age), tubular florets. JF

Eurybia divaricata
(Aster divaricatus)

ASTERACEAE | **white wood aster**

Aug–Oct, 1–2 ft. Erect, rhizomatous and colony-forming perennial found in moist to fairly dry forests and woodlands. Stems unbranched, somewhat zigzagged, smooth (hairy when newly emerged). Leaves petiolate, oval to lance-oval with heart-shaped to rounded base, to 7 in. long (reduced above), toothed and hairy; often withered by flowering. Flower heads in branched terminal clusters; heads about 1 in. wide, with 5–12 long, white ray florets (may be tinged lilac) encircling a center disk of yellow (turning red with age), tubular florets. BAS

Leucanthemum vulgare (*Chrysanthemum leucanthemum*)

ASTERACEAE | **oxeye daisy**

Apr–Oct, 1–3 ft. Erect-ascending, rhizomatous perennial found in fields, roadsides, pastures, and other disturbed areas. Native to Eurasia. Stems simple or forked near top, smooth to slightly hairy. Leaves basal and alternate, short-petioled, spoon-shaped, 1½–6 in. long (reduced and essentially sessile above), irregularly lobed and toothed, smooth. Flower heads solitary at top of stem, to 2 in. wide, with 13–35 white ray florets with rounded to square tips encircling a flat, yellow disk of tiny, tubular florets. RTW

Nabalus serpentarius (*Prenanthes serpentaria*)

ASTERACEAE | **lion's-foot**

Aug–Oct, 1½–5 ft. Erect perennial of moist to dry upland forests and woodlands. Stems branched above, reddish-purple, smooth or hairy. Leaves well distributed; lower leaves petiolate (often winged), oblong or elliptic-oblong and usually deeply divided or lobed, 2–8 in. long (smaller above), some reddish-purple, smooth to slightly hairy. Flower heads drooping from branches of open terminal panicle; heads cylindrical with 8–14 spreading, greenish-white to purplish ray florets surrounded by about 8 bristly-hairy, green (sometimes purplish) bracts. Fruit a tufted achene. BAS

Nabalus trifoliolatus (*Prenanthes trifoliolata*)

ASTERACEAE | **gall-of-the-earth**

Aug–Nov, 1–4 ft. Erect perennial of moist upland forests. Stems branched in inflorescence only, sometimes reddish-purple, smooth to slightly hairy. Leaves petiolate, evenly distributed on stem; lower leaves triangular or arrowhead-shaped, often deeply 3-lobed (lobes again divided) and 1¼–4 in. long, but smaller and progressively less divided upward. Flower heads drooping from short stalks of a narrow terminal panicle; cylindrical heads about ½ in. long, with 9–13 cream or yellowish ray florets surrounded by 6–9 pale green to purple-tinged and sometimes white- or black-dotted bracts. Fruit a tufted achene. BAS

Oclemena acuminata
(Aster acuminatus)

ASTERACEAE | **whorled aster**

Jul–Sep, 8–32 in. Erect, often colonial perennial found in spruce-fir forests, northern hardwood forests, mountain seepages and streambanks, and other cool, moist situations. Stems simple, hairy, slightly zigzagged and sticky. Leaves alternate (upper ones crowded and appearing whorled), short-petioled to sessile, oblong-lance-shaped, 2–6½ in. long, smooth or rough above, coarsely toothed. Flower heads on branches of an open, flattish panicle; heads about 2 in. wide and with 9–20 narrow, white ray florets encircling a small center disk of 10–35 yellow (aging to red) tubular florets. Fruit a tufted achene. BAS

Parthenium integrifolium

ASTERACEAE | **common wild quinine**

May–Oct, 1–3 ft. Erect perennial of dryish, sparsely wooded habitats, such as open forests and woodlands, barrens, and clearings. Stems 1–several from a crown, simple or branched above, smooth or hairy. Leaves petiolate, lance-elliptical, to 10 in. long (reduced and becoming sessile above), toothed and sometimes slightly lobed basally, rough-hairy. Flower heads in a flat-topped, branched terminal cluster; heads about ⅓ in. wide, with 5–6 very short-petaled, white ray florets encircling a center disk of many tiny, whitish-cream tubular florets. GMP

Pluchea foetida

ASTERACEAE | **stinking fleabane**

Jul–Oct, 1–3 ft. Erect annual/perennial of seasonally wet areas, coastal swamps, beaver ponds, ditches, other freshwater wetlands. Stems unbranched, purplish, hairy, gland-dotted. Stems and leaves give off an unpleasant odor when bruised or crushed. Leaves sessile with clasping bases, oval or oblong to lance-shaped, blunt-tipped, to 4½ in. long, thick, finely toothed, hairy, gland-dotted. Flower heads in dense clusters at end of stem and upper axillary branches; heads about ¼ in. tall and ⅓ in. wide, each with many tiny, creamy white tubular disk florets (no ray florets) closely surrounded by several series of hairy, pinkish, gland-dotted, pointy bracts. RTW

Sericocarpus asteroides

ASTERACEAE | **toothed white-topped aster**

Jun–Aug, 8–24 in. Erect perennial of dry woodlands, thin soils around rock outcrops, roadsides, sandhills, dry pinelands. Stems 1–several from a crown, slightly angled, branched in upper half, hairy. Lower leaves tapered to a winged petiole, oblong-oval to spoon-shaped, to about 4 in. long, toothed near tip and hairy; stem leaves alternate, fewer, sessile, smaller. Flower heads in dense clusters at ends of stems and branches; heads ½ in. wide, with 3–7 white ray florets encircling a center disk of 9–20 tiny, white to cream (or pink-tinged), tubular florets. Several series of whitish bracts with spreading, green tips surround the narrowly bell-shaped base of each head. WS

Solidago bicolor

ASTERACEAE | **silverrod**

Jul–Oct, 2–3 ft. Erect, rhizomatous perennial of dry upland forests, rocky woodlands, barrens, and road banks. Stems usually unbranched and hairy, may be angular. Leaves basal and alternate, petiolate (lower) to sessile (upper), oblong to oval, 1½–4 in. long (reduced above), toothed to entire, rough and hairy. Flower heads in a wandlike, leafy, terminal cluster that may branch; heads about ¼ in. wide, with 7–9 tiny, white to cream-colored ray florets encircling a center disk of tiny, cream-colored, tubular florets. Our only whitish goldenrod. RTW

Verbesina virginica

ASTERACEAE | **crownbeard**

Jul–Oct, 1½–8 ft. Erect perennial found in moist to dryish forests, especially over mafic or calcareous rocks. Stems 1–several from base, branched in inflorescence, winged, hairy. Leaves on winged petioles, oval or lance-shaped, to 5 in. long, often with wavy or toothed margins, hairy. Flower heads on hairy stalks in dense, branched terminal clusters; heads white, about ⅓ in. long, with about 5 oval ray florets (notched at tip) encircling a center disk of 8–12 tiny, 5-lobed tubular florets. RTW

Eupatorium linearifolium

ASTERACEAE | **narrowleaf bushy eupatorium**

Jul–Oct, 1–3 ft. Erect, bushy perennial of sandhill woodlands and sandy/peaty clearings. Stems several from a woody base, bushy-branched near the base and hairy. Leaves usually opposite, often subtending branches, sessile or subsessile, ascending, oblong to lance-oblong, 3/4–1½ in. long, minutely hairy and gland-dotted. Flower heads narrow, arranged in branching terminal cluster; heads cream-colored to brownish-white, about 1/3 in. long, with about 5 tiny, tubular florets. 1–2 series of tiny, lance-shaped bracts surround the base of each head. SG

Pycnanthemum tenuifolium

LAMIACEAE | **slender mountain-mint**

Jun–Sep, 1–2½ ft. Erect, rhizomatous perennial found in bogs, wet meadows, and moist to wet forests and clearings. Stems slender, 4-angled, bushy-branched, smooth. Leaves mostly sessile, linear, to 2 in. long, gland-dotted and with mintlike odor. Flowers crowded in dense, branching, flat-topped heads with small, white, hairy bracts in addition to flowers; each flower white to pale pink, less than 1/4 in. long, tubular opening to 2 spreading lips and with 2 purple anthers. RTW

Ageratina altissima (*Eupatorium rugosum*)

ASTERACEAE | **common white snakeroot**

Jul–Oct, 1½–4 ft. Erect perennial of moist, deciduous forests such as cove forests. Stems 1–several, many-branched, smooth to hairy, sometimes whitish. Leaves long-petioled, oval to lance-shaped and rounded to somewhat wedge-shaped at base, 2–7 in. long, with 3 major veins arising from base, toothed and smooth. Flower heads arranged in branching terminal and upper axillary clusters; heads white, about 1/3 in. tall, with 9–30 tubular disk florets surrounded by 2 series of narrow bracts. Protruding styles give heads a fuzzy appearance. BAS

Ageratina aromatica (*Eupatorium aromaticum*)

ASTERACEAE | **small-leaf white snakeroot**

Aug–Oct, 1–2½ ft. Erect, rhizomatous perennial of usually dry and often fire-maintained woodlands and forests; also sandhills and woodland edges. Stems simple or with loosely ascending branches above, smooth or finely hairy. Leaves petiolate, oval to diamond-shaped, 1½–3 in. long (reduced above), blunt-toothed. Flower heads arranged in flat- or round-topped clusters at tips of open-spreading branches; heads white, to ¼ in. wide, with about 15 disk florets surrounded by a row of 10 or more narrow, greenish bracts that are unequal in length. Protruding styles give heads a fuzzy appearance. BAS

Eclipta prostrata

ASTERACEAE | **yerba-de-tajo**

Jun–Nov, to 2 ft. Reclining to ascending (occasionally erect) annual of moist to wet disturbed areas, ditches, pondshores, and disturbed bottomlands. Stems sprawling, rooting at nodes, branching occasionally, often purplish, covered with stiff hairs that point upward. Leaves opposite (a few upper leaves may be alternate), sessile to short-petioled, lance-shaped, to 4 in. long, stiff-hairy. Flower heads in terminal and axillary clusters of 1–3; heads about ⅓ in. wide, with many narrow, white ray florets encircling a center of tiny, white, tubular florets with dark purple anthers. RTW

Eupatorium album

ASTERACEAE | **white-bracted thoroughwort**

Jun–Sep, to 3 ft. Erect perennial of dry woodlands and disturbed areas. Stems branched above (in inflorescence), hairy. Leaves mostly sessile, oval to lance-shaped, 1½–5 in. long, coarsely toothed, gland-dotted beneath and nearly smooth to rough-hairy above. Flower heads narrow, erect, fuzzy-appearing, in branching terminal cluster; heads about ⅓ in. tall, each with 4–5 tiny, white, 5-lobed, tubular disk florets with 2 protruding styles. A series of narrow green bracts with white, pointed tips surrounds the base of each head. BAS

Eupatorium glaucescens

ASTERACEAE | **broadleaf bushy eupatorium**

Jul–Oct, 1–2½ ft. Erect perennial of sandhills and other dry, sandy woodlands. Stems from a woody crown, usually much-branched from the base, minutely hairy. Leaves sessile, spreading to ascending, oblong-lance-shaped with tapered base, irregularly toothed in upper half, gland-dotted beneath, hairy. Flower heads narrow, erect, fuzzy-appearing, in terminal cluster, the branches of which are very hairy; heads about ⅓ in. long, each with about 5 tiny, bright white, 5-lobed, tubular florets with 2 protruding styles. A series of hairy, green, narrow bracts surrounds the base of each head. Flowers are notably whiter than those of other white eupatoriums. BAS

Eupatorium leucolepis

ASTERACEAE | **justiceweed**

Aug–Oct, 15–36 in. Erect perennial of savannas, seepage bogs, and depression ponds. Stems sparsely branched, hairy. Leaves mostly sessile, linear to lance-shaped, 1–3 in. long, often folded along the midrib, toothed or entire, hairy or gland-dotted. Flower heads small, in branching terminal cluster; heads white, under ½ in. tall, with 3–5 tubular disk florets surrounded by an overlapping series of tiny, narrow bracts with papery margins. BAS

Eupatorium mohrii

ASTERACEAE | **Mohr's eupatorium**

Aug–Oct, 2–3 ft. Erect perennial of moist savannas, pond margins, and other wet habitats. Stems simple or branched at the base into 2 or more aerial stems, densely branched toward the top, minutely hairy to rough-hairy. Leaves opposite and alternate, subsessile, narrowly elliptical to lance-shaped and tapering to the base, to 4 in. long, often coarsely toothed, hairy to smooth, dotted with glands beneath. Flower heads in narrow, branching terminal cluster; heads about ¼ in. long, with 5 white, tubular florets surrounded by 1–2 series of tiny, oblong-lance-shaped bracts. BAS

Eupatorium perfoliatum

ASTERACEAE | **boneset**

Aug–Oct, 3–4 ft. Erect, clump-forming perennial of marshes, swamps, bogs, wet pastures, and other wet habitats. Stems branched only in inflorescence, covered in long, spreading hairs. Leaves united at the base so stem appears to perforate them, lance-shaped with long tips, 2–7 in. long, conspicuously net-veined, finely toothed, smooth above, gland-dotted beneath. Flower heads arranged in flat-topped clusters; heads less than ¼ in. wide, with 7–14 white, 5-lobed tubular disk florets with protruding styles that give heads a fuzzy appearance. Whorls of tiny, gland-dotted, hairy, lance-shaped bracts surround the base of each head. GMP

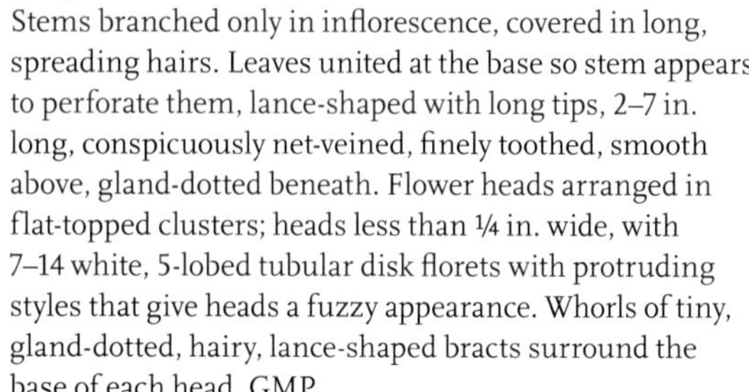

Eupatorium pilosum

ASTERACEAE | **ragged eupatorium**

Aug–Oct, 1–5 ft. Erect perennial of savannas, bogs, and other moist areas. Stems with 1–2 branches near the top, sometimes purplish-red-tinged, hairy and often rough. Leaves sessile to short-petioled, oval to oblong-lance-shaped, 1¼–3½ in. long, with prominent midvein, coarsely toothed and often with purplish margins. Flower heads arranged in short-branched, flattish clusters at stem tips; heads white, ¼ in. wide, with 5 tiny, tubular disk florets with protruding styles. A few series of narrow bracts surround the base of each head. BAS

Eupatorium pubescens
(E. rotundifolium var. *ovatum)*

ASTERACEAE | **inland roundleaf eupatorium**

Jul–Sep, 1–4 ft. Erect perennial of dry woodlands, woodland clearings and edges, and road banks. Stems sparsely branched above, hairy. Leaves sessile, oval with pointed tips and slightly rounded base, 1½–2 times long as wide, the principal pair of lateral veins diverging above the base of the midrib, sharp-toothed, very hairy above, hairy on veins beneath. Flower heads arranged in flattish clusters at branch tips, the branches and stalks hairy; heads white, with 5 tiny, tubular florets. A few series of tiny, narrow bracts surround the base of each head. BAS

Eupatorium rotundifolium

ASTERACEAE | **common roundleaf eupatorium**

Aug–Oct, 3–4½ ft. Erect perennial of savannas, seepage bogs, woodlands, interdune swales, old fields, roadsides. Stems 1–2 from a short crown, sparsely branched above and densely hairy, especially above. Leaves sessile, oval to triangular with somewhat rounded tip and nearly flat base, 1–1½ times long as wide, with the main pair of lateral veins diverging directly from the midrib base, round-toothed, rough-hairy above, gland-dotted and veiny beneath. Flower heads small, in clusters at branch tips, the branches and stalks hairy and glandular; heads about ¼ in. wide and with 5 white, tubular disk florets. A few series of tiny, pointed bracts surround the base of each head. BAS

Eupatorium semiserratum

ASTERACEAE | **smallflower thoroughwort**

Jul–Oct, 1½–5 ft. Erect perennial of swamp forests, seepage bogs, savannas, clay-based Carolina bays and other wetlands. Stems usually solitary and branched only in the inflorescence, densely hairy and sometimes glandular. Leaves opposite or in whorls of 3–4, elliptical to oblong-lance-shaped, with 3 primary veins, toothed, minutely hairy. Flower heads arranged in somewhat round-topped clusters at tips of branches; heads white, about ¼ in. long and with several tiny, tubular disk florets surrounded by several series of tiny bracts. BAS

Eupatorium serotinum

ASTERACEAE | **late eupatorium**

Aug–Oct, 3–6 ft. Erect perennial of interdune swales, tidal marshes, open forests, fields, powerline rights-of-way, and other open, disturbed areas. Stems much-branched above, often dark red, densely and finely hairy. Leaves petiolate, tending to droop downward, oval to lance-shaped, to 7 in. long, with 3 prominent veins, coarsely toothed, gland-dotted and smooth or short-hairy. Flower heads arranged in flat-topped clusters; heads white, about ¼ in. wide and with 9–15 tiny, white, tubular disk florets, each with 5 triangular corolla lobes and 2 protruding style branches. Several series of green and white bracts surround the base of each head. BAS

Eupatorium sessilifolium

ASTERACEAE | **sessile-leaf eupatorium**

Jul–Oct, 2–5 ft. Erect perennial of open upland woodlands and woodland borders, especially over calcareous or mafic substrates. Stems single or in clumps, branched near top, gland-dotted and smooth below inflorescence. Leaves sessile, lance-shaped, 3–6 in. long with long-tapering point, finely toothed, gland-dotted and smooth. Flower heads arranged in narrowly branched, flat-topped clusters; heads white, about 1/4 in. wide and with several tubular disk florets surrounded by several series of tiny, narrow bracts. BAS

Galinsoga quadriradiata

ASTERACEAE | **common Peruvian-daisy**

May–Nov, 6–24 in. Erect to ascending annual of roadsides, barnyards, and other disturbed areas. Native to Central and South America. Stems much-branched, densely hairy and often glandular. Leaves petiolate, oval, 1–2½ in. long, sharply and coarsely toothed and sparsely hairy. Flower heads on hairy stalks arising from upper leaf axils; heads about 1/4 in. wide, with 4–8 white, 3-toothed ray florets encircling a center disk composed of tiny, yellow tubular florets. RTW

Blephilia hirsuta

LAMIACEAE | **hairy woodmint**

May–Oct, 1–3 ft. Erect, rhizomatous perennial of rocky or alluvial forests, rich cove forests, northern hardwood forests up to at least 5000 ft. Stems 4-angled, branched above, usually densely covered with spreading hairs. Leaves long-petioled, lance-shaped to broadly oval, with pointed tips, 1½–3 in. long, toothed, sparsely hairy above, hairy beneath. Flowers in several dense, headlike clusters tiered along terminal spikes and surrounded by green, fringed bracts; each white or pale purple, 1/2 in. long, with tubular corolla split into 2 flaring lips, the upper narrow, the lower 3-lobed and purple-speckled; 2 long-protruding stamens. Calyx is tubular with hairy teeth. BAS

Hyptis alata

LAMIACEAE | **clustered bushmint**

May–Nov, 1–9 ft. Erect perennial found in wet pine savannas, margins of swamp forests, wet powerline rights-of-way, and ditches. Stems 4-angled, sometimes branched above, hairy on the angles; stem and leaves aromatic with a musky mint odor. Leaves mostly sessile, lance-shaped and tapering at both ends, 2–6 in. long, toothed. Flowers in domed heads, ½–1 in. wide, on long stalks emanating from leaf axils; each head rests on a series of small, leafy bracts. Flowers within heads white speckled with purple, about ¼ in. long, tubular and split into 2 flaring lips. BAS

Lycopus americanus

LAMIACEAE | **American bugleweed**

Jun–Nov, 1–3 ft. Erect to leaning, rhizomatous perennial of freshwater tidal marshes, floodplain forests, alluvial swamps, sandy/gravelly bars and shores. Stems 4-angled, ridged, simple or extensively branched, smooth or sparingly hairy. Leaves petiolate, lance- to elliptic-lance-shaped, 1¼–3 in. long, deeply toothed (less so upward), minutely hairy on veins beneath. Flowers in axillary heads; each white, less than ¼ in. long, short-tubular, with 4 spreading lobes. The light green, tubular, 5-lobed calyx is shorter than the corolla; there are 2 protruding stamens. Fruit a set of 4 nutlets forming a square inside the persistent calyx; calyx lobes exceed the nutlets. BAS

Lycopus rubellus

LAMIACEAE | **stalked bugleweed**

Jun–Nov, 1–4 ft. Erect tuberous perennial of marshes, swamp forests (often growing on logs and tree buttresses in flooded sloughs), bottomlands. Stems 4-angled, simple or branched, smooth to densely hairy. Leaves petiolate, lance-shaped, abruptly tapered, 2–4 in. long, often toothed from middle to tip, paler green beneath, usually smooth on both surfaces. Flowers in axillary heads (middle and upper stem); each white, less than ¼ in. long, with a short-tubular corolla with 4 lobes, a light green calyx with 4–5 narrow lobes, 2 slightly protruding stamens, and a pistil. Fruit a set of 4 nutlets forming a square inside the persistent calyx; calyx lobes exceed the nutlets. JG

Lycopus uniflorus

LAMIACEAE | **northern bugleweed**

Jul–Oct, 8–36 in. Erect, rhizomatous perennial of bogs, seeps, seepage swamps, alluvial forests, shores of depression ponds and beaver ponds. Stems 4-angled, few-branched, with lateral, tuber-producing stolons; smooth or sparsely hairy. Leaves in pairs at 90° to each other, short-petioled to subsessile, lance-shaped to oblong, ¾–3 in. long, toothed, hairy on veins beneath. Flowers in axillary heads, 1–2 blooming at once; each white, less than ¼ in. long, short-tubular, with 5 spreading lobes, 2 slightly protruding stamens, and a pistil. Fruit a set of 4 nutlets forming a square inside the persistent 5-lobed tubular calyx, which is shorter than the corolla tube. BAS

Lycopus virginicus

LAMIACEAE | **Virginia bugleweed**

Jun–Nov, 8–36 in. Erect, rhizomatous perennial of swamps, bottomlands, tidal marshes, and other wet habitats. Stems 4-angled, branched, sometimes with close-pressed hairs. Leaves lance-oval, tapering at the base to a winged petiole (upper leaves nearly sessile), to 4½ in. long, coarsely toothed, hairy. Flowers in axillary heads; each white, less than ¼ in. long, short-tubular, opening to 4 erect lobes; 2 stamens and a pistil are mostly within the corolla. The light green, tubular, 5-lobed calyx is shorter than the corolla tube. Fruit a set of 4 nutlets forming a square inside the persistent calyx. JS

Nepeta cataria

LAMIACEAE | **catnip**

Jul–Oct, 2–3 ft. Erect, naturalized perennial of fencerows, barnyards, and other disturbed areas. Native to Eurasia. Stems stout, 4-angled, branched, gray-green and densely furry. Leaves petiolate, oval to triangular with blunt or notched base, to 3 in. long, coarsely toothed, pale gray-green, white-hairy beneath; leaves release a strong scent when bruised. Flowers in spikelike, dense terminal and axillary heads; each flower white with purple or pink spots, ¼ in. long, tubular and split into 2 lips. GPF

Pycnanthemum flexuosum

LAMIACEAE | **savanna mountain-mint**

Jun–Sep, 1–3½ ft. Erect, rhizomatous perennial of moist to wet pine savannas, pocosin margins, mountain bogs, and seepage areas on low-elevation granite domes. Stems 4-angled, branched (ascending) above, covered with white hairs. Leaves petiolate, narrowly oblong to lance-shaped, with a few marginal teeth and 3–5 pairs of parallel veins starting at or below middle of blade, smooth or hairy on veins beneath, and with a faint mintlike odor. Flowers in flattened-round terminal and axillary heads with a bristly appearance; each white and purple-spotted, to ¼ in. long, tubular and opening to 2 spreading lips. The tubular calyx has 5 lobes with long, needlelike white tips. WS

Pycnanthemum muticum

LAMIACEAE | **short-toothed mountain-mint**

Jun–Aug, 1–3 ft. Erect, rhizomatous perennial of bogs, wet meadows, and moist to wet forests. Stems 4-angled, mostly unbranched, furry. Leaves short-petioled to sessile, oval to lance-shaped, 1½–3 in. long, finely toothed, finely hairy beneath; all parts with a strong minty fragrance. Flowers densely packed in flattened-round terminal and axillary clusters that sit on dusty-looking, leaflike bracts covered in white hairs; each flower white to pale pink and purple-spotted, about ¼ in. long, tubular, 2-lipped. Flowers produce copious nectar, attracting a wide variety of butterflies and other insects. PIP

Pycnanthemum pycnanthemoides

LAMIACEAE | **southern mountain-mint**

Jun–Aug, 3–6 ft. Erect, rhizomatous perennial of dry upland forests, rocky woodlands, forest borders and clearings, shale barrens. Stems 4-angled, loosely branched above, covered in dense curly hairs. Leaves petiolate, elliptical to narrowly oval, toothed, uppermost leaves whitish with dense, close-pressed hairs on upper surface; pungently minty when crushed. Flowers on white-furry leaflike bracts, densely packed in domed terminal and upper axillary heads; each white to pale lavender, less than ¼ in. long, tubular opening to 5 lobes, the 3 lower lobes spotted with purple. The tubular calyx has 5 narrowly triangular lobes. Abundant nectar for pollinators. BAS

Eupatorium hyssopifolium

ASTERACEAE | **hyssopleaf eupatorium**

Jul–Oct, 1–3 ft. Erect perennial of dry woodlands, dune grasslands and scrubs, bogs, damp to dry clearings, pastures, roadsides and other disturbed areas. Stems solitary or in small clumps, branched above, finely rough-hairy. Leaves in whorls of 3–4, sessile, linear, to 3¼ in. long; clusters of shorter leaves or short side branches in the leaf axils. Flower heads arranged in flattish clusters at branch tips; heads white or pinkish, with 5 tiny, tubular florets with protruding styles that give heads a fuzzy appearance. A series of 8–10 hairy, greenish-white bracts surrounds the base of each head. PIP

Eupatorium torreyanum

ASTERACEAE | **Torrey's eupatorium**

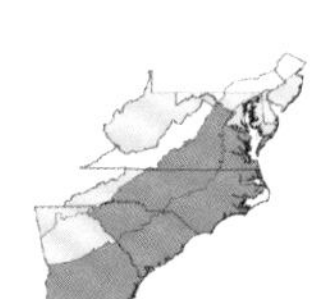

Jul–Oct, 2–4 ft. Erect perennial of dry woodlands, powerline rights-of-way, roadsides, and marshes. Stems mostly solitary, branched above, rough-hairy (especially above). Leaves in whorls of 3 or opposite, sessile, lance-shaped, 2–4½ in. long, rough-surfaced, with 3 prominent veins and widely spaced teeth. Flower heads arranged in flat-topped clusters at tips of branches; heads white, with several tiny, tubular disk florets with 5-lobed corollas. Several series of tiny, green and white bracts surround the base of each head. BAS

Chaptalia tomentosa

ASTERACEAE | **pineland daisy**

Dec–May, 4–16 in. Erect perennial of wet pine savannas and flatwoods, sandhill seeps, and wet streamhead margins. Stem a leafless, white-woolly flowering stalk arising from the center of a basal rosette. Leaves basal only, elliptical to oblong-lance-shaped, 2–7 in. long, smooth above and white-hairy beneath; a few widely spaced teeth sometimes present. Flower heads daisylike, solitary at top of stalk, nodding at first but soon erect; heads about 1½ in. wide, with narrow, white ray florets (may be pink or purple on lower surface) encircling a cream-colored central disk composed of tiny, tubular florets. RTW

Erigeron vernus

ASTERACEAE | **whitetop fleabane**

Mar–Jun, 18–24 in. Erect perennial/biennial from basal rosette, found in wet savannas, roadside ditches, seepages, and interdunal swales. Stem a flowering stalk emerging from the basal rosette, unbranched, hairy toward inflorescence. Basal leaves mostly entire and hairless, oval to nearly round (sometimes spoon-shaped or elliptic), ¾–5¾ in. long, fleshy; a few bracts on stem. Flower heads solitary, or in a loose branching cluster of 2–20 at top of flowering stalk; heads with 25–30 narrow, white (rarely lavender) ray florets encircling a yellow center disk composed of tiny, tubular florets. BAS

Eriocaulon compressum

ERIOCAULACEAE | **flattened pipewort**

Apr–Oct, 8–18 in. Erect, tufted aquatic perennial of ponds, lakes, and other depressions, also found in wetter places in pine flatwoods and pine savannas; normally submerged, with flowering stems extending above water. Stems 1–several flowering scapes, ridged lengthwise and slightly twisted, smooth. Leaves basal and weakly erect or lying on ground, linear-lance-shaped with narrowly pointed tip, 2–12 in. long, thin-textured. Flowers in compact, buttonlike, white heads about ½ in. wide topping each stem. Black dots scattered throughout the heads represent tips of bracts and stamens in the minute flowers. Flower heads compress easily. BAS, RTW

Eriocaulon decangulare

ERIOCAULACEAE | **ten-angled pipewort**

Jun–Oct, 12–32 in. Erect, densely tufted semi-aquatic perennial found in wet pine savannas and pine flatwoods, bogs, mafic fens and seeps, seasonally flooded ponds, and wind-tidal marshes. Stems 1–3 flowering scapes, ridged lengthwise and twisted, smooth. Leaves basal, ascending to erect, linear-needle-shaped, mostly 5–12 in. long, thick-textured and stiff. Flowers in compact, white, domed heads about ½ in. wide topping each stem and composed of minute flowers. Note that the head is hard (not compressible as in *E. compressum*). BAS

Lachnocaulon anceps

ERIOCAULACEAE | **common bogbutton**

May–Oct, 2–12 in. Erect, tufted perennial of moist to dry sands and moist peats in pinelands, sometimes locally abundant in open, disturbed areas where competition has been removed. Stems 1–several thin flowering scapes, ridged lengthwise and twisted in a spiral; covered with long, spreading hairs. Leaves basal and forming a mounded clump, linear and tapering to a point, 1–2½ in. long, smooth or hairy. Flowers in compact, buttonlike heads (domed or slightly flattened), about ¼ in. wide, topping each stem; white or grayish-white; tiny and hairy. BAS

Syngonanthus flavidulus

ERIOCAULACEAE | **bantam-buttons**

May–Oct, 4–11 in. Erect, tufted perennial of pine savannas, pine flatwoods, borders of pineland ponds and adjacent ditches. Stem (flowering scape) unbranched, sheathed at the base, glandular-hairy. Leaves basal and spreading-recurved, narrowly linear and tapering to a point, ¾–1¼ in. long, shiny and smooth to hairy. Flowers in compact, rounded, buttonlike heads topping each stem; heads about ¼–⅓ in. wide, yellowish-white aging to dull white or pale gray, tiny. RL

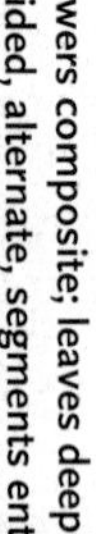

Dalea pinnata

FABACEAE | **summer farewell**

Aug–Nov, 2–3 ft. Erect perennial of sandhills and other dryish pinelands, especially in loamy sands. Stems 1–several from a single crown, branched above, green or red and smooth. Leaves petiolate, pinnately divided into 3–15 very narrow, thick leaflets less than ⅜ in. long with glandular dots. Flowers in compact heads at tips of branches and originating from a bright red bud; heads with 8–12 white flowers with prominent white stamens, all surrounded by reddish-brown bracts. MK

Achillea borealis (*A. millefolium*)

ASTERACEAE | **American yarrow**

Apr–Nov, 1–3 ft. Erect perennial of grassy balds, meadows, pastures, roadsides, and other disturbed areas. Stems simple or somewhat forking above, woolly-hairy. Basal leaves petiolate, stem leaves alternate and sessile; lance-shaped in outline, to 6 in. long, 2 times pinnately divided into linear segments in a 3-dimensional (not flat) arrangement, smooth to hairy. Flower heads arranged in flat-topped or rounded clusters on stiffly ascending, terminal stalks; heads less than 1/4 in. wide, consisting of 3–8 white (rarely pink) ray florets with rounded petals and 10–20 tiny tubular disk florets in the center. AMC

Anthemis arvensis

ASTERACEAE | **corn chamomile**

Apr–Jul, 4–32 in. Ascending to sprawling annual/biennial of roadsides and open, disturbed areas. Native to Europe. Stems usually weak and leaning, branched primarily near base, whitish-green to light reddish-green and woolly. Leaves short-petioled (flattened), broadly oval in outline, 3/4–2 in. long and deeply 2 times divided into linear segments, pale green and woolly. Flowers in 1- to 1½-in.-wide daisylike heads at tips of branches; heads with 10–18 white ray florets encircling a bright yellow, flattish center disk composed of tiny, tubular florets. Crushed flower heads give off a mild fragrance of pineapple. BMP

Anthemis cotula

ASTERACEAE | **stinking chamomile**

May–Jul, 12–20 in. Erect to ascending annual of fields, roadsides, and other open, disturbed areas. Native to Eurasia. Stems simple or bushy-branched (especially below), green or reddish, glandular and smooth or hairy. Leaves sessile, feathery (pinnately divided into linear segments), 1–2¼ in. long, slightly hairy, ill-scented when crushed. Flowers in ½- to 1-in.-wide daisylike heads at tips of branches; heads with 10–18 white ray florets encircling the bright yellow, domed center disk of tiny, tubular florets. KL

Eupatorium capillifolium

ASTERACEAE | **common dog-fennel**

Sep–Nov, 1½–6 ft. Robust and weedy, erect perennial found in disturbed soils of old fields and clearcuts in a range of moist to dry conditions. Stems 1–several from a somewhat woody crown, stout, branched above, reddish and hairy, the lower stem often with dead, brown leaves. Leaves alternate or opposite, crowded, 1–4 in. long, pinnately divided into threadlike segments, bright green, dotted with glands and emitting a pungent odor similar to fennel when crushed. Flower heads in multiple small clusters along drooping branches of the pyramind-shaped top of the plant; heads tiny, with 3–5 creamy white or purplish, tubular disk florets. Flowers mildly fragrant. PIP

Eupatorium compositifolium

ASTERACEAE | **coastal dog-fennel**

Sep–Dec, to 6½ ft. Erect perennial of sandy disturbed areas. Stems 1–several from a somewhat woody crown, stout, branched above, hairy. Leaves alternate or opposite, crowded, hairy, 1–4 in. long, divided into narrow, grayish-green segments. Flowers in many clusters of heads along branches; heads tiny, with white disk florets (rays absent) with protruding styles. AMC

Bidens alba var. *radiata* (*B. pilosa*)

ASTERACEAE | **hairy beggar-ticks**

Jan–Dec, 8–30 in. or taller. Erect or reclining annual/short-lived perennial of wet disturbed areas. Native to the Neotropics, invasive worldwide. Stems grooved, branched, rooting at lower nodes, smooth or soft-hairy. Leaves petiolate, mostly pinnately divided into 3–7, lance-shaped to oval, sharply toothed lobes; with soft, short hairs on both surfaces. Flower heads ½ in. wide with 2 series of bracts surrounding the bell-shaped base; solitary or in open, terminal cluster; each head with 5–8 white, broadly elliptical, toothed ray florets and a center disk of yellowish tubular florets. Fruit a 4-angled black achene, tapered at both ends, usually with 2–3 barbed awns. JG

Polymnia canadensis

ASTERACEAE | **white-flowered leafcup**

Jul–Oct, 2–6 ft. Erect perennial found in moist forests, particularly those over calcareous rocks. Stems simple or branched, densely hairy and with stalked glands, especially above. Leaves petiolate (sometimes winged and with large stipules), 10–16 in. long, deeply pinnately divided into 3–7 sharply pointed, coarsely toothed lobes (upper leaves may lack lobes). Flower heads in branched terminal and upper axillary clusters; heads ½ in. wide and with 5–8 white, oval ray florets with 3-toothed tips encircling a center disk of tiny, whitish-yellow, tubular florets with protruding yellow stamens. RTW

Croton argyranthemus

EUPHORBIACEAE | **sandhill croton**

Mar–Sep, 1½–2 ft. Erect perennial of deep sandy soils in sandhills, pine-oak scrub, and dry pinelands. Stems several from base of plant, branched, covered with reddish-brown scales. Leaves petiolate, oval or lance-shaped, to 2 in. long, green above, covered with minute silvery-white scales below. Flowers in spikelike, terminal racemes (¾–2 in. long), with male (higher) and female (lower) flowers separate; male flowers with 5 white petals and 10 stamens, female flowers fewer and with 5 greenish sepals and no petals. Fruit a round, 3-lobed capsule covered in minute silvery scales. Stem and leaves exude milky sap when bruised. AMC

Croton capitatus

EUPHORBIACEAE | **hogwort**

Jul–Oct, to 6 ft. Erect annual of fields, roadsides, and other open, disturbed habitats; often in barren, compacted soil. Stems stout, somewhat branched above, white or tawny, densely soft-woolly. Leaves petiolate, narrowly triangular to lance-shaped, densely soft-woolly, often loosely folded lengthwise into a boat shape. Flowers in separate male and female clusters at stem ends and from upper leaf axils, small and whitish-woolly; male flowers in short, dense spikes and with 5 sepals, 5 petals, and 10–15 stamens; female flowers in headlike clusters below the male spikes and composed of 6–12 sepals (petals absent) and 3 divided styles. BAS

Croton punctatus

EUPHORBIACEAE | **silverleaf croton**

May–Nov, 1–4 ft. Erect, shrubby annual/short-lived perennial of beach dunes and coastal grasslands; usually growing with *Uniola paniculata* and/or *Sporobolus pumilus*. Stems solitary or in large round clumps, semi-woody, with forking branches and covered with minute, star-shaped hairs with clear to reddish centers (seen under magnification). Leaves long-petioled, oval to elliptical, to 2½ in. long, grayish-green above with subtly rust-colored edges and star-shaped, rust-colored hairs beneath. Flowers in fuzzy clusters at stem ends, male and female separate; rust-colored and inconspicuous. Fruit a 3-lobed capsule, also with minute, star-shaped hairs. JG

Croton willdenowii

EUPHORBIACEAE | **broadleaf rushfoil**

Jun–Oct, 6–14 in. Erect to leaning annual of granite flatrocks and other rock outcrops, diabase and calcareous barrens, and disturbed, sandy soil. Stems branched, densely covered by silvery scales with reddish-brown centers. Leaves short-petioled to sessile, linear to elliptical, to 1½ in. long, folded during dry weather, upper surface green and covered with star-shaped hairs. Flowers in fuzzy clusters at stem ends, male and female separate; males at end of short spikes, with 5 tiny petals, 5 tiny sepals, and 5 stamens; females at base of spikes, with a tiny 3- to 5-lobed calyx and 2 divided styles. Fruit a tiny, elliptical capsule covered with star-shaped hairs. GPF

Euphorbia curtisii

EUPHORBIACEAE | **Curtis's spurge**

Mar–Jun, 8–15 in. Erect to ascending perennial of dry oak or pine-oak scrub of sandhills, pine-oak woodlands, and pine-oak savannas. Endemic to se U.S. Stems erect to ascending, branched, smooth, leaking milky sap when broken. Leaves short-petioled to sessile (with tiny stipules at the base), linear to elliptical, with prominent midvein and somewhat folded, sometimes sparsely hairy on the margins. Flowers in an open, terminal panicle; each greenish-white, less than ¼ in. wide, with 5 barely visible, semi-circular petal-like bracts attached to a green, cup-shaped receptacle where 5 tiny glands and reproductive organs are nestled. Fruit a tiny, rounded capsule. WS

Fallopia cilinodis

POLYGONACEAE | **fringed black bindweed**

Jun–Sep, to 6 ft. long. Herbaceous perennial vine of rock outcrops, glades, and open woodlands at high elevations. Stem trailing or twining (occasionally erect), often reddish, smooth or finely hairy. Leaves petiolate, with a fringed sheath (ocrea) where petiole joins stem, broadly oval or triangular with pointed tips and notched bases, finely hairy along wavy margins, dark green with conspicuous vein pattern above, often deeply reddish to maroon beneath. Flowers in loose, branching, axillary clusters; each white to greenish-white, less than 1/4 in. wide, with 5 spreading, oval to elliptical tepals (outer 3 faintly keeled), 6–8 white stamens, and a 3-parted style. JG

Fallopia convolvulus

POLYGONACEAE | **black bindweed**

May–Nov, to 3 ft. long. Herbaceous annual vine of fields, roadsides, fencerows, and other open, disturbed habitats. Native to Eurasia, widespread in NoAm. Stems trailing or vining, light green to reddish-green, hairless but with lines of rough bumps. Leaves widely spaced, petiolate and with a membranous sheath (ocrea) where petiole joins stem, arrowhead-shaped, 1–2½ in. long. Flowers in short, open, axillary racemes; each white inside, green or pinkish outside, less than 1/4 in. long, with 5 tepals (outer 3 slightly keeled) and 8 stamens surrounding a central green column (ovary and style). Fruit a black, 3-sided achene. A common agricultural weed. LADI

Fallopia scandens

POLYGONACEAE | **climbing buckwheat**

Jul–Oct, to 20 ft. Herbaceous perennial vine of moist to wet, open habitats, including floodplains, thickets, clearings, and meadows. Stems twining, sharply angled and rough-edged, often reddish with age. Leaves petiolate, with a membranous sheath (ocrea) where stalk joins stem (shed as leaf matures), oval to heart- or arrowhead-shaped, 2–5 in. long, semi-rough along margins and veins. Flowers in erect, unbranched axillary racemes, initially erect-spreading, drooping as fruit ripens; each white to light green, less than 1/4 in. long, with 5 tepals (outer 3 strongly winged with a pale ruffle), 8 greenish-white stamens, and a 3-parted style. Fruit a glossy black achene. BAS

Persicaria arifolia
(Polygonum arifolium)

POLYGONACEAE | **halberd-leaf tearthumb**

Jul–Nov, 2–6 ft. Reclining-scrambling annual/perennial of marshes, tidal swamps, floodplain pools, and wet thickets. Stems branched, ridged, the angles with hooked prickles. Leaves petiolate, with a prickled and hairy sheath (ocrea) where petiole joins stem, triangular with flaring basal lobes and sharp-pointed tip, 1–7 in. long, sparsely hairy above, with star-shaped hairs beneath. Flowers in short racemes, the stalk prickly, at stem tops and from upper leaf axils; flowers white to greenish or pink, less than ¼ in. long, with 5 oval to elliptical tepals. Fruit a broadly oval, brown achene. PIP

Persicaria hydropiperoides
(Polygonum hydropiperoides)

POLYGONACEAE | **waterpepper**

May–Nov, to 3 ft. Erect to sprawling perennial of swamp forests, streams, ditches. Stems often lean and form mats (rooting at nodes) but turn up at ends; occasionally branched, slightly hairy above, smooth below. Leaves short-petioled, with a fringed sheath (ocrea) where petiole joins stem, lance-shaped, 2–8 in. long (reduced above), smooth or hairy, lacking the red blotch of some *Persicaria* species. Flowers closely spaced in terminal and axillary spikes (to 3 in. long), greenish-white to pale pink, less than ¼ in. wide, with 5 ascending tepals united at their bases, 8 stamens, and a 3-parted style. PIP

Persicaria perfoliata
(Polygonum perfoliatum)

POLYGONACEAE | **Asiatic tearthumb**

Jun–Oct, to 10 ft. long or more. Climbing annual of disturbed forests, alluvial fields, roadsides, powerline rights-of-way, other disturbed areas. Native to Asia, introduced and spreading rapidly. Stems branched, clambering over other plants, covered with recurved barbs. Leaves long-petioled (petiole bearing recurved barbs), with an expanded, cup-shaped sheath (ocrea) where petiole joins stem, triangular, 1–3 in. long, pale or bluish-green, with recurved barbs beneath. Flowers clustered in short racemes arising from ocreae, greenish-white, less than ¼ in. long, usually closed. Fruit a blue, berrylike achene. AB, GPF

Persicaria punctata
(Polygonum punctatum)
POLYGONACEAE | **dotted smartweed**

Jul–Nov, 6–42 in. Erect-ascending annual/short-lived perennial of swamp forests, bottomlands, and marshes. Stems branched, smooth, gland-dotted. Leaves petiolate, with a fringed, brown, membranous sheath (ocrea) where petiole joins stem, lance-shaped, 1½–6 in. long, hairy on margins, lacking a red blotch, gland-dotted. Flowers irregularly spaced on erect-ascending spikes (2–6 in. tall), white to greenish-white, less than ¼ in. long, usually closed, and with 5 tepals that are gland-dotted. BAS

Persicaria sagittata
(Polygonum sagittatum)
POLYGONACEAE | **arrowleaf tearthumb**

May–Dec, 3–6 ft. Erect to sprawling annual/short-lived perennial of marshes, bogs, seeps, beaver ponds, and wet thickets. Stems sprawling over other plants, hollow and brittle, ridged, with recurved barbs on the ridges. Leaves petiolate to sessile, with a short-fringed and membranous sheath (ocrea) where petiole meets stem, lance-shaped with 2 "earlobes" at the base, 1–4 in. long, with fine hairs on margins and recurved barbs on the midvein beneath. Flowers in small, rounded clusters on stalks from upper leaf axils, white to pale pink, less than ¼ in. long, with 5 oval tepals. BAS

Persicaria setacea
(Polygonum setaceum)
POLYGONACEAE | **swamp smartweed**

Jul–Nov, 1½–4 ft. Erect perennial of swamp and bottomland forests, brackish and maritime swamps. Stems simple or branching from middle or upper nodes, slightly ridged, hairy. Leaves petiolate, with a long-fringed and hairy membranous sheath (ocrea) where petiole joins stem, lance-shaped to linear, 2¼–6 in. long, smooth or rough-hairy above and smooth or hairy beneath. Flowers in erect, dense spikes at ends of branches, greenish-white to pinkish, less than ¼ in. long, with 5 tepals that are joined at the base and usually not fully spreading. BAS

Persicaria virginiana (Polygonum virginianum)

POLYGONACEAE | **jumpseed**

Jun–Oct, 1½–4 ft. Erect perennial of floodplains and moist forests. Stems simple or branched, smooth. Leaves petiolate, with a short-fringed and membranous sheath (ocrea) where petiole meets stem, oval to lance-shaped with rounded base, 2½–6 in. long, usually hairy on both surfaces. Flowers widely spaced in a slender, terminal spike (to 14 in. long), white or greenish-white, about ¼ in. wide when open but often closed and curving downward from the spike stalk, with 4 pointed tepals and 4 stamens. PIP

Polygonum aviculare

POLYGONACEAE | **knotweed**

Mar–Nov, to 4 in. tall, 6 ft. long. Sprawling to erect annual (rarely a perennial) forming mats in bottomlands, marshes, roadsides, pavement cracks, and other disturbed areas. Native to Europe. Stems sprawling or loosely ascending, ribbed, much-branched, smooth. Leaves short-petioled, with a silvery membranous sheath (ocrea) where petiole joins stem, lance-shaped to elliptical, ½–2½ in. long, bluish-green. Flowers in axillary clusters of 2–8, white to greenish or pink-tinged, less than ¼ in. wide, with 5 subequal, flattish tepals that are green in the center with broad white or pinkish margins. Fruit a tiny, dark brown achene enclosed in persistent tepals. AB

Polygonum erectum

POLYGONACEAE | **erect knotweed**

Jun–Oct, 8–30 in. Erect-ascending annual of alluvial fields, streambanks, sand and gravel bars, and open, disturbed areas. Stems freely branched, hard and ribbed, with somewhat swollen nodes. Leaves short-petioled, with a silvery membranous sheath (ocrea) where petiole joins stem, elliptical to lance-shaped, ½–3 in. long, firm, yellowish-green. Flowers in sessile to short-stalked, axillary clusters of 1–5; flowers greenish-white (pink in bud), less than ¼ in. wide, with 5 green, oblong tepals with bluntly rounded tips and yellow to whitish margins. Fruit a tiny, brown achene. JG

Polygonum tenue

POLYGONACEAE | **pleatleaf knotweed**

Jun–Oct, 4–16 in. Erect-ascending annual of thin-soiled rocky woodlands, barrens, outcrops, dry sandy fields, roadsides. Stems stiff, angled, branches ascending, with somewhat swollen nodes, green to brownish, smooth or slightly rough. Leaves short-petioled, with a green to brownish membranous sheath (ocrea) where petiole joins stem, linear or narrowly lance-shaped, sharp-tipped, with a longitudinal furrow to either side of the midvein. Flowers single or in pairs in upper, bractlike leaf axils and ocreae; each white with green or pink, less than ¼ in. long, with 5 green, oblong-oval tepals with broad white or pinkish margins. Fruit a tiny, dark brown or black achene. AMC

Saururus cernuus

SAURURACEAE | **lizard's-tail**

May–Sep, 1–4 ft. Emergent, rhizomatous aquatic perennial of swamps, overwash pools in stream floodplains, freshwater and brackish tidal marshes, semipermanently inundated rocky bars and shores, beaver ponds and ditches; usually where water ponds seasonally or periodically. Stems simple or forked, hairy (sometimes smooth below). Leaves long-petioled and with a striped sheath, oval to lance-shaped with notched base, to 6¾ in. long, smooth. Flowers densely arranged in a 2- to 14-in.-long, erect spike that nods at the tip, white, about ¼ in. long, lacking petals or sepals but with 3–7 stamens and 3–4 carpels, fragrant. Fruit a tiny, somewhat fleshy capsule. RTW

Sparganium americanum

TYPHACEAE | **American bur-reed**

May–Sep, 1–3 ft. Erect, grasslike aquatic perennial, often growing in large patches at edge of water in streams, marshes, ponds, and pools. Stems stout, branching, zigzagging especially in the flowering stalk, smooth. Leaves narrow and grasslike, to 3 ft. long, spongy-thick and smooth. Flowers in round heads scattered along terminal stalk and side stalks, ½–1 in. wide; male flowering heads on upper part of the stem are smaller and greenish-yellow; female flowering heads are larger and bristly with radiating, white pistils. Fruit in compact bristly balls with tiny, dull brown, slightly flattened and beaked seed pods. BAS

Pachysandra procumbens

BUXACEAE | **Allegheny-spurge**

Mar–Apr, 6–10 in. Erect, rhizomatous-spreading perennial forming dense carpets in moist, rich woods. Stems short, fleshy, purplish-red, crowded with leaves. Leaves alternate (sometimes appearing whorled), oval to round, to 3 in. long, toothed above middle, semi-evergreen, blue-green mottled with white, smooth. Flowers in a spike (2–4 in. long) resembling a bottlebrush at the top of a separate flowering stem; white male tubular flowers are at the top and dominating; coral-pink female tubular flowers are at the bottom. RTW

Croton glandulosus var. *septentrionalis*

EUPHORBIACEAE | **sand croton**

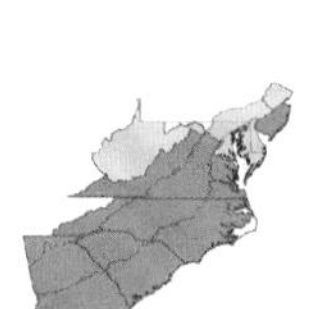

May–Oct, to 2 ft. Erect weedy annual of fields, roadsides, and other open, disturbed habitats. Species is widespread in tropical and subtropical U.S. Stems branched above, rough-hairy and glandular. Leaves petiolate, narrowly oblong to lance-shaped, to 3 in. long, coarsely toothed and with 1–2 large glands near the junction of petiole and blade. Flowers in separate male and female clusters at stem ends and from upper leaf axils, whitish; male flowers in short, dense spikes and with 4 sepals, 4 petals, and 7–9 stamens; female flowers in headlike clusters below male spikes and with 5 petals, 5 sepals, and 3 divided styles. Fruit an erect, 3-lobed capsule. SG

Alternanthera philoxeroides

AMARANTHACEAE | **alligator-weed**

Apr–Oct, 2–3 ft. Ascending to reclining aquatic perennial floating in dense mats on blackwater rivers, sloughs, ditches, ponds, and in very moist soil of ditches and shorelines. Native to the Neotropics. Stems stout, mostly hollow, often red-tinged, hairy at the nodes (from which it will root). Leaves in pairs, each pair widely spaced and at 90° to the next, sessile, the leaf base forming a sheath around stem at the node, linear to elliptical, 2–4 in. long, entire or obscurely toothed, smooth. Flowers in compact heads on long stalks from upper leaf nodes, white to off-white, tiny, with 5 ¼-in.-long sepals. A serious weed of natural areas. RTW

Froelichia floridana

AMARANTHACEAE | **Florida cottonseed**

Jun–Oct, 1½–6 ft. Erect annual of sandhills, sandy fields, and sandy roadsides. Stems wiry, unbranched or sparingly branched, covered with tangled woolly hairs. Leaves sessile, elliptical to lance-shaped, to 8 in. long, white along the margins, silky-hairy on both surfaces. Flowers in an often leaning, terminal spike as well as in several lateral spikes, white, less than ¼ in. long, conical, with 5 tiny tepals and covered with tangled, white cottony hairs. Fruit a seed with a cottony covering. BAS

Euphorbia maculata

EUPHORBIACEAE | **milk-purslane**

Jan–Dec, 2–4 in. Mat-forming annual of roadsides, fields, gardens, pavement cracks, disturbed areas. Stems branched, prostrate to 2 ft. wide, red, hairy; leak milky sap when broken. Leaves sessile, oval to oblong, ½ in. long, with a central red splotch, sparsely hairy. Tiny floral cups, solitary or in small, short-stalked axillary clusters, hold male and female flowers; cup rim with 4 white to pink, semi-circular, wavy-edged appendages that bear a greenish-red, thickened basal gland; anthers yellow, nearly indistinct; the single female flower in cup's center consists of a clump of styles atop a rounded ovary on a short stalk. Fruit a stalked, hairy, 3-lobed capsule. BAS

Euphorbia nutans

EUPHORBIACEAE | **eyebane**

May–Oct, 8–36 in. Erect to ascending annual of agricultural fields, gardens, waste places. Stems branched, reddish; leak milky sap when broken. Leaves mostly sessile, narrowly oval with asymmetric base, ½–1½ in. long, finely toothed, with occasional red markings. Stems and leaves hairy when new, becoming smooth. Tiny floral cups, in small, terminal (a few axillary) clusters, hold male and female flowers; cup rim with 4 white to pink, semi-circular appendages that bear a greenish-red, thickened basal gland; anthers yellow, nearly indistinct; the single central female flower consists of a clump of styles atop a rounded short-stalked ovary. Fruit a smooth, 3-lobed capsule. BAS

Euphorbia polygonifolia

EUPHORBIACEAE | **northern sandmat**

May–Oct, 2–4 in. Sprawling, mat-forming annual of dunes, upper beaches, dune blowouts, overwashes; prefers open sands with little competition. Stems branched, prostrate-spreading (to 12 in. wide), pale red and smooth; leak milky sap when broken. Leaves short-petioled, narrowly oblong with slightly asymmetric base, ¼–¾ in. long, medium green above, pale green beneath, smooth. Tiny floral cups mostly solitary in leaf axils, each rimmed with 4 nectar glands and 4 barely perceptible white appendages; within the cup are male flowers, each with 1 anther, and a single central female flower with a 3-part style atop a rounded ovary. Fruit a stalked, smooth, 3-lobed capsule. BAS

Plantago aristata

PLANTAGINACEAE | **buckhorn plantain**

Apr–Nov, to 6 in. Annual/short-lived perennial of disturbed areas, especially dry, barren, exposed soil, such as clay soils denuded by bulldozing. Stem a flowering stalk arising from a basal rosette. Leaves basal, linear, to 8 in. long, with conspicuous parallel veins and smooth or hairy. Flowers crowded in a slender, hairy spike at top of scape and among long, linear bracts; each flower whitish-green, less than ¼ in. wide, with 4 papery-translucent petals and 4 tiny green sepals. Introduced from farther west, though may be native in at least portions of our area. BAS

Plantago lanceolata

PLANTAGINACEAE | **English plantain**

Apr–Nov, 6–24 in. Erect perennial from a dense basal rosette, found in lawns, fields, roadsides, clearings, and other open, disturbed areas. Native to Eurasia. Stems 1 or more hairy, leafless flowering scapes. Leaves basal, narrowly elliptical or lance-shaped, 4–10 in. long, with 3–5 parallel veins, smooth to sparsely hairy. Flowers in a dense, conical spike ¾–2 in. long, at top of each scape; each flower white, less than ¼ in. wide, with a tiny corolla with 4 spreading lobes, 4 sepals, some papery bracts and, the most conspicuous feature, strongly protruding stamens. BAS

Plantago major

PLANTAGINACEAE | **common plantain**

May–Nov, 2–20 in. Erect perennial/annual of fields, lawns, roadsides, and other open, disturbed areas. Native to Europe, possibly ne NoAm. Stems 1–several from a 5- to 12-in.-wide basal rosette; smooth to finely hairy. Leaves on petioles that are green and rough-hairy at least at the base, oval, 2–5 in. long, with 5 parallel veins, smooth or sparsely hairy above, sometimes hairy on veins beneath. Flowers densely packed in a narrowly cylindrical spike occupying the upper 2/3 of each leafless scape; each greenish-white, tiny, with a papery corolla with 4 spreading, lance-shaped lobes, 4 keeled sepals, a pistil with a single white style, 4 stamens, and a green bract. KB

Plantago rugelii

PLANTAGINACEAE | **American plantain**

May–Nov, 6–10 in. Erect perennial of fields, lawns, roadsides, and other open, disturbed areas. Stems 1–several leafless, smooth flowering scapes arising from a low basal rosette. Leaves basal, on a thick petiole that is often purple-tinged at the base, oval, to 7½ in. long, with 5–9 parallel veins and wavy margins, smooth or sparsely rough-hairy. Flowers densely packed in a narrowly cylindrical spike occupying the upper 2/3 of each scape; each greenish-white, tiny, with a papery corolla with 4 lobes, 4 keeled sepals, a pistil with a single white style, 4 stamens, and a green bract. Fruit a brown, elongated capsule. JG

Hydrastis canadensis

HYDRASTIDACEAE | **goldenseal**

Apr–May, 10–15 in. Erect, rhizomatous perennial of moist (rarely drier), very nutrient-rich forests over circumneutral soils; often over calcareous or mafic rocks; can form large colonies after logging or other canopy disturbance. Stem a single, hairy flowering stalk. Leaves usually 1 large (petiolate) basal and 2 smaller (sessile), 1¼–4 in. wide, round; palmately divided into 3–9 toothed lobes, wrinkled. Flower solitary (or 2) on a stalk at top of stem, greenish-white, lacking petals, with a cluster of green ovaries surrounded by many white stamens. Fruit an inedible scarlet-red berry. Best known for the medicinal properties of its distinctive yellow rhizomes. AMC

Actaea pachypoda

RANUNCULACEAE | **doll's-eyes**

Mar–May, 1–2½ ft. Erect perennial found in heavy shade of rich, moist cove forests and bottomland forests. Stems simple and smooth. Leaves 2–3, each 2 times divided into 3 leaflets; leaflets to 2 in. long, variable in shape and lobing, with acute tips and coarsely toothed margins, smooth. Flowers in a compact raceme (to 3 in. long) on a smooth stem above leaves, each flower on a stalk that thickens and becomes red in fruit; flowers white, to ½ in. wide, with an ovary with stout style and numerous, prominent white stamens (plus several indistinct petals). Fruit a round, white berry with black center spot (suggesting dolls' eyes) on a coral-red stalk. RTW, WS

Actaea podocarpa *(Cimicifuga americana)*

RANUNCULACEAE | **late black-cohosh**

Jul–Sep, 3–5 ft. Erect perennial of rich cove forests and slopes, at mid to high elevations. Stems simple, usually smooth. Leaves petiolate, 2–3 times divided into 3 leaflets and then pinnately divided into toothed segments. Flowers in terminal, bottlebrush-like, branched racemes (to 20 in. long); creamy white, about ½ in. wide, with numerous white stamens and 3–8 stalked carpels. Fruit a flattened, stalked follicle. AMC

Actaea racemosa *(Cimicifuga racemosa)*

RANUNCULACEAE | **common black-cohosh**

May–Aug, 3–8 ft. Erect, rhizomatous perennial found in clearings in rich woods, usually on base-rich soils. Stems simple, smooth. Leaves petiolate, large and horizontal, 2–3 times ternately divided into 20–70 sharply pointed and coarsely toothed leaflets. Flowers in a tapering, erect spike, to 1 ft. long, on a tall, leafless, sometimes branched stalk held above foliage; white, to ½ in. wide, with 5 sepals that drop early, numerous bushy white stamens, and a single style. Flowers open in succession upward, so raceme remains in bloom for 2 weeks or more. Fruit an oval, firm-walled follicle. WS

Thalictrum clavatum

RANUNCULACEAE | **lady-rue**

May–Jul, 6–24 in. Erect perennial found in seepages and moist forests, on waterfall spray cliffs and brook banks. Stems slender, smooth. Leaves basal and alternate, twice divided into 3; the ultimate leaflets are oval to round, ½–1½ in. wide, lobed at the tip, blue-green above and white beneath. Flowers in an open, spreading panicle; each flower white, about ⅓ in. wide, pompom-shaped, lacking petals but with many flattened, white stamens and 5 diminutive to absent white sepals. Fruit a small, round head of 3–8 sickle-shaped achenes. JF

Thalictrum pubescens

RANUNCULACEAE | **common tall meadowrue**

May–Jul, 4–5 ft. Erect perennial of floodplain forests, alluvial and tidal swamps, streambanks, seeps, bogs, fens, wet meadows. Stems smooth to finely hairy. Leaves twice divided into round to oblong leaflets (¾–1½ in. long) usually with 2–5 lobes or teeth, finely hairy beneath. Flowers in a compound, round-topped panicle, male and female flowers on separate plants, though some perfect flowers may be present. Flowers erect, white to purplish, ¼ in. wide, with 4 tiny sepals, no petals; female flowers with multiple green to pinkish ovaries bearing straight or curved styles, male flowers with many bushy, white stamens. Fruit a small head of brownish-black, furry achenes. BAS

Thalictrum revolutum

RANUNCULACEAE | **skunk meadowrue**

May–Aug, 4–5 ft. Erect perennial of dry or barely moist forests, rocky woodlands, barrens, and outcrops on mafic or calcareous substrates; also in ultramafic woodlands, calcareous fens, and shell-marl ravines. Stems with a woody base, smooth. Leaves petiolate to sessile (upper), divided into 3 and then pinnately divided, the leaflets oblong to oval, mostly with 3 lobes, waxy upper surface and dotted with short-stalked glands beneath; skunklike odor when crushed. Flowers nodding in a large, loose panicle, mostly unisexual, with 4–5 tiny sepals (no petals); males with many white, bushy, drooping stamens, females with many green, erect ovaries bearing white, hooked stigmas. BAS

Trautvetteria caroliniensis

RANUNCULACEAE | **tassel-rue**

May–Aug, 1½–4 ft. Erect, rhizomatous perennial found along streambanks and in seepages, grassy balds, moist forests, and swamp forests (rarely in calcareous longleaf pine savanna ecotones). Stems branched, mostly smooth, erect. Leaves basal and alternate, petiolate, kidney-shaped, to 14 in. long and wide, palmately lobed into 5–11 sharply toothed segments (reduced and sessile upward). Flowers in a flat- to round-topped, short-branched terminal cluster, white to greenish, ½–1 in. wide, with 4 (sometimes 3 or 5) petal-like sepals and numerous long, white stamens clustered around a bright green, compound ovary. Fruit a cluster of plump, curve-beaked, fleshy seeds. WS

Aruncus dioicus

ROSACEAE | **eastern goat's-beard**

May–Jun, 3–6 ft. Erect perennial found in moist, nutrient-rich forests and woodland borders. Stems several from a root crown, arching upward. Leaves petiolate, to 20 in. long, 2–3 times divided into many long-pointed, sharply toothed, oval-lance-shaped leaflets. Flowers in an erect panicle (sometimes flopping over) with many spikelike branches, female and male flowers on separate plants; female flowers with 5 tiny, greenish-white petals and 3–4 pistils; male flowers with 5 tiny white petals and 15–20 stamens. Fruit a strongly curved, dry, tiny pod. WS

Sanguisorba canadensis

ROSACEAE | **Canada burnet**

Jun–Sep, 2–6 ft. Erect to ascending perennial of fens, seeps, seepage swamps, spray zones around waterfalls, other seepage wetlands, and wet meadows, usually over mafic/ultramafic or calcareous rocks. Stems simple or branched, mostly smooth. Leaves on petioles with coarsely toothed stipules, to 18 in. long, pinnately divided into 7–17 coarsely toothed, narrowly oblong leaflets (1–2½ in. long), often with a red rachis. Flowers densely packed in long-stalked, cylindrical terminal spikes (2–8 in. long), lower flowers blooming first; flowers white, each with a tiny calyx with 4 spreading lobes (no petals), 4 conspicuous stamens with long filaments, and a pistil. AMC

Astilbe biternata

SAXIFRAGACEAE | **Appalachian astilbe**

May–Jun, 3–6 ft. Coarse, erect perennial of moist cove forests, seepage slopes, and boulderfield forests. Stems several from a stout rhizome, somewhat glandular-hairy above. Leaves petiolate, 2 times ternately divided, with terminal leaflet 3-parted; leaflets heart-shaped to oval, long-tipped, sharply toothed, glandular-hairy on petioles and veins beneath. Flowers arranged in a pyramid-shaped, branching inflorescence held above leaves; male and female flowers on the same plant, with tiny white to yellowish white petals (petals mostly lacking in female flowers). Fruit a 2-sectioned capsule. RTW

Aralia nudicaulis

ARALIACEAE | **wild sarsaparilla**

May–Jul, 1–1½ ft. Erect perennial of upland forests and woodlands, usually in rocky and rather dry places, such as ridgetop forests. Stems underground and sending up a single leaf stalk and single flowering stalk, both of which may be red-tinged. Leaves 1(2), long-petioled, divided into 3 with each division pinnately divided into 3–5 oval to elliptical leaflets that are 2–5 in. long, finely toothed, and smooth. Flowers in 3 rounded umbels at end of stalk (may be hidden beneath leaf), greenish-white, less than ¼ in. wide, with 5 incurved petals, insignificant sepals, 5 protruding stamens, and a pistil with 5 styles. Fruit a round, dark blue berry. AMC

Burmannia capitata

BURMANNIACEAE | **white burmannia**

Jul–Nov, 1¼–6 in. Erect annual of pine savannas, bogs, and shores of Coastal Plain depression ponds. Stems very slender and threadlike, unbranched. Leaves tiny and scalelike, about ¼ in. long. Flowers 1–20 in a dense, headlike cluster at top of stem, creamy white (sometimes tinged yellow or green), about ¼ in. long, tubular with 6 lobes, the outer 3 triangular and usually curved inward. Can be found on seepage slopes with *B. biflora* and various pitcherplants, sundews, and orchids. FG

Baptisia perfoliata

FABACEAE | **catbells**

Apr–May, 1–3 ft. Erect to spreading perennial found in sandhills, river dunes, and longleaf pine woodlands. Stems branching, yellowish-green, with a white-waxy coating, smooth. Leaves sessile and seemingly pierced by the stem (perfoliate), oval to nearly round, 2–4 in. long, smooth. Flowers borne singly in leaf axils, yellow, 1/2 in. long, with typical pea-flower shape. Fruit a sturdy, round, inflated pod with short beak at the tip; green, drying to silvery-brown. JG

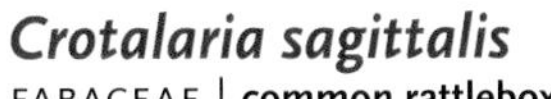

Crotalaria sagittalis

FABACEAE | **common rattlebox**

Jun–Aug, 6–15 in. Ascending to erect annual of dry woodlands, woodland edges, openings, and fields. Stems simple to bushy-branched, very hairy. Leaves on short petioles with a winged, double-tipped stipule at the base, elliptical to lance-shaped, 1–2½ in. long, hairy. Flowers in stalked racemes of 1–4, emerging opposite some upper leaves, yellow, 1/4–1/2 in. long, with typical pea-flower shape, including a large banner petal composed of 2 united petals. Fruit an inflated pod with pointy tip; when shaken, seeds rattle inside. JG

Crotalaria spectabilis

FABACEAE | **showy rattlebox**

Jul–Sep, 1½–6 ft. Erect annual of fields, roadsides, and disturbed areas. Native to s Asia. Stems coarse, ribbed, green or purplish, covered with stiff, sharp hairs. Leaves sessile and with lance-shaped stipules, oblong-oval (widest at the tip), 2–6 in. long, generally smooth above and densely hairy below. Flowers in terminal and axillary racemes, yellow, large (1 in. wide), with typical pea-flower shape; the calyx is tubular, and there are 2 persistent bracts at the base of the flower. Fruit a smooth, cylindrical pod. BAS

Rhynchosia reniformis

FABACEAE | **dollarweed**

Jun–Sep, 1–3 ft. Erect to ascending perennial of sandhills, dry woodlands, and sandy roadsides of the Coastal Plain. Stems unbranched, hairy. Leaves usually fewer than 6, alternate, long-petioled, round or kidney-shaped, 1–2 in. long, leathery with conspicuous netted veins and minute resinous dots. Flowers in short axillary and terminal racemes, yellow, about ½ in. long, with typical pea-flower shape, including an erect banner petal and calyx lobes about equal to the petals in length. Fruit a hairy, short, compressed pod. BAS

Cypripedium parviflorum

ORCHIDACEAE | **small yellow lady's-slipper**

Apr–Jun, 6–20 in. Erect perennial of rich, moist forests. Stem unbranched, with just a few leaves, densely hairy. Leaves 3–5, sessile and sheathing at the base, oval to lance-shaped, 2–7 in. long (reduced to bracts near flower), with prominent parallel veins, hairy. Flowers 1–2 at curved top of stem; yellow; ¾–2 in. long; with a pouchlike lower lip petal (the yellow "slipper"), 4 twisted greenish-yellow side tepals that are variously streaked with reddish-purple, and a single erect, broader tepal at the top, also greenish-yellow streaked with reddish-purple. Fruit a ribbed, elliptical capsule. RTW

Epidendrum conopseum *(E. magnoliae)*

ORCHIDACEAE | **green-fly orchid**

Jul–Oct, 2–11 in. Epiphytic perennial often found in large colonies, usually on relatively horizontal limbs of trees in blackwater river swamps and moist hardwood hammocks; rarely in crevices of Altamaha grit outcrops. Stems tufted, unbranched, smooth. Leaves 2–3, near end of stem, narrowly elliptical, 1–3 in. long, fleshy. Flowers 3–18 in a loose terminal raceme, pale green to bronze, about ¾ in. wide, with spreading, oblong-oval sepals and petals and a protruding, elongated, greenish-yellow reproductive column fused with a 3-lobed lip petal; strongly fragrant at night. FG

Platanthera integra (*Habenaria integra*)

ORCHIDACEAE | **yellow fringeless orchid**

Jul–Sep, 8–25 in. Erect perennial found in savannas in the Coastal Plain and bogs in the Mountains and Piedmont. Stems unbranched, smooth. Leaves (1–3) sessile with sheathing base, ascending-spreading, lance-oblong to lance-linear, to 12 in. long (reduced to bracts above), smooth. Flowers in a dense, cylindric-conical terminal raceme, golden yellow to pale orange, consisting of 2 petals and a sepal forming a curved hood, 2 winglike lateral sepals, a long lip petal that is either entire or wavy-margined, and a slender, tapering spur. Fruit an elliptical capsule. JF

Linaria vulgaris

PLANTAGINACEAE | **butter-and-eggs**

May–Nov, 1–2 ft. Erect, colonial perennial of fields, pastures, roadsides, and other open, disturbed areas. Native to Europe. Stems simple or with a few erect branches, smooth to sparingly hairy. Leaves crowded, alternate (lower leaves appearing whorled), linear, 1–2½ in. long, bluish-gray-green. Flowers in a dense terminal spike that elongates with time, yellow, ¾–1¼ in. long, tubular, with 2 elaborate lips and an elongated nectar spur that hangs downward; the upper lip is divided into 2 lobes that are folded upward, and the lower lip consists of 2 lobes that fold downward plus an orange-yellow "palate" that obstructs the opening to the throat of the corolla. AMC

Polygala cymosa

POLYGALACEAE | **tall pinebarren milkwort**

Apr–Aug, 1½–4 ft. Erect biennial of pond-cypress savannas, Coastal Plain depression ponds, clay-based Carolina bays, and other seasonally flooded habitats. Stems branched in inflorescence only, smooth. Leaves mostly basal, linear, to 5½ in. long; a few much smaller, alternate leaves on stem. Flowers in a flat-topped, terminal cluster, densely crowded toward tips of ascending branches, bright yellow, tiny, with 2 "wings" (sepals) and 3 joined petals forming a tiny tube with fringed tip. RTW

Polygala nana

POLYGALACEAE | **candyroot**

Feb–Jun (Oct), 4–6 in. Erect annual/biennial with prominent basal rosette, found in longleaf pine flatwoods, wet savannas and prairies, and other open, moist areas; often in patches of several plants. Stems usually branched from base, smooth. Leaves mostly basal, spoon-shaped, to 2 in. long, somewhat succulent and smooth; a few much smaller, alternate leaves on stem. Flowers densely packed into cylindrical terminal racemes, to 1½ in. long; flowers light yellow, about ½ in. wide, with 2 spreading "wings" (sepals) and 3 joined petals forming a tiny tube with fringed tip. Unlike most *Polygala* species, all the flowers bloom at the same time. Roots smell like wintergreen. AMC

Polygala ramosa

POLYGALACEAE | **short pinebarren milkwort**

Apr–Oct, 4–12 in. Erect annual/biennial of wet savannas, pocosin margins, streamhead ecotones, and bogs. Stems 1–several from crown, branched above, smooth. Basal leaves spoon-shaped, to 1½ in. long, often withering by second year; stem leaves alternate, linear, to ¾ in. long. Flowers on ascending branches of a flat-topped, branched terminal cluster; flowers bright yellow, less than ¼ in. long, with 2 spreading, elliptical "wings" with long-pointed tips (sepals) and 3 joined petals forming a tiny tube. Roots exude a spicy fragrance. RTW

Verbascum thapsus

SCROPHULARIACEAE | **common mullein**

Jun–Sep, 2–6 ft. Erect biennial of fields, roadsides, disturbed areas; sometimes weedy on rock outcrops; forms large basal rosette in first year. Native to Europe, established throughout NoAm. Stems unbranched, densely white-hairy. Leaves crowded, sessile with decurrent bases (suggesting wings on the stem), oval to oblong-lance-shaped, to 15 in. long (basal) but reduced up the stem, thick, entire to slightly toothed, densely hairy-woolly. Flowers in a dense, clublike terminal spike to 2 ft. long, yellow, ¾ in. wide, with 5 spreading, hairy, slightly unequal petals, 5 woolly sepals, and 5 hairy stamens with orange anthers. Fruit a rounded, downy capsule. BAS

Impatiens pallida

BALSAMINACEAE | **pale touch-me-not**

Jul–Sep, 2–6 ft. Erect to leaning annual of cove and other moist forests, streambanks, seepages, bogs, roadsides; can occur in dense stands. Stems succulent-watery, branched above, glossy and smooth. Leaves petiolate, oval, to 4 in. long, soft grayish-green with broadly toothed margins and a hairless, water-repellent surface. Flowers dangle on slender stalks from upper leaf axils; they are yellow (rarely creamy white), sometimes with reddish spots on the inside, 1–1½ in. long, cornucopia-like, with a backward-pointing spur and 2 lips, the lower larger and split into 2 lobes. Fruit a fleshy green capsule that bursts open, flinging turqouise-colored seeds. BAS

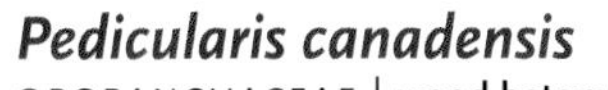

Pedicularis canadensis

OROBANCHACEAE | **wood betony**

Apr–May, 4–16 in. Low-growing perennial found in moist to dry forests and woodlands, and along streambanks. Stems very hairy and green, sometimes red-tinged; often forms small colonies. Basal leaves lance-shaped, to 6 in. long and 2 in. wide, lobed; stem leaves alternate, similar but smaller. Flowers in a dense spike to 2 in. long, which later elongates; yellow and purplish-red (occasionally all yellow or all red); tubular and split into 2 lips, the upper forming a slender hood that arches over the shorter lower lip. Fruit a lance-shaped capsule. Semi-parasitic. BAS

Viola hastata

VIOLACEAE | **spearleaf violet**

Mar–May, 3–12 in. Erect perennial of acid cove forests, dry to moist oak forests, and bluff forests. Stems unbranched and smooth. Leaves on petioles with variably shaped stipules, triangular with a long tip and flared at the base, 2–4 in. long, often with silvery blotches between the veins, smooth. Flowers solitary on slender stalks, bright yellow with purple veins and purple-tinged on the back, about ½ in. wide, with 5 unequal petals. Fruit an elliptical capsule. Closed, self-pollinating flowers often present. WS

Viola tripartita

VIOLACEAE | **three-part violet**

Mar–May, 5–15 in. Erect, rhizomatous perennial found on moist slopes and bottomlands, especially over mafic or calcareous rocks. Stems 1–2 from a single crown, hairy or smooth. Leaves on petioles with a pair of stipules at the base, diamond-shaped to triangular or oval, sometimes divided into 3 lance-shaped segments, with widely spaced teeth. Flowers on ascending stalks from leaf axils, bright yellow, to 3/4 in. wide, with 5 unequal petals; the 3 lowest petals have purplish-brown veins and the 2 lateral ones are bearded at the base. Fruit an elliptical capsule. Closed, self-pollinating flowers often present. RTW

Melampyrum lineare

OROBANCHACEAE | **cowwheat**

May–Jul, 4–16 in. Erect annual found on acidic, dry soils of woodlands and around rock outcrops. Stems finely branched and finely hairy. Leaves sessile or nearly so, linear to narrowly lance-shaped, to 2½ in. long and entire, though uppermost leaves often have teeth or lobes at the base. Flowers solitary in upper leaf axils but appearing paired, straw-colored, to ½ in. long, tubular and opening to 2 yellow lips, the lower slightly more prominent and 3-lobed. Fruit an oval capsule. Semi-parasitic on a variety of hosts. ER

Agastache nepetoides

LAMIACEAE | **yellow giant-hyssop**

Jul–Sep, 2–5 ft. Erect, rhizomatous perennial of woodlands and forests, generally over calcareous or mafic rocks. Stems distinctly 4-angled, sometimes branched above, mostly smooth. Leaves petiolate, oval or lance-oval, 1–5 in. long (reduced above), coarsely toothed, finely hairy beneath. Flowers densely packed, along with small green bracts, in terminal spikes to 4 in. long; flowers pale yellow, 3/8 in. long, the corolla tubular and divided into 2 lips: a nearly erect, 2-lobed upper lip and a 3-lobed lower lip (middle lobe largest). The green calyx also is tubular with 5 lobes; there are 4 long-protruding stamens. RTW

Collinsonia canadensis

LAMIACEAE | **northern horsebalm**

Jul–Sep, 2–3 ft. Erect to ascending perennial found in the understory of cove and other rich forests, especially over calcareous or mafic substrates. Ranges broadly over much of temperate e NoAm. Stems 4-angled, few-branched, mostly smooth. Leaves petiolate (upper ones nearly sessile), oval, 2–8 in. long, coarsely toothed, smooth. Flowers in a loose, wide-branching panicle, pale yellow, ½ in. long, tubular and 2-lipped (lower lip prominently fringed), with 2 long-protruding stamens and an elongated style. Plant gives off a lemony scent when bruised or crushed. LADI

Monarda punctata

LAMIACEAE | **eastern horse-mint**

Jul–Sep, 2–3 ft. Erect short-lived perennial of maritime forests, dry rocky or sandy woodlands, clearings, fields, and roadsides. Stems 4-angled, sparingly branched, brown to reddish-purple, with soft hairs beneath. Leaves petiolate, lance-shaped to narrowly elliptical, to 3½ in. long, with toothed margins and softly hairy. Flowers in 2–6 whorled clusters along upper reaches of stem, each whorl subtended by conspicuous whitish to pink-purple bracts. Flowers yellow, purple-spotted, to 1 in. long, tubular and split into 2 lips, the lower lip 3-lobed with a notched middle lobe, the upper longer than the stamens, strongly arched, and bearded at the tip. BAS

Aureolaria levigata

OROBANCHACEAE | **Appalachian oak-leech**

Aug–Sep, 1½–5 ft. Erect perennial of oak forests and woodlands, primarily in the Central/Southern Appalachians. Stems simple or with ascending branches above, smooth. Leaves opposite to subopposite, smooth, nearly sessile, 2–6 in. long, the lower ones narrowly lance-shaped to oval-lance and with toothed to entire margins (rarely lobed). Flowers on short, erect stalks in pairs on a terminal raceme; each flower rich yellow, about 1½ in. long, tubular, finely hairy within and with 5 spreading, rounded lobes. Fruit a smooth, oval capsule. Semi-parasitic on oaks. WS

Isotria medeoloides

ORCHIDACEAE | **small whorled pogonia**

May–Jun, 3–10 in. Erect perennial of acidic moist or dry to moist forests, in the Mountains and upper Piedmont usually with *Pinus strobus*. Stem unbranched, whitish-green with a powdery coating. Leaves in a whorl at top of stem where flowering stalk begins, elliptical to elliptic-oval, 1–2½ in. long, often drooping, light green. Flowers 1–2 on a stalk emerging from the center of the leaf whorl, with 3 green, spreading, linear-oblong sepals (½–1¼ in. long), 2 greenish-yellowish petals forming a hood, and a white, slightly downcurved lip petal with wavy-edged tip and greenish-yellow bumps (crests). Fruit a ribbed, elliptical capsule. JF

Isotria verticillata

ORCHIDACEAE | **large whorled pogonia**

Apr–Jul, 7–13 in. Erect perennial of acidic, moist-to-dry forests. Stem hollow, unbranched, purplish to reddish-brown, smooth. Leaves 5–6 in a whorl at top of stem where flowering stalk begins, oval to oblong-lance-shaped, to 3 in. long (enlarging as fruit develops). Flowers (1, rarely 2) on stalk emerging from center of leaf whorl, to 2 in. wide; each flower consists of 3 widely spreading, purplish-green, linear sepals (1⅓–2⅓ in. long), 2 greenish-yellow petals forming a small hood, and a yellowish to white, downcurved lip petal bearing a fleshy ridge in the middle and purple streaks on lateral lobes. Fruit an erect, ribbed, elliptical capsule. BAS

Pinguicula lutea

LENTIBULARIACEAE | **yellow butterwort**

Mar–May, to 10 in. Scapose, carnivorous perennial of Coastal Plain pine savannas and wet pine flatwoods, rarely extending inland to seepages and sandhill-pocosin ecotones in the fall-line Sandhills of SC. Stem a single, hairy flowering scape from 6-in.-wide basal leaf rosette. Leaves oval or oblong with curled-up margins, somewhat fleshy, yellowish-green and oily. Flowers held singly, terminally; each 1 in. wide, tubular, with 5 spreading, notched corolla lobes, a hairy lump at throat bottom, and a backward-pointing spur. Insects are trapped on the upper surface of leaves, which secrete a musty-smelling mucilage and digestive fluids. RTW

Viola rotundifolia

VIOLACEAE | **early yellow violet**

Mar–May, 3–6 in. Low-growing, rhizomatous perennial found in moist forests, particularly mountain coves. Stemless, with leaves and flower stalks arising from a rhizome. Leaves in a basal cluster and lying nearly flat on the ground, round to oval, 3/4–4 3/4 in. long, wavy-margined, slightly fleshy and glossy, with minute white hairs. Flowers several, each on a naked stalk, yellow to cream-yellow, 1/2–1 in. wide. Each flower with 5 unequal petals, the lowest largest and extending behind the flower in a spur, with purple veins on the lowest 3 petals, and the 2 lateral petals bearded at their base. Closed, self-pollinating flowers often present. WS

Baptisia cinerea

FABACEAE | **Carolina wild indigo**

Apr–Jun, 1–2 1/2 ft. Erect perennial of sandhills and other dry sandy woods, roadsides, and forest borders. A narrow endemic. Stems with a few wide-spreading branches, sometimes smooth but more often covered with close-pressed, gray hairs. Leaves petiolate, with conspicuous long, narrow stipules at the base; divided into 3 elliptical to oblong-oval leaflets, each 1 1/2–3 in. long and somewhat leathery. In fall, leaves do not drop but stay attached to the stems, the whole plant turning ashy gray. Flowers in (usually 1) terminal spike, bright yellow, 3/4–1 in. long, with typical pea-flower shape. Fruit a thick-walled, inflated, cylindrical pod. WS

Baptisia tinctoria

FABACEAE | **honesty-weed**

Apr–Aug, 2–3 ft. Erect, bushy perennial of sandhills, pine flatwoods, dry woodlands and woodland edges, ridges, roadsides. Stems bushy-branched, smooth to slightly hairy and with a bluish-white-waxy coating when young. Leaves short-petioled, divided into 3 oval (broader at tip and narrowing to base), often blue-green leaflets to 1 in. long and smooth. Flowers in open, few-flowered, terminal racemes; each flower yellow, 1/2 in. long, with typical pea-flower shape. Fruit a thin-walled, inflated, oval pod that turns black in winter. BAS

Chamaecrista fasciculata (*Cassia fasciculata*)

FABACEAE | **common partridge pea**

Jun–Sep, 6–22 in. Erect to sprawling annual with sensitive leaves, frequenting old fields, roadsides, and forest margins. Stems branched, light green to reddish-brown, smooth to minutely furry. Leaves petiolate, pinnately divided into 6–14 pairs of leaflets (each to 2/3 in. long) that react to touch by folding inward; there is a tiny, saucer-shaped gland on each petiole. Flowers on 1/2-in.-long stalks in small clusters from leaf axils, bright yellow, 1 in. wide, with 5 rounded to oblong-oval petals of unequal size bearing red markings at the base and 10 stamens. Fruit a flattened, brown seed pod. JED

Chamaecrista nictitans (*Cassia nictitans*)

FABACEAE | **common sensitive-plant**

Jun–Oct, 4–20 in. Erect to sprawling annual with sensitive leaves, growing in forests, woodlands, disturbed areas, pine savannas, and a wide variety of other habitats. Stems smooth or with close-pressed hairs. Leaves pinnately divided into 7–20 pairs of leaflets that react to touch by folding inward; there is a tiny, saucer- to umbrella-shaped gland on each petiole. Flowers solitary or in small clusters from leaf axils, on short stalks, less than 1/2 in. wide, with 5 bright yellow petals of unequal sizes and 5–8 stamens unequal and reddish. Fruit a flattened, brown seed pod. BAS

Crotalaria pallida

FABACEAE | **smooth rattlebox**

Jul–Sep, 3–5 ft. Erect annual/short-lived perennial of roadsides and fields. Native to Africa. Stems sometimes grooved, branched, pale green to reddish, hairy. Leaves on petioles with recurved, narrow stipules at the base; divided into 3 elliptical to oblong-oval leaflets, each 3/4–3 in. long (middle leaflet largest) and hairy above. Flowers on stalks in a terminal raceme, yellow with reddish-purple lines, with typical pea-flower shape, including a large erect banner petal. Fruit a hairy, cylindrical pod with a groove on 1 side and containing seeds that rattle when the pod is shaken. JG

Lotus corniculatus

FABACEAE | **birdsfoot-trefoil**

Jun–Sep, 1½–2 ft. Prostrate to erect perennial of fields, roadsides, and waste places. Native to Eurasia. Stems numerous and sprawling from a single root crown, somewhat branched, smooth to sparsely hairy. Leaves essentially sessile, pinnately divided into 5 oblong-lance-shaped leaflets, each to ¾ in. long, the lower 2 of which resemble stipules; smooth to somewhat hairy. Flowers in umbels of 3–12 on long stalks from upper leaf axils, yellow, ½ in. long, with typical pea-flower shape, including a pale green tubular calyx with long, narrow teeth. Fruit a cylindrical (sometimes flattened), linear pod. BAS

Rhynchosia difformis

FABACEAE | **twining snoutbean**

Jun–Aug, 3–6 ft. Mostly prostrate perennial that usually acts like a vine, trailing over the ground and other plants; found in sandhill woodlands and sandy clearings of the Coastal Plain. Stems angle-ribbed, furry with tawny hairs. Leaves on petioles with a pair of lance-shaped stipules, divided into 3 smooth to hairy, broadly oval to nearly round leaflets with conspicuous netted veins and inconspicuous resinous dots. Flowers in stalked racemes from leaf axils, yellow (sometimes with red or purple streaks), nearly ½ in. long, with typical pea-flower shape and a hairy, tubular calyx. Fruit a hairy, broad pod with hooked beak. BAS

Rhynchosia tomentosa

FABACEAE | **erect snoutbean**

Jun–Aug, 2–3 ft. Erect perennial of dry woodlands and forests, sandhills, and sandy clearings. Stems sometimes strongly angled, occasionally branched, very hairy. Leaves on petioles with a pair of linear-lance-shaped stipules, divided into 3 velvety-hairy, oval to elliptical leaflets, these to 2¾ in. long and with conspicuous, netted veins. Flowers in short terminal and axillary racemes, yellow, about ⅓ in. long, with typical pea-flower shape, including an erect banner petal and a hairy calyx tube nearly as long as the corolla. Fruit a hairy, compressed pod with blunt or short-beaked tip. RTW

Senna hebecarpa

FABACEAE | **northern wild senna**

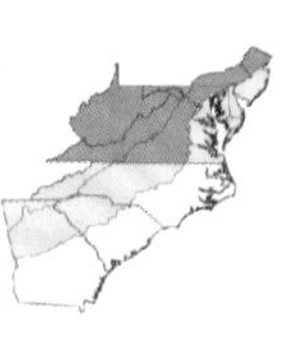

Jul–Aug, 1½–6 ft. Erect perennial of moist forests, meadows, riverbanks, open floodplain forests, and other open, wet habitats. Stems stout, mostly unbranched, slightly hairy above. Leaves petiolate, pinnately divided into 5–10 pairs of gray-green, oblong to elliptic-oblong leaflets, each to 2½ in. long. On the upper side of each petiole, near its base, is a small club-shaped, nectar-secreting gland. Flowers in terminal and upper axillary racemes or panicles, each ¾ in. wide, with 5 unequal yellow petals (aging to white), 5 sepals, 10 stamens with dark brown anthers, and a pistil with spreading white hairs. Fruit a hairy, dark brown (when mature), linear, segmented pod. RTW

Senna obtusifolia

FABACEAE | **coffeeweed**

Jul–Sep, 1–2½ ft. Erect, bushy annual of fields (especially soybean), roadsides, disturbed areas. Probably native to the Neotropics. Stems branched, often ridged; lower part often sprawling. Leaves petiolate, pinnately divided into 2–4 pairs of oblong-oval leaflets with bluntly rounded tips, each to 1½ in. long (terminal pair largest), smooth, pale beneath; slightly rank odor. Close to the lowest pair of leaflets is a small brown spikelike nectar gland. Flowers single or in pairs, nodding on stalks from upper leaf axils; each 1 in. wide, with 5 rounded and usually unequal petals, 5 light green folded sepals, and 10 stamens. Fruit a curved, slender, 4-sided pod. RTW

Stylosanthes biflora

FABACEAE | **pencil-flower**

Jun–Aug, 4–20 in. Erect to sprawling perennial of sandhills, dry to moist pine savannas and flatwoods, dry forests, woodlands, woodland borders, glades, barrens, and rock outcrops. Stems branched from the base, sometimes prostrate, usually covered with long, stiff, reddish hairs. Leaves on petioles with stipules that sheath the stem, divided into 3 elliptical to lance-shaped leaflets, each ½–1½ in. long with a sharp tip and usually very hairy. Flowers in terminal and axillary clusters of 2–6, yellow, about ⅓ in. long, with typical pea-flower shape, including an erect banner petal that is often streaked with red. Fruit a hairy, sessile, oval pod with 2 segments. WS

Zornia bracteata

FABACEAE | **viperina**

Jun–Aug, 8–22 in. long. Reclining, carpet-forming perennial of flatwoods, sandhills, and sandy roadsides. Stems mostly prostrate, much-branched, smooth. Leaves on long petioles with a pair of lobed stipules at the base, palmately divided into 4 lance-linear leaflets that are mostly smooth and spine-tipped. Flowers in erect, terminal spikes of 3–10 flowers, each subtended and partially covered by a pair of striate, oval bracts. Flowers yellow, less than ½ in. long, with typical pea-flower shape, including a large, erect banner petal that is red-streaked. Fruit a bristly, jointed pod with a beaked tip. BAS

Medicago lupulina

FABACEAE | **black medick**

Mar–Dec, to 2½ ft. Erect to reclining annual of agricultural fields, roadsides, and other open, disturbed areas. Native to Europe. Stems sprawling, 4-angled, branched and usually hairy. Leaves on petioles with a pair of oval to lance-shaped stipules, divided into 3 finely toothed, oval leaflets about ½ in. long; the center leaflet is stalked. Flowers in rounded heads about ¼ in. long, on stalks arising from leaf axils, yellow, less than ¼ in. long when fully open, with typical pea-flower shape. Fruit a tiny, kidney-shaped pod that turns black. JWH

Melilotus officinalis

FABACEAE | **yellow sweetclover**

Apr–Oct, 2–7 ft. Erect to leaning-sprawling biennial of fields, roadsides and other open, disturbed habitats. Native to Eurasia. Stems often lax, furrowed and angular (sometimes with red ribs in lower parts), branched, smooth to somewhat hairy. Leaves on petioles with a pair of lance-shaped stipules, divided into 3 oblong-oval leaflets, each about ⅓ in. long and toothed in the upper half. Flowers in long (to 6 in.) racemes on stalks from middle and upper leaf axils, often on only 1 side of the stalk; each flower yellow, to ⅓ in. long, angled downward, with typical pea-flower shape. Fruit a small, beaked, flattened pod. SG

Trifolium aureum

FABACEAE | **large hop clover**

May–Aug, 6–14 in. Erect to spreading annual/biennial of fields, roadsides, and disturbed areas. Native to Eurasia. Stems simple to much-branched, covered with flattened hairs. Leaves on petioles with stipules of about equal length, divided into 3 oblong-lance-shaped leaflets, each ½–¾ in. long and finely toothed (except near the base). Flowers densely packed into cylindric-oval clusters ½–¾ in. long; each flower yellow turning creamy and then rust-brown, tiny, with typical pea-flower shape. JG

Trifolium campestre

FABACEAE | **hop clover**

Apr–Oct, 2–12 in. Erect to sprawling annual of roadsides, fields, lawns, and disturbed areas. Native to Eurasia. Stems branched, hairy. Leaves on petioles with a pair of stipules at the base, pinnately divided into 3 oval leaflets, each about ½ in. long, finely toothed and smooth; the center leaflet is on a longer stalk. Flowers densely packed into short-cylindrical clusters about ½ in. wide, borne on hairy stalks from leaf axils; each flower yellow, tiny, with typical pea-flower shape, the banner petal with conspicuous grooves or veins. Fruit a tiny, 1-seeded pod. RTW

Trifolium dubium

FABACEAE | **little hop clover**

Apr–Oct, 2–8 in. Erect annual of roadsides, fields, lawns, and disturbed areas. Native to Eurasia. Stems simple to much-branched and hairy to smooth. Leaves on petioles with a pair of stipules, pinnately divided into 3 oblong-oval leaflets, each nearly ½ in. long, notched at the tip, on short to no stalklets, finely toothed and mostly smooth. Flowers densely packed into short-cylindrical clusters no more than ⅓ in. wide and borne on stalks from leaf axils; each flower is yellow, with typical pea-flower shape, the banner petal with a lengthwise fold. Fruit a 1-seeded pod. BAS

Corydalis flavula

FUMARIACEAE | **yellow fumewort**

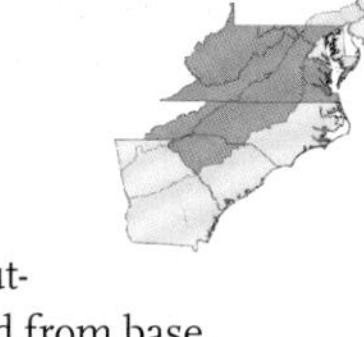

Mar–May, 4–12 in. Erect to reclining annual of rich moist forests, especially alluvial forests, as well as glades and outcrops over mafic rocks. Stems branched from base, reddish-green with a waxy coating. Leaves to 2 in. long, pinnately divided into 5–7 segments, which are further subdivided or lobed, the lobes minutely pointed at the tip; leaves pale green to bluish-green and smooth. Flowers in a short terminal raceme, clear yellow, ½ in. long, tubular and opening to 4 unequal lobes, the upper lobe with a toothed crest and backward-pointing spur. Fruit a slender, cylindrical capsule containing numerous shiny-black seeds. RTW

Aureolaria flava

OROBANCHACEAE | **smooth oak-leech**

Aug–Sep, 2–5 ft. Erect perennial found in oak forests and woodlands. Stems smooth, often purplish and unbranched or with several stiff, ascending branches above. Leaves opposite to subopposite, with a petiole-like tapered base, elliptic-lance-shaped to oval-lance, 2–6 in. long, at least lower ones deeply and irregularly divided, whitish beneath and smooth or finely hairy. Flowers on stout, ascending stalks in pairs along a terminal raceme, yellow, 1¼–1¾ in. long, tubular, smooth on the outside and densely furry within, with 5 spreading, broadly rounded lobes that are shorter than the tube. Fruit a smooth, oval capsule. Semi-parasitic on members of the white oak group. AWF

Aureolaria pectinata

OROBANCHACEAE | **southern oak-leech**

May–Sep, 1–3 ft. Erect to ascending annual found in turkey oak–dominated sandhills and other dry oak forests and woodlands. Stems bushy-branched. Basal leaves (on young plants) elliptical to lance-shaped, entire; stem leaves opposite, lance-shaped, to 2½ in. long, pinnately divided into 10 or 12 narrow, toothed segments. Flowers in a terminal raceme, bright yellow (sometimes red-tinged), about 1½ in. long, tubular, with 5 spreading, rounded lobes; 5 distinctive sepals are pinnately lobed. Fruit an oval capsule. Entire plant is glandular-hairy, sticky to the touch, and turns blackish in autumn. Semi-parasitic on oaks. WS

Aureolaria pedicularia

OROBANCHACEAE | **annual oak-leech**

Sep–Oct, 1–4 ft. Erect annual found in oak forests and woodlands. Stems much-branched, covered with glandular hairs, at least in lower portions. Leaves sessile to short-petioled, lance-shaped, 1–3 in. long, pinnately divided into many toothed or lobed segments, finely sticky-hairy. Flowers on ascending stalks in upper leaf axils (essentially a raceme), canary-yellow, about 1 in. long, tubular, finely hairy on the outside, marked with red on the inside and divided into 5 spreading, rounded lobes. Fruit a hairy, oval capsule. Semi-parasitic on oaks and heaths. BAS

Aureolaria virginica

OROBANCHACEAE | **downy oak-leech**

May–Jul, 1–5 ft. Tall, ascending perennial found in oak forests and woodlands. Stems unbranched or a few ascending branches above, downy (not glandular), often leaning on other plants. Leaves oval to lance-shaped, to 4¾ in. long with pointy tips, furry on both surfaces; lower leaves with a few large lobes but upper leaves entire or nearly so. Flowers on short stalks in pairs in a terminal raceme, canary-yellow, 1½ in. long, tubular, the corolla opening to 5 rounded lobes. Fruit an oval, rusty-pubescent capsule. Semi-parasitic on members of the white oak group. BAS

Seymeria cassioides

OROBANCHACEAE | **senna seymeria**

Aug–Oct, 2–3 ft. Erect annual of dry to moist pinelands, wet pine savannas, sandhills and other dry woodlands. Stems bushy-branched, smooth or finely hairy. Leaves short-petioled to sessile, to ¾ in. long, pinnately divided into many needlelike segments, pale green, often red-tinged. Flowers in leafy terminal racemes, pale yellow, ⅓ in. wide, with a short corolla tube with 5 spreading, unequal lobes (usually with a red basal triangle on the 3 lower lobes and a red basal splotch on the upper lobes), a 5-lobed bell-shaped-tubular calyx, and 4 protruding stamens. Buds and outside of petals lack hairs. Fruit an urn- or pear-shaped capsule. Parasitic on roots of pines. RTW

Seymeria pectinata

OROBANCHACEAE | **comb seymeria**

Jul–Oct, 1½–2 ft. Erect annual of dry pinelands and sandhills. Stems bushy-branched and covered with long hairs. Leaves short-petioled to sessile, to ¾ in. long, pinnately divided into many lance-shaped segments, light green and sometimes red-tinged. Flowers in leafy terminal racemes, pale yellow, about ⅓ in. wide, with a short corolla tube with 5 spreading, longer but unequal, very hairy lobes, a bell-shaped-tubular calyx with 5 linear-oblong lobes, and 4 protruding stamens with hairy filaments. Parasitic on roots of pines. KB

Utricularia subulata

LENTIBULARIACEAE | **slender bladderwort**

Mar–Jul or later, 1–8 in. Erect, carnivorous perennial of moist sands or peats in various kinds of acidic wetlands, including wet pine savannas and flatwoods, shores of dolines, borrow pits, and ditches. Stems underground with bladderlike traps on branchlets, sending up naked, wiry, often zigzagging flowering scapes. Leaves slender, sometimes divided into a few small segments, bladderless. Flowers 1–several per scape with a single bract at the base of each flower stalk, attached near its center; each flower yellow, about ⅓ in. long, tubular, with a smaller upper lip and a short, blunt, inconspicuous spur that is held close to the enlarged, 3-lobed lower lip. BAS

Lachnanthes caroliniana

HAEMODORACEAE | **redroot**

Jun–Sep, 1–3 ft. Erect perennial of wet savannas, pocosin edges, shores of Coastal Plain depression ponds and similar ponds in the mountains of VA, ditches, and other wet, disturbed places. Stems unbranched, hairy near top. Leaves mostly basal and overlapping, linear and pointed, parallel-veined, 18 in. long, ¾ in. wide; a few shorter, alternate, clasping leaves on stem. Flowers in a terminal, generally flat-topped cluster, each ⅓ in. long, with 3 erect petals (pale yellow on the inner surface, silvery-green and woolly on the outer), 3 less conspicuous sepals, 3 protruding stamens, and a style. Fruit a reddish, rounded capsule enclosed in persistent, furry tepals. BAS

Trillium luteum

TRILLIACEAE | **yellow toadshade**

Mar–Apr, 4–12 in. Erect perennial of moist cove forests over mafic or calcareous rocks; locally abundant in the vicinity of the Great Smoky Mountains. Stems stout, unbranched, green tinged with reddish-purple, smooth. Leaves 3 in a whorl at top of stem, sessile, triangular to oval, 2½–5 in. long, with dark and light green mottling, smooth. Flower solitary and sessile at top of stem in center of leaf whorl, yellow, with 3 erect narrow petals, 3 erect to spreading narrow green sepals, 6 erect yellow anthers, and a greenish-white ovary; may have a faint lemony scent. Fruit a maroon-red, 3-celled, fleshy capsule resembling a berry. WS

Xyris caroliniana

XYRIDACEAE | **pineland yellow-eyed grass**

Jun–Jul, 8–36 in. Scapose perennial from a clump of linear leaves, found in moist savannas and scrub oak sandhills. Stem minutely ridged or 2-ribbed, twisted. Leaves basal, to 20 in. long, spirally twisted and overlapping at the base, the outer ones short, scalelike and reddish-brown. Flowers in a short, conelike spike at top of stem, each bud concealed in a single yellowish to light brown (with green center), scalelike bract. Typically, a single yellow or white, 3-petaled flower opens at a time, usually in afternoon. GPF

Xyris torta

XYRIDACEAE | **mountain yellow-eyed grass**

Jun–Aug, 6–36 in. Scapose perennial from a clump of linear leaves, found in mountain bogs, marshes, ditches. Stem many-ribbed below, 2–4 ribs above, twisted, flexible, semi-flattened below flower spike. Leaves basal, ascending, less than ¼ in. wide, 8–20 in. long, spirally twisted, reddish-pink at base. Flowers in a short, terminal, conelike head composed of close-pressed, brown bracts; a single yellow flower, ¼ in. wide, emerges from each bract (only 1–2 flowers open at a time). Each flower has 3 ragged-tipped petals, 3 erect, yellow (fertile) stamens, and 3 hairy (sterile) stamens. Fruit a tiny, translucent, elliptical seed, 1 each held under the persistent bracts. AMC

Ludwigia alternifolia

ONAGRACEAE | **alternate-leaved seedbox**

May–Oct, 2–4 ft. Erect perennial of freshwater tidal marshes, ditches, and other open, wet places. Stems widely branched, red-tinged, smooth or hairy. Leaves tapering to a short (or no) petiole, lance-shaped, 2–4 in. long, smooth or hairy. Flowers solitary on short stalks from upper leaf axils, bright yellow, about 1/2 in. wide, with 4 rounded petals that soon drop, leaving 4 oval-triangular sepals nearly as long as the petals. Fruit a distinctive box-shaped capsule with a tiny pore at top; splits open when ripe, releasing numerous tiny seeds. BAS

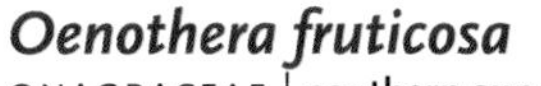

Oenothera fruticosa

ONAGRACEAE | **southern sundrops**

Apr–Aug, 1–2 ft. Erect perennial of dry forests and woodlands, glades, and rock outcrops. Stems simple or branched above, often tinged dark red, rough-hairy. Basal leaves form a rosette the first year and are oval to spoon-shaped; stem leaves are alternate, sessile or short-petioled, elliptical to lance-shaped, to 4 in. long. Flowers in compact, occasionally nodding clusters at tips of stems and solitary in axils of reduced leaves, lemon-yellow, about 2 in. wide, with 4 notch-tipped petals, 8 stamens, and a cross-shaped stigma. An elongated calyx tube consists of 4 spreading or reflexed sepals. Fruit a strongly 4-angled, club-shaped capsule. Flowers close at night. RTW

Oenothera biennis

ONAGRACEAE | **common evening-primrose**

Jun–Oct, 2–5 ft. Erect biennial/short-lived perennial found in fields, pastures, roadsides, and other disturbed areas. Stems unbranched, green to reddish-green, very leafy and furry-hairy. Basal leaves form a rosette the first year; second-year leaves alternate and mostly ascending on the stem, sessile to subsessile, lance-shaped, to 6 in. long, toothed or entire. Flowers arising from upper leaf axils, bright yellow, 1–2 1/2 in. wide, with 4 heart-shaped petals, an elongated calyx tube of 4 strongly reflexed sepals, 8 stamens, and a cross-shaped stigma. Fruit an ascending, lance-cylindrical capsule. Flowers open at dusk and are pollinated by sphinx moths. BAS

Oenothera humifusa

ONAGRACEAE | **seabeach evening-primrose**

May–Oct, 4–30 in. Trailing-leaning perennial found on coastal sand dunes. Stems simple or divergently branched from base, slightly woody at base and densely furry. Leaves sessile, oblong to oblong-lance-shaped or elliptical with sharp tips, to 3½ in. long, with some shallow teeth, gray-green and densely furry. Flowers sessile in upper leaf axils (these leaves reduced in size), bright yellow (becoming reddish with age), about 1 in. wide, with 4 notch-tipped petals, an elongated calyx tube with 4 reflexed and furry sepals, 8 stamens, and a cross-shaped stigma. Fruit a cylindrical, usually curved capsule. Flowers open in evening. BAS

Oenothera laciniata

ONAGRACEAE | **cutleaf evening-primrose**

Feb–Nov, 6–30 in. Erect to reclining annual/biennial found in fields, roadsides, and other dry, disturbed areas. Stems simple or branched near base, hairy. Leaves mostly sessile, elliptical to lance-shaped, to 4 in. long, irregularly toothed or lobed and hairy. Flowers borne singly on short stalks (or sessile) from upper leaf axils, pale yellow (becoming reddish with age), to 2 in. wide, with 4 heart-shaped petals, an elongated (to 1 in.) calyx tube with 4 reflexed sepals, 8 stamens, and a cross-shaped stigma. Fruit a linear-cylindrical, furry capsule that may be curved. Flowers bloom at night and are pollinated primarily by sphinx moths. BAS

Ludwigia decurrens

ONAGRACEAE | **wingstem water-primrose**

Jun–Oct, 1–7 ft. Erect annual/short-lived perennial found in swamp forests and ditches. Stems with 2 distinctive wings running between leaf nodes, often branched, smooth. Leaves mostly sessile, lance-shaped, to 7 in. long, thin and hairy or smooth. Flowers solitary in upper leaf axils of the slender branches, yellow, about ¾ in. wide, with 4 rounded, wavy-margined petals, 8 stamens, 4 triangular sepals visible between the petals, and an elongated ovary that is square in cross-section. Fruit a ribbed, reddish and hairy, narrowly cylindrical capsule with persistent sepals at the top. BAS

Rhexia lutea

MELASTOMATACEAE | **yellow meadow-beauty**

Apr–Jul, 4–18 in. Bushy, colonial perennial of wet pine flatwoods and savannas, seepage slopes, and bogs in the Coastal Plain. Stems 4-angled with subequal faces, branched, hairy. Leaves sessile, narrowly elliptical to lance-shaped, to 1¼ in. long, 3-veined, with toothed or entire margins, covered with stiff yellow hairs. Flowers on stalks from leaf axils, yellow, to 1 in. wide, with 4 broadly oval petals arising from a hairy, urn-shaped tube, and 8 stamens with straight yellow anthers. Fruit a ridged capsule enclosed in the urn-shaped tube. RTW

Galium verum

RUBIACEAE | **Our Lady's bedstraw**

May–Sep, 1–3 ft. Erect to ascending or sprawling, rhizomatous perennial of meadows, pastures, and roadsides. Native to Eurasia, Africa. Stems subtly 4-angled, branched in inflorescence, with a few short branches from nodes, and hairy. Leaves in whorls of 6–12, sessile, linear and sharp-tipped, to 1½ in. long, margins rolled downward, hairy. Flowers in a large, dense, pyramidal panicle, pale to golden yellow, less than ¼ in. wide, with 4 corolla lobes with pointed or blunt tips. SG

Barbarea verna

BRASSICACEAE | **early winter-cress**

Mar–Jun, 8–32 in. Biennial/perennial of fields and disturbed areas. Native to Eurasia. Stems branching from the base, mostly smooth. Basal leaves form a winter rosette and are up to 2½ in. long and deeply pinnately divided into 8–20 lobes; stem leaves alternate, also divided but smaller. Flowers in terminal and upper axillary racemes, yellow to pale yellow, composed of 4 tiny oblong-lance- to spoon-shaped petals forming a tube and spreading at their tips. Fruit a stalked, green, linear pod. SJB

Barbarea vulgaris

BRASSICACEAE | **common winter-cress**

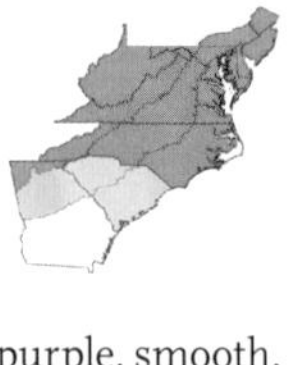

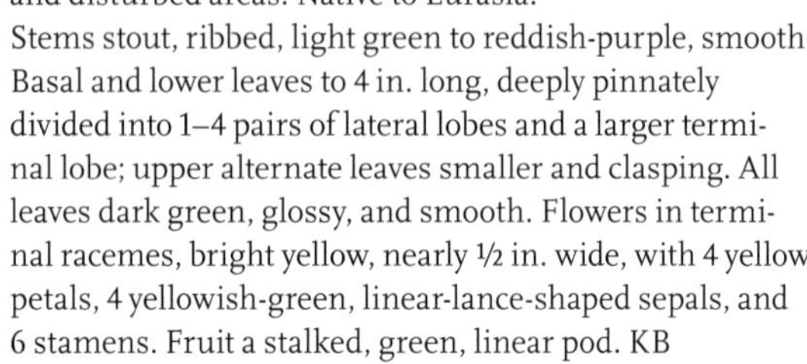

Apr–Jun, 1–2½ ft. Erect biennial/perennial from a basal rosette, found in fields and disturbed areas. Native to Eurasia. Stems stout, ribbed, light green to reddish-purple, smooth. Basal and lower leaves to 4 in. long, deeply pinnately divided into 1–4 pairs of lateral lobes and a larger terminal lobe; upper alternate leaves smaller and clasping. All leaves dark green, glossy, and smooth. Flowers in terminal racemes, bright yellow, nearly ½ in. wide, with 4 yellow petals, 4 yellowish-green, linear-lance-shaped sepals, and 6 stamens. Fruit a stalked, green, linear pod. KB

Brassica nigra

BRASSICACEAE | **black mustard**

May–Aug, 1½–6 ft. Erect annual of fields and disturbed areas. Native to Eurasia, widespread in NoAm. Stems branched, with scattered hairs below, smooth and white-waxy above. Leaves oblong-oval in outline, to 10 in. long, pinnately divided into pairs of toothed lateral lobes and a larger terminal lobe, often with short bristly hairs; upper leaves smaller and merely toothed or shallowly lobed. Flowers in narrow terminal racemes to 12 in. long (fruiting), yellow, about ⅓ in. wide, with 4 oblong-oval petals with blunt to rounded tips, 4 sepals (green, becoming yellow), several stamens, and a pistil. Fruit a thin, erect pod pressed close to the stem. KL

Brassica rapa

BRASSICACEAE | **field mustard**

Mar–Jun, 1–3 ft. Weedy annual of fields and disturbed areas. Native to Europe, naturalized in NoAm. Stems succulent, unbranched to branched above, mostly smooth, gray-green and white-waxy. Basal and lower leaves to 10 in. long, on winged petioles, pinnately divided into pairs of toothed lateral lobes and a larger terminal lobe; upper stem leaves smaller with clasping, ear-lobed bases. Flowers in erect-ascending terminal racemes that elongate as fruit matures, yellow, about ½ in. wide, with 4 rounded petals, 4 sepals, several stamens, and a pistil; blooming successively up the stem. Fruit a linear, ascending pod with narrowed tip. Cultivated as an oil crop and vegetable. RG

Raphanus raphanistrum

BRASSICACEAE | **jointed charlock**

Mar–Jun, 8–32 in. Erect annual of fields, roadsides, other disturbed areas. Native to Mediterranean Europe, found throughout NoAm, often as a cropland weed. Stems arise from a basal rosette, somewhat branched, usually very hairy. Basal leaves petiolate, oblong-elliptical, to 8 in. long, deeply lobed and divided, sparsely covered with bristly hairs; stem leaves few, alternate, similar to but smaller than basal leaves (some undivided). Flowers on ascending stalks in a terminal raceme, lower ones blooming first; each pale yellow, ½–¾ in. wide, with 4 spreading, prominently veined, broadly oblong-oval petals that eventually fade to white. Fruit a narrow, linear pod. BAS

Rorippa palustris

BRASSICACEAE | **marshcress**

May–Oct, 1–4 ft. Erect to ascending annual/biennial of marshes, bogs, and seeps. Stems 1–several from a basal rosette, stout, longitudinally ridged, branched, mostly smooth (may be hairy below). Leaves basal and alternate, petiolate (upper leaves winged to sessile), lance-shaped in outline but toothed to irregularly divided into a large terminal lobe and smaller lateral lobes, 2–8 in. long (reduced above), tinged with red, smooth. Flowers in terminal and upper axillary racemes, yellow, to ¼ in. wide, smooth, with 4 petals, 4 sepals, 6 stamens, and an ovary. Fruit a flattened, oval-linear pod. KB

Sisymbrium officinale

BRASSICACEAE | **hedge mustard**

May–Nov, 1–3 ft. Erect, weedy annual of fields, pastures, barnyards, and other disturbed areas. Native to Europe. Stems slightly hairy below, light green to purplish. Rosette of basal leaves forms first; these long-petioled, to 6 in. long, and pinnately lobed. Stem leaves alternate, short-petioled to sessile, roughly triangular, and smaller than basal leaves. Flowers on ascending stalks in slender terminal and upper axillary racemes, yellow, less than ¼ in. wide, with 4 yellow petals, 4 green to yellow sepals, a stout central style, and several stamens. Fruit a narrow, linear pod held close to the stem; pods form at bottom of racemes while upper flowers come into bloom. BAS

Chelidonium majus

PAPAVERACEAE | **greater-celandine**

Mar–Jul, 12–30 in. Erect to spreading biennial of moist slopes, shaded roadsides, rocky forests. Native to Eurasia. Stems ribbed, branched, covered with long white hairs (at least near base). Leaves basal and alternate, to 8 in. long, deeply divided into 3–9 bluntly toothed/lobed leaflets, blue-green to green. Flowers 3–8 in flattish umbels on upper stem, yellow, ¾ in. wide, with 4 broadly oval petals, a pair of narrow green sepals (these drop early), and numerous yellow stamens surrounding a stout green style, which elongates to rise above the stamens. Fruit an erect, slender, podlike capsule. Orange-yellow sap from broken stem and leaves can irritate skin and eyes. GPF

Stylophorum diphyllum

PAPAVERACEAE | **celandine-poppy**

Mar–Jun, 1–1½ ft. Erect, rhizomatous perennial of moist forests over calcareous rocks. Stems hairy, often white-waxy. Leaves basal and in a pair just below inflorescence, petiolate, broadly oblong to oval, to 6 in. long, pinnately divided almost to the midvein into 5–7 bluntly lobed/toothed segments, smooth above, silvery hairy beneath. Flowers 1–4 in a terminal umbel, 1¼–2¼ in. wide, with 4 overlapping round petals, 2 light green and very hairy sepals (these drop early), numerous golden yellow stamens, and an ovary with a single stout style and knobby stigma. Fruit a densely hairy, nodding, oval capsule. Stem and leaves exude yellow-orange sap when broken. AMC

Lithospermum canescens

BORAGINACEAE | **hoary puccoon**

Apr–May, 4–20 in. Densely furry, erect to leaning perennial found in dry woodlands and glades over calcareous or mafic rocks. Stems clumped and from a thickened taproot, simple or branched, densely leafy and hairy. Leaves sessile, the lower ones very short, the upper lance-shaped to narrowly oblong and up to 2 in. long by ½ in. wide, with a prominent central vein and densely hairy. Flowers bright yellow-orange in dense, sometimes coiled clusters at ends of upper branches, straightening as flowers open, each ½ in. wide, tubular, with 5 spreading, rounded lobes and 5 hairy, linear to lance-shaped, flattened sepals that are no more than ¼ in. long. Fruit a small, white nutlet. BAS

Lithospermum caroliniense

BORAGINACEAE | **Carolina puccoon**

Apr–Jun, 1–3 ft. Tufted, erect perennial found in sandhills and other sites with dry, sandy soils. Stems clumped, densely leafy, may be branched above, covered with scattered stiff hairs. Leaves ascending to spreading, linear-lance-shaped, to 2½ in. long, roughly hairy. Flowers in coiled, loose clusters terminating upper branches, these straightening as flowers open; each flower bright yellow-orange, about ¾ in. wide, the corolla tubular with 5 spreading, rounded lobes and the calyx hairy with 5 linear to lance-shaped and flattened sepals. Fruit a shiny, white nutlet. The stout, wooden taproot of this plant was once used as a source of dye. FG

Lithospermum virginianum

BORAGINACEAE | **Virginia marbleseed**

Apr–Sep, 8–32 in. Furry, erect perennial found in sandhill woodlands and shell middens in the outer Coastal Plain, and in woodlands and barrens over diabase and other mafic rocks in the Piedmont and low Mountains. Stems branched near top, covered with stiff, uni-directional hairs. Leaves sessile to short-petioled, oval to oblong, to 5 in. long, with 3 prominent veins, stiffly hairy. Flowers in coiled, leafy and hairy terminal spikes, which uncoil as flowers open; each flower pale yellow, about ⅓ in. long, tubular, with 5 ascending, pointed petals and a prominently protruding style. Calyx lobes also hairy. Fruit a tiny, faintly pitted, dull white nutlet. AH

Crocanthemum canadense (*Helianthemum canadense*)

CISTACEAE | **Canada sunrose**

Apr–Aug, 4–14 in. Erect perennial of fields, woodlands, forest edges, roadsides, and other disturbed areas. Stems unbranched or narrowly branched at flowering time, green or purplish-brown and slightly hairy. Leaves short-petioled to subsessile, narrowly oval, ¾–1½ in. long, densely hairy beneath, less hairy above. Flowers single (rarely 2) at stem tips, yellow, ¾–1¼ in. wide, with 5 petals and 10 or more orange-tipped stamens; later in the season, tight clusters of petal-less, self-pollinating flowers develop in leaf axils and at tips of branches. Fruit an oval capsule. BAS

Crocanthemum carolinianum (*Helianthemum carolinianum*)

CISTACEAE | **Carolina sunrose**

(Jan) Apr–May, to 1 ft. Erect perennial of fields, savannas, dry pine flatwoods, and scrubby woods. Stems arising from a basal rosette, branched from the base, very hairy. Basal leaves short-petioled, elliptical or spoon-shaped, to 2 in. long, hairy on both surfaces, often withered by flowering time; stem leaves alternate, similar to basal leaves but smaller. Flowers solitary at stem ends, yellow, about 1 in. wide, with 5 spreading, triangular petals that drop after one day, 6 hairy sepals (3 triangular, 3 linear), and many orange-tipped stamens. Fruit a round capsule. BAS

Crocanthemum propinquum

CISTACEAE | **creeping sunrose**

Jun–Jul, 4–12 in. Erect perennial of woodlands, rock outcrops, sandy barrens, fields. Stems multiple, wiry with short flattened hairs. Leaves petiolate, linear-spoon-shaped to oblong with narrow tapering base, ½–1¼ in. long, sparsely hairy above. Flowers long-stalked in terminal clusters of 2–6, yellow, ½ in. long, with 5 showy petals, 5 hairy sepals (2 narrow outer ones, 3 broader inner ones), and many orange-tipped stamens. Additional, self-pollinating flowers (pictured), produced Jul–Sep on erect branches, lack petals and are nearly sessile. Fruit an angular-oval capsule; capsules from self-pollinating flowers are smaller. GPF

Crocanthemum rosmarinifolium (*Helianthemum rosmarinifolium*)

CISTACEAE | **rosemary sunrose**

May–Jun, 8–18 in. Erect perennial of sandy roadsides and fields. Stems branched and covered with dense, short hairs that impart a pale gray-green cast. Leaves short-petioled, lance-shaped to broadly linear (almost needlelike), ⅝–1⅝ in. long, hairy above, woolly beneath. Flowers solitary or in small clusters, both terminal and axillary, pale yellow, about ¾ in. wide, with 5 triangular petals with wavy edges and 6 hairy sepals (2 different sizes). Many plants also (or only) produce later, self-pollinating flowers that lack petals. Fruit a smooth capsule. BAS

Linum floridanum

LINACEAE | **Florida yellow flax**

Jun–Oct, 1–2 ft. Erect perennial of longleaf pine savannas, flatwoods, and seepages. Stems 1–3, slender, branched above in inflorescence, smooth. Leaves alternate (lower ones may be opposite), numerous and overlapping, erect against the stem, linear, about ½ in. long. Flowers on short stalks from stiffly ascending branches, usually opening one at a time (per branch); each flower yellow, about 1 in. wide, with 5 oblong-oval petals with blunt, wavy-edged tips and 5 much shorter, lance-shaped sepals. Fruit a green, oval capsule with purplish tip. KB

Linum texanum

LINACEAE | **Texas yellow flax**

Jun–Oct, 8–28 in. Slender, erect perennial of dry open forests, woodlands, barrens, roadsides; sometimes in barren, periodically wet habitats. Stems 1–several in crowns, stiff, simple or branched (branches angled and spreading), whitish or pale green. Leaves alternate and opposite (lowermost), sessile, ascending to nearly erect, narrowly elliptical with pointed tip, to 1 in. long, stiff-firm, light green to bluish-green, smooth. Flowers in multiple elongated, terminal racemes; each flower yellow, about ⅓ in. wide, with 5 spreading oblong-oval petals, 5 light green to bluish-green and shorter sepals, 5 stamens, and a pistil. Fruit a tiny, nearly round capsule. BAS

Linum striatum

LINACEAE | **ridgestem yellow flax**

Jun–Oct, 1–4 ft. Erect perennial of bogs, seepages, streambanks, and other wet places, often growing in sphagnum. Stems several from a single crown, sometimes reclining at the base, narrowly ribbed, much branched. Leaves alternate above, opposite on lower half of stem (sometimes all opposite), sessile, ascending-erect, narrowly elliptical, to 1½ in. long, smooth. Flowers on stalks from nodes on the widely ascending, ribbed branches; each pale yellow, about ⅓ in. wide, with 5 spreading oval petals, and 5 smaller sepals. Fruit a tiny, round, slightly flattened capsule. JG

Linum virginianum

LINACEAE | **Virginia yellow flax**

Jun–Oct, 8–30 in. Erect to ascending perennial of dry forests, woodlands, clearings, and road banks. Stems 1–several from a crown, ribbed to slightly angled above, branched above in inflorescence. Leaves mostly alternate above and opposite below, sessile, erect and pressed close to stem, oblong-lance-shaped to narrowly elliptical, with a single prominent nerve leading to a tiny spine at the tip. Flowers on short stalks, scattered along and at ends of the ascending-spreading, thin branches; each pale yellow, 1/4–3/8 in. wide, with 5 oval petals with irregular margins and 5 smaller sepals. Fruit a small, rounded capsule. JG

Portulaca oleracea

PORTULACACEAE | **common purslane**

May–Nov, 3–6 in., to 2 ft. long. Succulent, mat-forming annual from a taproot, found in gardens, disturbed areas, and cracks in sidewalks. Apparently native to Asia, now cosmopolitan; evidence points to its pre-European presence in NoAm. Stems reddish-green, fleshy, smooth; runs across the ground, radiating from the center taproot. Leaves alternate or nearly opposite, spoon-shaped, 3/8–1 1/4 in. long, fleshy and smooth. Flowers sessile in leaf axils, yellow, about 1/4 in. wide, with 5 petals (sometimes 4 or 6); opening only in morning, withering later. Fruit a tiny, oval capsule. JG

Physalis walteri

SOLANACEAE | **dune ground-cherry**

May–Sep, 6–24 in. Spreading to prostrate or ascending perennial of seaside dunes, openings in maritime forests, sandhills (southward); rarely inland in disturbed areas. Stems several, unbranched or slightly branched. Leaves petiolate, oval to elliptical, 1–4 in. long; both leaves and stems covered with minute, star-shaped tufts of hairs. Flowers solitary and on stalks drooping from leaf axils, greenish-yellow with or without dark centers, 1/2–3/4 in. wide, funnel-shaped and with 5 flaring lobes, 5 fused hairy sepals, and 5 stamens with yellow anthers. Fruit a yellow or orange round berry enclosed by an expanded calyx, which matures to a papery husk. BAS

Abutilon theophrasti

MALVACEAE | **velvetleaf**

Jun–Oct, 2–4 ft. Coarse, erect annual of crop fields, roadsides, and other disturbed areas. Native to Asia, found throughout NoAm. Stems stout, branching, covered in velvety hairs. Leaves on stout petioles, heart-shaped to broadly oval with a long tip, 2–8 in. long, wavy-margined to obscurely toothed, velvety, and giving off a strong odor when crushed. Flowers solitary or in small, stalked axillary clusters; each flower yellow-orange, ½–1 in. wide, with 5 blunt-tipped petals that are united at the base, 5 furry triangular-oval calyx lobes, and multiple stamens clustered around the style. Fruit a stiff, capsule-like structure composed of a ring of flattened, beaked pods. TLJ

Sida elliottii

MALVACEAE | **Coastal Plain sida**

Jul–Oct, 1–3 ft. Erect to leaning perennial of sandy pine and pine-oak forests and clearings, sandy powerline rights-of-way; rarely in sandy alluvium. Stems tough to woody, branched, hairy. Leaves on petioles with conspicuous linear stipules, linear to narrowly oblong, ½–2 in. long, toothed, hairy above and smooth beneath. Flowers solitary or in small branching clusters arising from leaf axils, orange-yellow, 1 in. wide, with 5 widely oval-triangular petals with blunt to scalloped tips surrounding a central cluster of stamens (in 5 bundles) and styles. Fruit a ring of 7–10 joined podlike, 2-beaked, kidney-shaped segments surrounded by persistent, triangular calyx lobes. RTW

Sida rhombifolia

MALVACEAE | **arrowleaf sida**

Apr–Oct, 2–3 ft. Erect annual of roadsides, fields, gardens, and disturbed areas. Probably native to the Old World tropics, established in the se U.S. Stems tough-woody with stringy bark, branched, hairy. Leaves on short petioles with awn-shaped stipules at the base, elongate-diamond-shaped, to 3 in. long, toothed above the middle, densely hairy underneath. Flowers solitary on short stalks from leaf axils, yellow to cream-colored, about ¾ in. wide, with 5 asymmetric petals surrounding a central cluster of fused stamens and styles. Fruit a ring of 8–12 joined podlike, kidney-shaped segments, each with 1 beak, the ring surrounded by persistent, triangular calyx lobes. RTW

Sida spinosa

MALVACEAE | **prickly sida**

Jun–Nov, 1–3 ft. Erect annual of disturbed areas, especially wet fields. Native to the Neotropics and Paleotropics. Stems branched, covered with white hairs. Leaves on petioles with spinelike stipules at the base, oval-elliptical to lance-shaped, to 2 in. long, toothed, finely hairy beneath. Flowers single to several on short stalks arising from leaf axils, light yellow to orange-yellow, 1/3 in. wide, with 5 floppy, asymmetric petals and a fused column of 5 styles and numerous stamens. Fruit a ring of about 5 joined podlike, kidney-shaped segments, each with 2 beaks, the ring surrounded by persistent, triangular calyx lobes. RTW

Passiflora lutea

PASSIFLORACEAE | **eastern yellow passionflower**

May–Sep, to 15 ft. long. Herbaceous perennial vine of woodlands, forests, thickets. Stems trailing and climbing by tendrils, smooth to densely hairy. Leaves petiolate, 1–3 in. long, shallowly 3-lobed, often silver-gray-mottled, sparsely hairy beneath. Flowers 1–3 on axillary stalks, greenish-yellow, 1/2 in. wide, with 5 greenish, oblong sepals that are hairy on the outside, 5 slightly longer yellow-green petals, and a "crown" of green, threadlike segments (sometimes purple at the base) surrounding a central stalk supporting 5 stamens and a fleshy, green, 3-parted style. Fruit a green to black, oval or round berry. An excellent source of nectar for butterflies. RTW

Caltha palustris

RANUNCULACEAE | **cowslip**

Apr–Jun, 8–24 in. Mounded, somewhat succulent perennial found in bogs, wet meadows, seepage swamps, and on brook banks. Stems erect to reclining, hollow and fleshy, branched above, smooth. Leaves mostly basal, long-petioled, kidney-shaped and deeply notched at the base, 1–5 in. long, glossy, with toothed margins. Flowers in clusters of 1–3 at branch ends, rising above leaves, 1/2–1 1/2 in. wide, with 5–6 petal-like, bright yellow, glossy sepals surrounding a central cluster of bushy yellow stamens and a compound ovary. Fruit a cluster of flattened-oval follicles with tiny beaks. AMC

Ranunculus laxicaulis

RANUNCULACEAE | **Coastal Plain spearwort**

Mar–Sep, 6–20 in. Weakly erect to reclining annual of marshes, pond edges, swamps, and ditches. Stems slender, sometimes reclining and rooting at lower nodes, much branched, hairy becoming smooth. Leaves basal and alternate, petiolate, oval to oblong (basal) or linear-elliptical to lance-shaped (stem), to 2 in. long, entire or finely toothed. Flowers solitary on stalks from upper leaf axils, yellow, with 5 (sometimes more) clawed petals, 4–5 spreading (or reflexed) sepals that are shorter and rough-hairy on the outside, and a center of multiple yellow stamens around a green, compound ovary. Fruit a thimble-shaped cluster of tiny, oval achenes. JG

Ranunculus pusillus

RANUNCULACEAE | **low spearwort**

Apr–Jun, 4–20 in. Erect to ascending, colonial annual of marshes, ditches, depression pools, and other shallow seasonally flooded, muddy habitats. Stems weak, simple or loosely branched, smooth, sometimes with a white-waxy coating. Basal leaves petiolate (winged-clasping base), lance-oval, 1/3–1 in. long, entire; upper leaves alternate, short-petioled to sessile, linear to narrowly oblong, remotely toothed. Flowers in terminal and axillary racemes, pale yellow, less than 1/4 in. wide with 1–3 pale yellow petals, 5 slightly smaller yellowish-green sepals, and a central green, compound ovary ringed by a few stamens. Fruit a buttonlike clump of tiny, brown achenes. BAS

Geum radiatum

ROSACEAE | **cliff avens**

Jun–Aug, 8–20 in. Rhizomatous, federally endangered perennial of high-elevation summits, cliffs, and ledges (where not trampled), and open grassy balds. Stems mostly leafless and densely hairy flowering scapes. Leaves mostly basal, divided into a toothed, kidney-shaped terminal leaflet, 2 1/2–5 in. wide, and a pair of minor lateral leaflets, the petiole usually longer than the terminal leaflet. Flowers in a branching cluster, each on a short, glandular-hairy stalk, bright yellow, with 5 spreading, heart-shaped petals, 5 shorter lance-shaped sepals, and many stamens surrounding a cone-shaped compound ovary with elongated styles. Fruit a bristly, dome-shaped head of achenes. RTW

Physalis angulata

SOLANACEAE | **smooth ground-cherry**

Aug–Oct, 8–36 in. Erect-spreading annual of disturbed areas, open woodlands, and agricultural fields. Stems highly branched and usually smooth or with a few short hairs pressed against younger parts. Leaves petiolate, oval to lance-shaped, 1½–4 in. long, usually irregularly and coarsely toothed, smooth. Flowers solitary on stalks from leaf axils, yellow with slightly darkened center, about ½ in. wide, broadly funnel-shaped, with 5 triangular-tipped lobes and 5 fused, smooth to slightly hairy sepals; 5 stamens with bluish anthers are visible. Fruit a yellow, round berry enclosed by a 10-angled, purple-veined, expanded calyx, which matures to a papery husk. RWS, JS

Physalis heterophylla

SOLANACEAE | **clammy ground-cherry**

May–Sep, 8–35 in. Erect to reclining perennial of disturbed areas, dry rocky woodlands, and hammocks. Stems widely branched, covered with sticky-glandular hairs mixed with nonglandular hairs. Leaves petiolate, oval or triangular, 1–5 in. long, coarsely and irregularly toothed and densely hairy and sticky. Flowers solitary, drooping from leaf axils and divergent stems, yellow with brownish or purplish centers, funnel-shaped, with 5 very shallow lobes, 5 fused hairy sepals with triangular tips, and 5 stamens with yellow (rarely bluish) anthers. Fruit a yellow round berry loosely enclosed by a veined, expanded calyx, which matures to a papery husk. KJ

Physalis virginiana

SOLANACEAE | **Virginia ground-cherry**

Apr–Oct, 4–16 in. or taller. Erect perennial of dry woodlands, clearings and other disturbed areas. Stems sparsely branched and ascending, with long, soft hairs to shorter, stiff hairs. Leaves on winged petioles, oval to lance-shaped with a tapering base, 1–4 in. long, sparsely to abundantly short-hairy, with sparsely toothed, wavy, or entire margins. Flowers solitary and drooping on stalks from leaf axils, yellow with distinctly dark centers, ¾ in. wide, funnel-shaped, with 5 very shallow lobes, 5 fused hairy sepals, and 5 stamens, usually with yellow tips. Fruit an orange or red berry enclosed by a densely hairy, 5-angled expanded calyx, which matures to a papery husk. AMC

Asclepias obovata

APOCYNACEAE | **pineland milkweed**

Jun–Sep, 1–2½ ft. Erect perennial of sandy soils in pine and oak woods; occasionally in fields and on roadsides. Stem unbranched, furry; leaks milky sap when bruised. Leaves short-petioled to sessile, oval to elliptical, 1–3 in. long, thick, furry beneath. Flowers in dense clusters (1–1½ in. wide) on very short stalks from upper leaf axils, greenish-yellow, ½ in. long, with 5 strongly reflexed, pale green corolla lobes and a pink-tinged central crown surrounding the fused anthers and style. Fruit a follicle containing tufted seeds. AMC

Thyrsanthella difformis

APOCYNACEAE | **climbing dogbane**

May–Jul, to 20 ft. long. Herbaceous perennial vine of bottomlands, swamp and upland forests, marshes, woodlands. Stems slender, twining over other plants, reddish and smooth; lower portions woody. Leaves mostly sessile, narrowly lance-shaped to oval with a tapered point, 1½–3½ in. long (but widely variable in shape and size), smooth or hairy and deciduous. Flowers in stalked, branching clusters from leaf axils; each pale yellow with orange stripes in the throat, about ½ in. wide, with a short corolla tube that opens to 5 spreading, triangular-oval lobes. Fruit a drooping, slender green pod that twists as it dries, releasing tufted seeds. RTW

Hypericum canadense

HYPERICACEAE | **Canada St. John's-wort**

Jul–Sep, 4–24 in. Erect annual/perennial of bogs, seeps, fens, wet pine flatwoods and savannas, pond edges, and ditches. Stems slender, with ascending branches, smooth. Leaves sessile, linear or narrowly lance-shaped, to 1½ in. long, with 1–3 parallel veins on upper surface, smooth. Flowers in somewhat open, forked terminal cluster with linear bracts at the base; each flower yellow, to ¼ in. wide, with 5 spreading, oblong-lance-shaped petals, 5 linear to lance-shaped sepals at least as long as the petals and showing between them, and an erect bushy cluster of stamens and a pistil at the center. Fruit an erect, reddish, oval-conical capsule with persistent style. BAS

Hypericum denticulatum

HYPERICACEAE | **coppery St. John's-wort**

Jul–Sep, 8–24 in. Shrubby, erect-ascending perennial of savannas, wet pine flatwoods and adjacent ditches, borrow pits, blackwater stream shores. Stems often in clumps, slender, 4-angled, smooth, with glandular dots. Leaves sessile, ascending, linear to oblong-oval with rounded base, to 2 in. long, usually 1-veined, thick and firm, with translucent glandular dots on both surfaces. Flowers in an open or dense terminal cluster with narrowly lance-shaped bracts at the base; each flower coppery-yellow, ½ in. wide, with 5 oblong-oval petals, 5 shorter oval to lance-shaped sepals, and an erect bushy cluster of stamens and pistil at the center. Fruit a 1-celled, oval capsule. BAS

Hypericum drummondii

HYPERICACEAE | **Drummond's St. John's-wort**

Jul–Sep, 4–20 in. Erect, sometimes bushy annual of fields, dry clearings and woodlands, woodland borders, rock outcrops, barrens, and exposed, eroding sites. Stems rigid, with many ascending, wing-angled branches. Leaves sessile, linear to almost needlelike, to ¾ in. long, numerous and ascending, close but not pressed to stem. Flowers solitary in leaf axils on short stalks, scattered abundantly along leafy branches; each yellow, with 5 oblong-oval or asymmetrically-shaped petals (giving a pinwheel effect), 5 lance-shaped sepals (usually as long as or longer than petals), and an erect cluster of stamens and pistil in the center. Fruit an erect, reddish, oval capsule. BAS

Hypericum mutilum

HYPERICACEAE | **dwarf St. John's-wort**

Jun–Oct, 4–18 in. Erect, rhizomatous perennial of bogs, fens, marshes, shores, and other wet habitats. Stems reclining at the base; weak, slender, and diffusely branched above, the branches 4-angled. Leaves sessile with often clasping bases, oval to narrowly oblong with a bluntish tip, ½–1½ in. long, with 3–5 parallel veins and smooth. Flowers in loose, branching terminal clusters resting on a whorl of small leaflike bracts; each flower light orange-yellow, to ¼ in. wide, with 5 oblong petals, 5 narrower, pointed sepals of similar length, and an erect cluster of stamens and 3 styles in the center. Fruit a tiny, erect, oval capsule. BAS

Hypericum perforatum

HYPERICACEAE | **European St. John's-wort**

Jun–Sep, 1–2½ ft. Erect perennial from a woody base, found in fields, pastures, roadsides, woodland borders. Native to Europe. Stems tough, much-branched, with ridges leading from leaf bases, smooth. Leaves sessile with clasping bases, elliptical to linear-oblong, ¾–1½ in. long, with mostly translucent glandular dots (hand lens may be needed). Flowers many, in branching, sometimes flat-topped, leafy, terminal clusters; each flower bright yellow, ¾–1¼ in. wide, with 5 petals, which may have black spots along the margins, 5 shorter sepals, and an erect cluster of many bushy stamens and styles in the center. Fruit a brown or black, erect, oval capsule with a rough surface. RTW

Hypericum punctatum

HYPERICACEAE | **spotted St. John's-wort**

Jun–Sep, 1–2½ ft. Erect perennial with a somewhat woody base, found in wet to dry fields, woodlands, woodland borders and openings. Stems branched above, reddish and smooth but covered with tiny, black dots. Leaves sessile with clasping bases, oval or oblong, 1½–2½ in. long, blunt-tipped, with conspicuous black dots. Flowers at the ends of multiple short, ascending branches at top of plant; each bright yellow, ⅜–⅝ in. wide, with 5 petals that are conspicuously streaked and spotted with black, 5 shorter sepals, and an erect cluster of bushy stamens and styles in the center. Fruit a reddish, erect, oval capsule with 3 persistent styles. JG

Hypericum virgatum

HYPERICACEAE | **strict St. John's-wort**

Jun–Sep, 8–30 in. Erect perennial of alternately wet and dry hardpan forests and woodlands, rock outcrops, woodland borders, and clearings over mafic rock and glades. Stems slender, 4-angled, branched above. Leaves sessile, linear to lance-shaped with sharp tips, to 1¼ in. long, smooth, with tiny pitted dots beneath. Flowers in open, branching terminal cluster, with linear-lance-shaped bracts at the bottom; coppery-yellow, ⅓–½ in. wide, with 5 asymmetric petals, 5 narrower and shorter sepals, and an erect cluster of stamens and styles in the center. Fruit a reddish-green, erect, conical-oval capsule surrounded by persistent sepals and petals. BAS

Lysimachia ciliata

PRIMULACEAE | **fringed loosestrife**

May–Sep, 1–4 ft. Erect, rhizomatous perennial of moist forests, especially bottomlands and coves dominated by hardwoods. Stems slender or stout, usually branched, smooth or hairy only at nodes. Leaves short-petioled, oval to lance-shaped and rounded at the base, 1½–6 in. long, with a fringe of hairs on margins and on petiole. Flowers typically in whorls of 4 (may be solitary), nodding on long stalks from leaf axils; each flower yellow, to 1 in. wide, with 5 spreading, oval petals with red bases, sharply pointed tips, and lightly fringed margins. The 5 sepals have reddish veins. Fruit an oval capsule. AMC

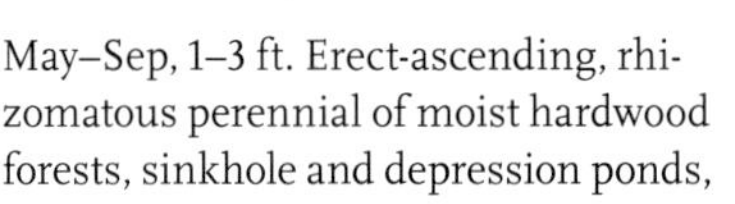

Lysimachia hybrida

PRIMULACEAE | **lowland loosestrife**

May–Sep, 1–3 ft. Erect-ascending, rhizomatous perennial of moist hardwood forests, sinkhole and depression ponds, wet meadows. Stems stout at the base, branched, smooth. Leaves opposite (rarely whorled), petiolate, lance-shaped and tapered at the base, 1–4 in. long; margins and lower petiole may be hairy. Flowers nodding on slender stalks arising from leaf axils, yellow, ½–1 in. wide, with 5 nearly round petals with ragged edges, narrowly pointed tips, and (often) reddish-brown splotches at the base, 5 shorter lance-shaped sepals, 5 stamens bearing brownish, crescent-shaped anthers, and a single, slender style. Fruit a rounded capsule. GPF

Lysimachia lanceolata

PRIMULACEAE | **lanceleaf loosestrife**

May–Aug, 1–2 ft. Erect-ascending, rhizomatous perennial found in moist to relatively dry forests, mafic or calcareous fens, bogs, forest edges, and road banks, primarily on circumneutral soils. Stems simple or with ascending branches, sometimes reclining and rooting at nodes. Leaves opposite (whorled near top), petiolate or sessile, linear to lance-shaped with tapering base, lighter green beneath when young; margins sometimes hairy. Flowers nod on slender stalks arising from upper leaf axils, 1–4 per axil; each flower yellow, about ¾ in. wide, with 5 spreading, round, ragged-edged petals with reddish bases, 5 lance-shaped sepals, and 5 yellowish-orange stamens. JF

Lysimachia nummularia

PRIMULACEAE | **creeping Jenny**

May–Aug, 2–4 in. to 2 ft. long. Prostrate, rhizomatous perennial found in lawns, pastures, seepages, and other moist, disturbed places. Native to Europe. Stems creeping, slender, often forming mats and rooting at nodes, smooth or with a few stalked glands. Leaves short-petioled, round, ½–1½ in. long, semi-evergreen, smooth and covered with tiny, red dots. Flowers on long stalks from leaf axils, usually 2 per axil, yellow, ¾–1¼ in. wide, with 5 ascending-spreading, oval petals finely speckled with red or black and 5 oval, pointed sepals with subtle keels. GPF

Lysimachia terrestris

PRIMULACEAE | **bog loosestrife**

May–Jul, 1–3 ft. Erect, rhizomatous perennial of bogs, wet meadows, swamp forests. Stems simple or loosely branched, smooth; cone-shaped. Leaves opposite to subopposite (rarely alternate), petioled to sessile, elliptical to lance-shaped, tapered at both ends, 1½–4 in. long, minutely black-dotted and smooth. Flowers held on ascending stalks in erect, crowded, terminal raceme 4–12 in. long; each ½–¾ in. wide, with 5 elliptic-oblong petals streaked/dotted with black and with 2 red basal patches, 5 oval to lance-shaped sepals, 5 stamens joined together at the base into a light green ring (glandular on the outside), and a green ovary with 1 style. Fruit a round to oval capsule. AMC

Lysimachia asperulifolia

PRIMULACEAE | **pocosin loosestrife**

May–Jun, 1–2½ ft. Erect, rhizomatous, federally endangered perennial of low and high pocosins, streamhead pocosins, savanna-pocosin ecotones, sandhill-pocosin ecotones; often forms colonies. Endemic to NC and SC. Stems slender, unbranched, smooth or with gland-tipped hairs in upper third. Leaves in whorls of 3(4), sessile, lance-shaped with sharp tip, to 1½ in. long, dark green, with margins slightly down-rolled and with gland-tipped hairs toward the base and along veins. Flowers produced mostly following fires, in a terminal raceme to 4 in. long; each yellow, ½ in. wide, with 5 spreading, lance-oval petals with pointy tips and gland-tipped hairs. JF

Lysimachia quadrifolia

PRIMULACEAE | **whorled loosestrife**

May–Aug, 1–3 ft. Erect, rhizomatous perennial of moist to very dry forests and openings, including pine savannas of the outer Coastal Plain. Stems stout to slender, rarely branched, hairy. Leaves in whorls of 4–5(2–7), sessile or short-petioled, elliptical to lance-shaped, 1½–4 in. long, with fringed-hairy margins and minute black dots on upper surface. Flowers nodding on slender stalks from leaf axils, 4–5 per node and held just above leaves; each yellow, ½ in. wide, with 5 pointed, oval petals streaked with black and red at the base, and slightly shorter, linear-lance-shaped sepals that are green with black dots/streaks. Fruit a round to oval capsule. BAS

Sarracenia flava

SARRACENIACEAE | **yellow pitcherplant**

Mar–Apr, 2–3 ft. Carnivorous perennial of wet pine savannas, seepage bogs, peat dome pocosins, peat-filled Carolina bays. Endemic to se U.S. Several leaves and a single flower stalk arise from underground stems. Leaves erect, yellowish-green pitchers (tubes that trap insects) with partially covered hooded opening; often streaked with red and with a narrow wing along length of pitcher. Long, flat, erect leaves (phyllodia) are produced in late summer. Flower solitary, nodding atop an erect stalk equal in height to pitchers, with 5 drooping yellow petals (2–3 in. long), 5 strongly curved triangular yellow sepals, and an umbrella-shaped structure in the center. WS, FG

Sarracenia minor

SARRACENIACEAE | **hooded pitcherplant**

(Jan) Mar–May, to 14 in. Carnivorous perennial of wet pine savannas, seepage slopes, bogs. Several leaves and a single flower stalk arise from underground stems. Leaves are erect, green pitchers (tubes that trap insects) tinged with red, embellished with white patches (opaque "windows") on upper parts and with a strongly curved hood, which covers the opening; a narrow wing runs along length of pitcher. Flower solitary, nodding from top of an erect stalk slightly shorter than pitchers; each with 5 drooping light yellow petals (1–2 in. long), 5 strongly curved triangular yellow sepals (sometimes reddening with age), and an umbrella-shaped structure in the center. RTW

Taenidia integerrima

APIACEAE | **yellow pimpernel**

Apr–May, 1–3 ft. Erect perennial of rocky, dry to dry-moist forests and woodlands over mafic or calcareous rocks. Stems slender, sparingly branched, dull green to reddish brown with whitish coating, smooth. Leaves on petioles with sheathing bases, 1–2 times ternately divided, the ultimate leaflets oval to oblong and about 1 in. long and smooth. Flowers in composite umbels 4–7 in. wide at ends of some branches, the 12–15 stalked umbellets widely spaced and containing about 12 flowers. Flowers yellow, tiny (less than ¼ in. wide), with 5 petals. Fruit a joined pair of oval, ridged seeds flattened on 1 side (pentagonal in cross-section). Has a light, celerylike odor. RTW

Oxalis dillenii

OXALIDACEAE | **southern yellow wood-sorrel**

Feb–Nov, 4–10 in. Tuft- or mat-forming perennial of roadsides, pastures, lawns, and a wide variety of other habitats. Stems erect to reclining, branched, with stiff hairs pressed against the stem. Leaves petiolate, divided into 3 cloverlike, heart-shaped leaflets about ½ in. wide each and often folded along the central vein (evenings and when cloudy); leaves smooth above with scattered hairs beneath. Flowers in umbels of 1–3, yellow, ½–1 in. wide, with 5 spreading oval petals, 5 sepals, and 10 stamens. Fruit an erect, cylindrical, 5-angled, pointed capsule, usually with short dense hairs that give it a grayish appearance. BAS

Oxalis grandis

OXALIDACEAE | **great yellow wood-sorrel**

May–Aug, 10–24 in., occasionally taller. Erect perennial of rich moist forests and rocky bluffs, often on calcareous substrates. Stems simple or sparingly branched, smooth or soft hairy. Leaves petiolate, divided into 3 cloverlike, heart-shaped leaflets, each ¾–2 in. wide and with a prominent fold along the midvein, usually with a narrow maroon line and tiny hairs on the margins. Flowers usually in clusters of 2–4, held above leaves; each flower yellow (may be red in the throat), about 1 in. wide, with 5 spreading, oblong petals, 5 sepals, and 10 stamens. Fruit a slender oval capsule, smooth or with spreading hairs. RTW

Oxalis stricta

OXALIDACEAE | **common yellow wood-sorrel**

Mar–Oct, 6–20 in. Erect-ascending (occasionally mat-forming) annual/short-lived perennial of disturbed areas, moist upland forests, floodplain forests. Stems simple or branched from base; with sparse to dense, spreading and often close-pressed hairs. Leaves petiolate (hairy), divided into 3 cloverlike, heart-shaped leaflets, each ½ in. long, often folded lengthwise along midvein; nearly smooth above, smooth to slightly hairy beneath. Flowers axillary in stalked, branching clusters of 3–15, as tall as or slightly above leaves; each ½ in. wide, with 5 spreading, oblong-lance-shaped petals, 5 sepals, and 10 stamens. Fruit an erect, 5-sided, sharp-tipped cylindrical capsule. WS

Foeniculum vulgare

APIACEAE | **fennel**

May–Aug, 3–5 ft. Erect-ascending perennial of fields, dredge spoil, old gardens, waste places, vacant lots, and roadsides. Native to Mediterranean Europe. Stems stout, branched, with a white-waxy coating, smooth. Leaves on petioles with sheathing bases, pinnately divided into numerous linear, almost threadlike segments and thus feathery-looking; leaves yellow-green and strongly anise-scented. Flowers in large, compound umbels at top of stem and from upper leaf axils; each flower yellow, less than ¼ in. wide, with 5 tiny, blunt petals. Fruit a joined pair of elliptic-oblong, highly ridged seeds. GPF

Pastinaca sativa

APIACEAE | **parsnip**

Jun–Jul, 3–5 ft. Erect, coarse perennial of fields and roadsides. Native to Europe. Stems stout, hollow, longitudinally ribbed, branched occasionally, smooth. Leaves on petioles with sheathing base, to 18 in. long (both leaves and petioles reduced above), 1–2 times pinnately divided into oval to elliptical leaflets, these to 3 in. long and toothed. Flowers in a flat-topped, compound umbel at top of stem and additional smaller umbels from upper leaf axils; each flower yellow, less than ¼ in. wide, with 5 initially incurved but eventually spreading petals and a prominent greenish-yellow nectar pad. Fruit a joined pair of elliptical, ridged seeds that are flat on 1 side. JG

Sanicula odorata

APIACEAE | **fragrant snakeroot**

May–Jun, 1–2½ ft. Erect perennial of rich, moist to semi-moist forests. Stems green, occasionally branched or pale reddish, smooth. Leaves basal; stem leaves alternate or opposite; lower leaves petiolate, to 5 in. long, palmately lobed/divided into 5 strongly toothed oblong to elliptical segments; middle and upper leaves smaller, mostly sessile, divided into 3 toothed leaflets. Flowers in spherical, ½-in-wide, terminal compound umbels of 3 perfect and several male flowers, all short-stalked, tiny, with 5 petals, 5 sepals, 5 exserted stamens, and a bristly ovary with a pair of long, curved styles. Fruit a round, burlike cluster of 2 bristly seeds. BAS

Thaspium barbinode

APIACEAE | **hairyjoint meadowparsnip**

Apr–May, 1–3½ ft. Erect perennial of moist forests. Stems slender, branched, hairy only at leaf nodes. Leaves alternate but mostly basal, on petioles with clasping, purple sheaths, to 12 in. long, ternately divided into 6 or 9 oval to linear segments that are toothed and hairy on the margins. Flowers in round-topped, compound umbels to 3 in. wide at ends of stem and branches and with 12–20 stalked umbellets. Each flower yellow to cream-colored, tiny, with 5 incurved petals, protruding stamens, and a divided protruding style. Fruit a joined pair of oval, winged seeds. RTW

Thaspium trifoliatum var. *aureum*

APIACEAE | **purple meadowparsnip**

Apr–May, 1–3 ft. Erect perennial of moist to dry upland forests and clearings. Stems occasionally branched, smooth. Basal leaves on petioles with a sheathing base, heart-shaped, 1–4 in. long and toothed; stem leaves alternate, also petiolate, ternately or pinnately divided into 3–5 leaflets that are oval to lance-shaped, toothed and smooth. Flowers in compound terminal umbels 1–3 in. wide, each with 6–12 stalked umbellets. Flowers yellow, tiny, with 5 petals, a short green to purplish-green calyx with 5 lobes, 5 stamens, and a 2-celled ovary with a pair of styles. Fruit a joined pair of elliptical, winged seeds. AMC

Zizia aptera

APIACEAE | **heartleaf golden-Alexanders**

Apr–May, 1–2½ ft. Erect perennial of moist forests, openings, and woodland edges. Stems slender, branched above, with longitudinal lines, smooth. Basal leaves petiolate, heart-shaped, 2–3 in. long, toothed, leathery and smooth; stem leaves alternate, reduced and gradually sessile upward, divided into 3 lobes or oval leaflets that are toothed. Flowers in compound umbels 2–3 in. wide, terminating the stem and branches, the 7–15 umbellets each having 10–20 flowers; each flower yellow, less than ¼ in. wide, with 5 incurved petals. Fruit a joined pair of ridged, oval seeds. RTW

Zizia aurea

APIACEAE | **common golden-Alexanders**

Apr–May, 1–2½ ft. Erect perennial of moist forests. Stems slender, branched above, with longitudinal lines, smooth. Leaves basal and alternate, petiolate (petioles shorter upward), pinnately divided into 3 or 5 lance-shaped to oval leaflets to 3 in. long each, the larger leaflets lobed and all margins toothed; shiny and smooth. Flowers in flat-topped, compound umbels 2–3 in. wide, terminating stem and branches and with around 12 umbellets each. Flowers stalked, except for the central one in each umbellet, bright yellow, less than ¼ in. wide, with 5 incurved petals, 5 protruding stamens, and a protruding, divided style. Fruit a joined pair of ridged, oval seeds. EO

Zizia trifoliata

APIACEAE | **mountain golden-Alexanders**

Apr–May, 1–3 ft. Erect perennial of moist forests, woodlands, woodland borders. Stems slender, with longitudinal lines, branched above, smooth. Leaves basal and alternate, petiolate (petioles reduced above), pinnately divided into 3–7 oval to lance-shaped leaflets (basal leaves usually with 3 leaflets), each leaflet to 2 in. long, coarsely serrate, leathery, shiny, smooth. Flowers in flat-topped compound umbels to 3 in. wide, at stem and branch ends, with 6–12 umbellets each, each with 4–12 flowers. Flowers golden yellow, less than ¼ in. wide, with 5 incurved petals, 5 protruding stamens, and a protruding, divided style. Fruit a joined pair of ridged, oval seeds. WS, RTW

Melothria pendula

CUCURBITACEAE | **creeping cucumber**

Jun–Nov, to 15 ft. long. Annual vine of bottomland forests, marshes, and moist roadsides and other disturbed areas. Stems slender, smooth, with coiled tendrils from leaf axils grabbing other vegetation. Leaves petiolate, round in outline but palmately 3- to 5-lobed, to 3 in. long and wide, rough-hairy. Male and female flowers separate, the female flowers solitary in leaf axils and male flowers smaller in few-flowered, long-stalked clusters. Flowers yellow, about 1/3 in. wide, with 5 shallowly notched corolla lobes. Fruit a speckled green or black, round to elliptical pod resembling a tiny watermelon. AMC

Ranunculus abortivus

RANUNCULACEAE | **kidneyleaf buttercup**

Feb–Jul, 1/2–2 ft. Erect annual/biennial of low fields, bottomlands, lawns, roadsides. Stems sometimes branched, smooth below. Basal leaves petiolate, heart- or kidney-shaped, 2 in. long, round-toothed; stem leaves alternate, mostly sessile, oblong-lance-shaped, irregularly divided or lobed, the lobes linear to spoon-shaped and entire to toothed; all leaves mostly smooth. Flowers terminal in groups of 1–3, about 1/4 in. wide, with 5 yellow, broadly lance-shaped to triangular petals, 5 larger green sepals, and a central cluster of green ovaries surrounded by a ring of stamens with bright yellow anthers. Fruit an oval cluster of tiny, flat, small-beaked achenes. RTW

Ranunculus acris

RANUNCULACEAE | **bitter buttercup**

May–Sep, 1–3 ft. Erect, rhizomatous perennial of pastures, fields, roadsides, and disturbed areas. Native to Europe. Stems hollow, with forking branches, hairy. Leaves mostly basal and low on the stem, alternate, petiolate, 3/4–2 in. long, deeply divided into 3–5 palmate lobes, which are further divided into smaller, narrow segments with sharp tips; upper leaves smaller and less divided. Flowers on branching stalks at top of plant, bright yellow, 3/4–1 1/4 in. wide, with 5 spreading, shiny, oval to round petals, 5 light green, spreading sepals, and a ring of yellow stamens surrounding a central cluster of light green pistils. Fruit a dense, round cluster of beaked achenes. JG

Ranunculus bulbosus

RANUNCULACEAE | **bulbous buttercup**

Apr–Jun, 8–24 in. Erect, clumped perennial of fields, pastures, lawns, roadsides, disturbed areas. Native to Europe. Stems from corm, bulbous at base, with forking branches, hairy. Basal leaves petiolate, 1–2 in. long, deeply divided into 3 further lobed/toothed segments (only the terminal segment stalked); stem leaves alternate, few, smaller, less divided. Flowers solitary on long stalks, 1–1¼ in. wide, with 5 yellowish-green, broadly lance-shaped, tightly reflexed sepals that are furry on the outside, 5–7 bright yellow, erect-spreading, oblong-oval petals, and a central cluster of ovaries surrounded by stamens. Fruit an oval cluster of tiny beaked achenes. RTW

Ranunculus septentrionalis

RANUNCULACEAE | **Carolina buttercup**

Mar–Aug, 4–6 in., or to 12 in. long. Erect to trailing perennial of swamps, swamp forests, wet woodlands, open marshy wetlands. Stems furry to spreading-hairy, prostrate after flowering. Leaves mostly basal, long-petioled, often reddish, divided into 3 oblong-oval to diamond-shaped leaflets cut into sharp-pointed lobes and teeth; terminal leaflet longer-stalked than the 2 laterals. Flowers solitary on ascending to erect stalks 2–5 in. long, bright yellow, ¾ in. wide, with 5–10 petals that are finely veined (nectar guides), 5 light green, reflexed sepals, numerous yellow stamens, and a central cluster of green pistils. Fruit a roundish cluster of flattened, beaked achenes. GPF

Ranunculus hispidus

RANUNCULACEAE | **hairy buttercup**

Mar–Jun, 1–2 ft. Erect to reclining, tufted perennial of rich moist forests, creek banks, semi-dry woodlands and forests, bottomlands. Stems weak, simple or branched, densely hairy. Leaves basal and alternate, petiolate, 1–5 in. long, nearly as wide, divided into 3 oval or diamond-shaped lobes/leaflets that are themselves further lobed or at least toothed. Flowers solitary on long, hairy, leafless stalks from upper leaf axils; each ¾–1¼ in. wide, with 5 oblong-oval bright yellow petals, 5 shorter yellowish to light green spreading sepals, and a center of many yellow stamens plus a green, compound ovary. Fruit an oblong cluster of teardrop-shaped, beaked achenes. RTW

Ranunculus parviflorus

RANUNCULACEAE | **smallflower buttercup**

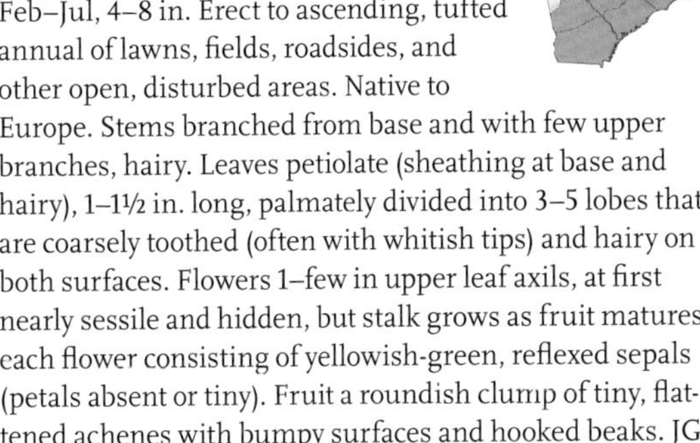

Feb–Jul, 4–8 in. Erect to ascending, tufted annual of lawns, fields, roadsides, and other open, disturbed areas. Native to Europe. Stems branched from base and with few upper branches, hairy. Leaves petiolate (sheathing at base and hairy), 1–1½ in. long, palmately divided into 3–5 lobes that are coarsely toothed (often with whitish tips) and hairy on both surfaces. Flowers 1–few in upper leaf axils, at first nearly sessile and hidden, but stalk grows as fruit matures; each flower consisting of yellowish-green, reflexed sepals (petals absent or tiny). Fruit a roundish clump of tiny, flattened achenes with bumpy surfaces and hooked beaks. JG

Ranunculus recurvatus

RANUNCULACEAE | **hooked buttercup**

Apr–Jul, 6–24 in. Erect to ascending perennial of cove and bottomland forests, moist slope forests, swamps. Stems 1–3, flexible, hairy. Leaves basal and alternate, petiolate, kidney-shaped to broadly oval, 4½ in. long and wide, divided into 3 toothed or further lobed, diamond-shaped to oval segments; upper surface dull with deeply etched veins, lower shiny, margins long-hairy. Flowers in stalked clusters of 2–5 from upper leaf axils, each ¼–½ in. wide, with 5 tiny, narrowly oblong, glossy yellow petals, 5 longer, whitish-green, hairy, recurved petals, and a central green, compound ovary ringed with stamens. Fruit a rounded cluster of flattened achenes with hook-beaked tips. RTW

Ranunculus sceleratus

RANUNCULACEAE | **cursed buttercup**

Apr–Sep, 4–20 in. Erect, succulent annual/short-lived perennial of marshes, ditches, stream margins. Stems hollow, freely branched, smooth. Basal and lower (alternate) leaves long-petioled, kidney-shaped, to 3 in. long and wide, 3- to 5-lobed with rounded teeth; upper leaves smaller, usually divided into 3 oblong segments. Flowers solitary, terminal and from upper leaf axils on furry stalks, each ¼ in. wide, with 3–5 shiny yellow, spreading, oblong petals, 3–5 yellow-green sepals (later recurving), and a green, compound ovary surrounded by a ring of yellow stamens. Fruit an elliptical to cylindrical cluster of tiny, yellowish achenes. JH

Agrimonia parviflora

ROSACEAE | **southern agrimony**

Jul–Sep, 2½–6 ft. Erect perennial of marshes, bottomland forests, wet pastures. Stems stout, unbranched, very hairy, glistening with tiny glands. Leaves on petioles with fan-shaped stipules; each to 18 in. long, pinnately divided into 7–19 lance-shaped, toothed leaflets that alternate on the rachis with much smaller, hairy leaflets that are copiously gland-dotted beneath. Flowers in a terminal spike (may be 1–2 shorter racemes in upper leaf axils), each less than ¼ in. wide, with 5 spreading, oblong-oval petals, a cup-shaped structure (ovary fused with calyx), and a central tuft of 5–7 stamens. Fruit a ridged, top-shaped achene bearing hooked bristles. KB

Agrimonia pubescens

ROSACEAE | **downy agrimony**

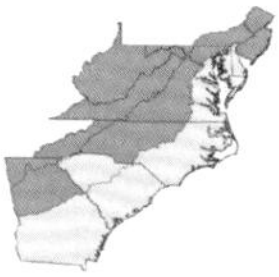

Jul–Sep, 1–4 ft. Erect perennial of semi-moist forests and woodlands, often in base-rich soils. Stems stout, hairy, solitary or few-branched. Leaves on petioles with lance-shaped stipules; pinnately divided into 5–13, toothed, lance-shaped to elliptical leaflets, rough or sparsely hairy above, velvety-hairy beneath, each 2–3 in. long, interspersed with pairs of much smaller leaflets. Flowers spaced along a hairy, terminal spike (may be 1–2 shorter racemes in upper leaf axils), each ¼ in. wide, with 5 spreading, oblong petals, a cup-shaped structure (ovary fused with calyx), and about 10 central stamens. Fruit a ridged, top-shaped achene with hooked bristles. SJB

Agrimonia rostellata

ROSACEAE | **woodland agrimony**

Jul–Aug, 1–2½ ft. Erect-ascending perennial of moist to wet forests and woodlands, often in base-rich soils. Stems 1–several, branched, sparsely hairy. Leaves pinnately divided into 3–9 (usually 5) toothed, oblong-oval leaflets, smooth to sparsely hairy above, gland-dotted beneath, with a pair of much smaller leaflets between each pair of major leaflets; terminal leaflet largest. Flowers spaced along a stalked-glandular, terminal spike (may be 1–2 shorter racemes in upper leaf axils), each ¼ in. wide, with 5 spreading petals, an ovary fused with calyx, and 10–15 central stamens. Fruit a ridged, top-shaped achene with hooked bristles and short glandular hairs. BAS

Geum fragarioides

ROSACEAE | **northern barren strawberry**

Mar–May, 3–36 in. Low, mat-forming perennial of moist to dry upland forests, rocky woodlands, bluffs, streambanks. Stems creeping, runnerlike rhizomes; leaves arise separately from flower stalks. Leaves erect, long-petioled, divided into 3 shallowly lobed and toothed, wedge-shaped leaflets, each 1–2 in. long, semi-evergreen. Flowers in a small cluster at the top of a separate stalk, about equal in height to the leaves; each flower yellow, slightly more than ½ in. wide, with 5 elliptical and round-tipped petals, 5 shorter lance-shaped sepals, and numerous stamens surrounding a green, aggregate ovary with multiple styles. Fruit a head of several finely hairy, tiny achenes. BAS

Geum vernum

ROSACEAE | **spring avens**

Apr–May, 1½–2 ft. Erect-ascending perennial of seepages, swamps, roadsides, and disturbed areas, probably both native and introduced from farther west. Stems occasionally branched, slightly hairy and shiny. Leaves basal and alternate, on petioles with toothed/lobed stipules at the base, simple or pinnately divided/lobed into 3–5 toothed segments, the basal leaves more often simple and round. Flowers at ends of branches from top of stem and from upper leaf axils, yellow, ¼ in. wide, with 5 small petals, 5 lance-shaped and longer sepals, and a dense cluster of pistils and stamens in the center. Fruit a round, bristly head of achenes. JG

Geum virginianum

ROSACEAE | **cream avens**

Jun–Aug, 1–3 ft. Erect-ascending perennial of bottomland, swamp, and moist slope forests, extending upslope to moist or even dry sites, especially over mafic rocks. Stems and leaves hairy. Basal and lower alternate leaves petiolate with leaflike stipules, from simple and oval to pinnately divided into 3–7 toothed/lobed segments; upper leaves smaller, lance-shaped to oval, simple or 3-lobed. Flowers 1–few in clusters, each pale yellow to creamy white, ¼–¾ in. wide, with 5 widely spaced, spreading, oblong-elliptical petals, 5 larger, spreading but soon reflexed, lance-triangular sepals, and a central cluster of pistils and stamens. Fruit a round, bristly head of achenes. SG

Potentilla argentea

ROSACEAE | **silvery cinquefoil**

May–Jul, to 20 in. Erect to sprawling perennial of dry fields, roadsides, and other disturbed areas. Native to Europe. Stems branched, covered with white woolly hairs. Upper leaves short-petioled, lower leaves long-petioled, palmately divided into 5–7 leaflets, these narrowly wedge-shaped, ½–2 in. long, with pointy lobes/teeth above the middle, hairy and green above, silvery woolly beneath. Flowers in branching clusters of 1–several, yellow, ¼–½ in. wide, with 5 triangular petals, 5 pointed hairy sepals of nearly equal length and visible between the petals, and 20 yellow stamens surrounding the conical yellow center. Fruit an aggregate of tiny achenes. JH

Potentilla canadensis

ROSACEAE | **running five-fingers**

Mar–May, 2–4 in. Low, creeping perennial of woodlands, forests, fields, lawns, and disturbed areas. Stems unbranched, covered with silvery silky hairs. Leaves petiolate, palmately divided into 5 wedge-shaped leaflets, these to 1½ in. long each, the rounded upper half coarsely toothed; all leaves with long, silky hairs beneath and smooth to hairy above. Flowers solitary, on stalks, the first arising from the axil of the first well-developed stem leaf, yellow, to ⅝ in. wide, with 5 rounded petals, 5 pointed hairy sepals, and many stamens encircling the yellow center. Fruit an aggregate of achenes. RTW

Potentilla indica (*Duchesnea indica*)

ROSACEAE | **mock-strawberry**

Feb–frost, 1–4 in. Low, creeping perennial of disturbed areas, lawns, gardens, and weedy clearings. Native to Asia. Stems often erect at first, becoming prostrate and creeping; covered with silky to stiff hairs. Leaves petiolate, divided into 3 oval leaflets, each about ¾–2 in. long, coarsely toothed, and sparsely hairy beneath. Flowers solitary on stalks from leaf axils, yellow, ½–1 in. wide, with 5 blunt-tipped oval petals, 5 pointed hairy sepals, and many stamens encircling the yellow center. Fruit an aggregate of tiny achenes on a red strawberry-like head; dry and bland to the taste. RTW

Potentilla norvegica

ROSACEAE | **rough cinquefoil**

May–frost, 1–3 ft. Erect to ascending annual/biennial/short-lived perennial of floodplain forests, alluvial openings, sandbars, pastures, fields, and disturbed areas, especially where moist. Stems mostly branched and hairy. Leaves basal and alternate, upper leaves sessile, lower leaves long-petioled; each leaf divided into 3 lance-shaped to oval leaflets 1–3 in. long, coarsely toothed and hairy. Flowers in wide-branching clusters, yellow, to ½ in. wide, with 5 vaguely heart-shaped petals, 5 slightly longer, hairy, triangular sepals, and 10–20 yellow stamens encircling the domed, yellow center. Fruit an aggregate of flattened achenes. BMP

Potentilla recta

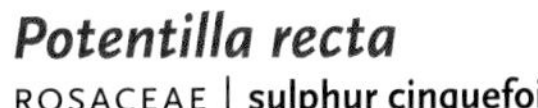

ROSACEAE | **sulphur cinquefoil**

Apr–Jul, 1–2½ ft. Erect to ascending perennial of fields, pastures, roadsides, and other disturbed areas. Native to Europe. Stems branching near top of plant, sometimes tinged with red, covered with white spreading hairs. Leaves sessile to petiolate, palmately divided into 5–9 narrowly lance-shaped leaflets (upper leaves smaller and with 3–5 leaflets), these 1¼–3½ in. long, coarsely toothed, and hairy. Flowers in flat-topped clusters, pale yellow, about ¾ in. wide, with 5 heart-shaped petals, 5 shorter, hairy, pointed sepals, and numerous yellow stamens with yellowish-brown tips encircling the yellow center. Fruit a dense aggregate of tiny, dark brown achenes. RTW

Potentilla simplex

ROSACEAE | **old-field five-fingers**

Apr–Jun, 4–16 in. Low, creeping perennial of woodlands, fields, and disturbed areas. Stems unbranched and hairy. Leaves petiolate, palmately divided into 5 narrowly oval leaflets, these ¾–3 in. long, sharply toothed except near the base, smooth above, and smooth to slightly hairy beneath. Flowers solitary on stalks, the first arising from the axil of the second well-developed stem leaf; each flower yellow, about ½ in. wide, with 5 rounded petals, 5 triangular hairy sepals, and many stamens encircling the yellow center. Fruit an aggregate of achenes. BAS

Hudsonia tomentosa

CISTACEAE | **woolly beach-heather**

May–Jul, 4–8 in. Low, evergreen, shrubby perennial forming dense, spreading mats on dunes, sand flats, and blowouts (DE, NC, VA), and in high-elevation quartzitic sandstone outcrops (WV). Stems somewhat woody, usually much-branched from below, grayish downy. Leaves crowded and pressed against the stem, scalelike to needlelike, less than 1/4 in. long, grayish, densely woolly. Flowers sessile (or on tiny stalks) and densely packed, along with leafy bracts, on the branches; each flower bright yellow, 1/4–3/8 in. wide, with 5 oval petals and many (9–18) stamens surrounding a single pistil in the center. Fruit a tiny, oval capsule. DPF

Hypopitys monotropa (*Monotropa hypopitys*)

ERICACEAE | **pinesap**

May–Oct, 2–8 in. Short, fleshy perennial of moist to dry deciduous forests. Stems usually several in a clump, fleshy, hairy; entire plant is yellow, tan, pink, red, or a combination of these colors. Leaves scalelike, clasped to stem. Flowers in a nodding terminal raceme, each flower about 1/2 in. long, urn-shaped, hairy, and with 4–5 petals and 10 stamens, but all parts held close together. Fruit a capsule that starts out nodding but becoming erect. Different color phases of this species occur at separate seasons. A mycoheterotroph (mostly of oaks or pines). Flowers are fragrant. BAS

Hypericum gentianoides

HYPERICACEAE | **orange-grass**

Jul–Oct, 6–20 in. Erect to ascending, bushy annual found on rock outcrops and in fields, woodland borders, eroding areas, pond margins, and pine flatwoods. Stems wiry, wing-angled, with many threadlike branches; main stem reddish brown and upper branches green. Leaves sessile, scalelike and tiny, pressed to stem or slightly angled outward. Flowers mostly sessile at branch tips and along branches at leaf nodes, yellow and less than 1/4 in. wide when open. Each flower with 5 lance-linear, blunt petals (which open only in sunlight), 5 slightly shorter, narrower sepals, and an erect cluster of stamens plus style in the center. Fruit a reddish-purple, slender-conical capsule. BAS

Uvularia grandiflora

COLCHICACEAE | **largeflower bellwort**

Apr–May, 8–24 in. Spring-flowering understory perennial found in cove forests and other moist, rich, forested sites. Stems 1 or more from a single root crown, smooth, branched and bearing 1–2 leaves below the branches. Leaves pierced by stem, elliptical to oval, drooping, smooth above and white-hairy beneath. Flowers 1–3 per stem/branch, golden yellow, 1–2 in. long, dangling on pendent stalks, with 6 slightly twisted tepals with smooth inner surfaces. Fruit an oval, 3-lobed capsule (triangular in cross-section). AMC

Uvularia perfoliata

COLCHICACEAE | **perfoliate bellwort**

Apr–May, 6–18 in. Spring-flowering understory perennial found in moist to fairly dry hardwood forests. Stems slender, smooth and waxy, branched above the lower few leaves. Leaves elliptical, 1½–4 in. long, smooth; distinctively pierced by the stem. Bell-shaped flowers solitary or in small clusters, dangling from downturned, slender stalks; each flower with 6 pale yellow to straw-colored, sharp-tipped tepals with tiny glandular, orange bumps on the inner surface. Fruit a short, 3-lobed capsule with 2 ridges on each lobe. RTW

Uvularia puberula

COLCHICACEAE | **Appalachian bellwort**

Mar–May, 4–18 in. Erect understory perennial found in dry to moist upland, acidic forests, up to about 5000 ft. Stems 1 or more from a single crown, slender, with 1–2 branches, lines of hairs running down the stem from leaf bases. Leaves sessile, elliptical, 1–3 in. long, with parallel veins, lustrous bright green. Flowers 1–3 per stem, dangling on downturned, slender stalks from leaf axils; each flower straw-yellow, ½–1 in. long, bell-shaped, with 6 tepals that are smooth on the inner surface. Fruit an elliptical, 3-sided capsule. BAS

Uvularia sessilifolia

COLCHICACEAE | **straw-lily**

Mar–May, 6–10 in. Erect to ascending, colonial understory perennial found in moist hardwood forests, on slopes, and in bottomlands. Stems smooth, once-branched; forms colonies via underground stolons. Leaves sessile, elliptical with pointed tips, 1½–3 in. long, pale beneath. A single flower hangs bell-like on a short stalk from an upper leaf axil; it is yellow- to cream-colored, about 1 in. long, and consists of 6 pointed tepals. Fruit a 3-sided, oval-elliptical capsule. WS

Prosartes lanuginosa (*Disporum lanuginosum*)

LILIACEAE | **yellow mandarin**

Apr–May, 1–2½ ft. Slightly leaning, erect perennial of moist, deciduous forests, especially mountain coves. Stems lightly red-tinted, with forked branches, softly hairy. Leaves sessile, oval to lance-shaped, 2–6 in. long, with prominent parallel veins, sparsely hairy on midrib and veins. Flowers dangling in small clusters from leaf axils, pale to greenish-yellow, 1–2 in. wide, bell-shaped and with 6 pointed tepals, 6 dangling stamens with yellow anthers, and a long style. Fruit a smooth, bright orange to red, oval berry. WS

Lophiola aurea

NARTHECIACEAE | **golden crest**

May–Jul, 1–2½ ft. Erect perennial of wet savannas, bogs, and marshes, and ditches adjacent to these natural habitats. Stems branched in inflorescence, woolly above. Leaves erect, sessile-clasping, linear, 3–12 in. long (decreasing upward), mostly smooth. Flowers in a woolly-hairy, open, multi-branched terminal cluster; each flower yellow, about ⅓ in. wide, consisting of 6 reflexed, lance-shaped tepals that are brownish-maroon on the inside and bear a yellow-fringed crest, 6 erect-spreading stamens, and a single ovary with a long style. Fruit an oval capsule. BAS

Polygonatum biflorum

RUSCACEAE | **small Solomon's-seal**

Apr–Jun, 1–5 ft. Erect-arching perennial of moist to dry forests. Stems unbranched, smooth with a waxy feel, sometimes with sheathing bracts at base. Leaves sessile or clasping, lance-shaped to elliptical, 2–8 in. long, with prominent parallel veins, smooth, waxy-white beneath. Flowers dangling below leaves on thin stalks from leaf axils, 1–5 (or more) flowers per axil, greenish-yellow to greenish-white, ½–¾ in. long, tubular and with 6 tepals with spreading tips. Fruit a blue-black, round berry. BAS

Polygonatum pubescens

RUSCACEAE | **downy Solomon's-seal**

Apr–Jun, 1–2½ ft. Erect-arching perennial of moist forests, especially cove forests, but also in montane oak forests. Stems unbranched and smooth; there are sheathing, papery bracts on the lower, leafless part of the stem. Leaves narrowly elliptical to oval, short-petioled, 1½–5 in. long, whitish and hairless above, with 3–9 finely hairy veins beneath. Flowers dangling below leaf from slender stalks originating in leaf axils (1–2 per axil), greenish-yellow, ⅜–½ in. long, tubular and with 6 short, pointed, spreading tepal lobes. Fruit a round, blue-black berry. BAS

Medeola virginiana

LILIACEAE | **Indian cucumber-root**

Apr–Jun, 8–24 in. Erect perennial from a tuberlike, horizontal rhizome, found in moist forests, usually on acidic soils. Stems wiry, unbranched, woolly-hairy when young. Leaves 5–11 in a whorl partway up the stem, with a second whorl of smaller, fewer leaves at the top; each leaf oblong-lance-shaped, to 6 in. long, glossy-green, smooth. Flowers 3–9 in a sessile umbel, each flower dangling just below the upper leaf whorl on a 1-in.-long stalk; each flower greenish-yellow, about ⅔ in. wide, with 6 strongly recurved tepals, 6 stamens, and a 3-branched style. Fruit a purple-black, roundish berry; the umbel of berries is held above the red-blazed leaf whorl when ripe. RTW

Eriogonum allenii

POLYGONACEAE | **shale-barren wild buckwheat**

Jul–Aug, 11–18 in. Erect, tufted perennial found in open and sunny situations on shale barrens and, rarely, sandstone barrens. Stems branched above, very furry. Basal leaves long-petioled, oval to oval-oblong, 2–5 in. long, fuzzy; stem leaves in whorls of 3–5, short-petioled, oval to oblong, 1–3 in. long (reduced above), fuzzy. Flowers in flat-topped compound umbels at ends of erect branches, each little cluster resting on a cup-like structure with triangular lobes, yellow, to 1⁄4 in. long, with 6 tepals and 9 stamens. GPF

Schoenolirion croceum

AGAVACEAE | **yellow sunnybell**

Mar–May, 8–14 in. Erect perennial from a bulb, found in wet pine savannas, bogs, seepage slopes, and seepages on granite flatrocks. Stems 1–2 flowering scapes from a tuft of grasslike leaves. Leaves primarily basal, linear, 8–13 in. long, fleshy, smooth. Flowers in a tall raceme at end of scape, bright yellow, less than 1⁄2 in. wide, with 6 oblong-lance-shaped tepals, 6 stamens, and a pistil. RTW

Hypoxis hirsuta

HYPOXIDACEAE | **eastern stargrass**

Mar–Jun, 4–8 in. Erect to reclining perennial from a corm, found in dry to moist forests, woodlands, clearings, and barrens. Stems unbranched and hairy. Leaves clustered at base of stem, with membranous sheaths, linear, 4–20 in. long, U-shaped in cross-section, stiff, with scattered white hairs. Flowers 2–7 in a loose, terminal umbel, yellow, 1⁄2–1 in. wide, with 6 spreading, lance-shaped and pointed tepals and a central yellow pistil surrounded by 6 yellow stamens. Fruit an elliptical capsule. BAS

Iris pseudacorus

IRIDACEAE | **yellow flag**

May–Jul, 3–4 ft. Erect, rhizomatous perennial of swamps, marshes, streams, pond edges, streambanks, tidal wetlands; typically forms large colonies. Native to Eurasia and Africa; cultivated as a water plant and widely naturalized; invasive in places. Stiff flowering stalks arise from crowded rhizomes at the soil surface. Leaves crowded at base of plant, linear-lance-shaped, stiff, to 3 ft. long and 1 in. wide, dark green, smooth. Flowers 4–12, produced toward top of stalk from nodes underlain by bracts, bright yellow, 3–4 in. wide, with 3 ornate, drooping, petal-like sepals bearing brown and violet lines and 3 erect, unmarked petals. RTW

Sisyrinchium rosulatum

IRIDACEAE | **annual blue-eyed-grass**

Apr–May, 6–14 in. Spreading-ascending, tufted annual found in lawns and on roadsides. Stems 1–several, flattened and smooth, arising from tuft of grasslike leaves; lacking the clump of dried leaf bases seen in some *Sisyrinchium* species. Leaves mostly basal, overlapping, linear and grasslike, to 14 in. long and less than 1/8 in. wide. Flowers borne singly at top of stems, yellow or white to lavender with a central yellow eye rimmed with purple, to 3/4 in. wide, with 6 tepals that may be pointy, rounded, or notched and bear a tiny tooth. Fruit a tan, round capsule. RTW

Clintonia borealis

LILIACEAE | **bluebead-lily**

May–Jun, 6–16 in. Erect perennial found in cool, moist forests, such as spruce-fir, northern hardwood, and (less commonly) red oak. Stem a smooth flowering scape. Leaves in a basal rosette, sessile, oval with pointed tips and strongly inset midvein, 5–12 in. long, shiny-green. Flowers 4–8 in an umbel terminating the slender, leafless flowering scape; each flower yellow, 1/2–3/4 in. wide, with 6 narrow tepals that are downy on the outside and 6 protruding stamens. Fruit a dark blue berry. WS

Erythronium americanum

LILIACEAE | **American trout lily**

Feb–Apr, 4–10 in. Colony-forming, early-blooming, scapose perennial of moist bottomland or slope forests, especially over mafic rocks. Stem a smooth, leafless, pink-tinged flowering scape. Leaves basal and spreading-ascending, sessile, lance-shaped, to 7 in. long, fleshy, and mottled with purplish-brown markings. Flower solitary, nodding at curved tip of scape, yellow, to 1 in. long, trumpet-shaped, with 6 spreading to reflexed and purple-spotted tepals (the 3 inner ones with tiny "ears" or pockets at the base) and 6 protruding stamens bearing long yellow (sometimes brown) anthers. Fruit a green, oval capsule held horizontally above the ground surface. RTW

Erythronium umbilicatum

LILIACEAE | **dimpled trout lily**

Jan–May, 4–10 in. Early-blooming, scapose perennial found in moist bottomland or slope forests, or in rather dry upland habitats. Stem a pink-tinged, leafless, and smooth flowering scape. Leaves basal, spreading-ascending, sessile, lance-shaped, to 7 in. long, fleshy, mottled with purplish-brown markings, and smooth. Flower solitary, nodding at curved tip of scape, yellow, to 1 in. long, trumpet-shaped, with 6 reflexed tepals with some purple spotting (but lacking the tiny "ears" of *E. americanum*) and 6 dangling stamens bearing long, brownish-purple anthers. Fruit a green, oval capsule with indentation at the end and typically lying on the ground. RTW

Aletris aurea

NARTHECIACEAE | **golden colic-root**

Apr–Jul, 7–26 in. Scapose perennial from a short, thick rhizome, found in pine savannas, seepage bogs, and pine flatwoods. Stem an unbranched, mostly naked (a few small, linear bracts) flowering scape that rises from the center of a leaf rosette. Leaves in a flattish basal rosette, elliptical to lance-shaped, ¾–3 in. long, bright green. Flowers in a single spikelike raceme at top of scape, yellow to orange-yellow, about ¼ in. long, tubular-cylindrical and lacking a constriction, nearly closed at the tip and granular on the outside. WS, BAS

Aletris lutea

NARTHECIACEAE | **yellow colic-root**

Mar–May, 1–3 ft. Scapose, rhizomatous perennial found in bogs and wet pine savannas at the southern end of our range. Stem an unbranched, mostly naked (a few small reddish-green bracts) flowering scape, rising from the center of a rosette. Leaves in a basal rosette, elliptical to lance-shaped, 2½–7 in. long, yellowish-green. Flowers in a spikelike raceme occupying a large portion of the scape, yellow, about ¾ in. long, cylindrical, composed of 6 fused petals that at full bloom flare into 6 triangular-pointed lobes; the tube has a granular-bumpy outer surface. Fruit a beaked, oval capsule containing tiny reddish-brown seeds. JG

Narthecium americanum

NARTHECIACEAE | **bog asphodel**

Jun–Jul, to 1½ ft. Erect, rhizomatous perennial with extremely restricted distribution in wet seepages and savannas. Stem a flowering scape (bearing a few small, linear bracts) that arises from a tuft of grasslike leaves. Leaves mostly in a basal rosette, linear and erect, 4–8 in. long, smooth. Flowers in a crowded raceme occupying the top 2½ in. of the scape, yellow, to ⅓ in. long, with 6 linear-lance-shaped tepals, 6 hairy stamens, and a single yellow-green, vase-shaped ovary. Fruit an oval, 3-celled capsule with a narrow beak. TOPO

Nuphar advena

NYMPHAEACEAE | **spatterdock**

Apr–Oct, about 6 in. above water. Aquatic perennial of lakes, depression ponds, old millponds, slow-flowing rivers (black- and brownwater), freshwater tidal marshes. Most widespread nuphar in e NoAm. Stem consists of a rhizome rooted in mud. Leaves floating or held above water on stout stalks, oval with a notched base, to 16 in. long, smooth. Flowers single on each stalk, held above water, yellow, 1–3 in. wide, cup-shaped; each flower consists of 6 (sometimes 5) thick, nearly round, yellow to green tepals, several rings of stamens, and a yellow, columnar pistil with flat top. Fruit an erect, oval capsule constricted at the top. BAS

Asparagus officinalis

ASPARAGACEAE | **asparagus**

Apr–Jun, 2½–6 ft. Erect, often clonal, rhizomatous perennial of fencerows, roadsides, disturbed areas. Native to Eurasia; commonly cultivated and escaped. Primary stem stout, semi-angular, branching, gray-green, smooth; secondary stems arise over time, ascending-spreading, slender. Leaves pressed close to stem, scalelike, triangular, light yellow to purple; along secondary stems and upper half of primary stem are whorls of 4–15 stemlets that resemble needlelike leaves. Flowers solitary or 2–3 in clusters; some female, some male, some perfect; axillary, on thin stalks; each ¾–1 in. long, bell-shaped, with 6 tepals recurved or straight at the tip. Fruit a red berry. BAS

Ficaria verna

RANUNCULACEAE | **fig buttercup**

Mar–May, 4–12 in. Erect to sprawling, naturalized perennial of disturbed rich forests and bottomlands, moist suburban forests and lawns. Native to Europe. Stems 1–several from lush basal rosette, succulent, smooth. Basal and lower (opposite) leaves petiolate, round to oval with notched base, ¾–2 in. long, shallowly round-toothed, semi-fleshy, smooth; upper alternate leaves similar in shape but smaller. Flowers solitary, terminal or in upper leaf axils, 1 in. wide, with 7–12 elliptical to oblong, shiny petals, 3 light green, oval sepals with blunt tips, and a center cluster of some 15 pistils ringed by about 30 stamens. Fruit a headlike cluster of beakless achenes. ER

Nelumbo lutea

NELUMBONACEAE | **yellow lotus**

Jun–Sep, to 3 ft. above water. Emergent or floating aquatic perennial of ponds, lakes, sluggish streams, freshwater tidal marshes. Flowers and leaves on separate stalks from thick rhizomes rooted in mud. Leaves usually above water, round with a depressed center where the petiole attaches below, 12–28 in. wide, with a waxy coating that repels water. Flowers solitary on stiff stalks raised above leaves and water, pale yellow, 8–12 in. wide, with numerous erect, oval to spoon-shaped tepals spirally arranged around numerous stamens and a central receptacle that resembles a shower head. Fruit an oval, nutlike seed found in the cavities of the enlarged receptacle. WS

Balduina angustifolia

ASTERACEAE | **sandhill honeycomb-head**

Jun–Nov, 1½–3 ft. Erect annual/biennial of sandhills and other dry, sandy soils. Stems branched, red-tinged, and gland-dotted. Leaves linear, to 2½ in. long, with inrolled edges; lower leaves withering by flowering time. Flowers in daisylike heads at ends of branches; heads yellow, 1–2 in. wide, with about 8 (5–13) ray florets with toothed tips surrounding a dome-shaped center composed of tiny disk florets. Several series of small, yellowish-green bracts surround the base of each head. BAS

Balduina uniflora

ASTERACEAE | **savanna honeycomb-head**

Jul–Sep, 1–3 ft. Erect perennial of wet pine savannas and sandhills. Stems ribbed, usually unbranched, hairy. Leaves basal and alternate-ascending on the stem, narrowly spoon-shaped, to 4 in. long (reduced above), slightly fleshy. Flower heads solitary and terminating stems, yellow, to 2 in. wide, with about 13 (5–22) ray florets with toothed tips encircling a low-domed center disk of yellow-orange tubular florets; several whorls of small, pointed green bracts surround the saucer-shaped base of each head. PIP

Bigelowia nudata (*Chondrophora nudata*)

ASTERACEAE | **rayless-goldenrod**

Aug–Oct, 1–2 ft. Erect perennial of moist to wet savannas, pine flatwoods, pocosin edges, and seepage slopes. Stems with ascending slender branches in upper third, smooth. Leaves basal, petiolate, oblong-lance-shaped, 2–6 in. long; a few smaller alternate, linear stem leaves also present; all leaves gland-dotted. Flower heads at tips of branches, forming a large, flat-topped cluster; heads less than ¼ in. wide, with 3–5 deep yellow, tubular disk florets. BAS

Chrysopsis gossypina

ASTERACEAE | **cottonleaf golden-aster**

Sep–Oct, to 3 ft. long. Sprawling biennial/short-lived perennial found in sandhills, coastal dunes, and other dry, sandy places. Stems lying on ground but turning up and erect near tips, densely covered with long white hairs. Leaves basal and alternate, lance- to oblong-lance-shaped with blunt or rounded tip, to 4 in. long (reduced above), densely covered with hairs. Flower heads on stalks on turned-up stem tips, 1½–2 in. wide, with 10–22 bright yellow ray florets encircling a center disk of many tiny, yellow tubular florets. Whorls of pointed green bracts, usually covered with white hairs (occasionally stalked glands), surround the base of each head. BAS

Chrysopsis mariana (*Heterotheca mariana*)

ASTERACEAE | **Maryland golden-aster**

Jun–Oct, 1–2 ft. Erect to ascending perennial of dry forests and woodlands, old fields, roadsides. Stems branched above in the inflorescence. Leaves basal and alternate, oblong-lance-shaped to elliptical, short-petioled or sessile, ¾–4½ in. long (stem leaves shorter); both stems and leaves covered with long white hairs. Flower heads in a dense, branched, terminal cluster; heads ¾–1½ in. wide, with 12–25 golden yellow ray florets encircling a darker yellow center disk of many tiny, tubular florets. Whorls of tiny, pointed green bracts bearing stalked glands surround the bell-shaped base of each head. BAS

Euthamia caroliniana

ASTERACEAE | **slender goldentop**

Aug–Dec, 1–3 ft. Erect, rhizomatous perennial of pine savannas, moist forests, ditches, pastures, and other disturbed areas. Stems unbranched, smooth to slightly hairy. Leaves linear, 1–2¾ in. long, somewhat drooping but ascending and smaller upward, gland-dotted; clusters of shorter leaves often grow in axils of the primary leaves. Flower heads in large, branched terminal clusters; heads ⅓ in. wide, with 7–16 short, yellow ray florets encircling a yellow center disk composed of several 5-lobed, tubular florets. BAS

Euthamia graminifolia

ASTERACEAE | **flat-top goldentop**

Aug–Oct, 2–3½ ft. Erect, rhizomatous perennial of moist to dry weedy situations, riverbanks, bottomlands, and bog margins. Stems branched above, with lines of fine, white hairs. Leaves sessile, narrowly lance-shaped, 1½–5 in. long, sparsely gland-dotted, sometimes with a few white hairs near the base of leaves and along the central vein beneath. Flower heads in a branched, often flat-topped, terminal cluster; heads less than ¼ in. wide, with 12–35 tiny, yellow ray florets encircling a few (4–13) yellow, tubular florets. BAS

Helenium amarum

ASTERACEAE | **bitterweed**

May–Dec, 1–2 ft. Erect annual from a taproot, found in overgrazed pastures, roadsides, urban areas; apparently introduced from farther west. Stems branched above, leafy, green to red-tinged, smooth. Leaves linear to nearly threadlike, to 3 in. long, often with clusters of smaller leaves in leaf axils, gland-dotted, and smooth. Flower heads at tips of branches; heads about ¾ in. wide, with 5–10 spreading to drooping, yellow, 3-toothed ray florets encircling a dome-shaped center disk composed of tiny, yellow tubular florets. Several green, drooping, pointed bracts surround the base of each head. Foliage very bitter; toxic to horses and cows in large quantities. BAS

Helianthus angustifolius

ASTERACEAE | **swamp sunflower**

Sep–frost, 1–6 ft. Erect perennial of savannas, ditches, marshes, and other wet habitats. Stems branched, leafy, and rough-hairy. Leaves alternate (upper) and opposite (lower), short-petioled to sessile, linear, to 8 in. long, with margins curled under, rough-hairy above and pale green and soft-hairy beneath. Flower heads solitary or in small clusters, 1½–3 in. wide, with 8–21 yellow ray florets encircling a center disk of reddish to purplish-brown tubular florets. Overlapping, narrow, pointed bracts surround the base of each head. Fruit a dark brown, rounded achene. BAS

Helianthus porteri (*Viguiera porteri*)

ASTERACEAE | **Confederate daisy**

Aug–Oct, 1½–3 ft. Erect, often colonial annual of shallow soils over granite on low-elevation granite domes or flatrocks. Stems rough-hairy. Leaves opposite below and alternate above, short-petioled to sessile, linear and tapering at both ends, to 4½ in. long, with fringed margins toward the base, and rough-hairy and gland-dotted above. Flower heads in small terminal clusters; heads 1½–2 in. wide, with 7–8 yellow ray florets encircling a center disk of yellow tubular florets. Overlapping, narrow, pointed bracts surround the base of each head. Fruit an achene. AMC

Heterotheca subaxillaris

ASTERACEAE | **dune camphorweed**

Jul–Oct (Jan), 2–6½ ft. Erect to sprawling annual/biennial (occasionally short-lived perennial) of coastal dunes and sand flats. Stems branched above, usually covered with long spreading hairs and stalked glands. Leaves sessile (clasping above), oval to oblong or lance-shaped, ¾–3½ in. long, entire or coarsely toothed, with scattered long hairs on margins, rough-hairy. Flower heads in diffusely branching terminal cluster; heads about 1 in. wide, with 15–30 narrow, yellow ray florets encircling a center disk of many yellow tubular florets. Several series of densely hairy-glandular, green, narrow bracts surround the cup-shaped base of each head. JG

Hieracium gronovii

ASTERACEAE | **beaked hawkweed**

Jul–Nov, 1–3 ft. Erect perennial of sandhills, dry forests, woodland margins, roadsides. Stems unbranched, very hairy especially at the base, oozing milky sap when broken. Leaves basal and alternate low on the stem (a few bract-like leaves above), short-petioled to sessile, elliptical to oblong-lance-shaped, to 4 in. long (reduced above), very hairy. Flower heads in a narrow, terminal cluster with alternate, glandular-hairy branches; heads ½–¾ in. wide, with 12–20 yellow, 3-toothed ray florets (no disk florets). A series of green or purplish, linear bracts surrounds the cylinder-shaped base of each head. BAS

Hieracium marianum

ASTERACEAE | **Maryland hawkweed**

May–Nov, 8–24 in. Erect perennial found in dry forests, woodland margins, and roadsides. Stems widely branched above, densely hairy below, leaking milky sap when broken. Leaves basal and alternate, oblong-lance-shaped, 1½–5 in. long (reduced above), basal leaves sometimes with purplish veins, hairy above. Flower heads at ends of branches in a flattish, terminal cluster; heads ½–¾ in. wide, with multiple yellow ray florets with squared-off tips (no disk florets). BAS

Hieracium scabrum

ASTERACEAE | **rough hawkweed**

Jul–Nov, 1–3½ ft. Erect perennial of dry forests, woodland margins, and roadsides. Stems thick, densely hairy, leaking milky sap when broken. Leaves sessile, oblong-lance-shaped to oval, 1–5 in. long (reduced and fewer above), mostly entire, lower surface paler than upper, hairy. Flower heads in elongated (to 1 ft.) terminal panicle; heads ½–1 in. wide, with 30–60 yellow ray florets with squared-off and toothed tips (no disk florets). Stalks and bracts surrounding the base of each head are covered with stalked glands. Fruit a fluffy cluster of cylindrical achenes with tufts of tawny hairs. GPF

Pityopsis adenolepis

ASTERACEAE | **Carolina silkgrass**

Jun–Oct, 8–18 in. Erect, rhizomatous perennial of dry woodlands, forests, and disturbed places. Stems branched in inflorescence, covered with a mixture of silky hairs and gland-tipped hairs. Leaves mostly toward stem bottom, linear-lance-shaped and parallel-veined, to 14 in. long (smaller upward), covered with silky hairs. Flower heads in widely branching terminal cluster; heads about ½ in. wide, with 8–13 yellow ray florets encircling a small center disk of 15–20 tiny, yellow tubular florets. Green, gland-covered bracts surround the cylindrical base of each head. AMC

Pityopsis graminifolia

ASTERACEAE | **narrowleaf silkgrass**

Jun–Oct, 11–30 in. Erect, tufted perennial of sandhills, dry woodlands and forests, road banks. Stems often with basal offshoots, branched above; upper stem sparsely glandular-hairy to smooth. Leaves mostly basal, a few alternate leaves above, linear-lance-shaped, 4–12 in. long (reduced above), covered with silvery-silky, close-pressed hairs. Flower heads on silky-hairy, sometimes glandular stalks in ascending upper branches; heads ½–1 in. wide, with 4–13 yellow ray florets encircling a center disk of 30–50 yellow tubular florets. Several unequal series of hairy bracts surround the bell-shaped base of each head. Highly variable; photo shows var. *latifolia*. BAS

Solidago odora

ASTERACEAE | **licorice goldenrod**

Jul–Oct, 2–3 ft. Erect to ascending perennial of dry forests and woodlands, especially dry Coastal Plain pinelands; inland, in glades, barrens, ridgetop pine-oak woodlands, and other dry, fire-maintained sites. Stems arching above, unbranched, with lines of hairs running up the stem between leaves. Leaves sessile, lance-shaped to elliptical, 1–4 in. long, mostly smooth and dotted with translucent glands; give off an aniselike fragrance when crushed. Flower heads in a roughly pyramid-shaped terminal panicle with short, arching branches; heads about ¼ in. wide, with 3–7 yellow ray florets encircling a small center disk of 4–7 yellow tubular florets. RTW

Solidago puberula

ASTERACEAE | **downy goldenrod**

Aug–Oct, 1–3 ft. Erect, rhizomatous perennial of bogs, wet meadows, wet pastures; also dry acidic soils of woodlands, barrens, and clearings. Stems with longitudinal lines, often purplish-red, unbranched, finely hairy. Leaves mostly basal, tapered to a winged petiole, spoon-shaped to oblong-oval, 2–6 in. long, toothed, finely hairy; stem leaves alternate, reduced above, usually entire. Flower heads densely clustered on short, ascending branches forming a narrow terminal array; heads ¼ in. long, with 9–16 yellow ray florets encircling a center disk of 6–15 small, yellow tubular florets. 3–4 series of tiny bracts surround the bell-shaped base of each head. GPF

Berlandiera pumila

ASTERACEAE | **eastern green-eyes**

May–Nov, 1½–3 ft. Erect perennial from thick, fleshy roots found in dry longleaf pine stands, sandhills, and roadsides. Stems 1–several from a crown, reddish, hairy. Leaves petiolate, oval to elliptical with a flat or heart-shaped base, 2½–5 in. long, round-toothed, densely furry beneath. Flower heads sunflowerlike, on stalks in a branching terminal cluster; heads about 2 in. wide, with (usually) 8 yellow, notched ray florets encircling a center disk of tiny, greenish, tubular florets that turn yellow or reddish. WS

Croptilon divaricatum (*Haplopappus divaricatus*)

ASTERACEAE | **scratch-daisy**

Jul–Nov, 1–4½ ft. Erect, taprooted annual found in sandy soils of fields, roadsides, and sandhill woodlands. Stems slender, branched above, covered with both glandular and nonglandular hairs. Leaves sessile but with narrowly tapered bases, linear to narrowly oblong-lance-shaped, to 4 in. long, rough-hairy, with a few spiny teeth. Flower heads at tips of widely spreading, glandular branches; heads about ¾ in. wide, with 7–11 yellow ray florets encircling the center disk of tiny, yellow tubular florets. Narrow bracts of varying lengths surround the cylindrical base of each head. AMC

Erechtites hieraciifolius

ASTERACEAE | **American burnweed**

Jul–Nov, to 8 ft. Erect annual found in disturbed soil in nearly all habitats except extremely dry ones. Stems grooved-striate, unbranched, smooth or hairy. Upper leaves clasping and lower subsessile, lance-shaped to oblong, to 8 in. long, sharply toothed or irregularly lobed, hairy or smooth. Flower heads in clusters at ends of upper-axillary stalks and terminating stem; heads about ¼ in. wide, ⅓ in. tall, cylindrical with a swollen base, with numerous, densely crowded, tiny, dull yellow or white disk florets. A tube composed of erect, narrow green bracts surrounds the head, nearly concealing the florets. Fruit a brown seed with a tuft of bright white hairs. BAS

Helenium autumnale

ASTERACEAE | **common sneezeweed**

Jul–Oct, 2–5 ft. Erect perennial of moist pastures, forests, woodlands, and forest edges. Stems wing-angled, simple or branched at terminus, hairy. Basal leaves withered by flowering, stem leaves sessile to clasping, elliptical to linear-lance-shaped, to 6 in. long, toothed or entire, hairy. Flower heads in branching terminal cluster; heads about 2 in. wide, with 10–21 spreading-drooping yellow, narrowly triangular and 3-toothed ray florets encircling a dome-shaped center disk composed of many yellow tubular florets. RTW

Helenium flexuosum

ASTERACEAE | **southern sneezeweed**

May–Aug, 1–3 ft. Erect perennial of moist forests, moist pastures, and riverbanks. Stems wing-angled, with stiffly ascending, leafy branches above, and rough-hairy. Leaves sessile (basal leaves petiolate), narrowly lance-shaped to oval, to 6 in. long (reduced above), wavy-margined, smooth or velvety-furry. Flower heads at ends of branches; heads 1½–2 in. wide, with 8–15 yellow, drooping, narrowly wedge-shaped and 3-toothed ray florets encircling a maroon-brown, ball-shaped central disk (about ½ in. tall) composed of many tubular florets. RTW

Helianthus annuus

ASTERACEAE | **common sunflower**

Jun–Oct, 2–10 ft. Stout, erect annual of disturbed areas. Native to the Plains states; often cultivated commercially and in gardens. Stems stout, branched, rough, and hairy. Leaves mostly alternate (except lowermost), long-petioled, oval, triangular or heart-shaped, 2–8 in. long, with 3 main veins, toothed, and with roughly stiff-hairy surfaces. Flower heads solitary or in open panicles; heads 3–6 in. wide, with 17–40 large, yellow ray florets encircling a large center disk of reddish-brown, purple, or yellow tubular florets. Overlapping oval bracts with long narrow tips surround the base of each head. Fruit a striped, finely hairy achene. BAS

Helianthus giganteus

ASTERACEAE | **giant sunflower**

Jul–Oct, 2–12 ft. Erect, rhizomatous perennial of bog edges, moist thickets, and ditches. Stems branching in upper third, green or reddish-purple, rough-hairy. Leaves mostly alternate, petiolate, lance-shaped, 2–8 in. long, pinnately veined, with toothed or nearly smooth margins, rough-hairy above and soft-hairy beneath. Flower heads several in loose clusters; heads 2–3 in. wide, with 10–20 yellow ray florets encircling a center disk of darker yellow tubular florets. Spreading and overlapping hairy, long, narrow bracts surround the base of each head. Fruit a blackish or mottled-brown, flattened, oblong achene. AMC

Helianthus grosseserratus

ASTERACEAE | **sawtooth sunflower**

Jul–Oct, 3–8 ft. Erect, rhizomatous, colonial perennial of roadsides, fencerows, clearings. Native farther west in NoAm. Stems simple to much-branched above, red- or purple-tinged, often with a whitish coating. Leaves alternate above, opposite below, petiolate (often winged), lance-shaped, to 8 in. long, coarsely toothed, stiffly hairy, pinnately veined, rough above, sometimes whitish beneath. Flower heads in small clusters or panicles; heads 2½–4 in. wide, with 10–20 yellow ray florets encircling a center disk of darker yellow tubular florets. Spreading, sharp-pointed, narrow bracts surround the base of each head. Fruit a mottled brown-and-black wedge-shaped achene. JG

Helianthus tuberosus

ASTERACEAE | **Jerusalem artichoke**

Jul–Oct, 3–11 ft. Erect perennial of rich bottomlands, streamsides, disturbed areas. Native farther west in NoAm, cultivated for its edible tubers. Stems branched occasionally above, light green to reddish-brown, rough-hairy. Leaves alternate above, sometimes opposite lower, on winged petioles (¾–4 in. long), oval to broadly lance-shaped, 3–9 in. long, 3-veined, toothed, rough-hairy above, with very short grayish hairs beneath. Flower heads numerous in flat-topped clusters; heads 2–4 in. wide, with 10–20 yellow ray florets encircling a center disk of yellow tubular florets. Overlapping, loosely ascending bracts surround the base of each head. Fruit a mottled-brown achene. PIP

Hieracium paniculatum

ASTERACEAE | **leafy hawkweed**

Jul–Oct, 1–3 ft. Erect perennial of dry to moist forests, especially along dirt roads. Stems hairy at the base, smooth above, leafy, leaking milky sap when broken. Leaves sessile, lance-shaped, 2–5 in. long, slightly toothed, smooth, solid green, lacking the purplish-red veins of some species in the genus. Flower heads on slender branches of a terminal panicle; heads ¼–½ in. wide, with 10–20 yellow ray florets with squared-off, toothed tips (no disk florets). BAS

Lactuca canadensis

ASTERACEAE | **American wild lettuce**

Jun–Nov, 4–10 ft. Erect annual/biennial of moist to dry forests, rocky woodlands, fields, roadsides, disturbed areas. Stems stout, unbranched, often purple-spotted, with a white-waxy coating, smooth or hairy, oozing milky sap when broken. Leaves with clasping bases, variable in shape, 4–12 in. long, the largest toothed or divided into narrow segments, dull whitish or shiny, mostly smooth. Flower heads numerous in tall, open-branching terminal cluster; heads ⅓ in. wide, with 15–20 yellow (purplish with age) ray florets with squared-off, toothed tips. Purple-tinged bracts surround the base of each head. Fruit a fluffy cluster of white-tufted, flattened achenes. BAS

Lactuca serriola

ASTERACEAE | **prickly lettuce**

Jun–Nov, 1–6½ ft. Erect annual/biennial of roadsides, pastures, and other disturbed places. Native to Europe. Stems stout, green or reddish-tan and white-waxy, smooth or with bristles below. Leaves sessile, oblong to spoon-shaped with lobed bases, often twisted at the base and thus oriented vertically, 2–6 in. long, pinnately lobed with spiny-toothed margins, spiny on midrib beneath. Flower heads in large, widely branched, pyramidal cluster at top of stem; heads about ⅓ in. wide, with 5–27 yellow ray florets with squared-off, toothed tips. Fruit a fluffy cluster of flattened, tufted achenes. BAS

Nabalus altissimus
(Prenanthes altissima)

ASTERACEAE | **tall rattlesnake-root**

Aug–Nov, 1½–6 ft. Erect perennial of moist to dry upland forests, well-drained alluvial forests and clearings. Stems branched and often zigzagged above, mostly smooth (sometimes hairy at base), leaking milky sap when broken. Leaves petiolate, triangular to lance-shaped, 1½–6 in. long, varying from a few teeth to deeply 3- to 5-lobed (lobes angular); also with milky sap. Flower heads drooping from short stalks of a terminal panicle; heads cylindrical, about ½ in. long, with 5 spreading to recurved, pale yellow or greenish-white ray florets surrounded by 5 smooth, pale green bracts. Fruit a tufted achene. AMC

Nabalus roanensis
(Prenanthes roanensis)

ASTERACEAE | **roan rattlesnake-root**

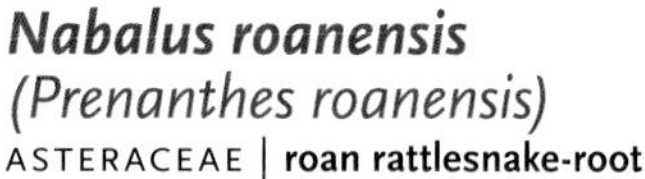

Aug–Oct, ½–3 ft. Erect perennial of high-elevation forests and grassy balds. Stems simple, green or purple, smooth below and with spreading hairs above. Leaves petiolate, evenly distributed along stem; lower and middle leaves triangular to arrowhead-shaped and 3-lobed (lobes angular) or unlobed, 1–5 in. long, sometimes purple-tinged, hairy or smooth. Flower heads drooping from short stalks on upper branches; heads cylindrical, about ½ in. long, with 5–13 greenish-yellow ray florets surrounded by 5 bristly-hairy, green bracts with dark tips. Fruit a tufted achene. LADI

Packera tomentosa

ASTERACEAE | **woolly ragwort**

Apr–Jun, 1–2 ft. Erect, colonial perennial of sandy roadsides, sandy woodlands and forests, granitic flatrocks and domes. Stems tufted, spreading via short rhizomes or stolons, unbranched (except in inflorescence), covered in cobwebby white fur. Basal leaves petiolate, nearly erect, oval to lance-shaped, to 5 in. long, round-toothed, with cobwebby hairs on one or both surfaces; stem leaves alternate, few, nearly sessile, shorter and narrower, lobed or toothed. Flower heads in branching terminal cluster; heads about 1 in. wide, with 10–13 bright yellow ray florets encircling a slightly domed central disk of tiny, yellow tubular florets. Fruit a small, tufted achene. BAS, AMC

Rudbeckia hirta

ASTERACEAE | **woodland black-eyed Susan**

May–Jul, 1–2½ ft. Erect to leaning biennial/short-lived perennial of dry woodlands, pastures, and roadsides. Stems simple or with a few branches from near the base; covered with stiff, white hairs. Leaves basal and alternate, petiolate, oval or lance-shaped, 3–12 in. long, sometimes toothed, grayish-green and rough-hairy; stem leaves sessile, gradually reduced in size upward, narrowly lance-shaped. Flower heads solitary at ends of stem and branches, 1½–4½ in. wide, with 8–16 dark yellow ray florets (¾–2 in. long) encircling a domed center disk of tiny brownish-purple tubular florets. RTW

Rugelia nudicaulis

ASTERACEAE | **Rugel's ragwort**

Jun–Aug, 11–18 in. Tufted perennial of high-elevation forests and openings, primarily in spruce-fir forests; extremely rare, known mostly from Great Smoky Mountains NP. Stems mostly naked flowering stalks from leaf rosette, cobwebby-hairy below, glandular-hairy above. Leaves mostly basal, petiolate, oval with pointed tip, 2–6 in. long, toothed, cobwebby-hairy; stem leaves alternate, few, much smaller, sessile. Flower heads nodding or held face-forward in a loosely branched terminal cluster. Heads to 1 in. wide, with tightly packed, pale yellow, tubular disk florets surrounded by a series of glandular-hairy, green, lance-linear bracts, which are slightly shorter than the florets. JS, JG

Solidago altissima

ASTERACEAE | **tall goldenrod**

Aug–Oct, 2–6½ ft. Erect, rhizomatous, colonial perennial of fields, roadsides, and other disturbed areas. Stems single or clumped, branched in inflorescence, hairy. Leaves alternate (no basal rosette), short-petioled to sessile, lance-shaped to elliptical, to 6 in. long, shallowly toothed to entire, hairy. Flower heads along the branches of a large, often leaning, pyramid-shaped panicle; heads about ⅓ in. wide, with 5–17 yellow ray florets surrounding a small, center disk of 2–9 yellow tubular florets. BAS

Solidago arguta

ASTERACEAE | **forest goldenrod**

Aug–Oct, 2–3 ft. Erect to arching, rhizomatous perennial of moist to dry upland forests, woodlands, barrens, clearings. Stems branched above, mostly smooth. Leaves basal and alternate, on winged petioles, elliptical to oval, 2–5 in. long (reduced and sessile above), toothed, smooth to slightly rough-hairy. Flower heads in an open, leafy, pyramidal array of branches at top of plant, the heads mostly on 1 side of each branch; heads with 2–8 small, yellow ray florets encircling a small center disk of 8–20 tiny, yellow tubular florets. 3–4 series of tiny bracts surround the cup-shaped base of each head. Several varieties in our region; var. *caroliniana* is pictured. BAS

Solidago caesia

ASTERACEAE | **axillary goldenrod**

Aug–Oct, 1–3 ft. Erect-ascending, rhizomatous perennial of moist forests. Stems arching, branched or unbranched, smooth, sometimes white-waxy or blue-green. Leaves alternate (no basal rosette), short-petioled to sessile, lance-shaped, to 4 in. long (reduced above), toothed, dark green, smooth to rough-hairy. Flower heads in small clusters in middle and upper leaf axils, about 1/4 in. wide, with 1–6 yellow ray florets encircling a small center disk of a few yellow tubular florets. BAS

Solidago canadensis

ASTERACEAE | **Canada goldenrod**

Aug–Oct, 2–5 ft. Erect perennial of alluvial clearings, riverbanks, fields, pastures, and roadsides. Stems unbranched, smooth below, sparsely hairy above; plant may lean with weight of flowers. Leaves alternate (no basal rosette), sessile, crowded, lance-shaped to lance-linear, 1–6 in. long, sharply toothed, with 2 veins parallel to the midvein, smooth to slightly rough above, hairy beneath along veins. Flower heads clustered along spreading-ascending, curving branches of a pyramid-shaped panicle, mostly on 1 side of each branch; heads to 1/8 in. long, with 8–14 yellow ray florets and just a few yellow tubular disk florets. RTW

Solidago curtisii

ASTERACEAE | **Curtis's goldenrod**

Sep–Oct, 1–3 ft. Erect, rhizomatous perennial of moist forested slopes, clearings, and rarely in mafic woodlands. Stems mostly unbranched, angled and grooved, smooth or sparsely hairy. Leaves alternate (no basal rosette), short-petioled to sessile, broadly lance-shaped with a long-tapering point, to 6 in. long, toothed and sparsely hairy. Flower heads in small axillary clusters; heads about 1/4 in. wide, with 2–4 yellow ray florets encircling a small center disk of 3–9 yellow tubular florets. 3–4 series of very narrow green bracts surround the narrowly bell-shaped base of each head. LADI

Solidago erecta

ASTERACEAE | **showy goldenrod**

Aug–Oct, 1–4 ft. Erect, rhizomatous perennial of dry woodlands and woodland borders, old fields, grassy balds, barrens, and roadsides. Stems unbranched, smooth (at least below inflorescence). Basal leaves oval to lance-shaped, to 12 in. long, toothed, hairy on margins and on the winged, tapering petiole; stem leaves alternate, smaller. Flower heads along short, widely spaced branches of a terminal spike; heads about 1/4 in. long, with 5–9 yellow ray florets encircling a small center disk of tiny, yellow tubular florets. RTW

Solidago fistulosa

ASTERACEAE | **hairy pineywoods goldenrod**

Aug–Nov, 1½–5 ft. Erect perennial of pocosins, swamp forests, wet savannas, wet pine flatwoods, maritime forests; often forms dense patches via stolons and rhizomes. Stems branched in inflorescence, mostly smooth below but densely furry above. Leaves sessile with somewhat clasping bases, crowded and ascending, narrowly elliptical, to 4 in. long, toothed to entire, rough-hairy above and hairy beneath. Flower heads on 1 side of the arching branches of a dense terminal panicle; heads about 1/4 in. long, with 5–9 yellow ray florets encircling a center disk of yellow tubular florets. 4–5 unequal series of tiny green bracts surround the narrowly bell-shaped base of each head. PIP

Solidago flexicaulis

ASTERACEAE | **zigzag goldenrod**

Aug–Oct, 1–3 ft. Erect-ascending, rhizomatous perennial of moist wooded slopes, especially over calcareous or mafic rocks. Stems slightly angled, usually unbranched, zigzagging between nodes, smooth to sparsely hairy. Leaves alternate (no basal rosette), wing-petioled, oval to lance-shaped with abruptly tapered base, 2½–5 in. long (reduced above), sharply toothed, hairy along midvein beneath. Flower heads in short racemelike clusters at stem end and in leaf axils; heads ⅛–¼ in. wide, with 1–5 tiny, yellow ray florets encircling a small disk of 4–8 tiny, yellow tubular florets. RTW

Solidago gigantea

ASTERACEAE | **smooth goldenrod**

Aug–Oct, 2–6½ ft. Erect, rhizomatous perennial of old fields, roadsides, streamside meadows, and bottomlands. Stems mostly unbranched, smooth below inflorescence, usually with a white-waxy coating. Leaves alternate (no basal rosette), short-petioled to sessile, narrowly elliptical to lance-shaped, 2–6 in. long, sharply toothed, with 3 prominent parallel veins, finely hairy to smooth beneath. Flower heads densely clustered on spreading-ascending branches of a pyramid-shaped terminal panicle; heads about ¼ in. long, with 9–15 yellow ray florets encircling a small center disk of 5–11 yellow tubular florets. BAS

Solidago glomerata

ASTERACEAE | **skunk goldenrod**

Aug–Oct, 1½–3 ft. Erect-ascending, rhizomatous perennial of high-elevation grassy and heath balds, rock outcrops, northern hardwood forests, spruce-fir forests. Endemic to w NC, e TN. Stems 1–5, hairy in inflorescence. Leaves basal and alternate, thick and fleshy. Basal and lower leaves on winged petioles, lance-shaped to elliptical, to 10 in. long, toothed; upper leaves sessile, narrowly lance-shaped, hairy-margined. Flower heads in leafy, racemelike terminal and axillary clusters; heads ½–¾ in. long, with 6–13 yellow ray florets encircling a center disk of 12–28 tiny, yellow tubular florets. Distinctive skunky odor is detectable without touching or bruising the plant. PIP

Solidago juncea

ASTERACEAE | **early goldenrod**

Jul–Sep, 1–3 ft. Erect, rhizomatous perennial of meadows, pastures, woodland borders, road banks. Stems unbranched, green to reddish, smooth or nearly so, may be obscurely angled. Leaves basal and alternate, sessile (upper) or on winged petioles (basal), oblong-lance-shaped to narrowly oval, to 8 in. long (basal larger), vaguely toothed or entire, often with hairs along margin. Flower heads in a terminal panicle, mostly on 1 side of the arching branches; heads 1⁄4 in. wide, with 7–13 yellow ray florets (often unevenly spaced) encircling a central disk of 8–12 tiny, yellow tubular florets. Tiny green bracts cover the narrowly bell-shaped base of each head. BAS

Solidago mexicana

ASTERACEAE | **southern seaside goldenrod**

Aug–Dec, 1½–6 ft. Erect-ascending, rhizomatous perennial of coastal dunes, dune slacks, maritime wet grasslands, tidal marshes. Stems unbranched, sparsely hairy in lines. Leaves basal and alternate, numerous, on winged petioles (those of basal and lower leaves sheathing the stem), oblong-lance-shaped to lance-shaped, 2–12 in. long (reduced above), with prominent midrib, fleshy-thick, smooth. Flower heads in conical to narrowly pyramidal array of branches, with heads mostly on 1 side of each branch; heads with 7–11 small, yellow ray florets encircling a small center disk of 10–16 yellow tubular florets. Light green bracts cover the base of each head. GPF

Solidago nemoralis

ASTERACEAE | **eastern gray goldenrod**

Jun–Oct, 1½–3 ft. Erect, rhizomatous perennial of woodlands, glades, barrens, road banks. Stems 1–6, unbranched, covered with short, white hairs; inflorescence may lean with weight of flowers. Leaves basal and alternate. Basal leaves on winged petioles (but not sheathing), oblong-spoon-shaped, 2–4 in. long, toothed and hairy; upper leaves sessile, smaller, hairy, and with tufts of tiny leaves in the axils. Flower heads along the nodding branches of a vaguely pyramidal terminal array, mostly on the upper side of each branch; heads about 1⁄4 in. wide, with 5–11 small, yellow ray florets encircling a center disk of a few tiny, yellow tubular florets. GMP

Solidago patula

ASTERACEAE | **northern roughleaf goldenrod**

Aug–Oct, 1½–5 ft. Erect, rhizomatous perennial of bogs, seepages over mafic rocks, and grassy balds. Stems sharply 4-angled (sometimes with wings), unbranched (except in inflorescence), smooth. Leaves basal and alternate, petiolate (some winged), elliptical, 4–12 in. long (becoming lance-shaped and smaller above), sharply toothed (uppermost leaves may be entire), rough above and smooth beneath; lower leaves may wither by bloom time. Flower heads in an open terminal panicle, mostly on 1 side of the arching-ascending branches; heads less than ¼ in. wide, with 5–12 small, yellow ray florets encircling a center disk of 5–15 tiny, yellow tubular florets. RTW

Solidago petiolaris

ASTERACEAE | **downy ragged goldenrod**

Aug–Nov, 3–5 ft. Erect perennial of upland forests and woodlands. Stems stout, minutely hairy (at least above). Leaves alternate (no basal rosette), sessile to short-petioled, elliptical and short-pointed, 1–3 in. long, shallowly toothed toward the tip or entire, smooth or rough-hairy above, hairy beneath. Flower heads on stiffly ascending branches of a terminal panicle, not limited to 1 side of each branch; heads with 7–9 yellow ray florets encircling a center disk of 10–16 tiny, yellow tubular florets. 3–4 series of tiny, green, lance-shaped bracts with recurved tips surround the bell-shaped base of each head. SH

Solidago pinetorum

ASTERACEAE | **pineywoods goldenrod**

Jul–Sep, 2–3 ft. Erect to ascending, rhizomatous perennial of dry woodlands, woodland borders, road banks, and dry pinelands. Stems obscurely angled, mostly smooth. Leaves basal and alternate, sessile, linear to lance-shaped (basal oblong-lance), 2½–6 in. long, sparingly toothed, and smooth; upper leaves smaller, spreading or reflexed. Flower heads abundant along the nodding branches of a vaguely pyramidal terminal array, mostly on the upper side of each branch; heads about ¼ in. wide, with 3–8 yellow ray florets encircling a center disk of 3–9 tiny, yellow tubular florets. 2–3 series of tiny green bracts surround the narrowly bell-shaped base of each head. BAS

Solidago rigida

ASTERACEAE | **bold goldenrod**

Aug–Oct, 2–5 ft. Erect perennial of glades, barrens, prairielike areas, over mafic or calcareous rocks, and in adjacent disturbed areas. Stems ridged or grooved, unbranched (except in inflorescence), covered with coarse, stiff hairs. Leaves ascending, petiolate below, sessile above, oval to diamond-shaped, 3–8 in. long (reduced above), with a prominent central vein, toothed or wavy-margined, densely hairy. Flower heads in a hairy, flat-topped, open-branching terminal array; heads to ½ in. wide, with 6–13 yellow ray florets encircling a center disk of 14–35 yellow tubular florets. 3–4 series of tiny green bracts surround the bell-shaped base of each head. RTW

Solidago rugosa

ASTERACEAE | **rough-leaf goldenrod**

Aug–Oct, 3–5 ft. Erect to ascending, rhizomatous perennial of floodplain forests and bogs, wet flatwoods, balds, clearings, meadows, upland forests. Stems few-branched, light green to brownish-red, spreading-hairy, at least above. Leaves numerous, crowded, lance-shaped to elliptical, 1–5 in. long (reduced above), with indented veins, toothed, rough to smooth above, smooth to hairy beneath. Flower heads in wide or racemelike terminal panicle, along (mostly) 1 side of arching branches; heads less than ¼ in. wide, with 3–13 yellow ray florets encircling a small center disk of yellow tubular florets. Yellowish-green bracts cover the narrowly bell-shaped base of each head. EO

Solidago sphacelata

ASTERACEAE | **limestone goldenrod**

Jul–Oct, 1½–3½ ft. Erect to ascending-arching perennial of dry rocky forests (usually over calcareous or mafic rocks) and rock outcrops. Stem usually 1, densely spreading-hairy. Basal leaves petiolate, slightly winged, heart-shaped (base may be only barely notched), 1½–4½ in. long, coarsely sharp-toothed, spreading-hairy; stem leaves alternate, short-petioled to sessile, oval to lance-shaped, reduced above. Flower heads terminal, clustered mainly along 1 side of each arching branch; heads ¼ in. long, with 3–6 yellow ray florets encircling a center disk of 3–6 tiny, yellow tubular florets. 2–3 series of tiny, unequal, oval bracts surround the base of each head. JG

Verbesina alternifolia

ASTERACEAE | **common wingstem**

Aug–Oct, 3–9 ft. Erect perennial found in alluvial forests, marshes, and floodplain pastures. Stems branched in inflorescence, usually winged, smooth or hairy. Leaves short-petioled to sessile, lance-shaped, to 10 in. long, usually toothed, rough-hairy. Flower heads in large, open, branching terminal cluster; heads to 2½ in. wide, with 2–10 drooping, yellow ray florets (⅓–1 in. long) encircling a domed center disk of greenish-yellow, tubular florets. Fruit a spherical head of sometimes winged achenes. RTW

Arnica acaulis

ASTERACEAE | **leopard's-bane**

Mar–Jun, 1–3 ft. Erect perennial of pine savannas, sandhills, clayey or sandy woodlands, powerline rights-of-way, road banks. Stem arising from basal rosette, with a few branches especially in inflorescence, densely glandular-hairy. Basal leaves broadly elliptical to oval, 1½–4 in. long, with 5–7 parallel veins prominent beneath, thick, densely furry above, less so beneath; a few smaller, opposite, ascending leaves occur on the stem. Flower heads 2–30 at ends of branches; heads yellow, 1–2 in. wide, with 10–15 ray florets with toothed tips encircling a central disk of tubular florets. A series of hairy, narrow, pointed green bracts surrounds the base of each head. BAS, WS

Borrichia frutescens

ASTERACEAE | **silver seaside oxeye**

Jan–Dec, ½–5 ft. Erect, bushy, colonial perennial of salt and brackish marshes, overwash flats, salt flats, disturbed tidal shores. Stems profusely branched, succulent, usually densely gray-hairy. Leaves spoon-shaped to lance-elliptical, to 3 in. long, succulent, gray-green, hairy. Daisylike flower heads held on stalks at ends of branches; heads about ⅔ in. wide, with 12–30 short, yellow ray florets encircling a central disk of tiny, yellow tubular florets interspersed with spiny bracts. A series of small, green bracts surrounds the base of each head. Many somewhat flattened, triangular seeds are packed into the brown, spiny, burlike remains of the flower head. BAS

Coreopsis linifolia

ASTERACEAE | **savanna coreopsis**

Jul–Oct, 1½–3½ ft. Erect to leaning perennial of pine savannas, sandhill seeps, and sandhill-pocosin ecotones. Stems ribbed, unbranched, smooth. Leaves basal and mostly opposite on the stem, petiolate (basal ones only), oblong-lance-shaped, to 7 in. long, stiff and thick, with minute dark dots beneath; reduced and bractlike above. Flower heads solitary at the end of the stem, to 2 in. wide, with 5–20 long, yellow ray florets with toothed tips encircling a dense center disk of tiny, dark red, 4-lobed tubular florets. Several series of small, pointed green bracts surround the base of the head, these sometimes streaked with red. WS

Krigia cespitosa

ASTERACEAE | **opposite-leaf dwarf-dandelion**

Mar–Jun, 4–18 in. Erect annual of fields, roadsides, and other disturbed places. Stem arising from a winter rosette, branching from the base, smooth, and often with a whitish coating; broken stems ooze milky sap. Leaves basal and more or less opposite on the stem, petiolate, linear-oblong, ½–5 in. long (reduced above). Flower heads solitary at ends of branches, about ½ in. wide, with 12–35 orange-yellow ray florets with squared-off, toothed tips. Narrow green bracts surround the bell-shaped base of each head. Fruit a fluffy cluster of tufted achenes. KB

Acanthospermum australe

ASTERACEAE | **Paraguay bur**

May–Nov, 1–5 ft. long. Prostrate-trailing, taprooted annual of disturbed areas. Native to South America. Stems prostrate, branching, usually rooting at nodes and short-hairy, at least toward stem ends. Leaves petiolate, oval to diamond-shaped, coarsely toothed, fleshy, gland-dotted. Flower heads solitary at ends of branches, about ¼ in. wide, with about 5 whitish-yellow ray florets in a ring around a few 5-lobed, tubular disk florets, all surrounded by a series of tiny bracts. Fruit a vaguely star-shaped (5-sided) nutlet covered with hooked prickles. BAS

Bidens cernua

ASTERACEAE | **nodding bur-marigold**

Aug–Oct, 1–3 ft. Erect to reclining annual of marshes, wet meadows, bogs, ditches. Stems simple or sparingly branched, usually smooth or with short rough hairs. Leaves sessile or clasping, lance-shaped, 1½–8 in. long, usually coarsely toothed, smooth. Flower heads on long stalks from upper leaf axils, starting out erect but later nodding; heads ½–1½ in. wide, with 6–8 yellow, elliptical ray florets with toothed tips (may be absent) encircling a center disk of yellow, 5-lobed tubular florets. 2 series of bracts, the inner yellow, the outer green and curling backward with age, surround the base of the head. Fruit an achene with 4 (or 2) barbed awns. GPF

Bidens laevis

ASTERACEAE | **showy bur-marigold**

Aug–Nov, 1–3 ft., occasionally to 7 ft. Erect annual/perennial of marshes, pond edges, streambanks, and ditches. Stems unbranched to freely branched and smooth. Leaves usually sessile, oval or lance-shaped, 1½–6 in. long, finely toothed and smooth. Flower heads 1–several terminating stem, erect or often nodding in age; heads 1½–2½ in. wide, with 7–8 yellow ray florets (at least as long as the outer bracts) encircling a slightly domed center disk of dark yellow, 5-lobed tubular florets. 2 series of bracts, the inner pale yellow and oval, the outer green and narrower, surround the base of each head. Fruit a flat or angled achene with 2–4 barbed awns. BAS

Chrysogonum virginianum

ASTERACEAE | **green-and-gold**

Mar–Jun, 2–10 in. Erect to spreading perennial of moist to fairly dry woodlands and forests. Stems branched, leafy, glandular, and hairy. Leaves petiolate, rounded to oval or oblong, 1–4 in. long, toothed or scalloped, hairy. Flower heads single or in pairs on erect stalks from leaf axils, ¾–1½ in. wide, with 5 yellow ray florets with 3-toothed tips encircling a center disk of 25–50 yellow-green tubular florets. BAS

Helianthus atrorubens

ASTERACEAE | **Appalachian sunflower**

Jul–Oct, 2½–6½ ft. Erect, rhizomatous perennial found in the dry soils of rocky, sandy, or clayey woodlands, pine savannas, road banks. Stems simple to few-branched, rough-hairy near base, with softer hairs toward the tip. Leaves mostly basal or on lower stems, opposite, on broadly winged petioles, oval to diamond-shaped, 2–8 in. long, toothed or scalloped, rough; upper stem leaves similar but fewer, smaller. Flower heads in small clusters; heads to 3 in. wide, with 10–15 yellow ray florets encircling a center disk of dark purple tubular florets. Overlapping oval or oblong bracts surround the base of each head. Fruit a dark brown, sparsely bristled, narrowly oval achene. WS

Helianthus decapetalus

ASTERACEAE | **forest sunflower**

Jul–Oct, 2–5 ft., occasionally to 8 ft. Erect, rhizomatous perennial of floodplain forests, moist upland woodlands and forests, and oak savannas. Stems simple or branched only below, smooth. Leaves opposite (uppermost leaves sometimes alternate) on narrowly winged petioles, broadly lance-shaped or oval, 3–8 in. long, thin or membranous, sharply toothed, rough above, light green and nearly hairless beneath. Flower heads solitary or in open clusters, 1½–3½ in. wide, with 8–15 yellow ray florets encircling a center disk of yellow tubular florets. Overlapping, spreading, long and slender bracts surround the base of each head. Fruit a dark, flattened, oblong achene. JP

Helianthus divaricatus

ASTERACEAE | **spreading sunflower**

Jun–Aug, 2–7 ft. Erect, rhizomatous perennial of moist to dry woodlands, forests, and forest edges and clearings. Stems simple or branched at the end, mostly smooth, often with a whitish coating. Leaves spreading horizontally, sessile, lance-shaped, 2–6 in. long, with 3 veins diverging from the base, toothed or entire, rough above or on both surfaces, lower surface soft-hairy. Flower heads in terminal clusters, 1½–3 in. wide, with 8–15 yellow ray florets encircling a center disk of darker yellow tubular florets. Overlapping, upwardly curving bracts surround the base of each head. Fruit a dark brown to blackish, flattened, oval achene. BAS

Helianthus hirsutus

ASTERACEAE | **hairy sunflower**

Jul–Oct, 2½–6 ft. Erect, rhizomatous perennial of dry open woodlands, prairies, and other sunny habitats. Stems simple or fork-branched above, light green to reddish-purple, covered with spreading hairs. Leaves in pairs at 90° to each other (may be a few alternate), short-petioled, lance-shaped, to 6½ in. long, with 3 conspicuous veins, usually hairy on both surfaces, sandpaper-like above. Flower heads solitary or in small clusters; heads 2–3 in. wide, with 8–15 yellow ray florets encircling a center disk of numerous yellow tubular florets. Spreading, green, narrow, pointed bracts surround the base of each head. Fruit a brown, narrowly oval, flattened achene. RTW

Helianthus microcephalus

ASTERACEAE | **small-headed sunflower**

Jul–Oct, 2–6½ ft., occasionally taller. Erect, rhizomatous perennial of dry woodlands, forests, barrens, clearings, and road banks. Stems branched above, dark greenish-purple, often with a whitish coating, smooth. Leaves mostly opposite, long-petioled, lance-shaped, 3–6 in. long, 3-veined, toothed but entire near the base, thin, rough-hairy above, resin-dotted and usually short-hairy beneath. Flower heads numerous on long slender stalks; heads 1–1½ in. wide, with 5–8 yellow ray florets encircling a center disk of darker yellow tubular florets. Overlapping, pointed green bracts surround the base of each head. Fruit a dark brown to blackish achene. EO

Helianthus strumosus

ASTERACEAE | **roughleaf sunflower**

Jul–Sep, 3–9 ft. Erect, rhizomatous perennial of dry woodlands, prairies, barrens, roadsides. Stems smooth (may be slightly hairy below flower head), often branched above and with a whitish coating. Leaves petiolate, lance-shaped or oval, 3–9 in. long, shallowly toothed, thick and firm, rough-hairy above, white-waxy or downy and resin-dotted beneath. Flower heads mostly solitary at ends of branches; heads 1½–2½ in. wide (may be up to 4 in.), with 8–15 yellow ray florets encircling a center disk of yellow tubular florets. Overlapping, spreading, narrow and pointed bracts with hairy margins surround the base of each head. Fruit a mottled light-and-dark-brown achene. PHA

Heliopsis helianthoides

ASTERACEAE | **eastern oxeye**

May–Oct, 2–5 ft. Erect, rhizomatous perennial of open forests, clearings, woodlands, and woodland borders. Stems simple or branched above, mostly smooth, and often with a white-waxy coating. Leaves petiolate, oval to lance-oval with tapered tip, 2–6 in. long, sharply toothed, often rough-surfaced above, slightly hairy beneath. Flower heads solitary on long stalks from upper leaf axils; heads 1½–3½ in. wide, with 8–16 bright yellow, linear-oblong ray florets with slightly notched tips encircling a domed center disk of 30 or more darker yellow-orange, 5-lobed tubular florets. PIP

Silphium perfoliatum

ASTERACEAE | **common cup-plant**

Jun–Aug, 4–8 ft. Coarse, erect perennial found in floodplain forests and openings; sometimes escaped from cultivation. Stems stout, 4-sided, unbranched, smooth, exuding a gummy sap when broken. Leaves sessile, at least the upper ones joined together at the base so that the stem appears to pierce each pair (with the resultant "cup" able to hold water), oval to broadly lance-shaped, 6–14 in. long, coarsely toothed, and rough-surfaced. Flower heads on stalks in branching terminal cluster; heads 2–3 in. wide, with 16–35 yellow ray florets encircling a center disk of darker yellow tubular florets. Fruit a thin, winged achene. GMP

Tetragonotheca helianthoides

ASTERACEAE | **pineland-ginseng**

Apr–Jul, 1–3 ft. Erect-ascending, tufted perennial of sandhills, longleaf pinelands and other sandy woodlands, open hammocks, and roadsides. Stems 1–few, sparsely branched, hairy. Leaves sessile with winged bases (lower leaves may be petiolate), elliptical to oval or diamond-shaped, 4–7 in. long, toothed. Flower heads solitary at stem tips; each head with 6–10 well-separated yellow ray florets encircling a flattish center disk of darker yellow tubular florets. Each head rests on 4 large, oval bracts that collectively suggest a square. WS

Verbesina occidentalis

ASTERACEAE | **southern crownbeard**

Aug–Sep, 3–10 ft. Erect perennial found in forests, woodlands, pastures, and roadsides, especially abundant in alluvial areas or upslope over mafic or calcareous rocks. Stems 4-winged, branched in inflorescence, minutely hairy above and smooth beneath. Leaves on winged petioles, broadly oval, 2½–9 in. long, shallowly toothed, hairy beneath. Flower heads in a large, open, branching terminal cluster; heads to 2½ in. wide, with 1–5 bright yellow ray florets (each to ¾ in. long) encircling a domed center disk of greenish-yellow tubular florets. Fruit a spherical head of achenes (lacking wings). RTW

Hieracium venosum

ASTERACEAE | **rattlesnakeweed**

Apr–Sep, 10–32 in. Erect, acaulescent, rhizomatous perennial of dry forests, woodland margins, and roadsides. Stems slender, arising from center of basal rosette, green or purple, mostly leafless, hairy at base. Leaves basal, elliptic-oblong with broadly rounded tip, 1½–6 in. long, green with reddish-purple veins, often with black dots above and reddish-purple beneath, hairy. Flower heads in wide-branching terminal cluster; heads ½–¾ in. wide, with many yellow ray florets with squared-off, toothed tips. Many green, glandular-hairy bracts surround the cylindrical base of each head. Fruit a fluffy cluster of achenes with pale yellow tufts of hair. BAS

Pilosella caespitosa (*Hieracium caespitosum*)

ASTERACEAE | **yellow king-devil**

May–Oct, 8–30 in. Erect, rhizomatous perennial of pastures, fields, roadsides, and grassy balds. Native to Europe. Stem a leafless flowering stalk arising from a basal rosette; densely hairy, with black-glandular hairs prominent on upper stem. Leaves basal, oblong-lance-shaped, 1½–6 in. long, with hairs along margins and on both surfaces. Flower heads 5–30 in a compact, terminal cluster; heads ½–¾ in. wide, with numerous yellow ray florets with squared-off, 5-toothed tips. Linear-oblong bracts covered with glandular, black hairs surround the base of each head. KB

Krigia dandelion

ASTERACEAE | **colonial dwarf-dandelion**

Apr–Jun, to 12 in. Erect perennial from fibrous roots with nodules, found in rocky woodlands and barrens, moist to semi-moist forests, roadsides, and other disturbed areas. Stems consist of mostly leafless flowering stalk(s) arising from a basal rosette, smooth and with a whitish coating, sometimes red-tinged, oozing milky sap when broken. Leaves basal, long-spoon-shaped to linear-lance-shaped with gradually narrowed base, 1–6 in. long, smooth, with margins toothed, lobed, or entire. Flower heads solitary at tip of stem, about 1 in. wide, with multiple orangish-yellow ray florets with squared-off, 5-toothed tips. Fruit a fluffy cluster of tufted achenes. BAS

Krigia montana

ASTERACEAE | **mountain dwarf-dandelion**

May–Sep, 4–15 in. Erect perennial of cliffs and rock outcrops at mid to high elevations. Stems branched near base, mostly leafless, oozing milky sap when broken. Leaves mostly basal, linear to lance-shaped, 1½–4 in. long, wider ones coarsely toothed or lobed near the base. Flower heads solitary at tips of branches, about 1 in. wide, with multiple yellow ray florets with squared-off, 5-toothed tips. Narrow green bracts surround the bell-shaped base of each head. Fruit a fluffy cluster of tufted achenes. AMC

Krigia virginica

ASTERACEAE | **Virginia dwarf-dandelion**

Feb–Nov, 1–12 in. Erect annual from a basal rosette, found in dry, open forests, rocky woodlands, roadsides, and disturbed areas. Stem consists of a flowering stalk arising from the center of the basal rosette; it may be branched, is glandular-hairy (especially above), and oozes milky sap when broken. Leaves mostly basal, oblong-lance-shaped to elliptical, to 5 in. long, sharply and irregularly lobed and toothed, usually hairy. Flower heads solitary at top of stem, about ½ in. wide, with many golden yellow ray florets with squared-off, 5-toothed tips. Narrow, green or red-tinged bracts surround the bell-shaped base of each head. Fruit a fluffy cluster of tufted achenes. FG

Tussilago farfara

ASTERACEAE | **coltsfoot**

Mar–Jun, 3–12 in. Erect perennial of roadsides, especially gravelly or shaley road banks or ditches, streamside gravel bars, and other disturbed areas. Native to Eurasia. Stems reddish and scaly with many clasping, lance-shaped bracts; hairy. Leaves mostly basal, long-petioled, broadly rounded with a notched base, 2–8 in. long and wide, palmately veined, scallop-edged, persistently white-woolly beneath; leaves develop after flowering. Flower heads solitary at stem tip; heads begin cylindrical but expand to 1–1¼ in. wide, consisting of numerous bright yellow ray florets and a smaller number of yellow tubular disk florets. Fruit a fluffy cluster of white-tufted seeds. RTW

Packera anonyma

ASTERACEAE | **Appalachian ragwort**

May–Jun, 1–2½ ft. Erect, rhizomatous perennial found on rock outcrops, rocky woodlands, and roadsides. Stems branched in inflorescence, smooth but hairy at the base and sometimes in leaf axils. Basal and lower (alternate) leaves petiolate, elliptical to lance-shaped, to 3½ in. long and finely toothed; upper stem leaves smaller, mostly sessile, and deeply toothed to pinnately lobed. Flower heads in a branching terminal cluster; heads about ¾ in. wide, with 8–13 yellow ray florets encircling a slightly domed center disk of tiny, yellow tubular florets. BAS

Packera aurea

ASTERACEAE | **golden ragwort**

Mar–Jun, 1–2 ft. Erect, rhizomatous perennial of moist forests, bottomlands, bogs, and streambanks. Stems 1–several, often tufted, branched in inflorescence, bearing cobwebby hairs when young but becoming smooth. Basal leaves petiolate, round to heart-shaped but with rounded tip, 1–2½ in. long, round-toothed, purple and sometimes furry beneath; stem leaves alternate, smaller, mostly sessile, elliptical to lance-shaped, pinnately lobed or toothed. Flower heads in branched, more or less flat-topped terminal cluster; heads ½–¾ in. wide, with 8–13 yellow ray florets encircling a slightly domed center disk of tiny, yellow tubular florets. Fruit a small, tufted achene. BAS

Packera glabella

ASTERACEAE | **butterweed**

Mar–Jun, 1–3 ft. Erect annual/biennial of swamp forests, bottomland forests, and cleared areas in bottomlands, often in mucky soils. Stems stout, hollow, branched in inflorescence, light green to reddish-green. Leaves petiolate, elliptical to oblong-lance-shaped, 2–8 in. long (reduced and sessile above), deeply lobed and the lobes nearly opposite (pinnate), irregular in shape, toothed. Flower heads in branched terminal clusters and smaller clusters from leaf axils; heads about ½ in. wide, with 5–15 yellow ray florets encircling a center disk of tiny, golden yellow tubular florets. Fruit a small, tufted achene. BAS

Packera obovata

ASTERACEAE | **roundleaf ragwort**

Apr–Jun, 8–28 in. Erect perennial of nutrient-rich forests and woodlands (dry or moist), usually over calcareous or mafic rocks. Stems branched in inflorescence, hairy when young, later smooth; often forming large colonies via stolons or creeping rhizomes. Basal leaves on winged petioles (sometimes cobwebby-hairy), broadly oval to rounded, 1½–4 in. long; stem leaves few, elliptical in outline, to 2½ in. long, variably pinnately lobed or toothed. Flower heads in a flat-topped, branching terminal cluster; heads ½–1 in. wide, with 8–16 yellow ray florets encircling a slightly domed central disk of tiny, orange-yellow, tubular florets. Fruit a small, tufted achene. RTW

Pyrrhopappus carolinianus

ASTERACEAE | **false-dandelion**

Mar–Jun or later, 6–20 in. Erect to ascending annual/biennial of both dry and moist forests, roadsides, meadows, and fields. Stems mostly smooth and leafless, with a few branches, leaking milky sap when broken. Leaves basal and (smaller) alternate, petiolate, oblong-lance-shaped, to 10 in. long, toothed or irregularly lobed, mostly smooth. Flower heads solitary at tips of stems and branches; heads to 2½ in. wide, with many lemon-yellow ray florets with squared-off, toothed tips (no disk florets); erect in the center are many slender, yellow styles, each enclosed by a sleeve of dark stamens. Fruit a tufted achene. BAS

Rudbeckia laciniata

ASTERACEAE | **cutleaf coneflower**

Jul–Oct, 3–7 ft. Erect, rhizomatous, colonial perennial of bottomlands, riverbanks, wet meadows, clearings, roadsides, moist upland forests. Stems branched, smooth, often with a white-waxy coating. Leaves petiolate (narrowly winged), drooping, lance-shaped to broadly oval in outline, to 18 in. long (reduced above), hairy beneath and rough above. Lower leaves pinnately divided into 5–many, toothed or lobed segments; upper leaves with fewer or no lobes. Flower heads solitary on long, erect stalks (ends of branches); heads to 1½ in. wide, with 5–13 drooping, yellow ray florets encircling a domed center disk of greenish-yellow tubular florets which enlarges with time. WS

Rudbeckia triloba

ASTERACEAE | **three-lobed coneflower**

Jul–Oct, 1–3 ft. Erect, rhizomatous perennial of moist forests and rock outcrops. Stems branched, often dark red, hairy. Leaves petiolate (lower leaves) to sessile, lance-shaped to oval, slightly to coarsely toothed, rough-textured from minute stiff hairs; some lower leaves divided into 3 lobes. Flower heads solitary (or 2) at tips of branches, 1½–2 in. wide, with 6–12 bright yellow, oblong ray florets encircling a brown to black, flattened-cone-shaped center disk of numerous tubular florets. RTW

Senecio vulgaris

ASTERACEAE | **common groundsel**

Mar–Jun, 4–16 in. Erect annual from a taproot, found on roadsides, fields, and other disturbed areas. Native to Eurasia. Stems branched, covered in cobwebby hairs, becoming smooth later. Leaves petiolate (lower) and sessile-clasping (upper), lance-shaped, 1–4 in. long, wavy margined to pinnately lobed (irregular, jagged lobes), and with margins curved downward, somewhat fleshy, smooth or hairy. Flower heads in dense, terminal clusters on short stalks; heads cylindrical, about ⅓ in. long, with many tiny, yellow tubular disk florets (no ray florets). Hairless, green, linear bracts with black tips tightly surround the head. Fruit a tufted, slender achene. RTW

Silphium compositum

ASTERACEAE | **kidneyleaf rosinweed**

May–Sep, 1½–8 ft. Erect perennial of dry woodlands, clearings, meadows, sandhills, road banks. Stems flexible and wandlike, smooth, often with a white-waxy coating. Leaves alternate but clustered near base of stem, long-petioled, oval to kidney-shaped but toothed to deeply pinnately lobed, to 14 in. long (reduced above), often with a red midvein, thick, smooth or hairy. Flower heads in a loosely forking, terminal cluster; heads to 2 in. wide, with 6–12 bright yellow ray florets encircling a center disk of 20 or more tiny, dull yellow, tubular florets. Several series of green, broadly oval bracts surround the cuplike base of each head. RTW

Smallanthus uvedalia

ASTERACEAE | **bearsfoot**

Jul–Oct, 3–10 ft. Erect perennial of moist forests, bottomland forests, disturbed places. Stems stout, branched above, smooth but with spreading hairs and glandular on branches. Leaves on winged petioles (these forming "cups" where they meet the stem), oval to triangular, to 14 in. long, rough-hairy above, finely hairy beneath, palmately lobed with lobes coarsely toothed. Flower heads in leafy, branching terminal cluster; heads to 3 in. wide, with 8–15 bright yellow ray florets with notched or toothed tips encircling a flattish center disk of 40–80 tiny, darker yellow tubular florets. 4–6 green, glandular-hairy oval bracts surround the saucer-shaped base of each head. BAS

Sonchus asper

ASTERACEAE | **prickly sow-thistle**

Mar–Jul, 1–5 ft. Erect annual of open, disturbed areas. Native to Europe. Stems reddish to dull green, often with longitudinal lines, sparingly branched above, smooth. Stems and leaves leak milky sap when broken. Leaves sessile with rounded basal lobes clasping the stem, lance- to oblong-lance-shaped, to 10 in. long, folded upward along the central vein, with conspicuously prickly-toothed margins, shiny and smooth. Flower heads in branching terminal cluster on a long stalk; heads ½–¾ in. wide, with numerous yellow ray florets. The urn-shaped base of the head is enclosed in dull green, lance-shaped bracts. Fruit a cluster of white-tufted achenes. BAS

Sonchus oleraceus

ASTERACEAE | **common sow-thistle**

May–Oct, ½–5 ft. Erect annual of roadsides, fields, pastures, and other open, disturbed areas. Native to Europe. Stems mostly unbranched, sometimes reddish-purple-tinged, usually smooth. Stems and leaves leak milky sap when broken. Leaves sessile with pointed basal lobes clasping the stem, oblong-oval to lance-shaped, 2–11 in. long, divided into several sharp-toothed segments, with a few prickles on the margins, smooth. Flower heads in small branching terminal cluster on a long stalk; heads about ¾ in. wide, with numerous yellow ray florets with blunt tips. Fruit a cluster of white-tufted achenes. RTW

Youngia japonica

ASTERACEAE | **Asiatic hawk's-beard**

Apr–Jun, 4–28 in. Taprooted annual of roadsides, trailsides, clearings. Native to se Asia; moving rapidly into minimally disturbed natural areas, open or shaded. Stems 1–several, may be reddish-purple-tinged, hairy below, smoother above. Leaves mostly basal but also reduced on the stem, petiolate, pale green tinted reddish-purple, oblong-lance-shaped, 2–5 in. long, quasi-pinnate with jagged edges, densely hairy, the hairs brownish and crinkled. Flower heads in branching terminal cluster, the closed heads fig-shaped, bright yellow, ⅓ in. wide, with 10–20 ray florets with squared-off, 5-toothed tips. A series of narrow green bracts with fleshy midribs surrounds each head. BAS

Coreopsis grandiflora

ASTERACEAE | **largeflower coreopsis**

May–Jun, 2–3 ft. Erect perennial of thin soils on rock outcrops, especially granitic flatrocks. Stems unbranched, smooth. Leaves petiolate, the lower ones lance-shaped and undivided, the middle and upper ones to 3 in. long and pinnately divided into several narrow segments, the center one being broadest. Flower heads solitary on naked, terminal stalks; heads 1½–2 in. wide, with 8 yellow ray florets with toothed tips encircling a dense center disk of yellow, 5-lobed tubular florets. 2 series of bracts, the inner straw-colored, the outer green, surround the base of each head. AMC

Coreopsis major

ASTERACEAE | **woodland coreopsis**

May–Aug, 2–3 ft. Erect, rhizomatous perennial of dry upland woodlands and forests, barrens, outcrops, clearings, and road banks. Stems unbranched, hairy. Leaves sessile, most divided into 3 oval to lance-shaped leaflets (to 4 in. long) and thus appearing to be 6 whorled leaves; hairy. Flower heads in a loose terminal cluster; heads 1½–3 in. wide, with 8 bright yellow ray florets encircling a dense center disk of many tiny, yellow tubular florets that age to maroon-red. 2 series of bracts surround the base of the head, the outer green and narrow, the inner yellowish-green, wider, and downcurved at the tips. BAS

Coreopsis pubescens

ASTERACEAE | **hairy coreopsis**

Jul–Sep, 2–4 ft. Erect perennial of forests, woodlands, and rock outcrops. Stems branched, leafy, often with spreading hairs. Leaves petiolate, oval to lance-shaped, to 4 in. long, often with 1–2 pairs of basal lobes, hairy to smooth. Flower heads solitary or several in a loose cluster at top of stem, about 2 in. wide, with yellow ray florets with notched/toothed tips encircling a dense center disk of yellow tubular florets. 2 series of bracts, inner and outer, surround the base of each head. Fruit an oval achene with 2 short, thin teeth at one end. Like all coreopsis, a nectar source for butterflies and seed food source for birds. WS

Coreopsis tripteris

ASTERACEAE | **tall coreopsis**

Jul–Sep, 4–6 ft. Erect, rhizomatous perennial of rich, moist woodlands and woodland borders, primarily over calcareous or mafic rocks or on nutrient-rich alluvium. Stems unbranched except in inflorescence, smooth and sometimes whitish. Leaves mostly opposite, petiolate or sessile, 1–4 in. long and divided into 3–5 linear to oblong-lance-shaped segments (uppermost leaves lance-shaped and undivided), margins sometimes rolled downward. Flower heads solitary on branches of an open, terminal cluster; heads yellow with dark centers, 1½–2 in. wide, with 8 yellow ray florets encircling a dense center of dark purple to maroon, tubular disk florets. ER

Bidens aristosa

ASTERACEAE | **midwestern tickseed-sunflower**

Aug–Nov, to 6 ft. Erect annual/biennial of marshes, wet meadows, and ditches. Stems much-branched, green or reddish and smooth or with fine, short hairs. Leaves petiolate, 1–6 in. long and pinnately divided into 5–7 lance-shaped or linear segments with pointed tips and toothed margins; segments sometimes again pinnately divided. Flower heads solitary or in small clusters; heads 2–3 in. wide, with about 8 yellow ray florets encircling a central disk of yellow tubular florets. 2 series of bracts, the inner membranous, the outer green, surround the base of the head. Fruit a flattened achene with 2 barbed awns that stick to fur and clothing. BAS

Bidens bipinnata

ASTERACEAE | **Spanish needles**

Jul–Oct, 1–5 ft. Erect annual of floodplains, disturbed areas, gardens, fields, roadsides, and ditches. Stems widely branched and smooth or minutely hairy. Leaves petiolate, 1½–8 in. long, 2–3 times pinnately divided into lance-shaped or oval segments with blunt teeth or lobes, mostly smooth; leaves resemble fern fronds. Flower heads on short to long stalks at ends of stems and branches; heads about ½ in. long, with 3–5 yellow, oval ray florets (often absent) encircling a center disk of dark yellow tubular florets. Fruit a very narrow, needlelike achene bearing 2–4 barbed awns. JG

Bidens discoidea

ASTERACEAE | **few-bracted beggar-ticks**

Aug–Nov, 1–3 ft., occasionally to 6 ft. Erect annual of floodplain forests and marshes. Stems slender, few- to bushy-branched, commonly red, smooth. Leaves long-petioled, 2–4¾ in. long, pinnately divided into 3–5 lance-shaped segments with long tapering tips (upper leaves may be undivided) and sharply toothed margins, mostly smooth. Flower heads on short to long stalks; heads ⅛–⅜ in. wide, rayless, with deep yellow to orange tubular disk florets. 2 series of bracts, the inner light or yellowish-green, the outer leaflike and green, surround the bell-shaped base of each head. Fruit a hairy achene bearing 2 very short, barbed awns (or awnless). BAS

Bidens frondosa

ASTERACEAE | **devil's beggar-ticks**

Jun–Oct, 1–4 ft. Erect annual of wet meadows, swamp forests, ditches. Stems branched in upper half, often purplish, mostly smooth. Leaves long-petioled, 1½–4½ in. long, pinnately divided into 3–5 lance-shaped, sharply toothed leaflets that taper to a sharp point; softly hairy beneath. Flower heads usually solitary, or in 2–3 stalked clusters; heads orange-yellow, ½–1 in. wide, with tiny, orange-yellow, 5-lobed tubular disk florets (rarely 1–3 yellow ray florets). 2 series of bracts, the inner brownish-green, erect and oval, the outer long, leaflike, and hairy-edged, surround the round to bell-shaped base of each head. Fruit a flat, dark brown achene with 2 barbed awns. AMC

Coreopsis lanceolata

ASTERACEAE | **longstalk coreopsis**

Apr–Jun, 1–2 ft. Erect to ascending, rhizomatous perennial of roadsides, fields, clearings, typically growing in clumps. Stems unbranched, with just 1–5 leaf nodes below the inflorescence, smooth or hairy. Leaves petiolate (upper leaves sessile), elliptical to oblong-lance-shaped, 3–6 in. long, pinnately lobed (upper) or with only 1–2 lateral lobes at the base (lower), smooth or sparsely hairy. Flower heads solitary or a few at the end of a naked, terminal stalk; heads 1–2 in. wide, with 8 yellow ray florets with toothed tips encircling a dense center disk of yellow tubular florets. 2 series of yellowish-green bracts surround the base of each head. BAS

Coreopsis tinctoria

ASTERACEAE | **calliopsis**

Jun–Sep, 1–3 ft. Erect, taprooted annual of roadsides and other disturbed places. Probably introduced from farther west. Stems unbranched, smooth. Leaves sessile and petiolate, smooth; basal and lower leaves once or twice pinnately lobed into linear segments to 2 in. long. Flower heads in a branched, terminal cluster; heads yellow with maroon centers, about 1½ in. wide, with 8 yellow ray florets with a reddish-brown band at the base and 3-toothed at tip, encirclng a dense center of tiny maroon or yellow, 4-lobed tubular florets. 2 series of bracts, inner and outer, surround the base of each head. KB

Coreopsis verticillata

ASTERACEAE | **threadleaf coreopsis**

May–Jul, 2–3 ft. Erect, rhizomatous perennial usually growing in clumps in dry sandy, rocky, or clayey woodlands and woodland borders. Stems unbranched except in inflorescence, smooth but with hairs at nodes. Leaves sessile, to 2½ in. long, divided into multiple threadlike segments, presenting a feathery appearance. Flower heads in diffusely branched, terminal cluster; heads yellow, 1–2 in. wide, with 8 ray florets with minutely toothed tips encircling a dense center disk of tiny tubular florets. 2 series of bracts, inner and outer, surround the base of each head. BAS

Hypochaeris radicata

ASTERACEAE | **spotted cat's-ear**

Apr–Oct, 1–2 ft. Erect perennial from a basal rosette, found on roadsides, lawns, fields, urban parks, and other disturbed areas. Native to Eurasia, widespread in NoAm. Stems solitary to many, leafless, sometimes branched in upper half, hairy at base. Leaves basal, oblong-lance-shaped, 2–6 in. long, coarsely toothed or lobed, densely stiff-hairy. Flower heads solitary at tips of stem and branches, about 1 in. wide, with yellow ray florets with squared-off and toothed tips (no disk florets); outer rays may be maroon on the outer surface. BAS

Taraxacum officinale

ASTERACEAE | **common dandelion**

Jan–Dec, 2–12 in. Erect perennial of lawns, urban areas, pastures, roadsides, trailsides; less commonly in various less disturbed habitats. Native to Eurasia. Stems 1–several hollow flowering scapes, light green, often reddish near base, smooth to hairy; leaking milky sap when broken. Leaves in a basal rosette, the blades narrowing into petioles, lance-shaped, 2–15 in. long, deeply divided into many sharp segments, sparsely hairy beneath and on midrib. Flower heads solitary at top of scapes, 1–2 in. wide, with numerous yellow, blunt-tipped ray florets; 2 series of linear-lance-shaped, green bracts surround the cylindrical base of each head, the outer ones recurved. RTW

Euphorbia cyparissias

EUPHORBIACEAE | **cypress spurge**

Mar–May, occasionally later, 6–12 in. Densely tufted, colonial perennial found in graveyards and on road banks and other disturbed sites. Native to Europe. Stems multiple from a creeping, horizontal rootstock; branched and smooth, with milky sap. Leaves crowded, alternate (opposite within inflorescence), sessile, often angled downward, narrowly linear or even needlelike, 3–12 in. long, pale green and smooth, exuding milky sap when broken. Flowers in a terminal, flat-topped, umbel-like cluster; each flower yellowish-green, tiny, inserted above 2 lime-yellow, oval, saucerlike bracts that turn red with age. Fruit a round, 3-lobed capsule with granular surface. JG

Tragia urens

EUPHORBIACEAE | **southeastern noseburn**

May–Oct, 8–19 in. Erect perennial of sandhills, sandy woodlands, and other woodlands. Stems usually branched, softly hairy. Leaves mostly alternate, sessile to short-petioled, narrowly elliptical to oblong-lance-shaped or linear with a tapered base, to 3½ in. long, entire (or with a few teeth), hairy. Flowers in terminal and upper axillary spikes, with 1–2 female flowers at the base of each spike and several male flowers above; flowers greenish-yellow to brownish, tiny, with 3–5 somewhat recurved sepals (petals lacking) and 2 stamens. Fruit a hairy, green, 3-lobed capsule with persistent styles at the top. BAS

Tragia urticifolia

EUPHORBIACEAE | **nettleleaf noseburn**

May–Oct, 1–2 ft. Erect, somewhat shrubby perennial found in dry woods and rocky areas, particularly in areas with high pH soil, over calcareous or mafic bedrock. Stems 1–several from the base, hairy. Leaves petiolate, triangular-lance-shaped with a notched base, to 2½ in. long, prominently toothed, covered in stinging hairs. Flowers in terminal and upper-axillary spikes, with 1–2 female flowers at the base of each spike and several male flowers above; flowers greenish-yellow to brownish, with 3–5 sepals and no petals. Fruit a green, 3-lobed capsule covered in stinging hairs and with persistent styles at the top. JG

Acorus calamus

ACORACEAE | **sweetflag**

May–Jun, 1–3½ ft. Stemless perennial found in marshes, wet meadows, and other wet areas. Native to Eurasia, widespread in e NoAm. Flowering stalk and leaves arise from a thick underground rhizome. Leaves 2-ranked and crowded basally, where they attach directly to the rhizome; linear and straplike, to 70 in. long, with a prominent pink or red central vein and crinkled margins. Flowers crowded in a stiff, linear-cylindrical spike (2–4 in. long) that is attached at an angle near the middle of a long, leaflike stem; flowers greenish-yellow (later brownish) and tiny. Crushed leaves and rhizomes have a distinctive sweet smell. BAS

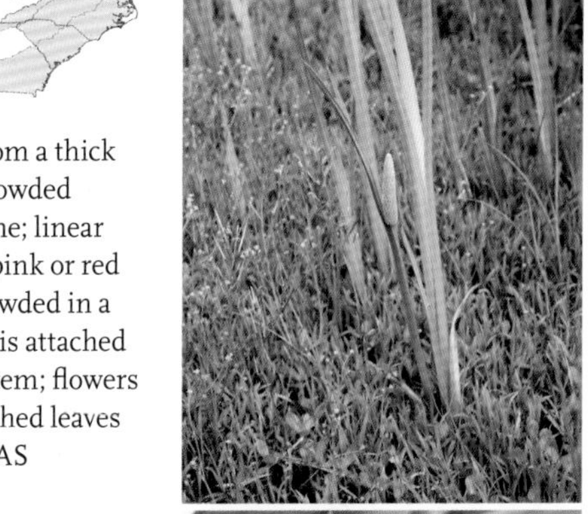

Orontium aquaticum

ARACEAE | **golden club**

Mar–Apr, 1–2 ft. Stemless, emergent perennial found on peaty soil in stagnant water (acidic to calcareous), including in blackwater streams, swamps, pools in low pocosins, freshwater tidal marshes. Leaves in a crowded cluster, appearing before the flowering stalk, floating on water or extended above, long-petioled, oval to elliptical, 4–12 in. long, with parallel veins, dark blue-green above and often with a waxy bloom that repels water, pale beneath. Flowers, numerous, bright yellow, tiny, on an elongated, cylindrical spadix at the end of a green and white clublike scape, extending above leaves and sometimes leaning. Fruits green, embedded in the fleshy spadix. WS

Peltandra virginica

ARACEAE | **green arrow-arum**

Apr–Jun, 8–22 in. Stemless, rhizomatous perennial of marshes, bogs, beaver ponds, pocosins, other stagnant wetland situations; tidal marshes. Leaves in a basal cluster, long-petioled, arrowhead-shaped with a major vein running parallel to the leaf margin, to 20 in. long and 12 in. wide, glossy-green above, pale beneath. Flowers tightly packed on an elongate, cylindrical spadix partly enclosed by a sheathlike, greenish-white spathe; flowers greenish-yellow to greenish-white, tiny, lacking petals and sepals. Male flowers above, sterile flowers in middle, female flowers below. Fruit a cluster of green, maturing to purplish-black, berries enclosed by base of spathe. BAS

Lupinus villosus

FABACEAE | **pink sandhill lupine**

Apr–May, 8–24 in. Erect, clumped annual/biennial of dry woodlands, sandy roadsides, and sandhills. Stems multiple from crown, sometimes sprawling, covered with long silvery-white hairs. Leaves clustered at base of stem and overwintering, petiolate, elliptical to oblong, 2½–6 in. long, covered with long silvery-white hairs. Flowers in crowded, erect terminal spikes 4–12 in. long; each flower pink or lavender, about ½ in. long, with typical pea-flower shape, including a banner petal that bears a large, maroon patch. Fruit an elongated, flattened pod densely covered with silvery-white hairs. AMC

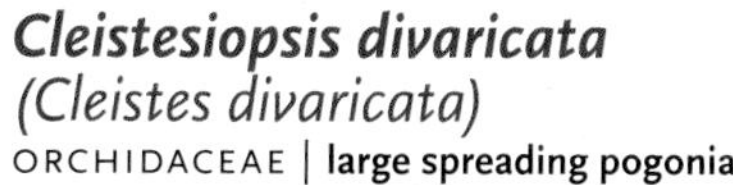

Cleistesiopsis divaricata (*Cleistes divaricata*)

ORCHIDACEAE | **large spreading pogonia**

May–Jul, 6–30 in. Erect perennial of pine savannas and Coastal Plain seepage bogs. Stems purplish below, smooth. Leaves 1–3 at midstem, erect, elliptical, to 8 in. long, waxy blue-green, smooth; there is usually a smaller leafy bract just below the flower. Flowers 1–2 at top of stem, facing slightly downward, with 3 long (to 2½ in.) flaring, maroon, linear sepals and a pink corolla tube splitting into 3 lobes, the lowest lobe with scalloped edges and purple-speckled and crested inside. Fruit an erect, cylindrical capsule. AMC

Platanthera grandiflora

ORCHIDACEAE | **large purple fringed orchid**

Jun–Jul, 1–4 ft. Erect perennial of bogs, seepages, and other moist places at high elevations. Stem somewhat fleshy, unbranched, smooth. Leaves lance-shaped to oval, 3–10 in. long (reduced above), with parallel veins and a central crease (keeled), smooth. Flowers 30–60 in a dense, cylindrical terminal raceme; each flower purple, ¾–1 in. long, with 2 petals and a sepal forming a flattish hood, 2 winglike lateral sepals, a 3-lobed lip petal (each lobe fanlike and prominently fringed), and a long, club-shaped spur. Fruit an elliptical capsule. WS

Pogonia ophioglossoides

ORCHIDACEAE | **rose pogonia**

Mar–Jun, 4–20 in. Erect perennial of savannas and bogs, especially in open peaty or gravelly situations. Stem unbranched, smooth. Leaves usually 1 about halfway up stem (may be 1–2 stalked leaves at base), sessile-clasping, lance-shaped, ascending, 1½–4 in. long, fleshy, smooth. Flowers 1–2 at top of stem above an erect, elliptical-oval leafy bract; each flower pink (rarely white), 1–2 in. wide and about ¾ in. long, with an erect sepal at the top, 2 spreading lateral sepals, and 2 petals (sometimes with darker pink veins) forming a hood over an unlobed but fringed lip petal bearing a showy crest of fleshy, yellow bristles. Fruit an elliptical capsule. WS

Asemeia grandiflora (*A. violacea*)

POLYGALACEAE | **showy milkwort**

(Dec) May–Jul, 8–20 in. Erect-spreading perennial of sandhills and the dry sandy soils of roadsides and fields. Stems 1–several from a taproot, usually branched, covered with close-pressed to spreading hairs. Leaves lance- to linear-lance-shaped, to 2 in. long, furry (at least on veins beneath). Flowers loosely spaced in a narrow, terminal raceme 2–5 in. long; flowers pink to rosy, about ½ in. wide, with 2 rounded "wings" (petal-like sepals) and, between them, 3 petals joined together to form a tube without a fringe at the tip. AMC

Polygala curtissii

POLYGALACEAE | **Appalachian milkwort**

Jun–Oct, 5–15 in. Erect annual of mafic barrens, old fields, thickets, and openings. Stems simple or branched above, smooth. Leaves linear to narrowly lance-shaped and pointed, ½–1¼ in. long. Flowers densely packed into erect, cylindrical terminal racemes ½–¾ in. long; each flower bright pink to rose-purple, about ¼ in. wide, with 2 spreading "wings" (sepals) and 3 joined petals forming a tiny tube with knobby tip. Green, slender, pointed bracts remain on the raceme after flowers wither. RTW

Polygala incarnata

POLYGALACEAE | **pink milkwort**

Apr–Nov, 6–18 in. Erect annual found in pine savannas, wet prairies, woodlands, old fields, and clearings. Stems stiff, slender, ribbed, simple or sparingly branched, waxy blue-green. Leaves widely spaced and close to stem, linear, to ½ in. long, fleshy, waxy blue-green. Flowers densely arranged in a short, erect terminal spike, opening from bottom upward; each flower dark pink, about ¼ in. long, with 2 narrow, pink "wing" sepals (plus 3 smaller, greenish ones), 2 pink and very narrow petals, and 1 pink, tubular, fringed petal. Fruit a round to egg-shaped, grooved capsule. RTW

Polygala mariana

POLYGALACEAE | **Maryland milkwort**

Jun–Oct, 6–16 in. Erect annual of bogs, pine savannas, and other open, wet habitats. Stems angled, simple or branched above, smooth. Leaves linear to narrowly lance-shaped with sharp tip, ½–1¼ in. long, smooth. Flowers densely arranged in oval to cylindrical terminal racemes; each flower pinkish-purple, tiny, with 2 pink, spreading, elliptical, pointy-tipped "wings" and 3 joined, greenish petals forming a tube with a yellow, knobby tip. PIP

Polygala polygama

POLYGALACEAE | **bitter milkwort**

Apr–Jul, 8–18 in. Erect biennial/short lived perennial found in sandhills, woodlands, and woodland openings and borders. Stems several from a crown, angled, unbranched, smooth. Leaves linear or oblong with sharply pointed tip, to 1½ in. long, smooth. Flowers loosely arranged along terminal racemes, pink to rosy-purple, about ½ in. wide, with 2 spreading elliptical "wings" (sepals) and 3 joined petals forming a tiny tube with fringed tip. Fruit an oval capsule. Also has non-opening white flowers growing on horizontal stems barely under or just above the ground surface. RTW

Polygala sanguinea

POLYGALACEAE | **blood milkwort**

May–Sep, 4–14 in. Erect annual of bogs, fens, seeps, woodlands, and woodland openings and borders. Stems simple to bushy-branched, smooth. Leaves linear to narrowly lance-shaped with pointy tip, ½–1½ in. long, smooth. Flowers densely crowded in cylindrical terminal racemes, about 1 in. long and ½ in. wide, reddish-purple to rose-pink (fading to greenish-white with age), less than ¼ in. long, with 2 spreading, oval "wings" (sepals) and 3 joined petals forming a tiny tube. RTW

Polygaloides paucifolia (*Polygala paucifolia*)

POLYGALACEAE | **gaywings**

Apr–Jun, 2–6 in. Low-growing, rhizomatous, colonial perennial found in moist to dry forests, mostly at mid to high elevations. Leaves clustered at top of smooth stem, oval, to 1½ in. long, with hairy margins and midvein. Flowers 1–4 from leaf axils at top of stem, dark pink (occasionally purple or white), ¾–1½ in. wide, with 2 pink, wide-spreading, oblong-oval "wings" (sepals) and a pink and white floral tube (3 joined petals) ending in a conspicuous pink or white fringe. Fruit a rounded, notched capsule. AMC

Lobelia cardinalis

CAMPANULACEAE | **cardinal flower**

May–Oct, 2–4 ft. Erect perennial of marshes, moist meadows, swamp forests, and streambanks. Stems stout, smooth, mostly unbranched. Leaves petiolate (petioles reduced above), lance-shaped to lance-oval, 4–5 in. long, with toothed margins and milky sap. Flowers in a tall, terminal spike; each flower brilliant red, with 2 spreading lips, the upper lip 2-lobed and with a protruding, gray-tipped filament tube, and the lower lip split into 3 long, lance-elliptical lobes. Fruit an oval to round capsule. Hummingbirds and long-tongued butterflies famously visit these flowers. JF, WS

Dicliptera brachiata

ACANTHACEAE | **branched foldwing**

Aug–Oct, 1–3 ft. Erect to leaning perennial of bottomland forests and shaded deposition bars along rivers and streams. Stems 6-angled, opposite-branched, hairy above, often with lines of hair on ridges/angles. Leaves long-petioled, lance-oval, ¾–5 in. long, thin, with tiny hairs along the margin. Flowers in small clusters from upper leaf axils, each subtended by a pair of leafy bracts; each flower pink or purple, nearly ½ in. long, with a narrow corolla tube opening to 2 somewhat recurved lobes (darker pink spots on upper lobe) and surrounded by 5 shorter, narrowly lance-shaped sepals; 2 stamens and a single long style visible. Fruit a slightly flattened, round capsule. RTW

Justicia americana

ACANTHACEAE | **American water-willow**

Jun–Oct, 1–3 ft. Rhizomatous, colonial perennial of shallow water in river and stream beds. Stems mostly simple, smooth, often rooting at nodes. Leaves opposite and ascending, sessile or short-petioled, narrowly elliptical and tapering to a long wedgelike base, 5 in. long or more. Flowers in dense, short spikes arising from upper leaf axils, in opposite pairs on the spike; each flower pale violet-pink to white, tubular but deeply cleft into 4–5 parts, the upper lip recurved and lower lip 3-lobed, marked with purple. Fruit a stalked, club-shaped capsule. BAS

Justicia ovata

ACANTHACEAE | **Coastal Plain water willow**

May–Jul, 1–3 ft. Rhizomatous, colonial perennial of swamps and marshes. Stems simple, smooth. Leaves sessile to short-petioled, in 4–7 pairs, elliptical to oval, 2–4 in. long. Flowers in a loose spike on a thin stem, becoming looser with time; each flower lavender-pink to white, ½–¾ in. long, tubular, with 2 lips, the bottom lip 3-lobed (middle lobe larger) and with a patch of dark pink-purple spotting, the upper lip slightly notched; there are 5 narrow sepals nearly as long as the corolla tube. Fruit a stalked, club-shaped capsule. RL

Clinopodium coccineum (*Calamintha coccinea*)

LAMIACEAE | **scarlet calamint**

Jan–Dec, 2–4 ft. Evergreen, somewhat shrubby erect-ascending perennial of sandhills and flatwoods. Stems wiry, vaguely 4-angled, loosely branched and hairy; older stems may have shredding bark. Leaves elliptical, to 3/4 in. long, with slightly rolled margins, gland-dotted, and mildly spicy-aromatic when crushed. Flowers on long, leaning terminal racemes, often favoring 1 side of the stalk; each flower red (rarely yellow), 1–2 in. long, tubular, split into 2 flaring lips, the upper lip notched at the tip and the lower 3-lobed and speckled with darker red; 4 anthers are usually visible. AMC

Cuphea viscosissima

LYTHRACEAE | **clammy cuphea**

Jul–Oct, 10–20 in. Erect, sticky-stemmed annual found in dry or wet places, especially over mafic or calcareous rocks. Stems branched, with a purple cast and covered with sticky hairs. Leaves petiolate, lance-shaped to oval, 3/4–2 in. long, covered with sticky hairs. Flowers solitary or paired in upper leaf axils, purple-red, to 1½ in. long, with 6 spreading purple petals of unequal size (2 long, 4 short), a sticky tubular calyx, and 12 stamens. Fruit an oval capsule opening along 1 side. BAS

Agalinis fasciculata

OROBANCHACEAE | **southeastern agalinis**

Jul–Oct, 1–3 ft. Erect to ascending annual found in sandhills, pine savannas, prairies, oak savannas, roadsides and other disturbed sandy areas. Stems slender, much-branched above, rough-hairy. Leaves linear, 1–2 in. long, rough-hairy on both surfaces. Flowers in terminal and axillary racemes, purplish-pink, 1 in. long or more, tubular with 5 spreading, rounded, slightly unequal lobes with furry margins; the corolla tube is purple-spotted and marked with 2 yellow streaks within, and the tubular calyx has 5 pointy-triangular lobes. Fruit a many-seeded, round capsule. WS

Agalinis linifolia

OROBANCHACEAE | **flaxleaf agalinis**

Aug–Sep, 2–4 ft. Erect to ascending, rhizomatous perennial of Coastal Plain depression ponds, cypress savannas, and wet pine savannas, sometimes found in standing water. Stems slender, unbranched or with a few erect branches, smooth. Leaves very narrow, mostly ascending, 1–2 in. long. Flowers on long, slender stalks in a terminal raceme, pale to dark pink, 1–1½ in. long, tubular and opening to 5 spreading, rounded lobes that are hairy on the margins; the throat of the tube is hairy and pale-spotted but lacking yellow lines. Fruit a narrowly oval capsule. PIP

Agalinis purpurea

OROBANCHACEAE | **common agalinis**

Aug–Oct, 1–4 ft. Erect to sprawling annual of woodlands, roadsides, open floodplain swamps and bogs, and other open habitats. Stems slender and wiry, 4-angled, branched above, dark green. Leaves linear, to 2½ in. long, dark green to purplish, with a conspicuous indented midvein. Flowers in a terminal raceme, pinkish-purple, to 1½ in. long, tubular and bell-shaped with 5 spreading, rounded lobes; within the corolla throat are purple spots, abundant white hairs, and 2 yellow streaks. Fruit a many-seeded, round capsule. AMC

Agalinis setacea

OROBANCHACEAE | **threadleaf agalinis**

Jul–Oct, 6–27 in. Erect to ascending, bushy annual found in sandhill woodlands, openings in other dry forests, and sandy roadsides. Stems slender, weakly angled, profusely bushy-branched, dull green suffused with purple, mostly smooth. Leaves narrowly linear to needlelike (no more than ¼ in. wide), to 1½ in. long, smooth. Flowers long-stalked and in terminal racemes, rose-pink, ½–1 in. long, tubular and opening to 5 erect or spreading, hairy lobes; densely long-hairy within the tube and with 2 yellow streaks and dark pink spots. The shorter, bell-shaped calyx has 5 triangular lobes. Fruit a many-seeded, round capsule. WS

Agalinis tenuifolia

OROBANCHACEAE | **slenderleaf agalinis**

Aug–Oct, 8–30 in. Erect annual found on wooded slopes, savannas, granitic outcrops, roadsides and other dry habitats. Stems slender, weakly angled, often profusely branched, dull green to red-purple, smooth to slightly hairy. Leaves linear to needlelike, ¾–2 in. long, sometimes darkened to reddish-purple, with a prominent midvein. Flowers in a branching, terminal raceme; each flower rose-pink, about ½ in. long, tubular and bell-shaped with 5 lobes, the bottom 3 spreading and the upper 2 flopping down to partly cover the corolla tube opening; white with pink spots and 2 yellow lines within the tube. Fruit a many-seeded, round capsule. BAS

Agastache scrophulariifolia

LAMIACEAE | **purple giant hyssop**

Jul–Sep, 4–6 ft. Erect, rhizomatous, clump-forming perennial of bottomlands and rich, moist woodlands and forests. Stems 4-angled, often reddish, branched above, smooth or with hairs on angles only. Leaves petiolate, lance-shaped or oval, base flattish to heart-shaped, 2–5 in. long, coarsely toothed; anise-scented when bruised. Flowers and small pinkish-white bracts densely packed in 6-in. terminal spikes; each flower pink or purplish, ½ in. long, tubular, the corolla with a nearly erect, 2-lobed upper lip and a 3-lobed lower lip (middle lobe largest); 4 long stamens protrude. The green calyx is tubular with 5 pink- or white-margined, narrow lobes. BAS

Clinopodium georgianum (*Calamintha georgiana*)

LAMIACEAE | **Georgia calamint**

Jul–Sep, 1–2 ft. Erect, shrubby perennial of longleaf pine sandhills, dry oak-hickory forests, and other dry, rocky or sandy woodlands. Stems woody, sometimes slightly 4-angled, branched and with the twigs hairy; older stems have tan, shredding bark. Leaves short-petioled, oval to elliptical, to 1½ in. long, toothed, gland-dotted and aromatic. Flowers in elongate, terminal clusters of 3–9 flowers mixed with leaflike bracts; each flower lavender to pale pink, about ½ in. long, tubular with 2 flaring lips, the upper notched and the lower 3-lobed and speckled with purple. FG

Clinopodium vulgare

LAMIACEAE | **wild basil**

Jul–Sep, 8–20 in. Erect-ascending perennial from short stolons or creeping rhizomes, found in pastures and forests, on road banks and thin soils around rock outcrops. Stems square, densely hairy. Leaves petiolate, oval or lance-shaped, 3⁄4–21⁄2 in. long, with prominent pinnate venation and finely hairy; faintly aromatic when crushed. Flowers in dense, hemispheric clusters whorled around upper leaf axils and stem top, typically with only a few blossoms open at a time; each pink (purple or white), 1⁄2 in. long, tubular, split into 2 lips, the upper 2-lobed, the lower 3-lobed with the center lobe largest and somewhat ruffled. A very hairy, tubular calyx persists in fruit. AMC

Cunila origanoides

LAMIACEAE | **American dittany**

Aug–Oct, 8–16 in. Sprawling perennial of dry rocky slopes, shale barrens, and other dry (often sloping) woodlands and barrens. Stems square, wiry verging on woody, branched, reddish-brown, soft-hairy in the upper half, smooth below. Leaves sessile or short-petioled, oval to lance-shaped, 3⁄4–11⁄2 in. long, with sparingly toothed margins, dotted with tiny glands. Flowers in clusters of 3–9 in upper leaf axils, pink or lavender with purple spots, 1⁄4 in. long, the corolla a hairy tube with 4 spreading lobes and 2 prominently protruding stamens; the calyx is tubular. Fruit 4 tiny, brown nutlets. Plant gives off a strong scent of oregano when bruised. BAS

Lamium amplexicaule

LAMIACEAE | **henbit**

Jan–Dec, 4–16 in. Sprawling to weakly erect annual of lawns, gardens, fields, pastures, roadsides, and disturbed areas. Native to Eurasia and n Africa. Stems 4-angled, branched from base, smooth or hairy; flower-bearing parts erect. Leaves petiolate (upper ones sessile and smaller), nearly round, to 1 in. long, with scalloped to shallowly lobed margins, hairy to smooth above. Flowers 6–10, clustered in upper axillary whorls underlain by clasping leaves; dark pink (or lighter); 1⁄2 in. long; tubular and split into 2 spreading lips, the upper arch-hooded and hairy, the lower 3-lobed, drooping and purple-spotted. The tubular-bell-shaped calyx has 5 teeth. JWH

Lamium purpureum

LAMIACEAE | **purple dead-nettle**

(Jan) Mar–Oct, to 2½ ft. long. Annual of lawns, fields, pastures, roadsides, and disturbed areas. Native to Eurasia. Stems 4-angled, hollow, sprawling and often branched at the base, erect above, slightly hairy. Leaves bristly-hairy: lower leaves long-petioled, pairs widely separated, round, to 2 in. long, bluntly toothed; upper leaves short-petioled, crowded, drooping, smaller, triangular, and purplish. Flowers clustered in upper axillary whorls of 3–6, each whorl underlain by leaflike bracts; flowers pink to purple, ½ in. long, tubular and split into 2 lips, the upper hooded and hairy, the lower lobed, paler, and purple-speckled. Tubular-bell-shaped calyx has 5 lobes. BAS

Monarda didyma

LAMIACEAE | **beebalm**

Jul–Oct, 2–4 ft. Erect, stoloniferous perennial of seepage slopes, boulder fields with abundant seepage, streambanks, bogs. Escapes from cultivation. Stems 4-angled, unbranched, sometimes hairy on angles. Leaves petiolate, oval to lance-triangular, 3–6 in. long, toothed, with hairy veins beneath; pungent odor when crushed. Flowers in crownlike terminal whorls (almost headlike) underlain by leafy red-tinted bracts. Flowers scarlet-red, 1–1½ in. long, narrowly tubular, split into 2 lips, the upper erect and arched, the lower split again into 3 lobes, the middle lobe notched and longest; 2 stamens protrude. RTW

Monarda fistulosa

LAMIACEAE | **Appalachian bergamot**

May–Sep, 2–5 ft. Erect, colonial-rhizomatous perennial of moist wooded slopes, roadsides, woodland edges, mostly in the Appalachians. Stems 4-angled, branched above, green to reddish-brown, often with hairs on the angles. Leaves petiolate, oval to broadly lance-shaped, to 4 in. long, toothed, often red- or purple-tinged, slightly hairy, releasing a pungent odor when crushed. Flowers in crownlike terminal whorls (almost headlike) up to 3 in. wide, surrounded by leafy bracts; flowers pink to lavender (or white), 1 in. long, tubular with 2 spreading lips, the upper lip straight with 2 projecting stamens, the lower split into 3 narrow lobes. Flowers in the center bloom first. RTW

Perilla frutescens

LAMIACEAE | **beefsteak-plant**

Aug–Oct, 1–3 ft. Erect colony-forming invasive annual of moist disturbed areas. Native to India. Stems stout, 4-angled and grooved, branched, sometimes purple-tinged, smooth or covered with downward-pointing hairs. Leaves petiolate, broadly oval with pointed tips, to 5 in. long, wrinkled, coarsely toothed, green to purplish-burgundy, aromatic. Flowers in long (to 6 in.) terminal and upper axillary racemes; each pink to pale purple, to 1/4 in. long, tubular, the corolla opening to a notched upper lip, notched lower lip, and 2 lateral lobes. The dark green-burgundy, densely hairy, toothed, tubular calyx is nearly as long as the corolla, and there are 4 pink-tipped stamens. BAS

Physostegia leptophylla

LAMIACEAE | **swamp obedient-plant**

May–Aug, 1–4 ft. Erect, rhizomatous perennial found in the wet muck of bottomland hardwood forests, swamps, freshwater or slightly brackish tidal marshes; rarely, wet savannas. Stems 4-angled, simple, smooth. Leaves petiolate (lower) to sessile and sometimes clasping (upper), lance-shaped, 1–4 in. long, wavy-margined. Flowers loosely spaced along a finely hairy/downy, terminal raceme; each lavender to reddish-violet, 1/2–1 in. long, tubular and inflated, with purple splotches within and opening to 2 lips, the lower lip 3-lobed. The tubular calyx is shorter, has 5 triangular lobes, and may be gland-dotted. KB

Physostegia purpurea

LAMIACEAE | **savanna obedient-plant**

May–Aug, 1–3 ft. Erect, rhizomatous perennial of wet savannas, savanna-swamp ecotones, and ditches adjacent to former pinelands. Stems 4-angled and ridged, simple, smooth. Leaves petiolate or sessile (may be clasping above), lance-shaped, to 6 in. long (reduced above, the uppermost pair often no larger than the floral bracts), bluntly toothed to entire. Flowers closely spaced along a purplish-red-tinged, finely hairy terminal raceme; each flower deep purple-pink, 1 1/2–2 in. long, inflated-tubular with darker splotches within and opening to 2 spreading lips, the lower lip 3-lobed. The purple-tinged, tubular calyx is shorter and finely hairy, with 5 triangular lobes. GMP

Physostegia virginiana

LAMIACEAE | **obedient plant**

Jul–Oct, 3–4 ft. Erect, colonial perennial of open or semi-open moist to wet habitats and disturbed areas; both native and escaped from cultivation. Stems multiple and scattered on long, horizontal rhizomes, 4-angled, unbranched, smooth. Leaves sessile to short-petioled, oblong-lance-shaped or elliptical, to 5 in. long, with sharply pointed and widely spaced teeth, smooth. Flowers closely spaced in 4 columns along a terminal raceme 2–10 in. long; each pink to purplish-pink (rarely white), 1 in. long, inflated-tubular, opening to 2 lips, the upper hooded, the lower 3-lobed. The shorter tubular calyx may be gland-dotted or covered in stalked glands. WS

Stachys latidens

LAMIACEAE | **broad-toothed hedge-nettle**

Jun–Aug, 1–3 ft. Erect perennial of moist forests in coves and on mountain slopes, mountain pastures, and forest edges. Stems 4-angled, unbranched, the angles with stiff, down-curved hairs. Leaves petiolate, oval to elliptical, 2½–6 in. long, coarsely toothed and sometimes purplish on the margins, smooth to slightly hairy. Flowers in whorls on terminal spikes, pink with purple streaking, ⅓–½ in. long, tubular and opening to 2 lips, the upper lip erect and concave, the lower spreading downward and 3-lobed. The finely hairy calyx tube, about half as long as the corolla tube, has 5 triangular lobes with sharp, needlelike tips and may be red-tinged. KB

Teucrium canadense

LAMIACEAE | **common germander**

May–Sep, 2–3 ft. Erect perennial of rich bottomlands, prairies, marshes. Stems stout, 4-angled, unbranched or with a few branches above, very hairy. Leaves petiolate (upper ones sessile), lance-oval to oblong, to 5 in. long, coarsely toothed, with deeply etched veins, hairy; releasing a strong odor when crushed. Flowers in conical terminal spikes, blooming from bottom up; each flower pale pink to whitish with dark pink spots, about ⅓ in. long, tubular and divided into 2 lips, the upper lip with 2 small, erect, horn-shaped lobes and the lower with a wide, downward-spreading center lobe and 2 narrow lateral lobes. Tiny, glandular hairs cover the corolla. RTW

Phryma leptostachya

PHRYMACEAE | **American lopseed**

Jun–Aug, 8–38 in. Erect, unbranched perennial of bottomland forests and nutrient-rich slopes; in the Coastal Plain primarily in places underlain by coquina limestone/marl. Stems smooth or hairy, swollen and purplish above each node. Leaves oval with round-toothed margins; pairs widely spaced. Flowers also in pairs, in racemes from axils of the upper 2 pairs of leaves; each slender corolla tube is divided into 2 lips, the upper pale purplish-pink, the lower purplish-white. The calyx is tubular-oval and strongly ribbed. Flowers held horizontally but soon become reflexed downward. Fruit an elliptical, light brown achene, distinctively reflexed. AMC

Chelone cuthbertii

PLANTAGINACEAE | **Cuthbert's turtlehead**

Jul–Sep, 16–39 in. Erect perennial of bogs, sphagnous swamps, and seeps. Stems simple or sparingly branched and smooth. Leaves sessile or nearly so, lance-shaped tapering to a sharp tip, 2–5 in. long, toothed. Flowers distinctly 4-ranked in dense terminal spikes and with leafy bracts that mostly conceal individual flower stalks; each purple to pinkish-purple, ¾–1¼ in. long, inflated-tubular with 2 lips (the lower yellow-bearded), 4 fertile stamens, and a single purple sterile stamen. Fruit an oval capsule. *Chelone* flowers produce large amounts of nectar, but the essentially closed lips seem to exclude all insects except large bees, which push their way in. AMC

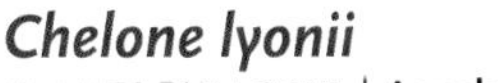

Chelone lyonii

PLANTAGINACEAE | **Appalachian turtlehead**

Jul–Sep, 15–39 in. Erect perennial of cove forests, spruce-fir forests, balds, and streambanks. Stems simple or sparingly branched, smooth. Leaves petiolate, 3–6 in. long, oval to lance-shaped, toothed. Flowers somewhat 4-ranked in dense terminal racemes and with leafy bracts mostly concealing individual flower stalks; each flower dark pink to purple, 1–1½ in. long, inflated-tubular with a broad arching upper lip, a lower lip with a yellow beard, 4 fertile stamens, and a single sterile stamen with a white or pink tip. Fruit a broadly oval capsule. WS

Chelone obliqua

PLANTAGINACEAE | **purple turtlehead**

Jul–Oct, 2–3 ft. Erect perennial of streambanks in floodplain forests and swamp forests. Stems simple or sparingly branched, smooth. Leaves petiolate, lance-shaped and tapering to a sharp tip, 3½–5½ in. long, and toothed. Flowers in dense terminal spikes, vaguely 4-ranked and with leafy bracts that mostly conceal individual flower stalks; each flower purple or reddish-purple, 1–1⅜ in. long, tubular and somewhat flattened, with a hoodlike upper lip, a lower lip bearing a white or yellowish beard, 4 fertile stamens, and a single white sterile stamen. Fruit an oval capsule. AMC

Penstemon australis

PLANTAGINACEAE | **southern beardtongue**

May–Jul, 8–28 in. Erect perennial of sandhills, flatwoods, dry hammocks, and dry sandy roadsides. Stems 1–several (not branched above the base), often tinged (or entirely) reddish-purple, usually hairy. Leaves sessile, lance-shaped, to 4 in. long, somewhat thick-firm, vaguely coarsely toothed, smooth to minutely hairy. Flowers in a moderately compact, terminal panicle, with branches angled upward; flowers pink to lavender-purple, to 1 in. long, tubular with 2 lips, the upper 2-lobed and slightly shorter than the lower, which is 3-lobed. Corolla throat white with purple lines and a barely protruding yellow-bearded "tongue." Flower parts often covered with glandular hairs. WS

Penstemon canescens

PLANTAGINACEAE | **Appalachian beardtongue**

May–Jul, 1–2½ ft. Erect perennial of woodlands, glades, forest edges, rocky woodlands, roadsides. Stems 1–several but not branched above base, covered with spreading hairs. Leaves sessile, elliptical-oblong to narrowly triangular (basal leaves broader), to 5½ in. long, toothed, hairy. Flowers in a moderately compact terminal panicle, with glandular-hairy branches angled upward; flowers pinkish-lavender, ½–1¼ in. long, the corolla tubular with 2 lips, the upper lip 2-lobed and slightly shorter than the lower, which is 3-lobed. Corolla throat white with purple lines inside and a barely protruding yellow-bearded tongue. RTW

Scrophularia marilandica

SCROPHULARIACEAE | **eastern figwort**

Jul–Oct, 1½–8 ft. Erect perennial of rich, moist to dry woodlands and forests, especially over mafic or calcareous rocks. Stems 4-sided and grooved, smooth beneath, glandular-hairy above. Leaves in pairs at 90° to each other, petiolate, oval to lance-shaped, 4½–10 in. long, toothed, smooth or hairy above, usually hairy beneath. Flowers in large, widely branching terminal panicle with glandular-hairy branches; each flower reddish-green outside and maroon inside, about ⅓ in. long, tubular and sac-shaped with a yellow downcurved lower lip and longer, 2-lobed, maroon upper lip. The style curves down over the lower lip. Fruit a shiny, round to oval capsule. RTW

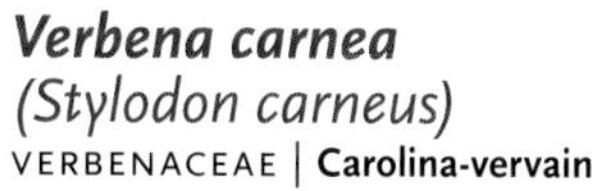

Verbena carnea (*Stylodon carneus*)

VERBENACEAE | **Carolina-vervain**

Apr–Jul, to 3 ft. Erect perennial found in sandhills and other sandy woodlands. Stems 4-angled, hairy. Leaves sessile, oval, to 3½ in. long (reduced above), toothed, with surfaces wrinkled-looking because of prominently impressed veins. Flowers in 1–5 loose terminal spikes to 16 in. long, the stem purple-tinged; each flower pink to lavender or white, about ¼ in. wide, the short corolla tube with 5 spreading lobes and a much shorter, purplish calyx. WS

Polygala brevifolia

POLYGALACEAE | **little-leaf milkwort**

Jun–Oct, 2–12 in. Erect annual of pine savannas, pocosin margins, and pocosin interiors after fire. Stems 4-angled, sparingly branched, smooth. Leaves in whorls of 4 (sometimes 3) or alternate, linear to oblong-lance-shaped and pointy-tipped, ½–1½ in. long, smooth. Flowers densely packed into erect, stalked, cylindrical terminal spikes to 2 in. long; each flower about ¼ in. wide, with 2 spreading, pink, green, and white triangular wings (sepals) and 3 joined petals forming an ascending green, pink, or yellow tube with a frilly opening. Tiny bracts below each flower persist after flower drops. PIP

Polygala cruciata

POLYGALACEAE | **drumheads**

Jun–Oct, 6–12 in. Erect annual of bogs and damp to wet soil of openings in savannas. Stems 4-angled, sparingly branched, smooth. Leaves in whorls of 4 (sometimes 3), linear to oblong-lance-shaped and pointy-tipped, to 2 in. long, with downcurved margins. Flowers densely packed into erect, cylindrical terminal spikes to 2 in. long; each flower about 1⁄3 in. wide, with 2 spreading, pink, green, and white triangular wings (sepals) and 3 joined petals forming an ascending green, pink, or yellow tube with a fringed tip. RTW

Calopogon tuberosus

ORCHIDACEAE | **common grass-pink**

Apr–Jul, 1–3 ft. Erect perennial of pine savannas, sandhill seeps, and floating peat mats; also in the Mountains in bogs. Stems slender, purplish-green, smooth. Leaves with sheathing bases, linear to lance-shaped, 9–20 in. long, folded lengthwise. Flowers 4–20 in a loose terminal raceme with a slight zigzag, only a few opening at a time; each flower rose-purple to pink (rarely white), about 1⁄2 in. wide, with 3 spreading, oval sepals, 2 spreading, oblong petals, an erect, T-shaped lip petal bearing a crest of gold and white hairs, and a protruding, spoon-shaped column supporting the reproductive parts. Fruit an elliptical capsule. Flowers are faintly fragrant. WS

Aplectrum hyemale

ORCHIDACEAE | **puttyroot**

May–Jun, 8–20 in. Erect perennial of rich, moist forests. Stem a stout, pale green to purple-green, leafless (with some tiny bracts) flowering stalk, emerging in spring separately from the leaves. Leaves 1 per plant, emerging in fall and lying on ground, oval, to 8 in. long, bluish-green with raised, white, parallel lines; withers by spring. Flowers 3–15 arranged in a loose raceme topping the scape; each highlighted with magenta, 3⁄4–1 in. long, with 3 narrowly oblong-lance-shaped sepals and 3 central unequal petals, 2 of which form a hood over the reproductive parts, and the lower a scallop-edged, pink and white lip. Fruit an elliptical capsule. AMC

Arethusa bulbosa

ORCHIDACEAE | **bog-rose**

May–Jul, to 14 in. Scapose perennial found in sphagnous bogs and seepage swamps. Stem a leafless scape (with a few bracts) arising from a bulbous corm before the solitary leaf emerges. Leaf basal, developing during and after flower opens, linear, obscurely pleated; there are several sheathed bracts on the flower scape as well. Flower solitary (rarely 2) and terminating the scape, pink to magenta (rarely white), 1–2 in. long, with 3 erect, narrowly oblong sepals rising above the upper 2 arched, hoodlike petals, and a drooping, elongated, pink and white lower lip petal with purple streaks and a tufted, yellowish crest. Fruit an erect, elliptical capsule. JF

Calopogon barbatus

ORCHIDACEAE | **bearded grass-pink**

Mar–Jun, 1 ft. while flowering, taller in fruit. Erect perennial of pine savannas, sandhill seeps, and pitcherplant bogs. Stems slender, smooth. Leaves 1–2, basal, erect, linear, to 8 in. long, folded lengthwise. Flowers 3–7 in a terminal raceme, most opening simultaneously, unscented; each flower dark pink (rarely white), about 1 in. wide, with 3 spreading sharp-tipped sepals, 2 spreading blunt-tipped petals, an erect T-shaped lip petal bearing a crest of golden hairs, and a protruding, spoon-shaped column holding the reproductive parts. Fruit an erect, elliptical capsule. AMC

Cypripedium acaule

ORCHIDACEAE | **pink lady's-slipper**

Apr–Jun, 6–20 in. Erect, scapose perennial of dry to moist, acid forests and woodlands, often under pines and other conifers, or oaks, sometimes forming extensive colonies. Stem consists of a hairy, leafless flowering stalk from the center of a small rosette of leaves. Leaves basal (usually 2), erect, sessile, elliptical to oblong, to 12 in. long, with raised parallel veins, and hairy. Flower solitary at top of scape, with a single green bract curving over it, pink, to 2½ in. long, with a pouch-shaped, lower lip petal (the pink "slipper") and 2 twisted, narrow, greenish-red petals to each side. Fruit a ribbed, elliptical capsule. BAS

Galearis spectabilis

ORCHIDACEAE | **showy orchid**

Apr–Jun, 2–9 in. Erect perennial found in rich, deciduous forests, most typically over calcareous or mafic rocks. Stem conspicuously angled, unbranched, succulent, and smooth. Leaves (typically 2) basal, oval to oblong, to 8 in. long, with a lengthwise center fold, fleshy, shiny and smooth. Flowers 2–12 in a terminal, spikelike raceme, each with a leafy bract beneath; each flower pink and white, about 1 in. long, with pink sepals and petals forming a hood over a longer, white, wavy-margined lip petal with a backward-projecting spur. Flowers mildly fragrant. WS

Amphicarpaea bracteata

FABACEAE | **hog-peanut**

Jul–Sep, 2–8 ft. Annual herbaceous vine of dry to moist forests and thickets, streambanks. Stem twining, sprawling, light green to reddish-green, hairy. Leaves on petioles with a pair of small stipules, 2–6 in. long, divided into 3 oval to diamond-shaped leaflets, each to 2½ in. long, smooth to sparsely hairy. Flowers 2–15 in long-stalked, nodding axillary racemes; each pale pink or lavender to white (often 2-toned), ½ in. long, tubular with 5 lobes; the shorter calyx tube has 4 teeth. Fruit a green pod containing 3–4 seeds. Closed, self-pollinating flowers produced on threadlike runners at ground level yield underground pods with edible seeds, hence the common name. RTW

Centrosema virginianum

FABACEAE | **spurred butterfly pea**

Jun–Aug, to 5 ft. long. Twining or climbing herbaceous perennial vine found in dry woodlands and openings. Stems trailing and twining over other plants, rough with tiny hairs. Leaves on petioles with tiny, lance-shaped stipules, divided into 3 oval to elliptical leaflets, each to 2¾ in. long and with conspicuous veins, especially beneath. Flowers 1–4 on slender stalks from leaf axils, pink or lavender, 1½–2 in. wide, with a typical pea-flower shape, including a large round and somewhat flattened banner petal; wings and keel petals are shorter and tightly curved to form a knob in the flower center. Fruit a narrow pod. RTW

Desmodium canescens

FABACEAE | **hoary tick-trefoil**

Jun–Oct, 2–4 ft. Erect to spreading perennial of agricultural fields, woodland borders, and open, disturbed areas. Stems 1–many from a single crown, unbranched, smooth below but densely hairy above. Leaves on petioles with hairy, clasping, oval stipules, divided into 3 hairy, oval leaflets with pointed tips. Flowers in branching, lax terminal and axillary spikes; each flower pinkish-purple turning green or white, about 1⁄4 in. long, with typical pea-flower shape and a furry calyx tube. Fruit a hairy, flattened pod with constrictions between 4–6 seeds. BAS

Desmodium ciliare

FABACEAE | **hairy small-leaf tick-trefoil**

Jun–Sep, 1–5 ft. Erect perennial of agricultural fields, dry woodland borders, and open, disturbed areas. Stems 1–several from a crown, branched in inflorescence, densely rough-hairy. Leaves on petioles with short, narrow stipules, divided into 3 densely furry, oval to elliptical leaflets, each to 1 1⁄4 in. long. Flowers long-stalked and loosely arranged on spreading branches, pinkish-purple, less than 1⁄4 in. long, with typical pea-flower shape, the erect banner petal bearing 2 green or yellow patches at the base. Fruit a hairy, flattened pod with constrictions between seeds (1–3). WS

Desmodium cuspidatum

FABACEAE | **large-bracted tick-trefoil**

Jun–Aug, 1–4 ft. Erect perennial of overgrown agricultural fields, rocky woodlands and woodland borders, and other open, disturbed areas. Stems 1–several from a crown, unbranched, smooth to slightly hairy. Leaves on petioles with lance-shaped stipules, divided into 3 oval leaflets that are pointed at the tip, bright green above, paler beneath, and mostly smooth. Flowers in sparse terminal racemes, pink, 1⁄4–1⁄2 in. long, with typical pea-flower shape. Fruit a hairy, flattened pod with constrictions between 3–7 seeds and covered with hooked hairs that stick to clothing and fur. BAS

Desmodium glabellum

FABACEAE | **tall tick-trefoil**

Jun–Sep, 2–4 ft. Erect to spreading perennial of various moist to dry habitats, including floodplain forests, open upland forests, woodlands, old fields, clearings, and roadsides. Stems 1–several from a crown, unbranched, covered in curly hairs. Leaves on petioles with tiny, triangular stipules, divided into 3 oval to elliptical leaflets that are 1–2 in. long, darker and less hairy above, paler and more hairy beneath. Flowers stalked and loosely arranged on spreading branches, purplish-pink, about 1⁄4 in. long, with typical pea-flower shape. Fruit a flattened pod with constrictions between 3–5 seeds and covered with hooked hairs that stick to clothing and fur. BAS

Desmodium laevigatum

FABACEAE | **smooth tick-trefoil**

Jun–Sep, 1–3 ft. Erect to reclining perennial of dry woodlands, clearings, old fields, and roadsides. Stems unbranched, smooth to minutely hairy. Leaves on long petioles with tiny, linear stipules, divided into 3 oval to oblong leaflets; leaflets shiny green and smooth above, pale and smooth or with hairs on the midrib beneath. Flowers in a long, terminal raceme (occasionally some branching); each flower pink to deep rose-pink, about 1⁄3 in. long, with typical pea-flower shape, the banner petal with 2 whitish-green spots near the base. Fruit a flattened pod with constrictions between 3–5 seeds and covered with hooked hairs that stick to clothing and fur. BAS

Desmodium lineatum

FABACEAE | **matted tick-trefoil**

Jun–Sep, 20–27 in. Mat-forming perennial of sandhills and other dry forests and woodlands, clearings, and roadsides. Stems prostrate, branched, marked with lines, usually densely furry. Leaves on petioles with short, lance-shaped stipules, and divided into 3 broadly oval to rounded leaflets with hairy margins but mostly smooth surfaces. Flowers in lax terminal and upper axillary panicles covered with hooked hairs, pale purple to reddish-purple, 1⁄4 in. long or less, with typical pea-flower shape. Fruit a flattened pod with constrictions between 2–4 seeds and covered with hooked hairs that stick to clothing and fur. BAS

Desmodium marilandicum

FABACEAE | **Maryland tick-trefoil**

Jun–Sep, 2–4 ft. Erect perennial of dry open forests, woodlands, clearings, old fields, and roadsides. Stems unbranched, smooth or sparsely hairy. Leaves on long petioles with short, linear stipules, and divided into 3 oval to nearly round leaflets; leaflets 1/2–1 1/2 in. long, darker green and smooth above, pale and mostly smooth beneath. Flowers on long stalks in loose racemes, pink, 1/4 in. long, with typical pea-flower shape. Fruit a flattened pod with constrictions between 2–4 seeds and covered with hooked hairs that stick to clothing and fur. BAS

Desmodium paniculatum

FABACEAE | **panicled-leaf tick-trefoil**

Jun–Sep, 1 1/2–3 1/2 ft. Erect perennial of fields, woodland borders, and disturbed areas. Stems several from the base, smooth to minutely hairy. Leaves petiolate, divided into 3 lance-linear to lance-shaped leaflets, each to 3 1/2 in. long, thin-textured, and smooth to sparsely hairy. Flowers in terminal panicles, the stalks usually covered with hooked hairs; each flower pink to rosy-pink, 1/4 in. long or slightly more, with typical pea-flower shape, the erect banner petal with 2 darker patches at the base. Fruit a flattened pod divided into 3–5 U-shaped segments and covered with hooked hairs that stick to clothing and fur. Common but variable. JF

Desmodium rotundifolium

FABACEAE | **roundleaf tick-trefoil**

Jun–Sep, 1 1/2–5 ft. long. Prostrate, mat-forming perennial of dry forests and woodlands. Stems trailing across the ground, densely furry. Leaves lie flat on ground, on petioles with oval stipules, divided into 3 round leaflets with hair on both surfaces, the terminal leaflet to about 2 in. long. Flowers in branching, usually axillary racemes; each flower dark pink to purplish, less than 1/2 in. long, with typical pea-flower shape, the banner petal with maroon markings at the base. Fruit a flattened pod divided into 3–6 nearly diamond-shaped segments and covered with hooked hairs that stick to clothing and fur. BAS

Desmodium strictum

FABACEAE | **pinebarren tick-trefoil**

Jul–Sep, 1½–3 ft. Erect perennial of sandhills and other dry woodlands such as turkey oak scrub. Stems round or angled in cross-section, branched, smooth to minutely hairy. Leaves petiolate, divided into 3 thick-textured, linear leaflets that are each 1–2 in. long and sparsely hairy. Flowers in a stiff terminal panicle composed of several ascending branches and covered with hooked hairs; each flower purplish-pink, about ¼ in. long, with typical pea-flower shape, the erect banner petal with 2 whitish patches near the base. Fruit a flattened pod divided into 1–4 U-shaped segments and covered with hooked hairs that stick to clothing and fur. BAS

Desmodium tenuifolium

FABACEAE | **slimleaf tick-trefoil**

Jul–Aug, 1½–3 ft. Erect to ascending perennial of wet pine flatwoods and savannas. Stems subtly angled, simple or branched from the base, smooth or sparsely and minutely hairy. Leaves petiolate, and divided into 3 thick-textured, linear leaflets, the terminal leaflet longer (to 2½ in.) than laterals; all leaflets with netted venation, minutely hairy above, sparsely hairy and pale beneath. Flowers on stalks to ⅓ in. long in a terminal panicle, pink to purplish, ¼ in. long or less, with typical pea-flower shape. Fruit a flattened pod divided into nearly round segments and covered with minute hairs. PIP

Desmodium viridiflorum

FABACEAE | **velvety tick-trefoil**

Jun–Sep, 2–5 ft. Erect to ascending perennial of fields, woodland borders, disturbed areas. Stems ridged and grooved, unbranched, usually covered with hooked hairs. Leaves petiolate, divided into 3 thick-textured, oval to diamond-shaped leaflets (the terminal one slightly larger) that are sparsely short-hairy above, densely long-hairy beneath. Flowers in a densely hairy, wide-branching terminal panicle; each pink to rose (turning green), ¼ in. long, with typical pea-flower shape, the erect banner petal with 2 greenish-white patches at the base. Fruit a flattened pod divided into 3–6 nearly diamond-shaped segments, covered with hooked hairs that stick to clothing and fur. KL

Erythrina herbacea

FABACEAE | **coral bean**

May–Jul, to 5 ft. Shrublike herbaceous perennial found in maritime forests, dry sandy woodlands, and sandhills in the outer Coastal Plain. Stems multiple, arising from a bulbous, woody base, and thorny. Leaves long-petioled, divided into 3 triangular leaflets, each leaflet to 4 in. long and 3-lobed; there are curved prickles beneath and on petioles. Flowers in a 12-in.-long spike at the top of a leafless stalk, blooming from the bottom up; each flower red, 1½–2½ in. long, tubular and curved upward. Fruit an elongated pod, scarlet seeds within. All parts, especially seeds, are toxic. AMC

Galactia regularis

FABACEAE | **eastern milkpea**

Jun–Sep, to 10 ft. long. Trailing to weakly climbing herbaceous perennial vine found in dry longleaf and pine-oak forests and woodlands. Stems may be many from a single rootstalk, prostrate or trailing, and with spreading or close-pressed hairs. Leaves petiolate, divided into 3 slightly leathery, elliptical to lance-shaped leaflets, each ¾–1½ in. long and smooth or hairy. Flowers in short racemes of 1–6 from leaf axils, dark pink or pink and white, about ½ in. long, with typical pea-flower shape, including a large, reflexed banner petal. Fruit a hairy, narrowly oblong pod. The larval host plant for Long-tailed Skipper, Gray Hairstreak, and Zarucco Duskywing butterflies. WS

Hylodesmum nudiflorum

FABACEAE | **naked tick-trefoil**

Jul–Aug, 4–12 in., flowering stem to 3 ft. Erect-ascending perennial of moist to dry upland forests. Stems bearing leaves are separate from flower-bearing stems and are unbranched and smooth to sparsely hairy. Leaves long-petioled, whorled and crowded toward stem top, divided into 3 oval or diamond-shaped leaflets, each to 3 in. long, green and sparsely hairy above, whitish and moderately hairy beneath. Flowers on leafless stalks in a terminal raceme, rose to purple (rarely white), about ½ in. long, with typical pea-flower shape. Fruit a flattened pod divided into 1–4 U-shaped segments and covered with hooked hairs that stick to clothing and fur. AWF

Kummerowia stipulacea

FABACEAE | **Korean-clover**

Jul–Sep, 4–22 in. Erect to prostrate annual of fields, roadsides, disturbed forests, other disturbed habitats. Native to e Asia. Stems much-branched, often reddish, very hairy. Leaves on ¼-in.-long petioles with papery, lance-oval stipules, divided into 3 oval leaflets; leaflets up to ½ in. long, with many closely spaced parallel veins and hairy margins. Flowers in dense, spikelike racemes from upper leaf axils, bicolored pink and white, with typical pea-flower shape, including an erect banner petal with darker pinkish-purple markings. Fruit a tiny, flattened, broadly oval pod with a short beak, covered at the base by the persistent calyx; contains a single seed. RTW

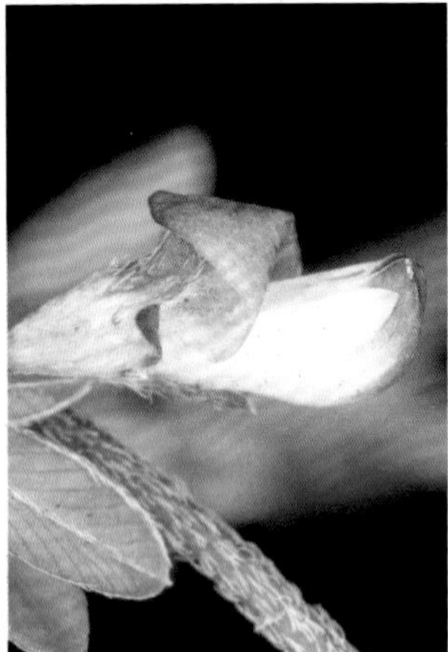

Kummerowia striata

FABACEAE | **Japanese-clover**

Jul–Sep, to 6 ft. long. Erect or decumbent annual of fields, roadsides, other disturbed areas. Native to e Asia. Stems diffusely branched, reddish-purple, hairy. Leaves on short petioles with papery, lance-oval stipules, divided into 3 oblong-elliptical leaflets, each ½–1 in. long with many closely spaced parallel veins, entire to slightly serrated, pale green beneath. Flowers 1–3 on short stalks from leaf axils, ¼ in. long, with typical pea-flower shape, the banner petal predominantly pink or purple with several dark purple veins near its base. Fruit a tiny, flattened, broadly oval pod with a short beak, covered at the base by the persistent calyx; contains a single seed. JG

Lathyrus hirsutus

FABACEAE | **Caley pea**

Apr–Jul, 1–2½ ft. Vinelike annual/biennial of roadsides, fields, and other open, disturbed habitats. Native to Europe. Stems ascending to sprawling, clinging by tendrils to adjacent vegetation for support, flattened and narrowly winged, often branched from the base, smooth. Leaves on flattened petioles with lobed stipules, divided into 2 lance-linear to oblong leaflets to 3½ in. long and with a branching tendril between, smooth. Flowers 1–3 in small racemes on stalks arising from leaf axils, purplish-pink and white, to ½ in. long, with typical pea-flower shape, the upper banner petal usually darker pink. Fruit a stiff-hairy, green (turning brown), flattened pod. JG

Lathyrus latifolius

FABACEAE | **everlasting pea**

May–Oct, 3–6 ft. long. Herbaceous perennial vine of roadsides, railroad rights-of-way, fencerows, fields, and other open, disturbed areas. Native to the Mediterranean region; cultivated in NoAm since the early 1700s, now widely naturalized. Stems sprawling or climbing, conspicuously winged, smooth. Leaves on winged petioles with lance-shaped stipules, divided into 2 thick-textured, lance-shaped to oval leaflets to 2 in. long, a branching tendril between them. Flowers 4–10 in dense racemes on axillary stalks, rose-pink (occasionally white), 1 in. long, with typical pea-flower shape, including a notched banner petal. Fruit a narrow, flattened, green (turning brown) pod. SG

Lespedeza bicolor

FABACEAE | **bicolor lespedeza**

Jun–Sep, 3–10 ft. Erect, deciduous shrub of forests, roadsides, wildlife food plots. Native to e Asia, brought to NoAm to control erosion and provide food and cover for upland game birds. Stems thick, ridged, loosely branched, stiff-hairy. Leaves on petioles with persistent, needlelike stipules, divided into 3 elliptical to broadly oval leaflets, each ⅓–1 in. long, blunt-tipped with a tiny point, rough-hairy. Flowers in small clusters from upper leaf axils and branch ends, rose-purple, ⅓–½ in. long, with typical pea-flower shape, including an erect banner petal marked with darker purple. Fruit a hairy, flattened, broadly elliptical pod with a long point and a single seed. BAS

Lespedeza repens

FABACEAE | **creeping lespedeza**

Jul–Sep, 1–3 ft. Trailing-reclining perennial of dry upland woodlands, clearings, and woodland borders. Stems few–many, slender, covered with straight, close-pressed hairs; form loose mats. Leaves well spaced, short-petioled, divided into 3 elliptical to oblong-oval leaflets, each to 1 in. long, blunt-tipped, and sparsely to densely hairy. Flowers in racemes of 4–6 on stalks from upper leaf axils, pale purple to pinkish-white, about ¼ in. long, with typical pea-flower shape, including an erect banner petal streaked with maroon. Fruit a flattened-elliptical pod with pointed tip and containing a single seed. JG

Lespedeza stuevei

FABACEAE | **velvety lespedeza**

Jul–Sep, 2–5 ft. Erect perennial of dry woodlands and woodland borders. Stems branched above, grayish-green, and covered with dense velvety hairs that spread outward. Leaves petiolate, divided into 3 elliptical to oblong leaflets, each to 1¼ in. long, hairy and gray-green on both surfaces. Flowers in dense racemes of 4–10 on short stalks from upper leaf axils, pink to violet, about ¼ in. long, with typical pea-flower shape, including an erect banner petal streaked with purple at the base. Fruit a hairy, flattened-elliptical pod containing a single seed. BAS

Lespedeza violacea (*L. intermedia*)

FABACEAE | **wand lespedeza**

Jul–Sep, 8–24 in. Erect perennial of dry woodlands and woodland borders. Stems with a few branches, light green to brown, usually with flattened hairs. Leaves petiolate, divided into 3 oval to oblong leaflets, each ½–1½ in. long, smooth above, hairy beneath. Flowers in dense racemes of 4–14 on stalks from upper leaf axils, violet, about ¼ in. long, with typical pea-flower shape, including an erect banner petal bearing a streaked, arch-shaped patch of dark rosy-purple. Fruit a minutely hairy, flattened, broadly oval pod containing a single seed. AMC

Lespedeza virginica

FABACEAE | **Virginia lespedeza**

Jul–Sep, 1–2½ ft. Erect perennial of sandhills, woodlands, and woodland borders. Stems 1–few, slender, with erect branches, smooth to hairy. Leaves crowded, short-petioled, divided into 3 narrowly elliptical or linear leaflets, each to 1 in. long and bearing a tiny point at the tip, typically covered in short, close-pressed hairs. Flowers in racemes of 4–10 on tiny stalks from upper leaf axils, rose-pink to purplish, about ¼ in. long, with typical pea-flower shape, including an erect banner petal with darker pink streaking; there are also inconspicuous closed flowers lower on the stem. Fruit a flattened, round to elliptical pod containing a single seed. BAS

Orbexilum psoralioides

FABACEAE | **eastern Sampson's-snakeroot**

May–Jul, 1–2½ ft. Erect to ascending perennial found in moist to dry longleaf pine savannas, loamy longleaf pine sandhills, and open woodlands. Stems ridged, branched mostly from base, generally rough-hairy. Leaves petiolate, divided into 3 narrowly elliptical or lance-shaped segments, hairy or smooth, and gland-dotted. Flowers in crowded, conical, long-stalked spikes at ends of branches; each flower pale purple (drying to tan), ¼ in. long or less, with typical pea-flower shape, the banner petal bearing a darker purple patch. WS

Phaseolus polystachios

FABACEAE | **wild bean**

Jul–Sep, 6–20 ft. long. Perennial vine that trails and twines over other plants, found in thickets near streams, upland woods, and disturbed areas. Stems slender, angled, hairy. Leaves petiolate, divided into 3 smooth to hairy (especially below) broadly oval leaflets, each 1–5 in. long and with a pointy tip. Flowers in numerous long-stalked racemes from leaf axils, pink to purple (sometimes white), about ⅓ in. long, resembling a typical pea-flower but with a very broad banner petal, 2 spreading wing petals, and a distinctively coiled keel petal in the center. Fruit a smooth, somewhat compressed, curved pod. RTW

Securigera varia

FABACEAE | **crown-vetch**

Jun–Nov, 1–3 ft. Trailing to ascending perennial of road banks, woodland borders, fields, rocky streambanks, disturbed floodplains. Native to Europe; may spread beyond erosion-control plantings, especially in alluvial habitats. Stems occasionally branched, smooth to sparsely hairy. Leaves 6 in. long, sessile with a pair of tiny stipules, pinnately divided into 11–25 oblong leaflets, ¾ in. long, smooth. Flowers in umbels, 10–25 on long stalks from upper leaf axils, each pink or white, ½ in. long, with typical pea-flower shape, including an erect banner petal that is often darker pink than the rest of the corolla. Fruit an erect, linear, 4-angled pod with 1–7 segments. ER

Strophostyles helvola

FABACEAE | **annual sand bean**

Jun–Sep, to 6 ft. long. Trailing herbaceous perennial vine of coastal dunes and beaches, dry sandy woodlands, disturbed areas. Stems slender, rough, with a few hairs. Leaves on petioles with stipules, divided into 3 1- to 2-in.-long, oval leaflets with tapering tips, the terminal leaflet stalked, the lateral leaflets with asymmetrical bases; smooth to sparsely hairy. Typical pea flowers in stalked, axillary clusters of up to 10 (2–3 in bloom at once); each pink, ½ in. wide, with an erect, flaring banner petal and a dark purplish spurlike projection on the keel petal that twists and curls back up at the tip. Fruit a slender round pod with a few close-pressed hairs. AMC

Strophostyles umbellata

FABACEAE | **perennial sand bean**

Jun–Oct, to 6 ft. long. Trailing herbaceous perennial vine of dry to moist, sandy or rocky woodlands, riverbanks, sandhills, savannas, disturbed areas. Stems green or purple, rough-hairy, slightly angled. Leaves petiolate with small, spreading-triangular stipules, divided into 3 slightly hairy, 1- to 2½-in.-long, oval to lance-oval leaflets with rounded to tapering tips. Typical pea flowers in stalked, axillary clusters of up to 10 (3–4 in bloom at once), dark pink, ¾ in. wide, with an erect, flaring banner petal and a dark purplish spurlike projection on the keel petal that twists and curls back up at the tip. Fruit a slender round pod with a few close-pressed hairs. RTW

Tephrosia florida

FABACEAE | **Florida hoarypea**

May–Jul, to 22 in. Prostrate to weakly erect perennial of pine savannas and other pinelands. Stems 1–several from a single crown, sparsely covered with short, gray hairs. Leaves long-petioled, 1–5 in. long, and pinnately divided into 7–9 elliptical to oblong leaflets, each about 1 in. long and covered with short whitish-gray hairs. Flowers in racemes of 2–20 on flattened stalks arising opposite leaves, the uppermost raceme appearing terminal; flowers pink or white turning maroon, ½–¾ in. long, with typical pea-flower shape but usually not opening completely. Fruit a hairy, flattened, and slightly curved pod. BAS

Tephrosia spicata

FABACEAE | **spiked hoarypea**

Jun–Aug, 2–3 ft. Reclining-sprawling to weakly erect perennial of dry, sandy woodlands and clearings. Stems 1–many from a single crown. Leaves on petioles less than ½ in. long, 1½–3 in. long, and pinnately divided into 7–17 elliptical to oblong leaflets, each to 1½ in. long and with a sharp tip. Flowers in stalked racemes of 2–20, arising opposite leaves (uppermost one appears terminal); flowers pink or white turning maroon, ½–¾ in. long, with typical pea-flower shape but usually not opening completely. Fruit a hairy, flattened, and slightly curved pod. Spreading rusty to tawny hairs conspicuously cover all parts of this plant. RTW

Tephrosia virginiana

FABACEAE | **Virginia goat's-rue**

May–Jun, 1–2 ft. Erect, clumped perennial of sandhills and other pinelands, xeric and rocky woodlands, forests, outcrops, shale barrens, dry road banks. Stems 1–several, unbranched to sparingly branched, usually covered with soft white hairs. Leaves on petioles with a pair of tiny stipules, 2–5 in. long, and pinnately divided into 13–23 elliptical to oblong 1-in. leaflets with a prominent central vein and soft grayish-white hairs beneath. Typical pea flowers crowded in erect, terminal racemes to 3 in. tall; each ¾ in. long, bicolored, with dark pink keel and wing petals and a pale yellow banner petal. Fruit a widely spreading, soft-hairy, narrowly cylindrical pod. BAS

Trifolium pratense

FABACEAE | **red clover**

Apr–Oct, 6–22 in. Erect to sprawling perennial of fields, roadsides, and other disturbed areas. Native to Europe. Stems sparsely branched, hairy. Leaves on petioles with a pair of large stipules, palmately divided into 3 oval to oblong-oval leaflets with hairy margins and a white or light green chevron mark on the upper surface. Flowers densely packed into sessile, pompom-like terminal clusters about 1 in. wide; each flower pink to purplish-pink (lighter or white toward base of the head), sessile, with typical pea-flower shape. RTW

Vicia sativa

FABACEAE | **common vetch**

Mar–Jun, 1–2½ ft. Erect-ascending annual of disturbed areas. Native to Mediterranean Europe. Stems ribbed, branched occasionally, light green, sparsely hairy, and leaning/creeping over other vegetation. Leaves petiolate with toothed stipules, pinnately divided into 5–6 pairs of oblong leaflets, each about ¾ in. long, with a branched tendril at the tip, smooth above. Flowers in groups of 1–2 in upper leaf axils, nearly sessile, pink, ¾ in. long, with typical pea-flower shape. RTW

Vicia villosa

FABACEAE | **winter vetch**

May–Sep, 1–3 ft. Sprawling annual/biennial of disturbed areas. Native to Europe. Stems ridged, occasionally branched, covered with spreading white hairs. Leaves petiolate, to 10 in. long and 2 in. wide, pinnately divided into 8–12 pairs of oblong-lance to linear leaflets with sharp tips, each with a tendril from the tip and with scattered white hairs. Flowers on slender, 1-sided racemes of 5–20 pairs of nodding flowers, from leaf axils and on often-purplish stalks covered with spreading hairs. Flowers pink to blue-violet, about ½–¾ in. long, tubular, with 5 petals and a hairy calyx that is united at the base. BAS

Tarenaya hassleriana

CLEOMACEAE | **spiderflower**

Jun–Nov, 3–5 ft. Erect annual of sandbars, riverbanks, disturbed areas. Native to South America, a common garden escape. Stems unbranched, glandular-hairy. Leaves petiolate with (usually) a pair of spines at the base, 6–8 in. wide, palmately divided into 5–7 glandular-hairy, finely toothed (or not), 2- to 2½-in.-long, oblong-lance-shaped leaflets; upper leaves sessile, not divided, smaller. Flowers in a large, leafy-bracted terminal raceme, blooming from the bottom up; each pink to white, 1–1½ in. wide, with 4 oblong-lance-shaped petals, 4 linear-lance-shaped and smaller sepals, 6 long-protruding stamens, and a pistil with a short style. Fruit a cylindrical seedpod. JG

Pueraria montana var. *lobata*

FABACEAE | **kudzu**

Jul–Oct, to 100 ft. long. Perennial twining vine, first promoted in the se U.S. to control erosion, now a conspicuous weed of waste areas, spreading into forests and toppling utility poles. Stems furry, becoming thick and woody, dying back in winter. Leaves long-petiolate with a pair of lobed, oval, basal stipules, divided into 3 oval to diamond-shaped lobed leaflets with marginal hairs and dense fur beneath. Flowers in hairy, stalked, pendent axillary racemes; each red-tinged purple, ½–¾ in. long, with typical pea-flower shape; scent is likened to artificial grape flavoring. Fruit a linear-oblong pod covered with reddish-brown hairs; rarely produces seeds in our area. RTW

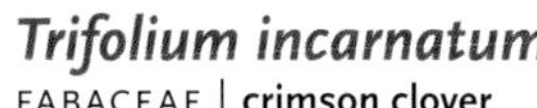

Trifolium incarnatum

FABACEAE | **crimson clover**

Apr–Sep, 11–25 in. Erect annual of fields, roadsides, and other disturbed areas. Native to the Mediterranean region, introduced for forage and soil improvement, now widespread in NoAm. Stems branched, soft-hairy. Leaves long-petioled, divided into 3 hairy, broadly oval, or heart-shaped leaflets, each to 1 in. long and finely toothed on the margin. Flowers in crowded, cylindrical or conical terminal spikes 1–2¼ in. tall; each flower bright red, about ½ in. long, with typical pea-flower shape. RTW

Capnoides sempervirens (*Corydalis sempervirens*)

FUMARIACEAE | **rock harlequin**

Apr–Aug, 11–32 in. Erect biennial of rock outcrops, especially granitic exfoliation domes but also quartzite, greenstone, and sandstone. Stems branched from base, sometimes red-tinged, smooth and with a white-waxy coating. Leaves petiolate (upper leaves nearly sessile), lacy, divided into 3–5 primary lobed segments (¼–¾ in. long), which are pale green and smooth. Flowers in an erect terminal raceme or panicle, pink and yellow, ½–¾ in. long, with a flattened-tubular corolla with a spur at the back and bright yellow lips at front. Fruit an erect, narrow cylindrical podlike capsule. Ants disperse the seeds. RTW

Dicentra eximia

FUMARIACEAE | **wild bleeding-heart**

Apr–Jul, 1–2 ft. Erect, rhizomatous perennial growing on cliffs, rocky slopes, and rock outcrops associated with rich, moist forests; may form mounds up to 3 ft. wide. An Appalachian endemic. Stems hollow at maturity, smooth. Leaves petiolate, oval in general outline, 2–8 in. long, finely divided into many pale green (white-waxy), toothed segments (fernlike). Flowers dangling from a panicle on a separate scape overtopping the leaves, magenta-pink (rarely white), 3/4 in. long, tubular with a flattened heart shape opening to 2 spreading-recurved lips facing downward. Fruit an oblong-oval capsule. WS

Leonurus cardiaca

LAMIACEAE | **motherwort**

May–Aug, 2–4 ft. Erect to ascending perennial of roadsides, pastures, other disturbed areas. Native to c Asia. Stems 1–several from crown, 4-angled and ridged, freely branched, sparsely hairy to smooth. Leaves petiolate, broadly oval in outline with wedge-shaped base, 2–4 in. long (upper leaves smaller, narrower), palmately divided into 3–5 sharp-pointed, toothed lobes; slightly rank odor. Flowers in axillary whorls, light pink to white, 1/3 in. long; the corolla tube opens to 2 lips, the upper prominent, hoodlike, and densely hairy on the outside, the lower 3-lobed and bearing purple spots. The tubular green calyx has 5 lance-shaped teeth and is slightly hairy. GPF

Utricularia purpurea

LENTIBULARIACEAE | **purple bladderwort**

May–Sep, 1–8 in. Erect but floating, aquatic, carnivorous perennial of ponds, ditches, and other sites with slow-moving water; may form small floating mats. Stems underwater, with wiry flowering scapes rising above water surface. Modified leaves underwater, opposite or in whorls of 5–7, divided into many narrow segments tipped with tiny bladderlike traps. Flowers in clusters of 1–5 at top of scape, dark pink to purple, about 1/2 in. long, tubular with a short, backward-pointing spur; the corolla tube opens to 2 lips, the lower lip with a yellow basal spot and divided into 3 lobes. RTW

Corallorhiza maculata

ORCHIDACEAE | **eastern spotted coralroot**

Jul, 8–20 in. Erect perennial of moist forests, including northern hardwood forests. Stem leafless, brownish-purple, smooth; a few sheathing bracts may be present. Flowers 10–30 in a narrow, terminal raceme and usually horizontally spreading. Each flower about ½ in. long, consisting of a prominent reddish-tan ovary with narrow, crimson-purple petals and sepals attached to its top; a lowest lip petal is larger and white with purple spots and scalloped edge. A mycoheterotroph. AMC

Corallorhiza odontorhiza

ORCHIDACEAE | **autumn coralroot**

Aug–Sep, 4–8 in. Erect perennial growing in the humus of some moist to dry forests, especially under oaks. Stem leafless, the base strongly thickened and bulbous; greenish to light brown tinged with purple. No true leaves; a few sheathing bracts may be present. Flowers in a terminal raceme 1–4½ in. long and horizontally spreading or nodding. The predominant flower part a red and greenish-yellow ovary about ¼ in. long; greenish-red petals and sepals form a short tube that often stays closed, though a white lower lip with purple spots may fold slightly outward. Fruit a drooping, oval capsule. A mycoheterotroph. AMC

Corallorhiza wisteriana

ORCHIDACEAE | **spring coralroot**

Apr–May, 4–17 in. Erect perennial of moist to dry forests, usually in base-rich soils. Stem leafless, the base strongly thickened and bulbous, yellowish-brown to reddish-purple, smooth. No true leaves; a few sheathing bracts may be present. Flowers 10–15 in a narrow terminal raceme and horizontally spreading, ascending, or drooping. Each flower about ⅓ in. long, consisting of a prominent greenish-red ovary with narrow, greenish-red petals and sepals attached to its top and forming a hood over a sharply drooping, white lip petal, which is larger and purple-spotted. A mycoheterotroph. RTW

Hexalectris spicata

ORCHIDACEAE | **crested coralroot**

Apr–Aug, 1–2½ ft. Erect perennial of dry forests and woodlands, especially over mafic or calcareous rocks, though sometimes in distinctly acidic situations. Stem unbranched, leafless, reddish-purple to brownish-pink, with a few purplish, sheathing bracts. Flowers in a narrow, spike-like raceme, purplish to yellowish-tan (or greenish), strongly striped with purple, about 1 in. wide, with 5 similar-looking spreading, oblong-lance-shaped sepals and petals with recurved tips plus an ornate, downcurved lip petal bearing 5–7 purple ridges (crests) and a wavy-edged tip. A mycoheterotroph. RTW

Cuthbertia graminea

COMMELINACEAE | **grassleaf roseling**

May–Jul, 4–16 in. Erect perennial of sandhills, sandy road banks and clearings, and dry, sandy woodlands of the Coastal Plain. Stems branched or freely forking, numerous, growing in a dense tuft, smooth or nearly so. Leaves linear and grasslike, the base of the leaf enclosing the stem in a fringed and hairy, tubular sheath; leaves to 9 in. long (often longer than stem) and smooth. Flowers in terminal clusters of 3–15, 1–2 opening and withering each day, bright pink, ¾ in. wide, composed of 3 triangular-oval petals and 6 hairy pink stamens. Fruit a nearly round capsule. PIP

Murdannia keisak

COMMELINACEAE | **marsh dewflower**

Sep–Oct, 8–59 in. Mat-forming, aggressively weedy, aquatic annual of streambanks, canals, ditches, freshwater marshes (tidal and non-tidal), swamp forests, and wet disturbed places. Native to Asia, widespread in the se U.S. Stems reclining or prostrate, freely forking or branched, extensively creeping and rooting at lower nodes. Leaves sessile with tubular sheaths bearing stiff hairs, linear to lance-shaped, ¾–2¾ in. long. Flowers solitary from upper leaf axils or sheaths, or in small clusters of 2–4; each flower pinkish or purplish-white, about ⅓ in. wide, with 3 oval petals and 6 bearded stamens (3 fertile and 3 non-fertile). Fruit an oval capsule. BAS

Trillium catesbaei

TRILLIACEAE | **Catesby's trillium**

Mar–Jun, 10–18 in. Erect perennial of bottomland forests, moist slopes, and cove forests. Stem single from an underground rhizome, unbranched, green to purplish, smooth. Leaves in a whorl of 3 at top of stem, short-petioled, elliptical, to 6 in. long. Flower solitary, held below leaves on a stalk emerging from center of leaf whorl, pink (rarely white), about 1½ in. wide, with 3 narrow, green-tinged-with-pink sepals, 3 wider and strongly recurved petals, 6 yellow stamens (twisted), and a white ovary. Fruit a greenish-white, oval, berrylike pod. JF

Trillium cuneatum

TRILLIACEAE | **sweet Betsy**

Jan–Apr, 6–11 in. Erect, often colonial perennial of rich cove forests, moist slopes, and bottomlands, usually over mafic or calcareous rocks. Stem stout, unbranched, smooth. Leaves 3, sessile and overlapping in a single whorl at top of stem, broadly oval to wedge-shaped, 3–7 in. long, with light and dark green mottling. Flower solitary and sessile at top center of leaf whorl, 1½–2¾ in. long, with 3 maroon to bronze (occasionally yellow), erect, narrow petals, 3 green and purple sepals, 6 linear maroon stamens, and a maroon ovary. Fruit a maroon-red, 3-celled, fleshy capsule resembling a berry. Flower scent variously described as spicy-fruity to "like a wet dog." RTW

Trillium erectum

TRILLIACEAE | **red trillium**

Apr–Jun, 6–24 in. Erect perennial of wooded slopes, usually at mid to high elevations. Stems unbranched, green to purple, smooth. Leaves 3 in a single whorl at top of plant, mostly sessile, broadly oval to diamond-shaped, 2–8 in. long and often wider, smooth. Flower solitary, held perpendicular to leaves on a long, erect stalk arising from center of leaf whorl; flower maroon or white (rarely pink, yellow, or green), 1½–3½ in. wide, consisting of 3 lance-shaped petals, 3 green and maroon sepals, 6 yellow or maroon anthers, and a maroon ovary. Fruit a dull purple-red, 3-celled, fleshy capsule resembling a berry. Flowers have a fishy fragrance. RTW

Trillium maculatum

TRILLIACEAE | **mottled trillium**

Feb–Apr, 5–16 in. Erect perennial of rich forests and floodplains, over calcareous materials such as coquina limestone/marl or on shell middens. Stems stout, unbranched, green to reddish-green, smooth. Leaves 3 in a whorl at top of stem, sessile, broadly oval, 3–6 in. long, with dark and light green mottling, smooth. Flower solitary and sessile at top of stem in center of leaf whorl, maroon or yellow, 1½–2¾ in. long, consisting of 3 erect narrow petals that are tapered at the base, 3 spreading, narrow, maroon or green sepals, 6 dark maroon anthers, and a dark purple ovary. Fruit a dark purple, 3-celled, fleshy capsule resembling a berry. Flower has a spicy-fruity fragrance. JF

Trillium sessile

TRILLIACEAE | **sessile trillium**

Mar–Apr, 4–12 in. Erect perennial of rich forests; in NC limited to very rich soils of natural levees and lower slopes along the Roanoke River. Stems stout, unbranched, smooth, often red-tinged. Leaves 3 in a whorl at top of stem, mostly sessile, broadly oval, 1½–4 in. long, with dark and light green mottling. Flower solitary and sessile in center of leaf whorl, erect, maroon, about 1½ in. tall, appearing closed. There are 3 narrowly elliptical petals, 3 ascending to spreading, green, lance-shaped sepals, 6 stamens, and a purple ovary. Fruit a dark purple, 3-celled, 6-angled, fleshy capsule resembling a berry. Flower has a musky fragrance. SJB

Trillium sulcatum

TRILLIACEAE | **southern red trillium**

Apr–May, 11–24 in. Erect perennial of coves and moist slopes. Stems stout, unbranched, smooth. Leaves 3 in a whorl at top of stem, sessile, broadly elliptical to nearly diamond-shaped, 5–7 in. long. Flower solitary on a long, erect stalk arising from center of leaf whorl; maroon (rarely cream-white). There are 3 spreading, oval, blunt-tipped petals with deeply incised veins, 3 green-suffused-with-purple, elliptical sepals, 6 stamens, and a round to pyramidal red ovary. Fruit a reddish, 3-celled, fleshy capsule resembling a berry. RTW

Trillium vaseyi

TRILLIACEAE | **sweet trillium**

Apr–Jun, 12–28 in. Erect perennial of cove and other rich forests; a Southern Appalachian endemic. Stems slender, unbranched, smooth. Leaves 3 in a whorl at top of stem, sessile, broadly oval to diamond-shaped with rounded angles, about 8 in. long. Flower solitary on a long stalk from center of leaf whorl, curved down below leaves; flower maroon (rarely white), to 4 in. wide, and consisting of 3 recurved, strongly overlapping oval petals, 3 spreading green sepals, 6 stamens with long anthers, and a purplish-black ovary. Fruit a dark reddish-maroon, fleshy, nearly round capsule resembling a berry. Flower has a pungent, roselike fragrance. JF

Cardamine douglassii

BRASSICACEAE | **purple cress**

Mar–Apr, 2–15 in. Erect, somewhat colonial perennial of nutrient-rich, moist forests, especially alluvial bottomlands, and nutrient-rich seepages. Stems unbranched, purple-tinged toward the base, hairy. Basal leaves petiolate, round (or nearly so), to 1 in. long, purple beneath; stem leaves (2–5) alternate, sessile or clasping, oval, to 2 in. long (reduced above), bluntly toothed or scalloped. Flowers on long stalks in a short terminal raceme, blooming from the bottom up; each pink to lavender (rarely white), ½–1 in. wide, with 4 oblong-oval petals, 4 shorter and hairy purple sepals, several stamens, and a single stout style. Fruit a thin, cylindrical pod. MK

Hesperis matronalis

BRASSICACEAE | **dame's rocket**

Apr–Aug, 2–3 ft. Erect, naturalized biennial/short-lived perennial found in bottomlands, moist forests, and along roadsides. Native to Europe. Stems much-branched above and hairy. Leaves short-petioled to sessile (above), 2–8 in. long, lance-shaped to narrowly oval, hairy, with small sharp teeth. Flowers on hairy stalks in 6- to 18-in.-long terminal and axillary racemes, pink to lavender (occasionally white), ¾–1 in. wide, with 4 spreading oblong petals and 4 linear-lance-shaped sepals (stamens and pistil not easily seen). Fruit an erect, slender, linear pod. Flowers very fragrant, especially in evening. JG

Chamaenerion angustifolium ssp. *circumvagum* (*C. danielsii*)

ONAGRACEAE | **fireweed**

Jul–Sep, 2–8 ft. Erect perennial of grassy balds, mountain fields, burned areas, roadsides. Stems unbranched, smooth below inflorescence. Leaves crowded, sessile, lance-shaped to elliptical, 2–8 in. long, slightly toothed or wavy. Flowers ascending to horizontal in a terminal raceme, blooming from the bottom up; each pinkish-purple, ¾–1 in. wide, with 4 spoon-shaped petals, 4 shorter, narrow, darker pink sepals, 8 white stamens with purple-brown tips, and a white style with 4 curled stigmas. Fruit an erect, purplish-red, slender pod containing white-tufted seeds. BAS

Epilobium coloratum

ONAGRACEAE | **eastern willow-herb**

Jun–Oct, 1–3 ft. Erect perennial of open floodplain forests, wet fields, meadows, ditches. Stems much-branched in upper half, with vertical lines of hairs on lower half. Leaves alternate (some may be opposite), short-petioled, lance-shaped, 4 in. long or more, sharply toothed, often with purplish veins or spots, smooth or minutely hairy along veins. Flowers usually numerous in an intricately branched panicle, light pink or white, ⅓ in. wide, with 4 notched petals attached to the top of a long-hairy, reddish-green calyx tube; calyx terminates in 4 lance-shaped sepals, which may be tinged purplish-pink. Fruit an elongated capsule, splitting to release tiny, tufted seeds. PIP

Oenothera speciosa

ONAGRACEAE | **pink-ladies**

Feb–Aug, 1–2 ft. Erect to sprawling, colonial perennial of roadsides and fields; introduced from farther west in the U.S. Stems slender, often slightly woody, smooth or hairy. Leaves short-petioled to sessile, linear to lance-shaped, to 3 in. long, irregularly toothed or lobed (basal leaves more so), hairy or smooth. Flowers borne singly on slender, downy stalks (or sessile) from upper leaf axils, pink to white with darker pink-red veins and yellow throat, 2–3½ in. wide, with 4 round petals, 8 prominent stamens, and a style with cross-shaped stigma; buds are spindle-shaped and nodding. Flowers open in evening. Often cultivated as a drought-hardy ornamental. AMC

Rhexia alifanus

MELASTOMATACEAE | **smooth meadow-beauty**

May–Sep, 1½–3 ft. Erect perennial of wet pine flatwoods, savannas, pocosin borders; more tolerant of merely moist (not saturated) soils than other rhexias. Stems 4-angled, usually unbranched, bluish-green, smooth. Leaves sessile, lance-shaped, tapered at both ends and pointing upward, to 2¾ in. long, with 3 conspicuous veins, bluish-green and smooth. Flowers in small terminal or upper axillary clusters, rosy-pink to purple, about 2 in. wide, with 4 spreading, asymmetric-oval petals arising from a glandular-hairy, urn-shaped tube; 8 stamens with curved yellow anthers conspicuously protrude from the corolla. Fruit a round capsule enclosed in the urn-shaped tube. RTW

Houstonia purpurea

RUBIACEAE | **summer bluet**

May–Jul, 4–12 in. Erect perennial of moist and dry woodlands and forests, road banks, thinner soils around rock outcrops, and a variety of disturbed sites. Stems 4-angled and narrowly winged, often furry. Leaves opposite (basal rosette barely evident at flowering), oval to lance-shaped, sessile, ½–1½ in. long, with 3–7 noticeable veins, and hairy at least along the veins. Flowers in small branching clusters at stem top or from upper axils, pale purple to white, to ¼ in. long, funnel-shaped with 4 spreading, pointed corolla lobes. Fruit a rounded, slightly compressed capsule. BAS

Rhexia aristosa

MELASTOMATACEAE | **awned meadow-beauty**

Jun–Sep, 16–28 in. Erect perennial of clay-based Carolina bays, depression meadows, dolines. Stems with a spongy-thickened base, 4-angled and narrowly winged, branched, covered with stiff hairs, especially at nodes. Leaves sessile, angled upward, linear to lance-shaped, 1 in. long, with 3 conspicuous veins and hair-tipped teeth. Flowers in small terminal clusters, purple to pinkish-lavender, ½–¾ in. long, with 4 asymmetric-oval petals spreading from an urn-shaped tube, which is rimmed with yellowish bristles, and 4 bristle-tipped, narrowly triangular sepal lobes; there are 8 stamens with yellow, curved anthers. Fruit a rounded capsule enclosed in the urn-shaped tube. AMC

Rhexia cubensis

MELASTOMATACEAE | **West Indian meadow-beauty**

Jun–Sep, 12–27 in. Erect perennial of dolines. Stems angled, with 4 markedly unequal faces, branched or unbranched, covered with coarse, stiff, glandular hairs. Leaves sessile, linear to narrowly elliptical, ¾–1½ in. long, with hair-tipped teeth, sparsely hairy. Flowers in few- to several-flowered clusters, lavender-rose to almost white, ⅝–¾ in. long, with 4 broadly triangular to oval petals arising from a glandular-hairy, urn-shaped tube (which is longer than the floral tube in other rhexias), and 8 stamens bearing curved yellow anthers. Fruit a round capsule. FG

Rhexia mariana

MELASTOMATACEAE | **Maryland meadow-beauty**

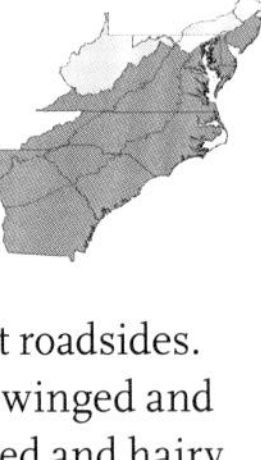

May–Oct, to 32 in. Erect, frequently colonial perennial of pine flatwoods, wet meadows, bog margins, ditches, and wet roadsides. Stems 4-angled, with the angles sometimes winged and faces markedly unequal at midstem; branched and hairy. Leaves sessile, elliptical to lance-shaped or narrowly oval, ¾–2½ in. long, 3 veined, finely toothed, hairy. Flowers in few-flowered, branching terminal clusters; each flower purplish to pale rose or white, to 2 in. wide, with 4 petals arising from a glandular-hairy, urn-shaped tube and 8 stamens bearing curved yellow anthers. Fruit a round capsule. RTW

Rhexia nashii

MELASTOMATACEAE | **hairy meadow-beauty**

May–Oct, 1–3 ft. Erect, often colonial perennial of wet pine flatwoods and savannas, pondshores, ditches, bogs, marshes, wet roadsides. Stems simple or branched, covered with scattered gland-tipped hairs. Leaves short-petioled to sessile, elliptical to broadly lance-shaped, 1–2½ in. long, finely toothed, and hairy. Flowers on branches from upper leaf axils, rosy pink, with 4 asymmetrical oblong-oval petals spreading from an urn-shaped tube, the petals and tube with gland-tipped hairs on the outer surface, and 8 stamens with yellow, curved anthers; the tube is rimmed with 4 narrowly triangular sepal lobes. Fruit a rounded capsule. BAS

Rhexia petiolata

MELASTOMATACEAE | **fringed meadow-beauty**

Jun–Sep, 6–20 in. Erect to ascending perennial of wet pine flatwoods and savannas, pocosin borders, ditches. Stems 4-angled, narrowly winged, unbranched or forked above, smooth. Leaves short-petioled, broadly elliptical to oval, about ¾ in. long, with 3 conspicuous veins and finely toothed, bristly margins; smooth or sparsely hairy and sometimes bristly above. Flowers single or in few-flowered terminal clusters, often upward-pointing; each purple to pink, to 1½ in. wide, with petals arising from a glandular-bristly, urn-shaped tube, and 8 stamens bearing straight yellow anthers. Fruit a round capsule. WS

Rhexia virginica

MELASTOMATACEAE | **Virginia meadow-beauty**

May–Oct, to 3 ft. Erect perennial of wet pine flatwoods and savannas, bogs, pondshores, ditches. Stems square, angles narrowly winged, usually unbranched except near apex, smooth to sparsely hairy, bristly at the nodes. Leaves sessile, broadly lance-shaped to oval, to 2¾ in. long, conspicuously 3-veined, sharply toothed, hairy along the margins, sometimes bristly. Flowers in branched terminal clusters and from upper leaf axils, pinkish-purple, 1–1½ in. wide, with broadly oval petals arising from a hairy or bristly urn-shaped tube, and 8 stamens with curved yellow anthers. Fruit a round capsule. The flowers are buzz-pollinated by bumblebees. RTW

Galium lanceolatum

RUBIACEAE | **lanceleaf wild licorice**

Jun–Jul, 12–28 in. Slender, erect to ascending perennial of moist to dry hardwood forests. Stems wiry, often branched from base or in inflorescence, smooth with some hairiness at nodes. Leaves in whorls of 4, sessile to short-petioled, elliptical to oval-lance-shaped, 1–3 in. long, with 3–5 prominent veins, and with margins and veins minutely hairy. Flowers sparse in a wide-branching terminal cluster, yellowish turning maroon-purple, less than ¼ in. wide, with 4 spreading, pointed corolla lobes. Fruit a green (turning black) capsule composed of 2 round lobes covered with curved bristles and containing 1 seed per lobe. JASA, EB

Galium latifolium

RUBIACEAE | **wideleaf bedstraw**

May–Aug, 10–22 in. Slender, erect to ascending perennial of moist hardwood forests. Stems wiry, simple or branched, smooth or with hairs at nodes. Leaves in whorls of 4, sessile, lance-shaped, 1–2 in. long, with 3 prominent veins, hairy on midrib and margins. Flowers in many-flowered, branching clusters from upper leaf axils, maroon to purple, less than 1⁄4 in. wide, consisting of 4 spreading, oblong-lance petals. Fruit a smooth capsule composed of 2 round lobes, only 1 lobe of which typically produces a seed. AMC

Galium pilosum

RUBIACEAE | **hairy bedstraw**

May–Aug, 6–30 in. Weakly ascending perennial of forests, woodland borders, and clearings, growing in tufts. Stems 4-angled, simple (branched in inflorescence), softly hairy. Leaves in whorls of 4, sessile, to 1 in. long, elliptic, with 3 prominent veins, glandular dots beneath, and hairy on both surfaces. Flowers on hairy stalks in terminal and upper axillary panicles, purple-maroon to greenish-white, less than 1⁄4 in. wide, with 4 pointed petals. Fruit a greenish-white (turning brownish-black) capsule composed of 2 rounded lobes covered with hooked bristles and containing 1 seed per lobe. Roots of this and other *Galium* species contain a substance sometimes used as a red dye. BAS

Galium sherardia (*Sherardia arvensis*)

RUBIACEAE | **blue field-madder**

Feb–Aug, 4–10 in. Erect to sprawling annual of lawns, roadsides, and other disturbed areas. Native to Europe. Stems 4-angled, branched, rough-hairy. Leaves in whorls of 4–6, linear to lance-shaped, with a sharp point at the tip and finely toothed margins. Flowers sessile in clusters at branch tips, pink to lavender, 1⁄8 in. long, tubular-funnel shaped with 4 spreading, pointed corolla lobes. Fruit an oval 2-ribbed capsule that splits in half. RTW

Stylisma aquatica

CONVOLVULACEAE | **water dawnflower**

Jun–Jul, 1½–6½ ft. long. Spreading-prostrate herbaceous perennial vine found in clay-based Carolina bays and wet savannas, margins of pineland ponds. Stems several to many, the basal portions appearing rhizomatous; often forming large mats. Leaves sessile, oblong, ¾–1¼ in. long, silky-hairy. Flowers in groups of 1–3 on long stalks (longer than leaves) from leaf axils, pale pink or purple, ⅓–½ in. long, the corolla bell- to funnel-shaped and composed of fused petals. At the base of the corolla are 5 leathery, lance-shaped sepals, and there are 5 stamens and a style that is split more than half its length. Fruit a 4-seeded capsule. JBG

Ipomoea purpurea

CONVOLVULACEAE | **common morning-glory**

Jul–Sep, to 10 ft. long. Herbaceous annual vine of fields, roadsides, sandbars, and other open, weedy areas. Native to the Neotropics. Stems twining or trailing, light brown to green, nearly smooth to hairy. Leaves petiolate, broadly heart-shaped, to 4 in. long and almost as broad, mostly smooth. Flowers in axillary clusters of 1–5, purple or blue to pink or white (sometimes variegated), 1½–2½ in. wide, with a tubular-funnel-shaped corolla and a much shorter calyx of hairy, lance-shaped sepals. Fruit a round capsule. Each flower blooms once, in the morning, and lasts a single day. BAS

Phemeranthus teretifolius (*Talinum teretifolium*)

MONTIACEAE | **Appalachian rock-pink**

May–Sep, 2–20 in. Delicate, ascending to erect perennial of outcrops and glades, especially where periodically wet from seepage. Stems fleshy and close to ground, reddish, smooth. Leaves sessile, crowded, linear and round in cross-section, 1–2½ in. long, fleshy, smooth. Flowers few in an open, 2- to 4-times forked, terminal cluster on a slender stalk above the leaves; each flower dark pink, about ½ in. wide, with 4–5 oval petals and 15–20 stamens (sepals drop early). Each flower opens in the afternoon for a day. Fruit an oval to elliptical capsule. BE

Portulaca pilosa

PORTULACACEAE | **kiss-me-quick**

May–Nov, to 10 in. long. Sprawling to erect, succulent annual of beaches, dune swales, pinelands, and disturbed sandy soils. Stems fleshy, often reddish, branched, with tufts of coarse hairs at leaf nodes and beneath flowers. Leaves mostly alternate, linear to lance-shaped, to 3 in. long, fleshy-succulent, sometimes red-tinged. Flowers usually solitary in leaf axils, pink or magenta, ¼–½ in. wide, with 5–7 oval petals with scalloped tips and many yellow stamens; petals drop after a few hours. BAS

Triodanis biflora (*Specularia biflora*)

CAMPANULACEAE | **small Venus' looking-glass**

Apr–Jun, 6–20 in. Erect annual of glades, roadsides, and other disturbed areas. Stems ridged, branched only at base. Leaves sessile but generally not clasping, elliptical to oval or oblong, to about 1 in. long, sometimes wavy-margined. Flowers in leaf axils, held close to stem, opening one at a time and most never opening, purple to pale lavender, about ½ in. wide with 5 widely spreading petals, 5 white stamens, and a 3-lobed stigma. Fruit an elliptical capsule. JS

Triodanis perfoliata (*Specularia perfoliata*)

CAMPANULACEAE | **Venus' looking-glass**

Apr–Jun, 4–12 in. Erect annual of glades, dry forests, roadsides, and other disturbed areas. Stem slender, unbranched, light green, and ridged, with a line of hairs on each ridge. Leaves clasping the stem, heart-shaped, to 1 in. long, wavy-margined. Flowers in groups of 1–3 in leaf axils along upper half of stem, the lower ones rarely opening. Flowers that do open are purple, ½ in. wide, with a short tubular corolla opening to 5 spreading lobes and a prominent pistil. Fruit an oblong to elliptical capsule. Stem and leaves leak milky sap when broken. RTW

Ipomoea coccinea

CONVOLVULACEAE | **scarlet creeper**

Aug–Dec, to 10 ft. long. Herbaceous annual vine of fields, roadsides, thickets, and streambanks. Stems twining and smooth. Leaves petiolate, heart-shaped or rarely lobed, to 4 in. long, with lower margins often weakly toothed, smooth. Flowers in axillary clusters, scarlet, often with a yellow throat, to 1 in. long and 1½ in. wide, narrowly funnel-shaped, with a long tube and flaring opening and with 5 protruding stamens. Fruit a nearly round capsule. RTW

Ipomoea sagittata

CONVOLVULACEAE | **saltmarsh morning-glory**

Jul–Sep, 6 ft. or longer. Herbaceous perennial vine of brackish marsh edges, moist thickets on barrier islands, and hammocks. Stems trailing or twining, smooth. Leaves petiolate, arrowhead-shaped with pointed or rounded basal lobes, 1½–3½ in. long. Flowers singular or in small clusters of 2–3, lavender-rose with darker throat, about 3 in. wide, tubular-funnel-shaped, with 5 shallow lobes at the rim, surrounded at the base by 5 leathery, elliptic-oblong sepals. Fruit a rounded capsule. PIP

Hylotelephium telephioides (*Sedum telephioides*)

CRASSULACEAE | **Allegheny live-forever**

Jul–Sep, 6–12 in. Erect to leaning perennial of rock outcrops, mostly at mid to high elevations (to 6500 ft.). Stems clumped, with semi-woody bases, branched in inflorescence, leafier above, often purple-tinged, smooth. Leaves alternate or opposite, short-petioled, oval, 1–3 in. long, shallowly toothed or entire, succulent, smooth. Flowers in branching terminal clusters; pale pink to pinkish-white, ¼ in. wide, with 5 spreading, lance-oval petals (green keels on the back) twice as long as the 5 sepals, a 5-parted ovary, and 5 stamens with pink anthers. Fruit a cluster of 5 erect capsules with spreading beaks. BAS

Hibiscus laevis

MALVACEAE | **smooth rose-mallow**

Jun–Aug, 2–11 ft. Tall, shrublike perennial of freshwater marshes, exposed riverbanks, and sandbars. Stems few to many arising from a crown, unbranched, smooth. Leaves long-petioled, arrowhead-shaped to lance-shaped and usually with 2 lobes at the base, to 6 in. long, with toothed margins and smooth. Flowers solitary on stalks arising from upper leaf axils, pink or white with a maroon center, to 5 in. wide, funnel-shaped, with 5 wide, veiny petals and a central tube of fused, reddish stamens surrounding the pistil. The flower rests on a whorl of green, linear bracts. RTW

Malva neglecta (M. rotundifolia)

MALVACEAE | **common mallow**

Apr–Nov, 6–24 in. Prostrate to ascending annual/biennial/short-lived perennial of pastures, roadsides, barnyards. Native to Europe. Stems trailing, branched from base, densely hairy. Leaves long-petioled, round and often notched at the base, 3/4–2 1/2 in. long, obscurely 5- to 9-lobed, toothed and fuzzy gray-green. Flowers 1–3 on stalks arising from leaf axils, pale pink or white, often with pale violet lines, 3/4 in. wide, with 5 ascending, oblong petals with slightly notched tips, a 5-lobed calyx, and a central column of numerous close-pressed stamens surrounding a pistil. Fruit a flattened-round, wheel-shaped capsule. GPF

Kosteletzkya pentacarpos

MALVACEAE | **seashore-mallow**

Jul–Oct, 1–5 ft. Erect, shrublike perennial of brackish to freshwater tidal marshes. Stems several, covered with branched hairs (as are leaves) and sometimes gray as a result. Leaves long-petiolate with linear stipules, heart-shaped to oval or triangular (upper leaves more lance-shaped), to 5 1/2 in. long, often lobed, coarsely toothed. Flowers in leafy axillary and terminal racemes, pink to lavender (occasionally white), to 3 in. wide, with 5 spreading oblong-oval petals and an erect tube of yellow stamens fused around a pistil. A whorl of linear, hairy bracts at the flower base surrounds a 5-lobed calyx. Fruit a 5-celled, flattened-round capsule. KB

Asclepias amplexicaulis

APOCYNACEAE | **clasping milkweed**

May–Jul, 2–3 ft. Erect perennial of sandhills and other dry woodlands. Stems stout, usually unbranched, smooth, with a white-waxy coating, leaking milky sap when bruised. Leaves in 2–6 pairs, sessile and clasping, oblong or widely oval to elliptical, 3–5 in. long, with a pink midrib, wavy-margined, smooth, with a white-waxy coating. Flowers 15–80 in a rounded, terminal umbel, smoky purple, about ½ in. long, with 5 strongly reflexed pinkish-green corolla lobes and a central crown surrounding the fused anthers and style. Fruit an erect, spindle-shaped pod containing many tufted brown seeds. WS

Asclepias cinerea

APOCYNACEAE | **Carolina milkweed**

Jun–Jul, 12–28 in. Erect to ascending perennial found in dry pine savannas and sandy uplands. Stems slender, unbranched, smooth, leaking milky sap when bruised. Leaves essentially sessile, linear, to 4 in. long, smooth. Flowers on long, slender, nodding stalks in a loose terminal umbel, pink to lavender, about ⅜ in. long, with 5 strongly reflexed, lavender corolla lobes and a pink central crown surrounding the fused anthers and style. Fruit an erect, slender, spindle-shaped follicle containing tufted seeds. AMC

Asclepias humistrata

APOCYNACEAE | **fleshy milkweed**

Apr–Jun, 1–2½ ft. Leaning to sprawling perennial of sandhills and other dry, sandy uplands. Stem unbranched, smooth, with a white-waxy coating; leaks milky sap when bruised. Leaves sessile-clasping, oval, to 4 in. long, thick, blue-green with pink veins, and smooth; curving upward when stem is sprawling on ground. Flowers on reddish-pink stalks in rounded, terminal and upper axillary umbels; each flower about ¾ in. long, with 5 strongly reflexed, dull pink corolla lobes and an erect pinkish-white central crown surrounding the fused anthers and style. Fruit an erect, spindle-shaped follicle containing tufted seeds. WS

Asclepias incarnata

APOCYNACEAE | **swamp milkweed**

Jul–Sep, 3–6 ft. Erect perennial of marshes, bogs, swamps, and banks of streams and ponds. Stems solitary or clustered, branched above, smooth to hairy. Stems and leaves exude milky sap when bruised. Leaves petiolate, lance-shaped to linear-oblong, 2–6 in. long, smooth to hairy. Flowers in umbels at stem and branch ends, dusty-pink to rose-purple (rarely white), fragrant, about ¼ in. wide, with 5 strongly reflexed corolla lobes and a central crown surrounding the fused anthers and style. Fruit a minutely hairy, spindle-shaped follicle containing tufted seeds. A host plant for Monarch butterflies. WS

Asclepias longifolia

APOCYNACEAE | **longleaf milkweed**

May–Jun, ½–2 ft. Erect perennial of coastal wet pine savannas and flatwoods. Stems solitary or clumped, unbranched, smooth or minutely hairy. Stems and leaves leak milky sap when bruised. Leaves sessile or nearly so, linear to linear-lance-shaped, 3–5 in. long, smooth or rough-hairy on veins beneath. Flowers on rough-hairy stalks in terminal and upper axillary umbels (10–30 flowers), rose-tinted greenish-white, about ⅜ in. long, with 5 strongly reflexed, pink/purple-tipped corolla lobes and a central crown composed of 5 "hoods" (no "horn") surrounding the fused anthers and style. Fruit an erect, slender, lance-shaped follicle containing tufted seeds. RTW

Asclepias michauxii

APOCYNACEAE | **Michaux's milkweed**

May–Aug, 4–16 in. Erect to reclining perennial of seeps in wet pine savannas and flatwoods and in drier, sandy uplands. Stems unbranched, purplish, with vertical lines of hairs; leak milky sap when bruised. Leaves mostly opposite, sessile, linear, 2–4½ in. long, smooth or sometimes with hairy veins beneath. Flowers in rounded terminal umbels, pink-tinged greenish-white, about ⅜ in. long, with 5 strongly reflexed corolla lobes and a central crown (the "horns" long and pointy) surrounding the fused anthers and style. Fruit a slender follicle containing tufted seeds. RTW

Asclepias purpurascens

APOCYNACEAE | **purple milkweed**

May–Jul, 1¼–3 ft. Erect perennial of moist bottomlands, swamp forests, prairies, woodlands. Stem solitary, minutely hairy or with lines of hairs between leaf nodes; leaks milky sap when bruised. Leaves (6+ pairs) petiolate, oval to elliptical or oval-oblong, 3–6½ in. long, with a pink central vein, the sides often curling up, smooth above, softly hairy beneath. Flowers in terminal cluster of 1–6 rounded umbels, each 2–3 in. wide; flowers deep purple to deep rose (greenish in bud), ¾ in. long, with 5 strongly reflexed corolla lobes and a lighter-colored central crown surrounding fused anthers and style. Fruit a furry, lance-shaped to oval follicle containing tufted seeds. WS

Asclepias rubra

APOCYNACEAE | **purple savanna milkweed**

Jun–Jul, 1½–4 ft. Erect perennial of pocosin ecotones, wet pine savannas, sandhill seeps, seepage swamps. Stem solitary, unbranched, with 3–5 leaf nodes, smooth or with hair in lines between nodes; leaks milky sap when bruised. Leaves sessile or nearly so, lance-shaped and round or weakly heart-shaped at the base, 3½–5 in. long, with wavy margins, sparsely hairy. Flowers in rounded terminal and upper axillary umbels about 1.5 in. wide; each flower dull red to pinkish-purple, ½–¾ in. long, with 5 strongly reflexed corolla lobes and a lighter-colored central crown surrounding the fused anthers and style. Fruit an erect, narrowly spindle-shaped follicle with tufted seeds. BAS

Asclepias syriaca

APOCYNACEAE | **common milkweed**

Jun–Aug, 3–6 ft. Conspicuous, coarse colonial perennial of unmowed fields and disturbed areas. Stem stout, unbranched, often furry; leaks milky sap when bruised. Leaves short-petioled, oval to oblong, 6–9 in. long, reddish central vein, soft-hairy beneath. Flowers on long stalks that often droop, in a globe-shaped terminal umbel and a few upper axillary umbels; each pale purple to rose-colored, with 5 strongly reflexed corolla lobes and a central crown surrounding fused anthers and style. Fruit a warty, somewhat furry, oval follicle containing tufted seeds. Fragrant; a well-known Monarch host plant, apparently expanding its range southward. RTW

Matelea obliqua

APOCYNACEAE | **limerock milkvine**

Jun–Jul, 4–5 ft. long. Herbaceous perennial vine of moist to dry forests, woodlands, barrens, and thickets over calcareous rocks. Stems climbing over other vegetation, hairy, leaking milky sap when broken. Leaves petiolate, widely heart-shaped with an abruptly tapered tip, 1½–6 in. long. Flowers in clusters of 10–50, on stalks from between leaf petiole pairs, the buds long-conical; flowers rose to light maroon (rarely dark maroon, green, or cream-colored), consisting of 5 ascending-spreading, narrow, pointed petals connected at the base, and a central "crown" containing the reproductive structures. Fruit a warty, oval to lance-shaped follicle. BAS

Triosteum perfoliatum

CAPRIFOLIACEAE | **perfoliate horse-gentian**

May–Jun, 2–4 ft. Coarse, erect perennial of woodlands and forests on circumneutral soils, particularly those over mafic or calcareous rocks. Stems unbranched, soft-hairy. Leaves in pairs at 90° to each other, and each pair joined at the base and encompassing the stem. Leaves broadly oval, 4–9 in. long, with slightly wavy edges and soft-hairy (especially beneath). Flowers solitary or in few-flowered clusters tucked into leaf axils, sessile, brownish-red, ⅜–½ in. long, tubular, with 5 rounded lobes, 5 downy narrow sepals that may be longer than the corolla, and a conspicuous light green style. Fruit a sessile, yellow, round to oval drupe. RTW

Atocion armeria (*Silene armeria*)

CARYOPHYLLACEAE | **sweet William catchfly**

Jun–Oct, 4–20 in. Erect annual of meadows, fields, and other disturbed areas. Native to Europe. Stems branched, smooth or sparsely hairy. Leaves sessile-clasping, ascending, oval to lance-shaped. Flowers in open or compact, branching terminal clusters; each flower magenta-pink to lavender, with 5 shallowly notched petals spreading outward from an inflated calyx tube bearing 10 prominent veins. Fruit an oblong to elliptical capsule encased in the persistent calyx tube. Flowers open in sunlight. SG

Dianthus armeria

CARYOPHYLLACEAE | **Deptford pink**

May–Sep, 6–24 in. Erect annual/biennial of fields, roadsides, and pastures. Native to Europe. Stems simple or with 1–2 slender branches from the base, knobby where paired leaves meet, hairy. Leaves joined at base by a stem-encircling sheath, linear or narrowly lance-shaped, 1–3 in. long, hairy. Flowers in narrow clusters at top of stem and from upper leaf axils, pink with white and darker pink spots, ½ in. wide, with 5 spreading petals that are toothed at the tip, these surrounded by 3 needlelike bracts. Fruit a narrow capsule. BAS

Silene antirrhina

CARYOPHYLLACEAE | **sleepy catchfly**

Apr–Jul, 8–30 in. Erect to ascending annual/biennial of fields and other disturbed areas. Stems branched, hairy, and with dark, sticky bands beneath upper leaf nodes. Leaves sessile and ascending, lance-shaped, 1–3 in. long. Flowers solitary or in sparse clusters at ends of branches, pink or lavender to white, ¼–⅜ in. wide, with 5 spreading, deeply notched petals emerging from the narrow end of an inflated, ribbed calyx tube. Fruit an oval capsule encased in the dry, inflated calyx tube. Flowers open in sunshine and close near evening. JG

Silene regia

CARYOPHYLLACEAE | **royal catchfly**

May–Sep, 2–4 ft. Erect to leaning perennial of dry prairies, calcareous woodlands, and rocky, open woods. Stems mostly unbranched, covered with fine white hairs. Leaves sessile, each pair perpendicular to the next, lance-shaped, to 5 in. long, with upper and lower surfaces covered with fine white hairs. Flowers in branching terminal clusters, bright red, ¾–1 in. wide, with 5 spreading, narrow petals (may be slightly toothed at the tip) and a 1-in.-long, tubular calyx that is longitudinally ridged and covered with sticky hairs. Protruding stamens bear gray anthers. Fruit an oval capsule. AMC

Silene virginica

CARYOPHYLLACEAE | **fire pink**

Apr–Jul, 1–1½ ft. Erect to leaning perennial of woodlands, rock outcrops, crevices in cliffs, and road banks. Stems branched from the plant base and covered with sticky hairs. Leaves petiolate (basal) and sessile (stem), elliptical to oblong-lance-shaped, 1–4 in. long, smooth. Flowers in an open, branching terminal cluster, red, about 1½ in. wide, with 5 spreading, deeply and unevenly notched petals with a ring of small, red teeth in their center, and a tubular calyx nearly 1 in. long and covered in sticky hairs. Fruit an elliptical capsule. WS

Sabatia angularis

GENTIANACEAE | **bitter-bloom**

Jun–Sep, 8–32 in. Erect annual/biennial of forests, woodlands, marshes, and fields, especially in base-rich situations. Stems 4-angled and winged, with opposite branches above middle, smooth. Leaves sessile-clasping, oval to lance-shaped, to 2 in. long, smooth; a basal rosette is sometimes present. Flowers on long stalks in terminal, opposite-branched panicles, rose-pink (occasionally white), 1½ in. wide, with 5 corolla lobes with basal markings that create a red-rimmed, yellow-green star shape in the flower center. A long style from the green ovary is split in 2 at the top. Fruit an angled, oval capsule. Flower buds have a distinctive "swirled" look. RTW

Sabatia campanulata

GENTIANACEAE | **slender marsh-pink**

Jun–Aug, 8–28 in. Erect to spreading perennial found in pine savannas, bogs, seeps, and fens. Stems strongly 4-angled and alternately branched; there may be several stems from a somewhat woody base. Leaves in a basal rosette and opposite (sessile) on stem; basal leaves oblong-oval and stem leaves linear and reduced above. Flowers in terminal panicles, dark pink (occasionally white), nearly 1½ in. wide, the petals connected at the base by a yellow-green eye; linear, needlelike sepals are about as long as petals. Fruit an elliptical capsule. RTW

Sabatia stellaris

GENTIANACEAE | **annual sea-pink**

Jul–Oct, 8–22 in. Erect annual from a shallow taproot typically found in brackish marshes and tidal flats. Stems usually square, often branched, smooth. Leaves sessile, narrowly elliptical to oblong, to 1 in. long; some basal leaves may be present. Flowers few to many in an open panicle, or solitary terminating the stem, pink (sometimes white), with 4–5 spreading oblong to oblong-oval petals with basal markings that create a red-rimmed yellow eye in the center of the flower and shorter, linear sepals. Fruit an elliptical to ovoid capsule. BAS

Triadenum virginicum

HYPERICACEAE | **marsh St. John's-wort**

Jul–Sep, 8–25 in. Erect, rhizomatous perennial of bogs, fens, tidal swamps and marshes, and other peaty wetlands. Stems simple or branched, often pinkish, smooth. Leaves sessile with clasping bases, elliptical to oblong, ¾–3½ in. long, sometimes with reddish margins, undersides with tiny pitted dots and a whitish coating. Flowers in terminal and upper axillary, branched clusters; each pinkish-purplish, ⅓–½ in. wide, with 5 ascending-spreading, lance-oblong petals with prominent reddish veins, 5 equal or shorter sepals, and a 3-celled ovary with 3 styles surrounded by an open ring of 9 stamens. Fruit an erect, oval to elliptical ovary with tapered tip and persistent styles. JED

Triadenum walteri

HYPERICACEAE | **Walter's marsh St. John's-wort**

Jul–Sep, 1–3 ft. Erect, rhizomatous perennial of alluvial, tidal, and maritime swamp forests, floodplain pools and ponds, and depression ponds and swamps. Stems bushy-branched, reddish, smooth. Leaves short-petioled, elliptical to oblong with rounded tips and tapered bases, to 6 in. long, the midvein often reddish and undersides with tiny, pitted, black and clear dots. Flowers in small terminal and upper axillary clusters, pale pink to salmon-colored, about ½ in. wide, with 5 pointed petals with pink veins, 5 smaller and narrower sepals, and 9 partially united stamens surrounding an ovary and 3 styles. Fruit a reddish-green, 3-celled, cylindrical capsule. GPF

Spigelia marilandica

LOGANIACEAE | **pinkroot**

May–Jun, 1–2 ft. Erect, clump-forming perennial of moist woods and streambanks, usually in circumneutral soils over limestone or other mafic rock. Stems wiry, unbranched, smooth. Leaves sessile, oval to lance-shaped, 2–4 in. long, smooth. Flowers in a terminal, 1-sided spike that curves slightly at the tip; each flower scarlet-red with yellow inner surface, to 2 in. long, erect-tubular, with 5 short, pointed, spreading corolla lobes and a protruding style. RTW

Claytonia caroliniana

MONTIACEAE | **Carolina spring-beauty**

Mar–May, 2–12 in. Delicate, erect perennial, somewhat colonial from a round underground corm, found in moist forests, especially northern hardwood forests and cove forests at mid to high elevations. Stems unbranched, smooth. Basal leaves petiolate, elliptical or spoon-shaped, 2–6 in. long, smooth; stem leaves oval to spoon-shaped, 1½–3 in. long, smooth. Flowers 6–20 in a loose terminal raceme, pink to white with darker pink stripes, ½ in. wide, with 5 spreading oval petals, 2 smaller oval sepals, and 5 stamens with pink anthers. Fruit a pyramidal to rounded capsule. Flowers close at night and on cloudy days. Plant withers shortly after seed capsules ripen. RTW

Claytonia virginica

MONTIACEAE | **spring-beauty**

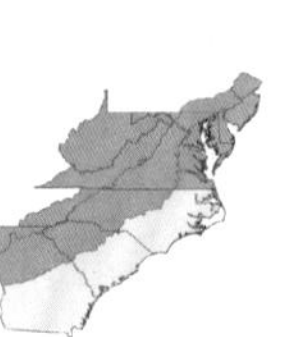

Feb–Apr, 4–6 in. Delicate, erect perennial, often colonial from a round underground corm, found in moist forests and well-drained floodplain forests. Stems unbranched, smooth. Leaves mostly in a single pair (a few basal leaves may be present), linear with indistinguishable petiole, 2–8 in. long, thick, smooth. Flowers 6–20 and erect or nodding in a small, open, terminal raceme; flowers pink to white with dark pink stripes, about ½ in. wide, with 5 oval petals, 2 blunt-tipped shorter sepals, and 5 stamens with pink anthers. Fruit an oval capsule. Like most spring ephemerals, plants disappear shortly after blooming. RTW

Phlox amoena

POLEMONIACEAE | **hairy phlox**

Apr–Jun, to 18 in. Erect or reclining perennial of dry woodlands and forests, road banks, sandhills. Stems unbranched (rarely weakly branched above) and very hairy. Leaves sessile, sometimes ascending, narrowly oblong to lance-shaped, 1–2 in. long, hairy on both surfaces, with long marginal hairs. Flowers in compact terminal clusters above hairy, leaflike bracts; each pink to red-purple (can be lavender to white) with a darker eye, ½–¾ in. wide, with 5 corolla lobes that flare abruptly outward from a hairless, narrow tube. The shorter calyx consists of 5 very hairy, narrowly lance-shaped sepals; hidden inside the corolla tube are 5 stamens. Fruit a papery oval capsule. BAS

Phlox carolina

POLEMONIACEAE | **Carolina phlox**

May–Jul, to 3 ft. Erect perennial of forests, woodlands, woodland borders, and barrens. Stems unbranched and smooth to softly hairy. Leaves sessile, 5–12 pairs, narrowly to widely lance-shaped, to 4½ in. long, with smooth margins and smooth to slightly hairy surface. Flowers in a loose, somewhat cylindrical terminal cluster, pink or magenta (rarely white), ½–1 in. wide, with 5 corolla lobes that flare abruptly outward from a hairless, narrow tube and 5 slightly protruding stamens. The cylindrical calyx consists of 5 lance-shaped sepals with overlapping margins. Fruit a rounded capsule. AMC

Phlox nivalis

POLEMONIACEAE | **pineland phlox**

Mar–Jun, 4–12 in. Spreading, mat-forming perennial of sandhills and other dry woodlands, road banks. Stems semi-woody and freely branched. Leaves opposite or in axillary clusters, sessile, stiffly linear, to 1 in. long, evergreen with bristly margins. Flowers in small clusters on erect-ascending stems, pink to lavender or white with a dark eye, 1 in. wide, with 5 corolla lobes that flare abruptly outward from a narrow, hairless tube and 5 partially fused, hairy, narrowly lance-shaped sepals, which are shorter than the corolla tube. Fruit a papery, nearly round capsule. FG

Phlox paniculata

POLEMONIACEAE | **garden phlox**

Jul–Sep, 1–5 ft. Erect, clump-forming perennial of streambanks, moist forests, woodlands, woodland borders. Stems unbranched, smooth or softly hairy above. Leaves short-petioled (or sessile upward), lance-shaped to oval, 2–6 in. long, conspicuously pinnately veined with a prominent marginal vein, usually smooth above, softly hairy beneath, margins finely hairy. Flowers in a dense pyramidal or dome-shaped terminal cluster; red-purple to pink, lavender, or white, ½–1 in. wide, with 5 lobes that flare abruptly outward from a hairy, narrow tube and 5 slightly protruding stamens. The shorter calyx tube has 5 needlelike lobes and may be glandular-hairy. Fruit an oval capsule. EO

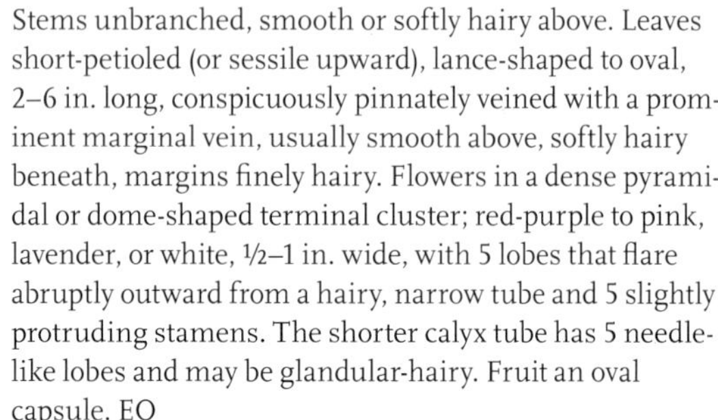

Phlox pilosa

POLEMONIACEAE | **downy phlox**

Mar–May, 8–22 in. Erect to ascending perennial of dry to moist woodlands and forests, and road banks. Stems unbranched and densely covered in soft, white hairs. Leaves sessile, narrowly lance-shaped to linear, to 3½ in. long; surfaces may be smooth or finely hairy and margins have small stiff hairs. Flowers in a branched terminal cluster, reddish-pink to pale purple, ½–¾ in. wide, with 5 corolla lobes that flare abruptly outward from a hairy or smooth, narrow tube. The calyx consists of 5 very hairy, narrow sepals with needlelike tips; 5 stamens are hidden in the corolla tube. Fruit an oval capsule. RTW

Phlox subulata

POLEMONIACEAE | **moss phlox**

Mar–May, 3–9 in., mats to 2 ft. wide. Spreading, mat-forming perennial of dry and exposed rock outcrops, rocky flood-scoured riversides, shale barrens, dry woodlands over a variety of rock types. Stems semi-woody, freely branched. Leaves opposite or in clusters in the nodes, sessile, linear to needlelike, to ¾ in. long, semi-evergreen and stiff. Flowers fragrant, in multiple small, loose clusters, purple or pink (occasionally white) with a darker eye, ½–1 in. wide, with 5 distinctly notched corolla lobes flaring from a hairy, narrow tube. The calyx consists of 5 glandular-hairy, narrow sepals; the 5 stamens barely protrude from the corolla tube. Fruit an oval capsule. TLJ

Verbena rigida

VERBENACEAE | **tuberous vervain**

Mar–Jul, 1–2 ft. Erect perennial of roadsides and other disturbed areas. Native to South America. Stems stiff, 4-angled and grooved, unbranched and hairy; spreads via stolons. Leaves sessile and clasping, lance-shaped, 2–4 in. long, coarsely toothed. Flowers in dense, cylindrical spikes 2–3 in. long and arranged in a wide-branching terminal cluster; each flower pink to purple, with a long (1/3 in. or more) tube opening to 5 spreading, notched lobes. RTW

Asclepias quadrifolia

APOCYNACEAE | **fourleaf milkweed**

May–Jun, 8–20 in. Erect perennial of moist to dryish forests and forest margins, usually on mafic or calcareous rocks. Stem solitary, unbranched, typically with 3 leaf-bearing nodes, hairy in lines between nodes; leaks milky sap when bruised. Leaves in a whorl of 4 at middle node, opposite above and below, petiolate, oval or lance-shaped, to 5 in. long, sparsely hairy on veins beneath. Flowers in a small, domed terminal umbel and often several upper axillary umbels; pale pink to greenish (rarely white), 1/2 in. long, with 5 spreading or reflexed corolla lobes and a central crown surrounding the fused anthers and style. Fruit a narrow, erect follicle containing tufted seeds. AMC

Drosera capillaris

DROSERACEAE | **pink sundew**

May–Aug, 1½–12 in. Low-growing, carnivorous annual/perennial found in pine savannas and other wet sandy or peaty sites. Stems are slender, smooth flowering scapes that emerge from a basal rosette to 4 in. wide. Leaves basal, petiolate, oblong to broadly spoon-shaped, reddish or greenish and covered with red, gland-tipped hairs that attract and trap insects. Flowers in a small cluster (2–20) nodding at the top of the flowering scape, light pink, about 1/2 in. wide, with 5 spreading, broadly oval petals. BAS

Drosera filiformis

DROSERACEAE | **threadleaf sundew**

May–Sep, 3–12 in. Carnivorous perennial found on the margins of clay-based Carolina bays and other natural pools in pinelands. Stems are slender, smooth flowering scapes that arise from a basal rosette. Leaves basal, erect-ascending, threadlike and unfurling from a fiddlehead shape, green or purplish, nearly as long as the flowering scape, and covered with gland-tipped, reddish hairs that attract and trap insects. Flowers 4–16 in a coiled, 1-sided raceme at the top of a leafless scape; each flower lavender-rose, 1/4–1/2 in. wide, consisting of 5 spreading, oval petals with lightly fringed edges. The raceme uncoils as fruits develop. Fruit an oval capsule. AMC

Sarracenia psittacina

SARRACENIACEAE | **parrot pitcherplant**

Mar–Jun, to 6 in. Carnivorous perennial of wet pine savannas and, less commonly, floating peat mats. Stems underground, sending up several pitchers and a single flower stalk per plant. Leaves usually lie on the ground in a rosette; they are narrow, green and red pitchers (tubes that trap insects), 3–12 in. long, with many white patches; each has a broad, curved wing on the upper side and a rounded hood (resembling a parrot head) nearly closing the opening. Flower solitary, nodding from an erect stalk taller than the pitchers, maroon, with drooping oblong petals (each 1–2 in. long), 5 strongly curved triangular sepals, and an umbrella-shaped structure in the center. AMC, RTW

Sarracenia purpurea var. *venosa*

SARRACENIACEAE | **southern purple pitcherplant**

Apr–May, to 14 in. Carnivorous perennial of wet pine savannas, sandhill seepage bogs, hillside seepage bogs. Stems underground, sending up several pitchers. Leaves are erect to leaning or reclining, green pitchers (tubes that trap insects), to 8 in. long, often tinged or veined with red or purple and inflated; the erect, flaring hood is kidney-shaped with a scalloped edge. Flowers solitary, nodding from a single, erect scape 8–15 in. tall; each maroon to red (rarely pink), with drooping oval petals (each 1–2 in. long), 5 spreading roundish sepals (reddish-purple), and an umbrella-shaped structure in the center. BAS

Sarracenia rubra

SARRACENIACEAE | **sweet pitcherplant**

Apr–May, to 16 in. Carnivorous perennial of bogs, pocosins, wet pine savannas, sandhills. Stems underground, sending up several pitchers and a single flower stalk per plant. Leaves are erect, slender, reddish to green pitchers (tubes that trap insects), 4–12 in. tall, with darker red veining above; the overhanging lid is roughly circular in shape and very red on the outside. Flowers solitary and nodding from a single, erect scape 6–20 in. tall and usually taller than the pitchers; each maroon to red, with 5 drooping oblong-oval petals (1–1½ in. long), 5 spreading maroon sepals, and a greenish umbrella-shaped structure in the center. WS

Ipomoea quamoclit

CONVOLVULACEAE | **cypress-vine**

Sep–Dec, 6–10 ft. Herbaceous annual vine of fields, hedgerows, and disturbed areas. Native to the Neotropics. Stems twining and smooth. Leaves petiolate, oval in outline, 2–4 in. long, pinnately divided into linear segments, giving the foliage a ferny appearance. Flowers in long-stalked, axillary clusters of 1–3, scarlet, ¾ in. wide, tubular with 5 spreading, triangular lobes at the opening making a 5-pointed star; white stamens and a style protrude from the tube. Fruit a round to oval capsule. AMC

Mimosa microphylla (*Schrankia microphylla*)

FABACEAE | **eastern sensitive-briar**

Jun–Sep, 3–6 ft. Trailing sprawling perennial of dry woodlands and forests (especially sandhills), disturbed areas. Stems weakly arching, covered with hooked hairs. Leaves petiolate, 2-times pinnately divided, the ultimate leaflets (9–12 pairs) oblong and sensitive to touch, folding up against each other; also folding at night and in overcast weather. Flowers many, in round, pompom-like clusters about ¾ in. wide, on stalks from leaf axils. The most noticeable flower parts are 8–10 prominent pink to rose-purple stamens with yellow anthers. Fruit a long, slender pod, densely covered with prickles. GMP

Thaspium trifoliatum

APIACEAE | **maroon meadow-parsnip**

Apr–May, 1–3 ft. Erect perennial of moist to dry upland forests and clearings. Stems slender, occasionally branched, often purple-tinged, smooth. Basal leaves on petioles with a sheathing base, heart-shaped, 1–4 in. long, toothed; stem leaves alternate, also petiolate, ternately or pinnately divided into 3–5 leaflets that are oval to lance-shaped, toothed, and smooth. Flowers in compound terminal umbels 1–3 in. wide, each with 6–12 stalked umbellets. Flowers maroon-red, tiny, with 5 petals, a short green to purplish-green calyx with 5 lobes, 5 stamens, and a 2-celled ovary with a pair of styles. Fruit a joined pair of elliptical, winged seeds. AMC

Geranium carolinianum

GERANIACEAE | **Carolina crane's-bill**

Mar–Jun, 4–24 in. Ascending to sprawling annual of fields, roadsides, lawns, pastures, gardens, and other disturbed areas. Stems reddish, branched, the branches often sprawling, and very hairy. Leaves petiolate, round to kidney-shaped, to 2 in. long and wide, palmately divided into 5–7 lobes that are further coarsely cleft, grayish-green, and hairy. Flowers on short, glandular-hairy stalks in clusters (occasionally solitary) at ends of branches, pale pink to white, to ⅓ in. wide, vaguely funnel-shaped and with 5 petals with shallowly notched tips and 5 hairy, narrowly oval sepals. Fruit a long-beaked capsule that splits into 5 pieces, curling upward. BAS

Geranium dissectum

GERANIACEAE | **cutleaf crane's-bill**

Apr–Aug, 6–24 in. Erect to spreading annual of roadsides, pastures, and other disturbed areas. Native to Europe, c Asia, and n Africa. Stems loosely branched, hairy. Leaves long-petioled (some upper leaves may be sessile), roundish and divided into 5–7 more or less deeply cleft lobes, these further dissected into linear segments; very hairy. Flowers in pairs, on stalks from leaf axils, dark pink, vaguely funnel-shaped, with 5 shallowly notched petals and 5 glandular-hairy sepals bearing a spine at the tip. Fruit a long-beaked capsule that splits into 5 pieces, curling upward. RTW

Geranium molle

GERANIACEAE | **dove's-foot crane's-bill**

Apr–Aug, 6–12 in. Weakly spreading-ascending, mounded annual of roadsides, pastures, and other open, disturbed areas. An aggressive weed, native to Europe and w Asia. Stems generally reddish, branched from the base, covered with soft hairs. Leaves petiolate (reddish), round in outline and divided into 5–11 oblong-oval lobes, which are usually further lobed/toothed and hairy. Flowers usually in clusters of 2 on stalks from leaf axils, magenta, about 1/3 in. wide, funnel-shaped, with 5 distinctly bilobed petals, 5 very hairy sepals, and stamens pressed close to the ovary and bearing purple anthers. Fruit a long-beaked capsule that splits into 5 pieces, curling upward. RTW

Hibiscus coccineus

MALVACEAE | **scarlet hibiscus**

Jul–Sep, 4–9 ft. Erect perennial of marshes, swamp forests, roadside swales. Presumably introduced from farther south, but sometimes appearing native; cultivated as an ornamental. Stems may be branched in upper portion, smooth. Leaves petiolate, round but palmately divided into 3–7 narrow segments that are shallowly toothed to entire and smooth. Flowers solitary on stalks arising from upper leaf axils, deep red, 6 in. wide, widely funnel-shaped, with 5 slightly creased, spreading, spoon-shaped petals and a central column of red stamens and style, all surrounded by 5 shorter, long-pointed sepals. Fruit an oval, 5-sectioned capsule with blunt tip and bumpy surface. GMP

Ipomopsis rubra

POLEMONIACEAE | **standing-cypress**

May–Aug, 2–6 ft. Erect biennial/short-lived perennial of sandhills, sand rims of Carolina bays, dolomitic glades and woodlands, dunes, road banks, and other disturbed areas. Has spread from cultivation in areas to the north. Stems simple, leafy, and hairy. Leaves crowded, to 1¼ in. long, pinnately divided into threadlike segments with bristle tips. Flowers in tall, leafy-bracted, terminal raceme, bright red (rarely yellow), to 1½ in. long, long-tubular, with 5 spreading, pointed lobes making a star at the tube opening; yellow dotted with red inside the tube. AMC

Aquilegia canadensis

RANUNCULACEAE | **eastern columbine**

Feb–Jun, 1–3 ft. Erect perennial of moist to dry habitats, including forests, woodlands, and rock outcrops (often on calcareous or mafic soils). Stems slender, branched, smooth or hairy. Leaves basal and alternate, petiolate, divided into 3 leaflets to 1½ in. long and wide, with each leaflet divided again into 3 toothed or lobed leaflets; white-waxy coating beneath. Flowers in an open panicle on slender stalks, red and yellow, 1 in. long, nodding so that the long spur at the base of each of 5 red petals points upward and the inner yellow parts point down; yellow stamens protrude and dangle. Fruit a narrow, 5-parted follicle with ascending-spreading persistent styles. RTW

Filipendula rubra

ROSACEAE | **queen-of-the-prairie**

Jun–Jul, 2–6 ft. Erect, rhizomatous and at times colony-forming perennial of fens, wet meadows, and seeps over mafic or calcareous rocks. Stems unbranched and mostly smooth. Leaves petiolate (petiole often red), to 2 ft. long (reduced above), mostly pinnately divided into 3–7 palmately or pinnately lobed and coarsely toothed leaflets, with much smaller leaflets scattered between. Flowers many, in a 6- to 9-in.-wide terminal panicle on a reddish-green stalk rising above leaves and blooming from the bottom up; each flower pink, about ⅓ in. wide, with 5 petals and numerous long white stamens with pink anthers. ER

Erodium cicutarium

GERANIACEAE | **heron's-bill**

Mar–Jun, 8–12 in. Erect to ascending annual/biennial of lawns and other open, disturbed areas. Native to Europe. Stems sprawling from a basal winter rosette, diffusely branched, red-tinged, white-hairy. Basal leaves on reddish petioles, to 8 in. long (stem leaves smaller), 2-times pinnately divided and further lobed, fernlike (rachises reddish); hairy. Flowers 4–12 in terminal umbels; each pink to purplish-pink, ½ in. wide, with 5 spreading-ascending, elliptical petals, 5 hairy green sepals, 10 stamens (5 fertile), and 5 united styles with purple stigmas in the center. Fruit a slender, beaklike capsule, eventually splitting into 5 seeds, each with a long, spiraled awn. JG

Geranium columbinum

GERANIACEAE | **long-stalk crane's-bill**

Apr–Jul, 6–26 in. Diffusely ascending to sprawling annual/biennial of roadsides, pastures, and other disturbed areas. Native to Europe. Stems several from the base, covered with hairs lying close to the stem. Leaves petiolate, kidney-shaped but palmately divided into 5–7 lobes, these again deeply and narrowly cleft into linear lobes; hairy, at least above. Flowers in pairs on stalks from leaf axils, purplish-pink, vaguely funnel-shaped, with 5 shallowly notched petals and 5 sepals with a spine at the tip. Fruit a long-beaked capsule that splits into 5 pieces, curling upward. KL

Geranium maculatum

GERANIACEAE | **wild geranium**

Apr–Jul, 8–24 in. Erect, rhizomatous perennial of moist to dry upland forests and well-drained floodplain forests, on acidic or strongly calcareous soils. Stems simple or branched above, somewhat to densely hairy. Leaves basal plus an opposite pair of stem leaves below the inflorescence, to 4 in. long, heart- to kidney-shaped and deeply divided into 3–7 lobes (often 5), which are again cleft, lobed, or toothed; leaves hairy above and on petiole. Flowers on hairy stalks, in a loose, branching terminal cluster; each rose-purple, 1–1½ in. wide, with 5 spreading, oval petals and 10 conspicuous stamens. Fruit a long-beaked capsule that splits into 5 pieces, curling upward. BAS

Glandularia aristigera (*G. pulchella*)

VERBENACEAE | **moss vervain**

Mar–Nov, to 12 in. long. Mat-forming annual/short-lived perennial found in pastures, along roadsides, and in other disturbed areas. Native to South America. Stems several from a woody crown, sprawling along ground, rooting at nodes; slightly hairy. Leaves to 1 in. long and finely divided into many narrow segments, gray-green. Flowers in dense terminal spikes, purple or pink (sometimes white) with a white eye, about 1 in. long and ½ in. wide, with a narrow tube opening into 5 spreading, strongly notched corolla lobes. JG

Oxalis violacea

OXALIDACEAE | **violet wood-sorrel**

Feb–Jun, 4–8 in. Low-growing perennial of dry to moist upland forests, well-drained floodplain forests. Stems essentially absent; leaves and flowering stalks emerge from stolons. Leaves long-petioled, divided into 3 heart-shaped leaflets (3⁄8–1 in. wide each), grayish-green with purplish markings, smooth; leaflets fold downward along midvein at night and in cloudy weather. Flowers 3–12 in a floppy umbel on a smooth scape, violet to pink with a white and green throat, 1⁄3 in. wide, with 5 oblong-oval petals, 5 sepals tipped with orange glands, and 10 stamens. Fruit a rounded or oval capsule that splits into 5 sections. Seeds have a fleshy pad (aril) that attracts ant dispersers. RTW

Monotropsis odorata

ERICACEAE | **Appalachian pigmy pipes**

Feb–Apr (Sep–Nov), 1–4 in. Erect perennial lacking chlorophyll that is rarely noticed in the leaf litter of dry to moist upland woods under oaks and pines, especially on slopes or bluffs with abundant heath species. Stems smooth and unbranched, light brownish-purple. Leaves scale-like, papery tan, and overlapping. Flowers 6–8 in a nodding terminal spike, pinkish-purple, 3⁄8 in. long or less, bell-shaped, with 5 persistent sepals and a corolla divided into 5 fleshy segments with whitish tips. Fruit an erect, round, purplish, multi-seeded berry. Flower scent is variously compared to cloves, nutmeg, cinnamon, and violets. A mycoheterotroph. AMC

Streptopus lanceolatus

LILIACEAE | **eastern rose mandarin**

Apr–Jun, 8–30 in. Erect to leaning perennial of moist forests at high elevations, especially spruce-fir and northern hardwood forests. Stems simple (forked-branched in older plants), zigzagged, sparsely fine-hairy, especially at leaf nodes. Leaves sessile and broadly rounded to nearly clasping at the base, lance-shaped to lance-oval, pointed at the tip and with dense, stiff hairs along margins. Flowers solitary (occasionally 2), dangling on thin, kinked stalks from leaf axils; each flower rose-purple, bell-shaped, with 6 recurved, lance-shaped tepals. Fruit a red, rounded, vaguely 3-lobed berry. WS

Lythrum salicaria

LYTHRACEAE | **purple loosestrife**

Jun–Sep, 4–10 ft. Stiff, erect perennial of swamps, marshes, and other wet places. Native to Eurasia; an extremely noxious weed, especially in the ne U.S. Stems 4-angled, branched from base, usually downy, becoming woody with age and often persisting through winter. Leaves opposite or in whorls of 3, sessile, lance-shaped with a nearly clasping base, 1–4 in. long, downy-hairy. Flowers densely packed in a terminal spike to 18 in. long, pink-purple, with 6 (sometimes 5) oblong-lance-shaped petals, a downy calyx tube, 8–12 stamens, and a style. Fruit a cylindrical, 2-sectioned, many-seeded capsule. BAS

Allium canadense

ALLIACEAE | **wild onion**

Apr–May, 8–24 in. Erect perennial of bottomland forests, pastures, and roadsides. Stem a smooth flowering scape from a bulb with fibrous covering. Leaves basal, ascending, grasslike, flattened and solid, 8–15 in. long. Flowers in a rounded, compact umbel that begins with a saclike, membranous covering, a dried remnant of which persists at the umbel base. Inflorescence consists of a mix of light green to reddish, oval bulbils along with several pinkish-lavender to white, long-stalked flowers, each to ½ in. wide and composed of 6 tepals, 6 stamens, and a light green ovary. RTW

Helonias bullata

HELONIADACEAE | **swamp pink**

Apr–May, 1–2 ft., taller at fruiting. Erect, stemless perennial, often forming dense patches in bogs; usually under dense shrubs in peaty soils, and in the VA Coastal Plain in acidic, sandy seepage swamps. A Federal Threatened species. A stout, hollow, smooth flowering scape arises from a large basal rosette and elongates markedly in fruit. Basal leaves elongate-spoon-shaped or lance-shaped, 3½–12 in. long, evergreen, and glossy; scalelike bracts on the flowering scape are alternate. Flowers in a dense cylindrical-cone-shaped raceme at top of scape, pink, about ¼ in. wide, with 6 tepals and 6 blue stamens, fragrant. Fruit a tiny, 3-lobed capsule. WS

Sabatia dodecandra

GENTIANACEAE | **large marsh rose-pink**

Jun–Aug, 12–27 in. Erect perennial from a short rhizome, found in brackish and freshwater tidal marshes. Stem vaguely 4-angled, with alternate branches above the middle, smooth. Leaves sessile, elliptical to lance-shaped, to 1½ in. long; a basal rosette of leaves is sometimes present. Flowers in an open, few-flowered panicle, bright pink, to 2 in. wide, consisting of 8–11 spreading, oblong-oval petals with basal markings that create a red-outlined yellow star in the flower center and 8–11 shorter, linear to spoon-shaped sepals. Fruit an ovoid to elliptical capsule. BAS

Sabatia gentianoides

GENTIANACEAE | **pinewoods rose gentian**

Jul–Aug, 6–20 in. Erect perennial of pine savannas and bogs. Stems vaguely 4-angled, branched above. Leaves linear, 1–4 in. long; elliptical to spoon-shaped basal leaves often present too. Flowers 1–5 in a compact terminal cluster, pink, about 1¼ in. wide, consisting of 10 oblong-lance-shaped petals with oblique tips and yellow at the base (making a yellow ring in the flower center), 10 linear to lance-shaped sepals, and prominent yellow anthers and a pistil. Fruit an elliptical to ovoid capsule. FG

Ampelaster carolinianus (*Aster carolinianus*)

ASTERACEAE | **climbing aster**

Sep–Dec, to 6+ ft. Robust, scrambling-sprawling perennial of coastal swamps, thickets, marshes, and streambanks. Stems weak, woody, branching and criss-crossing, hairy. Leaves with clasping bases, elliptical to lance-shaped, ¾–2 in. long, hairy at least beneath and rough on both surfaces. Flower heads in stalked clusters; heads with 50–70 purple-pink, narrow, ½- to ¾-in.-long ray florets encircling a center disk of yellow (turning red) tubular florets. Narrow, green and white bracts surround the cylindrical base of each head. BAS

Arctium minus

ASTERACEAE | **common burdock**

Jun–Nov, to 5 ft. Coarse, taprooted biennial of pastures, barnyards, roadsides, disturbed areas. Native to Eurasia. Stems stout, branched above, light green to reddish-green, with white-cobwebby hairs when young, becoming smooth. Basal leaves on hollow petioles, broadly oval, to 2 ft. long; smaller stem leaves alternate, petiolate, with heart-shaped bases, wavy-margined, dull green above, whitish-green-furry beneath. Flower heads in small clusters on branches, pink or purple, ¾–1 in. wide, with numerous tubular florets surrounded by many floral bracts with narrow, spine-like hooked tips; dark purple anthers sheath the white styles, which protrude from florets. PIP

Carphephorus bellidifolius

ASTERACEAE | **sandhill chaffhead**

Aug–Oct, 1–1¾ ft. Erect-ascending perennial of dry sandy forests and woodlands, primarily in the Sandhills region. Stems 1–several, smooth or short-hairy. Leaves basal (numerous) and alternate, petiolate, elliptical to oblong-lance-shaped with blunt tips, to 8 in. long (reduced and becoming sessile above), mostly smooth. Flower heads in much-branched terminal cluster as broad as it is long; heads ½–¾ in. wide, with 15–30 pink to purple, 5-lobed, tubular disk florets and protruding stamens. Several series of recurved, hairy-margined, green (tinged purple) bracts surround the bell-shaped base of each head. BAS

Carphephorus tomentosus

ASTERACEAE | **Carolina chaffhead**

Aug–Oct, 1–2 ft. Erect perennial of savannas, flatwoods, seepage slopes, sandy/boggy clearings, moist to dry sandhill woodlands. Endemic to se VA south to s GA. Stems 1–several, branched above, reddish-purple-tinged, usually densely hairy. Leaves basal and alternate, petiolate, narrowly elliptical to oblong, to 5 in. long (reduced and sessile above); stem leaves held close to stem. Flower heads at tips of ascending upper branches; heads about ½ in. wide, with 15–20 rosy-pink, 5-lobed, tubular disk florets (no rays) and protruding stamens. Several series of sticky-glandular, pointed, reddish-purple or green bracts surround the bell-shaped base of each head. BAS

Gamochaeta purpurea (*Gnaphalium purpureum*)

ASTERACEAE | **spoonleaf purple everlasting**

Mar–Sep, 4–15 in. Erect annual of fields, roadsides, pastures, and other open, weedy disturbed areas. Stems densely white-furry, sometimes bent from the base and then turning upward. Leaves basal and alternate, oblong-lance- to spoon-shaped, ⅓–2⅓ in. long, green, with cobwebby hairs above, white-furry beneath. Stem leaves may wither by flowering time. Flower heads in a leafy, cylindrical terminal spike that elongates and branches over time; heads tiny, with a group of minute yellowish- or purple-tipped tubular florets, packed tightly and surrounded by hairy, overlapping bracts that become brownish. BAS

Liatris cokeri

ASTERACEAE | **sandhills blazing-star**

Aug–Oct, to 2½ ft. Erect to ascending-arching perennial of turkey oak scrub and dry longleaf pinelands. Stems solitary or a few together, unbranched. Leaves numerous, linear, 2–7 in. long (reduced above), with dense tiny pits on both surfaces. Flower heads densely arranged along a spike, often along only 1 side; heads about ⅓ in. wide, sessile, composed of 4–9 pink, 5-lobed disk florets surrounded by purple bristles and with 2 style branches protruding. Green or purple-tinged bracts with resin dots near their tips tightly cover the cone-shaped base of each head. WS

Liatris elegans

ASTERACEAE | **elegant blazing-star**

Aug–Oct, 1–4 ft. Erect perennial found in sandhills and savannas. Stem unbranched, hairy. Leaves mostly clumped toward the base of the plant, linear, to 12 in. long (reduced above), gland-dotted, mostly smooth. Flower heads densely arranged along a spike; heads about 1 in. tall, sessile, composed of 4–5 pale pink to white, 5-lobed disk florets with protruding style branches. An inner series of hairy, pink-edged, petal-like bracts, plus an outer series of green bracts, surround the cylindrical base of each head. Fruit a cluster of small, tufted achenes. WS

Liatris pilosa

ASTERACEAE | **shaggy blazing-star**

Aug–Oct, 1–3 ft. Erect perennial of longleaf pine sandhills, pine barrens, shale barrens, other dry forests and woodlands, fields, road banks. Stems unbranched, with fine, dark green ridges; usually smooth (occasionally furry). Leaves basal (withered by flowering) and alternate, linear, 2–10 in. long (reduced above), gland-dotted, smooth but with scattered marginal hairs. Flower heads densely arranged along a spike; heads ½ in. tall, sessile or stalked, composed of 5–15 pinkish-purple, 5-lobed disk florets with protruding style branches and hairs within the tube. Purple-tinged bracts tightly cover the cylindrical base of each head. Fruit a cluster of tufted achenes. JG

Liatris spicata

ASTERACEAE | **florist's gayfeather**

Jul–Sep, 1–4 ft. Erect perennial of prairies, roadsides, seepages, bogs, moist to wet meadows, and grassy balds. Stems stiff, unbranched, usually smooth. Leaves linear, to 14 in. long (reduced above), smooth or hairy along midvein, sometimes with hairs along margins. Flower heads in a dense terminal spike; heads about ⅓ in. wide, sessile, with 4–14 pink, 5-lobed disk florets surrounded by purple bristles and with 2 style branches protruding. Green bracts tightly cover the cylindrical to bell-shaped base of each head. Fruit a cluster of small, tufted achenes. WS

Liatris squarrosa

ASTERACEAE | **scaly blazing-star**

May–Sep, 1–2½ ft. Erect perennial found in dry woodlands, glades, and barrens. Stems unbranched, hairy or smooth. Leaves broadly linear, 4–9 in. long (reduced above), mostly smooth. Flower heads sparsely arranged along a slightly zigzagged terminal spike; heads ½–¾ in. wide, composed of 10–60 purple-pink, 5-lobed disk florets surrounded by red, feathery bristles and with 2 protruding style branches. Spreading or erect, smooth or hairy, green bracts surround the cylindrical base of each head. Fruit a cluster of tufted achenes. WS

Liatris squarrulosa

ASTERACEAE | **Appalachian blazing-star**

Aug–Nov, 10–25 in. Erect perennial of diabase barrens, other glades and barrens, prairies, longleaf pine sandhills, open woodlands. Stems solitary, unbranched, hairy. Leaves numerous, the lower ones oblong-lance-shaped, 4–9 in. long (gradually reduced in size and linear above); may be rough-hairy. Flower heads in a short, terminal spike; heads ½ in. wide, angled away from stem, sessile or on very short stalks, with 11–20 purplish-pink, 5-lobed, tubular disk florets with 2 style branches protruding. Green (sometimes purple-tinged) bracts with slightly recurved tips surround the cylindrical to bell-shaped base of each head. Fruit a cluster of small, tufted achenes. RTW

Marshallia graminifolia

ASTERACEAE | **grassleaf Barbara's-buttons**

Jul–Oct, 1–1½ ft. Erect, sometimes clumped perennial of wet pine savannas and seepage slopes. Stems ridged, simple or sparingly branched. Leaves numerous and mostly basal; lower stem leaves erect, linear to narrowly elliptical (tapered at both ends) and 2–8 in. long; upper ones sparse, shorter and ascending. Flower heads solitary at tops of stems; heads about 1 in. wide, composed of pink to whitish tubular disk florets whose narrow lobes are twisted/curled. WS

Symphyotrichum novae-angliae

ASTERACEAE | **New England aster**

Sep–Oct, 3–4 ft. Erect, rhizomatous perennial of wet meadows, bogs, prairies. Stems 1–several, stout, spreading- to stiff-hairy, with stalked glands above. Leaves crowded, sessile with heart-shaped and clasping base, lance- to elliptic-lance-shaped, ¾–4¾ in. long, with slightly down-rolled margins, rough-hairy above, soft-hairy beneath. Flower heads in a short terminal panicle; heads ¾–1½ in. wide, with 45–100 violet-purple (rarely pink or white) narrow ray florets encircling a center disk of yellow tubular florets. Several series of sometimes purple-tinged, spreading, linear to lance-shaped bracts surround the bowl-shaped base of each head. Fruit a tan-tufted achene. RTW

Echinacea laevigata

ASTERACEAE | **smooth purple coneflower**

May–Jul, 1½–4 ft. Erect perennial of open woodlands and glades over mafic or calcareous rocks; rarely in pine-oak savannas over circumneutral clay sediments of the upper Coastal Plain. Stems simple, smooth, sometimes whitish. Leaves basal and alternate, petiolate (winged and purplish) to sessile, lance-oval to elliptical with pointed tips, 4–6 in. long, toothed, smooth beneath, smooth to slightly rough-hairy above. Flower heads solitary at stem end; heads to 4 in. wide, with 13–21 deep to pale pink, distinctively drooping ray florets encircling a domed center disk of tiny pink to yellowish-red tubular florets and spiny bracts. Fruit an erect, conelike seedhead. WS

Echinacea purpurea

ASTERACEAE | **eastern purple coneflower**

May–Oct, 1½–4 ft. Erect perennial of open woodlands and roadsides, sometimes persistent or spread from cultivation. Stems green with purple-brown streaks, occasionally branching, hairy. Leaves mostly basal, a few alternate (smaller), oval or lance-shaped with pointed tip, 2–10 in. long, toothed, rough-hairy on both surfaces. Flower heads solitary at stem ends; heads to 4 in. wide, with 8–21 dark pink to purple, somewhat drooping ray florets encircling a domed center disk of many maroon, tubular florets intermixed with orange-brown, spiny bracts. Fruit an erect, conelike seedhead. AMC

Elephantopus carolinianus

ASTERACEAE | **leafy elephant's-foot**

Aug–Nov, 1–3 ft. Erect perennial of moist to dry forests and woodlands. Stems simple or with forked branches above, very furry. Leaves on winged petioles (lower leaves) and sessile (upper), oval to elliptical or even diamond-shaped, 2–8 in. long (reduced above), shallowly toothed, furry beneath. Flower heads in clusters at tips of branches and surrounded below by unequal, triangular-oval bracts; heads lavender-pink, with 1–several tiny disk florets, each with 5 narrow corolla lobes. AMC

Pluchea baccharis (*P. rosea*)

ASTERACEAE | **marsh fleabane**

Jun–Jul, 1–2 ft. Erect perennial of wet savannas, natural ponds, Carolina bays, marshes, and ditches. Stems sometimes branched above, hairy, sometimes reddish, and with sticky glands. Leaves sessile, often clasping, oval to elliptic-oblong, to 2½ in. long, shallowly toothed (teeth with spiny tips), dusty gray-green, furry-glandular on both surfaces. Flower heads in dense clusters at top of stem and branching from leaf axils; heads about ⅓ in. wide, with tiny, rose-pink to purplish, tubular disk florets. Rose-pink to purplish, furry bracts tightly surround the base of each head. BAS

Pluchea camphorata

ASTERACEAE | **camphorweed**

Aug–Oct, 2–6½ ft. Erect annual/perennial found in bottomland sloughs, ditches, clay flatwoods, and other freshwater wetlands. Stems branched above, minutely hairy and glandular. Stems and leaves give off an unpleasant odor when bruised or crushed. Leaves petiolate, elliptical, to 6 in. long, toothed; covered with tiny, glistening glands. Flower heads in branching clusters at ends of branches; heads about ¼ in. long, with tiny, rose-pink disk florets (no ray florets) closely surrounded by several series of pinkish-purple, gland-dotted, pointy bracts. BAS

Pluchea odorata

ASTERACEAE | **saltmarsh fleabane**

Jul–Oct, 1–3 ft. Erect annual of salt and brackish marshes. Stems branched and covered with sticky, glandular hairs. Stems and leaves give off an unpleasant odor when bruised or crushed. Leaves short-petioled to sessile, oval with pointed tip, 1½–6 in. long, finely toothed, hairy beneath. Flower heads in mostly flat-topped, branching clusters at tips of stem and branches; heads ¼–⅜ in. wide, with tiny, pink to rosy purple tubular disk florets closely surrounded by several series of pinkish-purple, gland-dotted, pointy bracts. BAS

Trilisa odoratissima (*Carphephorus odoratissimus*)

ASTERACEAE | **deer's-tongue**

Jul–Oct, 1½–5 ft. Erect perennial of pine savannas, flatwoods. Stems branched in inflorescence, often reddish-purple, smooth, with a white-waxy coating. Leaves basal (mostly flat on ground) and alternate, sessile-clasping, spoon-shaped, 2–14 in. long, fleshy, sparsely toothed, with a large white midvein; upper stem leaves smaller. Flower heads in a flat-topped, branching terminal cluster; heads small, with 7–10 tiny, purplish-pink, 5-lobed tubular florets with 2 protruding style branches. Pointed, purplish bracts surround the narrowly bell-shaped base of each head. Gives off a pleasant vanilla scent when dried. RTW

Trilisa paniculata

ASTERACEAE | **hairy chaffhead**

Aug–Oct, 1–4 ft. Erect perennial of moist pine savannas and flatwoods. Stems branched in inflorescence, often reddish-purple, covered with spreading hairs. Leaves basal (mostly flat on ground) and alternate, essentially sessile, narrowly elliptical to spoon-shaped, 2–14 in. long, sparsely toothed, smooth; upper leaves much smaller and pressed up against the stem. Flower heads at tips of short branches of a cylindrical, branching terminal cluster; heads small, with 12–35 tiny, dark pinkish-purple, 5-lobed tubular florets with 2 protruding style branches. Tiny purple, gland-dotted (or hairy) bracts surround the narrowly bell-shaped base of each head. AMC

Vernonia acaulis

ASTERACEAE | **flatwoods ironweed**

Jun–Aug, 2–3 ft. Erect perennial of longleaf pine flatwoods, moist ecotones, moister sandhill situations in the Coastal Plain; in the Piedmont, in dry rocky woodlands, bluffs, barrens. Stems usually 1 per plant, branched above. Leaves mostly basal, elliptical to oblong-lance-shaped, 4–8 in. long, irregularly toothed, hairy; a few alternate stem leaves are linear to elliptical and much smaller. Flower heads arranged at tips of spreading-ascending branches; heads ½ in. wide, with 30–40 purple-magenta tubular florets with 5 spreading, narrow lobes. Several series of lance-shaped bracts surround the bell-shaped base of each head. Fruit a cluster of rusty-tufted achenes. BAS

Vernonia angustifolia

ASTERACEAE | **sandhill ironweed**

Jun–Sep, 2–4 ft. Erect perennial of longleaf pine sandhills. Stems 1–several per plant, branched above, hairy. Leaves numerous, linear, 2–5 in. long, with down-curled margins and scattered teeth, slightly rough-hairy. Flower heads on tips of branches of a flat-topped, terminal cluster; heads about ¾ in. wide, with 12–20 spreading, magenta tubular florets with 5 spreading, narrow lobes. Several series of purplish-green, narrow, pointed bracts surround the bell-shaped base of each head. Fruit a cluster of rusty-tufted achenes. RTW

Vernonia gigantea

ASTERACEAE | **giant ironweed**

Aug–Oct, 3–10 ft. Erect perennial of pastures, bottomlands, and streambanks. Stems stout, ribbed, hairy or smooth. Leaves lance-shaped, to 12 in. long, sharply toothed, typically rough-hairy beneath. Flower heads in large, loose, branched terminal clusters; heads magenta, about ¾ in. wide, consisting of 12–30 spreading tubular florets with 5 spreading linear corolla lobes and a protruding style. Tiny purplish-green, blunt-tipped bracts surround the bell-shaped base of each head. Fruit a cluster of rusty-tufted achenes. An excellent nectar source for butterflies and bees. RTW

Vernonia glauca

ASTERACEAE | **Appalachian ironweed**

Jun–Sep, 3–5 ft. Erect perennial of pastures, bottomlands, and streambanks. Stems branched in inflorescence, smooth or sparsely hairy, and with a white-waxy coating. Leaves alternate, on short petioles, oval to lance-shaped, toothed, dark green above and light green (usually with a white-waxy coating) beneath, minutely hairy. Flower heads in a branching terminal cluster; heads purple-magenta, with 30–48 spreading tubular florets with 5 narrow lobes. Tiny triangular to lance-shaped bracts surround the bell-shaped base of each head. Fruit a cluster of white- or straw-tufted, ridged achenes. An excellent nectar source for butterflies and bees. BAS

Vernonia noveboracensis

ASTERACEAE | **New York ironweed**

Jul–Oct, 3–7 ft. Erect perennial of pastures, bottomlands, and streambanks. Stems branched in inflorescence, rough-hairy. Leaves crowded, sessile, narrowly lance-shaped, 4–12 in. long, toothed to entire, slightly rough above, thinly hairy beneath; not appreciably lighter colored beneath. Flower heads in a wide and open, branching terminal cluster; heads purple, 1/4–1/2 in. wide, with 20–65 tubular florets with 5 spreading lobes. Tiny brownish-purple to greenish bracts with needlelike tips surround the urn-shaped base of each head. Fruit a cluster of purplish- to dark-tawny-tufted achenes. BAS

Coreopsis rosea

ASTERACEAE | **pink tickseed**

Jul–Sep, 1–2 ft. Erect, rhizomatous perennial growing in clumps in upland depression ponds in wet, sandy-peaty soils of the Inner Coastal Plain, and drawdown zones on banks of blackwater rivers in the Outer Coastal Plain. Stems simple to much-branched, smooth. Leaves subsessile, linear, and threadlike (occasionally with 2 lateral lobes), 1–2½ in. long. Flower heads in an open, terminal cluster; heads ½–1 in. wide, with 6–10 pink or white ray florets, each with 3 teeth at the tip, encircling a center disk of yellow tubular florets. BAS

Dipsacus fullonum

CAPRIFOLIACEAE | **teasel**

Jul–Sep, 1½–6½ ft. Erect biennial/perennial of roadsides, pastures, disturbed areas. Native to Europe, widespread in NoAm. Stems 1–several from the base, ridged, increasingly prickly upward. Leaves sessile, pairs joined at the base, lance-shaped, 4–16 in. long, with prominent midvein and prickles (especially beneath); basal leaves (dying in second year) are wrinkly and scallop-edged. Flower heads solitary on long stalks at top of stem; heads cone-shaped, 1¼–3½ in. long, with lavender to white tubular florets interspersed with spiny bracts. Long, narrow, prickly green bracts at base of head curve upward and form a cage around the persistent head. Fruit an angular achene. ER

Blephilia ciliata

LAMIACEAE | **downy woodmint**

May–Aug, 1–2½ ft. Erect, rhizomatous perennial of woodlands, meadows, forests, usually in circumneutral soils. Clump-forming, mostly unbranched; white hairs press against the 4-angled stem. Leaves petiolate (sessile above), oval to lance-shaped, to 3½ in. long, shallowly toothed or entire, sparsely hairy above, whitish-downy beneath, fragrant when crushed. Flowers in several dense, headlike clusters tiered along a terminal spike, each cluster resting on a whorl of fringed bracts; flowers pale pink to lavender, ⅓ in. long, tubular with 2 flaring lips, the upper narrow and the lower 3-lobed and speckled with purple; 2 long stamens protrude. The calyx is tubular and hairy. WS

Sclerolepis uniflora

ASTERACEAE | **pink bogbutton**

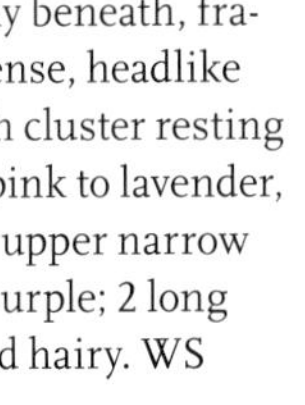

May–Aug, 4–16 in. Erect, colonial perennial found in shallow water and seepage wetlands, including sea-level fens, or on shores of clay-based Carolina bays, natural lakes, blackwater streams and swamps. Stems submerged-floating in shallow water or ascending-spreading on muddy shores, slender, mat-forming, and glandular. Leaves numerous in whorls of 3–6, sessile, linear to needlelike, ¼–1 in. long. Flower heads usually solitary at stem ends; heads ¼–½ in. wide, with about 50 purplish-pink or white tubular disk florets with protruding style branches. 2 series of narrow, glandular, green bracts enclose the bell-shaped base of each head. Fruit a dark brown to black achene. BAS

Eutrochium dubium (*Eupatorium dubium*)

ASTERACEAE | **three-nerved Joe-Pye-weed**

Jul–Oct, 3–4 ft. Erect perennial of swamp forests, pocosins, and other wet, acidic habitats. Stems unbranched, solid or hollow, purple-spotted or -tinted, sticky-hairy toward the top. Leaves in whorls of 3–4, petiolate, lance-shaped or oval with a wedge-shaped base, 2–6 in. long, sharply toothed, usually rough above and gland-dotted beneath. Flower heads in small clusters within a large branching terminal cluster; heads ¼–⅜ in. long, with 4–12 small, reddish-purple tubular florets. A nectar source for butterflies and hummingbirds. BAS

Eutrochium fistulosum
(Eupatorium fistulosum)

ASTERACEAE | **hollow-stem Joe-Pye-weed**

Jul–Oct, 5–8 ft. Erect perennial of moist forests, bottomlands, marshes, and ditches. Stems stout, hollow, unbranched, purplish (sometimes green below), and with a white-waxy coating. Leaves in whorls of 3–7, petiolate, narrowly elliptical or lance-shaped, to 10 in. long, toothed. Flower heads in small clusters within a large, domed terminal cluster; heads about ⅓ in. long, with 4–7 dull pinkish-purple disk florets (no ray florets) with protruding styles. Several series of narrow, overlapping bracts surround the base of each head. The mildly fragrant flowers are very attractive to butterflies. EO

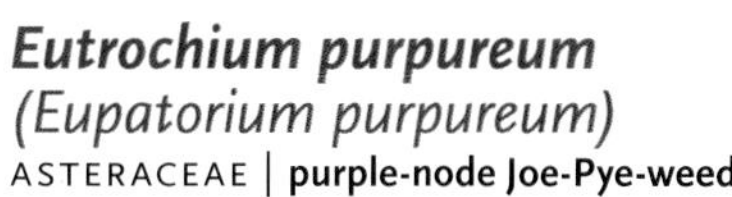

Eutrochium purpureum
(Eupatorium purpureum)

ASTERACEAE | **purple-node Joe-Pye-weed**

Jul–Oct, 3–6 ft. Erect perennial of usually moist upland forests. Stems solid (hollow at the base), unbranched, purple at the nodes, smooth. Leaves in whorls of 3–5, lance-shaped and tapered to a winged petiole, to 12 in. long, sharply toothed; may be slightly hairy or gland-dotted beneath. Flower heads in small clusters within a large, showy, domed terminal cluster; heads about ⅓ in. long, with 4–7 pinkish-purple or white, tubular disk florets (no ray florets) with protruding styles. Several series of narrow, overlapping bracts surround the base of each head. Plant and flowers sweetly vanilla-scented. GPF

Elephantopus elatus

ASTERACEAE | **southern elephant's-foot**

Aug–Sep, 1–4 ft. Erect perennial from a basal rosette, found in pine flatwoods and sandhills. Stems branched above, hairy, with no (or few) leaves. Basal leaves pressed flat against ground, oblong-lance-shaped with a blunt tip, to 12 in. long, toothed and hairy on both surfaces. Flower heads in clusters underlain by 3 hairy, green, heart-shaped bracts and held at tips of branches; heads lavender-pink, with several tiny disk florets, each divided into 5 narrow corolla lobes. Narrow, very hairy bracts enclose the base of each head. RTW

Elephantopus nudatus

ASTERACEAE | **Coastal Plain**
elephant's-foot

Jul–Sep, 8–24 in. Erect perennial from a basal rosette, found in woodlands and woodland borders, usually on fairly dry sites. Stems 1–3 per plant, widely branched above, hairy. Leaves basal, lying flat on the ground, elliptical to oblong-lance-shaped with bluntish tip, 6–12 in. long, round-toothed, sparsely hairy beneath. Flower heads in clusters underlain by 3 green, triangular bracts (each ½–¾ in. long) and held at tips of branches; heads pink to pale purple, about ½ in. wide, with several small disk florets, each divided into 5 narrow lobes. BAS, WS

Elephantopus tomentosus

ASTERACEAE | **common elephant's-foot**

Aug–Nov, 8–24 in. Erect perennial from a basal rosette, found in woodlands and woodland borders, usually on fairly dry sites. Stems essentially naked of leaves, branched above (in inflorescence), furry. Leaves basal, pressed flat against the ground, narrowly to broadly oblong-oval and rounded at the tip, 4–10 in. long, round-toothed, hairy. Flower heads in clusters underlain by 2–3 green, triangular bracts (each about ½ in. long) and held at tips of branches; heads lavender-pink, with several small disk florets, each divided into 5 narrow lobes. BAS

Centaurea stoebe ssp. *micranthos* (*C. maculosa*)

ASTERACEAE | **spotted knapweed**

Jun–Nov, 1–4 ft. Erect biennial/perennial of roadsides and other disturbed areas. Native to Europe; invasive. Stems wiry, branched, loosely gray-hairy. Leaves basal and alternate; lower leaves lance-shaped in outline and deeply divided into linear segments, 3–6 in. long (upper leaves smaller, entire or divided), gray-hairy (becoming smooth), gland-dotted. Flower heads numerous, stalked, on wide-spreading branches; heads pink to purple, ½–1 in. wide, with tubular disk florets (no rays). Tightly held bracts with fringed, black tips surround the oval to urn-shaped base of each head. AMC

Cirsium arvense

ASTERACEAE | **Canada thistle**

Jul–Nov, 1–3 ft. Erect, colonial perennial of pastures and other disturbed areas. Native to Europe. Stems slightly ridged, branched above, smooth. Leaves sessile or clasping, elliptical or lance-shaped, 3–7 in. long, pinnately lobed or toothed, bearing yellow spines on the margins, glossy green, sometimes hairy beneath. Flower heads 1–many at top of stem, pale pink or lavender, ½–¾ in. wide, with many disk florets, each with 5 threadlike lobes. Close-pressed, sharp-tipped, green to purple bracts surround the urn-shaped base of each head. Fruit a fluffy cluster of seeds, each with a tuft of tawny hairs. JG

Cirsium discolor

ASTERACEAE | **field thistle**

Aug–Nov, 2–8 ft. Erect biennial/perennial of pastures, floodplain forests, woodlands, clearings, thickets. Stems strongly furrowed, branched near the top, usually hairy. Leaves short-petioled to sessile, lance-shaped or oval, 4–10 in. long (reduced above), divided into sharp-tipped lobes, densely white-woolly beneath, with yellowish prickles on the margins. Flower heads 1–several at top of stem, subtended by bractlike leaves; heads 1½–2 in. wide, with numerous purple to white tubular florets, each with 5 threadlike lobes. Tightly held green and white, spiny bracts surround the urn-shaped base of each head. Fruit a fluffy cluster of white-tufted seeds. BAS

Cirsium horridulum

ASTERACEAE | **yellow thistle**

Mar–Jun, 3–8 ft. Erect biennial/short-lived perennial of roadsides, sandy clearings, pine savannas. Stems simple or short-branched, smooth to hairy. Leaves basal and alternate, oblong-lance-shaped to elliptical, to 16 in. long (smaller and clasping upward), hairy, lobed and toothed, with 1-in. marginal spines. Terminal flower heads (1–10) subtended by bractlike, sessile, spiny leaves; heads to 3½ in. long, with many reddish-purple or yellow to white tubular florets, each with 5 threadlike lobes. Tightly held, hairy-edged, green bracts surround the urn-shaped base of each head. Fruit a fluffy cluster of gray-tufted seeds. A larval host and nectar source for butterflies. BAS

Cirsium repandum

ASTERACEAE | **sandhill thistle**

May–Jul, to 2 ft. Erect biennial of longleaf pinelands, sandhills, other dry to very dry sandy habitats. Endemic to NC, SC; barely reaching se VA and the Augusta, GA, area. Stem (second year) simple or few-branched, covered with cobwebby hairs. Leaves basal (first year) and alternate, sessile, oblong-lance-shaped, 2½–6 in. long, irregularly lobed, wavy-margined, spiny, very hairy. Flower heads 1–5 at top of stem, 1½ in. wide, with many bright purple to purple-pink tubular florets, each with 5 threadlike lobes. Tightly held, short-spined green bracts surround the urn-shaped base of each head. Fruit a fluffy cluster of white-tufted seeds. BAS

Cirsium vulgare

ASTERACEAE | **bull thistle**

Jun–Nov, 3–6 ft. Erect biennial of meadows, pastures, disturbed areas. Native to Europe. Stems stout, semi-angular, occasionally branched, light green, covered in spreading white hairs. Leaves basal (first year) and alternate, elliptical to lance-shaped with long-tapering bases, to 7 in. long, pinnately lobed, the lobes armed with long spines, rough-surfaced above. Flower heads 1–several at top of stem, 1½–2 in. wide and fluffy, with many purplish-pink tubular florets, each with 5 threadlike lobes. Numerous prickly green bracts tapering to stiff, recurved points surround the urn-shaped base of each head. Fruit a fluffy cluster of seeds, each with a tuft of whitish hairs. RTW

Lactuca graminifolia

ASTERACEAE | **grassleaf lettuce**

Apr–Jul, 1½–3 ft. Erect-ascending biennial of moist to semi-dry pine-oak woodlands, forests, longleaf pine sandhills, sandy fields and roadsides. Stems unbranched, reddish, smooth; leak milky sap when broken. Leaves mostly basal and alternate, with clasping bases, linear to oblong-lance-shaped, 4–12 in. long (reduced above), irregularly lobed or toothed (upper ones entire), smooth. Flower heads in wide-branching cluster; heads nearly ½ in. wide, with 15–24 violet to blue ray florets with squared-off, toothed tips. Tightly held, lance-shaped, purple-tinged green bracts surround the cylindrical base of each head. Fruit a fluffy cluster of flattened, white-tufted achenes. BAS

Allium vineale

ALLIACEAE | **onion-grass**

May–Jun, 1–4 ft. Erect, scapose perennial from a bulb, frequenting lawns, pastures, and other disturbed places. Native to Eurasia. Stem a smooth flowering scape that becomes stiff over time. Leaves mostly basal, tubular and floppy, to 10 in. long; the few stem leaves are alternate. Flowers in a small umbel, to 2 in. across, at top of scape; each flower begins with a saclike, membranous covering that is pointed at the top, a dried remnant of which usually persists at the base of the umbel. The umbel contains a mixture of bulbils (often sprouting) and flowers, or all one or the other; flowers light purple, green, or white, with 6 erect to slightly spreading tepals. BAS

Persicaria pensylvanica

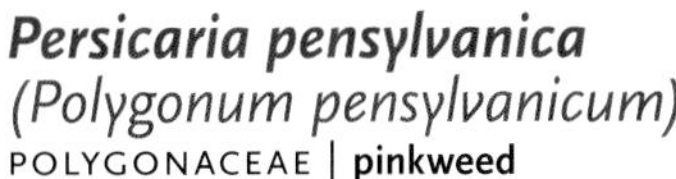

(Polygonum pensylvanicum)

POLYGONACEAE | **pinkweed**

May–Dec, 1–2 ft. Erect to sometimes prostrate annual of bottomlands, freshwater tidal marshes, depression ponds, wet fields, and ditches. Stems slightly zigzagged, simple or branched, smooth below, hairy to glandular hairy above. Leaves petiolate with a membranous sheath (ocrea) where petiole joins stem, lance-shaped, to 7 in. long, often with a reddish blotch and with hairy margins. Flowers in dense, cylindrical spikes on glandular stalks from leaf axils, pink to purplish, less than ¼ in. wide, with 5 tepals that are usually closed. BAS

Rumex acetosella

POLYGONACEAE | **red dock**

Mar–Sep, 4–16 in. Erect, rhizomatous perennial of pastures, fields, roadsides, rock outcrops, and grassy balds. Native to Eurasia. Stems single or in groups from basal rosette, 4-angled and ribbed, branched, smooth. Leaves petiolate with a brittle (soon shedding) sheath at base of stalk, lance-shaped, often with flaring lobes at base, ¾–2½ in. long, somewhat fleshy, and smooth. Flowers in a terminal cluster of narrow racemes, green becoming brownish-red, minute, with 6 tepals; male and female flowers on separate plants, males with 6 stamens and females with a 3-part, white, frilly pistil. Fruit a tiny, 3-sided achene. BAS

Rumex hastatulus

POLYGONACEAE | **heartwing dock**

Mar–Jun, to 2 ft. Erect annual/short-lived perennial of fields (especially sandy fields in the Coastal Plain), roadsides, disturbed areas. Stems 1–several, branched from base, angled, often with vertical stripes, reddish, smooth. Basal leaves petiolate, the stalk with a sheathing base, lance- to lance-oblong with 2 widely spreading, pointed lobes at base, the tip blunt; stem leaves entire; to 2½ in. long. Flowers in loose to densely arranged whorls of 3–6 along ascending, raceme-like branches, pinkish to red, ¼ in. long, with 6 roundish tepals with heart-shaped bases. Fruit a tiny, dark brown achene enclosed in 3 enlarged tepals that look like heart-shaped wings. BAS

Thalictrum coriaceum

RANUNCULACEAE | **Appalachian meadowrue**

May–Jul, 2–4 ft. Erect perennial found in the understory of moist to semi-dry forests, rich slope and floodplain forests; usually in moderately to strongly base-rich soils. A Central/Southern Appalachian endemic. Stems slender, smooth. Leaves short-petioled, thick, 2–4 times divided into 3; the ultimate leaflets oval to round, to 2 in. wide, with lobed or wavy tips. Flowers in a loose, widely branched, pyramid-shaped panicle, on separate male and female plants. Flowers consisting of 5 inconspicuous greenish-pink sepals and, in male flowers, dangling, maroon stamens bearing yellowish anthers, and in female flowers, maroon stigmas. Fruit a cluster of sickle-shaped achenes. KB

Commelina communis

COMMELINACEAE | **common dayflower**

May–Oct, 12–32 in. Erect to sprawling annual of bottomlands and disturbed ground; a common invader of rocky glades. Native to Asia. Stems branched, smooth, sometimes rooting at nodes. Leaves sessile-clasping with sheathing base, oval to lance-oval, 2–5 in. long, glossy and smooth. Flowers solitary in leaf axils, on a stalk with a folded bract below; each flower blue, ½–1 in. wide, with 2 large blue petals, 1 small white petal, 3 whitish-translucent sepals, 5–6 stamens, and a long white style. Each flower blooms during the morning for a single day. Fruit a rounded capsule. BAS

Commelina erecta

COMMELINACEAE | **erect dayflower**

Jun–Oct, to 2 ft. Erect to ascending perennial of dry openings and woodlands (especially in thin soil around rock outcrops), streambanks, riverbanks, moist forests. Stems simple or forked, succulent, hairy. Leaves sessile with a sheathing base fringed with white hairs, 4–6 in. long, smooth. Flowers single or clustered, ¾–1¼ in. wide, with 2 round blue (rarely white) petals, 1 tiny white petal, 3 purple stamens, 3 yellow stamens (one with a larger, butterfly-shaped anther), and a pistil with a slender style; a folded bract, 1–1½ in. long, is below each flower. Flowers open in morning, wither by afternoon. Fruit a small 3-celled capsule. RTW

Commelina virginica

COMMELINACEAE | **Virginia dayflower**

Jul–Oct, 8–34 in. Erect to ascending perennial of bottomlands, swamp forests, other moist to wet forests and forest edges. Stems branched or unbranched, relatively stout, smooth to slightly hairy. Leaves lance-shaped with long tapering tip, to 8 in. long, stiff-hairy above, smooth or finely hairy beneath, with tubular sheathing bases fringed with reddish or yellowish bristles. Flowers in crowded terminal clusters, each enclosed by a folded bract ½–1¼ in. long and wide; flowers blue, ¾ in. wide, with 3 kidney-shaped petals, the lower slightly smaller; stamens usually not hairy. Flowers open in morning, wither by afternoon. Fruit a small 3-celled capsule. FG

Lupinus diffusus

FABACEAE | **blue sandhill lupine**

Mar–May, 8–24 in. Erect and clumped short-lived perennial of sandhills and sandy roadsides. Stems branched from the base, covered with silky hairs. Leaves alternate but clustered at base of stem, petiolate, elliptical, 2½–6 in. long, covered with silky hairs. Flowers in erect, crowded terminal spikes, brilliant blue to purplish, with typical pea-flower shape, the banner petal bearing a white patch. Fruit an elongated, flattened pod. BAS

Linaria canadensis

PLANTAGINACEAE | **Canada toadflax**

Mar–Aug, 6–28 in. Slender, erect annual/biennial of a wide variety of dryish habitats, especially weedy in disturbed sites such as roadsides and fields but also common and apparently native in thin soil of rock outcrops. Stems 1–several, smooth; basal offshoots prostrate to trailing, forming overwintering rosettes. Basal leaves linear to oblong, to ⅓ in. long; stem leaves alternate, linear, to 1¼ in. long, smooth. Flowers in a narrow raceme, blue to purple, about ½ in. long, tubular, with a slender spur and opening to 2 lips, the upper lip 2-lobed and the larger lower lip 3-lobed; the white throat has 2 ridges. Fruit an oval capsule. BAS

Eichhornia crassipes

PONTEDERIACEAE | **water-hyacinth**

Jun–Sep, to 6 in. Free-floating aquatic perennial commonly used as an ornamental in water gardens and now invading ponds, ditches, and sluggish waterways throughout our region; highly invasive in warmer parts of the South, where it survives winter and can rapidly cover a pond or lake and choke waterways. Native to Brazil. Plants spread rapidly by stolons, forming dense mats of foliage. Leaves in a rosette, oval to round, glossy green, with inflated petioles that act as floats. Flowers 8–15 on erect spikes above foliage, blue to lilac (rarely white), with 6 oblong-oval and slightly unequal petals, the uppermost one with a yellow spot. JG

Pontederia cordata

PONTEDERIACEAE | **pickerelweed**

May–Oct, 1–4 ft. Erect perennial rooted in the mud of marshes, pondshores, lakeshores, and ditches. Stems unbranched, hollow, smooth. Leaves basal (plus 1 narrow, sheathing stem leaf), erect, long-petioled, narrowly oval to arrowhead-shaped, to 8¾ in. long, with many fine parallel veins, smooth. Flowers in a dense terminal spike, to 5 in. long, with a sheathing, spathelike bract below it; each flower blue-violet, about ½ in. wide, with a short corolla tube and 6 spreading, unequal lobes, the upper lobe bearing a yellow blotch, plus 6 stamens and 1 style. BAS

Lobelia elongata

CAMPANULACEAE | **longleaf lobelia**

Aug–Oct, 1–4 ft. Erect perennial of river and stream margins, floodplain forests, marshes, bogs, and pine savannas. Primarily a Coastal Plain endemic, rarely found inland (lower Piedmont, NC and SC). Stems mostly unbranched, smooth. Leaves lance-oval to lance-shaped, to 4 in. long, usually sharply toothed and smooth. Flowers in a mostly 1-sided, narrow, terminal spike, each on a short stalk with 2 narrow bracts at the base; each flower blue, tubular and opening to 2 spreading lips, the upper lip smaller and 2-lobed, the lower 3-lobed. The calyx is also tubular with 5 spreading, linear lobes. Fruit a rounded capsule. BAS

Lobelia georgiana

CAMPANULACEAE | **southern lobelia**

Aug–Oct, 1–3 ft. Erect perennial of swamps, floodplain forests, and other wet places. Stems unbranched, smooth (some hairs below). Leaves elliptic-oblong, to 3 in. long (reduced above), with scattered tiny teeth, whitish beneath. Flowers in a narrow terminal spike, each on a short stalk flanked by 2 small, narrow bracts; each flower pale blue, tubular and opening to 2 spreading lips, the upper lip smaller and 2-lobed, the lower 3-lobed. There are 5 prominently glandular-toothed calyx lobes. Fruit a rounded-dome-shaped capsule. GPF

Lobelia glandulosa

CAMPANULACEAE | **bog lobelia**

Sep–Dec, 1½–3 ft. Erect perennial of seepage slopes, pitcherplant bogs, streamhead margins, pine savannas, pine flatwoods, and margins of beaver ponds. Stems smooth to sparsely hairy. Leaves linear to narrowly lance-shaped, to 6 in. long, sessile, thick-textured, often with hardened teeth. Flowers few–20 in a 1-sided, narrow, terminal spike; each flower lavender-blue, 1 in. long, tubular and opening to 2 spreading lips, the upper lip smaller and 2-lobed, the lower 3-lobed with a patch of hairs inside at the base. The calyx is cup-shaped with 5 narrow, toothed or entire lobes. BAS

Lobelia inflata

CAMPANULACEAE | **Indian-tobacco**

Jul–Nov, 6–36 in. Slender, erect annual found in fields, meadows, open woodlands, and disturbed areas. Stems branched and hairy. Leaves mostly sessile, oval-oblong, to 3 in. long, toothed. Flowers in loose, narrow racemes terminating the stem and branches, each on a short stalk flanked by inconspicuous bracts. Flowers about ¼ in. long, pale blue, tubular and opening to 2 spreading lips, the upper lip divided into 2 sharp lobes, the lower into 3 sharp lobes. The tubular calyx is bell-shaped, veined, and has 5 sharp-pointed, lance-shaped lobes. BAS

Lobelia nuttallii

CAMPANULACEAE | **Nuttall's lobelia**

May–Nov, 8–30 in. Delicate, erect annual found in flatwoods, bogs, and savannas. Stems slender, simple or with ascending branches, hairy below. Leaves narrowly elliptical, to 1½ in. long; linear and smaller above, with tiny, callus-tipped teeth. Flowers in loose, narrow, terminal racemes, pale blue to whitish or lavender, less than 1 in. long, tubular and opening to 2 spreading lips, the upper lip divided into 2 narrow, erect lobes, the lower into 3 wider lobes. The tubular calyx is bell-shaped with 5 narrow, pointed lobes. Fruit a rounded capsule. AMC

Lobelia puberula

CAMPANULACEAE | **downy lobelia**

Jul–Oct, 2–4 ft. Erect perennial of forests and openings. Stems mostly unbranched, purple-tinged, and hairy. Leaves sessile, oval to lance-shaped, to 4½ in. long, the margins with tiny callus-tipped teeth, hairy. Flowers in a crowded terminal spike, each on a spreading-ascending short stalk flanked by 2 leaflike bracts; each flower purplish-blue, ½–1 in. long, tubular and opening to 2 spreading lips, the upper lip divided into 2 narrow, erect lobes, the lower lip divided into 3 wider lobes with white markings. The short-tubular calyx has 4 lance-shaped lobes. Fruit a rounded capsule. JF

Lobelia siphilitica

CAMPANULACEAE | **great blue lobelia**

Jul–Oct, 1½–4 ft. Showy, erect perennial of bottomlands, moist forests, ditches, wet meadows, and streambanks. Stems stout, leafy, sometimes branched above. Leaves sessile, oval to oblong-lance-shaped, 2–5 in. long, with rough hairs above. Flowers in a dense, narrow, terminal raceme, each on an ascending stalk flanked by 2 leafy bracts; flowers deep blue (rarely white), 1–1½ in. long, tubular and opening to 2 spreading lips, the upper lip split into 2 narrow, erect lobes, and the lower lip divided into 3 wider lobes with white marks at the base. Fruit an oval to round capsule. WS

Lobelia spicata

CAMPANULACEAE | **pale spiked lobelia**

May–Aug, 1–3 ft. Erect perennial of meadows, woodlands, and disturbed areas. Stems slender, angular, with rough hairs near the base; spreads by basal offshoots. Leaves mostly sessile, narrowly oval to lance-shaped, to 4½ in. long, often with widely spaced teeth. Flowers in a dense terminal spike, each on an ascending stalk flanked by 2 bracts; flowers pale blue to white, about ½ in. long, tubular and opening to 2 lips, the upper lip split into 2 narrow, erect lobes and separated by a tube of fused, grayish anthers, and the lower lip divided into 3 wider lobes. Fruit an oval to round capsule. BAS

Viola bicolor

VIOLACEAE | **field pansy**

Mar–Apr, 1½–12 in. Erect to reclining annual of dry open roadsides, lawns, other disturbed habitats; less commonly in dry rocky woodlands, barrens. Stems branched, nearly smooth. Leaves on petioles longer than the blade, with leafy, deeply lobed basal stipules; spoon-shaped (narrower upward), ¼–1¼ in. long, slightly toothed or entire, smooth. Flowers solitary on slender stalks from leaf axils, pale blue or white with dark veins and a yellow patch, about ½ in. wide, with 5 unequal petals, the lowest largest and extending behind the flower in a blunt spur and the 2 lateral petals bearded. Fruit an elliptical capsule. Closed, self-pollinating flowers often present. AMC

Viola labradorica

VIOLACEAE | **American dog-violet**

Mar–May, 2–8 in. Ascending perennial of moist alluvial woodlands and forests, seepage slopes, marl ravines, and hammocks. Stems usually several and clustered, unbranched, smooth. Leaves on petioles with sharply toothed stipules at the base, round to kidney-shaped or heart-shaped, ½–1½ in. long, with flattened teeth and smooth to slightly hairy above. Flowers solitary on stalks from leaf axils, light blue-violet to violet (or white), often lacking darker veins, ½–¾ in. wide, with 5 unequal petals, the lowest extending behind the flower in a stout spur and the 2 laterals bearded. Fruit an elliptical capsule. Closed, self-pollinating flowers often present. AMC

Viola rostrata

VIOLACEAE | **long-spurred violet**

Apr–Jun, to 10 in. Tufted, erect-ascending perennial found in acid cove forests and other moist forests, often under eastern hemlock (*Tsuga canadensis*). Stems several from a rhizome, smooth. Leaves on petioles with narrow, usually fringed stipules at the base; leaves heart-shaped to oval, ¾–2¾ in. long and wide, shallowly toothed, and mostly smooth (hairs on midvein). Flowers solitary on slender stalks from upper leaf axils, lavender or bluish-violet and streaked with dark purple, ½–1 in. wide, with 5 unequal petals, the lowest largest and extending behind the flower in a ¾-in.-long spur. Fruit an oval capsule. Closed, self-pollinating flowers often present. JF

Viola walteri

VIOLACEAE | **prostrate blue violet**

(Jan) Mar–May, to 4 in. Weakly ascending, mat-forming perennial of rich woodlands and forests, especially over mafic or calcareous rocks, becoming prostrate through the season, forming new rosettes. Stems 3–4, branched, finely hairy. Leaves petiolate, oval to rounded with a notched base and rounded tip, 1–2 in. long, finely toothed, silvery green with dark green or purplish veins above, solid purple beneath. Flowers on stalks from leaf axils, blue to violet with darker veins and white throat, to 1 in. wide, with 5 unequal petals, the 2 lateral and the lowermost bearded toward the base and the lowermost with a backward-pointing spur. Fruit an oval to elliptical capsule. FG

Trichostema brachiatum

LAMIACEAE | **false pennyroyal**

Aug–Sep, 6–15 in. Erect-ascending annual of shale barrens, outcrops of calcareous or mafic rock, diabase barrens, calcareous dry prairies, and disturbed rocky areas. Stems vaguely 4-angled, branched, very leafy, finely hairy or glandular-hairy. Leaves elliptical, 1–2 in. long, hairy and dotted with sessile glands; releasing a lemonlike odor when crushed. Flowers on glandular-hairy stalks from axils in upper, leafy branches, blue-purple, about 1/4 in. long, tubular and with 5 spreading lobes, the lowermost one only slightly longer. The hairy, bell-shaped calyx has 5 equal lobes, and there are 4 protruding stamens with straight filaments and blue anthers. Fruit a nutlet. AMC

Trichostema dichotomum

LAMIACEAE | **common blue curls**

Aug–Nov, 1–2 ft. Erect annual found in dry woodlands, disturbed areas, and on thin soils around rock outcrops. Stems 4-angled, branched, hairy and with abundant long-stalked glands. Leaves petiolate to sessile, elliptical and bluntly pointed, 1/2–2 1/2 in. long, minutely hairy and glandular. Flowers in a terminal panicle, with 2 leaflike bracts at the base of each 1- to 3-flowered stalk; each flower dark blue to purple, about 1/2 in. long, with 5 spreading lobes, the 4 upward-pointing ones similar in size and shape, and the longer downward-pointing lobe with a blue-purple-spotted white patch; 4 long stamens curl upward. RTW

Trichostema setaceum

LAMIACEAE | **narrowleaf blue curls**

Aug–Nov, 4–12 in. Erect annual of thin soils around rock outcrops, especially granite flatrocks, and dry sandy soils of the Coastal Plain. Stems 4-angled, branched, minutely hairy with scattered long hairs. Leaves short-petioled to sessile, linear and bluntly pointed, to 2 in. long, smooth. Flowers in a terminal panicle, with 2 leaflike bracts at the base of each 1- to 3-flowered stalk; each flower dark blue to purple, about 1⁄3 in. long, with 5 spreading lobes, the 4 upward-pointing ones similar in length to the downward-pointing lobe, which has a blue-purple-spotted white patch; 4 long stamens curl upward. FG

Lindernia dubia

LINDERNIACEAE | **yellowseed false pimpernel**

Jun–Sep, 4–8 in. Erect to leaning annual of interdune swales, sandbars, pondshores, freshwater tidal marshes and mud flats, alluvial swamps, and other seasonally flooded, wet sandy/muddy areas that experience water drawdown. Stems slender, 4-angled, much-branched, light green to reddish-green, smooth. Leaves sessile or short-petioled, elliptical to oblong-oval, to 1½ in. long. Flowers solitary in axils of upper leaves, pale violet to white, 1⁄3 in. long, tubular, the corolla with a 2-lobed upper lip, 3-lobed lower lip, 2 fertile stamens, 2 sterile stamens, and a single style; the shorter, sometimes reddish-green calyx has 5 linear lobes. Fruit an elliptical capsule. BAS

Glechoma hederacea

LAMIACEAE | **ground ivy**

Mar–Jun, to 2 ft. long. Prostrate, mat-forming perennial of lawns, gardens, and disturbed areas. Native to Eurasia. Stems 4-angled, creeping, turning upward at tips and rooting at nodes, smooth to rough-hairy. Leaves short-petioled, round to kidney- or heart-shaped, 1–2 in. long, with scalloped margins, smooth or hairy. Flowers in small clusters of 3–7 at the tips of stems, blue or bluish-violet to lavender, about ½ in. long, tubular and funnel-shaped, with 2 flaring lips, the upper lip small and 2-lobed, the lower larger, 3-lobed, spotted with purple, and hairy. RTW

Hedeoma pulegioides

LAMIACEAE | **American pennyroyal**

Jul–Oct, 4–16 in. Erect annual of dry woodlands, road banks, trails and woods roads. Stems round or 4-angled, branched, glandular-hairy. Leaves petiolate, oval-elliptical, to 1 in. long, with a few blunt teeth toward the tip, gland-dotted. Flowers in small whorls at leaf nodes, a pair of leafy bracts at the base of each flower; flowers light blue to lavender, less than 1/4 in. long, tubular and split into 2 lips, the upper lip 2-lobed and the lower 3-lobed and purple-spotted. The tubular calyx has 5 lobes and 13 prominent nerves; it becomes flask-shaped at maturity. AMC

Prunella vulgaris var. *lanceolata*

LAMIACEAE | **American self-heal**

Apr–Dec, 4–20 in. Prostrate to erect, tufted perennial found in bottomland forests, upland forests and woodlands, disturbed areas. Stems 4-angled, simple or branched, hairy, often with leafy basal offshoots. Leaves petiolate (upper leaves may be sessile), lance-shaped to oblong with wedge-shaped base, 3–5 times as long as wide, shallowly toothed or entire. Flowers in a short, dense terminal spike, each resting on an oval bract; each flower bluish-purple and white, about 1/2 in. long, tubular with a hooded upper lip and 3-lobed, fringed lower lip. BAS

Salvia azurea

LAMIACEAE | **azure sage**

Aug–Oct, 2–5 ft. Erect perennial of sandhills, hammocks, and dry sandy or rocky woodlands. Stems 1–several from a single crown, 4-angled, simple or branched above, hairy. Leaves narrowly elliptical to lance-shaped and tapering at both ends, to 3½ in. long, grayish-green, toothed, with short gray hairs; scent when crushed resembles culinary sage. Flowers in erect, loose, terminal spikes; each flower intense blue, 1/2–1 in. long, tubular and opening to 2 lips, the upper much smaller and hoodlike and the lower 3-lobed and (usually) with white stripes or smudges. The calyx is also tubular. BAS

Salvia urticifolia

LAMIACEAE | **nettle-leaf sage**

Apr–Jun, 6–30 in. Erect perennial from a thick rhizome found in woodlands and glades, usually over mafic or calcareous rocks. Stems square, slippery-hairy, and sometimes woody at the base. Leaves numerous, oval to diamond-shaped, the wedge-shaped base tapering to wings, coarsely toothed toward the tip but entire toward the base. Flowers in whorls along a spikelike raceme to 8 in. long, blue to violet, tubular and with 2 lips, the lower lip showy, cleft into 2 lobes, and with prominent white markings. The tubular calyx is also 2-lobed and with prominent nerves. RTW

Scutellaria elliptica

LAMIACEAE | **hairy skullcap**

May–Jun, 6–30 in. Erect perennial of moist to dry forests, woodlands, and barrens. Stems 4-angled, 1–3 per plant, simple or branched above, finely downy above. Leaves short-petioled, oval or diamond-shaped, to 3 in. long, toothed at least in the widest portion to tip. Flowers in an open terminal raceme or in upper leaf axils, bluish-purple (rarely white), to ¾ in. long, tubular and with an upper hoodlike, 3-lobed lip arched above a spreading and convex lower lip. As in all *Scutellaria* species, the calyx tube is 2-lobed, with a distinctive caplike projection on the upper lobe. RTW

Scutellaria incana

LAMIACEAE | **hoary skullcap**

Jun–Sep, 1–4 ft. Erect, clumped perennial of dry to moist upland forests and well-drained floodplain forests. Stems 1–many, bluntly 4-angled. Leaves petiolate, elliptical to oval, to 3 in. long, toothed, the upper surface smooth (except for young leaves), the lower whitish-green and finely hairy. Flowers in multiple erect, terminal, spikelike racemes to 6 in. long; each flower blue-violet, to ¾ in. long, erect and tubular, opening to 2 lips, the upper lip hoodlike with curled-back side margins and the lower larger and broader. Fruit a capsule. Var. *punctata,* which is distinguished from the type by being sparsely hairy only on leaf underside veins, is pictured. RTW

Scutellaria integrifolia

LAMIACEAE | **narrowleaf skullcap**

May–Jul, 1–2 ft. Erect perennial growing in wet pine savannas, seeps in forests, bottomlands, and other moist sites. Stems single to many from a slightly woody base, 4-angled, with arched-ascending branches above, densely hairy. Leaves petiolate, lower ones oval or triangular-oval, upper lance-shaped to narrowly elliptic, with blunt to acute tips and toothed to entire margins, hairy. Flowers in a terminal raceme up to 8 in. long; each flower bluish-purple, to 1 in. long, tubular, the corolla tube furry and with a hoodlike upper lip arched above a spreading lower lip, which is slightly notched, convex, and marked by 2 white bands. JF

Scutellaria lateriflora

LAMIACEAE | **tall blue skullcap**

Jul–Nov, 1–2½ ft. Erect to sprawling, rhizomatous and stoloniferous perennial found in alluvial forests, bogs, seeps, marshes, and pondshores. Stems 4-angled, light green to pale reddish-green, smooth to minutely furry on the angles. Leaves petiolate, oval to oval-lance-shaped with pointy tip, to 2¼ in. long, coarsely toothed, and with small hairs on veins. Flowers in several racemes on spreading upper branches, favoring 1 side of the raceme axis; each flower blue to pink (or white), to ⅓ in. long, tubular, the corolla tube furry and with a hoodlike, lobed upper lip arched above a spreading, convex lower lip, which is often white. GPF

Scutellaria serrata

LAMIACEAE | **showy skullcap**

May–Jun, 8–24 in. Erect, clumped perennial of rich, moist upland forests and well-drained alluvial forests. Stems 1–several, 4-angled, simple, smooth or sparsely hairy above. Leaves opposite but crowded toward top of stem (where they may appear whorled), petiolate, oval to roughly diamond-shaped, 1½–4 in. long, coarsely toothed and with a few hairs. Flowers erect-ascending in a 2- to 6-in.-long terminal raceme, blue-violet, about 1 in. long, tubular, opening to 2 lips, the upper lip hoodlike with curled-back side margins, and the spreading lower lip larger, broader, and notched. Fruit a capsule containing 2–4 nutlets. WS

Mazus pumilus

MAZACEAE | **Japanese mazus**

Dec–Oct, 2–7 in. Prostrate annual of lawns and sandy, rocky, or muddy shores and bars along lakes and rivers. Native to e Asia, naturalized in much of the U.S. Stems often several from a basal rosette, slender, smooth. Stem leaves opposite or alternate, short-petioled with slight wings, oblong-oval, ¾–2 in. long, toothed; basal leaves often larger and spoon-shaped. Flowers 2–10 in erect racemes, pale blue to blue-violet, ¼–½ in. long, tubular, with 2 lips, the lower lip longer, projecting, 3-lobed, and whitish marked with yellow spots, the upper lip violet. The calyx has 5 prominent, lance-shaped lobes. Fruit a round capsule enclosed by the persistent calyx. BAS

Buchnera floridana

OROBANCHACEAE | **Florida bluehearts**

Apr–Oct, 11–30 in. Erect perennial of pine savannas, flatwoods, seepage bogs, and sandy roadsides. Stems unbranched and rough-hairy below, smoother above. Leaves oblong-oval to lance-shaped (lower leaves) or linear (upper leaves), to nearly 3 in. long, prominently 3-veined, with a few blunt teeth, rough-hairy. Flowers in a loose terminal spike, bluish-purple to pink, about ½ in. long, tubular and opening to 5 spreading, slightly unequal lobes; the tubular calyx and corolla tube are covered with short white hairs. Semi-parasitic on roots of several grasses and woody plants, and dependent on regular fire. BAS

Mimulus alatus

PHRYMACEAE | **winged monkey-flower**

Jul–Nov, 1–4 ft. Erect, rhizomatous perennial of marshes, bottomlands, ditches, and seasonally flooded areas with drawdown during the growing season. Stems 4-angled, with wings on the angles. Leaves on winged petioles or sessile, lance-shaped to oval, tapering at the base, 2–5 in. long (reduced above), toothed, smooth. Flowers solitary on stalks from upper leaf axils, pale violet-blue or pink, 1 in. long, tubular and opening to 2 unequal lips, the upper lip erect and 2-lobed (each lobe often folded), the lower spreading and 3-lobed. A light green calyx tube is strongly 5-angled (winged) and has 5 short lobes. Fruit a capsule enclosed by the persistent calyx. BAS

Mimulus ringens

PHRYMACEAE | **Allegheny monkey-flower**

Jun–Sep, 6–36 in. Erect, rhizomatous perennial of wet habitats such as marshes, bogs, wet meadows, and bottomlands. Stem 4-angled but lacking the wings seen in *M. alatus*. Leaves lance-shaped to oval, sessile-clasping at the base, 2–5 in. long (reduced above), toothed. Flowers solitary on short stalks in upper leaf axils, blue to lavender with a yellow patch in the throat, tubular, opening to 2 lips, the upper erect and cleft into 2 lobes and the lower spreading and 3-lobed. The shorter calyx is also tubular and strongly angled. Fruit a capsule enclosed by the persistent calyx. WS

Veronica americana

PLANTAGINACEAE | **American speedwell**

May–Oct, 4–36 in. Semi-erect to creeping perennial of bogs, marshes, streamsides, wet meadows, and seeps. Stems usually branched, rooting at lower nodes, fleshy and smooth. Leaves short-petioled, lance-shaped to lance-oval, ¾–3 in. long, with toothed margins. Flowers in terminal and axillary racemes, blue-violet or white striped with purple, ¼–⅓ in. wide, with 4 tiny petals, 3 about equal in size, the other slightly smaller; 2 stamens and 1 style protrude from the green center. BMP

Veronica arvensis

PLANTAGINACEAE | **corn speedwell**

Mar–Sep, 2–8 in. Creeping to semi-erect annual of lawns, roadsides, and other disturbed areas. Native to Europe. Stems branched from below, hairy. Leaves mostly opposite, short-petioled or sessile, oval to nearly round, ¼–½ in. long, blunt-toothed, and hairy. Flowers solitary and sessile in leaf axils, blue with darker lines, less than ¼ in. wide, with 4 petals, 3 about equal in size, the other smaller; 2 stamens with white anthers and a single style protrude from the tiny, pale center. Fruit a tiny, heart-shaped capsule. BAS

Veronica hederifolia

PLANTAGINACEAE | **ivyleaf speedwell**

Mar–Jun, 2–14 in. Creeping to erect annual of moist, disturbed habitats such as lawns, fields, successional forests, and well-drained floodplain forests. Stems branched at the base, hairy. Leaves opposite (lower) and alternate (upper), petiolate, oval or kidney-shaped in outline but with 3–5 lobes, 1/4–3/4 in. long, bristly-hairy. Flowers solitary on short stalks from leaf axils, pale blue to light lavender and sometimes with darker lines, less than 1/2 in. wide, with 4 tiny petals, 3 about equal in size, the other slightly smaller. Fruit a heart-shaped capsule. RTW

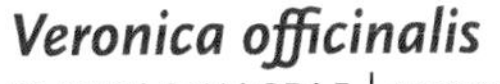

Veronica officinalis

PLANTAGINACEAE | **common speedwell**

May–Sep, 4–12 in. Creeping, mat-forming perennial of a wide range of disturbed and natural habitats, including lawns, roadsides, clearings, and moist to somewhat dry upland forests. Believed to be of mixed native and alien background. Stems mostly prostrate, with ascending branches, rooting at nodes, hairy. Leaves mostly opposite, short-petioled, oval or elliptical, 3/4–2 in. long, toothed and hairy. Flowers densely arranged in erect-ascending, glandular-hairy, axillary racemes; each flower lilac-blue to lavender and sometimes with darker lines, 1/4 in. wide, with 4 tiny petals, 3 about equal in size, the other slightly smaller. Fruit a tiny, flattened capsule. RTW

Veronica persica

PLANTAGINACEAE | **bird's-eye speedwell**

Mar–Oct, 4–12 in. Sprawling to ascending annual of lawns, fields, roadsides, and other disturbed areas. Native to Eurasia. Stems simple to profusely branched, often rooting at nodes, hairy. Leaves opposite (lower) and alternate (upper), short-petioled, oval to rounded, to 1/2 in. long, with coarsely toothed or scalloped margins, slightly hairy. Flowers solitary on short stalks from upper leaf axils, blue-violet but white toward the center (with darker lines), about 1/3 in. wide, with 4 tiny petals, 3 rounded, the other narrower; 2 stamens and 1 style protrude from a green center. Fruit a flattened, slightly heart-shaped capsule. RTW

Verbena simplex

VERBENACEAE | **narrowleaf vervain**

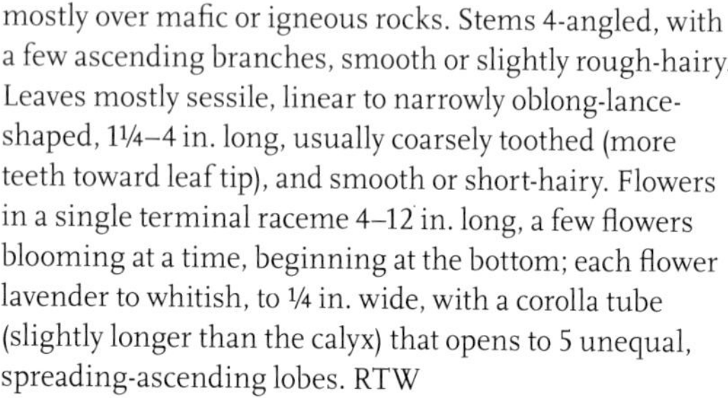

May–Sep, 8–26 in. Erect to ascending perennial of glades, rocky woodlands, forests, rock outcrops, and roadsides, mostly over mafic or igneous rocks. Stems 4-angled, with a few ascending branches, smooth or slightly rough-hairy. Leaves mostly sessile, linear to narrowly oblong-lance-shaped, 1¼–4 in. long, usually coarsely toothed (more teeth toward leaf tip), and smooth or short-hairy. Flowers in a single terminal raceme 4–12 in. long, a few flowers blooming at a time, beginning at the bottom; each flower lavender to whitish, to ¼ in. wide, with a corolla tube (slightly longer than the calyx) that opens to 5 unequal, spreading-ascending lobes. RTW

Pinguicula caerulea

LENTIBULARIACEAE | **blue butterwort**

Apr–May, to 8 in. Scapose, carnivorous perennial of pine savannas and wet pine flatwoods, mostly in the outer Coastal Plain, rarely extending inland to the fall-line Sandhills of NC and SC. Stem a single, hairy flowering scape from a 5-in.-wide basal rosette. Leaves oval with curled-up margins, fleshy, yellowish-green, oily. Flowers single, terminal, usually held at 90° to scape; pale blue to violet with darker veins, 1 in. wide, tubular, with 5 spreading, notched corolla lobes, a hairy lump on inside bottom of the throat, and a backward-pointing spur. Insects are trapped on the upper surface of leaves, which secrete a musty-smelling mucilage and digestive fluids. FG

Viola cucullata

VIOLACEAE | **bog violet**

Apr–Jun, 4–10 in. Tufted perennial of bogs, seeps, margins of spring branches. Stemless, rhizomes sprouting tufted crowns of leaves. Leaves in a basal cluster, long-petiolate with membranous, linear, whitish to greenish stipules; each leaf heart-shaped to nearly round or kidney-shaped, 1–4 in. long and wide, margins bluntly toothed, smooth. Flowers solitary on individual stalks to 7 in. long, pale blue to blue-violet (often darker toward center) with a white, purple-veined throat, ½–1½ in. wide, with 5 spreading petals, the 2 laterals with short, white, knobby hairs and the lowermost with a backward-pointing spur. Fruit an oblong-oval capsule. BAS

Viola hirsutula

VIOLACEAE | **southern woodland violet**

Feb–Apr, 1–8 in. Low-growing perennial of bottomlands, moist slopes, dry forests, and clearings. Stemless, the flowering scapes and leaves arising from a thick, fleshy rhizome. Leaves basal, on petioles with narrowly triangular, fringed stipules, oval to round with a broad heart-shaped base, to 4¾ in. long, margins toothed or smooth, upper surface with silvery-hairy patches, and often purple beneath. Flowers solitary on individual scapes, violet, 1–1¾ in. wide, with 5 petals; the 3 lower petals are white-throated and bear violet veins, and of these the 2 lateral ones are bearded and the lowermost has a backward-pointing spur. Fruit an oval capsule. RTW

Viola sagittata

VIOLACEAE | **arrowleaf violet**

Apr, 3–6 in. Low-growing, rhizomatous perennial of dry to moist forests and woodlands. Stemless, with leaves and flowering scape arising from the rhizome. Leaves basal, on purple-tinged petioles, lance-shaped or arrowhead-shaped with 2 lobes (which may be notched) at the base, 1½–4 in. long, wavy-margined or toothed, mostly smooth. Flowers solitary on naked scapes that are downcurved at the tip, violet-purple with a white center, about ¾ in. wide, with 5 spreading petals, the lowest with darker purple veins over the white patch and extended behind the flower in a spur. Fruit an oval capsule. Closed, self-pollinating flowers often present. RTW

Viola sororia

VIOLACEAE | **common blue violet**

Feb–Jun, 2–8 in. Erect, rhizomatous perennial of bottomlands, lawns, and moist forests. Stemless, with leaves and flower stalks arising from the rhizome. Leaves basal and ascending, on thick-fleshy petioles, heart- to kidney-shaped, 2–4 in. long, toothed or wavy-margined, and smooth or hairy. Flowers several, each on a naked stalk, deep violet to lavender (occasionally white) with darker veins and a whitish throat, about 1 in. wide, with 5 unequal petals, the lowest smooth and with a short backward-pointing spur, the 2 lateral ones bearded at the base. Fruit an oval capsule. Closed, self-pollinating flowers often present. RTW

Baptisia australis

FABACEAE | **blue wild indigo**

Apr–May, 2–3 ft. Erect, bushy perennial, typically found on riverbank scour areas and gravel bars, as well as disturbed areas, where it persists from cultivation. Stems several (more with age) from a woody base, branches angled upward, smooth, and with a white-waxy coating. Leaves on petioles with conspicuous stipules at the base, divided into 3 bluish-green, oval leaflets, each ½–3 in. long and smooth. Flowers in erect, terminal racemes to 12 in. long and extending well above foliage; each flower blue-violet, 1 in. long, with typical pea-flower shape. Fruit an inflated pod with pointed tip; turns charcoal-black when ripe. RTW

Clitoria mariana

FABACEAE | **Atlantic pigeonwings**

Jun–Aug, to 2 ft. long. Sprawling perennial of dry woodlands, openings, roadsides. Stems smooth and loosely ascending, often over other plants. Leaves on petioles with a pair of stipules at the base, divided into 3 oval to elliptical leaflets (middle leaflet on a stalk), smooth above, short-hairy beneath. Flowers in stalked clusters of 1–3 from leaf axils, pale blue to pinkish-lavender, 1–2 in. long, with typical pea-flower shape, including a significantly larger, showy petal marked with dark purple lines. The much shorter calyx is tubular. Fruit a linear-oblong, flattened pod tipped by the persistent style; upon splitting open, parts twist, revealing sticky seeds. WS

Lupinus perennis

FABACEAE | **sundial lupine**

Apr–May, 8–30 in. Erect, clumped perennial of sandhills, sandy roadsides, sandy or gravelly fields, and other dry, usually sandy, nutrient-poor habitats. Stems several from a crown, often reddish, smooth to densely hairy. Leaves long-petioled, palmately divided into 5–11 oblong to lance-shaped leaflets, which are ¾–2 in. long, smooth above, hairy beneath and on the margins. Flowers in erect terminal racemes 4–10 in. long; each flower blue-violet, about ½ in. long, with typical pea-flower shape, the banner petal bearing a purple-streaked, white patch. Fruit a densely hairy, flattened, linear-oblong pod. FG

Orbexilum lupinellus
(Psoralea lupinellus)

FABACEAE | **lupine scurfpea**

May–Jul, 1–2 ft. Erect perennial of Coastal Plain sandhills. A Coastal Plain endemic. Stems ribbed, branched from the base, somewhat hairy. Leaves palmately divided into 3–7 linear needlelike leaflets, each ¾–3 in. long and resin-dotted. Flowers in small, loose, long-stalked clusters from upper leaf axils; each flower blue-violet, about ¼ in. long, with typical pea-flower shape. Fruit a crescent-shaped pod with ridged surface and tiny beak. BAS

Pediomelum canescens
(Psoralea canescens)

FABACEAE | **buckroot**

May–Jul, 1–3 ft. Erect, bushy perennial of sandhills, pine flatwoods, and other sandy woodlands of the Coastal Plain. Stems much-branched, densely hairy. Leaves petiolate, divided (uppermost sometimes not divided) into 3 softly hairy, oval to elliptical leaflets, each 1–5 in. long and with rounded tips. Flowers in short, loosely few-flowered axillary racemes, mostly held perpendicular to the stalk; each flower dark blue to violet with yellow-green markings, ½ in. long, with typical pea-flower shape and a hairy, tubular calyx. Hairy stems, foliage, and calyces give plant a pale gray appearance. BAS

Medicago sativa

FABACEAE | **alfalfa**

Apr–Aug, 1–3 ft. Erect to decumbent annual of agricultural fields, roadsides, and other open, disturbed habitats. Native to Eurasia, widely cultivated as a forage crop. Stems branched, sparsely hairy, sometimes leaning. Leaves on petioles with a pair of lance-shaped stipules at the base, divided into 3 narrowly oval to linear leaflets, each ½–1¼ in. long (center leaflet tipped upward) and finely toothed toward the tip. Flowers in short, compact racemes of 5–30, on stalks from leaf axils; each flower blue-violet (rarely white), ¼–½ in. long, with typical pea-flower shape. Fruit a coiled pod. JF

Aconitum uncinatum

RANUNCULACEAE | **eastern blue monkshood**

Aug–Oct, 2–5 ft. Erect to sprawling perennial of seepages, moist meadows, cove forests, and other moist forests. Stems arising from tuberlike root, slender and weak (often leaning on other plants), branching, smooth to minutely hairy. Leaves petiolate, about 4 in. long and wide, palmately and deeply divided into 3–5 coarsely toothed segments. Flowers in loose panicles from upper leaf axils and stem ends, blue to purple, 1–2 in. long, with 5 petal-like sepals—the uppermost one shaped like a hood or helmet—enclosing 2 smaller blue petals. Fruit a beaked, elliptical follicle. All parts are toxic, yielding a drug that has been used to treat neuralgia and sciatica. RTW

Delphinium carolinianum

RANUNCULACEAE | **Carolina larkspur**

May–Jul, 1–5 ft. Erect perennial of rocky woodlands, granite outcrops, Altamaha grit outcrops, and moist sandy woodlands associated with longleaf pine. Stems mostly unbranched, sometimes with a reddish base, hairy. Leaves basal and alternate, petiolate, roundish in outline, to 4 in. long, divided into many hairy, linear segments. Flowers in a terminal raceme above leaves, blue-violet (sometimes white), ¾ in. wide, tubular, with 5 curving-spreading petal-like sepals and a 1-in. spur extending behind and upward. 4 less showy, united petals in the center cover stamens and carpels, and the lowest ones are bearded. Fruit a 3-celled, cylindrical follicle. BAS

Delphinium exaltatum

RANUNCULACEAE | **tall larkspur**

Jul–Sep, 3–6 ft. Erect perennial of dry to moist soils over calcareous or mafic rocks, usually in the open or in partial sun. Stems slender, smooth below the inflorescence. Leaves petiolate, palmately divided into 3–5 long-toothed lobes, deep green above and pale green beneath. Flowers in loose, wandlike, terminal raceme with some branching below; each flower pale to medium blue (occasionally pink or white), to 1 in. long, with 5 furry, petal-like sepals, the upper elongated into a distinctive spur; 4 reduced petals are enclosed within the sepals. Fruit an erect, strongly 3-parted follicle. All parts are poisonous. JS

Delphinium tricorne

RANUNCULACEAE | **dwarf larkspur**

Mar–May, 12–20 in. Erect perennial found in rich, moist forests, especially over mafic or calcareous rocks; less commonly on very fertile alluvial deposits. Stems stout, fleshy, unbranched. Leaves mostly basal, petiolate, to 4 in. long and wide, deeply palmately divided into 5–7 lobes, these in turn divided into 2–3 shallow lobes; leaves sparsely hairy. Flowers in an open, terminal raceme, blue-purple to pink or white, 3⁄4–1 in. long, with 5 petal-like sepals, the upper sepal prolonged into a curved nectar spur behind the flower and the others spreading outward; 4 small, inner petals surround a whitish opening that leads to the spur. Fruit a strongly 3-parted follicle. WS

Salvia lyrata

LAMIACEAE | **lyreleaf sage**

Mar–Jun, 1–2 ft. Erect, weedy perennial of lawns, woodlands, roadsides, floodplains, and calcareous barrens. Stems 4-angled, simple or branched from the base, slightly hairy. Leaves primarily basal, petiolate, oblong-oval in outline, pinnately lobed and suggesting a lyre shape, toothed, often tinged or marked with dark reddish-purple, slightly hairy (sometimes smooth). Flowers in widely spaced whorls in a loose, terminal spike (additional flowers may occur on branches subtended by small leaves); each flower pale blue to lavender, 1⁄2–11⁄4 in. long, tubular and opening to 2 gaping lips, the upper entire or 2-lobed and the lower 3-lobed. RTW

Viola brittoniana

VIOLACEAE | **northern coastal violet**

Apr–May, 2–8 in. Erect perennial of seeps, bogs, brackish areas and other sites with low sphagnous ground. Stemless; flowering stalk and leaves arise from a thick rhizome. Leaves basal, on long petioles with narrow basal stipules, oval to triangular-oval, 11⁄2–4 in. long and usually wider, variably divided into 5–15 irregular lobes, the central lobe usually largest. Flowers solitary on slender stalks, lavender-blue or violet with a conspicuous white center, 3⁄4–11⁄4 in. wide, with 5 unequal petals, the lowest largest and extending behind in a short spur, the 2 laterals bearded. Fruit a cylindric-oval capsule. Closed, self-pollinating flowers often present. BAS

Viola palmata

VIOLACEAE | **early blue violet**

Apr–Jun, 4–8 in. Low-growing perennial of moist to dry forests. Stemless; leaves and flowering scape arise from a rhizome. Leaves basal, on petioles with narrowly lance-shaped and fringed (rarely entire) stipules, 2–4¾ in. long; early leaves round, oval, or heart-shaped; later leaves palmately divided into 3–11 irregular lobes, variously toothed; generally hairy, may be smooth. Flowers solitary on naked scapes, violet-blue or white streaked with violet, ½–1½ in. wide, with 5 spreading petals, the 2 lateral ones densely bearded, the lowest bearded or smooth and extending behind the flower in a spur. Fruit an oval capsule. Closed, self-pollinating flowers often present. RTW

Viola pedata

VIOLACEAE | **bird's-foot violet**

Mar–Jun, 2–8 in. Erect perennial of dry rocky or sandy forests, woodlands, glades, and road banks. Stemless, with flowering stalk and leaves arising from a rhizome. Leaves basal, petiolate, 1–2 in. long, palmately divided into 5–11 narrow lobes, which are often toothed at the tip; usually smooth. Flowers solitary on slender stalks, blue-violet or lavender, ¾–1¾ in. wide, with 5 wide-spreading petals, the lowest largest and extending behind the flower in a blunt spur and bearing a white patch and dark veins. 5 conspicuous orange stamens project from the corolla throat. Fruit an elliptical capsule. No closed, self-pollinating flowers. MHV

Viola septemloba

VIOLACEAE | **southern coastal violet**

Mar–May, 2–10 in. Low-growing perennial of sandy, dry, or seasonally wet pinelands. Stemless, the flowering scapes and leaves arising from a thick, vertical rhizome. Leaves basal, on long petioles with small linear stipules at the base; early leaves round to oval or heart-shaped; mature leaves divided into 3–11 narrow lobes, to 2 in. long, smooth. Flowers solitary on individual slender scapes, purple with a white throat and darker purple veins, ¾–1½ in. wide, with 5 spreading petals, the lower 3 with a patch of hair at the base and the lowermost with a spur extending behind the flower. Fruit an elliptical capsule. Closed, self-pollinating flowers are present. RTW

Tradescantia ohiensis

COMMELINACEAE | **smooth spiderwort**

Apr–Jul, 1–4 ft. Erect to ascending, clump-forming perennial of woodlands and forests, alluvial bottoms, meadows, and other open, disturbed areas. Stems branched, somewhat succulent, smooth, and with a whitish coating. Leaves sessile with smooth (sometimes hairy) sheathing bases, linear or lance-shaped, to 18 in. long, bluish-green and smooth. Flowers in terminal clusters underlain by 2 leaf-like, spreading-drooping, sharp-pointed bracts up to 3 in. long; each flower blue to purple or rose (rarely white), with 3 oval petals and 6 hairy stamens bearing bright yellow anthers. Flower stalks are hairless. Fruit a 3-celled, oval capsule. RTW

Tradescantia subaspera

COMMELINACEAE | **zigzag spiderwort**

Jun–Jul, 1½–3 ft. Clump-forming, ascending perennial of dry to moist woodlands, forests, and hammocks. Stems sparingly branched, somewhat zigzag, smooth or hairy. Leaves sessile with tubular, sheathing bases, narrowly lance-shaped to oval-lance-shaped, to 12 in. long, smooth or hairy, with the upper surface a darker green than the lower. Flowers in terminal clusters with a long leaflike bract spread beneath, blue or light purple (rarely white), about 1 in. wide, with 3 petals and 6 hairy blue stamens bearing yellow anthers. Fruit a nearly round, 3-celled capsule. JF

Tradescantia virginiana

COMMELINACEAE | **Virginia spiderwort**

Apr–Jul, 6–20 in. Erect to ascending, clump-forming perennial of nutrient-rich, moist to dry forests and rocky woodlands, and well-drained floodplain forests. Stems branched, somewhat succulent, smooth or sparsely hairy. Leaves sessile with hairy sheathing bases, linear to lance-shaped, 5–15 in. long, smooth. Flowers in terminal clusters with a pair of long, leaflike bracts with pointy tips spread beneath; each flower blue or purple (occasionally rose or white), about 1 in. wide, with 3 spreading oval petals, 3 hairy sepals, and 6 hairy stamens. Individual flower stalks are hairy. Fruit a 3-celled, oval capsule. BAS

Burmannia biflora

BURMANNIACEAE | **violet burmannia**

Aug–Nov, 1–7 in. Erect annual of pine savannas, bogs, and shores of Coastal Plain depression ponds; usually in full sun. Stems slender, unbranched, smooth. Leaves tiny and scalelike. Flowers 1–10 on short stalks at top of stem, bluish-violet, less than 1/4 in. wide, tubular and pointing upward, with 3 flaring "wings" and ending in 6 green to yellow-green, tiny, pointed lobes. AMC

Houstonia caerulea

RUBIACEAE | **Quaker ladies**

(Jan) Apr–Jul, 2–6 in. Tufted, erect perennial of forests, woodlands, openings, lawns, and a wide variety of disturbed sites. Stems thin, sparingly branched, smooth. Leaves mostly basal in rosettes, petiolate, spoon- to oblong-lance-shaped, less than 1/2 in. long, smooth to slightly hairy; opposite stem leaves narrower and mostly sessile. Flowers solitary at stem tips or in upper axils, 1/4–3/4 in. wide, pale blue to violet with yellow center, with a short corolla tube and 4 spreading, slightly pointed lobes. Fruit a 2-celled, green, slightly compressed and round capsule. JF

Houstonia pusilla

RUBIACEAE | **tiny bluet**

Mar–Apr, 1–4 in. Slender, erect annual of woodlands, lawns, cemeteries, and other disturbed sites. Stems thin with ascending branches, some slightly reddish, smooth. Leaves mostly basal in rosettes (a few opposite stem leaves), oval to lance-shaped, about 1/4 in. long. Flowers solitary and terminal or from upper axils, lavender with darker or red center, about 1/4 in. wide, with a short corolla tube and 4 spreading, pointed lobes. Fruit a round, slightly compressed, 2-celled capsule. AMC

Houstonia serpyllifolia

RUBIACEAE | **Appalachian bluet**

Mar–Jul, 4–7 in. Prostrate, mat-forming perennial of streambanks, grassy balds, moist forests, seepy rock outcrops, spray cliffs, and moist disturbed areas. A Central/Southern Appalachian endemic. Stems very slender, diffusely branched, creeping and rooting at nodes, smooth. Leaves short-petioled, oval to round, to ¼ in. long. Flowers solitary on erect, threadlike stalks, blue with yellow-white center, to ½ in. wide, with a short corolla tube and 4 spreading, bluntly pointed lobes. Fruit tiny, green, flattened, and 2-sectioned capsule. JF

Amsonia ciliata

APOCYNACEAE | **sandhills bluestar**

Apr–May, 1–2 ft. Clump-forming, erect to ascending perennial growing in sandhills and other sandy woodlands. Stems and new leaves with a fringe of hairs, hence the epithet. Leaves crowded all the way up the stem, sessile, narrow and almost needlelike, to 3 in. long, turning yellow-bronze in the fall. Flowers in a loose cluster at top of stem, pale blue, ½ in. wide, with a ½-in.-long thin tube that opens into a 5-lobed "star" with a white or pale yellow center. Fruit a pair of erect, green, slender follicles. WS

Amsonia tabernaemontana

APOCYNACEAE | **eastern bluestar**

Apr–May, 1–3 ft. Slender, erect perennial found in floodplain forests and moist, rich slope forests. Stems 1–several from a single root crown, unbranched, smooth. Leaves occurring all the way up the stem, short-petioled, narrowly oval to lance-shaped, 2½–5 in. long, smooth. Flowers in a pyramidal terminal panicle, powder-blue, ¾ in. wide, star-shaped, with a ¼-in.-long tube topped with white hairs that splits into 5 spreading, narrow, blunt-tipped corolla lobes; the calyx is short, with triangular lobes. Fruit a pair of erect, green, slender follicles. Leaves turn golden yellow in fall. RTW

Andersonglossum virginianum (*Cynoglossum virginianum*)

BORAGINACEAE | **wild comfrey**

Apr–Jun, 11–30 in. Erect perennial of moist deciduous forests. Stems stout, unbranched, with few leaves and covered in bristly hairs. Leaves mostly basal, petiolate, oval to elliptical, to 10 in. long, stiff-hairy; the few stem leaves are alternate, sessile and clasping, and smaller. Flowers in 1–4 coiled racemes branching off at the top of the stem, these lengthening and straightening as flowers open and fruit matures. Flowers pale blue or white, about 3/4 in. wide, with a short corolla tube that opens to 5 overlapping lobes and a shorter, hairy, 5-parted calyx. Fruit a cluster of 4 bristly nutlets. BAS

Echium vulgare

BORAGINACEAE | **viper's bugloss**

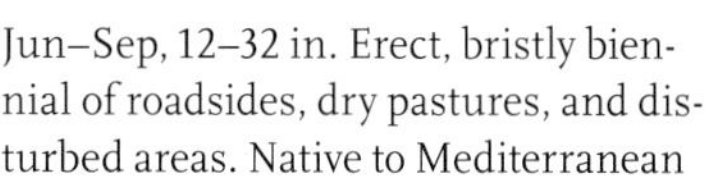

Jun–Sep, 12–32 in. Erect, bristly biennial of roadsides, dry pastures, and disturbed areas. Native to Mediterranean Europe, widespread in NoAm. Stem unbranched and covered with stiff, spreading hairs. Leaves sessile, oblong to lance-shaped, 3/4–5½ in. long (reduced above), hairy. Flowers in bristly, coiled racemes that branch off the stem, bright blue to blue-violet (pink in bud), ½ in. long, tubular to funnel-shaped, with 5 rounded lobes and 4 red stamens. Fruit an oval-oblong nutlet. Abundant bristles make this plant painful to touch. JF

Mertensia virginica

BORAGINACEAE | **Virginia bluebells**

Mar–May, 12–28 in. Erect to ascending perennial of rich, moist, alluvial floodplain forests and thickets; sometimes colonial and seen in large masses. Stems branched above, smooth. Leaves short-petioled to sessile, oval-elliptical to spoon-shaped, to 2½ in. long (basal ones biggest), gray-green. Flowers nodding in bractless, coiled racemes terminating the stem and branches; each pink in bud, turning blue (occasionally white), funnel-shaped with a distinctly long tube that is densely furry at the base and opens to a shallowly undulate bell with 5 small folds. Anthers and style are prominently visible in the corolla throat. Fruit a small nutlet with wrinkled surface. RTW

Myosotis laxa

BORAGINACEAE | **tufted forget-me-not**

May–Oct, 4–16 in. Short-lived perennial/annual growing in marshes and on streambanks and seeps. Branching stems are sparsely to moderately covered in close-pressed hairs, lower portions often reclining. Leaves petiolate (upper leaves sessile), lance-oblong to somewhat spoon-shaped, ½–3 in. long (reduced above). Flowers in a long, coiled terminal raceme (in bud) that elongates as flowers bloom, blue, to ¼ in. wide, tubular with 5 spreading oval lobes, each with a yellow-colored swollen spot at the base, creating a yellow center to each flower. DASM

Hydrolea quadrivalvis

HYDROLEACEAE | **waterpod**

Jun–Sep, to 1½ ft. Erect to spreading aquatic perennial of cypress-gum and other swamp forests, backwater sloughs, marshes, ditches. Stems stout, succulent, branched; upper stem with stiff spreading hairs, lower trailing and rooting at nodes to form mats. Leaves short-petioled to sessile, elliptical to lance-shaped, 2–5 in. long, smooth to sparsely hairy; spines to ½ in. long in some leaf axils. Flowers in small clusters in upper leaf axils, blue or bluish-purple, broadly bell-shaped, with 5 oval petals, 5 narrow sepals bearing spreading hairs (like those on stem), 5 stamens, and a green ovary in the center. Fruit a round capsule surrounded by persistent calyx. PIP

Campanula americana

CAMPANULACEAE | **tall bellflower**

Jun–Sep, 1½–6 ft. Erect annual/biennial of moist to fairly dry forests, especially those over mafic or calcareous rocks. Stems stout, slightly wing-angled, smooth to somewhat hairy. Leaves on winged petioles, lance-shaped, to 6 in. long, with toothed and slightly hairy margins, and rough-hairy on upper surfaces. Flowers in a leafy-bracted terminal spike (some branching possible), blue or bluish-purple, to 1 in. wide, with 5 spreading, sharp-pointed petals that are fused at the base and with a white ring in the center; a long style with curved-up tip protrudes from the center. Fruit a cylindrical capsule. WS

Campanula divaricata

CAMPANULACEAE | **Appalachian bellflower**

Jul–Oct, 8–30 in. Delicate, erect perennial of wooded slopes, cliffs, talus slopes, and trail banks. A Central/Southern Appalachian endemic. Stems smooth, slender, with spreading-drooping branches; often grows in clumps. Leaves short-petioled to sessile, lance-oval, to 3 in. long, coarsely toothed. Flowers numerous in a loose, open panicle, pale blue-violet on dangling stalks, bell-shaped, with 5 petals with recurved tips, a cup-shaped (green) calyx tube with 5 spreading narrow lobes, and a protruding style. Fruit a tiny top-shaped capsule. RTW

Wahlenbergia marginata

CAMPANULACEAE | **southern rockbell**

Feb–Dec, 1–2 ft. Erect perennial of sandy soils along roadsides and in fields. Native to e Asia and Oceania. Stems several in a clump, slender, branched, red-tinged, smooth. Leaves mostly near base of stem, alternate, linear to lance-shaped, to 1½ in. long (reduced to bracts above), with toothed to wavy margins, smooth. Flowers solitary at ends of branches, blue, ½ in. wide, tubular with 5 spreading, pointed corolla lobes and a cylindrical calyx with 5 narrow, erect, pointed lobes situated below the corolla. Fruit an erect, cylindrical, red capsule with persistent calyx lobes. BAS

Nicandra physalodes

SOLANACEAE | **shoo-fly plant**

Jul–Sep, 2–5 ft. Erect annual of cultivated fields, roadsides, and other disturbed places. Native to Peru. Stems stout, angled or distinctly ridged, branched above, succulent, mostly smooth. Leaves ascending, petiolate, oval or lance-shaped, 1½–8 in. long, coarsely and unevenly toothed or scalloped, mostly smooth. Flowers solitary in axils of upper leaves, on short, erect or nodding stalks; each flower light blue to lavender, 1–1½ in. wide, trumpet-shaped with 5 shallow lobes, white inside the throat, where there are 5 stamens and a single pistil. The calyx is prominently 5-lobed and 5-angled. Fruit a round, dry berry enclosed in the persistent calyx. KB

Ruellia caroliniensis

ACANTHACEAE | **Carolina wild petunia**

May–Sep, 1–2 ft. Erect perennial of dry to moist forests and woodlands. Stems simple (occasionally branched above), furry with light-colored hairs; leaves closer together on upper stem. Leaves petiolate, oval to oblong-oval, 1½–4 in. long, furry. Flowers in sessile clusters of 2–4 flowers each in upper leaf axils, 1–2 in. long, lavender-blue to lilac, trumpet-shaped with 5 broad, spreading lobes that are prominently creased; 5 calyx segments are prominently narrow and pointy. Fruit a narrow, somewhat flattened oval capsule. WS

Ruellia humilis

ACANTHACEAE | **low wild petunia**

May–Sep, 4–15 in. Erect, almost bushy perennial found in calcareous or mafic glades and in woodlands and prairies. Stems with long, arched and sometimes reclining branches from the base; hairy. Leaves mostly sessile, elliptical to oval, slightly leathery. Flowers single and sessile, or in several few-flowered clusters in the upper 4–8 leaf axils; each flower blue to lilac (rarely white), 1–2 in. long, funnel-shaped with 5 broad, spreading corolla lobes that are prominently creased. 5 shorter calyx segments are narrowly awl-shaped. Fruit a narrow, somewhat flattened, oval capsule. RTW

Ruellia strepens

ACANTHACEAE | **limestone wild petunia**

May–Oct, 1–3 ft. Erect perennial of floodplain forests, alluvial swamps, and riverbanks in the Mountains and Piedmont, as well as calcareous forests and seepage swamps in the Coastal Plain. Stems slightly 4-angled, occasionally branched, smooth to minutely hairy. Leaves petiolate, oval, 4 in. long, thin-textured. Flowers 1–several in middle and upper leaf axils, nearly sessile, pale blue-violet, about 2 in. long, tubular and trumpet-shaped, with 5 broad, spreading corolla lobes that are prominently creased and 5 shorter, slightly hairy, lance-shaped calyx lobes. Each flower/cluster is subtended by 2 oval leafy bracts. Fruit a narrow, somewhat flattened, oval capsule. BAS

Vinca minor

APOCYNACEAE | **common periwinkle**

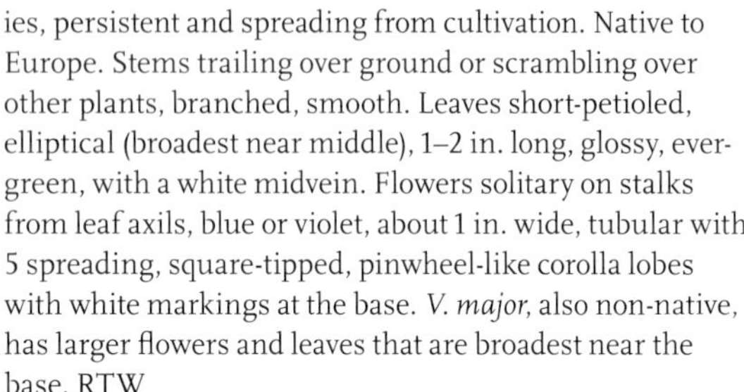

Apr–Jun, 4–8 in. Trailing, colonial perennial found in disturbed areas, especially around old house sites and cemeteries, persistent and spreading from cultivation. Native to Europe. Stems trailing over ground or scrambling over other plants, branched, smooth. Leaves short-petioled, elliptical (broadest near middle), 1–2 in. long, glossy, evergreen, with a white midvein. Flowers solitary on stalks from leaf axils, blue or violet, about 1 in. wide, tubular with 5 spreading, square-tipped, pinwheel-like corolla lobes with white markings at the base. *V. major*, also non-native, has larger flowers and leaves that are broadest near the base. RTW

Gentiana autumnalis

GENTIANACEAE | **pinebarren gentian**

Sep–Jan, 6–24 in. Erect perennial of longleaf pine savannas, pine flatwoods, sandhills, and pine barrens in a variety of sites from moist to very dry; in se VA, NC, and SC nearly always associated with *Pinus palustris* and/or *Aristida stricta*. Stem smooth, rarely branched. Leaves few, linear to narrowly oblong-lance-shaped, 2–3 in. long, and curved parallel to ground. Flowers solitary (rarely 2–3) and terminal, deep blue and spotted/streaked with bronze-green inside, to 2 in. long, funnel-shaped, with the corolla tube divided into 4–5 spreading lobes with pleats in between. Fruit an elliptical capsule. WS

Gentiana catesbaei

GENTIANACEAE | **Coastal Plain gentian**

Sep–Nov, 1–2 ft. Erect perennial found in pocosins, moist longleaf pine savanna edges, edges of moist hardwood forests, and bluff seepages. Stems unbranched, slightly rough, hairy. Leaves sessile, elliptical to lance-shaped, to 3 in. long, with minutely rough-hairy margins. Flowers essentially sessile in dense clusters of 1–9 at top of stem and in upper leaf axils; each flower blue to blue-violet (with darker stripes, inside and out), about 1½ in. long, tubular and vase-shaped, opening to 4–5 ascending, rounded or short-triangular lobes, which are connected to each other with fringed pleats. Fruit an elliptical capsule. WS

Gentiana decora

GENTIANACEAE | **Appalachian gentian**

Sep–Oct, 11–25 in. Erect perennial of dry and dry-moist, acidic forests, especially mixed oak, oak/heath, and northern red oak forests. Stems ridged, unbranched, densely hairy (especially on ridges). Leaves in 6–8 pairs below inflorescence, sessile to short-petioled, elliptical to oval, to 4 in. long. Flowers 2–12 in a leafy, compact, terminal cluster; each flower white streaked with blue or purple, 1–2 in. long, tubular, the corolla split into 5 lobes at the opening and surrounded by a shorter, cup-shaped calyx tube, which is densely hairy and split into 5 linear, pointed lobes. Fruit an elliptical capsule. AMC

Gentiana saponaria

GENTIANACEAE | **soapwort gentian**

Sep–Nov, 8–24 in. Erect, sometimes sprawling, perennial of bogs, marshes, wet hardwood forests, and other moist to wet habitats. Stems unbranched, smooth or minutely rough. Leaves sessile, elliptical, to 3½ in. long, with prominent center vein, glossy, and sometimes minutely rough-hairy. Flowers sessile in a leafy, compact terminal cluster (additional small clusters may be in upper leaf axils); each flower purplish-blue, 1–2 in. long, tubular and bottle-shaped, with the 5 short lobes at the corolla tip typically closed. A green, cup-shaped calyx with 5 lance-shaped lobes surrounds the base of each flower. Fruit an elliptical capsule. AMC

Gentiana villosa

GENTIANACEAE | **striped gentian**

Aug–Nov, 8–22 in. Erect, sometimes clumped perennial of upland forests and sandhill-pocosin ecotones. Stems 1–several from a single crown, unbranched, smooth. Leaves sessile to short-petioled, elliptical to oblong-lance-shaped, to 4 in. long, glossy and smooth. Flowers 2–several in leafy, compact terminal cluster, greenish- or yellowish-white striped or tinged with purple, 1–2 in. long, tubular, with 5 triangular lobes that are erect or closed over the opening. A green, cup-shaped calyx with 5 irregular, linear lobes surrounds the base of each flower. Fruit an elliptical to oblong capsule. WS

Gentianella quinquefolia

GENTIANACEAE | **Appalachian gentianella**

Aug–Oct, 6–20 in. Erect annual/biennial of dry to semi-moist forests, woodlands, clearings, meadows; often over mafic or calcareous rock at lower elevations but tolerant of a range of soil chemistries at higher elevations. Stems simple or sparingly branched, wing-angled. Leaves in pairs at 90° to each other, sessile to clasping, oval, to 3 in. long, with 4–5 conspicuous parallel veins. Flowers stiffly erect in terminal and axillary clusters, violet-blue or lilac (occasionally greenish-white) with fine purple veins, ¾ in. long, tubular, the corolla with 5 triangular lobes (usually closed and forming a point) surrounded by a short green calyx tube with 5 slender teeth. JF

Phlox divaricata

POLEMONIACEAE | **eastern blue phlox**

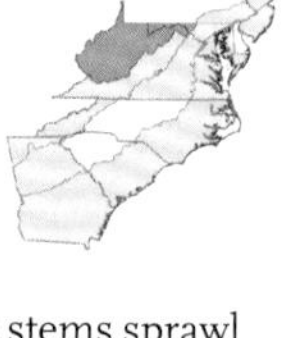

Apr–Jun, to 20 in. Erect to reclining perennial of moist deciduous forests in circumneutral soils. Stems unbranched, hairy, often glandular-sticky; nonflowering stems sprawl on ground and root at nodes. Leaves sessile, narrowly lance-shaped to oval, 1–2 in. long, sparsely hairy, wth small stiff marginal hairs. Flowers fragrant, in a loose, flattish terminal cluster, pale blue to lavender or red-purple, with a darker eye, ¾–1 in. wide, the 5 semi-spoon-shaped lobes flaring outward from a hairless, narrow tube. The calyx consists of 5 glandular-hairy, purplish, very narrow sepals; 5 stamens are hidden inside the corolla tube. Fruit an oval capsule. RTW

Verbena brasiliensis

VERBENACEAE | **Brazilian vervain**

May–Oct, to 8 ft. Erect annual/perennial of roadsides, old fields, clearings, and other disturbed areas. Native to South America. Stems solitary or several from the base, sharply 4-angled and grooved, rough-hairy on the angles. Leaves sessile or short-petioled, elliptical, 1½–4 in. long, sharply toothed, with bristly veins beneath. Flowers in compact, cylindrical spikes to 2 in. long, arranged in a wide-branching terminal cluster; each flower bluish-purple to pink, tiny, with a hairy tube opening to 5 ascending, minute lobes. The slightly shorter calyx is also hairy. BAS

Verbena hastata

VERBENACEAE | **common vervain**

Jun–Oct, 1½–5 ft. Erect perennial of fens, marshes, bogs, meadows, calcareous spring marshes, riverbanks, and low fields. Stems 4-sided and grooved, rough-hairy. Leaves petiolate, lance-shaped or narrowly oval, sometimes with lobes at the base, 1½–7 in. long, coarsely to doubly toothed, rough-hairy. Flowers in dense, elongate-pointy, erect spikes at ends of branches of a candelabra-like terminal cluster, lower flowers blooming first; each flower blue to violet, less than ¼ in. wide, tubular, opening to 5 spreading, minute lobes. TLJ

Verbena officinalis

VERBENACEAE | **European vervain**

Jun–Oct, 8–45 in. Erect to ascending perennial of disturbed areas and riverbanks. Native to Europe. Stems 4-angled, branched, mostly smooth. Leaves petiolate (grooved), oval to oblong-oval, ¾–2½ in. long, 1–2 times pinnately lobed, with wavy or toothed margins, rough-hairy. Flowers in very narrow, long (to 7½ in.), erect spikes in a wide-branching terminal cluster, the rachis with stalked glands; each flower blue or purple to lilac to white, tubular, opening into 5 spreading, notched lobes, the corolla twice as long as the calyx. JG

Limonium carolinianum

PLUMBAGINACEAE | **Carolina sea-lavender**

Aug–Oct, 8–28 in. Erect perennial found in tidal marshes, especially on salt flats. Stems wide-branched and smooth. Leaves in a basal rosette, petiolate, broadly oval to spoon-shaped, 2–12 in. long, with a prominent midvein, leathery-fleshy, and smooth. Flowers along 1 side of each of the stiffly forking branches, creating a fanlike effect; each flower lavender-blue to pink, ¼ in. long, with 5 overlapping, rounded petals and a reddish, 5-lobed calyx. JED

Ipomoea hederacea

CONVOLVULACEAE | **ivyleaf morning-glory**

Jul–Dec, to 6 ft. long. Herbaceous annual vine of fields, roadsides, gardens, and other disturbed areas. Stems twining and hairy. Leaves on light green to dull red petioles, heart-shaped and deeply indented at the base, or deeply 3-lobed with rounded sinuses and pointed lobes, to 5 in. long, and sparsely hairy. Flowers in clusters of 1–3, sky-blue quickly changing to rose-purple and with a white throat, 1–2 in. wide, the corolla tubular and funnel-shaped and the calyx with densely hairy sepals abruptly tapering to 5 linear tips. Fruit a nearly round capsule. Each flower is open for only a few hours, from morning to early afternoon. RTW

Polemonium reptans

POLEMONIACEAE | **spreading Jacob's-ladder**

Apr–Jun, 6–18 in. Erect to spreading, semi-colonial perennial of moist, rich forests. Stems clustered or tufted, often leaning, branched, smooth to slightly hairy. Leaves on petioles that are U-shaped in cross-section, to 8 in. long, pinnately divided into 5–17 narrowly elliptical to oval or oblong leaflets (each ¾–1¼ in. long), the pairs well spaced. Flowers in an open-branching terminal cluster, nodding, blue to purplish, ⅔ in. wide, bell-shaped, with 5 rounded petals, a short-tubular calyx (sometimes reddish) with 5 triangular teeth, 5 stamens with white anthers, and a pistil with slender white style split into 3 at its tip. Fruit a 3-celled, oval capsule. WS

Solanum dulcamara

SOLANACEAE | **climbing nightshade**

May–Nov, 2–8 ft. long. Clambering perennial vine of disturbed habitats, sometimes of natural areas. Native to Europe. Stems sprawling or climbing, branched, purple and slightly hairy when young, becoming brown and woody with age. Stem and leaves have a strong odor when bruised. Leaves on minutely winged petioles, arrowhead-shaped with 2 basal lobes, to nearly 4 in. long, mostly smooth. Flowers in a few drooping clusters of 6–20 from stems or axils of leaves, purple or violet, with petals bent backward and away from a central "cone" of united stamens. Fruit a shiny, oval berry that starts out green and turns scarlet when ripe. ER

Phacelia bipinnatifida

HYDROPHYLLACEAE | **fernleaf phacelia**

Apr–May, 1–2 ft. Erect biennial of moist, hardwood forests, especially rich cove forests, boulderfield forests, and moist cliffs and outcrops in those areas. Stems branched, especially above, and covered with gland-tipped hairs. Leaves on glandular-hairy petioles, broadly triangular to oval in outline, to 3 in. long, pinnately divided into 3–7 toothed segments and hairy on both surfaces. Flowers on hairy stalks in branching terminal clusters, lavender-blue with a white throat, about ½ in. wide, the short bell-shaped corolla spreading into 5 broadly rounded lobes. Fruit a tiny, round capsule. RTW

Phacelia dubia

HYDROPHYLLACEAE | **smallflower phacelia**

Apr–May, 8–16 in. Erect to spreading annual of floodplain forests, rocky forests, fields, roadsides, granitic flatrocks. Stems simple or branched, a mix of rough-hairy and glandular-hairy. Basal leaves petiolate, simple or resembling the divided stem leaves; stem leaves alternate, the uppermost sessile, smaller, pinnately divided into 1–5 pairs of lance-shaped to oval segments, the terminal segment 3-lobed. Flowers in loose, branching terminal clusters of 5–15; each pale blue to white, ¼ in. wide, the corolla bowl-shaped, the 5 spreading, round lobes with fuzzy back surfaces; 5 hairy stamens with purple anthers are visible. Fruit a tiny capsule. BAS

Passiflora incarnata

PASSIFLORACEAE | **purple passionflower**

May–Aug, to 12 ft. Herbaceous perennial vine of roadsides, fencerows, thickets, fields. Erect, trailing, or climbing by tightly coiled tendrils. Leaves petiolate, palmately 3-lobed (rarely 5-lobed), 2½ to 8 in. long, toothed, thick, leathery, smooth or with short, soft hairs beneath. Flowers solitary (rarely 2) on short axillary stalks, 2½ in. wide, showy, complex: 5 oblong sepals with hornlike extensions, green outside, white inside; 5 sepal-like petals, except white or purplish and lacking horns; a "crown" of purple and white thread-like segments; and a central stalk supporting 5 stamens and a fleshy, green, 3-parted style. Fruit a yellowish-green, oval berry. RTW

Camassia scilloides

AGAVACEAE | **eastern camas lily**

Apr–May, 1–2 ft. Scapose perennial from a bulb, growing in moist, open forests, sometimes on slopes and natural levees, usually over circumneutral soils. Stem a naked flowering stalk. Leaves in a basal clump, straplike, 10–18 in. long. Flowers in a terminal raceme 5–7 in. long, light lavender to blue, to 1 in. wide, with 6 linear-elliptical tepals with 3 veins, 6 prominent yellow stamens, and a green ovary with style. Fruit a 3-sectioned, round capsule containing shiny black seeds. Native Americans and early settlers used the bulbs of this plant for food. RTW

Muscari neglectum

HYACINTHACEAE | **grape-hyacinth**

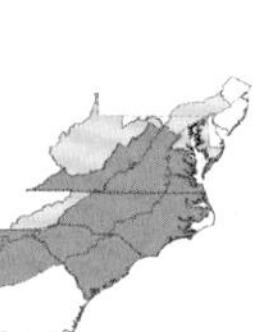

Mar–May, 2–9 in. Bulbous perennial, cultivated as an ornamental and persistent and naturalized in lawns, old fields, suburban woodlands, and disturbed areas. Native to Eurasia. Stem a smooth flowering scape arising from a rosette of leaves. Leaves basal, linear, nearly round in cross-section, 4–10 in. long. Flowers in a dense, oval-conical raceme at top of scape, resembling a cluster of grapes; each flower nodding, blue to violet (rarely white), 1⁄4 in. long or less, tubular and urn-shaped, with minute, white curved lobes at the opening. JWH

Iris cristata

IRIDACEAE | **dwarf crested iris**

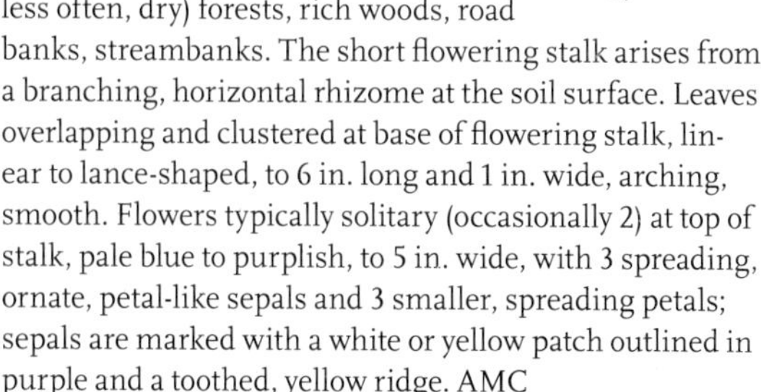

Apr–May, 4–6 in. Low-growing, rhizomatous, colonial perennial of moist (and less often, dry) forests, rich woods, road banks, streambanks. The short flowering stalk arises from a branching, horizontal rhizome at the soil surface. Leaves overlapping and clustered at base of flowering stalk, linear to lance-shaped, to 6 in. long and 1 in. wide, arching, smooth. Flowers typically solitary (occasionally 2) at top of stalk, pale blue to purplish, to 5 in. wide, with 3 spreading, ornate, petal-like sepals and 3 smaller, spreading petals; sepals are marked with a white or yellow patch outlined in purple and a toothed, yellow ridge. AMC

Iris germanica

IRIDACEAE | **fleur-de-lys**

Apr–May, 2–3 ft. Erect, rhizomatous perennial of roadsides, old home sites, and ditches; cultivated and rarely persistent or escaped. Native to Europe. The stiff flowering stalk, branching once or twice above the middle, arises from a branching, tuberous, horizontal rhizome at soil surface. Leaves mostly basal, in 2 ranks, linear-lance-shaped, to 2 ft. long, light green and smooth. Flowers about 6, produced on the flowering stalk from nodes underlain by bracts; each flower pale purple to purple-lilac or whitish, with 3 ornate, yellow- to brown-veined, drooping, petal-like sepals with white bases and yellow beards, and 3 simpler, erect petals. TLJ

Iris verna

IRIDACEAE | **Coastal Plain dwarf iris**

Mar–May, 3–6 in. Low-growing, rhizomatous perennial found in coastal longleaf pine sandhills and dry rocky-sandy woodlands and roadsides. Stems consist of creeping rhizomes, not usually visible at the soil surface, from which a few leaves and a flowering stalk emerge. Leaves overlapping, linear and sheathing, to 4 in. long and 1/3 in. wide or less, stiff and smooth; often emerging after flowers. Flowers 1–2 at top of short, stiff stalk; bluish to violet; with 3 spreading-drooping, petal-like sepals marked down the middle with a bold, bumpy, yellow stripe with white edges, and 3 erect, spoon-shaped, unmarked petals. Fruit a 3-angled, elliptical to oblong capsule. RTW

Sisyrinchium angustifolium

IRIDACEAE | **narrowleaf blue-eyed-grass**

Mar–Jun, 8–12 in. Erect, tufted perennial of moist to dry woodlands, upland forests, floodplain forests, meadows, sandhill swales. Stem flattened and narrowly winged, flexible and sometimes leaning, smooth, the base lacking fibrous remains of old leaves. Leaves mostly basal, overlapping, linear and grasslike, to 14 in. long and less than 1/8 in. wide. Flowers (just a few) in a single small cluster at top of scape, blue (occasionally white), less than 1/2 in. wide, consisting of 6 spreading tepals with rounded or notched tips and a tiny toothlike extension. Yellow markings at the base of each tepal create a yellow center in the blue “star.” Fruit a round capsule. JF

Sisyrinchium atlanticum

IRIDACEAE | **Atlantic blue-eyed-grass**

Mar–Jun, 8–18 in. Erect, tufted perennial of dry, sandy or rocky woodlands, clearings, roadsides, and dunes; occasionally in damp, open habitats. Stem flattened and narrowly winged, branching and sometimes bending at 1–2 nodes, smooth, the base lacking fibrous remains of old leaves. Leaves mostly basal, overlapping, linear and grasslike, to 14 in. long, firm and pale bluish-green. Flowers (usually 2) in a single small cluster at top of scape, blue-violet, 1/2–3/4 in. wide, consisting of 6 spreading tepals with rounded or notched tips and a tiny toothlike extension. Yellow markings at the base of each tepal create a yellow center in the blue "star." Fruit a round capsule. AMC

Sisyrinchium mucronatum

IRIDACEAE | **needle-tip blue-eyed-grass**

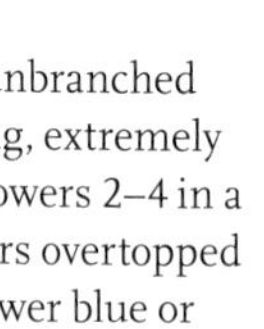

Apr–Jun, 4–16 in. Erect, tufted perennial of dry forests, dry rocky woodlands, clearings, and fields. Stems slender and wiry, scarcely winged as in other sisyrinchiums, unbranched and smooth. Leaves mostly basal, overlapping, extremely narrow-linear and grasslike, 4–8 in. long. Flowers 2–4 in a single small cluster at top of scape, the flowers overtopped by a short, erect, sharp-tipped bract; each flower blue or violet, 1/2–3/4 in. wide, consisting of 6 spreading tepals with rounded tips and a tiny toothlike extension. Yellow markings at the base of each tepal create a yellow center in the blue "star." Fruit a round capsule. BAS

Sisyrinchium nashii

IRIDACEAE | **Nash's blue-eyed grass**

Apr–Jun, 8–19 in. Erect, tufted perennial of dryish woodlands and forests. Stem flattened and narrowly winged, few-branched, dull green, and with smooth margins; tufts of old, dried leaves remain at the base. Leaves mostly basal, overlapping, linear and grasslike, to 12 in. long, dull green, and with smooth margins. Flowers (just a few) in a single, small cluster at top of scape; each flower blue to purple, 1/2–1 in. wide, consisting of 6 spreading tepals with rounded or notched tips and a tiny toothlike extension. Yellow markings at the base of each tepal create a yellow center in the blue "star." Fruit a tan to beige, roundish capsule. JG

Hepatica americana

RANUNCULACEAE | **round-lobed hepatica**

Feb–May, 2–7 in. Low-growing, stemless perennial of moist to dry upland forests, rocky woodlands, well-drained flood-plain forests. Leaves petiolate, kidney-shaped, to 2¾ in. long and 4 in. wide, divided into 3 broadly rounded lobes, leathery, usually variegated (2-tone green or green and purple-brown), emerging densely hairy, becoming smooth and turning bronze in late summer and persisting into winter. Flowers solitary on hairy scapes, blue-lavender (occasionally white), nearly 1 in. wide, with 5–12 petal-like sepals surrounding a green, conical, compound ovary and bushy stamens; 3 green, oval, hairy bracts sit just below flower. Fruit a cluster of tiny, beaked achenes. WS

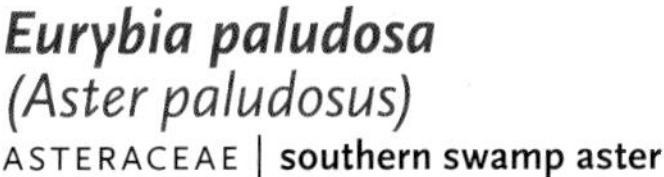

Eurybia paludosa
(Aster paludosus)

ASTERACEAE | **southern swamp aster**

Jul–Oct, 1–2½ ft. Weakly erect perennial of wet pine savannas and sandhill seeps. Stem branched above, sometimes tinged red, mostly smooth. Leaves basal (usually withering by flowering) and alternate, linear to narrowly lance-shaped, to 12 in. long (stem leaves smaller), with hardened margins. Flower heads in a relatively flat-topped, branching terminal cluster; heads 1–1¼ in. wide, with violet- to lavender-blue, very narrow ray florets encircling a yellow center disk composed of tubular florets. Slightly recurved and minutely hairy bracts surround the base of each head. AMC

Ionactis linariifolia
(Aster linariifolius)

ASTERACEAE | **stiff-leaved aster**

Jul–Nov, 1–1½ ft. Erect perennial of dry savannas, sandhills, flatwoods, prairielike openings, glades, barrens, rock outcrops, road banks. Stems few to many forming dense tussocks, greenish-yellow to reddish, hairy. Leaves alternate (appearing whorled), sessile, linear, to 1½ in. long, stiffly spreading, shiny dark green above, paler below, rough-hairy. Flower heads 1–many on short branches near top of stem; heads 1 in. wide, with 7–20 violet ray florets encircling a center disk of yellow tubular florets. Several series of green and white bracts surround the cylindrical base of each head. BAS

Symphyotrichum concolor

ASTERACEAE | **eastern silvery aster**

Sep–Oct, 1½–4 ft. Erect to ascending perennial of dry longleaf pine sandhills, Piedmont woodlands, forest edges, road banks. Stems 1–several, often leaning on other plants, unbranched, silky-hairy. Leaves crowded, sessile, elliptical, ½–1½ in. long (reduced above), covered with silvery-silky close-pressed hairs. Flower heads in a narrow panicle or cylindrical raceme to about 8 in. long; heads about 1 in. wide, with 8–18 blue to violet (rarely pink) narrow ray florets encircling a center disk of many yellow tubular florets. Several series of hairy, green-tipped bracts closely surround the bell-shaped to cylindrical base of each head. Fruit a tiny, white-tufted achene. WS

Symphyotrichum grandiflorum

ASTERACEAE | **big-headed aster**

Sep–Nov, 2–3 ft. Erect, rhizomatous, colonial perennial of dry woodlands, forest edges, road banks, powerline rights-of-way. Stem stiff, hairy, branched, with 30+ nodes below the inflorescence. Leaves sessile with heart-shaped clasping base, lance-shaped to oblong or linear, ⅓–2½ in. long (reduced above), rough-hairy; lower leaves wither early. Flower heads in a terminal panicle; heads 1–1¼ in. wide, with 20–30 narrow, violet ray florets encircling a center disk of 25–35 yellow (becoming reddish-purple) tubular florets. Several series of spreading or reflexed, spoon- to oblong-lance-shaped bracts surround the bell-shaped base of each head. Fruit a tan-tufted achene. EO

Symphyotrichum patens

ASTERACEAE | **late purple aster**

Aug–Nov, 1–3 ft. Erect to sprawling, rhizomatous, colonial perennial of dry upland forests, clearings, road banks. Stems slender, hairy, unbranched, with 12–30 leaf nodes below the inflorescence. Leaves with a heart-shaped clasping base, oval or lance-shaped, 1–6 in. long (reduced above); lower leaves wither early. Flower heads solitary at ends of branchlets; heads 1–1½ in. wide, with 15–25 blue to violet or purple, narrow ray florets encircling a center disk of yellow (turning reddish) tubular florets. Several series of glandular-sticky, oblong bracts with green and spreading tips surround the top- to bell-shaped base of each head. Fruit a tan-tufted achene. BAS

Symphyotrichum walteri

ASTERACEAE | **Walter's aster**

Oct–Dec, 1–3 ft. Erect to sprawling, rhizomatous, colonial perennial of savannas, sandhills, pine flatwoods. Stems 1–several, branched, smooth to slightly hairy. Leaves sessile-clasping, spreading or turned down at the tip, oblong-lance-shaped to triangular, to 1¼ in. long (reduced to bracts above and on branches); lower leaves wither early. Flower heads in a diffuse panicle; heads about ½ in. wide, with 11–26 pale bluish-purple, narrow ray florets encircling a center disk of yellow tubular florets. Several series of oblong-lance-shaped, pointy bracts, whitish with a diamond-shaped green patch, surround the bell-shaped base of each head. Fruit a tan-tufted achene. BAS

Eryngium aquaticum

APIACEAE | **marsh eryngo**

Jul–Sep, 1–4 ft. Coarse, erect aquatic perennial/biennial of freshwater or brackish tidal marshes. Stems thick, longitudinally ridged, branched above, whitish-green. Leaves petiolate, linear to lance-shaped, 4–8 in. long, sometimes finely toothed (upper leaves smaller and more toothed or spiny-lobed), with notably netted veins. Flowers in dense, compact, thimble-shaped heads surrounded by a whorl of large, spiny-toothed bracts; flowers pale blue, tiny and tubular with 5 petals, 5 stamens, and a divided style. JP

Eryngium integrifolium

APIACEAE | **savanna eryngo**

Aug–Oct, 1–2 ft. Erect perennial of savannas, pine flatwoods, seepages, and other moist, nutrient-poor places. Stems branched above, smooth. Leaves subsessile, oval to lance-shaped, 1–2¾ in. long, coarsely toothed; upper leaves smaller, nearly linear and sometimes weakly lobed. Flowers in compact, thimble-shaped heads less than ½ in. wide and resting on a whorl of stiff, spiny bracts; flowers greenish-blue to blue (white in bud), less than ¼ in. wide, tubular, with 5 tiny lobes, long blue stamens, and a divided style. BAS

Erigeron pulchellus

ASTERACEAE | **Robin's-plantain**

Apr–Jun, 1½–2 ft. Erect, stoloniferous perennial of moist slopes, coves, limestone bluffs, moist to dry woodlands and clearings, trail margins, road banks. Stems hollow and soft, unbranched, covered with spreading hairs. Basal leaves in a rosette, spoon-shaped, 2–6 in. long, with scalloped to bluntly toothed margins and hairy; stem leaves sparse, alternate, sessile-clasping, oval to lance-shaped, shorter. Flower heads daisylike, 1–12 at top of stem; heads to 1½ in. wide, with 50–100 pale violet, threadlike ray florets encircling a yellow center disk of tiny, tubular florets. Several whorls of hairy, narrow, pointed green bracts surround the base of each head. JF

Eurybia macrophylla

ASTERACEAE | **big-leaved aster**

Jul–Oct, 1–3½ ft. Erect, rhizomatous, colonial perennial of moist to dryish forests, mostly at mid to high elevations, particularly in red oak forests on ridge tops. Stems unbranched or sparingly branched, rough-hairy or smooth. Leaves basal and alternate, on winged petioles (stem leaves sessile), oval with heart-shaped base, to 12 in. long (much reduced above), toothed, rough above, smooth or hairy beneath; basal leaves wither by flowering. Flower heads in branched, terminal clusters; heads about 1¼ in. wide, with 9–20 narrow, pale violet to white ray florets encircling a center disk of pale yellow (turning dark red with age) tubular florets. BAS

Symphyotrichum novi-belgii

ASTERACEAE | **New York aster**

Aug–Sep, 1–4 ft. Erect to sprawling, rhizomatous perennial of wet pine savannas, interdune swales, swamps, marshes. Stems 1–several, often reddish, sometimes hairy in lines. Leaves short-petioled to sessile, lance-shaped to elliptical or linear, 1½–6 in. long, with down-rolled margins and sharp to rounded teeth. Flower heads in a diffuse panicle; heads ¾–1¼ in. wide, with 20–50 blue-violet (rarely pink or white) ray florets encircling a center disk of yellow (turning reddish) tubular florets. Several series of oblong-lance-shaped to linear greenish bracts with spreading to recurved tips surround the bowl- to bell-shaped base of each head. Fruit an off-white-tufted achene. BAS

Symphyotrichum prenanthoides

ASTERACEAE | **zigzag aster**

Aug–Oct, 1–4 ft. Erect, rhizomatous, colonial perennial of moist upland forests, floodplain forests, road banks. Stems zigzagged between nodes, smooth below, finely hairy above. Leaves on winged petioles, clasping, lance-shaped, 2½–6 in. long, sharply toothed in the middle, rough to smooth above, smooth or loosely hairy along midrib beneath. Flower heads in a leafy-bracted terminal panicle; heads 1–1½ in. wide, with 20–35 pale blue or violet (rarely white), narrow ray florets encircling a center disk of yellow tubular florets. Several whorls of sharp-tipped bracts surround the bell-shaped base of each head, their tips recurved-spreading. Fruit a yellow-tufted achene. TOPO

Symphyotrichum puniceum

ASTERACEAE | **swamp aster**

Sep–Oct, 3–7 ft. Erect, rhizomatous perennial of bogs, seeps, ditches, wet meadows. Stems 1–several, stout, reddish-purple, smooth to densely spreading-hairy (particularly above). Leaves sessile-clasping, oblong to lance-shaped, 2–6½ in. long, entire to slightly toothed, rough and sometimes hairy above, smooth to slightly hairy beneath; lower leaves wither by flowering. Flower heads in a many-headed panicle; heads 1 in. wide, with 20–50 light violet-blue to purple (rarely white), narrow ray florets encircling a center disk of yellow to red tubular florets. 2 series of spreading to ascending (outer series looser), linear bracts surround the bell-shaped base of each head. GMP

Symphyotrichum undulatum

ASTERACEAE | **wavyleaf aster**

Aug–Nov, 2–5 ft. Erect to spreading-ascending, rhizomatous perennial of dry forests, woodlands, glades, road banks. Stems 1–several, stiff, densely hairy. Lower leaves on clasping winged petioles with a basal flare (upper leaves clasping without a petiole), oval to lance-oval, 1½–6 in. long, toothed or entire, rough above, downy beneath. Flower heads in a panicle (sometimes racemelike); heads ¾ in. wide, with 8–20 light blue or violet (rarely white), narrow ray florets and a center disk of yellow or reddish tubular florets. Several series of unequal bracts with (often) purple tips surround the bell-shaped base of each head. Fruit an achene with cream-colored tuft of hairs. CL

Conoclinium coelestinum (*Eupatorium coelestinum*)

ASTERACEAE | **blue mistflower**

Jul–Oct, 1–3 ft. Erect, rhizomatous, colonial perennial of floodplain forests, moist to wet meadows, old fields, and other moist to wet disturbed areas, especially ditches. Stems branched, sometimes red-tinged, very hairy. Leaves petiolate, oval to triangular, to 4 in. long, with 3 main veins from the base, thin, blunt-toothed, and hairy or smooth. Flower heads at ends of short branches, making a nearly flat terminal cluster (to 4 in. wide); heads blue to lavender and fuzzy-looking, the tiny tubular florets (about 1/4 in. long) with protruding style branches. BAS

Eryngium prostratum

APIACEAE | **creeping eryngo**

May–Nov, 2–3 in., to 16 in. long. Sprawling to weakly ascending, mat-forming perennial of floodplain forests, bogs, pond margins, moist ditches and lawns, other moist, open habitats. Definitely native southward, perhaps only recently spread to the northern parts of our area. Stems longitudinally ribbed, branched, rooting at nodes. Leaves long-petioled (lower leaves) to sessile (upper), oval to lance-shaped, to 2¾ in. long, sometimes 3-lobed and toothed, smooth. Flowers in dense, cylindrical heads on stalks from leaf axils, each head resting on 5–10 linear-oblong, drooping bracts; flowers blue, less than 1/4 in. wide, with 5 tiny petals and long, bluish-purple stamens. RTW

Cichorium intybus

ASTERACEAE | **chicory**

May–Nov, 1–3 ft. Erect perennial from a long taproot, found on roadsides, fencerows, vacant lots, and other disturbed areas. Native to Europe. Stems branched, hairy, exuding milky sap when broken. Basal leaves numerous, short-petioled to sessile, lance-shaped, 3–10 in. long, deeply divided into sharp segments; stem leaves few, alternate, partly clasping, smaller and undivided. Flower heads in small, nearly sessile clusters along upper stem and branches; heads 1–1½ in. wide, with 15–20 blue (rarely lavender) ray florets with small teeth at the tips (no disk florets). RTW

Cyanus segetum
(Centaurea cyanus)

ASTERACEAE | **bachelor's-buttons**

Apr–Sep, 1–3 ft. Erect annual of roadsides and other disturbed areas. Native to Mediterranean Europe. Stems slender, with long-ascending branches and covered with silky, white hairs. Leaves linear-grasslike, to 6 in. long, lower ones pinnately lobed, gray-hairy. Flower heads on tips of branches, blue (may be white, pink, or purple), to 2 in. wide, with 25–35 spreading, tubular disk florets that seem like petals (no ray florets), the largest toothed at the tip. Several series of green, purple-fringed bracts surround the bell-shaped base of the head. BAS

Lactuca biennis

ASTERACEAE | **tall blue lettuce**

Aug–Nov, 3–15 ft. Erect annual/biennial of pastures, roadsides, forest edges, thickets. Stems unbranched, often purple-tinged, smooth to sparsely hairy, oozing milky sap when broken. Leaves on winged petioles, lance- to arrowhead-shaped, 4–12 in. long, with several wide, coarsely toothed, pointy-tipped lobes; upper leaves smaller, sessile, less divided. All leaves smooth or with hairs on veins beneath. Flower heads in terminal cluster; heads nearly ½ in. wide, with 15–30 pale blue to whitish ray florets with squared-off, toothed tips. Tightly held, hairless, often purple-tipped bracts surround the cylindrical base of each head. Fruit a fluffy cluster of tufted achenes. BAS

Lactuca floridana

ASTERACEAE | **woodland lettuce**

Aug–Nov, 1½–6½ ft. Erect-ascending annual/biennial of well-drained floodplains, moist to semi-dry upland forests, thickets, clearings. Stems unbranched, purplish-green, smooth, oozing milky sap when broken. Leaves sessile-clasping above, petiolate below, lance-shaped to triangular, to 8 in. long, toothed or lobed (the terminal lobe usually triangular), smooth, with hairs on veins beneath. Flower heads in wide-branching terminal cluster; heads less than ½ in. wide, with 11–27 pale blue to lavender ray florets with squared-off, toothed tips. Narrow, purple-tipped bracts surround the cylindrical base of each head. Fruit a fluffy cluster of flattened, white-tufted achenes. AMC

Platanthera ciliaris
(Habenaria ciliaris)

ORCHIDACEAE | **orange fringed orchid**

Jul–Sep, 10–28 in. Erect perennial of sunny, moist sites in savannas, rights-of-way, meadows, pastures, and bogs. Stems unbranched, smooth. Leaves sessile-clasping, strongly ascending, lance-shaped, 2–12 in. long (reduced above) and folded lengthwise (keeled). Flowers 30–60 in a dense, cylindrical terminal raceme with leafy bracts, orange, about 1½ in. long, with 2 upper petals and a sepal forming a hood, 2 additional winglike sepals, and a deeply fringed lip petal bearing a mostly straight spur about 1 in. long. Fruit a semi-erect, elliptical capsule. RTW

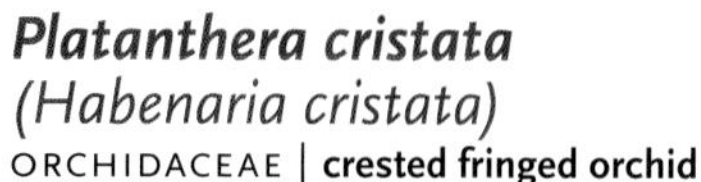

Platanthera cristata
(Habenaria cristata)

ORCHIDACEAE | **crested fringed orchid**

Jun–Sep, 8–18 in. Erect perennial of savannas, bogs, seepage slopes, and moist powerline clearings and roadsides. Stem unbranched, smooth. Leaves sessile, lance-shaped, 2–8 in. long (reduced above), with parallel veins and a central crease (keeled), smooth. Flowers in a dense, somewhat cone-shaped terminal raceme with leafy bracts, orange, with 2 upper petals and a sepal forming a hood, 2 additional winglike sepals, and a deeply fringed lip petal bearing a mostly straight spur no more than ½ in. long. Fruit a semi-erect, elliptical capsule. AMC

Polygala lutea

POLYGALACEAE | **orange milkwort**

Feb–Nov, 6–12 in. Erect-ascending biennial/short-lived perennial of wet savannas, ditches, bogs, boggy clearings, and other wet areas. Stems simple or few-branched, smooth. Leaves basal and alternate, spatula-shaped, to 2½ in. long, somewhat succulent and smooth. Flowers densely packed into erect, cylindrical terminal racemes; each flower bright orange (drying yellow), about ½ in. wide, with 2 oval pointy-tipped wings (sepals) and 3 joined petals forming a tiny tube with fringed tip. RTW

Impatiens capensis

BALSAMINACEAE | **orange jewelweed**

May–Nov, 3–5 ft. Erect to leaning annual of cove and other moist forests, bottomlands, streambanks, and bogs. Can occur in dense stands. Stems succulent-watery, branched above, glossy and smooth. Leaves petiolate, oval, to 5 in. long, with broadly toothed margins, soft grayish-green, with a hairless, water-repellent surface. Flowers dangle on individual slender stalks from leaf axils; each flower orange-yellow with reddish-brown spots, about 1 in. long, cornucopia-shaped, with a backward-pointing spur and 2 lips, the lower lip larger and split into 2 lobes. Fruit a fleshy green capsule that bursts open, flinging turquoise-colored seeds. BAS

Sesbania vesicaria (*Glottidium vesicarium*)

FABACEAE | **bagpod**

Jul–Sep, 6–10 ft. Shrubby, erect annual of marshes, ditches, and other disturbed wet areas. Stems with mostly horizontal branches, light green turning woody, and silky-hairy turning smooth. Leaves petiolate, 4–8 in. long and pinnately divided into 10–20 pairs of oblong leaflets with bluntly rounded ends bearing a short, pointy tooth. Flowers in drooping spikes 4 in. long from upper leaf axils, orange to yellowish, about 3/4 in. long, with typical pea-flower shape, the 2-lobed banner petal often with a sunburst pattern at the base. Fruit a flattened, usually 2-seeded pod with needlelike tip. RTW

Castilleja coccinea

OROBANCHACEAE | **eastern Indian-paintbrush**

Apr–Jun, 1–2 ft. Erect annual/biennial of woodlands, fens, barrens, rock outcrops, meadows, wet pastures, grassy openings, usually over mafic rocks. Stems unbranched, purple-tinged, hairy. Basal leaves linear or oblong-oval to elliptical, 1–3 in. long; stem leaves to 3 in. long, divided into 3–5 linear or oblong segments. Flowers in a dense terminal spike, with showy orange-red, hairy, 3- to 5-lobed bracts that are more prominent than the greenish-yellow flowers. The corolla is tubular with 2 lips, one much longer than the other and enclosing the stamens; the 2-lobed, tubular calyx may be reddish. Fruit an oblong, pointed capsule. Semi-parasitic on a variety of hosts. BAS

Papaver dubium

PAPAVERACEAE | **long-headed poppy**

Apr–Jul, 1–2 ft. Erect annual from a taproot, found in fields, roadsides, other disturbed areas. Native to Europe, sw Asia. Stems simple or branching, stiff-hairy, leaking milky sap when broken. Leaves basal and alternate, petiolate to sessile-clasping, oval to elliptic, 1½–3½ in. long, pinnately divided into toothed lobes, hairy. Flowers solitary at top of stem (may nod in bud but erect in bloom), orange-red and often darker in the center, 1½–2 in. wide, with 4 overlapping round petals, 2 sepals (these drop early), numerous stamens, and a large reddish-green ovary with 7–9 stigmas in a radiating array on its top. Fruit a green, ribbed, narrowly oval capsule that elongates and turns brown. JWH

Asclepias tuberosa

APOCYNACEAE | **butterfly milkweed**

May–Aug, 1–3 ft. Erect to ascending perennial of woodland margins, roadsides, pastures. Stems often several from a single woody taproot, mostly unbranched, sometimes reddish-purple-tinged, rough with stiff hairs. Leaves short-petioled, narrowly oblong to lance-shaped, to 4 in. long, hairy. Flowers in terminal and upper axillary compound umbels, orange or reddish-orange, about ½ in. long, consisting of 5 strongly reflexed corolla lobes and a central crown surrounding the fused anthers and style. Fruit an erect, narrowly spindle-shaped follicle containing tufted seeds. Sap is clear, not milky. Nectar-rich flowers attract many pollinators. BAS

Modiola caroliniana

MALVACEAE | **bristly-mallow**

Mar–Jul, to 2½ ft. Prostrate annual/biennial of lawns, roadsides, disturbed areas, and pondshores. Native to South America and probably adventive in our area. Stems sprawling, branched, often rooting at nodes, hairy. Leaves long-petioled, to 2¾ in. long, with 3–7 toothed lobes, slightly hairy. Flowers solitary on stalks arising from leaf axils, reddish-orange to purple-red, ⅓ in. wide, consisting of 5 oval petals around a center of 10–30 yellow stamens and red styles. Fruit a flat ring of 15–25 joined bristly, podlike, kidney-shaped segments. KB

Asclepias lanceolata

APOCYNACEAE | **few-flower milkweed**

Jun–Aug, 2–3 ft. Erect perennial of swamps, fresh to slightly brackish marshes, and wet pine savannas. Stem slender, unbranched, reddish-tinged, and smooth; leaks milky sap when bruised. Leaves short-petioled, linear to narrowly lance-shaped, 4–10 in. long, thick and firm, smooth; leak milky sap when bruised. Flowers in somewhat sparse terminal umbels, reddish-orange, about 3/4 in. long, consisting of 5 strongly reflexed corolla lobes and a lighter-colored central crown surrounding the fused anthers and style. Fruit an erect, narrowly spindle-shaped follicle containing tufted seeds. RTW

Lysimachia arvensis (*Anagallis arvensis*)

PRIMULACEAE | **common pimpernel**

Apr–Nov, 4–12 in. Ascending-sprawling annual of fields, roadsides, and many other disturbed areas. Native to Europe. Stems generally 4-angled, wide-branched, smooth. Leaves sessile, crowded, oval, 1/4–1 in. long. Flowers solitary on long, thin stalks from upper leaf axils, orange (occasionally blue), 1/4 in. wide, consisting of 5 spreading, oval-round petals with reddish-purple bases and 5 reddish-purple stamens (with yellow anthers) surrounding the ovary. Flowers close in overcast weather. AMC

Lilium catesbaei

LILIACEAE | **pine lily**

Jun–Sep, 1–3 ft. Erect perennial from a bulb found in moist pine savannas and sandhill seeps. Stems unbranched, smooth. Leaves alternate (some basal leaves may be present), sessile, pressed against stem, narrowly elliptic, 1–3 in. long (reduced above), smooth. Flowers solitary (occasionally 2) and erect at top of stem, 3–4 in. wide, orange-red to red-purple, with purple-spotted yellow patches at the base of each of 6 recurved-drooping, long-pointed, clawed tepals; 6 long yellow-red stamens and an erect pistil sit in the flower center. Fruit an erect, oval capsule. WS

Lilium canadense

LILIACEAE | **Canada lily**

Jun–Jul, 2–6 ft. Erect perennial from a bulb, found in wet meadows, clearings, coves, and seepages. Stems unbranched, smooth. Leaves in 6–11 whorls of 4–15 leaves each (a few alternate leaves may be present), linear-elliptical to lance-shaped, sessile, 3–7 in. long, rough with minute spines on margins and the veins beneath. Flowers 5 or more, nodding on long stalks branching from top of stem, orange-red to yellow with purple-brown spots within, trumpet-shaped and consisting of 6 recurved tepals, 6 stamens with red anthers, and a central pistil. Fruit an erect, oval, 3-celled capsule. AMC

Lilium grayi

LILIACEAE | **Gray's lily**

Jun–Jul, 2–5 ft. Erect perennial from a bulb, found in bogs, seepages, grassy balds, moist forests, and wet meadows, at mid to high elevations. A rare Southern Appalachian endemic. Stems unbranched, smooth. Leaves in 3–8 whorls of 3–11 leaves each, sessile, elliptical to lance-shaped, 1–5 in. long, rough on the margins and veins beneath. Flowers 1–9 on long stalks branching off from top of stem, slightly nodding to perpendicular to stem, deep red-orange, spotted with purple and lighter red within (becoming yellow at the throat), trumpet-shaped, to 2 in. long, consisting of 6 very slightly recurved tepals. Fruit an erect, oval capsule. WS

Lilium michauxii

LILIACEAE | **Carolina lily**

Jul–Aug, 1½–3½ ft. Erect perennial from a bulb, found in dry upland forests on ridges and slopes. Stems unbranched, smooth. Leaves in 1–4 whorls of 3–15 leaves each (a few alternate leaves), sessile, oblong-oval or oblong-lance-shaped, to 4½ in. long (reduced above), fleshy-thick, pale beneath, smooth. Flowers 1–4 nodding on long stalks arising from top of stem, orange, trumpet-shaped, with 6 strongly recurved tepals, which are yellow and maroon-spotted toward the base. 6 dangling stamens with rust-colored anthers cluster around the pistil. Fruit an oval capsule. Flowers strongly fragrant. RTW

Lilium philadelphicum

LILIACEAE | **wood lily**

Jun–Jul, 1–3 ft. Erect perennial from a bulb, found in grassy balds, moist to wet meadows (especially in thin soils over rock), open woodlands. Stems unbranched, smooth. Leaves in 3–6 whorls of 4–9 leaves each (a few alternate leaves), sessile, lance-shaped, 1–4 in. long, smooth but rough-margined. Flowers 1–5 erect on terminal stalks, red-orange (sometimes yellow) with basal maroon spots, 1½–3 in. wide, trumpet shaped, consisting of 6 spreading, lance-shaped tepals with generally pointed tip and tapering to a narrow base with rolled edges. In the center are 6 stamens with reddish-orange filaments and a reddish-orange style from a green ovary. Fruit a rounded capsule. RTW

Lilium pyrophilum

LILIACEAE | **sandhills bog lily**

Jul–Aug, 3–5 ft. Erect perennial from a bulb, found in peaty seepage bogs in the Sandhills region and peaty swamp margins in the upper Coastal Plain. Stems unbranched, smooth. Leaves in 1–12 whorls of 3–11 leaves each (with numerous scattered alternate leaves), sessile, ascending, narrowly elliptic, 1–4 in. long, densely rough-hairy on the margins and veins beneath. Flowers 1–7 nodding at tips of stalks arising from top of stem, red-orange to dusky red with a yellowish center and magenta spots, consisting of 6 lance-shaped, strongly recurved tepals with narrowed bases but no claws, and 6 dangling rust-red stamens and a pistil. Fruit an oval capsule. BAS

Lilium superbum

LILIACEAE | **Turk's-cap lily**

Jul–Aug, 3–7 ft. Erect perennial from a bulb, found in cove forests, moist ravines, blackwater stream swamps, Coastal Plain bogs. Stems unbranched, smooth. Leaves in 6–24 whorls of 3–8 (or more) leaves each (some alternate too), sessile, lance-shaped to narrowly elliptic, to 10 in. long, smooth. Flowers 3–30 (or more) in a pyramidal terminal raceme, dangling from long stalks; each flower yellow-orange to reddish with many brown-purple spots, 3–5 in. wide, consisting of 6 strongly recurved, lance-shaped tepals with green nectaries at their base and 6 stamens with rust-colored anthers. Fruit an oval capsule. RTW

Hemerocallis fulva

HEMEROCALLIDACEAE | **orange daylily**

May–Jul, 1½–5 ft. Weakly erect, colonial perennial of old homesites, streambanks, suburban woodlands, lawns, waste places. Native to Asia, frequently escapes cultivation to semi-natural habitats. Flowering scape usually splits into 2 near top. Leaves in basal cluster, linear, to 3 ft. long (1 in. wide) and arching, smooth; a few smaller, bractlike leaves are on the scape. Flowers in a fork-branched, terminal raceme, orange to yellow or reddish (yellow throat), to 6 in. wide, funnel-shaped, consisting of 6 recurved, long and narrow tepals whose edges are crimped. 6 stamens and a short stigma are visible in the flower throat. Does not fruit in our area. BAS

Iris domestica

IRIDACEAE | **blackberry-lily**

Jun–Aug, 1–3 ft. Erect-ascending, rhizomatous perennial of dry woodlands, edges of granitic flatrocks, suburban areas. Native to e Asia. Stems branched near top. Leaves mostly basal, overlapping in a fan-shaped arrangement, with clasping bases and a white-waxy coating, 1–2 ft. long; smaller bractlike leaves are scattered on flowering scape. Flowers terminal in groups of 3–6, each group originating from a modified leaf (spathe) about ½ in. long; flowers orange to orange-yellow mottled with red or purple, to 2 in. wide, with 6 elliptical to oblong tepals that spread from the top of a green ovary. Fruit an oval capsule, splitting to reveal a cluster of shiny black seeds. KB

Pilosella aurantiaca

ASTERACEAE | **orange hawkweed**

May–Aug, 5–18 in. Erect, stoloniferous perennial of pastures, roadsides, other open, disturbed sites. Native to Europe. Stem a flowering stalk from a basal rosette (1–2 small alternate leaves on the stem), densely covered with black-glandular hairs, especially the upper stem. Basal leaves petiolate, oblong-lance-shaped to narrowly elliptic, 2–6 in. long, long-hairy, exuding a milky sap when broken. Flower heads 5–20 in a compact, terminal cluster; heads about ¾ in. wide and consisting of numerous deep orange ray florets (yellow toward center of head) with squared-off, 5-toothed tips. Linear bracts covered with glandular, black hairs surround the base of each head. BAS

Gaillardia pulchella

ASTERACEAE | **blanket-flower**

Apr–Dec, 1–2 ft. Bushy annual/short-lived perennial of dunes, sandy flats behind dunes, and roadsides on barrier islands. Stems much-branched, hairy, becoming woody late in the season. Leaves linear to spoon-shaped, to 3 in. long, fleshy, often toothed or lobed, gray-green, and hairy. Flower heads daisylike on stalks, about 2½ in. wide, consisting of 8–14 orange and yellow, 3-toothed ray florets encircling a center disk of small, red, tubular florets. The flowers attract butterflies. BAS

Dactylorhiza viridis

ORCHIDACEAE | **frog orchid**

Apr–Jun, 4–20 in. Erect perennial of moist woods and seepage swamps. Stem unbranched, smooth. Native across Eurasia and NoAm, from AK to NC; one of the widest global distributions of any orchid. Leaves sessile, oval, 2–5 in. long and smooth; becoming smaller, lance-shaped, and sharper-tipped up the stem. Flowers in spikelike terminal raceme, each resting on a narrow, green bract that is longer than the flower; flowers green (sometimes purple-tinged), ¼–½ in. wide, with hoodlike petals and sepals and a long, dangling, notched lower lip petal. Fruit an erect, ribbed, oval capsule. JF

Epipactis helleborine

ORCHIDACEAE | **broadleaf helleborine**

Jun–Sep, 10–30 in. Erect perennial of moist and dry-moist forests. Native to Europe, increasingly common in se Canada and ne U.S. Stem unbranched, light green, short-hairy. Leaves sessile-clasping, oval to lance-elliptic, 1½–6 in. long, smooth, with prominent parallel veins. Flowers 3–50 in spikelike terminal raceme, pale yellowish-green to pink, ½–¾ in. wide, consisting of a lower lip petal forming a bowl with constriction near the tip (often purplish-brown on the inside), 2 broadly oval lateral petals that flare outward above a yellowish center column, and 3 light green sepals with purplish streaks forming a triangle behind the flower. Fruit a ribbed, elliptical capsule. AMC

Habenaria repens

ORCHIDACEAE | **floating orchid**

Apr–Nov, 4–20 in. Erect perennial of blackwater swamps, pools, and banks of creeks and rivers, often found in floating mats of vegetation. Stems unbranched, leafy and smooth. Leaves sessile-clasping, lance-shaped, to 10 in. long (reduced above), with prominent parallel veins, thick and fleshy. Flowers in a crowded, spikelike terminal raceme, each with a leaflike bract; flowers green, about ½ in. wide, with 3 sepals and 3 petals that are divided into very narrow segments, making the bloom resemble a spider; a slender spur curves below each flower. At night flowers emit a strong vanilla fragrance that attracts moth pollinators. FG

Malaxis unifolia

ORCHIDACEAE | **green adder's-mouth**

Jun–Aug, 1–20 in. Erect perennial, often rooted in moss, of bogs and moist forested slopes; in the Sandhills, in longleaf pine/oak-hickory forests. Native from Labrador and Newfoundland to Mexico; uncommon within its extremely wide range. Stem with thickened base, unbranched, smooth. Leaves usually 1, sessile-clasping, oval, to 4 in. long, with parallel veins, glossy, and smooth. Flowers (to 50) in a terminal raceme, most densely clustered toward the top, green, less than 1⁄4 in. wide, consisting of 3 tiny, narrow sepals and 2 recurved, linear, lateral petals plus a triangular, fork-tipped lip petal. AMC

Platanthera flava (*Habenaria flava*)

ORCHIDACEAE | **southern rein orchid**

Mar–Sep, 6–24 in. Erect perennial of shaded wet places, such as swampy forests. Stem unbranched, smooth. Leaves 2–3, sessile-sheathing, lance-shaped, 2–8 in. long (reduced to bracts above), with parallel veins and smooth. Flowers 10–40 in a narrow, spikelike terminal raceme, with a linear, sharp-tipped bract below each flower; flowers yellowish-green, 1⁄4 in. wide, with 2 upper petals and a sepal forming a hood, 2 lateral winglike sepals, and a lip petal with a distinct bump near its base; there is also a club-shaped spur. Fruit a semi-erect, elliptical capsule. AMC

Cubelium concolor (*Hybanthus concolor*)

VIOLACEAE | **green-violet**

Apr–Jun, 1–3 ft. Erect perennial of very nutrient-rich and moist forests, especially over calcareous substrates. Stems solitary or clustered, from a crown of fibrous roots, smooth (may be hairy above). Leaves present throughout stem, petiolate, elliptical to oval-oblong, 3½–7 in. long, veiny and hairy or smooth. Flowers in groups of 1–3, dangling on short stalks from axils of midstem leaves, green, about 1⁄4 in. long, with 5 small petals with upturned tips and 5 narrow, arching sepals. Closed, self-pollinating flowers also are present. BAS

Listera smallii

ORCHIDACEAE | **Appalachian twayblade**

Jun–Jul, 3–8 in. A Central/Southern Appalachian endemic of shaded swamps and wet slopes, nearly always beneath *Rhododendron maximum*. Stem unbranched, green to reddish-purple, smooth below (hairy in inflorescence). Leaves usually 2, sessile, broadly oval, ¾–1¼ in. long, with parallel venation, dark green (sometimes bronze), smooth. Flowers 3–15 in a terminal raceme, the raceme stem and individual flower stalks glandular-hairy; each flower green to greenish-bronze, to ¼ in. long, consisting of 3 tiny sepals and 2 similar upper petals, all recurved, and a spreading, triangular lower lip petal that is divided into 2 bluntish, toothed lobes. Fruit an oval capsule. AMC

Tillandsia usneoides

BROMELIACEAE | **Spanish moss**

Apr–Jun, to 10 ft. Perennial with inconspicuous flowers, growing in cascading masses in branches of trees, especially in swamps, and elsewhere where humidity is high enough. Stems silvery-gray, stringlike, covered with gray scales. Leaves linear and curling, to 1½ in. long, mostly indistinguishable from stems. Flowers solitary on short stems from leaf axils, green to yellowish-green, about ⅓ in. long, tubular but with 3 spreading, oblong-lance-shaped petals. Fruit a tan, 3-lobed capsule containing plumed seeds. Not parasitic; uses tree as support and absorbs water and some nutrients from air but also photosynthesizes. AMC

Croomia pauciflora

STEMONACEAE | **smallflower croomia**

Apr–May, 6–12 in. Erect, often colonial perennial of moist bluff forests, often growing with American beech (*Fagus grandifolia*) and American basswood (*Tilia americana*). Stems somewhat fleshy, smooth. Leaves alternate but appearing whorled because they are clustered atop the stem, petiolate, broadly oval, 4–7 in. long, with prominent parallel veins. Flowers in small stalked clusters arising from leaf axils and hanging down below leaves, yellowish-green (may be purple-tinged), about ⅓ in. wide, with 4 spreading, lance-shaped tepals and 4 thick, erect, reddish-maroon anthers closely pressed to the green ovary. Fruit a roundish capsule. BAS, FG

Ludwigia palustris

ONAGRACEAE | **common water-purslane**

May–Nov, 3–12 in. Sprawling, mat-forming perennial of moist to wet disturbed areas; plants seem to float in shallow water. Stems somewhat succulent, reddish, smooth to slightly hairy, rooting at nodes. Leaves on winged petioles, oval to elliptical with a blunt tip, to 1½ in. long, often reddish-green, smooth. Flowers borne in the leaf axils, whitish-green, tiny, lacking petals but with 4 triangular sepals and 4 noticeable white-tipped stamens above a cube-shaped, 4-angled ovary. Fruit a tiny pale green, cube-shaped capsule with darker green stripes on the angles and persistent sepals at the top. BAS

Chrysosplenium americanum

SAXIFRAGACEAE | **golden saxifrage**

Mar–Jun, 2–12 in. Creeping, mat-forming perennial found in shaded, rocky, gravelly, or mossy seeps and seepage swamps. Stems forking and creeping, with some reddish tint. Leaves mostly opposite, short-petioled, round to widely oval, to ½ in. long, shallowly lobed or toothed. Flowers mostly solitary at ends of branches or in upper leaf axils, inconspicuous, yellowish-green with a ring of 4 or 8 red anthers. Fruit a tiny, 2-lobed capsule. AMC

Frasera caroliniensis

GENTIANACEAE | **American columbo**

May–Jul, 3–9 ft. Infrequently seen perennial of rich forests over mafic or calcareous rocks, upper slopes of cove forests, floodplain forests. Basal rosette only for 5–15 years, finally produces a flowering stalk, then dies. Flowering stem unbranched, stout, smooth. Basal leaves oblong-elliptical, 14 in. long, 4 in. wide; stem leaves in whorls of 4–5 (reduced above). Flowers many in a narrowly pyramidal panicle, greenish-white with purple specks, ¾–1¼ in. wide, with 4(5) spreading oblong-lance-shaped petals, 4(5) linear-lance sepals, 4(5) spreading stamens, and an ovary with a single style. On the lower middle of each petal is a conspicuous fringed, green nectar pad. RTW

Asclepias connivens

APOCYNACEAE | **largeflower milkweed**

Jul–Aug, 1–3 ft. Erect, often leaning perennial of wet pine flatwoods. Stem stout, unbranched, hairy; leaks milky sap when bruised. Leaves mostly sessile, oblong to narrowly lance-shaped, to 2¾ in. long, somewhat white-waxy, and slightly hairy. Flowers in small terminal and upper axillary umbels, greenish-white, about ¾ in. long and more rounded-looking than flowers of other milkweeds, with 5 strongly reflexed corolla lobes (greenish) and 5 "hoods" (greenish-white) that arch over the fused anthers and style. Fruit a follicle containing tufted seeds. FG

Asclepias exaltata

APOCYNACEAE | **poke milkweed**

Jun–Jul, 2–6 ft. Erect perennial of moist forests, forest margins, roadsides. Stem light green to purplish, unbranched, mostly smooth; leaks milky sap when bruised. Leaves petiolate, broadly oval to lance-oval, 3–8 in. long, thin-textured, smooth (midrib beneath may be hairy). Flowers on long, drooping stalks in terminal umbel and several upper axillary umbels; each flower green and pink, ¼ in. wide, ½ in. long, with 5 strongly reflexed green or pale purple corolla lobes and a central crown surrounding the fused anthers and style. Fruit an erect, spindle-shaped follicle containing tufted seeds. The nectar attracts many butterflies, and the plant hosts Monarch larvae. RTW

Asclepias tomentosa

APOCYNACEAE | **sandhills milkweed**

May–Jun, 7–19 in. Erect to ascending perennial of longleaf pine sandhills, turkey oak barrens, and clearings. Stems stiff, unbranched, and velvety-hairy; leak milky sap when bruised. Leaves petiolate, lance-shaped to broadly elliptical, 2–3½ in. long, with wavy margins, covered with velvety (short) hairs. Flowers in 2–6 umbels from upper leaf axils, pale green to yellowish-green, 1½–2 in. wide, consisting of 5 spreading corolla lobes with pink-tinged upcurved tips and a central crown surrounding the fused anthers and style. Fruit a follicle containing tufted seeds. AMC

Asclepias viridiflora

APOCYNACEAE | **green milkweed**

May–Aug, to 2½ ft. Erect to ascending perennial of open woodlands, woodland edges, barrens and glades, especially over mafic or calcareous rocks. Stem solitary, unbranched; leaks milky sap when bruised. Leaves rounded to lance-shaped, 4 in. long, 1¾ in. wide, leathery, with a white midvein and wavy margins, thinly hairy beneath. Flowers in several dense (15–30 flowers), rounded, nodding umbels on short stalks from upper leaf axils; each pale green (yellowish-green to purplish with age), ½ in. long, with 5 strongly reflexed corolla lobes, 5 erect "hoods," and a central column of fused anthers and style. Fruit a cylindric-linear follicle containing tawny-tufted seeds. AMC

Gonolobus suberosus

APOCYNACEAE | **eastern anglepod**

Jun–Aug, climbs to 15 ft. Herbaceous perennial vine of moist to wet forests and thickets on floodplains and streambanks, as well as occasionally in moist upland forests. Stems twining over other plants, branched, hairy; may be reddish. Leaves petiolate, spade-shaped with notched base, 2½–6 in. long, dark green and crinkly, minutely hairy. Flowers in small axillary clusters of 3–9, the buds notably cone-shaped; each flower green to yellowish with a purple center, consisting of 5 stiff-spreading, waxy, lance-shaped corolla lobes and a complex, fleshy "crown" structure in the center. Fruit a stiff, oval pod with sharp-angled edges. BAS

Paronychia canadensis

CARYOPHYLLACEAE | **Canada whitlow-wort**

Jun–Oct, 3–16 in. Erect, bushy-branched annual of dry rocky woods and shale barrens. Stems with finely forked branches, smooth. Leaves short-petioled, elliptical to oval with blunt tips, ¼–1 in. long, covered with dark glandular dots. Flowers 1–2 and sessile in the axils of leaflike bracts, greenish-white, tiny, cup-shaped, consisting of 5 petal-like sepals with a green to brownish midvein and whitish edges, 5 stamens, and 2 short styles. Fruit a reddish-brown, rounded capsule with persistent sepals. GPF

Scleranthus annuus

CARYOPHYLLACEAE | **annual knawel**

Mar–Oct, 2–8 in. Erect to spreading annual/biennial of fields, ditches, roadsides, and other disturbed areas. Native to Europe. Stems branched and with fine, short hairs. Leaves sessile, with membranous, fused bases, linear to awl-shaped, 1/4–3/4 in. long. Flowers in panicle-like terminal clusters, or solitary from leaf or branch axils; each flower greenish, less than 1/4 in. long, lacking petals and with 5 sharp, lance-shaped sepals. Fruit an oval, membranous bladder enclosed by a hardened, cuplike structure formed by the fusion of the sepals. BAS

Heuchera americana

SAXIFRAGACEAE | **American alumroot**

Apr–Aug, 6–10 in. Erect perennial of rocky forests and rock outcrops, particularly where soils are subacidic to circumneutral. Flowering stems arising from a basal rosette, unbranched, somewhat sticky-hairy. Leaves long-petioled, round to oval and notched at the base, 1–4 in. long, shallowly palmately divided into 5–9 variously sized, toothed lobes, thick-textured, often white-mottled; smooth or hairy. Flowers in a narrow, loose, terminal panicle, greenish-white to pink, 1/4 in. long or less, consisting of 5 tiny petals attached to a tiny, sticky-hairy cup-shaped calyx with minute segments. There are 5 protruding stamens. Fruit an oval capsule with 2 persistent styles. LADI

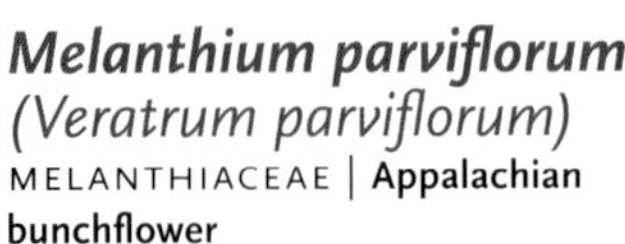

Melanthium parviflorum (*Veratrum parviflorum*)

MELANTHIACEAE | **Appalachian bunchflower**

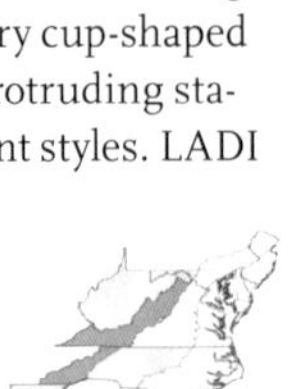

Jul–Sep, 1–5 ft. Erect perennial of moist (sometimes drier) hardwood forests, most frequent in oak forests at mid elevations. Stems mostly unbranched, hollow, thickened at the base, hairy. Basal leaves petiolate, elliptical to oblong-oval, 7–14 in. long, with prominent parallel veins, slightly pleated and smooth; stem leaves few, alternate, much reduced. Flowers in an open panicle, 8–30 in. long, green, about 1/2 in. wide, consisting of 6 spreading, oval to diamond-shaped, hairless tepals that taper at the base but are not truly clawed. Fruit a 3-lobed capsule with 3 persistent, beaklike styles. AMC

Veratrum viride

MELANTHIACEAE | **cornhusk lily**

Jun–Aug, 1–5 ft. Erect perennial from a short vertical rhizome arising from a bulb. Stems stout, unbranched, hollow, crowded with leaves, smooth. Leaves attached to stem with tubular sheaths, oval to elliptic, 6–11 in. long (reduced above), with prominent parallel veins and pleats. Flowers arranged in a pyramidal, freely branched panicle, the lowest branches subtended by leafy bracts; each flower yellowish-green, about ½ in. wide, consisting of 6 elliptic, spreading tepals with fringed margins. Fruit a short, oval 3-lobed capsule with persistent styles. Often observed as large patches of nonflowering plants. WS, BAS

Caulophyllum thalictroides

BERBERIDACEAE | **blue cohosh**

Apr–May, 1–3 ft. Erect perennial of rich, deciduous forests. Stem smooth with a blue-green tint and white-waxy coating. Leaves 1(2), petiolate, divided into many stalked, veiny, oval leaflets that are 1–3 in. long and irregularly toothed/lobed, blue-green, and with a waxy coating. Flowers in a branched terminal cluster, yellowish-green to brownish-green, ¼ in. wide, consisting of 6 sepals with nectar glands at the base (no real petals), 6 stamens, and a prominent ovary. Fruit a conspicuous pair of deep blue, fleshy seeds. RTW

Xanthium strumarium

ASTERACEAE | **cocklebur**

Jul–Nov, 1–6 ft. Erect to ascending annual of disturbed ground, roadsides, pastures, barnyards, and beaches. Stems thick and ridged, branched, often reddish or speckled with purple, smooth or with hairs pressed to stem. Leaves alternate (lowermost may be opposite), on long reddish-green petioles, triangular-oval to nearly round, 2–6 in. long, with 3–5 irregularly toothed lobes, slightly rough above. Flower heads in clusters of 2–4 in leaf axils; heads rounded to cylindrical and consisting of minute, greenish-white male or female disk florets interspersed with spines. Fruit a spiny, cylindrical bur. BAS

Artemisia ludoviciana

ASTERACEAE | **prairie sage**

Aug–Nov, 2–3 ft. Erect, rhizomatous, colony-forming perennial of dry roadsides, fields, other disturbed areas. Believed to be native to w NoAm, adventive in e NoAm. Stems stiff, branched above, gray-green, white-hairy (at least above). Leaves sessile, linear to lance-elliptic, 1–4 in. long, coarsely few-lobed or pinnately lobed, densely white-hairy (sometimes becoming smooth above with age), aromatic when crushed. Flower heads arranged in elongate terminal panicles and racemes; heads erect to nodding, whitish- to yellowish-green, less than 1/4 in. wide, each consisting of tightly clustered tiny tubular florets surrounded by a series of overlapping, gray-green bracts. RWS

Artemisia vulgaris

ASTERACEAE | **common mugwort**

Jul–Nov, 2–6 ft. Erect, rhizomatous, colony-forming perennial of roadsides, pastures, other disturbed areas. Native to Eurasia. Stems simple or branched above, often reddish-brown, smooth to slightly hairy. Leaves petiolate, broadly lance-shaped to oval or linear, 1–5 in. long, divided into irregular, lance-shaped segments, often with 1–2 small "earlobes" at the base, green above, white-woolly beneath, aromatic. Flower heads small and arranged in a large panicle of leafy spikes; heads whitish- to yellowish-green, less than 1/4 in. wide, each consisting of tightly clustered tiny disk florets surrounded by a series of narrow bracts. GPF

Ambrosia artemisiifolia

ASTERACEAE | **annual ragweed**

Aug–Nov, 1–6 ft. Erect, often bushy, taprooted annual of roadsides, gardens, disturbed ground, thin soils on rock outcrops. Stems simple to branched, sometimes reddish, smooth to rough-hairy. Leaves opposite below, alternate above, oval to elliptical, 1–4 in. long, 2 times divided into narrow, blunt-tipped lobes, gland-dotted, and with a pungent odor when crushed, smooth. Male flowers in small, green, nodding, cup-shaped heads arranged in spikes (1–4 in. long) at tips of branches; female flowers tiny, in round, green clusters in upper leaf axils, each cluster with 1–3 flowers surrounded by tiny bracts. Male flowers release large amounts of allergy-provoking pollen. BAS

Ambrosia trifida

ASTERACEAE | **giant ragweed**

Jul–Nov, 3–12 ft. Erect, taprooted annual of floodplains, moist pastures, and disturbed ground. Stems stout, freely branched, covered with white hairs. Leaves petiolate (often with wings), broadly oval to elliptical with long-pointy tips, 3–12 in. long, often palmately divided into 3–5 lobes, toothed, and rough-surfaced. Male flowers in tiny, nodding, saucer-shaped heads less than 1/4 in. wide and arranged in terminal spikes 3–6 in. long; female flowers tiny, in axils of upper, bractlike leaves. BAS

Amaranthus cannabinus

AMARANTHACEAE | **water-hemp**

Jul–Dec, 2–7 ft. Erect to reclining, fleshy annual found in salt, brackish, and freshwater tidal marshes, especially along the banks of tidal guts. Stems stout, branched, reddish below, ridged, smooth. Leaves petiolate, narrowly lance-shaped to linear, 2–6 in. long, smooth. Flowers in narrow spikes at top of stem and from upper leaf axils, green, less than 1/4 in. long, lacking petals and with 3 tiny bracts surrounding each flower; male and female flowers separate. Fruit a seed surrounded by a dark reddish-brown, wrinkled membrane. BAS

Amaranthus hybridus

AMARANTHACEAE | **green amaranth**

Jul–Oct, 2–6 ft. Erect annual of disturbed areas. Apparently native in e NoAm, but original distribution is obscured by its very weedy nature. Stems branching, reddish at least at base, scaly-hairy in inflorescence. Leaves long-petioled, oval to diamond-shaped, 1–5 in. long, hairy underneath. Flowers clustered in narrow spikes at top of plant and in leaf axils, green to purplish, minute, each with 3 long, spinelike bracts at the base. Fruit a dark brown seed surrounded by a wrinkled membrane. JG

Amaranthus pumilus

AMARANTHACEAE | **seabeach amaranth**

Jul–Nov, 4–10 in. Prostrate to ascending annual of sea beaches, foredunes, island end flats; rarely, sound-side beaches. Stems fleshy, branching from the base, reddish, smooth; larger plants may contain over 100 stems branching from the center, forming a mat of more than 3 ft. Leaves clustered toward ends of branches, petiolate, round to oval with decurrent base and shallow notch at the tip, ½–¾ in. long, fleshy, margins slightly wavy, smooth. Flowers in conspicuous clusters in leaf axils, reddish-green, minute, with yellow stamens in male flowers protruding at peak flowering. Fruit a shiny black seed surrounded by a dark, wrinkled membrane. MK

Amaranthus spinosus

AMARANTHACEAE | **spiny amaranth**

Jul–Oct, 3–4 ft. Erect to ascending weedy annual of fields, gardens, roadsides, barnyards, and pastures. Native to the Neotropics. Stems bushy-branched, ridged, reddish, and smooth. Leaves long-petioled, broadly oval, smooth, with 2 long spines at each leaf node. Flowers in separate clusters by sex: female in clusters in leaf axils, and male in elongated, nodding spikes at top of stem; each flower greenish-white, minute, consisting of 5 tepals and 3 shorter bracts. Fruit a blackish-brown seed surrounded by a membrane. BAS

Amaranthus viridis

AMARANTHACEAE | **slender amaranth**

Jun–Oct, 1–3 ft. Erect to ascending annual of disturbed areas. Native to South America. Stems often ridged and reddish, branched, smooth. Leaves petiolate, oval to diamond-shaped with rounded to pointed tip, 2–3 in. long, smooth. Flowers clustered along slender, usually branching terminal and upper axillary spikes that are often interrupted; flowers green tinged with red, less than ¼ in. long and consisting of 3 tiny tepals; male and female flowers separate. Fruit a faintly wrinkled, oval capsule partly enclosed in the persistent tepals. JG

Suaeda linearis

CHENOPODIACEAE | **southern sea-blite**

Aug–Dec, 6–36 in. Erect to ascending annual of island end flats, marsh edges, and brackish flats. Stems profusely branched, woody at the base, green or red and smooth. Leaves sessile, linear and sharp-pointed, 1/8–2 in. long, succulent, green or red, and smooth. Flowers in small clusters in the axils of a leafy spike to 5 in. long; each flower green, red, pink, or yellow and tiny, lacking petals but with 5 red or green, keeled sepals. Fruit an achene. GPF

Phyllanthus caroliniensis

PHYLLANTHACEAE | **Carolina leaf-flower**

Jul–Nov, 5–18 in. Erect-spreading annual of roadsides, moist woodlands, forests, fields, and seasonally wet, muddy places. Stems slender, with many long, arching-ascending branches; green to reddish and smooth. Leaves 2-ranked on the stem, short-petioled, elliptical to oval or oblong-oval, to 3/4 in. long, smooth. Flowers in clusters of 2–4 in leaf axils, greenish-white, about 1/8 in. wide, consisting of 6 calyx lobes (no petals) and a round ovary (female flower) or 3 stamens (male flower). Fruit a tiny, flattened-round, 3-celled capsule. PHA

Rumex crispus

POLYGONACEAE | **curly dock**

Mar–Jun, 1–5 ft. Erect biennial/perennial from a taproot, found in disturbed areas, such as pastures, fields, and roadsides. Native to Europe. Stems thick, branched above, often reddish, smooth. Leaves basal and alternate, petiolate with the stalk sheathing at base, lance-shaped, 2–12 in. long (stem leaves smaller), with undulating margins, and sometimes red-tinged. Flowers in whorled clusters on tall, narrow, branching racemes at top of plant; each flower yellowish-green to reddish, 1/4 in. long, consisting of 6 oval tepals, the 3 inner ones remaining attached to fruit. Fruit a tiny, brown achene enclosed in 3 papery, green or reddish, heart-shaped wings. BAS

Rumex obtusifolius

POLYGONACEAE | **bitter dock**

Apr–Aug, 2–3½ ft. Erect taprooted perennial of pastures, barnyards, disturbed areas. Native to Europe. Stem single, ribbed, branched in inflorescence, smooth. Basal leaves petiolate, oblong-oval, to 1 ft. long, wavy-margined; stem leaves lance-shaped, shorter. Flowers short-stalked in terminal cluster to 1 ft. long, in well-spaced whorls; flowers drooping, reddish-green, about ¼ in. long, consisting of 6 tepals (3 inner, 3 outer); male flowers have 6 stamens and dull yellow inner tepals; female (pistillate) flowers usually have reddish inner tepals. Fruit a tiny achene enclosed in 3 enlarged, triangular-oval tepals with 2–4 teeth on their margins. SJB

Parietaria pensylvanica

URTICACEAE | **rock pellitory**

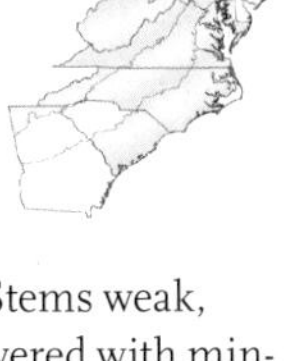

Apr–Oct, 4–16 in. Erect to ascending annual of calcareous shale barrens, rich floodplain soils, and thin soils at the base of calcareous or subcalcareous cliffs. Stems weak, 4-angled, simple or sparingly branched, covered with minute hairs. Leaves petiolate, elliptical to lance-shaped, to 3½ in. long, finely hairy. Flowers in small, sessile clusters in middle and upper leaf axils, each flower surrounded by several hairy, green, linear bracts; flowers either male, female, or perfect (male and female), and all may occur in a single cluster. All flowers with 4 green sepals and no petals; male flowers with 4 stamens and female with an ovary bearing a style. Fruit an oval achene. JG

Chenopodium album

CHENOPODIACEAE | **lamb's-quarters**

Jun–Nov, 1–10 ft. Erect annual of disturbed soils and gardens. Stems branching, with lengthwise grooves, bluish-green (sometimes with red or purple stripes), covered with fine, white, mealy powder. Leaves long-petioled, triangular or diamond- to lance-shaped, to 5 in. long, with margins irregularly toothed or lobed; younger leaves have white mealy coating. Flowers in small balls densely clustered along 1- to 7-in.-long spikes arising from axils of upper leaves; flowers mealy whitish-green, with 5 keeled and pointed sepals that largely cover the fruit at maturity. Fruit a smooth-surfaced achene. JG

Dysphania ambrosioides (*Chenopodium ambrosioides*)

CHENOPODIACEAE | **Mexican tea**

Aug–Nov, 1–4½ ft. Erect to ascending annual/short-lived perennial of gardens, fields, streambanks, roadsides, and other open, disturbed areas. Native to the Neotropics, possibly southern parts of NoAm. Stems angular or grooved, branching, sticky-hairy, with glandular resin dots. Leaves petiolate, lance-shaped, 1–3 in. long (reduced above), prominently toothed to entire, gland-dotted, and with a smell like kerosene. Flowers in dense axillary and terminal, leafy-bracted, ascending spikes; flowers green or reddish, tiny, closed, consisting of 3–5 sepals. Fruit a tiny, glossy, dark brown achene. GPF

Acalypha gracilens

EUPHORBIACEAE | **shortstalk copperleaf**

Jun–Nov, to 2½ ft. Erect annual of woodlands, prairies, and open, disturbed areas. Stems branched and very hairy. Leaves short-petioled, oval to oblong, to 2½ in. long, with 3 prominent veins, toothed, hairy on the margins, sparsely hairy above. Flowers clustered in spikes from upper leaf axils, yellowish-green, tiny, consisting of translucent sepals; male flowers at tip of each spike and fewer female flowers at the base, where there is a large, leafy bract with short, triangular, hairy-margined lobes bearing tiny, stalked glands. Fruit a tiny, hairy, 3-lobed capsule. JG

Acalypha ostryifolia

EUPHORBIACEAE | **pineland threeseed mercury**

Jun–Nov, 1–2½ ft. Erect annual of roadsides, fields, and disturbed alluvial soil. Stems branched, fuzzy to hairy. Leaves long-petioled, oval with heart-shaped base, to 4 in. long, finely toothed; petioles and blades somewhat hairy. Flowers in spikes from leaf axils (male) and terminating the stem (female); male flowers less than ¼ in. wide, consisting of 4 green to translucent white sepals and several white stamens; female flowers ¼ in. wide, consisting of several white, long, branching styles, a spiny, green ovary, and a surrounding floral bract with several narrow lobes. Fruit a softly prickly, 3-lobed capsule. KB

Acalypha rhomboidea

EUPHORBIACEAE | **rhombic copperleaf**

Jun–Nov, 6–24 in. Erect annual of floodplain forests, swamp hammocks, seasonally exposed bars and shores, alluvial clearings and fields, roadsides and other weedy, disturbed habitats. Stems usually simple, with lines of fine white hairs. Leaves long-petioled, oval to diamond- or lance-shaped, to 3½ in. long, with bluntly toothed margins and conspicuous pinnate venation. Flowers in axillary spikes with female flowers below and male above, though most are hidden by a surrounding green bract that is shallowly cut into 5–11 oblong to lance-shaped lobes bearing glandular hairs; flowers lack petals and sepals. Fruit a small, hairy, 3-lobed capsule. BAS

Acalypha virginica

EUPHORBIACEAE | **Virginia copperleaf**

Jun–Nov, 6–24 in. Erect annual of dry oak-hickory forests, woodlands, barrens, outcrops, clearings, riverside prairies, and weedy, disturbed habitats. Stems usually simple, occasionally red, densely hairy. Leaves long-petioled, elliptical to lance-shaped, to 3 in. long, with round-toothed margins, sparsely hairy. Flowers in axillary clusters, each resting on a leaflike bract; male flowers less than ¼ in. wide, consisting of a 4-lobed calyx, no petals, and several stamens; female flowers ¼ in. wide, consisting of insignificant sepals, no petals, and a 3-valved, round ovary with short divided styles. Fruit a tiny, hairy, 3-lobed capsule. GPF

Stillingia sylvatica

EUPHORBIACEAE | **queen's-delight**

May–Jul, 1–2½ ft. Erect to ascending perennial found in sandhills and (mostly) Coastal Plain dry woodlands. Stems often branched from the base, yellow-green, smooth. Leaves angled upward, short-petioled to sessile, elliptic, to 3½ in. long, finely toothed (each tooth with a tiny, red gland), glossy smooth. Flowers in a terminal spike, a few female flowers occupying the base and many male flowers above; flowers yellowish-green, with a round, cupped nectar gland to each side of each flower. Fruit a sessile, green, 3-lobed capsule. RTW

Fatoua villosa

MORACEAE | **crabweed**

Jul–Nov, ½–4 ft. Erect annual of disturbed areas, vegetable and flower gardens, landscaped areas around buildings. Native to Asia. Stems branched, light green, darkening with age, sometimes reddish-purple at base, with hooked hairs; exude oil-like odor when bruised. Leaves petiolate, triangular, with prominent veins, toothed and hairy. Flowers in sessile, feathery clusters about ¾ in. wide in leaf axils and resting on a small leaflike bract; flowers light green to purple but turning brown and minute. Fruit a cluster of tiny, oval achenes. RTW

Laportea canadensis

URTICACEAE | **Canada woodnettle**

May–Aug, 1–3½ ft. Erect perennial of moist, nutrient-rich forests and seepage swamps; especially abundant in cove forests in the Mountains and bottomlands in the Piedmont. Stems stout, covered with stinging hairs. Leaves long-petioled, oval and with long pointed tips, 2–6 in. long, with prominent veins, sharply toothed. Male and female flowers in separate branching clusters arising from leaf axils. Female flowers toward the top of the plant, with 4 tiny, greenish-white sepals; male flowers with 5 sepals (no petals). Fruit an achene containing a shiny black seed. BAS

Euphorbia ipecacuanhae

EUPHORBIACEAE | **Carolina ipecac**

Feb–Jun, 6–12 in. Reclining to ascending perennial of dry, barren sands in sandhills, woodlands, clearings, and other sandy sites. Stems several, with forked branches, smooth (rarely hairy), often reddish. Leaves sessile, linear to broadly oval with blunt bases, ½–2½ in. long, with smooth, often reddish margins, and fleshy. Flowers at ends of branches or axillary, appearing solitary but actually composed of a small, cuplike structure with yellowish-green, semi-circular lobes and containing minute male and female flowers and nectar glands. Fruit a rounded, 3-lobed capsule. BAS

Euphorbia dentata

EUPHORBIACEAE | **toothed spurge**

Jul–Oct, 9–24 in. Erect annual found in hedgerows, thickets, railroad cinders, disturbed areas. Native to w NoAm. Stems sparingly branched, short-hairy. Leaves opposite or alternate, crowded along upper stem, petiolate, lance- to diamond-shaped (verging on oval), ¾–3 in. long, coarsely toothed, sometimes red-spotted; exude milky sap when torn. Flowers in compact, flat-topped terminal clusters ¾–2 in. wide, each subtended by a few leaflike bracts that are white or pinkish-red tinged; clusters hold a mix of ripening fruits and the minute, yellowish-green cuplike structures containing female and male flowers, which lack petals and sepals. Fruit a rounded, 3-lobed capsule. KB

Boehmeria cylindrica

URTICACEAE | **false-nettle**

Jul–Aug, 2–5 ft. Erect perennial commonly seen in swamp forests, bottomlands, bogs, marshes, and ditches. Stems usually several in a clump arising from a woody crown, 4-angled or round, unbranched and light green, usually smooth, and definitely lacking stinging hairs. Leaves opposite, sometimes alternate, long-petioled, oval, to 4 in. long, with 3 noticeable veins, coarsely toothed. Flowers in ascending, dense spikes arising from leaf axils, each usually with a small leaf at the tip; male and female flowers often on separate spikes. Flowers green or greenish-white, minute, and in small, dense, ball-shaped heads. Fruit a small achene. BAS

Pilea pumila

URTICACEAE | **Canada clearweed**

Aug–Sep, 4–24 in. Erect annual found in swamp forests, bottomlands, freshwater marshes, tidal marshes, and disturbed wet ground. Stems succulent, sometimes slightly ribbed, pale green to reddish-green and nearly translucent, smooth; no stinging hairs. Leaves long-petioled, oval, ¾–4 in. long, with 3 prominent veins, coarsely toothed, smooth. Flowers in narrow, somewhat horizontal, 1-in.-long racemes from upper leaf axils; flowers greenish-white to greenish-yellow, less than ¼ in. wide, male and female flowers separate, female flowers with 3 sepals and 1 pistil, males with 4 sepals and 4 stamens. Fruit a straw-colored to green achene. LADI

Urtica gracilis

URTICACEAE | **American stinging nettle**

May–Jul, 2–7 ft. Erect perennial of bottomland forests and edges, particularly over limestone or mafic rocks. Stems stout, ridged, mostly unbranched, covered with stiff white hairs that can penetrate the skin and sting. Leaves slightly downward-drooping, on long petioles with a pair of linear stipules at the base, coarsely toothed, upper surfaces heavily veined and smooth, lower surfaces covered in stinging hairs. Flowers in longish, spreading or drooping, branched clusters from axils of middle and upper leaves; flowers whitish-green, less than 1/4 in. wide, consisting of 4 green sepals and 4 white stamens (male) or 4 green sepals and an ovary (female). GPF

Callitriche heterophylla

PLANTAGINACEAE | **common water-starwort**

Mar–Nov, 2–15 in. long. Tufted aquatic perennial of pools, impoundments, upland depression ponds, slow-moving streams, ditches. Stems slender and compressed, elongating in deep water, with parts floating at the surface. Submerged leaves linear, to 1 in. long, with 1 major vein; floating and upper leaves crowded into tufts, broadly spoon-shaped, with 3–5 major veins. Flowers 1–3, inconspicuous in leaf axils; each green, resting on 2 small bracts, lacking petals/sepals and with either a single stamen or single, 4-celled ovary. Flowers of *Callitriche* species can be pollinated by wind when above the water surface or by water when floating at the surface or even when submerged. JG

Thalictrum dioicum

RANUNCULACEAE | **early meadowrue**

Apr–May, 12–30 in. Erect perennial of seepages, shaded outcrops in moist to dryish forests, shell-marl ravines. Stems unbranched, smooth, waxy-coated. Leaves long-petioled, divided into 3 leaflets, which are again divided into 3–5 leaflets; ultimate leaflets round to kidney-shaped, round-lobed, drooping at flowering, pale to purplish green, smooth. Flowers in terminal and axillary panicles, male and female flowers on separate plants. Flowers 1/4 in. wide, males with straw-colored to purple sepals and dangling yellowish-green stamens, females with greenish-purple sepals and spreading, slender, purple stigmas. Fruit a cluster of 3–8 hook-beaked, elliptical achenes. BAS

Aphanes australis (*Alchemilla microcarpa*)

ROSACEAE | **parsley-piert**

Mar–May, 1–4 in. Prostrate to ascending annual of lawns, fields, pastures, and roadsides. Native to Europe. Stems simple or branching from the base, hairy. Leaves sessile to very short-petioled, ¾–3 in. long, round to fan-shaped, deeply palmately lobed and each segment deeply 3-toothed and furry. Flowers in sessile clusters of 3–7 in leaf axils, yellowish-green, tiny, consisting of 4 sepals (no petals). BE

Arisaema dracontium

ARACEAE | **green dragon**

May–Jun, 1–2 ft. Erect perennial of bottomlands and floodplains, occasionally found in uplands over mafic rocks. Leaf single, basal, on a long petiole (to 20 in.), forked and divided into 5–15 elliptical leaflets arranged on a semi-circular axis. Flowers in a yellowish-green, long-tipped spadix terminating a separate stalk and partially enclosed by a pale green, leaflike spathe; flowers minute, lacking petals and sepals. A plant may have all female, all male, or both kinds of flowers, in which case female flowers are lowest on the spadix. Fruit a cluster of orange-red berries in a conical head at tip of spadix. RG

Arisaema triphyllum

ARACEAE | **Jack-in-the-pulpit**

Mar–Apr, 1–2 ft. Erect, scapose perennial of moist hardwood forests and bottomlands. Flowering scape unbranched, smooth, separate from leaf stalks. Leaves 1–2, each divided into 3–5 oval or lance-shaped leaflets that are 2–7 in. long, whitish underneath, smooth and glossy. Flowers minute, sessile, and densely clustered on a green or yellow spadix, which is enclosed and hooded by an ornate white- or purple-striped green spathe; flowers lack petals and sepals, and a plant may have all female, all male, or both kinds of flowers (all-male plants tend to be smaller). Fruit a cluster of bright red berries in a conical head at tip of spadix. AMC, WS

Salicornia bigelovii

CHENOPODIACEAE | **dwarf glasswort**

Jul–Oct, 2–16 in. Erect annual of salt pannes in coastal marshes. Stems single or much-branched, green to red, succulent, narrower than flowering spikes. Leaves absent or minute, opposite, scaly or needlelike with a tiny, sharp tooth at the tip. Flowers in branched, erect, terminal spikes; minute and sunken or immersed in the thick, segmented spikes, whose segments are thicker than they are long. Fruit an achene. AMC

Salicornia virginica

CHENOPODIACEAE | **samphire**

Jul–Oct, to 15 in. Erect annual of salt pannes in coastal marshes. Stems single to much-branched (lower branches sometimes prostrate), succulent, narrower than flowering spikes, turning red to yellow or orange in autumn. Leaves below the flowering spikes, minute, scaly, and rounded-fleshy, lacking a sharp tip. Flowers in erect, branched terminal spikes; the flowers minute and sunken or immersed in the thick, segmented spike, whose segments are thicker than they are long. Fruit an achene. AMC

Brown Flowers

Endodeca serpentaria (*Aristolochia serpentaria*)

ARISTOLOCHIACEAE | **Virginia snakeroot**

May–Jun, 4–24 in. Rhizomatous perennial of dry to mesic forests; ranges into drier situations over base-rich substrates but may be more restricted to mesic situations over acidic substrate. Stems smooth to hairy, sometimes trailing. Leaves petiolate, narrowly lance-shaped to somewhat oval and the base lobed, suggestive of an arrowhead in shape, 2–6 in. long. Flowers solitary on a weak-stemmed lower branch, maroon-brown to greenish-purplish, ½–¾ in. long, tubular, with a sharp curve and a constriction below the flaring mouth, hairy. Roots have a strong turpentine odor when bruised. AMC

Listera australis (*Neottia bifolia*)

ORCHIDACEAE | **southern twayblade**

Feb–Jul, 3–8 in. Erect perennial of swamps, second terraces in floodplain forests, and borders of seeps. Stem unbranched, purplish, smooth below (hairy in inflorescence). Leaves usually 2, sessile, oval, ½–1¼ in. long, with parallel venation, dark green, and smooth. Flowers 5–25 in a terminal raceme, the raceme stem and individual flower stalks with short hairs; each flower purplish-brown to reddish-green, to ¼ in. long, consisting of 2 tiny sepals and 2 upper petals that are concave and recurved and an elongated lower lip petal forked into 2 linear lobes that taper to points. Fruit a slender, ovoid capsule. AMC

Liparis liliifolia

ORCHIDACEAE | **brown widelip orchid**

May–Jul, to 1 ft. Erect perennial, sometimes growing on other plants, of moist forests and floodplains. Stems stout, angled to almost winged, bright green, smooth. Leaves 2, oval with a blunt tip, to 7 in. long, with a prominent center fold, lightly fleshy, glossy, and smooth. Flowers 5–30 on slender purple stalks in a terminal raceme, opening from the bottom up; each flower about 1 in. wide, consisting of 3 spreading, greenish-white, linear sepals (about ½ in. long), 2 drooping, purple, needle-thin (about ½ in. long) lateral petals, and a protruding, purplish-brown, triangular-oval lip petal at the bottom. Fruit an elliptical capsule. AMC

Tipularia discolor

ORCHIDACEAE | **cranefly orchid**

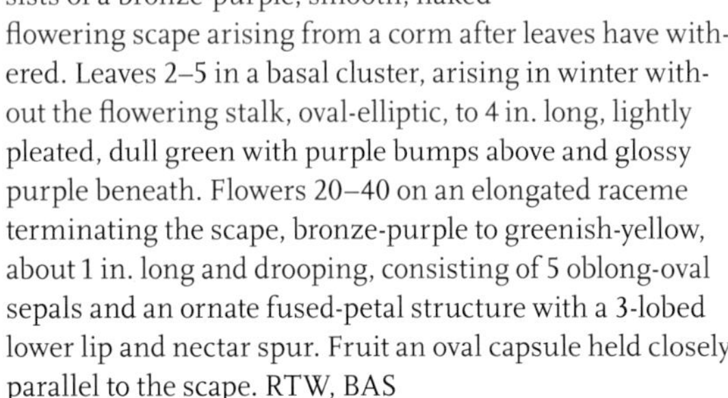

Jun–Sep, 4–20 in. Erect perennial found in moist to fairly dry forests. Stem consists of a bronze-purple, smooth, naked flowering scape arising from a corm after leaves have withered. Leaves 2–5 in a basal cluster, arising in winter without the flowering stalk, oval-elliptic, to 4 in. long, lightly pleated, dull green with purple bumps above and glossy purple beneath. Flowers 20–40 on an elongated raceme terminating the scape, bronze-purple to greenish-yellow, about 1 in. long and drooping, consisting of 5 oblong-oval sepals and an ornate fused-petal structure with a 3-lobed lower lip and nectar spur. Fruit an oval capsule held closely parallel to the scape. RTW, BAS

Apios americana

FABACEAE | **common groundnut**

Jun–Sep, to 12 ft. Twining herbaceous perennial vine found in marshes (tidal and non-tidal), wet thickets, bottomland forests, and along streambanks. Stems twining and climbing over other plants, smooth. Leaves petiolate, 4–8 in. long and divided into 5–7 oval to lance-shaped leaflets, each up to about 2 in. long and smooth. Typical pea flowers in dense, raceme-like clusters to 6 in. long from leaf axils; each flower maroon, about ½ in. wide, with a folded pinkish-brown banner petal, 2 maroon wing petals, and a twisted, maroon keel petal; fragrant. Fruit a green pod. A host plant for the Silver-spotted Skipper. BAS

Epifagus virginiana

OROBANCHACEAE | **beechdrops**

Aug–Nov, 4–18 in. Erect, clumped perennial lacking chlorophyll, found under beech trees (*Fagus grandifolia*) in moist to dry forests. Stems stiff, sometimes branched, cream or tan-colored (often with purple streaks), bearing small brownish scales rather than leaves. Stems darken with age and persist through winter. Flowers of 2 types tucked into the scales: closed budlike flowers on lower parts of the stem, and open tubular flowers with 4 short, flaring lobes in upper parts. Both are cream-colored, heavily streaked with purple-brown. Fruit (produced only by closed flowers) an oval capsule filled with minute seeds. An obligate parasite on beech tree roots. AWF

Asarum canadense

ARISTOLOCHIACEAE | **Canada wild ginger**

Apr–May, 2–8 in. Rhizomatous, creeping, stemless perennial of rich deciduous forests, usually on circumneutral soils. Leaves paired and on long furry petioles, heart-shaped with a deeply notched base, 2–6 in. long, thin-textured, downy-hairy. Flower solitary, borne on a hairy, stout stalk emerging from the base of the leaf petioles, maroon-brown-green, consisting of a fleshy tube with hairy inner surface and 3 flaring triangular-pointed lobes. The flower is usually hidden beneath the leaves, in the leaf litter. Fruit a fleshy capsule crowned by the persistent calyx. Leaves and stems emit a gingerlike aroma when torn or crushed. AMC

Hexastylis arifolia (*Asarum arifolium*)

ARISTOLOCHIACEAE | **arrowleaf heartleaf**

Mar–May, 2–6 in. Low-growing, stemless perennial from short, stout rhizomes; found in dry to moist deciduous forests, primarily in the Coastal Plain and Piedmont. Leaves on long petioles, triangular to arrowhead-shaped, to 8 in. long and 6 in. wide, often variegated, evergreen-leathery, and smooth; exude a spicy smell when torn. Flowers arise from the underground stem/rhizome on stalks so short, they are often hidden beneath leaf litter; they are dark brownish-purple inside, purplish or greenish outside, urn-shaped, with 3 short, spreading triangular-pointy lobes, and fleshy-firm. Fruit a round, fleshy capsule. BAS

Hexastylis heterophylla

ARISTOLOCHIACEAE | **variable-leafheartleaf**

Mar–May, 2–6 in. Low-growing, stemless perennial of slopes and bluffs in dry to moist forests, usually associated with *Kalmia latifolia*. A Southern Appalachian endemic. Leaves from a rhizome, long-petioled, triangular-heart-shaped, 1–4 in. long and wide, usually not variegated, evergreen-leathery, with a spicy smell when torn. Flowers from the rhizome, so short-stalked that they are often hidden beneath leaf litter; each dark red- or purplish-brown and reticulate-ridged inside, greenish or purplish outside, and fleshy-firm, weakly bell-shaped with 3 spreading-ascending triangular lobes, the lobes often mottled with white or green. Fruit a round, fleshy capsule. JF, BAS

Hexastylis minor

ARISTOLOCHIACEAE | **little heartleaf**

Feb–May, 3–6 in. Low-growing, stemless, rhizomatous perennial of upland or moist forests. Endemic to the Piedmont and adjacent Coastal Plain and mountains of VA, NC, and SC. Leaves long-petioled, heart- to kidney-shaped, 1½–3 in. long, variegated, evergreen-leathery, with a spicy smell when torn. Flowers on such short stalks that they are often hidden beneath leaf litter; each maroon-brown, ½ in. long, weakly bell-shaped, and prominently flared at or above the middle of the tube, with strongly spreading, widely triangular lobes (often white-mottled), firm-fleshy, and prominently ridged-reticulate within. Fruit a round, fleshy capsule. BAS

Hexastylis shuttleworthii (*Asarum shuttleworthii*)

ARISTOLOCHIACEAE | **largeflower heartleaf**

Apr–Jul, 4–8 in. Low-growing, stemless, rhizomatous perennial found on acidic soils in deciduous and deciduous-coniferous forests, often along creeks under *Rhododendron maximum*. A Southern Appalachian endemic. Leaves long-petioled, heart-shaped, to 4 in. long, usually lighter green along veins, firm and evergreen-glossy, releasing a spicy smell when torn. Flowers short-stalked, often hidden beneath leaf litter, solid maroon-brown on the outside, mottled maroon-brown inside, fleshy-firm, to 1½ in. long, tubular and cup-shaped, with 3 spreading, widely triangular lobes. Fruit a round, fleshy capsule. AMC

Hexastylis sorriei (*Asarum sorriei*)

ARISTOLOCHIACEAE | **sandhill heartleaf**

Mar–Apr, 3–6 in. Low-growing, stemless, rhizomatous perennial of seepage bogs and pocosins, typically in association with *Osmundastrum cinnamomeum*, *Sarracenia rubra*, and *Sphagnum* species. Leaves (2–8) petiolate, heart-shaped, variegated to not variegated. Flowers solitary, 2–4 per plant, maroon-brown but white to greenish-white at the base, less than 1 in. long, cylindric-tubular, with 3 triangular, somewhat spreading lobes, thin-fleshy, and longitudinally ridged and reticulated inside tube. Fruit a round, fleshy capsule. BAS

Hexastylis virginica (*Asarum virginicum*)

ARISTOLOCHIACEAE | **Virginia heartleaf**

Apr–Jun, 4–8 in. Low-growing, stemless, rhizomatous perennial of mesic to dry upland forests, usually found on extremely acidic soils. Leaves heart-shaped, 1–3 in. long, glossy-evergreen, usually variegated; they release a spicy smell when torn. Flowers on such short stalks that they are often hidden beneath leaf litter. They are mottled maroon-brown, tubular and urn-shaped, slightly flared toward the opening, with 3 widely triangular, erect to ascending lobes; within they are fleshy-firm and prominently reticulate-ridged. Fruit a round, fleshy capsule. AWF

Matelea carolinensis

APOCYNACEAE | **Carolina spinypod**

Apr–Jun, 4–5 ft. long. Herbaceous perennial vine found in moist to dry, nutrient-rich forests. Stems slender, climbing over other vegetation, hairy, leaking milky sap when broken. Leaves petiolate, widely heart-shaped with the basal lobes sometimes overlapping, 2–4 in. long, minutely hairy. Flowers in clusters of 5–10, on stalks from between leaf petiole pairs, brown-purple to maroon (rarely yellowish), about ¾ in. wide, consisting of 5 minutely hairy, widely spreading to slightly recurved, elliptic-oblong petals with rounded tips, and a central "crown" that encloses the reproductive structures. Fruit a spiny, oval to lance-shaped follicle. BAS

Agave virginica

AGAVACEAE | **eastern false-aloe**

May–Aug, 3–6 ft. Succulent perennial of dry woodlands over mafic or calcareous rocks, sandhill woodlands, dry road banks; also found in shallow soil associated with granite flatrocks, diabase glades, limestone and dolomite barrens and glades. Leaves ascending to widely spreading, straplike, to 20 in. long, somewhat folded longitudinally, succulent, pale green and sometimes purple-spotted. Flowers very fragrant, night-blooming, 10–60 in a spike at the top of a tall, thick stem rising from the center of the basal rosette, pale greenish-tan, about 1 in. long, tubular with 6 linear lobes and 6 purple-speckled stamens. Fruit a cylindrical, 3-lobed capsule. GMP, AMC

Brasenia schreberi

CABOMBACEAE | **water-shield**

Jun–Oct, held just above water. Aquatic perennial of lakes, ponds, sluggish streams, floodplain oxbow ponds, and beaver ponds. Stems usually submerged (occasionally floating), slender, reddish and coated with a thick layer of clear jelly. Leaves on stalk attached to center of blade, floating, elliptic, to 5 in. long and 3 in. wide, upper surface green, lower surface and stalk maroon-red and coated with layer of clear jelly. Flowers solitary, held above water surface on red stems, reddish-brown, about 1 in. wide, consisting of 6 recurved tepals, a cluster of erect, pinkish-purple stamens, and a pink ovary. BAS

Lechea minor

CISTACEAE | **thymeleaf pinweed**

Jul–Aug, 4–28 in. Erect to ascending perennial of savannas, sandhills, pine-oak woodlands, sandy, disturbed places. Stems from basal shoots of previous season; abundantly branched, hairy. Stem leaves alternate or opposite or whorled, sessile or short-petioled, oblong to narrowly lance-shaped, 1/4–1/2 in. long, smooth, short-hairy on margins and midrib beneath. Leaves on basal shoots opposite or whorled, oval or broadly elliptic, to 1/4 in. long; may be softly long-hairy. Flowers in compact clusters or short racemes, reddish-brown, the 3 petals mostly shorter than the enclosing minute calyx and rarely seen open. Fruit an erect, oval capsule protruding above enclosing sepals. BAS

Lechea mucronata

CISTACEAE | **hairy pinweed**

Jun–Aug, 8–36 in. Erect to ascending perennial of open dry habitats, sandhills, dunes, dry hammocks, and woodlands. Stem leaves alternate on upper branches and opposite or whorled below, petiolate, elliptic, 3/8–1 1/4 in. long, with sparse hairs above and long spreading hairs beneath. Leaves on basal shoots small and crowded, to 5/8 in. long, smooth above but with long, shaggy hairs on midvein and margins. Flowers densely clustered on short, ascending, axillary branches; each flower maroon-brown, minute, consisting of 3 tiny petals and 5 slightly longer green sepals, the inner 3 keeled (boat-shaped). Fruit a round capsule surrounded by persistent sepals. BAS

Lechea racemulosa

CISTACEAE | **Virginia pinweed**

Jun–Aug, 4–32 in. Erect perennial of dry pine woodlands, other woodlands, forest edges, and old fields. Stem leaves alternate to opposite, short-petioled to sessile, linear-lance-shaped, 1/4–3/4 in. long, smooth except for short hairs on margins and midrib beneath. Leaves on basal shoots often whorled and a little wider and shorter. Flowers in a loose panicle with ascending branches occupying the upper half of the plant, reddish-brown, tiny, consisting of 3 petals that are mostly concealed by the sepals and rarely spreading. Fruit a slender elliptical to narrowly pear-shaped capsule partially enclosed by the persistent calyx. BE

Lechea sessiliflora

CISTACEAE | **pineland pinweed**

Jul–Aug, 4–39 in. Prostrate to erect perennial of sandhills, dry flatwoods, sandy roadsides, and coastal scrub and dunes. A Coastal Plain endemic. Stems prostrate to flaring out from the base, many-branched, covered with hairs that are pressed against the stem. Leaves short-petioled, linear to linear-elliptic, to 3/8 in. long, smooth above, with soft short hairs beneath. Flowers in short panicles, reddish-brown, less than 1/4 in. wide, consisting of 3 tiny petals and 5 sepals. Fruit an elliptical capsule, less than 1/4 in. long, surrounded by 5 hairy sepals and capped by reddish-brown fringed stigmas. BAS

Lechea tenuifolia

CISTACEAE | **narrowleaf pinweed**

Jun–Aug, 4–15 in. Mat forming, bushy perennial of dry pine-oak forests, dry roadsides, and other openings. Stems with short, spreading branches and covered with fine, ascending hairs. Stem leaves alternate, 1/4–3/4 in. long, needle-thin and more than 10 times as long as wide, sparsely hairy beneath; on basal shoots, leaves linear, to 3 in. long, and crowded on the stem. Flowers on numerous spreading axillary branches in the upper half of the plant, brown or reddish, 1/4 in. long or less, with 3 tiny petals that are shorter than the 5 sepals. Fruit an oval capsule, completely enclosed by the hairy sepals. GPF

Symplocarpus foetidus

ARACEAE | **skunk cabbage**

Jan–Apr, 1–2 ft. Strong-smelling, low, fleshy perennial of seepage-fed bogs and non-alluvial swamps. Stem a thick, underground rhizome that sends up the fleshy inflorescence and, later, the leaves. Leaves basal and clustered, emerging after flowers, petioles lengthening over time, broadly oval, 6–24 in. long, with netted veins and entire margins; smells like cabbage when bruised. Flowers completely cover a short-stalked, round to oval spadix that is mostly enclosed by a reddish-purple-mottled, fleshy spathe with in-rolled margins. Flowers purplish-brown or yellowish-green, consisting of 4 perianth segments. Fruit a cluster of fleshy berries embedded in the spadix. TLJ

Typha angustifolia

TYPHACEAE | **narrowleaf cattail**

May–Jul, 3–5 ft. Emergent aquatic perennial of brackish to freshwater marshes and swamps, usually tidal, and also inland in non-tidal wetlands (where it is probably introduced); often forms colonies. Stems stout, stiff, unbranched. Leaves mostly basal and overlapping, linear, 1½–5 ft. long and ½ in. wide, the inner surface flat to slightly concave. Flowers tiny, densely packed in a cylindrical terminal spike broken into 2 sections with a gap between, the lower all female flowers, and the upper all male; female flowers start out pale green and become dark brown; male flowers yellowish-brown. Fruit numerous minute nutlets with fluffy white tufts. JED

Typha latifolia

TYPHACEAE | **broadleaf cattail**

May–Jul, 5–10 ft. Emergent aquatic perennial of freshwater ponds, lakes, ditches, and marshes, including freshwater tidal marshes; forms dense colonies. Stems stout, stiff, unbranched. Leaves mostly basal and overlapping, linear, to 10 ft. long and 1 in. wide, loosely twisted, more or less flat, smooth. Flowers tiny, densely packed in a cylindrical terminal spike broken into 2 sections without a gap between, the lower all female, the upper all male, both sections to 7 in. long; female flowers start out pale green, mature dark brown; male flowers yellowish-brown. Fruit numerous minute nutlets tufted with fluffy tawny hairs at maturity (pictured). BAS

GLOSSARY

achene. A more or less small, dry fruit that does not split open at maturity (is indehiscent), with a typically thin, close-fitting wall surrounding a single seed.

acidic. Applied to soils and rocks having low levels of basic (base-cation) minerals, such as calcium, magnesium, and potassium; indicative of low fertility.

adventive. Introduced but not naturalized, or only locally established.

alternate. Positioned singly at different heights on the stem; one leaf occurring at each node. (Compare with **opposite** and **whorled**.)

annual. Normally living one year or less; growing, reproducing, and dying within one cycle of seasons. Also used as a noun.

anther. The pollen-producing portion of the stamen, typically borne at the tip of a stalk or filament.

aquatic. Living in water; a plant that spends its entire life cycle in water.

ascending. Spreading at the base and then curving upward to an angle of 45° or less relative to the bearing structure.

axil. The point of the upper angle formed between the axis of a stem and any part (usually a leaf) arising from it.

axillary. On the stem just above the point of attachment of a leaf (or leaf scar) or branch; borne in the axil of a leaf or branch.

basal. At or very near the base of a plant structure.

basic. Applied to soils and rocks having high levels of basic (base-cation) minerals, such as calcium, magnesium, and potassium; indicative of high fertility.

berry. A fleshy fruit that does not split open at maturity, with few or more seeds (rarely just one), the seeds without a stony covering; the flesh may be more or less homogenous or with the outer portion more firm or leathery. (Compare with **drupe**.)

biennial. Normally living two years; germinating or forming and growing vegetatively during one cycle of seasons, then reproducing sexually and dying during the following one. Also used as a noun.

bilateral (also, **bilaterally symmetric**). Divisible into two essentially equal portions along only one plane. Used to describe flower form. (Compare with **radial**.)

brackish. Of or pertaining to water having a salt concentration of 0.5–30 parts per thousand.

bract. A modified, usually reduced leaf, often occurring at the base of a flower or inflorescence.

bulbil (also, **bulblet**). A small bulb or bulb-like body produced on aboveground parts of a plant, or also arising around a parent bulb.

calcareous. Applied to soil and rocks having relatively high levels of calcium; e.g., limestone, siltstone, dolomite.

calyx. Collective term for all the sepals of a flower; the outer perianth whorl. (Compare with **corolla**.)

capsule. A dry fruit that opens (dehisces) in any of various ways at maturity to release few to many seeds.

carpel. The basic ovule-bearing unit of flowers, thought to be evolutionarily derived from an infolded leaflike structure; equivalent to a simple pistil or a division of a compound pistil.

circumneutral. Applied to soils and rocks having moderate levels of basic (base-cation) minerals, such as calcium, magnesium, and potassium; indicative of moderate fertility.

claw. The long, narrow, petiole-like base of the sepals or petal in some species.

corm. A short, solid, vertical, usually underground, enlarged stem with leaves that are dry and scalelike or absent; serves as a food-storage organ.

corolla. The collective term for all the petals of a flower; the inner perianth whorl. (Compare with **calyx**.)

deciduous. Falling at the end of one growing season, as the leaves of non-evergreen trees; not evergreen. (Compare with **evergreen**.)

disjunct. Applied to a species with a discontinuous distribution. Also used as a noun.

disk floret. The tiny, often tubular flowers located in the center of a flower head in members of the aster family (Asteraceae).

drupe. A fleshy fruit that does not split open at maturity (indehiscent), with a soft outer wall and one or more hard inner stone(s) each usually containing a single seed, as cherries and plums. (Compare with **berry**.)

elliptical. Widest near the middle, with convex sides tapering equally toward both ends; in the shape of an ellipse or narrow oval. (Compare with **oblong** and **oval**.)

emergent. With part(s) of plant aerial and part(s) submersed; rising out of the water above the surface.

endemic. (adj.) Of a species or taxonomic group, restricted to a particular geographic region or habitat type; (n.) a taxon so restricted.

entire. With relatively smooth margins that lack teeth, spines, or other projections; with a continuous margin.

erect. Growing essentially in a vertical position; applied to whole plant or individual organs (fruit, petals, etc.).

evergreen. Bearing green leaves through the winter and into the next growing season; persisting two or more growing seasons; not deciduous. (Compare with **deciduous**.)

felsic. Containing light-colored silicate minerals rich in silicon, oxygen, aluminum, sodium, and potassium (e.g., quartz, muscovite, orthoclase); usually applied to igneous (and some metamorphic) rocks.

follicle. A usually dry fruit, with one interior chamber or locule, and splitting open (dehiscing) lengthwise along a single line, as in milkweed (*Asclepias*).

herbaceous. Having little or no living portion of the shoot persisting aboveground from one growing season to the next, the aboveground portion being composed of relatively soft, non-woody tissue.

incurved. Curved inward or upward.

indehiscent. Not opening up along a seam (such as would happen in certain fruits or anthers).

inflorescence. A flower cluster; the mode or pattern of flower bearing; the arrangement of flowers on the floral axis.

invasive. A non-native plant that infests and persists in natural habitats.

keeled. With a vertical ridge or keel.

lance-shaped (leaf or fruit). Several times longer than broad, widest near the base and tapering to a point at the apex.

mafic. Applied to rocks containing large amounts of dark-colored silicate minerals rich in magnesium and iron; e.g., serpentine, gabbro, diabase, greenstone.

mesic. Of intermediate moisture conditions (i.e., moist and well drained).

midvein (also, **midrib**). A main or primary vein running lengthwise down the center of a leaf or leaflike structure; a continuation of the leaf stalk (petiole); the midrib.

mycoheterotroph. A plant that is mycoheterotrophic, that is, lacks chlorophyll and obtains all or part of its food from the roots of other plants via obligate associations with fungi rather than from photosynthesis.

node. The portion of a stem where leaves and/or branches arise; often recognizable by the presence of one or more buds.

nutlet. A small nut.

oblong. Shaped more or less like a rectangular prism that is two to four times longer than wide.

opposite. Positioned in pairs along the stem, the members of each pair at the same level across from one another; two leaves occurring at each node. (Compare with **alternate** and **whorled**.)

oval. Broadly elliptical, the width more than one-half the length; with the outline of an egg.

ovary. The lower portion of a pistil where ovules are borne; often distinguishable from the rest of the pistil by its larger circumference.

palmately divided/compound/lobed. With three or more leaflets, lobes, or other structures arising from a common point and diverging from one another; arranged or structured in a hand-like pattern. (Compare with **pinnately divided**.)

panicle. A branched raceme, the main axis either determinate or indeterminate, and the lateral branches raceme-like; more loosely, a much-branched inflorescence of various types.

parasitic. Living in or on an organism of a different species and deriving nutrients from it.

perennial. Normally living more than two years, with no definite limit to its life span. Also used as a noun.

perfect. With both male (stamens) and female (carpels or pistils) reproductive parts in the flower.

perianth. The collective term for the outer sterile parts of a flower, comprising the calyx (sepals) and the corolla (petals) when both whorls are present.

petiole. The stalk of a leaf.

petiolate. With a leaf stalk (petiole).

pinnately divided/compound/lobed. With several leaflets, lobes, or other structures positioned along and on either side of a central axis; arranged or structured in a feather-like pattern. (Compare with **palmately divided**.)

pistil. The female or ovule-bearing organ of a flower, typically composed of an ovary, style, and stigma.

pod. A dry fruit enclosing a hollow space containing one or more seeds; opens along a seam.

raceme. An elongate, indeterminate inflorescence with stalked flowers borne singly along an unbranched main axis or rachis. (Compare with **panicle** and **spike**.)

radial (also, **radially symmetric**). Divisible into two essentially equal portions along more than one plane. Used to describe flower form. (Compare with **bilateral**.)

ray floret. The petal-like flowers that form the outer ring of flower heads in many members of the aster family (Asteraceae).

recurved. Curved outward or downward.

reflexed. Bent backward or downward.

rhizomatous. Having rhizomes.

rhizome. An underground, usually horizontal stem, often resembling a root but bearing nodes (points where leaves and/or branches can arise).

saprophytic. Obtaining nourishment from dead organic matter; saprophyte (n.). (Compare with **parasitic**.)

scape. A leafless flowering stem (with or without a few scale leaves), arising from an underground stem and, usually, from the middle of a basal rosette of leaves.

scapose. With a solitary leafless flowering stem (see **scape**), usually arising from a basal rosette.

schizocarp. A dry fruit with two or more interior chambers (locules), splitting open along the partitions between chambers and separating into indehiscent, usually one-seeded segments (mericarps), as in the carrot family (Apiaceae) and maples (*Acer*).

sepal. A unit or segment of the outermost floral envelope or calyx of a flower; usually green and leaflike. (Compare with **petal**.)

sessile. Without a stalk, positioned directly against the bearing structure. (Compare with **petiolate**.)

siliceous. Applied to rocks that consist largely or almost entirely of silicon dioxide (SiO_2).

simple (leaf or stem). Undivided, as a leaf blade that is not separated into distinct leaflets or lobes; for the purposes of the Key to Wildflowers, not cut more than halfway to the leaf's midrib or the leaf's base.

smooth. With an even surface; not rough to the touch; also, hairless.

spadix. An inflorescence with small, stalkless (sessile) flowers more or less embedded in a thick, fleshy, unbranched axis or rachis, the whole inflorescence subtended and sometimes partially enclosed by a specialized bract or spathe.

spathe. An often large, sometimes colored and flowerlike bract subtending and sometimes partially enclosing an inflorescence, as in Jack-in-the-pulpit (*Arisaema triphyllum*).

spike. A usually indeterminate, elongate inflorescence with unstalked (sessile) flowers arranged singly along an unbranched axis or rachis.

spoon-shaped. Referring to a leaf (or petal or sepal) that is broadly rounded at the tip and narrowed at the base.

spreading. Extending outward horizontally, or upward at an angle between 45° and 90° relative to the bearing structure.

spur. A hollow, slender, saclike appendage of a petal or sepal (or the corolla or calyx); also, a short shoot bearing leaves or flowers and fruits.

stamen. The male reproductive organ in a flower that produces and releases pollen, composed of an anther usually borne on a stalk (filament).

stigma. The pollen-receptive region at the tip of a pistil.

stipule. A relatively small, typically leaflike structure occurring at the base of a leaf stalk (petiole), usually one of a pair; stipules are sometimes in the form of spines, scales, or glands.

stolon. A slender horizontal stem—at or just above the surface of the ground—that gives rise to a new plant at its tip or from axillary branches.

stoloniferous. Bearing stolons.

tendril. Long, slender, coiling plant organ, adapted for climbing. Formed by modification of a part of a plant, such as a stem, leaf, or leaflet.

tepal. A member or segment of perianth in which the parts are not differentiated into distinct sepals and petals.

ternately divided/compound. In threes, as a leaf which is divided into three leaflets.

umbel. An inflorescence in which individual flower stalks arise from a single point and are approximately of equal length. In a compound umbel, this branching is repeated.

umbellet. The secondary umbel in a compound umbel.

whorled. With three or more leaves positioned on the stem at the same level; three or more leaves occurring at each node. (Compare with **alternate** and **opposite**.)

wing/winged. Having one or more elongate, relatively thin protrusions or appendages that loosely resemble wings, as in the twigs of winged elm (*Ulmus alata*).

xeric. Dry, drought-prone.

RESOURCES FOR LEARNING MORE

You may find that your interest in plants has grown beyond this guide. If so, wonderful! Perhaps you've encountered a species not included here, or you are interested in a wildflower in a group whose identification requires examination of details beyond those we were able to cover. In such cases, botanists identify plants with the aid of dichotomous keys (simple decision trees) and detailed technical descriptions found in botanical manuals or floras, and by comparing their find to known and identified specimens in herbaria.

Today we have resources for plant identification that were unimaginable a few decades ago, when technical botanical manuals for large regions of the country (the Northeast, the Southeast), manuals for a few states, and a few, very limited field guides were the only available options. At the time of this writing, new regional manuals are available, and many states have published geographically focused manuals/floras. In addition, online resources—websites, apps, and search engines—make plant identification and the search for additional information about a wildflower species easier than ever. Here we list some currently available resources, recognizing that additional ones will continue to appear.

Regional and State Floras and Botanical Manuals

Flora of North America Editorial Committee. 1991– . *Flora of North America North of Mexico*. Oxford University Press. At 30 volumes (of which about 20 have been published) this is obviously not a field manual! But as a landmark technical treatment of the native and naturalized plants of North America, the *Flora of North America* is one of the most important and authoritative library references for the flora of our continent. Like most of the other floras or manuals listed here, it has dichotomous keys, technical descriptions, maps (of distribution by U.S. state and Canadian province), and (for some species) line drawings.

Gleason, H. A., and A. Cronquist. 1991. *Manual of Vascular Plants of Northeastern United States and Adjacent Canada*. New York Botanical Garden, Bronx. The standard technical botanical manual for the northeastern United States since its publication in 1991. Its compact format is handy to carry in the field, but it lacks maps and line-drawings, and some of its taxonomy and nomenclature is dated.

Haines, A. A. 2011. *New England Wildflower Society's Flora Novae Angliae: A Manual for the Identification of Native and Naturalized Higher Vascular Plants of New England*. New England Wildflower Society and Yale University Press, New Haven, CT. While its area of coverage is entirely non-overlapping with the area of this guide, it is a modern flora with good keys that can be helpful in the northern parts of our coverage area.

Holmgren, N. H. 1998. *Illustrated Companion to Gleason and Cronquist's Manual: Illustrations of the Vascular Plants of Northeastern United States and Adjacent Canada*. New York Botanical Garden, Bronx. This companion volume to Gleason and Cronquist (1991) consists (only!) of black-and-white line drawings of the species treated. It is a large and heavy book.

Naczi, R. F. C., ed. [in progress]. *New Manual*

of Vascular Plants of Northeastern United States and Adjacent Canada. New York Botanical Garden Press, Bronx. An effort to update the classic *Manual* by Gleason and Cronquist; some plant family treatments are already available (70, as of early 2018). It will eventually be published as a single-volume manual. Relative to this field guide, it covers the states from Virginia northward (Virginia, West Virginia, Maryland, Delaware, Pennsylvania, and New Jersey).

Radford, A. E., H. E. Ahles, and C. R. Bell. 1968. *Manual of the Vascular Flora of the Carolinas*. University of North Carolina Press, Chapel Hill. The "Green Book" was a go-to resource for generations of botanists in the southeastern and mid-Atlantic United States and remains a very valuable resource, with county dot maps for each species and classic line drawings for about a third of the covered species. Fifty years of research and discovery since its publication has rendered some of its taxonomy and nomenclature obsolete.

Rhoads, A. F., and T. A. Block. 2007. *The Plants of Pennsylvania*, 2d ed. University of Pennsylvania Press, Philadelphia. This manual will be especially useful in the northern part of the area covered by this guide: Pennsylvania, New Jersey, Maryland, Delaware, and the District of Columbia.

Weakley, A. S. 2018. *Flora of the Southern and Mid-Atlantic States*. NC Botanical Garden, Chapel Hill, NC. This flora covers over 8000 species, including the entire area of this field guide, providing identification keys, distribution maps, detailed synonymy (reference to other names used for the species), nativity and origin, phenology (flowering and fruiting dates), and ecological and rarity information for each species. It is periodically issued in pdf and print versions and is available from the UNC Herbarium (herbarium.unc.edu/).

Weakley, A. S., C. L. Ludwig, and J. F. Townsend. 2012. *Flora of Virginia*. Bland Crowder, ed. Foundation of the Flora of Virginia Project, Inc., Richmond. Botanical Research Institute of Texas Press, Fort Worth. This flora covers the native and naturalized plants of Virginia, with keys, descriptions, line drawings, and introductory chapters about the state and its botany, ecology, and botanical exploration. It also offers useful coverage for an area beyond Virginia, especially northern North Carolina, West Virginia, the District of Columbia, Maryland, Delaware, and southern Pennsylvania. An especially welcome feature for the interested botanical explorer is a short chapter by Gary P. Fleming, "Learning the Virginia Flora: 50 Sites for Productive Field Botany."

Apps

FloraQuest. Available only on Apple devices (iOS). It is essentially an "app version" of the Weakley *Flora of the Southern and Mid-Atlantic States*, with some enhancements made possible by digital format, such as a clickable and visual glossary of terms, "key filtering" by geography (one can set one's location, and the keys automatically simplify based on the plants plausibly present in that region, improving the likelihood of "smooth keying"), and some photographs and drawings.

Flora of Virginia. Available on Apple (iOS) and Android operating devices. While it is customized for Virginia, this app is useful in a broader area, especially northern North Carolina, West Virginia, the District of Columbia, Maryland, Delaware, and southern Pennsylvania. It includes nearly all the content of the print *Flora of Virginia* but adds an intuitive and visual identification system (multiple access key), which selects possible identifications based on entered characteristics; for example, if one chooses the combination of "non-aster dicot," "blue flowers," "blooming in April," "alternate leaves," and "leaf margins serrate," the 3164 species in Virginia reduce to 18 possibilities.

iNaturalist. iNaturalist is a citizen-science application available as a smartphone or desktop/laptop app. The enrolled user can post observations of plants and animals from pictures taken on a smartphone or camera; those observations are then available to other users for identification, comment, discussion, and scientific use. In 2017, iNaturalist introduced a "machine learning" module in the app, which endeavors to identify the organism in the photo based on the similarity of the image to known and correctly identified images previously in iNaturalist and the "location plausibility" of the observation. Other users also engage with posted observations and interact to come to "team" identifications. The user can also access identified photographs of a particular wildflower species, and see a map of the locations where that plant has been seen.

Web Resources

We list only a few recommendations for what is a dynamic and expanding set of resources for learning about native and naturalized plants of your area. Many of these sites will provide one or several types of information you might want: identification aids, photographs, detailed distribution data, detailed conservation information, etc.

Biota of North America Program: bonap.org

Flora of North America: efloras.org/flora_page.aspx?flora_id=1

Go Botany (New England Wild Flower Society): gobotany.newenglandwild.org

Native and Naturalized Plants of the Carolinas and Georgia: namethatplant.net

Natural Heritage Programs (by state): natureserve.org/natureserve-network/united-states

NatureServe Explorer: explorer.natureserve.org

North Carolina Botanical Garden: ncbg.unc.edu

Southeastern U.S. Plant Identification Resource: southeasternflora.com

USDA Plants: plants.usda.gov/java/

PHOTOGRAPHERS

Photographer credits are indicated by initials at the end of each photo caption or species description. Use the following list to identify individual photographers. All photographers retain rights to their photographs. Those with initials NCBG are in the collections of the North Carolina Botanical Garden.

AB	Ashley Bradford
AH	Arthur Haines
AMC	Alan M. Cressler
AWF	Ann Walter-Fromson
BAS	Bruce A. Sorrie
BE	Bryan England
BH	Bill Hubick
BMP	Bruce Patterson
CL	Chris Liloia, NCBG
DASM	David G. Smith
DPF	Dorothy P. Fields
EB	Edwin Bridges
EO	Emily Oglesby, NCBG
ER	Evan Raskin
FG	Floyd A. Griffiths
GMP	Grant Morrow Parkins, NCBG
GPF	Gary P. Fleming
JASA	Jason Sachs
JB	Jim Brighton
JBG	Janet Gray
JED	Jacob Dakar, NCBG
JF	Jim Fowler
JG	John Gwaltney
JH	John Hayden
JP	Jennifer Peterson, NCBG
JS	Jennifer Stanley
JWH	J. W. Hardin, NCBG
KB	Keith Bradley
KJ	Kirsten Johnson
KL	Kenneth Lawless
LADI	Layla Dishman
LMC	Laura M. Cotterman, NCBG
MHV	Maurice H. Vaughan
MK	Mike Kunz, NCBG
PHA	Pat & Herb Amyx
PIP	Jeffrey S. Pippen
RG	Rob Gardner, NCBG
RL	Richard LeBlond
RTW	Richard & Teresa Ware
RWS	R. W. Smith, Lady Bird Johnson Wildflower Center
SG	Stan Gilliam
SH	Sonnia Hill
SJB	Steven Baskauf
TLJ	Tracie L. Jeffries
TOPO	Tom Potterfield
WS	Will Stuart

INDEX

ABOUT THE AUTHORS

John Cotterman

Laura Cotterman has worked as both a professional botanist and an editor. She received an M.S. in plant ecology from NC State University and a B.S. in biology from Vassar College. She began her career as a seasonal botanist/ecologist for the N.C. Plant Conservation Program and then a botanist/data manager for the N.C. Natural Heritage Program. She was publications and publicity coordinator for the North Carolina Botanical Garden from 2003 to 2014.

Jennifer Peterson

Damon Waitt has broad responsibility for overall leadership and management of the North Carolina Botanical Garden and for ensuring that the garden fulfills its mission to inspire understanding, appreciation, and conservation of plants and to advance a sustainable relationship between people and nature. Waitt holds a Ph.D. in botany from the University of Texas in Austin, an M.S. in botany from Louisiana State University Baton Rouge, and a B.S. in biology from Tulane University.

Julie P. Tuttle

Alan Weakley is a plant taxonomist, community ecologist, and conservationist specializing in the southeastern United States. He holds a Ph.D. from Duke University and a B.A. from UNC-Chapel Hill. He has worked as botanist and ecologist for the N.C. Natural Heritage Program, and as regional and chief ecologist for The Nature Conservancy and NatureServe. Since 2002, he has served as director of the UNC Herbarium, a department of the North Carolina Botanical Garden.

LEAF FORM

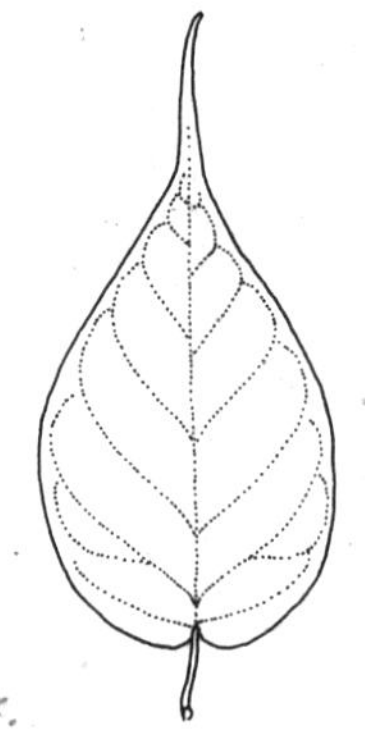

simple

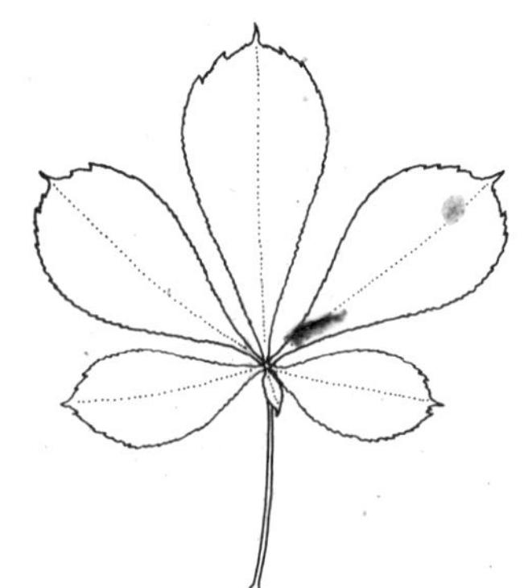

palmately divided/compound

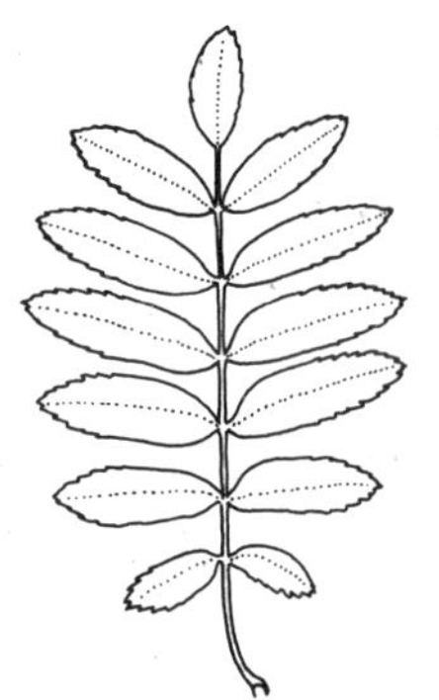

pinnately divided/compound

LEAF SHAPE

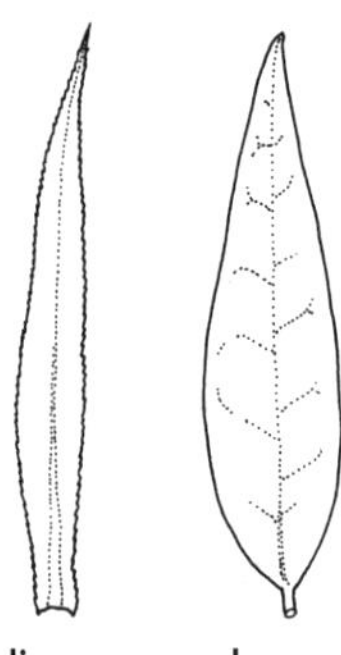

linear lance

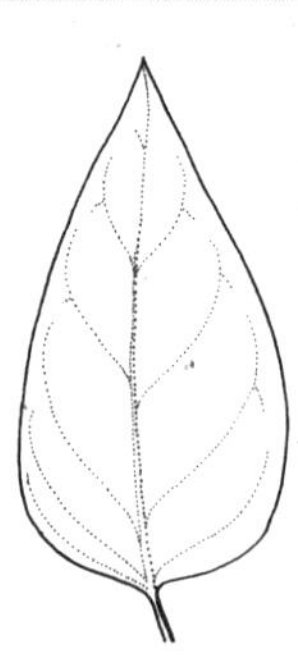

oval

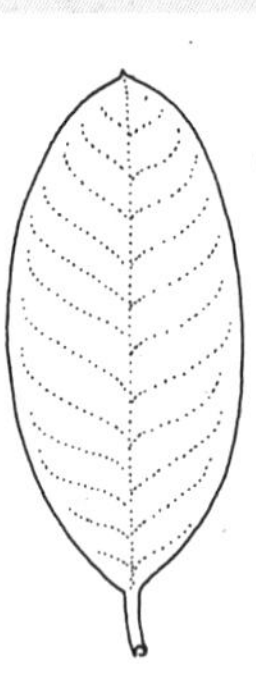

elliptical

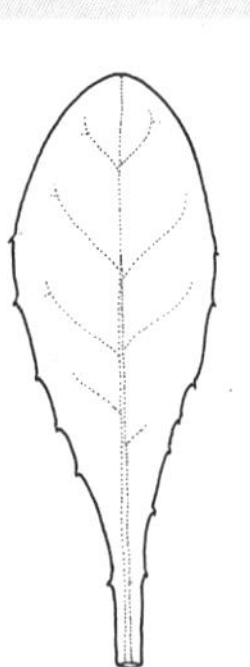

spoon

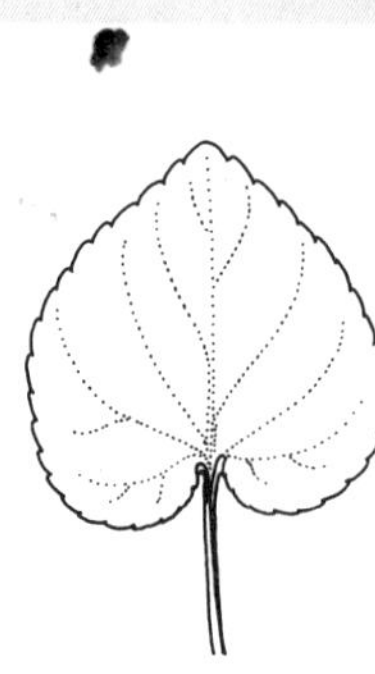

heart

LEAF MARGINS

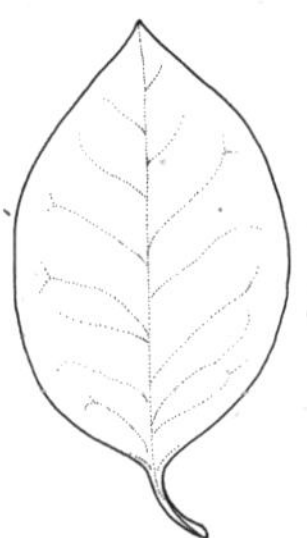

entire

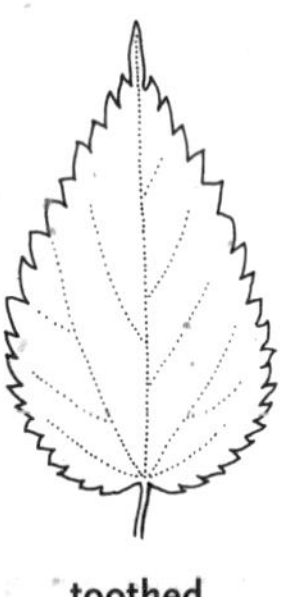

toothed

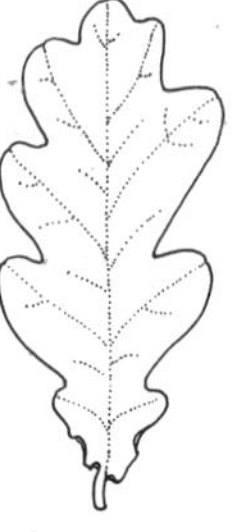

lobed

LEAF ARRANGEMENT

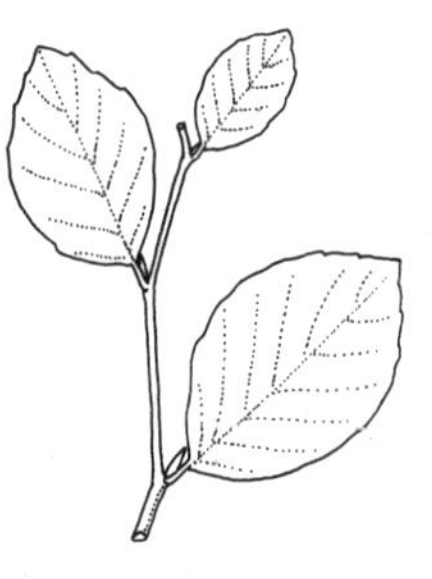

alternate